REPORT

ON THE DEPREDATIONS

COMMITTED BY

THE THUG GANGS

OF

UPPER AND CENTRAL INDIA

REPORT

ON THE DEPREDATIONS

COMMITTED BY

THE THUG GANGS

OF

UPPER AND CENTRAL INDIA

WILLIAM HENRY SLEEMAN

GYAN

Published by

Gyan Publishing House
5, Ansari Road
Daryaganj, New Delhi-110002
Phone: 011-47034999, 9811692060
E-mail: books@gyanbooks.com

Distribution Network
gyanbooks.com
India, USA, Canada, UK, Australia

ISBN: 978-93-7133-426-6 (PB)

First Published, 1840

2nd Impression 2025

Printed at: Gyan Press, Delhi.

REPORT ON THE DEPREDATIONS COMMITTED BY THE THUG GANGS OF UPPER AND CENTRAL INDIA

Author: WILLIAM HENRY SLEEMAN

REPORT

ON THE DEPREDATIONS

COMMITTED BY

THE THUG GANGS

OF

UPPER AND CENTRAL INDIA,

FROM THE

COLD SEASON OF 1836-37, DOWN TO THEIR GRADUAL SUPPRESSION, UNDER THE OPERATION OF THE MEASURES ADOPTED AGAINST THEM BY THE

SUPREME GOVERNMENT,

IN THE YEAR 1839.

By MAJOR SLEEMAN,

Commissioner for the Suppression of Thuggee and Dacoitee.

CALCUTTA:

G. H. HUTTMANN, BENGAL MILY. ORPHAN PRESS.

1840.

CONTENTS.

A

PREFACE.

WITH the exception of the Narratives of the depredations of the gangs who resided in Furruckabad, Cawnpore and the other Districts between the rivers Ganges and Jumna, this Report was all prepared and sent to the Press before the end of 1838. That part of the work had been confided to Captain Charles Brown, but he was unable to complete it in consequence of the pressure of other duties. Captain Reynolds kindly undertook and completed these Narratives in the early part of the present year (1840); and the delay has enabled me to add considerably to the table which exhibits the results of the trials in all parts of India; and to correct the list of Thugs still at large up to the present day. It would have been inconvenient to strike out the names of those who had died or been otherwise disposed of in the interval, as the list had for the most part been printed off before these corrections reached Calcutta; and a list of the names of such persons has been substituted. Many of those who are still borne on this list have no doubt died, though we have not been able to ascertain their death.

The only parts of India in which there are any Thugs still at large and not entered in these lists, are, I believe, the Eastern districts of Bengal, where we have reason to believe that the crime still prevails to a small extent; and Midnapore, where Captain Vallancey and Mr. Ewart have recently discovered some traces of an isolated colony or two who are supposed to depredate between Midnapore and

Nagpore, along the road leading from Calcutta to Bombay. Measures are being taken to put down these associations should they, on further inquiry, be found really to exist. The gangs who committed the numerous murders along the coast from Jugurnath to Vizagapatam have been put down by the active and most able exertions of Mr. Ewart and Captain Vallancey, which have left only two of their able-bodied members still at large. These gangs were from an isolated colony settled in the hilly parts of the Cuttack District, which would, no doubt, soon have sent out its branch establishments to other parts had they been left undisturbed. They are Hindoos by caste and are known by the name of Goalahs; but whence they came originally, or whence they derived their system of murder, has not yet been discovered.

After trying long in vain to trace the murderers of the numerous travellers whose bodies had been found along the coast, Captain Vallancey succeeded in arresting a gang of twelve persons with the property of some travellers whom they had recently murdered upon them; and making a judicious use of the information of some of the party, who volunteered their services as King's evidences, upon the usual conditions of exemption from the punishments of death and transportation beyond seas for all past offences, and having the advantage of the aid of a Magistrate of great energy and sagacity in Mr. Ewart, and the support of an able Commissioner in Mr. Mills, he has been enabled to effect the arrest and conviction of the whole of the gangs, with the exception of two members of no great note. At least so far as our present information extends these gangs are unconnected with any others, and these two are the only members of these gangs left at large. It may possibly be found hereafter that they were connected with the colonies who are supposed to reside in Midnapore; and even with others in that quarter of India to which our operations have but lately been extended. I shall give the narrative of the successful pursuits after these gangs in Captain Vallancey's and Mr. Ewart's own words. Captain Vallancey says, in a Memoir published in the *Madras United Service Journal*—

"After the Vizagapatam Thugs were all apprehended, several murders, which had occurred between Chicacole and Ganjam, were brought to my notice; and from the appearance of the bodies, when found, I was satisfied they were the handy work of Thugs. I had previously closely questioned my approvers, from the Vizagapatam Thugs, as to their knowledge of any colonies of Thugs in the Ganjam District, but they uniformly asserted that none to their knowledge existed. However two of the oldest of them told me, that when they were quite young lads, (but after their initiation,) when out on an expedition with their fathers, they fell in with a party of fellows, calling themselves Pundah Brahmins, but who were Thugs; that in concert with them they had murdered some merchants travelling south, with a quantity of silks. They had never met with them since then, neither did they know where they resided, consequently there was little or no probability of their recognizing any of them, should they now fall in with them on the roads. From the middle of 1837 to the middle of 1839, I had constant reports of murders; it therefore appeared that either my approvers were playing me false, and that more of their own fraternity were at large, or else that some Bengal Thugs had found their way down to the coast: else that, or the story about the Pundah Brahmin Thugs, was correct, and that they were the murderers.

"During these two years I kept my parties constantly on the look out on the roads in the Ganjam District, and even extended my reach as far north as Cuttack, but without success, as the murders still continued. At length, in September last year, one of my parties met in this district a gang of twelve fellows, calling themselves Pundah Brahmins, travelling the country with the consecrated rice of Jugurnath, but the property found upon their persons placed it beyond a doubt that they were the Thugs, I was so anxiously searching for. Just at this period the attention of the Magistrates of South and Centre Cuttack, was aroused to the fact that Thugs had visited their districts, as human bodies partly decomposed, were discovered in four or five places along the roads; they offered rewards and exerted themselves to find out the perpetrators, but without effect.

" The would-be Brahmins I had apprehended, described themselves as inhabitants of Koordah in South Cuttack, or the Pooree District. After mature enquiry, they were proved to be a party of the low caste, called Goalahs, and inhabitants of a small village on the western border of the Pooree District. In a short time I succeeded in making some of them approvers, and obtained a knowledge of their history. This colony has existed in the Pooree District for generations; they appear ignorant how the system of Thuggee came amongst them. The secret has been confined to their own clan, strangers never having been admitted; though I believe, they are acquainted with other classes who carry on Thuggee. The initiated of this caste amount to forty-two; but there are a dozen young hands ready to be admitted. These fellows have been most determined murderers; all castes were alike to them—they spared neither sex. As yet I am only acquainted with some of their expeditions.

" About three years since, in 1837, a gang of twenty-seven murdered a party of twelve travellers, close to Munsoorcota, amongst whom were some of Rajah Chundoo

Loll's people proceeding to Jugurnath, with his yearly gift to the Temple. By the Rajah's account, property to the amount of 10,000 Rupees, must have been taken by the Thugs. On the expedition on which the party was apprehended they had murdered seventeen persons. They were seized shortly after they had committed the last murder, and had just turned homewards. Doubtless, had they been allowed to proceed, this would not have been the last. On an expedition as far as Chicacole, about two years since, they murdered twenty people; about four years ago they murdered eight merchants on the banks of the Mahanuddy, and robbed them of 4,000 Rupees. A few months previous to the above, at another spot on the same river, they murdered thirteen travellers at one blow, and last year the eight travellers, whose bodies were found by the Pooree Police, as before mentioned. In 1836, two Government peons, of the Vizagapatam Zillah, escorting 700 Rupees for the repairs of the Stree Poormum Pagoda, not far from Chicacole, were missed; their bodies were afterwards found buried within half a mile of the Pagoda; they were murdered by the Goalah Thugs. In 1833, four pearl merchants from the Cuddapah District, were found by a relation, murdered a stage or two north of Chicacole, they were also killed by the Goalah Thugs, and about a thousand rupees worth of pearls stolen.

"These Thugs were for years protected by a petty independent Rajah on the western border of the Pooree District, but in late years his exactions became so severe, that they quitted his territory, and found shelter in the villages in which the body of them were arrested, under the protection of a Serbarakar, or Revenue officer, who was well acquainted with their practices, and well paid for his protection; this man is to be brought to trial for his connexion with the Thugs.

" I have now given you, in as brief a manner as possible, the history of those colonies of Thugs, which I have been especially employed in suppressing. Hereafter my exertions are chiefly to be confined to the Cuttack District; and I have some information which leads me to believe that ere long, I shall be able to trace out more colonies in that quarter.

" The day that sees this far-spread evil completely eradicated from India, and known only in name, will greatly tend to immortalize British rule in the East.

Mr. Ewart says in a letter addressed to me on the 22d of August last—

" No. 105.

" To Major Sleeman, &c. &c.

" Sir,—You ask for a narrative of proceedings against this colony. The successful issue must primarily be attributed to Captain Vallancey's judicious dispositions for watching the great thoroughfare to the southward, by which a clue was obtained requiring little exertion or sagacity, but a knowledge of localities of this district to obtain important results.

" The party posted at Kunchelogundum, 40 miles south of Ganjam, by Captain Vallancey, in the end of September 1839, detained 12 persons, of whom 10 called themselves Pundahs, and two were said to be the servants of the party. On 3d October, Captain Vallancey sent me the examinations, taken by the Mootsuddy, of two of the party who had absconded,—and intimated his intention of proceeding to examine the detenus. He omitted to send a description of the runaways; and the statement given in the examinations were too vague to make any use of; but there were inconsistencies relating to localities which satisfied me they were false. I wrote to Captain Vallancey for information of a more precise nature ; and on receipt of a demi-official letter from him, dated from Kunchelo, October 10th, I perceived that the most effectual plan would be for me to go myself and ask the men a few questions.

" Taking advantage of my offices being closed for three days, I went to Kunchelo. The circumstance of the habits, appearance and dialect of the people of the hilly and level parts of the districts being so different, as mentioned in para. 9 of my letter to you No. 165, dated 21st July, and the inconsistencies and ignorance of the plain country betrayed by the captives in replying to my questions, excited my suspicions that they were from the hills. On my return to Pooree the Deputy Collector, in charge of the Estate of Khoordah, had arrived with his annual accounts, and on being made acquainted with my suspicions he informed me, that my predecessor, Mr. Wilkinson, had suspected some persons of the Goalah tribe of practising Thuggee: and had caused the apprehension of several of them in March 1836, on their return from a journey, with a quantity of very suspicious property. But there was no information of any travellers being missed, nor any claimants to the property—the persons apprehended were, therefore, released; and the property was restored to them after the lapse of some months. The Deputy Collector informed me, that some of the suspected persons had two residences, one in villages of Gurh Seekoh, a sub-division of Khoordah; the other in Rupoor, which is contiguous to that part of Khoordah. Rupoor being held under the Provisions of Section 31, Regulation XII. of 1805, I was apprehensive that the Rajah might found a complaint on a sudden incursion of a party of Police; and that the ordinary course of a Purwannah to him would frustrate my object; nor could I be confident, that he did not harbour the Thugs, and connive at their mal-practices.

" I directed the Deputy Collector to return immediately to Khoordah, giving him an authority to require a body of Police, and of the Khoordah Paik Company; and to set out from Khoordah a particular evening, so as to surround the Goalah villages at dawn before any one could have any intimation of his plans. I gave him also a description of the two runaways, and of the remaining ten captives, instructing him first to try to apprehend those two, then to ascertain whether any persons answering the descriptions were absent from home, and to search every place where he found cause to suspect there was any property that had been obtained by improper means.

To have a simultaneous search in Khoordah Rupoor, I so timed my arrival after midnight at Tanghey, a Police station on the skirts of that Estate, where a detachment of the Khoordah Paik Corps is stationed, that no one had any idea of my approach; and I proceeded immediately with some Police and Sepoys of the Paik Company to surround and search the Goalah villages in Rupoor. My information was, however, very imperfect; and by the time I had ascertained that I had gone to the wrong villages the intelligence of my visit had spread, and I obtained no results. The Deputy Collector succeeded in capturing the two runaways; and obtained evidence, that they had left their houses with ten others, answering the descriptions of those detained by Captain Vallancey, whose true names he of course ascertained. The only suspicious property he found was a piece of cloth such as is only made in the districts of the Northern Sircars, viz. Ganjam, &c. That was found upon a boy, the son of the man who was supposed, and afterwards proved, to be the leader of the captured party.

" After examining the two retaken and the youth, I set the latter at liberty; and sent the two accompanied by the

Commissary of their village Putbas Putnaick, to Vizagapatam. The two recaptured persons were at once recognised by Captain Vallancey's people; and the Commissary recognised and gave the true names of the other ten.

"This Commissary, although frequently, attending my Court, and, as he afterwards said, entertaining strong suspicions that the Goalahs had robbed the travellers' party of the 1400 rupees and murdered them, never spoke to me on the subject until the three persons sent in by the Deputy Collector were being examined. He is now under examination before Captain Vallancey on a charge of harbouring Thugs.

"At Kunchelo I had carefully examined all the property found upon the captives: it was a heterogenous mass. Among it were some gold ear and nose ornaments, and a very diminutive silver spoon somewhat peculiar. On 19th October, Beero Naik, a resident of a village, eight miles North of Pooree, gave a petition for an enquiry regarding his uncle and cousin who had gone to Berhampore, near Ganjam, and had sold their brass wares to the amount of 310 rupees, and set out on their return home; but the traces of their progress were lost in the Ganjam district. He described as having been in their possession ornaments and a spoon, such as I have mentioned above. I had not spoken of these articles to any one, and it was not probable any information regarding them could have reached Pooree. I immediately sent the petitioner with a letter to the Magistrate of Ganjam, requesting a search might be instituted for the bodies; and that the petitioner might afterwards be forwarded to Captain Vallancey. The petitioner at once recognised the property; and afterwards by the aid of the approvers the remains of the two men were found. This is the case on which the first commitment was made; and on which six persons have been executed.

"While Captain Vallancey was drawing from the approvers all the information he could relative to their fraternity, I also was obtaining some which put me in possession of the names of all the members of the three gangs, and of their connections. Having no information on which to base any charge, I waited until the receipt of a letter from Captain Vallancey, dated 6th December, informing me, that he had sufficient evidence to warrant the arrest of seventeen persons whose names were given, and whom he believed to be the whole. Being apprehensive that unless all were taken at the same time, the others of whose connection with the gangs I had very sufficient information, would escape, I at once issued warrants for the arrest of all. Another letter from Captain Vallancey, dated 16th December, furnished a supplementary list, comprising ten of those whose arrest I had ordered on my own responsibility, and two others whom I had not heard of.

"The party sent to effect the arrests surrounded the villages before dawn, but unfortunately some of those sought were in raised platforms in their fields watching their crops, and seeing the picquets outside were deterred from entering their villages. However all those wanted were taken, except three, of whom, one, a Sirdar, has been since sent in by the Rupoor Rajah. The other two are still at large. I have received no confirmation of the suspicion entertained by Captain Vallancey, alluded to in the P. S. to my letter, No. 165, dated 21st July; nor have I any further positive information regarding any other Thugs.

"I am now collecting information to form a Register of all the Goalahs in the districts, and of the families with which they have intermarried, and all other particulars relating to this offset of the race of Hindoos, of whose designation or existence even I had no knowledge a year ago. I am led to suppose they come from the South.

(Signed) JAMES EWART,
Magistrate.

Pooree (alias Jugurnath,) 22*d August*, 1840.

Except in the parts I have mentioned (Eastern Bengal between Midnapore, Nagpore and Cuttack) and in Oude, I believe the roads are now from one end of India to the other, free from the depredations of Thug gangs; but there are many leaders and leading members of the old gangs still at large; and some of them may perhaps be in situations which enable them occasionally to destroy solitary travellers though they have for the most part I believe found service in the military and police establishments of Native Chiefs. All these persons would return to their old trade, and teach it to their sons, and to the needy and dissolute of their neighbourhood, and thus re-organise their gangs should our pursuit be soon relaxed. To prevent the system from rising again it will be indispensably necessary to keep up the pursuit for some years till all these leaders and leading members of the old gangs die, or become too old to return to their old trade. Under the pressure of this pursuit their sons will take to honest industry, seeing no prospect of being able to follow successfully that of their ancestors.

I intended to reserve what I had to state regarding the suppression of the gangs in the South of India till I could offer narratives of their proceedings similar to those here given of the depredations of the gangs of Upper and Central India; but I cannot deny myself the gratification of here inserting the account which Captain Vallancey has given of the suppression of gangs along the Coromandel Coast, and that which I have lately received from Captain Malcolm of the result of our measures in the dominions of the Nizam of Hydrabad. Captain Malcolm's letter is addressed to Captain Reynolds, through whom I had expressed some apprehensions that the system still prevailed in those dominions. The exertions of Captains Elwall, Lumley and Burrows throughout the other parts of Southern India, including the Districts of the Bombay Presidency and the Territories of Mysore, have been equally successful; but neither of these Officers has given me a connected narrative of proceedings that I could add to this volume.

To the Editor of the United Service Gazette.

(Written by Capt. Vallancey.)

Sir,—My object in addressing you, is, to give a short account of the different colonies of Thugs that have infested the Cuddapah and Chittoor Districts, the Northern Circars and Orissa; it being desirable that the public should be made acquainted with the ramifications of this dreadful system, and the operations going on for its entire suppression in Southern India.

From 1823 to 1836 a large body, of what are termed Arcottee Thugs, under four famous leaders—Sheik Ahmed, Emam Sahib, Hoonoor Sahib, and Hyder Khan,—had been located in villages in the Masulipatam District from Moongal, on the Hyderabad border, to a village one stage north of Ellore. Most of these Thugs, more particularly the leaders, maintained excellent characters in their villages for being industrious cultivators. For the space of thirteen years, these gangs carried on their murders with impunity on all the principal roads of the country within three hundred miles from of their villages. They extended their expeditions West, as far as Hyderabad—South as far as Cuddapah—South-west to Gooty, and Hunde Anantipoor—and North as far as Chicacole. On several of those expeditions they obtained large sums of money. One of their first prizes, after settling in the Bundah Districts, was a sum of 14,000 Rupees by the murder of five persons, the property of a merchant of Bunder, who was forwarding it to Hyderabad. About fourteen years since, when on an expedition in the direction of Gooty, they murdered four persons and obtained a prize of 6,000 Rupees, which money belonged to a merchant of Cuddapah. Again, not far from the same place a year afterwards, they fell in with five treasure carriers, by the murder of whom they gained another prize of 8,000 Rupees. Ten years since, within a stage of Chicacole, they surprised a Mogul horse merchant, with four people, whom they murdered and secured property to the amount of 3,000 Rupees. In 1835, on an expedition towards Hyderabad, they obtained a booty of 4,000 Rupees; murdering the four treasure carriers. These form but a small portion of the murders perpetrated by these miscreants. From an account I have by me of murders disclosed to me, I find that from 1823 up to the time of the arrest of these gangs they had committed sixty murders, by which 170 persons became their victims, and property to the amount of half a lac of Rupees came into their hands. These Thugs might have continued unmolested to this day, had not an approver of the Deccan Thugs, with Captain Reynolds, at Hingolee, disclosed their existence and place of residence. Shortly afterwards, nearly the whole colony, which comprised 60 members, were apprehended. They are now under trial at Vizagapatam.

By the seizure of these gangs, a knowledge of the existence of a colony of Mussulman Thugs in the Vizagapatam District was gained. They had, twice or thrice, been met with, on the roads, by the Bundah Thugs, and thus they became acquainted. To them alone was their existence known. How this colony had become planted in this part of India, the Arcottee Thugs could give no information; but when I had got the whole of them into safe custody, I soon made myself conversant with their history. About twenty years ago they numbered between 60 and 70; though at the time of this arrest they were reduced to twelve. The grandfathers of the oldest of them, with a number of others, had come from Hindoostan; they were originally under three leaders; and appear never to have admitted strangers amongst them. Of late years many of the young hands, after their initiation, became Sepoys, and are now in various Regiments, in which I have ascertained they bear good character. One of this fraternity, an expert strangler, who was lately hung at Vizagapatam, was formerly a Sepoy in the 41st Regiment, and when his Corps was in the Northern Circars, and stationed at Samulcottah, he used to join his brethren, and taking a couple of parades leave, would go off with them on the road, join in murders, and return. These Thugs had never fallen in with large prize. They were most inveterate murderers, sparing neither sex or age; nor did they pay any respect to those castes, which other classes of Thugs thought it an heinous offence to murder. They seldom troubled themselves with omens, and the pick-axe was not held in any veneration; in fact they were considered by the Arcottees, an ill-omened set of Thugs. They never extended their expeditions to the South, beyond Rajamundry, or to the North beyond Chicacole, but nevertheless, their murders within this space were numerous. From the year 1825 up to the time of their arrest in

1835, they perpetrated 40 murders, comprising eighty persons.

These Thugs had reigned undisturbed in the Northern Provinces, doubtless for more than a hundred years, and a fearful number of victims must have fallen by their hands. All of them have now been tried; some of them have been hung, others have been sentenced to confinement for life, but one or two, I am sorry to say, have been set at large, and enjoy a liberty they do not merit, but as they were not principals, I hope that no evil will result from the leniency shewn them.

Again, from the Bundah Thugs, I became acquainted with two parties of Thugs, one residing in the Cuddapah, the other in the Chittoor Zillah. These in the Cuddapah Districts, were more or less connected with the Mysore Thugs; they were under two famous leaders, and numbered about 25 persons. These, with one or two exceptions, have been apprehended, tried, and finally sentenced.

Their operations are not well known to me, as they were sent to the Assistant at Bangalore, and there tried.

Of this, however, I am aware that their ancestors had been located for many generations in the Southern Districts and pursued their dreadful practices almost without let or hindrance.

The colony in the Chittoor District numbered twelve persons. At their heads was an old Approver named Madar Khan. He was one of the Approvers, made by the Magistrate of Chittoor in 1812. At that time these, wretches abounded in the Chittoor, Arcot and Salem Districts. After the attack they made upon them, the generality of them quitted those Districts, but some four or five remained in the Chittoor District whom Madar Khan rejoined. They inducted their offspring into the fraternity, and in 1837, they numbered a dozen. The whole of them were apprehended by me. The old hands were recognised by the Approvers, but the persons of the younger men were not known. It appears that this colony had kept themselves entirely distinct, and had not communicated with any of the gangs in their quarters of the South, therefore their proceedings of late years were entirely unknown, and the leader, Madar Khan, trusting to his former pardon, would make no disclosures. One of the old hands, a Mahratta, acknowledged that they still followed their old system, yet nothing could induce him to divulge the history of his later life. The consequence of this was, the release of the younger hands, who are now at large in the Chittoor District, the others, however, have been duly cared for. I must now return to the North.

(Copy.)

No. 124.

From Captain Malcolm,

To Captain P. A. Reynolds,

Superintendent, &c. &c.

Sir,—At the period at which I was permanently appointed as an Extra Assistant, to aid you in your operations in the Deccan, and which, as you may remember, was in the early part of 1836, the whole of the Districts of the Nizam's Territories to the North of the Godavery, had, by your exertions, been almost entirely cleared of the gangs of Thugs, which had so long infested the principal roads leading towards Hindoostan, Jaulnah, Husungabad, and Nagpore; while the seizure of several of the leading Thugs in the vicinity of Hydrabad and Goolburgah had opened sources of information which, there was reason to hope, would, if properly followed out, lead to the detection of the gangs of Sheikh Daood, in the city of Hydrabad; Loondar Nubbee and Ghouse Mahomed towards Wurrungul; Nunhoo Boolakee and Salut Khan towards Shorapore and the Dooab; and the remnants of Lungooteean's followers, who after the arrest of their leader by you, had, it was supposed, collected under Bhagwaroo and others, in the vicinity of Afzulpore and Beder.

The prosecution of these enquiries you were pleased to entrust to me, and as Hingolee was inconveniently situated for their prosecution, I proceeded via Naudair and Dighoor, direct to Hydrabad, where I was led to believe, I should most probably hear of some of the parties I was in search of. I was accompanied on my route by a small party of approvers; and through their means effected the arrest of a few Thugs of little note, who had hitherto eluded pursuit through their comparative insignificance, and their having fled for concealment to a part of the country little traversed by your parties.

As was to be expected, the arrest of these men led to no beneficial results; and for some time after my arrival at Hydrabad, my endeavours to gain a clue to the haunts of the Telingana Thugs proved ineffectual. One morning, however, I was surprised by three men, apparently Mussulman Peadahs, rushing into the Residency, and throwing themselves at my feet. On enquiry what had led them to adopt such a proceeding, they confessed themselves to be the well known leaders Dhoomdee, Moheeoodeen, and Sheikh Hajeè, and stated, that the unremitting pursuit which had been kept up after them by your parties, had rendered escape hopeless, and life a burden; and that they had in consequence determined on giving themselves up in the expectation of being admitted approvers, and sharing in the rewards offered by Government, for the apprehension of several of their companions whose haunts they were ready to betray.

A compliance with their wishes led immediately to the arrest of three leaders, Daood, Moheeoodeen 2d, and Nunhoo Bolakee, with whom they had been recently on an expedition; and eventually to that of several others, of whom I was in search in the neighbourhood of Hydrabad. The Thugs above alluded to, when apprehended, were out on an expedition, in which they had murdered several travellers, only a few days before their arrest; and one of the men who gave themselves up to me, was dressed in the clothes of an inhabitant of Hydrabad, whom he had murdered within a few stages of this place, where the body had been left disposed of in such a careless manner, that it did not escape detection above a few hours.

While I was personally engaged in the arrest of the Hydrabad Thugs, and the examination of the Arcot Thugs made over to me by the Magistrate of Guntoor—the parties I had despatched towards Goolburgah and Afzulpore were completely foiled in their pursuit by the determined hostility evinced towards them by the adherents of Shumsool Dowrah and other Jageerdars. As I conceive it necessary that I should be on the spot to superintend our proceedings in that part of the country where the Thugs had always met with more open support than in any other portion of the Nizam's Dominions, I proceeded to Goolburgah, where I had ordered all the parties to join me; and from thence made an attack on a gang which was known to have taken refuge in the vicinity of Kulleeanee. My people were on this occasion violently opposed by the inhabitants; and it was only by open force and at the risk of their lives, that they succeeded in overpowering their opponents, and making themselves masters of the persons of 33 Thugs, for some of whom large rewards had been offered by Government.

Most of the Thugs arrested on the above occasion had recently been engaged in a protracted expedition in which they had traversed nearly the whole extent of the Nizam's Territories from North to South—had perpetrated 17 distinct cases of murder, in which 22 individuals lost their lives; and had succeeded in regaining their homes, with a booty composed of gold lace valued at six thousand rupees, the greater portion of this, estimated at five thousand rupees, I succeeded in recovering, and on my return to Hydrabad, had the satisfaction of restoring it to the owners.

These proceedings left only one gang of Thugs, whom I had reason to believe were still actually engaged in Thuggee. This was a small party under Jaffier, composed principally of his sons and relatives, who had some years before left the vicinity of Kullumnoory, and taken up their haunts in the neighbourhood of Rajahpett. The father and one of his sons fell early into my hands; and the remainder of the gang would have shared the same fate had not the local authorities of a village, into which they were pursued, shut the gates in the face of my party, and allowed the Thugs to escape. Upwards of three years have elapsed since this occurred; and though the Nizam's Government inflicted a severe punishment on all concerned, which I was in hopes might have led to their apprehension, and an unremitting search has ever since been maintained, they have hitherto eluded pursuit; and the chance of discovering their retreat becomes in consequence every day less. With the exception of the remains of this gang, I know of no other which could possibly collect three initiated Thugs; and I apprehend they themselves have either fled into the Company's Territories, or found refuge in some of the most uninhabited tracts of this country on the banks of the Godavery to the Eastward of Nirmull.

Having effected the arrest of the principal Jemadars and the dispersion of the gangs of Thugs which had escaped your operations, in the manner described above, my attention was directed to the adoption of measures for eventually hunting down such of the fugitives as were scattered over the country seeking concealment in the most unfrequented Districts. This I have from experience found to be a most difficult task, as I have in almost every case met with the same difficulties in arresting a single individual as in tracing and apprehending the whole of a gang composed of a number of Thugs. These men seemed to know by intuition the persons who would afford them protection; and while they avoided the Taloogs of Hoosain Dost Khan and others, who had afforded me previous assistance, they were sure to be heard of in villages belonging to Jageerdars or Desmooks, who were known to pay little or no obedience to the orders of Government.

No analogy exists between the proceedings in the Thug Department, within the Territories of the Honorable Company, or any other well regulated State, and those which are carried on in the Nizam's Dominions, in which no system of Police can be said to exist. In the former the parties charged with this duty are armed with a warrant before which the gates of every village are thrown open; and the Police, if not aiding or furthering the object on which they are employed, dare not openly at any rate throw any obstacles in their way.

In the Nizam's Territories however the case is very different. A few of the principal Taloogdars, such as Hoosain Dost Khan and Ameer Nowaz ad Dowlah, evince the greatest readiness to afford me prompt assistance whenever called on by Government to do so. Their authority however does not extend to the villages held on military and other rent-free tenures with which their Districts are studded, and the Potails of which effect to attend to no orders, but those emanating from their immediate superiors. The consequences frequently are, that when a Thug is traced into a village of this class, the gates are shut in the face of the pursuing party, or should they have been allowed to enter from ignorance of the object of their visit, the Government orders when produced are treated with the utmost contempt, and if the party do not quietly take their departure they are generally forced to do so by the armed men stationed at the place on the part of the Jageerdars, or by the armed villagers themselves. Serious collisions have in consequence arisen in which several of my men have at times been severely wounded, and at others treated with the greatest indignity. In bringing these cases to the notice of the local Government, I have always received the greatest support from the present Resident, Major General Fraser, and peremptory orders have, in consequence of his remonstrances, been issued to the authorities to put a stop to such outrages: beyond this however little has been done by the Government, as in the majority of cases these orders have been disregarded, and the existing state of affairs is such as to render it obvious, that after the failure of one or two orders no good would result from pressing the matter any further, as by so doing the Government, whose willingness to do what is necessary cannot be questioned, would in the end perhaps be driven to confess its inability to carry its orders into effect; and to avoid such a result, might hereafter when applied to, withhold under some pretext or another the ready aid which it now affords, and which in many cases is of essential use to me in my proceedings.

With these difficulties to contend against it will not I hope be deemed surprizing that the number of Thugs arrested by me in the course of my operations have been so small. The total number in question amounts to 155, among whom however will be found the names of almost every leader of note, who had escaped your parties. The importance of these captures, and the amount of property of which they had possessed themselves at one of the last murders perpetrated in the Deccan by Thugs, may be estimated by the fact that the sums received at different times by me from the Government of India as rewards for the apprehension of the leaders alone, together with the value of the booty which it was my good fortune to recover and restore to its lawful owners, amounts in all to 10,000 rupees.

At an early stage of my proceedings I had made a request to the local authorities to give me immediate information of the sudden disappearance of any individual within their Districts, or the discovery of any dead bodies which there was reason to apprehend were those of travellers who had fallen into the hands of Thugs; and at a subsequent period a requisition to the same effect was made at my suggestion by the Resident to the Nizam's Government. I had recourse to this measure as one of precautions to enable me in the event of any of the fugitive Thugs venturing out on an expedition to gain the earliest intimation of their movements. I felt convinced from the opportunities which my position as a Superintendent of Police gave me of making enquiries of the numerous Marwarees who are in the habit of travelling from this to their native country, and from other sources, that the high and more frequented roads were perfectly free; but I could not feel assured, that such was the case in the less frequented parts of the country, where my parties had seldom occasion to go, and where, except by the above means, I could not ascertain if there was any reason to apprehend that any body of Thugs were on the move.

The total disappearance of dead bodies however for a period of three years, combined with the concurrent testimony of all the native authorities and travellers with whom I had an opportunity of conversing on these matters, had latterly convinced me that our most sanguine expectations had been attained in the complete suppression of a system which had for ages past been one of the heaviest curses that has fallen to the lot of any nation. Impressed with this belief, and congratulating myself on the share which it had been my good fortune to take, in bringing about this most desirable result, I leave it to the General Superintendent to conceive the feelings of deep mortification I experienced on the receipt of his communication of the 23d of July last.

Under this impression immediately on the receipt of his letter I addressed a communication (No. 1) to the Resident, Major General Fraser, requesting him to aid me in obtaining the necessary reports from the Nizam's Government, the Brigadier Commanding the Hydrabad Subsidiary Force, and the Officers Commanding the several Divisions of the Nizam's Army, to place it beyond the possibility of a doubt whether or not the Thugs had again commenced their operations in the Nizam's Dominions. Being personally acquainted with several of the most respectable Taloogdars in charge of extensive districts in the Nizam's Dominions, I, at the same time, addressed a communication to them to the same effect. The manner in which these parties have responded to my call, and the decided tone in which they express their opinion, that the system of Thuggee has been completely eradicated, will, I am confident, prove as gratifying to the General Superintendent as it has to myself.

I would particularly draw his attention to the documents which comprise the papers marked No. 1, as I conceive a better idea may be formed from them of the actual state of the case in connection with the existence of Thuggee, than from a perusal of the returns furnished by the Officers Commanding the Hydrabad Subsidiary Force, and the Divisions of the Nizam's Army, satisfactory as the latter undoubtedly are in as far as regards the impunity now enjoyed by our troops from the attacks of Thugs while proceeding to their houses on furlough.

I pass over the reply received from the Minister, as it contains merely an intimation, that during a period of twelve months none of the local authorities had brought to his notice the fact of dead bodies having been found in their Districts, or of travellers having suddenly disappeared, and proceed to notice those of the following from Taloogdars, viz. Mr. Dighton, Pestonjee Merjee, Hoosain Dost Khan, and Ameer Nuwaz-od Doulut, as I conceive from their superior intelligence and the better system of Police which they have introduced into their Districts, their statements may be implicitly relied on; and that it is very improbable that any murders could have occurred within the limits of their jurisdiction without their having been brought to their knowledge by their subordinate Officers. Independent of the above reasons I was induced to address myself to these individuals from a consideration, that their Districts which in the aggregate comprise one-third of the Nizam's Territories in value and extent, are situated in almost every portion of the sphere allotted to my supervision. Mr. Dighton has the management of large tracts of country in Telingana, comprising among others, the Taloogs of Maiduck, Khummum, Nulgoonda, and the Zemindaree of Jutpole towards Kurnool. Hoosain Dost Khan farms or holds in charge from Government the Districts of Nirmul, Digloor, Wurwal, Rajoorah, and Goolburgah. To the extreme West of the Nizam's Territories, on the Frontiers of the Bombay Presidency, lie the Districts of Bheer, Mominabad, &c., which comprise the Taloogs and Jageer of Ameer Nuwaz-od Dowlah; while to the North West Berar, Bala and Paeen Ghaut, are situated, the extensive Districts entrusted to the charge of Pestonjee Merjee.

I have been thus particular in describing the position of these Districts to enable the General Superintendent to trace their extent on the Map of the Nizam's Dominions, as I conceive situated as they are in every quarter, the absence of all dead bodies, and the sudden disappearance of no travellers within their limits, afford strong grounds of belief, that such is also the case throughout the whole of the Nizam's Territories.

The General Superintendent will perceive, from Mr. Dighton's letter which stands the first in the file of replies received from the above individuals, that within the last twelve months the perpetrators of every case of murder occurring within his Districts had been traced and punished: that no instance had been brought to his notice during the same period of any traveller or other individual having been suddenly missed; and that from the above circumstances and the general testimony of natives from other parts of the country, he had every reason to believe, that the system of Thuggee was entirely suppressed not only within his own Districts, but "*equally so throughout the Nizam's Dominions.*"

Pestonjee Merjee's letter (of which I have given a literal copy) is equally satisfactory, and proves, that within his extensive jurisdiction there is no reason to apprehend that the system, eradicated by your exertions in Berar previously to my assuming charge of the Department, had again been renewed. Only one instance has been brought to my notice of a dead body of a traveller having been found in Berar, which the local authorities had reported to me under the erroneous impression that he had fallen by the hands of Thugs. The unfortunate man was afterwards ascertained to be an inhabitant of Kamptee; and from the circumstance of no marks of violence having been discovered on the throat, his clothes and money being found untouched, and the circumstance occurring during the hot weather, it was apparent that he had not been murdered by Thugs, but had probably died from a stroke of the sun or the effects of sickness.

The next letter to which I shall refer is the reply furnished by Hoosain Dost Khan. The General Superintendent will perceive from it that since the date on which I addressed a communication to that effect several years ago, not a single instance has been brought to his notice of the occurrence of murders supposed to have been the work of Thugs. I would particularly beg to draw your attention to the concluding paragraph of this letter in which the gratitude of the people is feelingly expressed for the boon which the result of our proceedings have conferred on them, and is illustrative of the change in sentiment which the line of conduct pursued by you and followed up by myself, has effected on a bigoted Mussulman, who at the outset of our proceedings was one of the most bitter and prejudiced opponents we had to deal with! Hoosain Dost Khan's actions now keep pace with his professions; and it affords me much gratification to bear testimony to the disinterested assistance I have always experienced from him, and to which I am in a great measure indebted for the complete success which has always attended any proceedings within his Districts.

The statement made by Ameer Nuwaz-od Dowlah is so much in accordance with those which precede it, that I shall not notice it any further than to state, that it confirms the impression entertained by the other Taloogdars as to the total suppression of Thuggee. The discovery of one dead body is, I perceive, reported by his Naibs to Ameer Nuwaz-od Dowlah; but as only a small portion of the corpse of the traveller has been discovered it is difficult to form a conjecture as to the mode in which the unfortunate man met his death. From the circumstance however of some of the clothes still adhering to the body of which it would have been denuded had a party of Thugs been engaged in the murder, and the jungly nature of the country, it is not improbable that the traveller may have been destroyed by a Tiger,* died from exposure to the sun, or been killed by highway robbers, who are but too frequently to be met with on the high roads in this country.

The document to which I shall next call the attention of the General Superintendent are the returns furnished at my requisition by the Brigadier Commanding the Hydrabad Subsidiary Force, and the Officers Commanding the different Divisions of His Highness the Nizam's Regular Army, for the purpose of ascertaining if there was reason to believe that any of the men proceeding on furlough had fallen into the hands of Thugs. The Troops composing these Forces, inclusive of all ranks, amount to a body of 18,000 fighting men, and are at present cantoned at the Stations of Secunderabad, Jalnah, Ahmednuggur, Satara, Asseerghur, Boloram, Mucktul, Hingolee, Ellichpoor, Aurungabad and Mominabad. The five first Stations enumerated above are occupied by the Hydrabad Subsidiary Force, and the remainder by the Corps in the Nizam's Army. I mention the localities of the different cantonments to enable the General Superintendent to see at one

* The remains of the individual were found near the lair of a Tiger.

glance the extent of country which the men proceeding on furlough must pass over to and from their homes, the Madras Sepoys on their way to the Carnatic and Northern Circars, and the Hindoostan men, who compose the majority of the Nizam's Army, to Oude, Bundelcund and other Districts in the North of India, whence the Bengal Army draws its recruits.

Referring to the returns (marked No. 2) from the different Corps in the Hydrabad Subsidiary Force the General Superintendent will perceive, that in no instance have the Commanding Officers of Corps attributed the circumstance of men who have proceeded on furlough not having rejoined Head Quarters to their having fallen into the hands of Thugs. Out of the whole force it appears that only three men have been struck off in consequence of not having joined at the expiration of their furlough. All of these men had received an extension of furlough to enable them to rejoin, two on account of sickness, and the third (though no reason is assigned) probably on the same account. I shall take steps to ascertain the fate of these men, but with reference to the remarks made by their Commanding Officers there is every reason to believe they died a natural death or have deserted. Men who have been a short time in the service, when they proceed the first time on furlough, do so frequently for the purpose of getting married; and being persuaded to remain at home are in consequence struck off for desertion. This will probably be found to be the case with the Sepoy from the 29th Regiment referred to in the return from that Corps."*

* *Translation of a letter addressed by Major General Fraser, Resident at Hydrabad, to Rajah Chundoo Lall, His Highness the Nizam's Minister, dated 4th August,* 1840.

With a view to ascertain whether the system of Thuggee is suppressed or not, a communication was on a former occasion addressed to you to

In 1830, Mr. George Swinton, who was then Chief Secretary to the Supreme Government of India, and our best support which in the cause Mr. F. C. Smith and I had undertaken, wrote to him to say that he feared success

request that orders might be issued to the Local Authorities to the effect that whenever the dead bodies of travellers were found within the limits of their Districts whom they had reason to believe had fallen by the hands of Thugs, intimation of the same should be immediately given to Government for the purpose of being communicated to me. I now therefore address myself to you, to acquaint me, whether within the period of the last twelve months any of the Local Authorities have brought to your notice the fact of the dead bodies of travellers having been found within their Districts—if such has been the case have the goodness to inform me of the place and the circumstance under which the murder is supposed to have occurred : also have the goodness to state if within the period above mentioned any of the Local Authorities have written to inform you of the sudden disappearance of any traveller, or of the existence of Thugs in His Highness the Nizam's Territories.

You will oblige me much by giving the information above required.

(True Translation,)

(Signed) D. A. MALCOLM,
Assistant Resident.

Translation of a Note from His Highness the Nizam's Minister, in reply, received 4th August, 1840.

I have been favored with your note of this date (here recapitulates the contents).

Within the period of the last twelve months none of the Local Authorities have written to me accounts of persons being murdered, or the existence of Thugs. Had Thugs existed or persons been murdered, they would certainly have done so.

(True Translation,)

(Signed) D. A. MALCOLM,
Assistant Resident.

To H. DIGHTON, ESQUIRE,
&c. &c. &c.

SIR,—Being anxious to ascertain to what extent the system of Thuggee may still prevail within the Nizam's Territories, I take the liberty of

must be considered as altogether unattainable, for he had been given to understand by those who appeared to be well informed upon the subject, that the evil had taken deep root in all parts of India, and extended itself to almost every village community. There were certainly at that

addressing you with the hope you will have the goodness to furnish me at your earliest convenience with information on the following points:

1. The number of dead bodies discovered during the last twelve months within the Taloogs entrusted to you, which there is reason to believe are those of travellers who have been murdered by Thugs, such being easily distinguished from the bodies of men who have been murdered by highway robbers, from the circumstances of their generally being dug up by Jackalls from the beds of Nullahs and Ravines where they have been slightly buried, and offering no marks of violence, with the exception of those inflicted about the throat by the roomal, or cloth with which they have been strangled.

2. Any particular instances which may have been brought to your notice during the above period, of travellers or other individuals having been suddenly missed, whose disappearance is, in your opinion, suspicious.

In furnishing me with the information above solicited, I beg you will do me the favor to state your opinion, whether from your experience as the Superintendent of a large tract of country, you have reason to believe that the system of Thuggee, formerly so rife throughout the whole of the Nizam's Territories, has been entirely suppressed; or that you have come to the conclusion from the circumstance of dead bodies being discovered within your District, and from the otherwise unaccountable disappearance of travellers and others, that gangs of these murderers are still carrying on their depredations in the Deccan.

(Signed) D. A. Malcolm, *Captain*, &c. &c.

Hydrabad, 5th August, 1840.

The same to Pestonjee Merjee, Esq.

To Captain D. A. Malcolm,

Assistant Resident.

Sir,—I have the honor to ackowledge the receipt of your letter of the 5th August, and I have much pleasure in returning replies to the Queries therein put to me.

time very few Districts in India without their resident gangs of Thugs; and in some almost every village community was more or less tainted with the system, while there was not one District free from their depredations. No man aware of the fearful extent of the evil could ever have

1. During the last twelve months no dead bodies have been discovered in the Taloogs under my charge, which there was reason to believe, were those murdered by Thugs, those found were unburied, and the murderers of each have been seized and punished.

Secondly. No instance has been brought to my notice during the above period, of travellers, or other individuals, having been suddenly missed.

2. I am happy to state to you, that from the circumstances of no dead bodies having been discovered, which were not fully accounted for, in the Districts under my Superintendence, I have every reason to believe that the system of Thuggee is entirely suppressed in those Districts; and from the general observations of Natives, from other parts of the country, I should say it was equally so, throughout the Nizam's dominions.

(Signed) H. DIGHTON.

Camp, 14th August, 1840.

To CAPTAIN D. A. MALCOLM,

&c. &c. &c.

SIR,—I have the honor to acknowledge the receipt of your letter of this day's date requesting me to state whether the syatem of Thuggee is still carrying on in the Nizam's Territory, or if it has been already suppressed.

In reply I beg leave to inform you that in the Taloogas entrusted to me by the Nizam's Government, there does not appear any depredations of the Thugs, and to the best of my knowledge, I believe that during the last twelve months no travellers or other individuals were suddenly missed or fallen victims to them. I frequently get information from my several Naibs in the Taloog about the case of murders which were only caused from affrays, robberies, burglaries, &c., and not a single instance was known from which it would lead to suppose to have been done by the violence of the Thugs; and from this reason I have no doubt to believe that the Thuggee system in the Deccan must have been suppressed.

(Signed) PESTONJEE MERJEE.

Hydrabad, 5th August, 1840.

expected to see so much progress made in its suppression within so short a time; because no man could have calculated upon those many extraordinary combinations of circumstances upon which our success has chiefly depended, combinations which it behoves us gratefully to acknow-

Translation of a letter addressed by Captain D. A. Malcolm to Hoossain Dost Khan, Taloogdar of the Purgunnah of Degloor, Kundhar, Rajonah, Goolburgah, Wurwoly, &c &c., under date the 6th August 1840.

After compliments.—On a former occasion I wrote to you to request that in the event of the dead body of any traveller being discovered within the boundaries of any Kusbah or Hamlet under your jurisdiction, and it appearing that the said traveller had fallen by the hand of Thugs, you would acquaint me with the same. I now write to request that if within the period of the last twelve months the body of any traveller should have been discovered within your Districts, you will have the kindness to communicate to me all the particulars you may be able to obtain regarding it. I do not require, however, any information regarding such persons as may have been killed by highway robbers or decoits. Should you likewise in the above period have received accounts of any traveller having disappeared on any particular road, or in regard to the existence or otherwise of Thugs, have the kindness also to give me information on these points.

True Translantion,

(Signed) D. A. Malcolm, *Captain.*

Translation of a letter in reply from Hoossain Dost Khan, dated 17*th August*, 1840.

After compliments and repetition of the purport of Captain Malcolm's letter of the 6th instant.

On a former occasion you made a particular request on the above subject, and in compliance with your wishes I particularly enjoined the Naibs and Taloogdars in my service of the necessity of giving me the earliest intimation of the murder of travellers by Thugs; but up to this date no report has been made to me from any of the Naibs of any murders committed by Thugs. Upon the receipt of your present communication, I again addressed orders to the Taloogdars to furnish me with correct information on the above points. Replies under the seal of the Naibs of Digloor, Kundahr, Rajoora, Wurwal, Moodhul, Benoola, Goolburgah, Chircholee and Neermul, &c. have since reached me, stating, that within the last

ledge as providential interpositions for the benefit of the people entrusted to our rule—interpositions which these people themselves firmly believe will never be wanting to

year not a single instance of murder by Thugs, whether occurring in villages or on the roads, has been known.

Seeing that the best arrangements in this matter have been made, the whole of the inhabitants of the country, and Travellers have been emancipated from the fear of Thugs, day and night they raise their hands in prayer to state that in the days of Kings by-gone, no such peace and comfort existed. Thanks to Almighty God, the power of conferring this great boon, a source of great renown has been conferred on you from the begining of the world, in order that this matter should be so arranged. Where are the murdered men? How can there be any, when you do not even hear the slightest allusion to Thugs. The whole world are giving thanks for this. Many ill-disposed persons however following evil courses, such as Surdar Naiks, Putils, collect together for the purpose of theft, and commit dacoities in the country. I have stated the above for your information.

True Translation,

(Signed) D. A. Malcolm,

Captain, Asst. Resdt.

Translation of a further Letter received from Ameer Nuwozoodowlah,
10*th Rujjeeb*, 1256 *Hijree.*

After compliments.—On a former occasion, I in compliance with your request, instructed my Naibs to report to me any case of the discovery of dead bodies within the last twelve months, supposed to have been murdered by Thugs, and the existence of Thugs in any part of the District. I have now received replies from the Naibs to the effect, that within the period above referred to, no dead bodies of murdered travellers have been discovered, and that they have no knowledge of any Thugs. This is the purport of the letters I have received from various places.

From what the Naib of Kony Doroor writes, I have learnt that about eight days ago, within the limits of the village of Soumowah, in the pergunnah of the same name, belonging in Jageer to Meer Assudally, the dead body of a man was discovered near the haunts of a tiger. When persons went to enquire into the case, they found only the leg of a man, the rest of the body having been eaten by wild animals. A piece of rope and a blanket were found near the body. It could not be ascertained by

rulers, whose measures are honestly intended and wisely designed for the good of their subjects.

W. H. SLEEMAN.

Moradabad, 23*d November*, 1840.

whom the man was killed, or if he had been destroyed by a tiger, nor was it discovered to what caste he belonged, or who he was. No discoveries have as yet been made regarding him, or are likely to be brought to light hereafter. I enclose a Translation of the Mahratta letter, received from the Naib on the above subject, dated 1st Rujjeeb, 1256 Hijree.

True Translation,

(Sd.) D. A. Malcolm.

INTRODUCTION.

1. I was anxious to place on record, in an authentic shape, the proceedings of the Thug associations in all parts of India from the year 1827 down to their gradual suppression under our operations, which commenced with Major Borthwick, Col. Stewart, Mr. F. C. Smith and myself, under the auspices of Lord William Bentinck, in the year 1829;* and with this view, and with the aid of the late Lieutenant Briggs and Mr. McLeod, I prepared myself a narrative

* In 1826 a large gang of Thugs was arrested by Major Wardlow, on their way back from the Duckun across the valley of the Nurbudda; and sent by him to Mr. Charles Fraser, who had then the civil charge of the district of Jubulpore. He conducted the preliminary enquiries with great ability; and the whole were finally tried and convicted by Mr. Wilder. A still larger gang had been arrested in passing across the same valley towards the Duckun by General Adams and Major Macpherson in 1820, but all, except one individual, were afterwards released for want of the same skill in the peliminary enquiries. A still larger gang of one hundred and fifteen was arrested by Mr. Molony in 1823, in passing across the same valley on their return from the Duckun. They were committed by me for trial before Mr. F. C. Smith, and all convicted. These were, however, all isolated cases; and not otherwise connected with the subsequent plan of operations than as furnishing useful sources of information for our guidance.

of those of the gangs which resided between the rivers Nerbudda, Jumna and Sutlege, and often extended their depredations into the countries south of the Nerbudda and east of the Jumna. The narratives of the proceedings of the Oude gangs I left to Captain Paton, and that of the gangs of the districts between the Ganges and Jumna to Lieutenant Charles Brown. The bodies of several of the parties murdered have, in every one of the expeditions here narrated, been exhumed, and the records of the inquest held upon them by the local authorities, produced as evidence at the trial of the murderers ; and the general correctness of the record may I believe be entirely relied upon. I have a skeleton map upon a large scale of all India, shewing the lines of the several expeditions herein narrated, with the places where the bodies of murdered travellers have been exhumed ; and I had intended that this map should form a part of the present report, but I have been deterred from a dread of the expense.

2. The task of preparing such narratives as are here given—of conducting all those preliminary enquiries, which enable us to fix the dates of the particular cases of murder that are tried at the sessions, to place them in their proper position, and to connect them with those which have gone before, and those which have

followed in the same expeditions, is one of very great difficulty. An approver may be strictly correct in describing all the circumstances of a particular murder; and four approvers, examined at the same time in different parts of the country may agree in all the principal points; and yet they may all differ as to the expedition in which it took place. In the narrative of every one it may form one of a totally different series of murders. One believes it to have taken place on their advance; and places it as a link in the chain of murders perpetrated as they were going to Bombay—another believes it to have taken place on their return, and links it with the murders perpetrated on their way back—a third places it in the expedition in which they got the camel load of Spanish dollars; and a fourth declares that it was in that which took place the year after, and gave them the doubloons; and the only way to settle the point is, to bring them all four together, that they may compare recollected circumstances, which at last place it in its proper position. In describing these expeditions, the approvers can speak only as to seasons and religious festivals: like all natives of the lower or uneducated orders, they retain no recollection of dates—an event was before or after the festivals of the Mohurrum, the Hooly, the Dusseyrah or the Ramleela—it was in one or other of the four months of the rains, the cold season or the hot season—before or after the seige of Bhurtpore, or some other remarkable event. They will often describe with wonderful accuracy, a murder perpetrated many years ago, which made a strong impression upon their minds—the place of the murder and burial—the age, character, appearance and names of the different people murdered—their place of residence, the place whence they came, the friends to whom they were going, all shall be found on enquiry precisely as described by them in their narratives; and yet they will be often found to have placed this murder, so admirably described, in an expedition that really took place two years before or two years after that murder.

3. We often find it extremely difficult to verify, by a reference to the friends of the deceased, a murder that has been correctly described in these narratives; and we are very often obliged to authorize the local authorities to give a pledge, that they shall not be summoned to give evidence in a court of justice, before we can induce their nearest relatives to acknowledge that the deceased actually disappeared, and answered the description given of them by the murderers. No less often have we been obliged to give a similar pledge to bankers, whose money had been taken from murdered

treasure-bearers, before they could be prevailed upon to acknowledge that their money had been lost; or allow a reference to be made to their books. They all know that they shall not be able to recover any of the lost property, they feel no resentment against the murderers, whom they all consider as instruments in the hands of God—and they have no desire to make the sacrifice required to promote the ends of justice—" If similar losses are predestined, they " will take place in spite of all sacrifices; and " if not predestined, no sacrifices are required " to prevent them."

4. In a letter under date the 22d of October 1838, Captain Whiteford, an officer of my department at Berhampore, states, " I am preparing for another sessions, and have twenty-one " cases complete, with the exception of a few " witnesses to the defence. In one case, the " proprietors of the money taken from the murdered treasure-bearers, respectable bankers, " have been found; but they are now so much " in the habit of denying that they have ever " sustained any loss, that even in this case we " may have to commit the prisoners upon the " general charge, under Act XXX. of 1836." I will here mention one among a hundred instances that stand recorded in my office of the difficulties we have to encounter in getting men

to disclose what they know regarding these cases of murder. In November 1835, on my way from Jubulpore to Agra, I had to pass through the town of Dumoh, five stages from Jubulpore on the road to Saugor. Lieutenant Brown, of my department, accompained me that far for the purpose of investigating a case of murder which had taken place at the village of Soojuna, a few miles from that place. The case was this: One day in the cold season of 1814, a gang of two hundred Thugs encamped in the groves at Hindoreea on that road. The next morning about sunrise seven persons, well armed with swords and matchlocks, passed by the groves, bearing treasure to the amount of four thousand five hundred rupees, from Motee Kocheea, a banker at Jubulpore, to his correspondents at Banda. The value of their burthens was immediately discovered by these keen-eyed *sportsmen;* and Kesuree and Dirgpaul, Subahdars (who have since been hung at Jubulpore) and Feringheea Jemadar, three of the principal leaders, with forty of their stoutest and fleetest followers, were immediately selected for the pursuit. They followed them unperceived for several miles, till they had seen them pass through the village of Soojuna, beyond which they knew the road passed through a deep water-course well suited to their purpose. Here they suddenly closed in upon them, and put them all to death with their swords, before they could prepare for resistance. Just as they had done their work, and were preparing to make off with their booty, a Tanner, of Soojuna, came up with his buffaloe ; and to prevent his giving the alarm too soon, they put him to death also. A heavy shower of rain came on, during which no person was seen on the road, and the party, leaving the bodies unburied, made off with their booty, and rejoined the main body at the place appointed. When the rain ceased, some females left Soojuna on their way to Huttah, and finding the mangled bodies in the water-course, returned and reported the circumstance to their friends. All the people of the village men, women and children, went to look at the bodies ; and that of the Tanner was burned by his friends with all the usual ceremonies, while the rest were left to be eaten by jackals, dogs and vultures, who generally make short work of such things in India.

5. Some of the prisoners who had been concerned in this affair still remained untried in the Jubulpore Jail, and we thought it desirable to bring the case to trial if we could find the narratives of the approvers confirmed by the evidence of the villagers. These approvers, in describing the murder, agreed in all the material points except that of the number of persons killed, some

affirming that eight were put to death, while others declared that there were only seven.—Lieutenant Brown was suddenly called back from Dumoh, and unable, in consequence, to go himself to the village of Soojuna; he sent on an intelligent native officer with Feringeea, who pointed out the spot where the bodies had been left exposed. All the men of the village were assembled, but they all said it must be a mistake—that the murder of so many persons could never have taken place without their knowledge; and that they had none of them ever seen the bodies or heard any thing about them. We examined some of the oldest men at Dumoh upon the subject, and they told us that they had never heard of the murder of these seven men, but that they well remembered another that took place some few years before the time we mentioned, at Abhana, a few stages nearer Jubulpore. Seventeen treasure-bearers, who lodged during the night in the grove near that town on their way from Jubulpore to Saugor, were set upon by a large gang of Thugs, who strangled sixteen of them. The seventeenth laid hold of the noose before it could be brought to bear upon his throat, pulled down the villain who held it, and made good his way to the town. The native chief of the town, Rajah Durk Sing, went as fast as he could to the spot with all the followers he could collect; but he found nothing but the sixteen naked bodies lying on the ground among the trees with their eyes apparently starting out of their sockets: the Thugs had all made off with their treasure, and all the Rajah's efforts to trace them were fruitless.

6. Lieutenant Brown knew that the people of the village were all well acquainted with the circumstances of this murder, and pretended ignorance merely from the dread that they might be summoned to give evidence at the trial of the murderers in some distant court; and some months afterwards he wrote to the officer in the civil charge of the district in which the village lay, to request that he would give them full assurance that their presence would never be required in any court but his own. Mr. Doolan, the assistant to that officer, happened to be going through Soojuna from Saugor on deputation at that time; and when he encamped at the village he sent for all the old men of the place, and told them that if they would tell him the whole truth, he pledged himself that they should never be summoned to any other court to give evidence. They then took him to the spot, pointed out to him the places where the bodies had been found, and mentioned the circumstances of the tanner having been killed with the treasure-bearers, and buried afterwards by his friends, which accounted for the difference in the depo-

sitions of the approvers, for some had in the confusion of putting the treasure-bearers to death and seizing upon their treasure, never seen the poor tanner or heard of him. He had been quietly put to death by those who remained in the rear, to prevent the main actors in the scene from being interrupted in their work by travellers coming up behind.

7. All Lieut. Brown's attempts to discover the banker to whom the treasure which these poor men were carrying, or the friends of these men, were vain, till he pledged himself that they should none of them be summoned to the court to give evidence at the trial, a pledge he was enabled to give, after the prisoners had confessed their crimes, and been convicted and sentenced for other murders. The banker upon this pledge came forward with his books, which gave the date of the murder, the amount of the treasure lost, and the names of the seven persons who were carrying it and had been murdered. The friends of the murdered persons were then found, but neither they nor the banker would have willingly come forward without this pledge, though the courts in which the case was to be tried were not more than a mile from their doors. Such are some of the minor difficulties that we have to contend with in the suppression of this horrible system.

8. In my narratives I have included nearly all the expeditions made and murders perpetrated within the time specified by the gangs who resided in the Gwalior and Bundelcund states, Eastern Malwa and the Saugor and Nerbudda territories; and the late Lieutenant Briggs included in his narratives nearly all those perpetrated by the Kanthal gangs that resided in the western Malwa. But he was unable to complete any narratives of the expeditions of the Sooseea gangs, who resided in the Rajpootana states, and confined their depredations chiefly to those states and to the province of Gozerat. They were very numerous, but of recent origin; and the system had not yet attained among them that maturity which enabled the older gangs to extend their depredations every year with impunity into the remotest parts of India. They contented themselves with occasionally joining the larger gangs as they passed through Rajpootana into Gozerat, Khandeish, Malwa and the Delhie territories; or depredating independantly in small parties upon the roads that passed through their own countries. Their expeditions were generally very short; and these parties, small as they were, were often repeatedly re-organized in the course of one season; and it was found almost impossible to form any satisfactory narratives of their proceedings. Like the older associations they have, I believe,

been nearly all suppressed under our operations, and through the great exertions of this very talented and most excellent public officer whose death I have lately had to lament.*

* The following two letters may gratify the friends of this worthy young man, should this volume ever fall into their hands :—

To MAJOR W. H. SLEEMAN,

General Superintendant, Jubulpore.

Sir,

It is with feelings of deep concern, that I have to report for your information, the death of your Assistant Lieutenant W. T. Briggs, which melancholy event was caused by an attack of Cholera Morbus, and took place yesterday about noon in my camp at Nyagaon, a short stage west of Boondee.

2. As you are fully as well acquainted as I am, with the high qualifications of the deceased, and with his able and zealous public services, I need not dwell on the loss which the Government of India has sustained by his death.

I have the honor to be, &c.

(Signed) N. ALVES,

Agent Govr. General.

Rajpootana Agency, Camp Jehazpore, 1st May, 1831.

No. 694.

To W. H. MACNAGHTEN, Esq.,

Secretary to the Government of India.

Sir,

I have the honor to forward the copy of a letter I have received from Lieut.-Col. Alves, the Governor General's Agent in Rajpootana, communicating the death of Lieut. Briggs, a young officer of great promise, to whose exertions we have been greatly indebted.

2. He succeeded Mr. D. F. McLeod of the Civil Service in that field in the beginning of 1835. At that time we had been able to

9. Lieut. Brown has included in his narratives of the expeditions of the Dooab gangs nearly all the murders perpetrated, within the time specified, by all those who reside in the districts situated between the Ganges and the Jumna; but Captain Paton has not recorded in his narratives even the greater part of the murders perpetrated within that time by the gangs that resided in Oude. I may give his reason in his own words.—"Regarding the num-" "ber of men murdered within the last ten years" "in the kingdom of Oude, so far as they are" "detailed by the three approvers, Ramzan,

discover very little of the history of a very extensive class of Thugs denominated Sooseeas, who, in the course of four generations, had spread themselves over all Rajpootana. We knew them, as we then knew the river Thugs of Bengal, merely by the reports of other gangs who had occasionally fallen in and served for a time with them in passing through these states towards Gozerat and the Delhi territories. The sagacity, activity and *unweärying* industry of this young officer soon made us acquainted with their history and proceedings; and by his conciliatory spirit and amiable deportment, he everywhere secured us the cordial support and co-operation of the local authorities in the duty of arresting and bringing to justice the members of this class, and those of the older gangs from the Dooab, Gwalior and Bundelcund states, who had emigrated into Rajpootana. I have never had under me an officer on whose judgment, temper and industry I could more entirely rely; and there are few situations in which these qualities are more essentially necessary than in that which he has filled under me.

(Signed) W. H. SLEEMAN,

General Superintendant.

Genl. Supt's Office,
Jubulpore, 14*th May,* 1838.

" Dhoosoo and Imambux, in the abstract en-" closed, my impression is that they do not nar-" rate a tithe of the assassinations perpetrated " by the Thugs in their various expeditions; " but I found it a most perplexing labour, to se-" parate one expedition from another where the " route followed one month by any specific " gang, was perhaps in the following month in " part followed by a portion of the same " gang increased or diminished by the addi-" tion or retirement of members. The most " correct method of ascertaining the extent " of assassination would be to assemble all " the approvers, that they might correct each " other's errors and memories; but whilst the " trials are pending I could not thus assem-" ble the approvers, or allow them to narrate " those murders in the hearing of each other, " because in many of those murders these ap-" provers were to appear separately before the " Resident as witnesses, as they had appeared " before me; and had they heard the narration " of an expedition by any of the witnesses in " that particular case, they would have been " able to make their own depositions in the " trial correspond with what they had heard " narrated." After the trials were over, the narratives of other approvers were added, and all taken with great care and under proper checks; but still the whole murders recorded in them are but a small portion of the murders that were actually perpetrated in the kingdom of Oude within the time embraced by them.

10. It should be remarked that the gangs of Thugs who resided in the kingdom of Oude, unlike those who resided in other parts, generally confined their depredations to that country ; and their expeditions were, in consequence, generally less extensive and more frequent. It should also be remarked, that the murders perpetrated by these gangs in that kingdom, were but a part and often a small part of the whole, as the gangs from the Dooab, and those from Behar, were in the habit every year of visiting that country.

11. Maps similar to the one here given by Captain Paton for the kingdom of Oude, shewing the principal beles, or places of murder, have been given by several other officers for the division of country under their respective superintendence ; but I have thought it sufficient to add this one to the present volume, and to publish it without the addition of the very elaborate index prepared by Captain Paton, to show the number of murders which each of the men examined, had witnessed at each of the beles named. In forwarding to me this map, Captain Paton observes,—" It has occurred to me that

" the vast number of places of Thug murders, or " beles, put down in my map of Oude, and de- " noted by the black spots, may stagger the " belief of many, and lead to the conclusion, " that those fatal spots may have no existence " in reality, and may be merely the idle asser- " tions of Thug approvers vaunting of their " infamous assassinations. Now if you think it " worth while, it might perhaps be well to test " the truth of that map by a very simple process, " namely, by placing it before you, and calling " in Ouseyree, Kadir, Mooradun, Daveedeen, " Persaud, and other notorious Thugs, who " are known to be well acquainted with all the " high roads in Oude, and fixing upon any of " the high roads in the map, ask them to des- " cribe the most noted beles between any of the " towns or large villages. It strikes me that in " almost every case you will find that those " named by me in the map will be indicated by " them. The Resident here, Colonel Low, tested " a few places in this way, and found them cor- " rect; but then the approvers questioned by " him were those from whose information the " map had been formed by me."

12. I sent Captain Paton's map as I received it to Lieutenant Brown, who had charge of the approvers at Jubulpore, and requested that he would examine all those from the kingdom of

Oude, and those from the districts between the Ganges and the Jumna, who had been most in the habit of crossing the Ganges and depredating within that kingdom, and ascertain whether the places mentioned by them as the most *approved places of murder* (matubar beles) upon some of the principal roads, corresponded with those entered as such in this map. He did so, and they almost invariably named the same places as those inserted by Captain Paton; and had Lieutenant Brown been required to make a map upon the same scale from their information without any reference whatever to that of Captain Paton, I have no doubt that they would have been almost exactly alike, so well are those *sporting places*, known to all the Thugs who are accustomed to *hunt* over the same ground. If one of these men has not himself been present at a murder at any one particular bele, he never passes it without being told by his companions of the many murders they have seen there, of the remarkable circumstances that attended them, and of the booty they and their associates acquired from them.*

* I will not deny myself the gratification of publishing the enclosed letter from Captain McSherry:

Meerut, Decr. 1835.

To CAPTAIN SLEEMAN,

General Superintendant, &c. &c. &c.

Sir,

I do myself the honor to state that no native commissioned officer nor sepoy belonging to the 30th Regt. N. I. has this year lost his life by Thugs.

In forwarding the enclosed document I beg to mention, that the security from Thugs, with which the Oude territory may now be traversed, has frequently been observed to me by officers and men, natives of that country, and of whom there are upwards of four hundred

13. Except in some parts of Bengal where this system of murder was more extensively practised on the great rivers than on the high roads; and the Concan or coast of Malabar below the ghats, to which the gangs seldom penetrated; these beles, or favorite places of murder, abounded as much I believe in every part of India as in the kingdom of Oude. There were some districts in which no gangs resided, such as Khandeish and Rohilcund; but they were as much infested by them as any other parts of India, during the eight months of the year that they remained absent from their homes; and though a gang generally abstained from murder within the district in which their families resided, such district was never exempted from the depredations of gangs from other districts; and thus the annually returning tide of murder swept unsparingly over the whole face of India, included between the river Sutlege, the sea coast, and the Himmaleh mountains. Except in the districts of the Madras coast, extending from Cuttack down to Masulipatam, I am disposed to think that there is not at this time any

in the ranks of the regiment under my command. The men going on leave of absence proceed in large parties until they reach the frontiers of Oude, when many, in seeking their villages in remote situations, become solitary travellers, peculiarly obnoxious to the designs of Thugs; and the safety with which under such circumstances the sepoys may at present journey over a country formerly so much infested, has become a theme of their (I may say with truth) admiration.

I have, &c. &c.

(Signed) T. McSHERRY, *Capt.*

Commanding 30*th Regt. N. I.*

considerable organized gang of these assassins left in any part of India, to depredate either upon the rivers or upon the roads; but where so very many of their members are still at large, it is impossible to doubt, that they occasionally commit murders; as the greater part of these members have never learnt any trade, and will certainly never follow any other while they can, with any chance of success, pursue this.* The greater part of those who have eluded our pursuit have found an asylum in the service of native chiefs, and become members of their civil and military establishments; but they will quit those establishments and return to their old trade as soon as they find our pursuit relaxed. The qualities which gave them most influence among their fraternity are precisely those which endear them most to their new masters and companions; and while we find it easy to get from a native chief a Thug who is not worth having, because he can do no mischief if left alone, we

* I am preparing a report of a new class of offenders, who have of late years been extensively and successfully engaged in the murder of indigent parents for the sake of their children whom they sell to prostitutes and others at a high price when it is known that their parents can never come back to reclaim them. This system has not yet, I believe, been extended beyond the upper Dooab, the Dehlie territory, and Rajpootana and Alwur States; and I am in great hopes that the very active and able exertions of Lieutenant Mills, in the suppression of this system, will, at no distant period, be crowned with entire success.

find it extremely difficult to obtain from him any of those influential characters who could recreate their gangs in any part of India if left unmolested for a few seasons.

14. A Government that has effected so great a good over so vast an extent of country, inhabited by so many millions of our fellow creatures, in so short a time, and with the infliction of so very small a portion of suffering to the innocent, is assuredly entitled to the gratitude of the great mass of the people subject to its dominion; and I believe the great mass of the people do every where feel grateful for the benefit received, whatever may be said of the feelings of those territorial chiefs who have co-operated or acquiesced in our measures with reluctance. Mr. Smith, Major Borthwick, Colonel Stewart, Mr. Charles Fraser, and all those public officers who have assisted and are assisting the Government in effecting so great an object, will, I hope, always recollect the share they have had in the work with feelings of pride and pleasure.

Captain Reynolds will, I trust, at no distant period, with the aid of the other officers of the department employed in that quarter, be able to furnish an authentic narrative of the depredations of the gangs of southern India who were scarcely ever known to extend their expeditions across the river Nerbudda. They all however derived their origin, by descent or initiation, from the members of the old Thug clans of northern India, who, from time to time, emigrated into southern India, and there confined the trade almost exclusively to their own families, and to the sons of murdered parents adopted and brought up among them. We shall I hope some day have a similar narrative of the depredations of the gangs of Bengal and Behar; but this work must necessarily be retarded by the heavy loss we have sustained in that quarter in the death of a very able public officer and most estimable man, Captain N. Lowis, who is supposed to have perished with his three children on his way back from Sincapore to Calcutta in October last, on board the bark *Haídee.* In no man have I ever found united more of the qualifications requisite for the efficient performance of the duties entrusted to him than in Captain Lowis; and I shall here venture to give a memorandum on the system of river Thuggee in Bengal, drawn up by him only a few days before he embarked for Sincapore in April last. It was written in haste, and in the hurry of preparation for his voyage, and with a mind oppressed by his own indisposition and by his anxiety for an amiable and suffering wife, whom he attended to the grave only a few days before he embarked to return with her children.

Though he has not left one child to read this my humble testimony to his merits and eminently successful exertions in the cause of humanity, he has other relations to whom it will, I hope, prove gratifying.

MEMORANDUM ON RIVER THUGGEE IN BENGAL, BY CAPTAIN N. LOWIS.

" I reached Berhampore, and entered on my duties in the end of March 1836; and up to that period we had no knowledge of the state of Thuggee in Bengal, beyond the fact, that the crime existed to a great extent; and what vague and scanty information we possessed had been gleaned from the depositions of approvers of the western gangs, who either had, or pretended to have practised with the river Thugs.

" Of the list of Thugs at large made out from these sources, there were not probably six existing river Thugs; and they were for the most part deposed to by Emam Khan and Somun Khan, who, with their celebrated leader Jhowlee Khan (the fair) had on some occasions, joined the Bengal gangs. Of the Thugs thus denounced, two, Nooroddeen and Shookooroddeen, father and son, were arrested at their home at

Geereea, near Moorshedabad, at the very outset of my operations; and with them a man of the name of Sheikh Jagun was apprehended, supposed to be a son of Nooroddeen's. This man was detained till it was clearly proved that he was of different parentage, when the order was written for his discharge. Before it could be issued, however, I received a message from him, offering to be of service if I would ensure his escape from capital punishment—he was sent for and confessed—denouncing a number of Bengal Thugs, with whom he declared that he had many years before been engaged in a murder near Sooty; but that under the influence of fear he had fled. He stated that the gang was embarked on three boats, and comprised Thugs of a Mussulman gang from Bancoorah; of Kaets from Burdwan; and of the Maloo, or fishermen cast, from the north-western part of the Moorshedabad district. About this time my attention had been drawn to the supposed existence of a formidable gang of Mussulman Thugs, at the town of Bancoorah, by a letter from Mr. Stockwell to Major Sleeman, the General Superintendent. Through the kindness of the former gentleman, I obtained a copy of the proceedings in a case in which a large body of Mahomedans of that place had been denounced as Thugs, by one of their followers. These men I found had been arrested and sent to Jubulpore; and, on looking over their names, I discovered that many of them were mentioned in the depositions of Sheikh Jagun. At the period also of this man's confession, I received a communication from Mr. Skipwith, the Magistrate of Burdwan, with whom I had had some correspondence regarding some supposed Thugs in his zillah, stating that his Nazir, Gholam Alli, had furnished him with a list of persons whom he could prove to be Thugs. I found that the names of many of these persons also occurred in Jagun's deposition. By the time Jagun's confession reach Jubulpore, several of the Bancoorah Mussulmen had at length pleaded guilty* to being Thugs on the usual conditions, and been admit-

* Note by W. H. S.—For this we were entirely indebted to Lieutenant Charles Brown, under whose management these Bancoorah men had been placed by me.

These men had been arrested in Naraenpore, (a village in the Bancoorah district in Bengal, whose population consisted almost exclusively of Thugs) soon after their return from an expedition down through Cuttack to the temple of Juggurnath, during which they had perpetrated numerous murders.* One of the party turned King's evidence, and his statements were confirmed by a reference to the local authorities along the road; but as all the rest sturdily denied their guilt, the proof was not sufficient for their commitment, and they were sentenced to imprisonment on a requisition of security. Mr. Stockwell, the Commissioner in the Cuttack Districts, was soon after appointed to those of Allahabad, where he mentioned the circumstance to Mr. Wilson, who sent for the proceedings, and reported the circumstance to Mr. Smith and myself. The local authorities were prevailed upon to send them to Jubulpore, where they were, under the judicious management of Lieutenant Brown, induced to disclose, and offer their services. Nineteen, out of the twenty-one, were Thugs, and the other two Thug capitalists, who made advances

* The perpetrators of these murders have been since providentially discovered by Captain Vallancey. They are a small association of Thugs which have sprung up in Orissa, and never yet connected themselves with a gang from any other part. How they sprung we do not yet exactly know, but it seems clear that they are of recent origin, and that they have not had time to increase and throw off branches. By the vigilance and able exertions of the Magistrate, Mr. Ewart, who happily took immediate advantage of the information elicited by Captain Vallancey from a gang of this colony which he arrested immediately after the murder of several travellers, all the male adults of this Colony were secured, with the exception of two, who have fled the country. The property of murdered persons was found upon the gang and recognized by their surviving friends, and the bodies of their recent victims exhumed.

ted approvers. He was at once denounced by them as an old and practised Thug, who had repeatedly been engaged in murders with them; and the persons mentioned in the Burdwan Nazir's list were almost to a man included in that made out from their depositions. Feeling that I had now safe ground to act upon, I had all the suspected persons sent to me by Mr. Skipwith, to whose zealous co-operation I have been often and much indebted. Most of them were recognized as Thugs by Sheikh Jagun. I was now possessed of ample information; and arrested many of the persons deposed to by the Bancoorah men at Jubulpore. Among others Nuffer Sircar, said by them to be a Jemadar, was seized. When I came to examine him he seemed so utterly surprised at the amount of knowledge I possessed regarding the fraternity, that he begged to be allowed to confess, and tell me all he knew. This he did, and that without having a moment's intercourse with any person, but the soldiers of his guard. His confession comprised every single individual denounced by the Bancoorah approvers at Jubulpore; by Jagun at Moorshedabad; and those sent to by Mr. Skipwith. Nuffur Sircar was sent with an escort to apprehend the Thugs of his own neighbourhood;

to the Thugs when they entered upon their expeditions, and received payment with high interest when they returned. These two have been released on security for their future good behavior.

and during his absence six of the Bancoorah approvers, who had been sent to me from Jubulpore, arrived in two parties by different routes; and they individually recognized a great part of the Thugs who had, in the mean time, come in; and none of whom they could possibly have seen for nearly six years.

"Almost immediately after my arrival at Berhampore, three Bengallies were arrested at Derriapore, beyond Monghyr, by the Police of that district, and sent to Mr. Lang the Magistrate. It appeared that one of them, by name Madhub, had arrived at the Serai with a large sum of money in the hollow of a joint of bamboo. A short time afterwards two others, called Gunga Hurree Mitter and Kunhaye, made their appearance in pursuit of the first, accusing him of having stolen the money from their boat. Madhub retorted that they were Thugs, and wanted to murder him: this squabble excited suspicion, and ended in the result I have just mentioned, the arrest of all three. Within a day or two after this, two Bengallee boats of suspicious characters, full of people, with a large quantity of property of various sorts, and a considerable sum of money hidden in the hollow of bamboos, were seized at the town of Bar, between Monghyr and Patna. Gunga Hurree Mitter, the man above mentioned, in his examination before the

Magistrate, although protesting his own innocence, had allowed that he was acquainted with the persons of some of the Bengal Thugs; and he was in consequence sent by Mr. Lang with a guard to meet the persons who had been arrested in the boats. He immediately recognized most of them as Thugs; and on the way to Bar he had found a third boat empty in charge of the Zemindar of Ponaruk, which he pronounced immediately to be a Thug boat, and a man was seized in the house of this Zemindar with a bundle containing bobbin nett, balls of thread, and other suspicious property. He had, it appeared, been accompanied by four other men who made off on the first alarm. Immediately after the return of all these people to Monghyr, Mr. Lang received intelligence that four travelling merchants with English goods, such as lace, bobbin nett, &c. had disappeared close to the several places where all these men had been apprehended. The master of the four men had himself been attacked with the small pox, and obliged in consequence to hire a carriage, while his followers proceeded on foot with their packs. Mr. Lang very fairly concluded, that all the persons arrested, being evidently of the same class, having cognizance of each other—being all seized under suspicious circumstances, one of them with what seemed to be the property of the missing men, and near the very spot where there was every reason to believe that a foul murder had been committed, were of the gang, and all alike guilty. It was of course an object of importance in the absence of all, save presumptive evidence, to induce one of the prisoners to become witness on the part of Government against his associates in guilt. Gunga Hurree was the only one who appeared at all practicable ; but he, although evidently willing to be of use, most positively denied all knowledge of the murder in question, and protested that he had not accompanied the crew of the two boats, but had been travelling with a party on three boats, which he offered to search for. He was sent to seek for them, but his want of success only confirmed Mr. Lang in his belief that he was playing him false. I had been in communication with Mr. Lang regarding these men ; and was well aware that very many of the party, Gunga Hurree among the rest, were notorious Thugs ; and at this stage of the proceedings I requested that in case there were not sufficient evidence to prosecute them to conviction, they might be made over to me.* This was done ; and very soon after their arrival, Gunga Hurree confessed to a

* The following correspondence took place on that occasion between the Commissioner of Revenue and Circuit, Mr. Nisbet, and the Magistrate Mr. Lang.

W. H. S.

life spent in the commission of the most frightful murders as a river Thug, and he was admitted

No. 272.

To H. NISBET, Esq.,

Offg. Commissioner of Circuit for the 12th Division.

Sir,

I now have the honor to forward for your information a statement in Persian, shewing the particulars relative to the apprehension of several individuals in this district on suspicion of River murder and Thuggee, as requested in your letter of the 17th instant.

2. The statement is not as clearly drawn out as it might have been; but I have not had it altered, considering it desirable to forward for your consideration the whole of the papers connected with the business, though the proceedings are far from being brought to a close, in consequence of an application from Captain Lowis of Berhampore, that the people should be sent down to him, he having clear proof of a case of Thuggee against one of the party, *Muthoor Ghose;* and several of the others being mentioned in his lists.

3. You will perceive that more than suspicion now attaches to the defendants, with regard to their proceedings in this district; and that they have made away with four box pedlars on the river between Durriapore and Soorujgurah, having robbed them of money and property, amounting to 300 rupees.

4. From the circumstances connected with the apprehension of Gunga Hurree, Madhub, Chinibus, Kunnai, Sooklaul Zumeendar of Poonaruck, and others apprehended at that place, I was inclined to think that they were the perpetrators of this horrible crime; and it was my intention to have detained them here, and to have sent off Muttoor Ghose and the seventeen other defendants, apprehended in two boats by the Darogah of Durriapore, and who were merely detained here on suspicion, to Captain Lowis, with a request that he would not release any of them without giving me previous information; in fact, I had actually started them off for Berhampore, but they were detained at the ghat by adverse winds, when the day

as an approver. He still however denied all knowledge of the murder of the four mer-

before yesterday the Soorujgurrah Darogah brought me three witnesses, who deposed to their having seen the defendant's boats No. 2 and 3, at Oolypore ghat, where the missing box pedlars went on board them; and they recognized Muthoor Ghose, Gunga Hurree, Kunnai, Madhub and Chinibus as of the party.

5. Now if the evidence of these witnesses is to be believed, the whole of the defendants are more or less clearly convicted of having been concerned in this atrocious crime; and though I do not exactly credit what they say with regard to their recognizing the particular boats, it is not at all improbable that they may have seen the box pedlars go on board two boats manned by Bengallees, and that they may even have remarked Gunga Hurree and Muthoor Ghose and some others. The two I have mentioned are men of most peculiar and horrible countenances.

6. I have not been able to persuade any of the defendants to turn King's evidence. Gunga Hurree, who is no doubt one of the leaders, has as much as acknowledged that he is a Thug; but he will not give evidence sufficient to convict the defendants, and entitle himself to a pardon. Were you to offer him one, he might act differently. I have not spoken to him on the subject since evidence has been obtained to the box men having gone on board the boats.

7. You may perhaps be surprized that Ruffaint Oolah was not detained when he first mentioned that his companions were missing. The fact was that there was never any suspicion at the time what had taken place; and it was not till after Chinibus had been apprehended with English lace and balls of cotton in his possession, that on comparing dates, &c. &c. it struck me that the defendants in my custody must have made away with them.

8. You will perceive that Gunga Hurree and Madhub are stated by the Magistate of Burdwan and Beerbhoom, to be men of notorious bad character; and there is no doubt but a similar report with regard to the others will shortly be received. Since writing the

chants; but stated that the gang which he had accompanied on the three boats had committed

above, a report has been received from Burdwan, from which it appears, that all the defendants from that district are known to be river murderers. The report is with the case, for they all came from the same part of the country; and what they have stated in their defence is altogether contradictory and evidently false.

I have, &c.
(Signed) A. LANG,
Offg. Joint Magistrate.

Monghyr,
Fouzdarree Adawlut,
30*th June*, 1836.

No. 367.

To A. LANG, Esq.,
Acting Joint Magistrate, Monghyr.

Sir,

I have read and attentively considered the case of River Thugs apprehended by the Police under your orders; and the accompanying copy of a letter, addressed by me to the Register of the Nizamut Adawlut, will let you into my views regarding it.

2. The case, like others of the kind that I have seen, is a most painful one; just light enough in it to show that a fearful and horrible crime has been committed; and yet insufficient to admit of its ascertained authors being brought to condign punishment.

3. There is no doubt in my mind, that the monsters you have now in custody, took the lives of the four ill-fated Bengallee traders; but it is sad to think, that the proof you have obtained does not bring home the atrocious act with such clearness and precision as to give any hope of conviction if those miscreants are put on their trial for the specific act of murder.

4. My wish would be to commit them as *Thugs*. Of their being so, I think there is proof sufficient to satisfy the most fastidious judgment; and conviction to this extent, if either reason or humanity mingles with the constitution of the laws, ought to ensure condign punishment against such wretches.

upwards of fifty murders between Moorshedabad and Bar; and that they had last put to death

5. It will be of great consequence to you to obtain the evidence of Refayut Oollah, though you already have very clearly ascertained the point of time and place up to which the unfortunate travellers were publicly seen and conversed with.

6. If the reply of the Nizamut Adawlut is favorable to my view of the case, the whole of the Bengallee prisoners will be committed as "being Thugs; and taken while in the prosecution of their murderous employment."

7. Leekraj Sookaul, Motee Mullah, Chooney Mullah, Boodhoo Sykulgur, will be committed as accessaries and abettors of the principal culprits.

8. Should, unfortunately, the opinion of the Court be averse to the commitment on this ground, I would then send the whole of the Bengallees, ironed and properly guarded, to Captain Lowis, with a copy of all such parts of the proceedings held by yourself and your officers, as relate to them. I have no doubt that their crimes will meet with some retribution through his agency.

9. Leekraj, &c. will, upon the supposition of the transmission of the rest, become liable to the poor redress of being put under requisition of security, as infamous characters, and in league with the worst description of public criminals.

10. Your two Thanadars of Soorujgurrah and Durriapore have, I think, shewn a very laudable diligence in the long and arduous enquiries which they have had to conduct. I should be inclined to consider favorably their claim to a reward; but it will be as well to await the issue of the case before proposing any of this kind in their behalf.

I have, &c. &c.

(Signed) H. NISBET,
Offg. Commissioner of Circuit.

Commissioner's Office,
12th Division, Bhagulpore,
the 12th July, 1836.

P. S. The File of your proceedings is herewith returned.

three treasure-bearers of the Zemindar of Oleepoor, and obtained as a plunder 500 rupees. He added, that there was a Mussulman Thug in my jail, Sheikh Gholamee, who probably knew of the crime I was so anxious to trace; as he had met him at Bhagulpore when returning from an expedition under Ramchunder Sein and

To the Register of the Nizamut Adawlut,
Fort William.

Sir,

I beg the favor of your obtaining the Court's opinion on the following point, which is of importance to the issue of a case on which my orders are now called for.

2. Is then the fact of being Thugs by profession, and being actually engaged in this cruel and murderous vocation, without a specific charge of attempting or destroying life, sufficient to warrant the commitment of a set of criminals for trial at the Sessions; and ought it to ensure such miscreants a commensurate sentence?

3. The provisions of Regulation VIII. of 1818, I considered futile and absurd for dealing with wretches of this description.

4. The great prevalence of this fearful species of crime: the secrecy and facility with which it works—and the lamentable degree of difficulty that attends its detection; conspire, in my judgment, to call for the fullest extension of legal vengeance against it.

5. The blood of hundreds of miserable victims shed where no pitying eye or succouring hand was nigh to rescue, calls out of the ground for retribution!

6. It is my opinion that satisfactory proof of the detestable livelihood of these enemies of mankind should be sufficient to warrant their receiving the utmost sentence short of death, that the Law will warrant.

several other notorious Jemadars, and it was their boat he had pointed out to Mr. Lang's people at Ponaruck—I sent for Sheikh Golamee, and he was immediately induced to confess by his kinsmen, the Bancoorah approvers from Jubulpore who had by this time arrived. He deposed to a long and murderous expedition; and stated that the boat in question was indeed theirs, but he denied all knowledge of the unfortunate boxmen. About this time a very notorious Thug Jemadar, Sonatun Dass, was arrested by me in the Burdwan District. On his arrival he begged me to spare him on condition of his giving me very valuable information. I admitted him an approver on the usual conditions of exemption from the punishments of death and transportation, and he wound up a confession of twenty years spent in murder, by stating, that he had accompanied the party seized on the boats so far as Bar, from which, place, he and four others (who had in the mean

7. The occasion which has led to this reference is one in which justice, humanity, and the due execution of the Laws, are deeply concerned. I therefore deprecate delay; and respectfully solicit that the subject of my communication may have the Court's earliest attention.

I have, &c. &c.

(Signed) H. NISBET,

Offg. Commissioner of Circuit.

Comr.'s Office, 12th Dn.
Bhagulpore,
12th July, 1836.

W H. SLEEMAN.

time been apprehended by me at their homes) had fled. These men he pointed out at once when the prisoners were all shown to him, indicating, as one of the four, the man who had been seized alone in the house of the Zemindar of Ponaruck, with the thread, &c. To my great surprize however neither did Sonatun Dass' confession contain any notice of the four men; and I began to be extremely perplexed. As my only seeming chance I now decided on separating the members of the gangs, and sent to Chuprah, two members of the party who had been seized on the two boats at Bar, Bhowanee, a Jemadar, and Ishur Higra. With them I sent Madhub, who had been apprehended with Gunga Hurree Mitter and Hurree Ghose, a Thug who was deposed to by Sheikh Gholamee as having been of his party.

"These men with several others who accompanied them all confessed to Captain Ramsay at Chuprah, were admitted approvers by him on the usual condition and ordered back to me at Berhampore.

"The moment Sonatun Doss learned that Bhowanee and Ishur Higra had confessed and become approvers, he, before their return made a full confession of the murder of the four unfortunate merchants, which from fear he had hitherto suppressed; and on their arrival, Bhowanee and Ishur Higra fully confirmed his statement of this case. Mahdub's confession corroborated that of Gunga Hurree; and it was clearly proved, that the three treasure-bearers were missed at the very spot, and with the very sum, deposed to. I may add as another extraordinary circumstance, that eight or ten months after these confessions, the three boats which Gunga Hurree's gang had abandoned, on hearing from one of their confederates of the arrest of the gang on the two boats at Bar, and which I had been so long searching for in vain, were accidently discovered by one of our Nujeebs going in charge of prisoners to Chuprah. He saw three empty Bengallee boats lying at a village on the bank of the Ganges near Hadjepore in Tirhoot; and on enquiry, learned that they had been left by a body of men pretending to be pilgrims, who promised to come back, but never did so. He reported the circumstance to me and I sent for the boats which were fully identified. The difficulty in tracing these boats had arisen from this, that all the approvers were absent from the party when the gang fled from the boats and knew not where they had been left. Hurree Ghose's deposition in every respect confirmed that of Gholamee, and established what the latter suppressed, but now admitted to be the fact, that his relation Sheikh

Nehal Jemadar had also been of the party. Gunga Hurree and Madhub both mentioned having met near Bhagulpore a fourth gang in two boats, under Jewun and Gunesh Jemadars, both of whom had been seized and were afterwards admitted as approvers; and thus the seeming casual arrest of the three Thugs at Durriapore became the providential means of securing correct information of four gangs; and I have no doubt of bringing to conviction one hundred and twenty of these monsters, by whom, on the last expeditions, nearly one hundred of their fellow creatures had been pitilessly destroyed.

"In the list of Thugs sent to me from Jubulpore, deposed by the Bancoorah approvers, was a very notorious Jemadar, *Ramlochun Sein.* I sought for him long without success; and although I had arrested his maternal uncle, Sunker Sircar, the greatest of the Bengal leaders, I could obtain no tidings of him. His house in the Burdwan District had been searched in vain. One morning when sitting in Court, a Bengallee petition was given into my hands from a man outside, my Sheristadar proceeded to read it to me as usual aloud, and it appeared to be from a person of the name of *Ramlochun Sein* complaining that his house had been most unjustly searched by my orders. I sent for him, and he appeared to be an exceedingly decent looking man—was a good Persian scholar, and handed several official perwannahs (warrants) proving that he had been employed in the Collectorate at Bancoorah, and as Ameen of the European bazar at Bèrhampore, and in other offices. I examined him closely, although I thought that some unhappy mistake might have occurred. He declared that he never had travelled; and that he had no relationship with any person of the name of Sunker Sircar. This was unfortunate for him, for Sunker happened to be at that moment heavily ironed in my guard; and there was another prisoner also in jail whom I knew to be a brother-in-law of the *Ramlochun Sein* I was in search of. They were sent for; and both immediately claimed the petitioner as their kinsman. He was the man and had failed in trying too bold a ruse. He was one of the party I sent to Chuprah. He was admitted an approver, and is by far the most valuable I have. He is a man of extraordinary ability; and he had actually been employed in the way he mentioned. He was a great leader; and, although a young man, had been at work for 15 years. When any thing occurred to excite alarm in the pursuit of Thuggee, he managed, from his scholarship, to get some appointment in which he kept quiet, till the storm blew over. His intelligence has enabled him fully to appreciate the strength of our system; and the folly of practising deceit, when sooner or later it is sure to be detected.

"There was another extraordinary coincidence with the commencement of our operations in Bengal. One of the first letters I received after my arrival at Berhampore, from my brother Mr. John Lowis, who was at the time Commissioner of Circuit in the Dacca Division, conveyed to me the notice of a case of river Thuggee which had just been tried at Dacca, and the gang prosecuted to conviction by Mr. Martin, Magistrate of Furreedpore. Of the Thugs of those districts we had, up to that period, absolutely no knowledge whatever. I received the two men who had been admitted King's evidences: they confessed and were admitted approvers. The convicted Thugs were made over to me by order of the Hon'ble the Governor of Bengal; and many approvers were obtained from among them: thus securing to us the necessary information at the very time when alone it could be serviceable. There can be no doubt that had there been no Officer of our Department on the spot to graft our system upon the events described, that they would have been lost as means of enlarged good altogether. The gang arrested at Monghyr would have found security without difficulty; and the Dacca King's evidences would soon have been at their old work again, had they been turned loose upon a district swarming as theirs then did, with Thugs, for one of them was a most important leader. It is impossible, in a narrative diffuse like this, to preserve with sufficient impressiveness the very remarkable coincidence of these circumstances.

"There is only one more occurrence which seems to deserve particular notice. In October last I sent a party of Nujeebs with four approvers, towards Cuttack, for the purpose of making investigation on the spot as to several murders of an old date that had taken place on that road. By the time I speak of, the alarm had been so thoroughly given that it had become exceedingly difficult to make any arrests.

Indeed so hopeless did search for the fugitive Thugs appear, that the Officer was instructed not to occupy himself in it; but as usual he was provided with a list of Thugs still at large, and a warrant for their apprehension should he happen to fall in with them. One day while the party was engaged in making a plan of the locality of a murder deposed to by one of the approvers, four Thugs of great note came up along the road, and were immediately recognized by the approvers, some of whom were their kinsmen, and seized. Two of these men,

Nuddeea Chand Sircar and Casseenath Bukshee, were noted leaders; and Jugmohun Doss, a Chaur ;* and Huradhun Sircar, a brother of the

* *Note by Capt. Lowis.*—The Chaur is a strangler: he knows the incantations and prepares poojahs too for any one else to offer. He strangles in every murder, takes the omens when present, and is a man of very great consequence. There was only nine in the whole of my districts, five of whom have been seized.

The following memorandum of a conversation on the subject of a Chaur was sent to me by Captain Lowis :

Substance of conversation with Ramlochun Sein and Nuffez Sircar, Jemadars.

Q. How many Chaurs are there now ?—A. Khittoo, Sircar of Aimah ; Churn Doss, Byragee ; Teluk Ghose, his brother Kishenpershaud Ghose, who is also a great Jemadar ; and Jugmohun Doss : the others are all dead.

Q. Who were the others ?—A. Bullai Sircar, Jemadar Rampersaud Sircar, Jemadar Allum Doss Kaet and Allum Doss Byragee ; Mohun Sein, Anund Haldar (Buneea), Puteet Haldar (Buneea), Teekaram Sircar, Deendyal Haldar (Buneea), and Kishen Haldar (Buneea). We have heard also that Sartuk Mooseeb of Bancoorah was one, and there were several among the Mussulmans of Bancoorah.

Q. How is a Chaur initiated ?—A. We do not know the munters (incantations) nor the nature of the poojah (religious rites,)—they are very sacred and may not be witnessed by any but the Chaurs : the expence too is great, and used formerly to be much greater—four, five, or six old Chaurs are required to initiate a new one. There are first two poojahs held in some very private place in the jungles,—never in a house ; and at these none but Chaurs are present. Afterwards a third poojah (also confined to the Chaurs) is held in the fields near home ; and then a fourth at the house of the initiated, or his patron ; and to this last only are admitted such other Thugs as may be especially invited. We never were present.

first named leader. These men had all been of the same expedition with Gunga Hurree,

Q. Is there any particular ceremony performed before or after the murder?—A. In the evening or at night after a murder the Chaur takes nine cowries which he washes in the river; and then while he performs the poojah (holy rites) places them in the hands of some other man. He takes a pān leaf which he spreads and uses instead of the toolsee, and performs poojah; consecrating the gamcha (strangling cloth), he puts the pān leaf in a lotah, (brass jug) full of water, and wraps up the gamcha on a kutora, (brass cup) which he places over the lotah. No other person but the Chaur is allowed to touch them; and while the poojah (religious ceremony) is going on all must keep themselves pure: none but the Chaurs know the munters, (incantations) used in this poojah. In the morning the Chaur drinks the water in the lotah, and washes the gamcha. The nine cowries which he had, after the poojah, taken again from the person who held them, he puts by: no one else may touch them. After the cowries of three or four affairs are collected he buys with them sweetmeats, and eats them. Should any of the cowries be lost it is considered a dreadfully bad omen, and all return home. The poojah we have described we call the gol larajoo.

Q. What other poojahs have you!—A. Suppose we have made 100 rupees by a murder, two rupees five annas would be laid aside for the poojah, of which sum two rupees would go to meet the expense of goor, liquor, &c. and five annas be offered to the goddess Davey Mai: after the completion of the poojah the goor, &c. are eaten by all; and till its completion all must fast, and avoid pollution: this poojah is called the dansh marani.

Q. Have you any other?—A. Sometimes we keep the proceeds of several affairs for a grand poojah, when sweetmeats and liquor are offered to the goddess Davey Mai.

Q. Have you always a Chaur with you?—A. We kaets always have one if possible. The Jemadars of other castes, such as Sham Sircar (Kotal), Bhippoo Pundit, Jewun Haldar, Rugonauth (Kotal) have no Chaurs; and they perform all the poojahs themselves.

noticed above; and from the time of their leaving the boats they had been engaged in unceasing flight, between Burdwan, Hoogly, Juggernauth, Sulkeea and Jessore, then back to Juggernauth, where they were going for the third time when apprehended. They had committed upwards of eight murders in their flight. All this I learned from Casseenath Bukshee, who confessed, and was admitted an approver on the usual conditions the day after he arrived. He also informed me of the reasons for leaving their boats on the expedition with Gunga Hurree. Casseenath Bukshee was detached with a guard two days after he confessed, for the apprehension of Sreemunt Sircar, an elder brother of Nuddeea Chand's, and Nund Coomar Dass, both very noted Thugs, and who had been practising with them just previous to their apprehension. In this he was

Q. Have the Eastern Thugs of Dacca, &c. any Chaurs?—A. We do not know, we never meet them; and know nothing of them: they keep to their own rivers. We have heard that Ramtonoo Mojumdar of Jessore, always had one: he used to go west.

Q. When a Chaur is on board can any one else perform the poojah?—A. No one else dare even touch the sweetmeats, &c. used in it!

Q. What symbol is worshipped in the dansh marani and the chaka poojahs, the sword (gheel) or the gamcha, strangling cloth?—A. On an expedition the gamcha is always the symbol used—at home, before setting out, we use the sword.

(Signed) N. LOWIS, *A. G. S.*

W. H. SLEEMAN.

successful, having seized them at Sulkeea, opposite Calcutta. It may be well to mention some circumstances which seem to me peculiar to this horrid system in Bengal. The Western Thugs appear to have been rapidly falling off from the practice and usages of their fathers; and to have constantly committed crimes against their system, such as murdering women, &c. to which they themselves attribute all their misfortunes. In no one known instance have the Bengallees offended in this way: they are, and consider themselves the purest of all Thugs; and this I think may well be turned to account: that the crime should have been attacked, and I hope stricken down, if our proceedings be followed up, where the Thugs had no one reason to assign which could satisfy their superstition as a reason for their misfortune.

"I would notice also the extraordinary audacity and success with which the river Thugs seem to commit their murders—I know of repeated instances in which ten, eleven and twelve persons have been put to death by boat's crews, varying from only fourteen to sixteen in number. I am credibly informed that last year seven men were murdered at one instant by a crew of nine Thugs. In very many instances, too, the persons put to death were sepahees, generally west-country men, who are notoriously a far stronger and braver race than the inhabitants of Bengal.* The small size of the

* *Note by W. H. S.*—In April 1828, two non-commissioned Officers and eight Sipahees of the 52d Regiment of Native Infantry, then commanded by Colonel Dunlop, and stationed at Chittagong, having been transferred to the Invalid establishment, embarked on board a boat near Comilla in the Tipperah District, to proceed up the river Ganges to Allahabad, leaving on the bank a little serving boy whom the boatmen refused to take. Soon after they had embarked they were all strangled; and the boy who had unperceived by the boatmen, followed them along the bank, became aware of their fate returned to the Regiment, and related the circumstances of the murder. Many boatmen were taken up on suspicion by the Magistrate of the District Mr. Thompson; but they were all soon released as the boy's recognition was very unsatisfactory; and it has since been discovered by Lieutenant Sleeman employed in that quarter, that they were all really innocent men. Twelve more Sipahees of this Regiment were strangled by the river Thugs while it was stationed at Chittagong. In the year 1819, a native Commissioned Officer and sixteen Sipahees belonging to the 37th Regiment Native Infantry, were murdered at one time in two boats on the Ganges, as stated in the following letter, and afterwards ascertained by Captain Lowis.

Agra, *9th November*, 1836.

Sir,

I have the honor to acknowledge your letter, dated 1st of Sepember 1836, enquiring whether the Native Officers and men of the Regiment under my command have rejoined from Furlough. In reply, I beg to state that all (with the exception of one or two, satisfactorily accounted for) have safely rejoined from leave of absence; indeed I may add that within the last eight or nine years no casualties have occurred during the absence of men from their Regiment, with the exception of the Thuggee affair of 1829 near Lucknow, which has already been brought under the cognizance of your department. From my own experience I am happy to state, that of late years murders by Thugs are far less frequent than formerly, which I entirely attribute to the active and vigorous measures adopted for the detection and punishment of the offenders.

boats, too, is another extraordinary circumstance; so much so that some of the murders stated

With reference to your circular of September 1835, I beg to state the following particulars of a heavy loss which occurred so far back as 1819.

In the month of April 1819, the Native Commissioned Officer and sixteen Sipahees mentioned in the margin, left Berhampore, where the Regiment was stationed, and proceeded by land to Mussau, about eight coss from Sukree Gully on the Ganges. At that place a boat was lying to, which belonged ostensibly to a Bengalee Baboo, who stated to the men, that he was going to Benares for the purpose of performing pooja (worship) and invited them to accompany him, for the sake of their protection.

A Sipahee of the name of Berinch Sing, transferred afterwards as a Havildar to the 53d Regiment by G. O., 31st October 1827, went on board the boat: but as there was not sufficient room for him he returned immediately; also a Naek Deerga Singh, transferred in 1820 as a Havildar to the 2d Battalion of the 1st now 4th Regiment Native Infantry, who fortunately came back for the same reason.

On the return of the above two men from Furlough, they mentioned the circumstance of these seventeen individuals going on board the boat, where it was supposed they had been murdered, as they never reached their respective homes; nor have they ever since been heard of. *(a)*

Having but lately returned from Cuttack, where the Regiment had been employed on service, these men had accumulated considerable sums of money, which they were carrying with them.

I have, &c.

Signed J. HERRING, *Major,*
Commanding 37th Regt. N. I.

To Capt. W. H. SLEEMAN,
Genl. Supt., &c. &c. Mussoorie.

(a) Note by W. H. S.—The case of 1829, to which Major Herring alludes, being an interesting one, I shall venture to describe it. A

to have been committed upon them would seem incredible, on any but evidence, which it is im-

Havildar and four Sipahees from the 37th Regiment, then stationed at Kurnaul, were proceeding together to their homes near Lucknow, when they fell in with a gang of Thugs, who pretended to have escorted an European Officer to Futtehgur, and to be on their way to their homes in the neighbourhood of those of the party. They spent the night at Julalpore; and as the party were anxious to make the most of their furlough, they made long marches; and, as usual, left the place with the gang long before day-light. The gang, pretending to be on escort duty, was armed, while the Sipahees, not half the number, were without their arms. They had gone on about two miles when the Havildar had some vague suspicion of danger, and unperceived sat down on the long grass by the side of the road—the party had not advanced fifty paces from him when the signal was given and the Sipahees were strangled. The Havildar heard their stifled screams, crawled to the village of Khujolee, and brought the Police to the spot where he found the dead bodies of his companions, and had them taken to Lucknow; but all search for the murderers was fruitless.

In the beginning of 1835, one of this gang, then with me at Jubulpore, described this case, and stated that till they counted the dead bodies when about to bury them, they had supposed the whole five to be murdered. Finding one had made his escape in a mysterious manner, they were alarmed and ran off, leaving the bodies unburied. I made the necessary reference to Lucknow, and found the bodies had been discovered, and the statement so far confirmed; but I had no hope of ever being able to discover the survivor of the party. Some months after this, the Havildar, mentioning to his Commanding Officer at Nusseerabad, the narrow escape he had once had near Julalpore in Oude from the hand of Thugs, was sent to Lieutenant Briggs of my department then at the station; and he described the circumstances just as they had been described to me, stating "that "if he were to live to eternity, the recollection of the horror of that "moment, when his poor companions had been strangled within a "few paces of him and within his hearing, would make him shudder." Lieutenant Briggs forwarded his deposition to me: and, as the rest

possible to resist—it is only another proof of the exceeding dexterity of the murderers. I have as yet been unable to carry any trace of the crime from the Burdwan and Bancoorah Districts (in both of which it abounds) into Hooghly and towards Calcutta, where, prima facie, it might be supposed to exist to a large extent. The approvers of the districts above named have always positively denied any knowledge of Thuggee in this direction ; but state, that it probably exists. From their ignorance we might argue its non-existence, but for an extraordinary circumstance which I have met with in the history of two other Thug clans, I found that a very formidable gang of the Maloo caste, under Jewun and Guness, which acted principally from the head of the Jelinghy and the north-eastern frontier of Moorshedabad, were in strict alliance with a gang of their own caste in Pubna ; and had besides many Mahommedan and other adherents in that zillah and Nuddeea. They almost invariably practised up the river Ganges as far west as Chuprah.

"I discovered that there was another most formidable gang of Pubna Thugs of the Kaet

of the gang had now been secured, and others had been admitted as King's evidence at Lucknow and Cawnpore, the case was sufficiently complete for trial, and the witnesses being sent to Lucknow, it has been there tried by the Resident.

W. H. SLEEMAN.

cast, with a few Mussulman followers, who invariably acted with the Thugs of Dacca, Furreedpore and Mymensing, haunting the Ganges lower down between Comillah and Bhugwangolah, and the other minor streams; and it is sufficiently proved, I think, that the two classes of Pubna Thugs had no knowledge of each other: so great was this mutual ignorance, that Suroop Dutt, a great leader of the eastern gangs, acted for several years as Ghat-mangy of Bhugwangolah, and used there constantly to embark victims on the boats of his comrades, and join them in murders, without the Thugs of Jewun's gang, who constantly embarked from that place, being even aware of his existence. Of these facts, singular as they appear, there can be no doubt; for Jewun, his brother, and his cousin Guness, and Netun Jemadars, and several other leaders of their gangs, are now approvers; and there are also approvers from both clans of the Pubna Thugs, and the eastern gangs, from none of whom can it be discovered that there was any intercourse between these distinct clans of murderers though residing in the same district; this may teach us the danger of considering that we have finally eradicated a crime much of which may be every where lying hidden from us. Thus the fullest information regarding the gang of Jewun and his brother would have given no indication of the existence of Thuggee in the adjoining districts.* It is right to state that Mr. Mills, when Joint Magistrate of Pubna, many years ago, obtained information regarding nearly every Thug of every class in his district; he seized and brought them to trial on grounds which, with our present light on the system, would have sufficed for the conviction of all. I cannot imagine how they came to be thought deficient even then; and it is melancholy to reflect, that the exertions of this excellent officer should have been defeated, and a large proportion of these wretches sent back to their work of murder without even the precaution of placing them under the surveillance of the Police. To conclude, there seems no doubt but that this horrid crime has been fostered by nearly all classes in the community—the landholders, the native officers of our courts, the police and village authorities—all I think have been more or less guilty; my meaning is not of course that every member of these classes—but that individuals varying in number in each class, were concerned. The Foujdaree Police gomastahs† have in many instances been

* *Note by W. H. S.*—When Captain Lowis speaks of *the existence of Thuggee* in this paper, he must be understood to mean, the residence of Thug associations within the districts indicated; and not the depredation of such associations, who extended their depredations through every district around their abodes.

† I know not what Police officers bear this designation in Bengal; but conclude that they are subordinate police reporters; or petty police supervisors. W. H S.

practising Thugs; and the chowkedars, or village watchmen, frequently so. It is much to be feared that men so respectable in position as to make it seem almost incredible that they should give protection to such criminals, have in fact done so; for it appears out of the question, that the total population of a village should be Thugs engaged in the regular practice of Thuggee, and several of them frequently apprehended on the gravest suspicion of that crime, without the cognizance of the Zemindars, (landholders.) This is the case with Aimaparah; and nearly so with Secoor in Burdwan; and in some villages in all the districts where Thuggee exists.*

(Signed) N. LOWIS.

Calcutta, 19*th April*, 1838.

I shall conclude this introduction, which has run into much greater length than I had intended, by a short report of his proceedings in the province of Behar, drawn up for me on the occasion of my visit to his district in December last.

* One hundred and fifty-three (153) of the prisoners arrested by Captain Lowis have been tried by Mr. Charles Garstin, and his proceedings submitted for the revision and final orders of the Sudder Nizamut Adawlut. I am afraid their orders will not be out in time to admit of my giving the result of these trials in this Report.

To MAJOR SLEEMAN,

GENERAL SUPERINTENDENT.

SIR,

On receiving charge of the approvers you sent me from Jubulpore I left Mirzapore on the 8th December 1835; and in the hope of being able to arrest some of the gangs then infesting the roads from the southward to Gorruckpore and Fyzabad, I proceeded by hasty marches to the latter place, from whence, with four approvers, I travelled along the Gorruckpore road, and sent Subadar Major Rostum Khan with three others along that leading to Chupra. Neither of us were fortunate enough to meet any of the persons we were in search of; indeed I was told by Radhai Raee, a noted leader I apprehended some time afterwards, that the Thugs were aware of my object and destination as soon as I quitted Mirzapore. On reaching the station of Gorruckpore I was told by Buctawur approver, that there were a number of his former associates there in the jail. Mr. Currie, then Magistrate of the district, taking Buctawur into the jail shewed him about seven hundred prisoners, seated in rows for the purpose, and desired him to point out the Thugs.

After a careful examination he denounced two, Ghassee Khan and Boul Khan Thug leaders, and several others as followers. He failed however in recognising several other Thugs who were then in the jail; but their countenances had undergone so much change from long confinement, that this was not to be wondered at, although he had accompanied them all for many years in different Thug excursions. As I was anxious to get some Thug approvers in addition to those you sent me, only two of the number being well acquainted with the Thugs of Behar, I requested Mr. Currie to have the two leaders abovenamed confronted with Buctawur in court, which he was kind enough to do. Boul Khan stoutly denied his guilt; but Ghassee Khan, on seeing there was now no chance of his immediate release, admitted that he was not only a Thug but one of their leaders. He was then made over to me; and I was returning home to my tents when Buctawur expressed a wish to speak to me in private. Taking him aside, I was told that he had heard a native officer of the court send off an express to the Kusseea Thana Police station to give notice of our approach, as Dilawur Khan, a leader of Thugs, was there in the police at Kusseea as a Chaprassie (belted attendant) and a great friend of the Thanadars of that place, who, with his (Dilawur's) assistance, used to arrest Thugs and release them or otherwise, according to the fee they might be able and willing to give him. This Thanadar, Buctawur added, was a relation and friend of Hursuhaee, the Nazir of the Magistrate's Court at Gorruckpore. I did not then give any credit to Buctawur's assertion, conceiving it likely that he owed the Thanadar a grudge for former annoyances. However, on my arrival at Kusseea, a few days afterwards, I found that not only was Dilawur Khan, as Buctawur had stated, a Chaprassie attached to the Thana, but that his brothers, Dookhee and Futtoo, two noted Thugs, both resided there, as well as the wives and female relatives of several other Thugs then in jail, who were extremely useful as spies or messengers to convey information. On asking for the Thanadar I found he had that morning gone off a distance of some cos to make some investigation. This made me suspect he had only gone out of the way to avoid troublesome enquiries. I sent a messenger for him, and told him to say I should await his arrival. He made his appearance next evening, and denied he knew either Dookhee or Futtoo, but admitted that Dilawur Khan was a Chaprassie attached to his Thana; and said the late Mr. Armstrong had appointed him: moreover, that he had then just gone to Moozufferpoor to give evidence in a case of murder. Although the different Thug women, when examined before the Thanadar, all accused him of keeping Dilawur's brothers, Dookhee and Futtoo in his employ, he persisted in his denial of any knowledge of them, but promised if they ever visited the Thana he would immediately arrest them. I need hardly add they were both in the course of a few days sent to Gorruckpore. From Kusseea I sent a letter through the different Thanas to Mr. Gough, the Magistrate at Moozufferpore, requesting him to arrest Dilawur Khan. Mr. Gough afterwards told me, that after recording Dilawur's evidence, which he thought of a very suspicious nature, he got away his sword from him; and told him I had written to have him arrested as he was a Thug; and that on looking over a list of Thugs sent from Jubulpore he perceived his name mentioned in it as a leader of note. Dilawur became extremely indignant, and swore he was falsely accused; that he was not a Thug; and did not even know what Thuggee was. On his arrival in my Camp he was recognized by a relation of his own, Shumshere Khan approver, from Jubulpore, as well as by all the others then present. I then offered to recommend him to you as an approver on the usual conditions; but he persisted in his denial of being a Thug. Sometime afterwards he was sent to Jubulpore; where, after making a full confession, and detailing innumerable murders he had been engaged in, he was admitted an approver on the usual conditions.

His two brothers, Dookhee and Futtoo, were forwarded to me by the Magistrate at Gorruckpore. Dookhee, when he saw that his brother had been sent to Jubulpore, that Thugs who had never before been in the hands of the police were daily arriving from my detached parties, and that matters had now assumed a serious aspect, requested I would recommend him as an approver. He made a full confession, and was eventually made an approver; when he not only corroborated the statement made by Bucktawur at Gorruckpore, but added, that Chardee Lall, the Kusseea Darogah, used to levy contributions on all the Thugs, who, to conciliate him, were in the habit of presenting to him, *as a nuzzur*, any nice or costly articles obtained from their victims; that he himself resided at the Thanah, and had frequently seen different articles brought by the Thugs to Chardee Lall.

In the jail at this station I found two notorious Thugs, Buxoo and Mouzzim; the former a noted leader, and the latter a very old "Bhurtote," or strangler. On their being first confronted with the approvers, who not only mentioned their names, but those of all their relatives, they denied that they knew, or had ever seen the approvers; and, turning up their eyes to heaven called their god and their prophet to witness, that they were innocent and oppressed men. They said that Mr. Luke, the Magistrate, had kept them in confinement for upwards of a year, for no offence whatever, but merely on the accusation of a bitter enemy. I was then much in want of their services, and had them several times before me; and after much difficulty I succeeded in making Buxoo believe, that if he made a full and free confession he should be exempted from the punishments of death and transportation, and not *flogged*, which he seemed to be still more in dread of. He frequently told me, that with us nothing was certain; that we Europeans made all sorts of promises to gain our immediate object, and afterwards broke them; and constantly referred me to what Ghassee, Joothee, and Afreen had suffered from having given evidence in the case of murder of Mr. Pringle's Mussalchee in 1827. On this murder he had himself been tried and acquitted. I shortly afterwards detached both him and Mouzzim to arrest the Thugs whose names were in the lists you sent me from Jubulpore.

By the accompanying returns you will observe, that up to this date a hundred and sixty-one Thugs have been arrested, and that thirty-eight now remain on the lists for seizure; of this number five are undergoing sentence of imprisonment for fourteen years in the Bhagulpore jail; their time will expire on the 28th January 1839.

I have, &c. &c.

(Signed) W. M. RAMSAY,
Assist. Genl. Supt.

Chupra, 24*th Decr*. 1837.

W. H. SLEEMAN.

EXPEDITIONS

OF THE

GUALIOR AND BUNDELCUND GANGS,

FOR 1826-27.

Report of an Expedition to the Deckan from November 1826 *to March* 1827, *of several gangs under Feringeea, Chotee, and other leaders, amounting to three hundred and seventy Thugs, from Gualior, Bundelcund and the Dooab.*

1. Feringeea, with a gang of thirteen Thugs, left his home in Gorha, in Jhansee, and set out for the Deckan. At a village two coss from Jhandagow, they met Sheik Mungoo, (since hung at Jhoura) Gungadeen, (hung at Jhoura) Surjhun Ahier, and Ajubee (hung), with a gang of one hundred Thugs. Among the rest was Kunhae Approver. The gangs united next day and returned to Jhandagon, where they met three Musselmen Rokureeas, Kazies of Bhundere. The next morning Sorjun Jemadar and Makun, with forty Thugs, followed them, and the next morning at a nullah between Murode and Akajerie put them to death and buried their bodies unde rstones in the nullah, —rejoined the other gang the day after at Maghulka Surae.

2. The gang after this affair proceeded to Peeputthone, in Bhopaul, where they meet at the Pass three Sikhs en route from Chimpaneer to Bhopaul, and taking them on two coss on the road to Bhopaul, put them to death, and buried their bodies in a nullah. They then proceeded to Bhysa, in Bhopaul.

3. Leaving Bhysa the next morning, they crossed the Nerbudda, and went to little Chimpaneer, encamping on the banks of the river outside the village. Here they fell in with a Chowdheree Brahmin, four attendants and a barber. The Chowdheree was from the Bazar of Colonel Seyers' Cantonment, and with his attendants, had a purwanna from Colonel Seyers. Feringeea leaving the gang with the travellers re-crossed the river and proceeded to Sehud Deo, half a coss from the Camp, and met Bhimmee, Omraow, Buduloo, Bukut and Heera Mussulman, with a gang of one hundred Thugs, and made over the six men to them. They were all put to death the day after at the Bhawra Ghâtee Pass, by a party of twenty-six men detached under Bhimmee and Omraow, who, after the murder, crossed the Nerbudda and proceeded to Chimpaneer, where they overtook Feringeea, and advanced with him after his own gang, which was two or three stages in advance, while their own gang was two or three in the rear.

4. On reaching a village south of Hurda, they met a Sepahee whom they murdered at their encampment. Dheera, who died in the Saugor Jail, put him to death, and the body was buried under the mangoe-tree in a deep grave, to the east of the village. Feringeea demanded the share of all his gang of Thugs in the booty from the two affairs, which they declined giving, and offered the share for fourteen who had left home with Feringeea; he took nothing from the first affair, but four rupees from the Sepahee's effects.

5. Feringeea after the last affair left Bhimmee's gang and rejoined his own, at a village the other side of Singeea Deo, encamped under tamarind-trees. Behorena (who died in Jail at Hydrabad), Bhawanee (hung), and Tejna, with a gang of thirty-five Thugs, had joined them from the Deckan, and were accompanied by one Havildar, five Sepa-

hees, and three Marwaries. Maharaj Patuck, (who drowned himself) joined them with fourteen Thugs from Indore, having crossed the Nerbudda at Budulana. About eight at night the whole nine travellers were strangled in their beds, and the bodies were buried in a small nullah in a rice field near some bamboo trees. These bodies were exhumed by a party from Saugor.

6. In the morning they set out for the Deckan, and were overtaken by Bhimmee and Omrow at the Khurooa nullah in the Asseer district, the gangs united, and were more than two hundred and fifty Thugs. A Thug from the gang under Chutter Jemadar and other leaders at Burhampore, came up and gave intelligence to Feringeea that at the village of Jamuneea, seven coss distant, his gang had got nine Marwaries and required assistance. Feringeea with his gang left Bhimmee's, and proceeded westward and reached Jamuneea, encamped near the gangs of Chotee and Chutter, consisting of sixty Thugs, in a grove, who had with them nine Marwarie shop-keepers (one woman and a boy.) In the morning they all set out with them on the road to Indore, and encamped at the village of Bhosawur or Sursode, in Nemawur, in a grove to the south of the village on the bank of a nullah. In the evening they were all strangled and the bodies buried under the tamarind trees in two graves near the camp. These bodies have been taken up in the presence of the Local Authorities.

7. After the last affair they proceeded to and reached Dhorecote in five days. Feringeea, with thirty of the gang, lodged in the Bazar, and the rest were encamped outside of the village on the bank of a nullah to the north. In the Bazar they found eight Pythans and a woman, one was Kalee Khan, a Havildar of Motie Tuwala's Resala at Indore, whom they enveigled to accompany them the next

morning. Eight coss distant and at a nullah eight coss from Dharcote, and four coss from Dhoree, they were put to death and buried in the nullah under some stones.

8. After this affair they proceeded to a village the other side of Amulnair in the Dhooleea district, and encamped in a grove outside to the west. Here they met two Hindoos (a Sepahee and his relation,) whom they strangled at night in the Camp.

9. The gang proceeded to Dholeea and thence to Jokur, where they passed three days in the festivities of the Holee. After burning the Holee they set out and soon after fell in with two Mahrattas,—on reaching a nullah one coss from Jokur, they strangled them and buried their bodies in the bed of the nullah.

10. After the murder of those two men, the gangs proceeded with the intention of passing on to Kopurgow, through Moligaon, but while they were resting at a well two coss from Jokur, soon after daylight, they heard the call of a wolf, and struck off to the right on the road to Chundone. At night Feringeea, with a party of twenty, left the gang and returned to Maligaon to await the evils threatened by the omen. Here they again met with Bhimmee and Budulo's gang, who had with them four treasure bearers on their way from Poonah to Indore. They returned the next day to Jokur, where they were joined by Chotee and a party of forty-five more from the large gang, who had heard of those treasure bearers from two of Bhimmee's men who had come to see their relations at Jokur. The four treasure bearers were joined by two weavers and a hurcara, and the whole seven were murdered at a Bowlie, about one coss north of Jokur; some of the bodies were thrown into the Bowlie, and the others buried in an adjacent field, where they were soon afterwards found by the Local Authorities. Feringeea and

Bhimmee's gang, after this affair, returned to their respective homes, while Chotee and his party rejoined their friends at Chandore.

A total of forty-nine men and two women were murdered in this expedition.

Proceedings of the gang under Bhimmee, Budoloo and others.

1. In the month of October 1826, Murlee, Budoloo, his brother, (hung at Saugor) Bhimmee, Heera, Laek, Beju Sing, (dead) and Muneeram, (hung at Saugor) left the village of Muletura in Gualior for the Deckan,—reached the village of Myapoor, where they met Bukut Jemadar, who joined them: they proceeded to Bhilsa. On reaching Sahadeo, they were joined by Omrow and Durroo with fifty followers. • Feringeea with Makun and Gungadeen, had left Gorha on an expedition to the Deckan and crossed the Nerbudda river. During the day one Brahmin Chowdree, two Brahmin servants, two Bunneeas and a barber came up: a party of twenty-six Thugs were sent with them. They killed the whole the day after at the Bhowra Ghatee Pass, and buried the bodies under some stones. The next morning they proceeded towards Hurda, south of the Nerbudda.

2. On reaching Heerimghatee, in an open plain, they fell in with two Seikhs, whom they put to death. They crossed the Nurbudda, and the fourth day after this affair reached Hurdah and were joined by the rest of the gang.

3. Having overtaken the gang under Feringeea and other leaders at Singeea Deo, they soon separated from them again and went by regular stages to Muslah, in Ourungabad, and halted outside of the village under some trees. Two hours before dark a Mehratta traveller came

up, and one hour after dark they strangled him, and threw the body into a ruined well.

4. Left Muslah and reached Daburee in Ourungabad, and from thence came on the Ourungabad road, and the third day after arrived at a village called Borjwala. Some Thugs occupied the Bastion or Bhorj, and some lodged in a Fuqueer's Takeea. In the evening two travellers came up and lodged in the Bastion. Four hours after dark they were killed and buried on the spot.

5. After this affair they reached Ourungabad the third day and thence were proceeding towards the Deckan, when about one and half coss from Ourungabad they met Jeychund Rajpoot (now in Saugor Jail), with six Thugs, Gurhoo Lodhee (hung at Saugor) and Gunnaram Aheer (hung at Jowa), who joined them, and the third day about two coss from Beejapoor they fell in with two travellers, who went on with them to Bejapoor where they halted in a grove outside the village, on the bank of a river,—one hour after dark they were strangled and the bodies buried under some mangoe trees.

6. After this affair they proceeded to Kopergow and halted outside the village under some trees to the east. The villagers recognised some of the Thugs, gave information to the Amil, who ordered them all to be seized, but released them the next morning. Oomrow, with fifty Thugs, proceeded on the Poonah road, agreeing to meet again at Maligaon, seventeen coss north of the place. The rest went through Ewla, five coss from which, at a village, they halted and lodged in some of the Buneeah's shops. Two hours before dark four men of the Jat caste, treasure bearers, came up. In the morning two men were sent on with them, and they halted at noon at Mallagaon: the gang encamped three coss distant, and were joined by the party that had separated at Kopurgaon, proceeded to

Mallagaon and halted outside the village. In the morning, when the treasure bearers left the place, they were followed by the gang to a village called Jokur, where the treasure bearers halted in the bazar, and the gang remained outside at a gun-shot distance under some trees,—the treasure bearers were here joined by two weavers and a hurcara; and the Thugs having been joined by Chotee and Feringeea, with sixty-five Thugs from the other gangs, put the whole seven to death.

A total of twenty men murdered in this expedition.

Proceedings of the part of the gang under Chotee and Chutter Jemadars, and others.

1. Chotee Brahmin, with a gang of twenty-five Thugs, assembled at Tegra in Sumthur, and having found the omens favourable, opened their expedition. Their first stage was to the village of Hurda, in the Jhansee district, where they fell in with Chutter and others; and eleven days after with Husnoo, on the boundaries of Sirdhora, in the Gwalior territory. They arrived in fifteen days at Rheilie in the Bhopaul territory, where they met five Brahmins from Hurda on their way to Bhopaul. Chotee prevailed on them to travel with them, and they murdered them at a water-course as they crossed, and buried the bodies.

2. Continuing their march the next morning they crossed the Nerbudda, overtook one Pundit and three Rajpoots, residents of Timmurnee, in the Hurda district, proceeding from Hurda to Boorhanpoor, and strangled them at a nullah, four coss south of Hurdee, and buried their bodies in the bed of the stream.

3. They then proceeded by regular stages to Ourungabad, halted one day there, and returned to Boorhanpore in

ten days,—shortly afterwards, met eight shop-keepers and one woman from Ourungabad en route to Kishengurh. They induced them to travel with them the next morning and brought them via Boargaon to Timmurneea, in the district of Asseergurh. Here they met Feringeea, Gungadeen and Makun, and one hundred and ninty-seven Thugs from Gwalior, Bundelcund and the Dooab, they joined, and the gang then amounted to two hundred and sixty. They all set out with the travellers for Sirsode, in the district of Nemawur, and encamped in a mangoe grove, on the bank of a nullah, two hundred yards south of the village, strangled them while sleeping in their beds, and interred their bodies securely in the nullah.

4. After this affair they set out in the direction of Candeish, and arrived at Dhorecote in five days, where they joined in the murder of Kalee Khan Havildar, one woman and seven men, as before described. They remained at Dhooreea one day, and proceeded via Choprah to Chandere, which they reached in fifteen days, having on the road perpetrated the murders already described. After the murder of the treasure bearers at Jokur, they proceeded towards Ourungabad, and on arriving at Pudora, in the Mulkapore district, Gungadeen and Makun, with one hundred and twenty five men, went in the direction of Poonah, and several men returned home. The remainder of the gang, which then consisted of sixty Thugs, proceeded to Ourungabad, and thence towards Dhooleea. They were resting a short distance from Ourungabad, when Emambux, a Havildar (Serjeant) in a Regiment there, brought them seven Sepoys and one Havildar proceeding to Dowarka, and entrusted them to their care. They set out with the Havildar and seven Sepoys, and strangled them at a deserted village and buried their bodies securely.

5. After this affair they came on to a hamlet, a short distance from Ewla, and again met Makun, Gungadeen, and the party who had proceeded on an expedition to Poonah. They all went to Ewla, where the Police officer arrested eight of the principal men, but released them after fifteen days, on their delivering up their property. During their confinement all the gang dispersed, except twenty men of Makun's, and twenty of Chotee's, who remained to hear the result of their imprisonment. On being released they joined this party and proceeded to Mallagaon, where they fell in with six Facqueers and two Seapoys, from Poonah en route to Agra, and prevailed on them to accompany them to Dhooleea, ten coss from Mallagaon. Here the gang encamped in separate parties : during the day, two Seapoys arrived from Poonah en route to Bhurtpore, and Chotee prevailed on them to halt with them. They were strangled in their beds during the night, without the other eight travellers being aware of it, and their bodies buried on the bank of a nullah. They were afterwards dug up by the jackalls, and the circumstance reported to the Officer Commanding at Dhooleea.

6. They set out with eight men the following morning on the Oojein road, and murdered them at a nullah about a coss from Dhooleea, and buried them securely in the bed of the nullah.

7. After this affair, they went to a village three coss distant, and after dividing the spoils of the two last murders, Makun, with twenty men, returned to Dhooleea for the purpose of giving Hoormut Khan, a Sipahee of the Provincial Corps, a share of the Dhooleeah affair, he being aware of the perpetration of it. They, while encamped at Dhooleea, fell in with Jeea Lall Pundit and four attendants from the Concan on their way to Gwalior, proceeded with them to Loharree in Kandeish, and the fol-

lowing morning murdered them a coss and a half from the village, in a dry nullah, while on the march, and intered their bodies securely. After dividing the spoils of this affair the gang separated and returned to their homes. The whole of this expedition was completed in six months.

A total of forty men and one woman murdered during this expedition.

Proceedings of part of the gangs under Soorjun the Cowherd, Kemla the Weaver, and Hurnagur Brahmin.

1. A gang of forty Thugs under Kemla, Soorjun the Cowherd, Soghur, Hurnagur and other leaders from Joractera, in the Gwalior territory, and went on to Mogul-ka-Serai, where they fell in with four Sepahees whom they took on and murdered. The bodies were covered over with stones in the bed of a water-course.

2. Passing through Bhopaul they were overtaken by a Goosaen and two Brinjarahs in the bed of a rivulet, where they put them to death immediately, and buried their bodies under the stones.

3. Crossed the Nerbudda, and going on to Bhoregow, in the Aseergur district, fell in with five Mahratta travellers from Gwalior, and taking them on to Idelabad murdered them, on leaving that place the following morning, in a water-course, and buried their bodies in the sand.

4. Passed through Hingolee to Girgow, where they fell in with two Shop-keepers, on their way from Hydrabad to Nagpore, and two Troopers on their way from Ourungabad to Hydrabad. These travellers lodged with the Thugs in a grove outside the village, about midnight preparations were made for strangling them, but Soorjun Jemadar

bungled in his attempt upon one of the Sowars who got up and made off towards the village calling out lustily for help. The villagers ran towards the spot, and the whole gang made off. The greater part made their escape, and joining the gang of Chotee, assisted in the murders at Serjeindeo, Nursode and Malagow, already described. Eleven of the gang lost their way in the dark, and when day broke found themselves close to the grove again. They found all the villagers looking at the bodies of the two Shop-keepers who were dead; and listening to the two Troopers who had escaped. They tried to appear as travellers just come in from a journey, but were recognized by the Sowars, who pointed them out to the people as the murderers. They were secured and sent to the European authorities in the Cantonment at Hingolee, where they remained several years in confinement, but were at last released as the Hydradad Government did not like the expense of feeding them every day; and they all, as a matter of course, returned to their trade of murder.

A total of fourteen men murdered in this expedition.

Report of an Expedition through Malnea by gangs from Gwalior and Bundelcund, in the year 1826-27, *under Aman Subahdar and others.*

1. Aman Sobahdar, with eighty Thugs from Sindouse, Soper and other places, left Alumpore, Indore, and reached Palee, where he met Chutter Jemadar with eighteen, and murdered three men at Raghdownd,—sent by Hurree Ram Seth.

2. The gang proceeded to Madhoorajpore, where they murdered seven Hindoos. Aman Sing, on his way back with fifty men, came to Tuppa, where he met Zoolfakar

with twenty, and Noor Khan with eleven, on their way from their homes in Bejana, in Tehree, through Saugor.

3. Zalim Jemadar, with seven men, went to Bhopaul, where he met Esuree Jemadar with eight men. They proceeded to Saugoree in Indore, where they murdered two Sepahees on their way from Bombay to Cawnpore.

4. Proceeding on to Mhow, they met four men six coss east of it, whom they murdered on the spot.

5. Arrived at Raghoogur, where they met seven Sepahees on their way from Bombay to Allahabad, took them on to Tuppa, where they found, besides Aman and the above Thugs, Roshun Jemadar with fifteen from Saugor; soon after came up Bohurena Jemadar with ten, Zoolfakar (hung at Saugor) with sixteen, Ashraff Jemadar with five, and Soopureea with ten. In the morning all set out with the travellers, except Zoolfakar approver and a few others—soon after four other men came up from Mhow, and Zoolfakar sent on with them Purumna, who induced them to go on fast and overtake the others. The whole eleven were killed at a Ghautee, one coss and a half from Tuppa on this side.

6. After this affair they went back to Dittora, where they met two Sepahees on their way from Barodah to Cawnpore, whom they murdered at the Thapa.

7. Aman then proceeded to Indore, all the rest came back towards Saugor. At Khillode, near Bhilsa, they fell in with six men on their way from Mhow to Cawnpore—coming on this side of Khillode to a nullah they strangled them.

8. Returning towards Indore, at a village a little on the other side of Peepla, met three men on their way from Mhow to Cawnpore, and killed them at the Thapa.

9. Coming back through Peepala to a village near the Nuddee-walagow, they were seen by a Dawk hurcara, and from fright Noorkhan, Zalim and Ashraff went toward

Indore. Zoolfakar, Bohorena and Esuree, came towards Saugor with a Kafila, arrived at Kondee, where they met two Sepahees from Mhow to the Dooab and killed them in the morning. Whilst in the act two Dawk hurcaras came up, whom the Thugs believed to be of their party until they had advanced a little, when their mistake was discovered. They then dispersed and returned to their homes.

10. Noor Khan left Zalim and Ashraff at Indore and went home. The latter went to Saugor where they met a man and a boy, took them to Kutora and murdered them a quarter of a coss on, in the morning, and then returned home.

11. Aman went from Tuppa to Indore, thence to Mahesur, where he met Chotee Jemadar on his way back from the Dhooleea affair, with twenty-four men, joined and killed three men between Mohcsur and Indore.

12. On arriving at Mhow they met a Havildar and three Sepahees, took them on to Samnere in Indore for the night, and murdered them a quarter of a coss on the other side next morning.

13. Proceeded to Oojein and there met Chutter, (hung at Saugor) with Sohur, Parumsook and thirty Thugs, they joined and enveigled a man with two camels, whom they killed at their encampment. Went back to Oojein and got a man with a mare and colt—two shop-keepers who knew Aman, called out they were Thugs and would kill the man, on hearing this the gang dispersed and returned home leaving only Aman and Chutter with fifteen Thugs, who went to Kotah.

14. At Kotah they met a Havildar and two Sepoys whom they murdered and buried under a Bur tree, and then returned home.

A total of three men murdered in this expedition.

Report of an Expedition through Malwa by gangs from Bundelcund, under Sheik Macul, Noorkhan, Khaleel and other leaders in 1826-27.

1. Inaeut left his home at Ghateearee in Jhansee with twenty men; at Mohlie near Saugor, met Khuleel (hung) with twenty men, Noorkhan with twenty, Lal Mahomud five, Booda, (transported) Ghureea (hung 1832) five, Dhurum Khan (hung 1832) ten. All joined and passed through Saugor to Sehora, where they murdered a Sipahee in their encampment.

2. Proceeded to the Taptee river, five coss this side of Bhilsa, to a village where they met two travellers, whom they killed in the encampment.

3. Going on to Bhilsa they met Esuree Jemadar with forty Thugs, Esagur Mahadeo approver, who resided in Bhopaul with nine, and Kurreem (hung at Saugor) with ten, total one hundred and fifty Thugs. Going through Ashta to a village on the other side spent the night. On proceeding they met a woman and a boy whom they murdered and buried on the spot.

4. Going on to Hondee this side of Tuppa, Kurreem brought to them an old woman and her two sons Nujeebs of Bhopaul, whom they murdered at night and buried there.

5. They then went to the Mhow Cantonments, and were sitting at a stream on this side, when they heard a crow call whilst flying, and they all returned to Raghogurh, where they overtook two Sepahees, whom they murdered next day in camp.

6. Came on to Koturee in Bhopaul and fell in with Hurlal Kaet and his wife, whom they murdered the following morning. Came to Bhilsa and there dispersed and returned to their homes.

A total of nine men and three women murdered in this expedition.

Report of an Expedition into Rajpootana by gangs from the Gwalior Territories, under Shere Khan, Rostum Khan, and other leaders, in 1826-7.

1. Aman Mussulman (hung at Saugor) with fifteen Thugs, left his home in Kurreawlee, in Gwalior, and went to Naea Sheher, thence to Mahabeer, where they met a traveller on his way from Gwalior to Jodepore and murdered him.

2. Came to Naea Sheher and thence to Tiktolee in Jypore, where they met Peera, son of Aman approver, with Mr. Briggs and five Thugs—joined and went to Sama in Jypore. Here they met Shere Khan Jemadar with sixteen Thugs, in all thirty-six Went to Bumbhola, one coss from which they murdered a traveller.

3. They reached Kondee in Jypoor, where they met five travellers, whom they took on one coss and murdered.

4. Went to Madhorajpore and met Suknundun Thug (died in Saugor Jail) who told them of the Dholeea affair. Shere Khan went to Jypore, Aman remained three days at Madhorajpore, when three travellers came up, whom they murdered the next morning long after sunrise.

5. On the road they fell in with another traveller, came on with him to a village, a little on the Jypore side of Charsoo, and killed him next morning.

6. At Charsoo overtook two Sepahees whom they carried on to Salpore and murdered next morning.

7. Came to Bhowunbas, in Jypore, and met three men whom they murdered next morning one coss from the place.

8. Arrived at Naea Sheher, where they met a servant of the Jeypore Rajah whom they murdered.

9. Went to Kawata, where they met Roostum Khan approver with seven Thugs; joined and went to Jypore; returned to Kawata, thence to Kagreebag, where they met two Troopers whom they murdered. After this a dispute arose between Aman and Roostum Khan, the former went home and Roostum Khan took the road to Jypore.

A total of nineteen men murdered in this expedition.

Total—Two hundred and four men and six women murdered during the different expeditions this season.

Names of the Principal Leaders of the Gangs engaged in the foregoing Expeditions for 1826-27.

Names of Leaders.	Caste.	Resident.	Remarks.	No. of Thugs.
Feringeea,	Brahmin,	Gwalior,	Approver,	20
Makun Jemadar,	Lodhee,	Sumthur,	Hung at Jowra in December 1829,	40
Gungadeen,	Ditto,	Ditto,	Ditto ditto,	30
Sheik Mungoo,	Mussulman,	Jhansee,	Died at his home,	30
Purusram,	Lodhee,	Ditto,	Died at Jubulpore, March 1838,	15
Persaud,	Ditto,	Ditto,	Hung at Saugor in June 30 1832,	16
Rajee Khan,	Mussulman,	Ditto,	Ditto Jowra in 1829,	5
Ajubee,	Brahmin,	Indore,	Ditto Saugor, June 1832,	14
Chotee,	Ditto,	Jhansee,	Approver,	30
Chutter Jemadar,	Aheer,	Gwalior,	Hung at Saugor, June 1832,	10
Achroo,	Komar,	Indore,	Ditto ditto,	5
Bhowanee,	Lodhee,	Gwalior,	Hung at Jowra, December 1829,	12
Hurnagur,	Brahmin,	Jhansee,	Approver (died March 1838,)	13
Sooghur,	Lodhee,	Ditto,	Ditto.	
Purumsook,	Buneea,	Etawa,	Ditto,	
Buduloo Jemadar,	Lodhee,	Jhansee,	Hung at Saugor, June 1832,	
Morlee,	Ditto,	Ditto,	Approver,	
Munneeram,	Ditto,	Gwalior	Hung at Saugor, June 1832,	
Oomrao,	Ditto,	Ditto,	Ditto Jowra, December 1829,	
Heera,	Mussulman,	Jhansee,	Approver,	7
Laek,	Aheer,	Gwalior,	Ditto,	
Bijee Sing,	Ditto,	Ditto,	Killed by a Zemindar in the Gwalior Territory in 1833,	
Durroo Jemadar,	Lodhee,	Ditto,	Hung at Jowra in 1830,	40
Bhimmee ditto,	Ditto,	Ditto,	Approver,	18
Bukhut,	Rajpoot,	Indore,	Ditto,	18
Kinher Bygna,	Brahmin,	Gwalior,	Ditto,	7
Joychund,	Rajpoot,	Ditto,	Died in Saugor Jail, 12th November, 1831,	7
Kehreea,	Lodhee,	Jhansee,	Ditto, 1832,	7
Khanjoo,	Aheer,	Jhansee,	Died in Saugor Jail, 19th November, 1831,	14

Names of Leaders.	Caste.	Resident.	Remarks.	No. of Thugs.
Bukut,	Lodhee,	Sumthur,	Hung at Saugor, 23d June, 1832,	10
Gunesh,	Ditto,	Ditto,	Ditto 30th June, 1832,	12
Maharaj Patuk,	Brahmin,	Ditto,	Drowned himself near Saugor after his arrest, 1832,	8
Munohur ditto,	Ditto,	Ditto,	Cut his own throat after his arrest, 1835,	7
Amann Sobahdar,	Ditto,	Jhansee,	Died at his home in 1828,	80
Chuttee Jemadar,	Ditto,	Ditto,	Hung at Saugor 9th July, 1832,	18
Zoolfakar ditto,	Mussulman,	Ditto,	Approver,	20
Noorkhan ditto,	Ditto,	Ditto,	Hung at Jubulpore 16th April, 1835,	11
Zalim ditto.	Ditto,	Tehree,	Died at his home in 1833,	7
Esuree ditto,	Brahmin,	Gwalior,	At large,	8
Roshun ditto,	Mussulman,	Jhansee,	Hung at Saugor 10th August, 1832,	15
Zoolfukar,	Ditto,	Saugor,	Ditto ditto,	15
Buhorena Jemadar,	Lodhee,	Huttah,	Died in Hydrabad Jail,	15
Ashraf,	Mussulman,	Gwalior,	At large,	5
Puramna,	Ditto,	Ditto,	Hung at Saugor 30th June, 1832,	
Khuleel,	Ditto,	Jhansee,	Ditto ditto,	20
Gurreeba,	Ditto,	Ditto,	Ditto ditto,	5
Dhurm Khan,	Ditto,	Saugor,	Ditto 10th August, 1832,	10
Inaent	Ditto,	Jhansee.	Approver,	20
Noor Khan,	Ditto,	Ditto,	Hung at Jubulpore,	20
Boodha,	Ditto,	Ditto,	Transported from Saugor in 1832,	10
Lall Mahomed,	Ditto,	Ditto,	Approver,	5
Mahadeo,	Rajpoot,	Bhopaul,	Ditto,	9
Curreem Jemadar,	Mussulman,	Ditto,	Hung at Saugor in 1832,	10
Aman ditto,	Ditto,	Gwalior,	Ditto ditto,	15
Shere Khan ditto,	Ditto,	Bhurtpore,	Ditto ditto,	16
Rostum Khan,	Ditto,	Dholepore,	Approver,	7
Hurnagur,	Lodhee,		Ditto,	
Soorjun,	Cowherd,	Gwalior,	At large,	
Humula,	Weaver,	Ditto,	Approver,	
Soghur,	Lodhee,	Ditto,	Ditto,	

EXPEDITIONS

OF THE

KANDEISH AND BERAR GANGS,

IN 1827-28.

Report of an Expedition into Kandeish and Berar by a Gang of sixty Thugs under Chotee and Sheik Nungoo from Gwalior in 1827-28.

1. Chotee approver, and Sheik Nungoo (died) with sixty Thugs left Poora, in Jhansee, and on their arrival at Sarora murdered a traveller proceeding to Jhansee.

2. On nearly reaching Bhopaul they met three Brahmins, whom they murdered on the spot.

3. Crossed the Nerbudda at the Chimpaneer Ghat—at a village called Hutteea, near Ourungabad, they murdered a Hindoo.

4. Went through Ourungabad to Walagow, there met a Havildar of the barber caste and five Sepahees. In the evening came to Jokur, and in the morning killed them near the place where the treasure bearers were killed the year before.

5. When between Jokur and Dholeea they met a Sepahee of the shepherd caste, whom they killed in the jungles.

6. Passed through Dholeea and lodged in a village—a coss distant on the road to Indore, met a Byragee, whom they murdered at the Thapa.

7. Leaving in the morning the Thapa they fell in with three Marwarie travellers, whom they murdered.

8. Reached a village on the banks of the Taptee—met four travellers and killed them at the Thapa.

9. Reached Choupra and met a Marwarie, whom they murdered between Choupra and Dhoreea.

10. Came to Dhoree, where they met three Marwaries, whom they took on one coss and then murdered.

11. Coming to a river a coss further on, three treasure bearers overtook them, refused to give the cowries to the Chokee Police, who reproached them, saying "that if the treasure was taken they would come down upon them." The gang hearing this followed up, and in the jungles two coss further on, they rushed upon and strangled them.

12. Came on to Khurgore Bateesa in Indore, divided and dispersed. Sheik Nungoo was seized by Brareelal Seth a month after he came home, and Chotee, three or four months after, went to enquire after his family who had been seized, and remained with him.

A total of twenty-seven men murdered in this expedition.

Report of an Expedition into Malwa, Kandeish and Berar, by Gangs under Zoolfakar and other Leaders from Bundelcund in 1827-28.

1. Zoolfakar approver, with twelve, and Pahar (dead) four, left Parwaha, in Jhansee, and went to Jumal Bagree, in Bhilsa; there met Noorkhan Jemadar and came to Ratgurh, where they killed two Mussulmen.

2. Went to Jumal Bagree and there met Esuree Jemadar with fourteen, and proceeded to Bindola, in Bhopaul, where they murdered two Sepahees.

3. Went to Sehore, thence to Dittora, where they met Zalim (dead) with twenty, Roshun fifteen, Dhurm Khan five, Lalmahomed five—all proceeded to Khillode, where they murdered a tailor.

4. Went to Choona Bhutta, in Indore, where they met a Sepahee whom they murdered at Hurda.

5. Came to Burwalagow, there met one Havildar and three Sepahees on their way from Cawnpore to Bombay; took them to Akleepore and killed them.

6. Zalim, Roshun and Gholab, went to Burkhera, where they killed a Goosaen and his servant, and got forty gold coins, but refused to give any share to five of Zoolfakar's men who were with them. Went on to Ashta after much altercation—Zoolfakar and his party had followed up the five and came to Burkhera, where they remained, while Zalim and his party went on to Ashta.

7. At Burkhera three carpenters and a woman joined and proceeded with them to Nadeewalagow, where they were murdered.

8. Went to Kotaree and were joined by Zalim and the rest, and came to Imlaha, where Zoolfakar, Noorkhan, Puhur and Esuree left the party on their way home—at Kotara, three stages east of Saugor, they met and killed a Sepahee from Bombay—after this affair they returned home.

9. Zalim, Roshun and the others crossed the Nerbudda at Chimpaneer and went to Burhanpoor, where they met Munnohur Patuk (who lately cut his own throat), Purus Ram (still at large), Maharaj Patuk (who lately drowned himself), Doroughna and Bukut Moreea, with one hundred and twenty-five, and proceeded towards Bohergow, met with two travellers, whom they murdered at Tiktolee on the Taptee.

10. Went to Edulabad, where they met nine treasure bearers with money from Dhunraj Seth and killed them at

Barwaghat—thence went home. Persaud was soon after seized by Beharee Loll Seth.

A total of twenty-seven men and one woman murdered in this expedition.

Report of an Expedition into Malwa, Gozerat, Kandeish and Berar, by Gangs from Gwalior, Bundelcund and the Saugor Districts in 1827-28.

1. Feringeea left Gorha with twenty-five Thugs and went to Moghul ka Serai, where they met two Marhattas, whom they killed after taking them on a coss and a half.

2. Went to Tuppa, in Indore, and there met Chotab with five Thugs and five other Thugs—all came to Raghoogur, where they met two Mahrattas and a Marwarie, on their way from Saugor to Indore. Soper Sing came up with fifteen Thugs and three travellers (one a bird-catcher and two shop-keepers), on their way from Indore to Patna, killed them all at night and buried them near a Bowlie.

3. Soper Sing and ten of his party came to Bhilsa. Feringeea with his twenty-five, and five of Soper Sing's, crossed the Nerbudda at the Puglana Ghat, and proceeded towards Samneer, near which they fell in with three Sipahees in search of service, killed them at mid-day in the jungles and left the bodies exposed.

4. Went to Kurajgow Kurinjee and fell in with a traveller going south. Eight coss further, on the Hydrabad road, they killed him and buried him under the walls of a mut.

5. Went through Omroutee to Larun Kurnajee, and in the camp in the grove killed a traveller that they took on

with them from Bam, also a thief that was going off with 1100 rupees of Dhunroj Seith's from Parowtee, and had hidden himself under graves where Feringeea found him.

6. Went to Busum and met Sheik Meerun the Great, (deceased) and Sahib Khan of Kakurwalla, Kalee Khan and Kurreem (hung at Saugor with fifty Thugs). Went altogether to Nandair, met five travellers, and murdered them at their encampment.

7. Sahib Khan returned home and the others went to Rovegow, where they met nine travellers, took them on one and a half coss, and killed them before daylight.

8. Went to Hydrabad, where they met a Brahmin and two Rajpoots, in the Bhegan Bazar, at the bridge of the Hoosa Nuddee, killed them at their lodgings and buried them near the bridge.

9. Went to Gungakhera and there met three Marwaries, took them on a stage on the Holwa road, and then killed them. Immediately on leaving the village one of the travellers fell from his horse and they strangled him immediately, and afterwards the other two. Left the bodies exposed as they had not reached the appointed Bele.

10. Went to Pururreea, in Holwa, and fell in with a Subahdar, five Sepahees and one woman, whom they murdered at their encampment.

11. Thence to Doregow, where they met three Pundits and a Byragee, mounted on a pony, plastered over with sugar and covered with flies. Drove off the Fakir and killed the other three.

12. On leaving Doregow, the Byragee again joined them and went on in their company to Raojana, where they met six Khutries with cloth, on their way from Bombay to Nagpore, joined them at Kodhunkhere and came to Raojana. The Faqueer was still with them, so they drove him

off with stones, and he lodged in the village. Killed the six men in camp and buried them in the grove.

13. The Byragee again joined them and came to Mana, where they fell in with two Kahars and a Sepahee, leaving him here, they came towards the place chosen for the murder and when near it, were again joined by the Byragee. Losing all patience with him, they gave Mithoo, one of the gang, five rupees to murder him and take the sin upon himself. All four were strangled (the Byragee among the rest) and they were surprised to find upon him one maund and three seers of Coral, 350 strings of small Pearls, 15 of large Pearls and a gilded Necklace.

14. Came to Omrowtee, thence intended going to Arungabad. On leaving the former, they fell in with two men, took them on to Nadgow and there killed them in camp. They were treasure bearers, and had with them 4000 rupees worth of silver.

15. Went to Kuragow and thence were on their way towards Omrowtee, when at a nullah they fell in with four men with two bullocks laden with copper pice, killed them there, and buried their bodies slightly. After this affair Kalee Khan and Kurreem went home. The rest came on through Burhanpore to Indore, where they met Bhyroo, Bhowanee and Ramla Jemadar with sixty Thugs, in different bodies.

16. Aeera, brother of Jowahir, brought three Marwaries, and they were put into the house occupied by one part of the gang, where they were killed and buried.

17. Remained one day when Feringeea inveigled four Marwaries, and brought them to the other party encamped at the bank of the river, where they were killed.

18. Leaving Indore they fell in with four travellers, and going on with them one stage on the road to Dhar, killed them at the encampment.

19. Feringeea, with his party, after this affair, came through Saugor to Chutterpore, where he heard that the people of Dhunraj Seth were in pursuit of him, and with seventeen Thugs he went back through Saugor to Kondee where he met two travellers. Took them on to a place chosen a coss distant and put them to death.

20. Thence went to Raghoogur, where they fell in with Bhajjoo with five Thugs, and Bohorena five. Leaving that place next day together, fell in with Sheik Inaent with thirty Thugs from Ghateeara—Inaent's party at Dorgown murdered a Chuprassie, his chuprass or breast-plate was buried with the body.

21. Came to Dubohee, near Bhilsa, where he met Zoolfakar (hung at Saugor) and Sheik Lall (afterwards hung at Saugor) with twenty Thugs. There they met a Sepahee and killed him at the Thappa, and halted the next day. Another came up from Joonagur to Saugor, and he was killed at the same place.

22. After this affair the whole fifty went on to Baroda, and there all got sick, and came back to Bheelpore, where they fell in with two Kahars and killed them at the encampment. Thence proceeded to Oodeepore, in the Dhar Pergunnah.

23. Here they fell in with three Sepahees and another man, who was made over to them for safety by the Lohars of Oodeepore. One coss on this side of the town they killed them next morning, and rested at the village one coss the other side of Dhar.

24. Here they met an Elephant driver of the Oodeepoor Rajah, and murdered him in camp the same night at a village called Amjhera.

25. Came on through Mhow to a village, a little the other side of Raghoogur, where they fell in with three Kahars, coming on next morning a coss,

they murdered them on the road near the town of Raghogurh.

26. After this affair they came on through Ashta to a village one coss on this side, where they fell in with a Havildar, one Jylal Sepoy, and a relation of theirs. Came on with them next morning to a place a coss on this side of the village where they were killed. Soon after this Zoolfakar and Sheik Lall left Inaent and returned home with their gangs. He went off and joined Feringeea.

27. Soon after they had joined parties, Roshun and Dhurmkhan (both hung at Saugor) came up and told them of the Peerwahaghat affair, said the police were close after them, and went to their homes. Some of Inaent's party returned home with them, and he had only twenty-one left, Feringeea had seventeen and Bujjoo and Bohorena had ten. They all came back to the river near Peepala from fear of the Police, and there fell in with two Sepahees, one woman and a relation, they brought them on to Peepala, where they were all four put to death in camp.

28. After the last affair they came to a village called Jhundawala, where a Kahar joined them, whom they murdered in their encampment.

29. After this they came on to Tuppa and were leaving that place next morning, when Heera Singh Havildar, a Sepahee, the wife of Mukka Sing Subadar and the wife of Heera Sing Havildar, joined them, and came on to a village a coss and half on the other side of Ashta,—coming on with them the next morning towards Ashta, they put them to death and then came on to Khenjarra.

30. At this last place they fell in with two Sepahees on their way to their homes at Husooa Futtehpore, and put them to death in the camp.

31. After this, Inaent and his party, with Madhoo and Bhowanee from Feringeea's, came in advance. At Manoru they fell in with two Sepahees, whom they put to death next morning, one coss east of the village.

32. After this affair, Inaent and his party came on through Saugor to Korsalee in Chutterpore, where he fell in with two Sepahees, killed them in camp and then went to their homes. Feringeea came on after them to Saugor, whence he proceeded to his home in Tehree.

A total of one hundred men and five women murdered in this expedition.

Report of an Expedition into Malwa and Rajpootana by Gangs under Oman Subahdar, and other Leaders, from the Gwalior Territories, in 1827-28.

1. Amaun Jemadar, Mussulman, (hung at Saugor 1832), father of Golab and Kaen Khan approvers, with nine Thugs, left Kerowlie and reached Peepara in Jypore, where he fell in with Aman Subahdar, Brahmin, with twenty Thugs. He had a Rajpoot with him, went on with them next day to Hunoomangow, and thence going on the following morning half a coss, killed and buried him under a Bur tree.

2. Went to Charso, where they fell in with two travellers,—came on with them to Gurawassee, and leaving that place the next morning, killed them on the road to Agra half a coss.

3. Went through Dehwas to Neweree, where they fell in with three Chuprassies going to Agra on business—came on with them to Powae, leaving this place next morning they killed them at a water-course one and a half coss distant.

4. Went back to Charsoo, where they fell in with a man with a buffaloe, went with him to Bhowras, and taking him on one and a half coss, next morning killed him.

5. Proceeded to Burwasagow where they fell in with three travellers, and accompanied them for four days—on the fourth they reached Kotepotlee, and going on with them the next morning, murdered them in the Alwar territory.

6. Returned towards Jypore and reached Gorha, where they fell in with a Kourutbee, (carrier of Ganges water) and going on with him to Nawla, killed him at the encampment.

7. Went to Jypore and thence towards Jogneer—on the road they fell in with another Kourutbee, and killed him at their encampment near a village on the road.

8. Went to Sambur, where they fell in with two men, and taking them on to a village called Kohgow, killed them at their encampment.

9. Went to Mirtha and thence towards Palee, when they fell in with a Byragee, murdered him at a village near Palee, and thence proceeded to Palee.

10. Here they met two Chumars, who pretended to be of the Jat caste, and coming on with them next morning two coss, killed them. They knew their caste by finding the tools of Chumars upon them.

11. Went back towards Jypore, and on the road met a Rajpoot. At a village before they reached Joudpore, they put him to death in camp, and returned towards Jypore.

12. At a village they met a traveller, whom they induced to set out at night, and killed him at a place seven coss distant.

13. Went through Sambur to Jypore. Here fell in with two travellers, took them on to a place two coss on

the road to Delhie, and there murdered them, and reached Newaree.

14. Here they fell in with a man with two Camels, going on with him six coss to a village on the road to Jypore, they put him to death.

15. Went to Bhugwunt and met a traveller, whom they killed the next morning at a place one coss from Bhugwuntgow on the road to Naea Sheher.

16. Came to Naea Sheher and met four Hindoos, encamped one day with them at Malana, they met at a village Kirowhe, and going on with them the following morning, killed them near the village of Mohlee in Kerowhe.

17. Went to Koochalgow and thence to Naea Sheher—met two Musselmen—went to Borhana, and going on with them half a coss the next morning put them to death.

18. After this affair they went through Mallana to Borondee, where they feasted with Buljeet Sing, an old acquaintance of theirs, for fifteen days, and then went to Gurawas, where they met Rostum Khan approver, with twelve Thugs, who had inveigled two Shop-keepers and a woman; going on with them one night, and the next morning went half a coss further and put them to death.

19. Going on three coss on the Delhie road after the last murder, they fell in with another Shop-keeper and his wife, and killed them at their encamping ground.

After this affair they dispersed and returned to their respectives homes, and this was the last expedition of the most noted Thug of his day, "Aman Subahdar," the cousin of Feringeea approver.

A total of thirty-four men and two women murdered in this expedition.

Report of an Expedition into Malwa and Khandeish by Gangs from Bundelcund and Gwalior, under Budaloo, Muneeram and others, in 1827-28.

1. Budaloo Jemadar with twelve, Munnee Ram eight, left Puchodrun in Gwalior. Mootee, brother of Kaleea Sing approver, with eight, Purmsook approver eight, and Bazkhan approver four, left Narae in Gwalior—all united and went to Surora, thence to Bhilsa, met two travellers, came on with them from Bhilsa to Moreea, where they killed them, and then went to Jehawur.

2. At Jehawur they met three Sepahees, having inveigled them to their camp, put them to death.

3. Going on through Tappa to a village on the other side, they met a Havildar and four companions, and coming on with them the next morning half a coss this side of Tappa, put them to death.

4. Going on to a village a coss on this side of Raghogur, they met a Rajpoot from Mhow and a Mussulman from Indore, on their way to Shajehanpore, in Rohilcund, and murdered them at night in camp.

5. Went to Para through the Mhow cantonments, and there they met Dirgpaul Subahdar with forty Thugs, Bhimma Jemadar twenty, Chutter Aheer twenty-five, Bukut approver twenty, Jungalee twenty, Kunhye approver sixteen, and Khosala sixteen. They had with them Lall Sing Subahdar and his family, consisting of nine persons. They travelled with them two days, and the third put them all to death except the two children, boys of one and a half years old.

6. Went to Dabohee, and Budaloo had a dispute. Budaloo, Purmsookh, Sakal and Bazkhan separated and went to Joudpore in the Barodah district, where they fell in with a Sepahee and his wife and a relative,

they encamped with the gang, and were at night put to death.

7. The next day Dhurum Khan Jemadar came up with nine Thugs on his way from Indore, he had murdered two Seikhs on their way from Lahore to Nagpore at Samneer. After this, he brought another traveller and murdered him in camp at Joudpore, after he joined Budaloo and his party.

8. Went to Ameergur and leaving that place next morning met seven men, and taking them to the place where they had put Lall Sing Subahdar to death, they murdered them.

9. Going to the village of Burree in the Barodah district, they fell in with Makhun Jemadar, Omrow Gungadeen, Bajee Khan and Bhawanee Sing with fifteen Thugs. All joined, making a gang of two hundred. Three Sepahees from Bombay and three Pundits from Barodah came up and encamped with them, and at night they were all killed.

10. After this affair Budaloo, Munneeram, Bhujjoo, Purmsookh, Sooklal and Bazkhan returned towards Indore and met Chutter Jemadar with twenty-five, all joined and came on together to a village on the other side of Dhar, here they inveigled five Sepahees who came on with them to Dhar—leaving Dhar next morning they killed them a coss on this side, and came on to the Mhow cantonments. Three of the friends of the murdered men had come on before them and meeting Purmsook Misser, asked what he had done with their friends—hearing this, all that could made off, but eleven were taken, and four of the fugitives were arrested afterwards near Bhopaul. After examination at Indore the Thugs were all released in February 1828. The property of the murdered persons was found on them, but they would not point out the bodies.

11. Makun, Gungadeen and the others, after they had separated from the rest, went to Dabargow and met five men on their way from Khumnat to Bhopaul; they killed them in camp.

12. Went through Barodah to Ahmedabad, where they met eight travellers whom they brought to the village of Peepala, and leaving that place with them next morning, they killed them a coss and a half on this side.

13. They returned to Barodah and thence took the road to Burnagur and Noulee, when they met a Banker with four attendants on the road from Noulee to Nathdwara, and two stages from Burnagur, on the road to Nathdwara, killed them.

14. Went to Nathdwara where they fell in with three travellers—they took them on a distance of twenty-two coss on the road to Ojean and then killed them.

15. They came towards Humeergurh, and on the road fell in with eight travellers on their way from Hydrabad to Joudpore, and killed them.

16. They all encamped together at the village of Dhukola, and were engaged in cooking, when three Troopers came up, and suspecting who they were got the assistance of the people of the village and fort, and seized above one hundred—twenty or thirty only of the Gang managed to escape.

17. Mootee Dirgpaul, Bhimmee, Bhujjoo, Joychund, Ajub, Chutter Aheer, Bukut approver, Jungulee, Kunhye, and Khoosalu, in all two hundred, went on to Barodah together, and there Motee, Joychund, Bhimmee and Ajub with eighty Thugs, separated and went to Broach, where they met a traveller and put him to death.

18. Went to Dhurumpore, where they met three travellers, and bringing them on two coss, killed them, and went on to Peth.

19. Here they met three Byragees, and taking them on one stage put them to death.

20. Went to Nasick and remained three days, the third day fell in with three Sepahees, and, taking them five coss on the Poonah road, killed them in camp.

21. Going on three stages more on the road to Poonah they met three treasure-bearers, and following them up a coss, put them to death. The bodies were left exposed, and they made off as fast as they could to a village on the other side of Bhilsa; here Motee and Bhimmee quarrelled, and separating, each returned to his home.

22. Ajub and Joychund Bilhas met two Rajpoots and a Brahmin (Sepahees), whom they murdered five and a half coss distant on the road to Dhoree.

23. After this affair they came to the river Aukee Jhankee, where they fell in with three Rajpoots and a Byragee. They left that place in the evening, and put them to death on the road within the boundaries of Dhoree, quarter of a coss the other side, and spent the night at Dhoree.

24. Here they fell in with five Rajpoots and one Byragee, coming on with them to a village three coss from Dhoree, they all dined together, after which they continued their journey and put them to death three coss from the village on the road to Indore—came to Indore, and thence all returned to their respective homes.

A total of ninety-five men and three women murdered in this expedition.

Report of an Expedition into Malwa and Gozerat by Gangs from Gwalior, Bundelcund and the Dooab, under Makun, Gungadeen and other Leaders in 1827-28.

1. These three gangs assembled at Omrow Sing's house at Mulaitera in Gwalior, and the neighbourhood, when Mundun Jemadar and his Mussulman Gang preceded Omrow Sing's and Makun's fifteen days; Makun's Gang left Mulaitera, proceeded from Jhansee to Seronje in three stages, and on the night of their arrival murdered a traveller who had taken up his quarters with them at the Pundwakee Bowlie.

2. They proceeded the following morning, and about half way to the first stage they came to a river where they saw four Sepahees cooking their dinner, whom they murdered with some difficulty, and plundered of their property.

3. After the murder of the four Sepahees, going on towards Indore, they met four strolling players whom they induced to join them on the pretence, that they would see their performance at the next stage. They were murdered at a well-known Temple and Bowlee near Bhopaul.

4. Their next stage was to the Pawn nullah, a short distance from Bhopaul, where a division of the plundered property took place, and four men were detached to their homes with all that was not required for immediate use, with instructions to rejoin in the vicinity of Indore. They continued their march the next morning, and had proceeded about a coss when they fell in with a party of twenty or twenty-five brother Phansegars, chiefly Mussulmen, who had inveigled two water carriers.

5. They were preparing to leave the village, where they had lodged during the night, when two Brahmins came up from Poonah én-route to Hindoostan, whom they murdered and robbed of their property.

6. They next proceeded to Rajghur in the Dewas Pergunnah, where they fell in with a Subahdar and two Sepahees of the Company's Service, and murdered them.

7. On the same night they met with and murdered a Gardener from the cantonments of Mhow.

8. The following morning, passing by the cantonment of Mhow, they arrived at a place called Dhar in four stages; remained there three days, for their four friends whom they had despatched to their homes with the booty—during their stay at Dhar a Mussulman joined them and was murdered.

9. Quitting Dhar for Baroda, they proceeded by short stages until they were joined by their absent friends at Barahitty; here they met a Banker and four Sepahees attendants, with a Bullock and Pony én-route to Baroda, whom they accompanied three or four stages and then murdered them.

10. In three stages they arrived at Oodeypore, where they met an European gentleman on his way to Mhow from Bombay, they studiously avoided him—he proceeded next morning with a number of travellers, who had sought his protection, and they took the road to Baroda. On the fourth or fifth stage from Oodeypore fell in with Dirgpal Subahdar Brahmin, and his gang on their return from Baroda—they encamped that night with them and prosecuted on the following morning their respective routes; when they arrived at Muckary they met five Company's Sepahees from Bombay, and murdered them.

11. They proceeded by short stages and arrived at Doobha—here they met a Brahmin and Mussulman from Doobha and Mahygaon, whom they murdered.

12. After the above murder they went to Baroda where they found Mundun and his Mussulman gang, who had

preceded them fifteen days and had perpetrated the following murders. Having passed the village of Dutteea about six coss distant, they murdered a Mahomedan Priest.

13. The gang having arrived at Oojein proceeded towards Baroda, and about five coss from the town they murdered a Barber and Byragee or Hindoo mendicant.

14. Mundun Jemadar and his Mussulman gang joined the gangs of Mukun and Omrow, and the three gangs leaving Baroda, proceeded towards Broach, and arrived within seven coss of it on the day of the Holey festival, which they celebrated with due solemnity. At this place they met two Mussulmen and a Byragee whom they murdered.

15. After this murder they struck off the Broach road, and proceeded via Jaonuggur and Dwarka to Pihawud, where they met four travellers proceeding to Baroda with considerable property, and as they would in all probability reach it the same night, the gang detached twenty-five of the most expert Thugs, who came up with them a short distance from the Cantonments and murdered them; but, much to their mortification, they found the subjects of their pursuit to be poor stone-cutters, with their working implements tied up in bundles.

16. The men detached on this expedition having rejoined, they all again took the Baroda road and fell in with some horse dealers, and their horses, but from the difficulty of disposing of so many bodies on so frequented a road, and as much time had already been spent in their consultation, they deemed it advisable to forego their designs; the same night they were molested by thieves and lost some property. They left it in the morning and having reached Baroda set out for Hindoostan—about two coss on the first stage they met three travellers and murdered them.

17. Their next march brought them to the village or town of Dhuboy, where they fell in with four Pedlars whom they murdered.

18. Having left Dubhoy, they met six Palanquin bearers, two women and two children, whom they persuaded to accompany them—they arrived at the end of their march and having taken temporary possession of a Temple, no opportunity offered for effecting their designs. They started however next morning in company with the bearers, and murdered them, having despatched a party the previous evening for the preparation of their graves.

19. After this murder they encamped on the banks of the river Mahie in four separate parties, where four travellers from Baroda, én-route to Bhopaul, arrived, and encamped near one of them whom they murdered.

20. Their next stage was Oodeipore, where they met a number of hackeries laden with Opium, under an escort of Sepahees, one of whom remarking that some men of a similar caste had been apprehended at the Cantonment of Mhow, they became considerably alarmed and occupied a position in a retired spot in a jungle near a fountain. Makhun Jemadar, having occasion to go to the Bazar, fell in with a party of horsemen from Baroda, with a Palanquin and some Sepahees—on one of them remarking that Makhun wore a necklace very like one his brother wore, Makhun Jemadar became greatly agitated and immediately rejoining his gang related to them what had occurred, upon which the whole party quitted the place and proceeded many coss on the Jubbooa road. At Jubbooa Omrow Sing and his gang quitted the others and preceded them on the Rutlam road a short distance. Their first stage was Jhillawud, and Makun with his party were a short distance in the rear. At Jhillawud, the gangs again met, but Omrow and his followers again quitted on the

following morning, while Makun and the others halted there at a Bowlie outside the town—here they found a Banker and his four attendants cooking, who immediately, from the expensive ornaments and clothes upon them, became the objects of their attention and design; but the travellers proceeding on their journey after their meal escaped them, but fell in with Omrow Sing's party, who murdered them.

21. Makun's and Nundun's gangs quitted Jhillawud and proceeded towards Rutlam, where they met two or three of the advanced party from whom they learnt of the despatch of the Banker and attendants, who had proved a most valuable prize—Makun and Nundun Jemadars took the Peeplodah road to avoid Jourah and the residence of Captain Borthwick. Omrow Sing and his gang had also deviated from their route for the same purpose. The three gangs again met at Doodah, one stage beyond Jourah, and proceeded together via Mundisair—about five coss, they halted near a village under a large tree where stands a Fakeer's temple, and there meeting a Mussulman traveller they murdered him.

22. Having continued their march in the morning they went a short distance, and after some consultation dispatched Rutting Ram and a party of men to their homes, in charge of the plunder they had acquired, he left them accordingly at the next stage. They then took the road to Neemuch, and halted for a day at the north side of the Cantonments, where they fell in with four travellers whom they murdered.

23. Two or three stages further they met another traveller whom they also murdered.

24. At Tangawa four Shop-keepers came in their way and met with the same fate. This was their last affair—when they arrived at Dikallah, Captain Borthwick, having

heard of their proceedings, detached a party of horse to apprehend them. The horsemen came upon the gangs unawares while encamped outside a village, and accused them of stealing Opium; they were glad to have an opportunity of clearing themselves of this unfounded accusation, so accompanied the horsemen to the village for the purpose of being examined; immediately on their arrival, they were secured and taken to Captain Borthwick, of whom seventy-nine were made prisoners—viz. five made approvers—seventy-four tried by Colonel Stewart (Resident at Hydrabad), thirty-nine condemned to death, twenty-one to imprisonment for life, eleven to limited imprisonment, and three acquitted. Total seventy-nine.

A total of seventy-three men and four women murdered in this expedition.

Report of an Expedition into Berar and Khandeish made by Gangs from the Saugor and Nerbudda Districts, under Lall Khan, Mudee Khan and others, in 1827-28.

1. They left their homes in the District of Nursingpore on the Nerbudda river and reached Oomroutee in thirteen days and then went towards Aurungabad, about a coss from which place they met a Kular and his wife on their way from Nagpore to Jaulna; came on the following morning, and lodged that night with them. The next morning they proceeded to Moortagapore via Boregow to Lakunwara, and encamped outside the village, and were joined by Bhow Jemadar, Lodhee and eight followers. They set out with the travellers next morning and murdered them at the spot selected, and buried their bodies in a nullah.

2. After this affair they took the Lakunwara road, and while examining the booty acquired in the last affair, were joined by Monowur, Lall Mahomed, Sahoo and fourteen others, and came to Lakunwara together—left it in the morning, and at a Pass a coss distant met two travellers whom they murdered and buried.

3. They reached Jaulna in three days after this affair, where the parties separated. Kurreem Khan and Monowur Jemadars with thirty, proceeded towards Aurungabad, while Bhow Jemadar and eight followers proceeded towards Nandair. The gang under Kurreem Khan and Monowur reached Aurungabad in five days without meeting any travellers, and then went to Dholeea together and encamped at a temple, and there met Ruheem Khan who joined their gang. They proceeded with six travellers whom they met at Dholeea, viz. two men, three women and one girl, to a village about two coss off, where they halted. Then set out from this place about midnight and murdered them as they were going along, and buried their bodies in the jungles. They reached Burhanpore in eight days, where they divided the spoils of the last affair and were joined there by two hundred and fifty Thugs under the following leaders—Chotee Brahmin, Bhoree, Brickbam, Soorjun, Kurreem Khan, Bundgee who were flying away from the Gurgowders' district, in consequence of a traveller having effected his escape out of a party whom they were murdering. They all halted four days without meeting any travellers; when Chotee and Munaur Jemadars returned to their respective homes with their followers. Shaik Kurreem with fourteen Thugs, and Bundgee, started for Oomroutee, and reached it in seven days, from whence Sheik Kurreem with his fourteen Thugs went towards their homes, and Bundgee Jemadar and his six Thugs went to the Deckan.

4. Shaik Kurreem and his gang fell in with three men and one girl at Synegaon, and travelled with them five days; having succeeded in gaining their confidence, on the fifth day they encamped at a village the other side of the river Amneer—started with the travellers in the morning and murdered them between Amneer and the village at which they encamped and buried their bodies in a nullah.

A total of eight men, five women, and one girl murdered in this expedition.

Total—Three hundred and sixty four men, twenty women and one girl murdered during the different expeditions this season.

Names of the Principal Leaders of the Gangs engaged in the foregoing Expeditions for 1827-28.

No.	Names of Leaders.	Cast.	Resident.	Remarks.	No. of Thugs.
	Chotee Jemadar,	Brahmin,	Jhansee,	Approver,	30
	Sheik Nungoo,	Mussulman,		Died at his home in 1829,	30
	Jalim,	Ditto,	Tehree,	Ditto 1833,	20
	Lall Mahomed,	Ditto,	Jhansee,	Approver,	5
5	Ashraff,	Ditto,	Gwalior,	At large,	0
	Dhurum Khan,	Ditto,	Saugor,	Hung at Saugor in 1832,	5
	Khuleel Khan,	Ditto,	Jhansee,	Ditto ditto,	8
	Roshun Jemadar,	Ditto,	Ditto,	Ditto ditto,	15
	Madaree,	Ditto,	Ditto,	Hung at Jubulpore in 1830,	4
10	Ghureeba,	Ditto,	Ditto,	Hung at Saugor in 1832,	3
	Monohur,	Brahmin,	Sumthur,	Died in 1833,	6
	Purusram,	Lodhee,	Jhansee,	Died in March 1838,	20
	Mohraj,	Brahmin,	Sumthur,	Drowned himself after his arrest in 1832,	5
	Persaud,	Lodhee,	Jhansee,	Hung at Saugor 30th June 1833,	15
15	Bukhut,	Brahmin,	Ditto,	At large,	5
	Dorogna,	Mussulman,	Ditto,	Died in Jubulpore Jail in 1835,	4
	Feringeea,	Brahmin,	Gwalior,	Approver,	25
	Gholab Jemadar,	Mussulman,	Seronje,	Transported in 1832,	5
	Sooper Sing alias Khan Mahomed,	Ditto,	Gwalior,	Hung at Saugor in 1832,	15
20	Sheik Meerun,	Ditto,	Hydrabad,	Died at home in 1837,	20
	Sahib Khan Jemadar,	Ditto,	Ditto,	Approver,	10
	Kalee Khan, Do.	Ditto,	Ditto,	At large,	10
	Kureem,	Ditto,	Bhopaul,	Hung at Saugor in 1832,	10
	Bhyroo,	Ditto,	Seronje,	Hung at Jowra in 1829,	20
25	Bhowaneea,	Sooseea,	Pertabgurh,	Ditto 1830,	20

	Ramla,	Sooseea,	Pertabgurh,	Approver,	20
	Buhoreena,	Lodhee,	Huttah,	Died in Hydrabad Jail in 1832,	5
	Sheik Inaeut Jemadar,	Mussulman,	Jhansee,	Approver,	30
	Sheik Lall,	Ditto,	Saugor,	Hung at Saugor in 1833,	10
30	Zoolfakar,	Ditto,	Ditto,	Ditto 1832,	10
	Munohur,	Ditto,	Jhansee,	Approver,	
	Beejoee,	Ditto,	Bandah,	Died in Saugor Jail in 1832,	2
	Bhula,	Buneea,	Jhalone,	Approver,	10
	Bhowanee,	Lodhee,	Ditto,	Ditto,	10
35	Dumee Jemadar,	Ditto,	Cawnpore,	Died in Furukabad Jail,	30
	Chutter,	Aheer,	Ditto,	Hung at Jubulpore in 1836,	10
	Zoolfakar Jemadar,	Mussulman,	Puna,	Approver,	12
	Pahar ditto,	Ditto,	Jhansee,	Died at his home in 1830,	4
	Noorkhan ditto,	Ditto,	Ditto,	Hung at Jubulpore in 1835,	10
40	Essuree ditto,	Brahmin,	Bhopaul,	At large,	14
	Gholab alias Bhushra ditto,	Mussulman,	Peethoreea,	Hung at Saugor in 1832,	25
	Aman ditto,	Ditto,	Gwalior,	Ditto ditto,	9
	Aman Subahdar,	Brahmin,	Jhansee	Died at home in 1828,	20
	Rustum Khan Jemadar,	Mussulman,	Dholepore,	Approver,	12
45	Budloo Jemadar,	Lodhee,	Jhansee,	Hung at Saugor in 1832,	12
	Muneeram,	Ditto,	Ditto,	Ditto ditto,	8
	Motee Jemadar,	Ditto,	Ditto,	Ditto ditto.	8
	Dhokal alias Purumsook,	Brahmin,	Gwalior,	Ditto ditto,	8
	Baz Khan,	Mussulman,	Sumthur,	Approver,	4
50	Dirgpaul Subahdar,	Brahmin,	Gwalior,	Hung at Saugor in 1832,	40
	Bhimee Jemadar,	Lodhee,	Ditto,	Approver,	20
	Joychund ditto,	Rajpoot,	Ditto,	Died in Saugor Jail in 1831,	13
	Ajub ditto,	Brahmin,	Indore,	Hung at Saugor in 1832,	20
	Chutter Jemadar,	Aheer,	Gwalior,	Hung at Saugor in 1832,	25
55	Bukut ditto,	Rajpoot,	Indore,	Approver,	20
	Junglee,	Mussulman,	Gwalior,	Transported in 1832,	20

No.	Names of Leaders.	Cast.	Resident.	Remarks.	No. of Thugs.
	Kunhye Jemadar,	Aheer,	Ditto,	Killed by a Zemindar in the Gwalior Territory in 1833,	16
	Khosala,	Mussulman,	Ditto,	Transported from Saugor in 1832,	16
	Soorjun,	Aheer,	Ditto,	At large,	
60	Uchroo,	Koomhar,	Duteea,	Hung at Saugor in 1832,	
	Dhurum Khan,	Mussulman,	Gwalior,	Died at Surohee ditto,	9
	Makhun Jemadar,	Lodhee,	Sumthur,	Hung at Jowra, December 1829,	40
	Gungadeen,	Ditto,	Ditto,	Ditto ditto,	35
	Omrow,	Ditto,	Etawa,	Transported from Saugor in 1829,	30
65	Rujee Khan,	Mussulman,	Jhansee,	Hung at Jowra, December 1829,	5
	Bhowanee Jemadar.	Lodhee,	Gwalior,	Ditto ditto,	40
	Chuttee ditto,	Brahmin,	Jhansee,	Hung at Saugor in 1832,	25
	Kurreem Khan,	Mussulman,	Jubulpore,	Approver,	
	Lal Khan,	Ditto,	Ditto,	Transported from Saugor in 1832,	
70	Mudee Khan,	Ditto,	Ditto,	Hung at Saugor in ditto,	
	Bhoree,	Ditto,	Ditto,	Ditto ditto in ditto,	
	Roshun Khan,	Ditto,	Ditto,	Died in Saugor Jail in 1832,	
73	Monowur,	Ditto,	Ditto,	Approver,	

EXPEDITIONS

OF THE

MALWA AND KHANDEISH GANGS,

IN 1828-29.

Report of an Expedition into Malwa and Khandeish by some Gangs from Bundelcund and Gwalior, amounting to one hundred and twenty persons, under Bhujjoo, Khoshal, Khoorkoo and Dulsah, in the year 1828-29.

1. Bhujjoo Jemadar with eight Thugs, and Khoshal with eighteen, left their homes, and proceeding through Bhilsa crossed the Nerbudda at Chimpanee and reached Berhanpore; here Khorkoo Jemadar with forty, and Dulsa with thirty, joined them—they proceeded through Aurungabad, Lahoree and Bamboree, to within four stages of Poonah, without killing any one. They returned to Ankee Jhankee, two stages beyond Dholeea, where they met two Rajpoots—leaving that place before day light next morning, they put them to death at a place a coss and a half from their encampment on the road to Dholeea.

2. After this they came to Walagon, where they met a Rajpoot, and bringing him to the village of Rae, spent the night there—proceeding about one coss next morning, before day light they killed him.

3. The gang came on to Dholeea, where, in February 1829, they fell in with seven Treasure Bearers. They

followed them and reached Amulnair, and thence to Choupara, on the Taptee, to Dhoree, without getting the Treasure Bearers into their power. On the fourth day the Rokureeas reached Dharee, about ten in the morning, and cooked their dinner on the bank of the river. The Thugs did the same at a distance. After they had dined, the Treasure Bearers went on about mid-day, and two coss from the place, about 2 P. M., the Thugs overtook them in a jungle and killed them; but they only found six, one having gone on—they left the bodies exposed and made off with the Treasure—fifteen of them were seized by the Police of the country under Captain Hodges, the Magistrate of Kandeish, and the remainder reached their homes in safety.

A total of nine men murdered in this expedition.

Report of an Expedition made in Berar and Khandeish by some Gangs from Bundelcund and Gwalior, amounting to two hundred and twenty, under Feeringeea, Phoolsa, Tijjun, Buhorena, Gungadeen, Hurreea and others.

1. Feringeea with twenty-three, Phoolsa thirteen, Tijjun twenty-four, left their homes at Gorha in Jhansee, and at Bhilsa met Buhorena with five, making a gang of sixty-five Thugs. They crossed the Nerbudda at Kherepore, and reached Roojana in Deogur, on the road to Nagpore. There they met a traveller, inveigled him to their camp from the village, and murdered him. Phoolsa was arrested by the people of the village.

2. The gang went on to Omrowtee, and on the road they met Rambuksh, Rae Sing, and Heera approver, on their way back from the Dhoree affair, who recommended

them to fly, as the Police was in pursuit. They went on to Omrowtee from this place. Tijjun twenty, and Buhorena five, left the gang and returned. Feringeea went on to Nadgow to Sonee; where he met five men on their way back to Lucknow, with Images and Busts for sale—with them were Gungadeen with seven, Hureea approver five, Lall Khan, Jemadar, eight, and Adhar, Jemadar, five. All united and came with the travellers to Bham, leaving that place the next morning, they killed them at a place half a coss distant.

3. After this affair they went to Mungrook; leaving that place the next day, on the road to Hydrabad they met Tilokee Sing Havildar and four Sipahees on their way to Singheerampoor, in Jhansee. Returned with them the next day and killed them at a place two coss distant.

4. After the last affair they went to Phaleegow, on the road to Hydrabad, where they met two Hindoos and five Mussulmen—coming on with them to a place two coss north of Phaleegow, they put them to death.

5. Proceeded to Phandegow, where they met Hosein Khan, Jemadar, with ten, and Sheik Kurreem, approver, with twenty—coming on with four travellers. These four men were killed at the encampment.

6. Went through Nandair to Gungakhere, where they met three travellers—took them on to Sehloo, and leaving that place next morning murdered them.

7. Went to Jhalna, and on preparing to set out the next morning, four men came up and accompanied them to a village between Jhalna and Boregow, and leaving that place the following morning killed them.

8. After this affair they came to Barora, a village on the road to Omrowtee, where they fell in with four men, whom they killed next morning, one and a half coss on the road to Lakunwara.

9. They then proceeded on the Omrowtee road to Basum where they met three men—leaving the place with them the next day they killed them one coss distant.

10. Coming on they met six men, whom they accompanied to a village six or seven coss from Basum, and leaving this next morning they killed them at one and a half coss on the road to Purureea.

11. The gang proceeded to Soonee, where they met four Kowrutties. They were Sepahees who had taken that disguise for security—coming on next day they killed them half a coss from Soonee.

12. After the last affair they went to Omrowtee, where they met two travellers,—came on to a village seven coss from Omrowtee on the Nagpore road, and put them to death in camp.

13. Returned to Omrowtee and there met Zoolfakar (hung at Saugor) with seven men, all joined and went to Burwulagow, on the road to Hydrabad, where they met a Punditanee and two attendants. Took them on to Boregow, and leaving that next morning put them to death about one coss distant.

14. They reached Korinja and there met four Seiks—leaving this place next day they killed them at a place one coss this side.

15. The gang returned to Omrowtee where they fell in with Mojahid Khan (hung at Jubulpore 1835,) with twenty, Kalee Khan (still at large) with eight: all united, and brought nine travellers to Mojhuree, where they killed them.

16. After the last affair the men of the Deccan returned towards Hydrabad, and Feringeea and followers came to Meinpanee, in Baitool, where they fell in with two Hindoos and a Mussulman, and coming on a coss with them next morning they killed them.

17. After this the gangs dispersed and returned home, except Feringeea and two followers, who came to Saugor and there met Ghasee Khan Duffadar, with three companions. They left Saugor with these three men, and in three days reached Kheree in Churkaree territory, on the road to Calpee. There they met Zoolfakar Approver with nineteen, on his way from his home at Purwaha in Jhansee —Zoolfakar had murdered a Tailor, his wife, son and daughter at Kuneara, in the Myhere territory,—they were on their way from Allahabad to Nagpore.

18. All the gang, except those who returned home, went to Jeitpore, where they fell in with one Mussulman, whom they took on half a coss and then murdered.

19. They went to Khopnewaree, where they met a man on his way from Mhow—taking him to a nullah one coss distant, next morning they killed him.

20. After this they came to the village of Jumaneea, close by the Sudder Bazar at Saugor, where they met two Mussulmen Merchants, with horses for sale, from Bhopaul. They killed them at their encampment and buried their bodies under a hill at some distance.

21. After this affair Hyaut and Noorkhan returned home and Zoolfakar and his men went on to Rahtgurh, where they met a Kahar, and taking him on, a coss and a half, next day, towards Saugor, killed him. Afraid of the search for Thugs on that road they came back to Khyra, in Churkaree, where they met Feringeea, who pointed out his companions (Ghasee Khan Duffadar and his companions) as a good prize. They went on with them to Chutterpore, where they met Omeda and Sewdeen Sing Jemadars, they all joined and proceeded with the travellers to Jytpore, and thence taking them on half a coss put them to death, after which they dispersed and returned to their homes.

A total of seventy-seven men and three women murdered in this expedition.

Report of an Expedition made into Bundelcund and the Saugor Territories by some Gangs from Bundelcund and Gwalior, to the amount of two hundred, under Inaeut, Zalim, Ashroff, Bukut, Bheeka and others, in the year 1829.

1. Inaeut with twenty Thugs, Zalim ten, and Ashroff ten, left Guteara, in Jhansee, and going to Mundula, in Punna, killed two Shop-keepers going to Punna with cloth.

2. Came on to Biseynee, Bukut Jemadar (hung at Saugor), Bukut 2d (transported), Bikha (still at large), and Bhugee Lodhee (transported), with a gang of twenty-four Thugs. They had with them four Sepahees. The whole united and went on with them half a coss on the road to Khopnewaree and put them to death.

3. They returned to Biseynee, where they fell in with three Treasure Bearers, and leaving Biseynee with them put them to death—after this affair they returned to their homes.

4. Inaeut had been at home only four days when Bhola Buneea Approver came to him with a party of four Thugs, and they opened a second expedition. Inaeut had twenty, Lall Mahomed six, and Bhola four. They came to Biseynee, where they fell in with Bhowanee, the son of Mukka, with forty Thugs. Soon after they had joined a Moonshee, by name Bhowanee Sing, came, upon his way, from Soonee, they went to Jhoojhar Ghat, where he was put to death with his four companions.

5. Went thence to Chutterpore, where they fell in with two Hindoos and a Mussulman, Sepahees, on their way to

the Dooab—they went on with them to Sitaree, a little west of Jytpore, and going on with them next morning put them to death.

6. Thence went to Loghasee, where they fell in with three other Sepahees on their way home, they took them on to Jytpore, where they met Khuluk Jemadar, Bhowanee, son of Runna, Dhokul Jemadar, Noorkhan and others, with a gang of sixty Thugs. All made a gang of one hundred and fifty, and going on with the Sepahees, half a coss from Jytpore, put them to death.

7. After this some went to their homes, but Inaeut, Peer Mahomed and Lall Mahomed came to Goolgunge with a party of forty, and there met two Pundits taking cloths to Jhansee—going on with them to Khurgapore, in Tehree, and half a coss from that place on the Jhansee road, they put them to death.

8. They came to Khopnewarree, in Punna, and there met two travellers going to the Dooab. Deeba Buneea joined them with four men—and going on one coss from Khopnewarree, put them to death.

9. Going on one coss on the road to Punnah, they met two men, a Buneea and his companion—going on with them to the boundary of Muhoba village, they killed them.

10. After this affair Inaeut went home. Bhola Buneea soon after came again to Inaeut, and they proceeded together. Inaeut with twenty men and Bhola with five, they reached Biseynee. Here they met a man from Nehreepunguree, in Banda, who had been to see his son at Jubulpore, and had arrived near his home. They took him on half a coss on the road to Khopa and put him to death.

11. They returned and came through Biseynee to Shuhgurh, where they fell in with Gholab, alias Koman, and nine, Bhika, son of Sunum, with five, Bodha two, and

Khyratee with three. All united, and soon after a man came up with a camel and a Sepahee—they took them to Pareyna, in Punna, and put them to death.

12. Went back to Khopa where Bhikah, Lall Mahomed and Bhoda left them, and returned to their homes—on their way they fell in at Hadjeegur, with two treasure bearers, and there murdered them.

13. Inaeut was joined at Khopa by Rambuksh, son of Punna, with five Thugs, Meherban five, Persaud five and Dhokul five. All united and came to Biseynee—here two Blacksmiths, two Shop-keepers and a Trooper came up. They took them on some distance on the Khopa road and murdered them.

14. They proceeded through Punna to Sohawul, where they met three travellers on their way to the Dooab. Inaeut sent on twenty Thugs with Esuree, who took them on two coss, east of Kothee Sohawul, and killed them. Inaeut and the rest came to Sunkur Killa, in Oocheyra, where they met a traveller and put him to death at night in camp. After this they went to Myhere and there met Bhukun Khan with eight followers.

15. Proceeded to Sewagunge, on the road from Jubulpore to Mirzapore, here the twenty men rejoined them, Inaeut was soon after seized by some approvers from Jubulpore, going with the 73rd to Bandah. Rambuksh, Dibba, Miherban, Persaud and Esuree fled towards Mirzapore, and at Oomerpatun killed six Goosaens from Elichpore to Benares.

16. After the arrest of Inaeut, Chand Khan and Dulelee, his brother, with Bhekun Khan (approver) fled to Belehree with all his gang, and there fell in with two Kawrutties, two Tailors and a woman. Took them on to Biseynee, where two other travellers joined them, and they took the whole seven on to the nullah, where they had

murdered five men on the road to Khopa, and there put them to death—after this affair they returned home.

A total of fifty-two men and one woman murdered in this expedition.

Report of an Expedition made by a Gang of seventy Thugs from Bundelcund and Gwalior under Buduloo, Purmsook, Muneeram, Heera, Rambuksh and Chotee, in the year 1829.

1. Buduloo, Purmsook, Muneeram, Heera and Rambuksh with fifty Thugs from Bundelcund, crossed the Nurbudda, at Chiepanee, and proceeded to Boorhanpore and thence to Chowka Phoolmaree, where they fell in with a traveller. Taking him on one coss and a half they killed him. This is the man whose sitrengees were brought to Saugor.

2. They went to Aurungabad, where they fell in with two Rajpoots going from that place to Naggur, they took them on two coss and put them to death and went on to Naggur.

3. At Naggur they fell in with three travellers. They took them on two coss, put them to death and went on to Poonah. From a village four coss this side of Poonah, they retraced their steps and struck off on the road to Nasick.

4. At Nasick they met Chotee, who had escaped from Beharee Lall Seith and reached that place with a gang of twenty Thugs. He had gone to Barodah and there killed a Rajpoot.

5. At Nasick the gangs joined and fell in with two travellers. Taking them on one and a half coss, they killed them and thence Chotee returned to Nasick, while the rest went to Barodah and thence to Tuppa.

6. At Tuppa they fell in with Soorut Sing Tomandar and four attendants. One and a half coss from Tuppa, on the road to Echawur, they put them to death. After this they dispersed and returned to their respective homes.

7. Chotee fell in with two women at Nasick in search of service—he accompanied them to a village, one stage on the other side of Nasick, and killed them both.

8. They returned through Nasick to Barodah, where they fell in with two Rajpoots, one Lodhee and one Aheer. They went on with them to Chanee, where they killed all four in camp.

9. After this affair they went on to the banks of the Mehee river in Guzerat, whence they returned to the Khyra cantonments—here they fell in with two men on their way to Bhurtpore—going on with them to a village two coss distant, they killed them.

10. They went back to Barodah where they fell in with five Sepahees—came on with them to Makhunee where they murdered them in their camp. After this affair they heard of the execution of Makhun, Gungadeen and their gang at Jowra, and in alarm returned to their respective homes.

A total of twenty-seven men killed in this expedition.

Report of an Expedition into Berar by a gang of forty Thugs, under Bhodae, Bukut, Moreea, Soorjun Aheer, Jowahir, Nunhooa Weaver, and Mandhata, in the year 1829.

1. Bodhee (hung at Saugor), Bukut, Moreea, Soorjun Aheer, Jowahir, Nunhooa and Mandhata with forty Thugs from Jhansee and Gwalior, set out and reached Rughoogur in Bhopaul, where they met two travellers, took them on one coss on the road to Jowra, and there put them to death.

2. After this they crossed the Nerbudda river at the Pugulana Ghat and reached Omrowtee, where they found four men in search of service—they took them to Bham, pretending to be able to get service for them—and thence going on half a coss put them to death.

They came back to Bham and were dividing the booty when the people of Dunraj Seith came and arrested twenty-two of the gang, the rest escaped. They remained in confinement four months when they heard that orders had been sent from Jubulpore for them, and dreading the consequences of coming here, they broke their prison and got off. They were not in irons and remained merely to negociate for the cost of their release.

Dirgpal Subahdar had returned from his expedition into Guzerat, and having had a dispute with his associates he went to Narain Raw, Subah of Gwalior, and got a guard to seize Durroo and Motee—having heard this, these two men fled and came in the same character to Jubulpore whence Durroo got a guard and arrested Dirgpal and Ramchund. Durroo and these two men were sent from Jubulpore to Jowra, where Durroo was hung and Dirgpal sent to Gwalior and released. He was again seized in 1831, and executed at Saugor in 1832.

A total of six men murdered in this expedition.

Report of an Expedition into Rajpootana by some gangs under Bhimmee, Saadut Khan and other Jemadars, with a gang of Thugs, in the year 1828-29.

1. Eight years ago, Bhimmee Jemadar with twenty-two Thugs, after observing the usual omens, left their homes in the Jhansee district on a Thuggee expedition. They

reached Secundra, four coss from Jypore, in ten days, where they met Saadut Khan, (approver) Aman, Setar Khan, (hung) Bheka and Chundee Jemadars, (still at large). Shortly after this they fell in with four travellers, two Hindoo Blacksmiths and two women from Jypore en route to Allahabad—Bejee Sing Jemadar acted as Sothai or inveigler, and won their confidence, and they proceeded in their company next morning. After proceeding a short distance, east of the village of Mangouh, they were all strangled, and their bodies buried in the sand, but were exhumed by the wild beasts a few days afterwards and discovered by the civil authorities.

2. After this affair they proceeded to Leik in Jypore, and while encamped outside the city, Bigae Sing introduced a traveller to them—a party of the gang set out with him in the morning and effected their designs on him after proceeding about a coss on the Agra road, and rejoined the main gang.

3. They then arrived at Jypore in five days, where Setar Khan won the confidence of two travellers en route to Bhurtpore. They left this place with them next morning, and murdered them on arriving at a mangoe grove, one coss distant.

4. They struck off to the Delhie road and while resting near a nullah, were overtaken by three travellers, Mussulmen, proceeding from Neemuch to Delhie, accompanied them to a mangoe tope, three coss from Achreole, and, after the congregation they found assembled there had been dispersed, they strangled them and interred their bodies in an adjacent field.

5. On the following morning they reached Achreole, and while encamped in the Serai, were joined by Peearjee Jemadar, with twenty-two Thugs, of the Soseea caste. Shortly after four Rajpoots from Gwalior came up én-

route to Lahore, who had with them two horses about 400 rupees value. Gholab Khan afterwards inveigled three more travellers, one a Sewar belonging to a Corps of Local Horse, returning from leave, and the other two from Jyepore, en-route to Kurnal. The same day Sutar Khan won the confidence of six more travellers, two Bheesties (or water carriers), one Mussulman and three Hindoos from the Dekhan, en-route to Delhi. Gholab Khan set out with the three travellers in the Delhi direction, and after descending a Pass, two coss from Achrole, killed them in a heavy jungle, threw their bodies into a nullah and covered them over with stones.

6. Sutar Khan and forty Thugs set out with the six travellers shortly after Gholab Khan and his party; and on arriving at the spot where the above murder was perpetrated, the travellers became alarmed at seeing the Sewar's horse without its owner and ran off, but the gang followed, soon after overtook and strangled them; when brought their bodies to the place where the three men had been interred. These bodies were discovered by the local authorities. Bhimee Jemadar then set out with his own gang and the remaining four travellers; but were obliged to forego their intentions on account of the lateness in leaving their ground, and they consequently proceeded to Munear Thana, where the parties who had preceded them were encamped. Having previously taken the precaution to leave two Thugs, Kudar Buksha and Mungra Sooseea, near the place where the nine men were murdered, to give them intelligence in case the bodies should be discovered. In the evening they detached seven men to bury them more securely; but before these men reached the place, they saw a concourse of people collected round the dead bodies, and lost no time in giving the gang intelligence, and they immediately made off, leaving their four victims behind unhurt,

they halted at the Ghasee Thana, and divided the spoils acquired on the expedition; after which the Sooseea Thugs left the gang, and the remainder proceeded via Ulroul and Rujghur to Dhoosa, whence Laek and Doorjun (approvers) went to their homes, and the remainder toward Jypore. They halted at Lallsoute, where they met Bhowaneea (nose cut) and Omna Dacoits, who informed the Police of their being Thugs, and caused their apprehension: but they obtained their release after delivering up their property.

A total of seventeen men and two women murdered in this expedition.

Report of an Expedition into Rajpootana by a gang of Thugs under Chutter, Ameer Allee, Imamee, and Kalee Khan, in January 1829.

1. At half a coss distant from the village of Sasmere, they met two shopkeepers on their way from Indore—halted with them during the night, and, going on with them next morning, murdered them at a water course a short distance from the village.

2. They then went towards the Mukundeea Pass, there met two travellers from Indore, halted with them during the night, and the next morning went on with them to Burnoon, in the Khotah territory—set out again at day break next morning, and murdered them under a tree. They next proceeded to Lukheree and Niea Sheher, in the Jypore territory, and there met a party of six Koeleea Thugs,—

3. Whom they joined, and formed a gang of thirteen. They then went to Milana, thence towards Indore—on the road met four Brahmins, went on with them to Khosalghur,

where they passed the night; started the next morning, and murdered them, about a coss and half distant, in the plain.

4. After this affair the Koeleea Thugs returned to their homes, to spend the Hooley festival. Two months after this expedition, in the month of March 1829, Imamee opened another expedition with a party of twenty-six Thugs, and proceeded to Garwasa, in the Jypore territory, there met two Bunjarus, set out with them next morning, and murdered them near a water course, a coss from the village—proceeded to the village and sent back four men to bury their bodies securely.

5. Proceeded on the road to Dhoosa; the following morning halted at a village one and a half coss distant, there fell in with a traveller, murdered him about midnight and afterwards proceeded to Dhoosa.

6. There met an Affghan; proceeded with him towards Lalsont; halted at a village—left it about midnight, strangled him at the banks of a water course, and went on to Lalsont.

7. At Lalsont they met a Sepahee, proceeded with him to the next stage and encamped there—left it about midnight, and murdered him on the march.

8. Then took the road to Agra, and while halted at a Chokie, fell in with a Duffadar and three Nujeebs—halted with them at a village; proceeded towards Dholpore Baree the next morning, and strangled them in a nullah; got from them four Bullocks, which they disposed of.

9. Went towards Nugora and met a traveller a short distance this side of the village, on his way home from Neemuch, and murdered him.

10. From Nagura went to Madhoorajpore and were then joined by five Soosea Thugs, and soon after fell in with nine travellers on their way home—set out from Madhoorajpore in company with the travellers towards Jypore, and murdered them about one coss from the town.

11. Halted that day at a village where they were joined by five travellers on their way to their homes,—came on with them to Gararwas, and, leaving that place before day light, murdered them in the open plain, and buried their bodies in a water course which they, in the dark, took for the Bele selected by their people for the murder. It proved however to be a place much frequented by the villagers—on discovering their mistake they sent back some of their party to see whether the bodies might be discovered; and they found that they had been dug up by jackalls, and that a concourse of people had collected round them. They returned forthwith to the gang, who immediately dispersed but rendezvoused some days afterwards at Karowlie, where a division of the plunder took place, the Soosea Thugs did not rejoin them.

12. On the road to Karowlie, they fell in with a Chuprassee of the Insurance office, on his return to Calcutta from Mhow, where he had delivered some books to Captain Burns on the 20th July 1829—he encamped with them at Rujooghur, and going on with them next morning, he was murdered.

13. They then came to Peepala and then to Tuppa; there met a Havildar, two Sepahees and two of their relations going to their homes in Oude; they induced them to join their party and encamped with them at Konoee in the Bhopaul territory; started with them the following morning and murdered them half a coss from the village. This was their last affair. Of the men present in this expedition fifteen were soon after apprehended, of whom five were executed; three made approvers, and the remainder sentenced to imprisonment for life.

A total of thirty-eight men murdered in this expedition.

A total of two hundred and twenty-six men and six women murdered during the different expeditions this season.

Names of the Principal Leaders of the Gangs engaged in the foregoing Expeditions for 1829.

No.	Names of the Leaders.	Caste.	Resident.	Remarks.	No. of Thugs.
1	Sooper Sing,	Mussulman,	Gwalior,	Hung at Saugor in 1832,	20
2	Khoosala,	Ditto,	Ditto,	Transported from Saugor 1832,	10
3	Dulsa Jemadar,	Ditto,	Ditto,	Died at his home in 1830,	10
4	Khoorkooa ditto,	Ditto,	Ditto,	Transported from Saugor in 1832,	40
5	Rae Sing ditto,	Ditto,	Jhansee,	Hung at Saugor in 1832,	30
6	Purumna ditto,	Ditto,	Cawnpore,	Ditto ditto,	8
7	Kullooa ditto,	Lohar,	Candeish,	At large,	6
8	Nungoo ditto,	Barber,	Bundelcund,	Ditto,	6
9	Feringeea ditto,	Brahmin,	Gwalior,	Approver,	23
10	Tejun ditto,	Ditto,	Ditto,	Hung at Saugor in 1832,	24
11	Phoolsa ditto,	Ditto,	Ditto,	Approver,	13
12	Buhorena ditto,	Lodhee,	Huttah,	Died in Hydrabad Jail in 1832,	5
13	Heera ditto,	Aheer,	Gwalior,	Approver, died 1832,	
14	Gungadeen,	Lodhee,	Sumthur,	Hung at Jowra in December 1829,	7
15	Hureea,	Rajpoot,	Hingolee,	Approver,	5
16	Lal Khan,	Mussulman,	Calpee,	Hung at Saugor in 1832,	8
17	Adhur,	Rajpoot,	Baitool,	Ditto ditto,	5
18	Hoosain Khan Jemadar,	Mussulman,	Hydrabad,	Hung at Jubulpore in July 1835,	10
19	Sheik Meerun ditto,	Ditto,	Ditto,	Approver, died in 1837,	20
20	Zoolfakar ditto,	Ditto,	Saugor,	Hung at Saugor in 1832,	7
21	Mojahet Khan ditto,	Ditto,	Hydrabad,	Hung at Jubulpore in 1835,	20
22	Fureed Khan ditto,	Ditto,	Ditto,	Ditto ditto,	20
23	Kalee Khan ditto,	Ditto,	Ditto,	Died in Jubulpore Jail in 1835,	8
24	Zoolfukar ditto,	Ditto,	Punna,	Approver,	19
25	Noorkhan,	Ditto,	Jhansee,	Hung at Jubulpore in 1835,	

No.	Names of Leaders.	Caste.	Resident.	Remarks.	No. of Thugs.
26	Omed Jemadar,	Lodhee,	Cawnpore,	Hung at Saugor in 1832,	9
27	Sewdeen ditto,	Ditto,	Ditto,	Approver,	9
28	Inaeut ditto,	Mussulman,	Jhansee,	Ditto,	20
29	Zalim ditto,	Ditto,	Tehree,	Died at his home in 1835,	10
30	Ashraff,	Ditto,	Gwalior,	At large,	10
31	Bukut Jemadar,	Lodhee,	Sumthur,	Hung at Saugor in 1832,	6
32	Bukut ditto,	Brahmin,	Gwalior.	Transported from Saugor in 1832,	6
33	Bheka ditto,	Mussulman	Jhansee,	At large,	6
34	Bhugee ditto,	Lodhee,	Cawnpore,	Died in Saugor Jail in 1833,	6
35	Khuluk ditto,	Ditto,	Ditto,	Hung at Saugor in 1833,	20
36	Bhowanee,	Ditto,	Jhalone,	Approver,	10
37	Dhokul,	Ditto,	Cawnpore,	Hung at Saugor in 1833,	20
38	Bhola Buneea,	Buneea,	Jhalone,	Approver,	5
39	Kohman,	Mussulman,	Jhansee,	Ditto,	9
40	Boodha,	Ditto,	Ditto,	Transported from Saugor in 1832,	2
41	Khyratee,	Ditto,	Saugor,	Died in Saugor Jail ditto,	3
42	Rambux,	Lodhee,	Feruckabad,	Approver,	5
43	Persaud,	Ditto,	Ditto,	Ditto,	5
44	Deeba,	Buneea,	Ditto,	Ditto,	5
45	Mihrban,	Lodhee,	Cawnpore,	Ditto,	5
46	Esuree,	Ditto,	Ditto,	Ditto,	5
47	Dhunooa,	Ditto,	Ditto,	Hung at Jubulpore in 1836,	10
48	Hurlal,	Ditto,	Ditto,	Hung at Saugor in 1833,	10
49	Bhikhun Khan,	Mussulman,	Calpee,	Approver,	8
50	Chand Khan,	Ditto,	Jhansee,	Hung at Saugor in 1832,	
51	Dulele Khan,	Ditto,	Ditto,	Ditto ditto,	
52	Budloo Jemadar,	Lodhee,	Ditto,	Ditto ditto,	10

53	Purumsookh,	Brahmin,	Gwalior,	Hung at Saugor in 1832,	10
54	Muneeram,	Lodhee,	Jhansee,	Ditto ditto,	10
55	Heera.	Aheer,	Ditto,	Approver, died ditto,	10
56	Rambux Jemadar,	Brahmin,	Gwalior,	At large,	10
57	Chotee ditto,	Ditto,	Jhansee,	Approver,	20
58	Bhudai ditto,	Ditto,	Ditto,	Hung at Saugor in 1832,	5
59	Bukut Moreea,	Ditto,	Gwalior,	At large,	5
60	Soorjun,	Aheer,	Ditto,	Ditto,	5
61	Jowahir,	Rajpoot,	Indore,	Approver,	10
62	Nunhooa,	Kolee,	Gwalior,	Ditto,	5
63	Mandhata,	Lodhee,	Etawah,	Ditto,	10
64	Dirgpaul Sobahdar,	Brahmin,	Gwalior,	Hung at Saugor in 1832,	
65	Motee Jemadar,	Lodhee,	Ditto,	Ditto ditto,	
66	Durroo ditto,	Mussulman,	Sindouse,	Hung at Jowra in 1830,	
67	Sutar Khan,	Ditto,	Dholepore,	Hung at Saugor in 1832,	22
68	Bhimee Jemadar,	Lodhee,	Gwalior,	Approver,	
69	Sahadut ditto,	Mussulman,	Ditto,	Ditto,	22
70	Peearjee ditto,	Naik,	Jeypore,	Ditto,	
71	Ainan ditto,	Mussulman,	Gwalior,	Hung at Saugor in 1832,	
72	Chutter ditto,	Aheer,	Ditto,	Ditto ditto,	
73	Kunhye ditto,	Ditto,	Ditto,	Died in Joudpore 1833,	
74	Kulooa,	Rajpoot,	Ditto,	Killed by a Zemindar in attempting to arrest him at Gwalior in 1835,	20
75	Bhika Jemadar,	Mewatee,	Ditto,	At large,	
76	Kalee Khan,	Mussulman,	Koel,	Hung 1837,	
77	Emamee,	Ditto,	Gwalior,	Approver,	
78	Ameer Allee,	Ditto,	Ditto,	Ditto,	
79	Punoo,	Ditto,	Ditto,	Ditto,	
80	Kalee Khan,	Ditto,	Nursingpore,	Died in Saugor Jail in 1832,	
81	Chutter,	Aheer,	Gwalior,	Hung at Saugor ditto,	
82	Chudamee,	Mussulman,	Nursingpore,	Ditto ditto,	

EXPEDITIONS

OF

GANGS UNDER SEVERAL LEADERS,

IN 1829-30.

Report of an Expedition under Feringeea, Budaloo, Muneeram, Zoolfakar, Noorkhan, Mahomed Buksh, Punna, Alee Khan and others, in the year 1829-30.

1. Feringeea set out from his home at Gorha with twenty-five Thugs, and reached Morheea, where he fell in with Budaloo and Muneeram with sixty, and together they went to Bahadoorpore, where they fell in with Hussun Alee Moonshee and five attendants, on their way from Barodah to the Dooab. They brought them on one coss and a half next morning, and killed them.

2. After this affair Budaloo, Muneeram, and their gang returned home, and Feringeea went to Dooraha, where he fell in with four Brahmins, and taking them on half a coss put them to death.

3. After this they crossed the Nerbudda river, and went to Omrowtee, where they fell in with a Shopkeeper; taking him on one and a half coss they put him to death.

4. Re-crossed the Nerbudda and came to Bhopaul, thence to Gharuspore; here they fell in with three travellers on their way to Saugor; coming on with them one and a half coss, they murdered them between Gharuspore and

Bagrode, and came on to Sehora—here they met Zoolfakar with ten, on their way from Biseynee after the arrest of Sheik Macub, which he had heard of from Chinna the weaver.

5. The gang united and went to Bagdae, where they fell in with four travellers—they took them on three coss, killed them, and went on to Bhopaul, where they met Noorkhan with nine Thugs.

6. At Bhopaul they fell in with a Parsee Merchant of Saugor, his attendant and two shopkeepers—they came on with them to Goolgunge Amaree, and leaving that place next morning, put them to death.

7. They then came to Khoree Khunjara, where they fell in with five travellers, and coming on with them, put them to death between Khumpara and Manora. They were three men and two women.

8. After this the gang came to Bilehra, four coss from Saugor, on the road to Hoshungabad through Seremow, where they fell in with Mahomed Buksh and twelve Thugs. He had heard from Bhola Bunnea of the arrest of Makul at Sewagunge. They went to Ranepore, on the road to Bhopaul, together; there met two travellers on their way to Bhopaul and killed them in camp.

9. They then went to Selwanee, and there Zoolfakar's mare, to their great surprise and consternation, dropped a foal, and put them all under the Etuk. Going on to the Doha-ghatee, they fell in with a Tailor, whom they put to death on the spot. Zoolfakar returned home with Mahomed Buksh. Feringeea and his party of thirty-six went to Murdheea in Bhilsa, where twenty-four of the gang were arrested by a guard from Jubulpore, and the rest got home.

10. Zoolfakar and his party fell in with four bearers at Bagrode, and killed them on the banks of a river. Thence came through Saugor to Chaterpore.

11. At Chaterpore, they fell in with two men from Saugor to Banda, and killed them at their encampment.

12. Went after this to Gunoora, where they fell in with Purumna and Alee Khan with sixteen Thugs. The united gang went to Jytpore, where they fell in with two travellers, took them on a quarter of a coss from Jytpore, put them to death, and then came back to Mulhera. Here Dhurum Khan and Chand Khan, brothers of Inaeut, met them with a party of ten and a traveller.

13. At Mulhera, they murdered this traveller during the night, and the united gang came to Chaterpore.

14. At Chaterpore they fell in with two travellers and took them on to Mahoba, where they met with Bheekan Khan and came to Beseynee. Feringeea, who had gone home with sixteen Thugs—the united gang went on to Mahoba with the travellers and leaving that place next morning took them two coss on the road to Bandah and murdered them.

15. After this affair Zoolfakar and Noor Khan went home with their parties. Chand Khan and Bheekun Khan came to Beseynee. Feringeea, who had gone home from Bhilsa after the arrest of his gang, found that his family had been seized and sent to Jubulpore, and with Rumma and Durroea came in search of a gang to Beseynee and found the party, and another of eight Lodhee Thugs, making in all a gang of thirty. Five Byragees came up with a Sepahee. Taking them on the road to Kohpa, they put them to death at the place the other people had been murdered before.

16. Going on to the Jhoojhar Ghat, Feringeea was taken up on suspicion and the rest made off. He remained two days in confinement and then got off and rejoined the party of Bheekun Khan and ten Thugs at Dhunora in Saugor. They went on to Chanee in the Rhat Pergunnah,

Humeerpore District, where they fell in with a servant of the Police Thana. They took him on one coss and put him to death. Feringeea soon after this affair was arrested by a guard from Jubulpore.

Having ascertained precisely Feringeea's residence in the Jhansee territory, I sent a guard to secure him. It reached his house at midnight, but he heard their whispers, and got out at a back door, leaving an English blunderbuss and pistol loaded on his bed, which the guard found warm when they entered. They brought these arms back to me at Jubulpore, with the mother, wife, child and brother of the fugitive. They arrived at Jubulpore the day before Feringeea's foster brother, Jhurhoo, was to be hung, with ten others of his gang arrested at Bhilsa. He entreated to be allowed to see them; and in the morning, just before going to the scaffold, the interview took place before me. He fell at the old woman's feet, and begged that she would relieve him from the obligations of the milk with which she had nourished him, and the care with which she had cherished him from infancy, as he was about to die before he could fulfill any of them. She placed her hands on his head, and he knelt, and she said she forgave him all, and bid him die like a man.

I knew Feringeea would not go far while links so dear to him were in my hands; and I sent off a second guard to Jhansee. It was found that he divided his time between five villages in which resided the friends and relations of prisoners in the Jubulpore Jail, who could manage occasionally to get him some information regarding his family. He never slept two successive nights in the same village; and having ascertained, by means of spies, the precise house in each village in which he slept, the guard determined to search the whole in one night. They had concealed themselves at Burwa Saugor, eight miles from the nearest of these villages during their search. Soon after night-fall they set out; and not finding him in the first, they seized the proprietor of the house, bound and left him under two sentries, and went on two miles to the next. Not finding him there, they seized and bound the proprietor and left him under two sentries, and went on to Jomun Sagura, the third village, eight miles distant. Not finding him, they seized the proprietor of the house, Soghur, the son of Kuleean Sing, an approver, in the Jubulpore Jail. Him they took on with them six miles to the fourth village, Kisrae, which they reached as the day began to break. Five hundred rupees had been offered for his apprehension, and this village was their last hope, as the alarm would be given before they could reach the fifth. Leaving the remnant of the guard outside the village, Dhun Sing, a young approver, the son of Busuntee, went to the house accompanied by only Soghur. Finding Feringeea was within, they rushed in upon him; and, supposing the house to be surrounded by soldiers, he suffered himself to be bound without resistance by these two boys, both of whom he was strong enough to have strangled: all who had been seized in the other villages, were now released, and the guard brought the prisoner to me at Saugor in December 1830. A servant of the Jhansee Rajah was with the guard during the whole time.

A total of forty-six men and two women murdered in this expedition.

Report by Mr. McLeod of a Thug Expedition between the months of October 1829 *and April or May* 1830, *by a gang of Thugs under Bhimmee, Kunhye and Chutter Jemadars, called the Churus Expedition. Vide Mr. McLeod's letter of* 21*st March,* 1834.

1. This gang of Thugs, twenty six in number, left their homes in October 1829 under Bhimmee, Kunhye and Chutter, and proceeded through Myapoor Ghat to the village of Suptowra, where another gang of eleven, under Bhijjoe, joined them and murdered two travellers between Bhopawur and Para.

2. This occurred whilst on the road from Oojein to Para. There were three travellers, one of whom died shortly after joining them and before the murder of the other two.

3. They proceeded from Para to Barodah, whence they brought two pastry cooks and murdered them at Bheelagaon, then went to Jhubboogaon.

4. At this place they murdered a man of the Kahar caste, and passed on towards Jeypore.

5. Passing through Jeypore to Amjhara, they were joined by forty Malwa Thugs, under Bhowanee and other leaders, and six from Omutwarah, under Alee Bahadoor. Here the parties of Chutter Jemadar, Mungulcea, his son, and Bhijjoo left them: the remainder went through Dubohee to Meergaon, and murdered a Faqueer.

6. The gang passed through the city of Baroda, and Channee and Mureeabad to Doorkha, where they murdered a Byragee.

7. Proceeding to a village a few coss south of Doorkha, they murdered two cloth merchants, whose bodies are said to have been laid bare by wild animals.

8. Going on towards Bhimnauth, they murdered a Byragee and threw his body into the water. He was proceeding to the Ginnar Fair with articles for sale.

9. Went on through Dhundhokha to Bhimnauth, and a coss from this place, murdered two Mussulmen travellers.

10. From Bhimnauth on the road to Bhonugur, they murdered three Mussulmen, and obtained three guns, which fell to the shares of Bhowan, Khemla and Laek—the latter sold his to a Sepahee of the Pitawund Choukie.

11. The gang proceeded to Jytpore on the road to Gunnar, and eight coss from Jytpore, they murdered five Byrâgees.

12. They now proceeded to Joonagur, and on the 4th March 1830, murdered four Byragees at a village between Dhooreea and Ghudeyra.

13. They reached Joonagur in ten days, and proceeding to a village six coss on the Bunkarneer road, they murdered two Sepahees and a woman—one of the Sepahees was named Jokhoo Sing.

14. Passing through Bunkurneer, they went on to Khat, near which place they murdered two Mussulmen on their way from Lucknow to Scind. The property obtained was conveyed to Cambay for a part of the gang.

15. Leaving Cambay, they murdered two Hindoos and a Mussulman, six coss on the road to Baroda. The Thugs were here nearly discovered by one of the victim's screaming; but a camel being made to roar drowned his voice.

16. They proceeded through Bhorswul to Baroda, where they were joined by a man dressed as a Byragee, whom they murdered at Bhillanda. The gang then set out eastward to their homes.

17. At Deohuttee, they were joined by two Comedians, whom they murdered one coss eastward of that place.

18. They halted next day at a grove of Mangoe trees, near a village, one coss from Bhopawur. The man who guarded this grove was persuaded to join them, and at a village one coss east of Bhopawur, they murdered him.

19. Coming on through Shojawulpore, they murdered a man who had joined them from Oojein. Here Bhimmee, taking one of the rupees, obtained for the bullock, into the bazar for change, proving a bad one, the whole gang were arrested. They were however released, by Poonoa producing a Persian perwanah, said to have been given him by an Officer at Goonah. In the above expedition thirty-nine persons were murdered and robbed.

A total of thirty-eight men and one woman murdered in this expedition.

The last Expeditions of the Bundelcund gang of Sheikh Inaeut and his brothers on the roads between Saugor and Calpee in the latter end of 1830.

In May 1830, six months after the arrest of their principal leader (Sheik Inaeut,) a small gang of about twenty Bundelcund Thugs, under his brother Chand Khan, Bhola, Phoolsa and Nijabut, collected at Guteearee in Jhansee, and took the auspices on the bank of the Dusan river, which flows within one hundred yards of the village. Finding the omens favorable, they opened the expedition by going on to the village of Buseela, where they passed the night, and thence went on to the town of Chatterpore, on the road to Saugor, where they met four other Thugs, agreeably to appointment. From Chatterpore, they struck off from the Saugor road towards that from Jubulpore to Mirzapore, and at Shahnagur they fell in with a Tamborine player and his wife, with an infant daughter at her breast, on their way from Elichpore to Futtehpore, on the Ganges. Soon after they were joined by a Mussulman and his wife and son, a lad of about five years of age, a Brahmin and a Guala, and going on with them to Biseynee, they were overtaken by five other travellers, all men, on their way from Nagpore to the Dooab. On the road from Biseynee to Banda, they murdered the Tamborine player, his wife and child, and the Guala; but lost all the rest in an attempt to divide the parties into three for the convenience of putting them to death. Going on to Chatterpore they divided the booty.

Going on next day, they fell in with two Brahmins and a Rajpoot on their way home on furlough from the Duckan. They had been travelling with them three days before they could prevail upon them to set out before day break, as they had heard of numerous murders on these roads, and were on their guard. On the second day several of the gang were taken up by the police, and told so plausible a story, and looked so very respectable, that the officer of the guard released them all, apologised for having detained them, and gave them a letter for his friend, the head native officer of police in the town of Calpee, with whom they pretended to be intimately acquainted. Seeing all this, the three Soldiers were prevailed on the next morning to set out with them earlier than usual, and all were strangled in a water-course on the road.

Passing through Chatterpore, they fell in on the road to Calpee with three carriers of Ganges water. They persuaded them that they had made a propitiatory vow to feed holy men, and as they were Brahmins, and employed in so holy an office, they should take advantage of the occasion and give them a feast. They accepted the invitation, lodged and feasted with them that night, and going on with them the next morning, were all three strangled in a water-course and their bodies buried in the bed of the stream.

Going on to a grove on the great road in the territory of Bejawur, they fell in with three travellers on their way from Mahidpore in Malwa to Cawnpore. Returning with them through Chatterpore, they put them to death in a water-course near Jenjura, while they sat smoking and talking with them about the execution of the Thugs, whom they had assisted in arresting, and seen hung at Joura by Major Borthwick.

Going on to a Bowlie between Chatterpore and Kopnawaree they met a guard of Sipahees on their return from escorting prisoners from Indore to Humeerpore. After a little conversation the Sipahees told them, that they appeared to be very much like the Thugs whom they had been lately escorting, they ran off to Chatterpore and in the street met one of the guards from Saugor. Hurnagur, one of the approvers with the guard, recognized Dulele, one of the brothers of Sheikh Inaeut, and seized him; and some others of the gang were soon after secured and brought to Jubulpore.

The gang returned to their homes, but soon after opened another expedition on the bank of the same river near Gutteearee, and came on to the shrine of a Faqueer outside the village of Kullowa on the road from Calpee to Saugor. Here they lodged for the night and found an old Brahmin who had been confined in the shrine, for several days, by sickness. He was on his way from the Mhow Cantonment to the Doab, and the Thugs pretending to be going to the same place offered him a seat upon one of their ponies. He gladly accepted it being anxious to get home to his family. Going on with him the next morning, they put him to death and buried his body in a field of millet.

The body was dug up the same morning by jackalls and discovered by the villagers; and the gang hearing of it from travellers on the road became alarmed, and took another road. On reaching the bank of a tank at

Kopnawaree they lodged near the temple dedicated to Hurdoul Lala, and soon after a man passed them on his way from Chatterpore with a bag of copper pice on his shoulder which they took for silver money. Fifteen of the gang followed the man, and as he crossed a water-course they rushed in upon him and stabbed him in several places with knives and swords, and flung the body in among some bushes, and made off with the bag to their homes. The poor man was still living when discovered by some travellers, who got him taken to Chatterpore by the people of Kopnawaree, and he there survived his wounds three days, and described the manner in which he had been wounded and robbed.

A total of ten men, one woman and one child murdered in this expedition.

A total of ninety-four men and four women and one child murdered during the different expeditions this season.

Names of the Principal Leaders of the Gangs engaged in the foregoing Expeditions for 1829-30.

No.	Names of Leaders.	Caste.	Resident.	Remarks.	No. of Thugs.
1	Feringeea Jemadar,	Brahmin,	Gwalior,	Approver,	25
	Budaloo,	Lodhee,	Jhansee,	Hung at Saugor 1832,	60
	Muneeram,	Ditto,	Ditto,	Ditto,	
	Zoolfakar,	Mussulman,	Ditto,	Approver,	10
5	Noorkhan,	Ditto,	Ditto,	Hung at Jubulpore in 1835,	9
	Mahomud Buksh,	Ditto,	Ditto,	Approver,	12
	Purumna,	Ditto,	Cawnpore,	Hung at Saugor in 1832,	
	Allee Khan,	Ditto,	Agra,	Ditto ditto,	16
	Dhurum Khan,	Ditto,	Jhansee,	Approver,	
10	Chand Khan,	Ditto,	Ditto,	Hung at Saugor in 1832,	10
	Bheekun Khan,	Ditto,	Calpee,	Approver,	
	Rumma,	Rajpoot,	Gwalior,	Ditto,	
	Durroo,	Lodhee,	Jhansee,	Hung at Jowra in 1830,	
	Bhimmee,	Ditto,	Gwalior,	Approver,	
15	Kinhur Benguna,	Brahmin,	Ditto,	Ditto,	
	Chuttur Jemadar,	Aheer,	Ditto,	Hung at Saugor in 1832,	
	Bhijjoe,	Mussulman,	Banda,	Died in Saugor Jail 1832,	11
	Bhowanee,	Lodhee,	Jhalone,	Approver,	40
	Allee Bahadoor,	Moslem,	Seronje,	Approver at Jowra,	6
20	Munguleea,	Aheer,	Gwalior,	At large,	
	Bhowun Jemadar,	Naik,	Seronje,	Hung at Jowra 1830,	
	Khemla,	Moslem,	Malwa,	Approver,	
	Laek,	Aheer,	Gwalior,	Ditto,	
	Sheik Inaeut,	Moslem,	Chunar,	Ditto,	
25	Bhola,	Bunneea,	Jhalone,	Ditto,	
	Phoolsa,	Brahmin,	Gwalior,	Ditto,	
27	Nijabut,	Moslem,	Jhansee,	Ditto,	

EXPEDITIONS

OF THE

BUNDELCUND GANGS,

IN 1830-31.

Narrative of an Expedition from Bundelcund into Gozerat under Budeloo, Munneeram and others, in the months of December 1830, *and January and February* 1831.

1. In December 1830, about forty Thugs under different leaders from Bundelcund and the Dooab, assembled at the village of Mauch, in the pergunnah of Kuroulee, and thence proceeded together towards Madhoorajpore. About two coss east of that place, they fell in with two Cowherds on their way from Maukunpore, where they had been on a pilgrimage, to Ajmere. These men halted with the gang in the grove at Madhoorajpore, and at night were strangled and buried on the spot. The property found on them consisted of four rupees, three brass utensils and a bullock.

2. Next morning the gang proceeded towards Ajmere, and at the village of Chourae, they fell in with two Brahmins on their way to Madhoorajpore. Rambuksh prevailed on them to join the party at their halting ground, where both of them were strangled at night, and their bodies buried near the tank under a tamarind tree. The only property found on them was one brass thalee and two lootahs. After this ten of the gang, residents of Kohel and the vicinity, left them and went towards Jypore; the rest continued their route, next morning, to Ajmere.

3. They were joined on the road by a horseman, and his servant, on foot, who went on with them to Kishengur, but did not halt till they reached a village about a coss distant on the Ajmere road, where these men were strangled on the bank of a nullah under a Peepul tree. They found on them 10 Rupees in money and some clothes, which they divided, but the horse they let go, to avoid suspicion; the bodies were buried on the spot. Next morning they continued their journey towards Ajmere.

4. About three coss from that place, they met three Mussulmen going from Ajmere, in search of service, and prevailed on them to return on promise of securing them service with their friends—halted with them at a village of Gwalior, about one coss from Ajmere, with the intention of strangling them there, but they could not get an opportunity. Next morning they took them on to Ajmere, where the travellers after paying their devotions at a shrine of one of their saints—went on with the gang to the bank of a river about four coss from Ajmere, and one coss from the village of Pokhur, where they encamped under some trees. At night they were all three strangled, and the bodies buried at some distance from the spot. They found on them fifty rupees in money, a gun, a shield, two swords and some clothes. The next morning they proceeded towards Basunugur in Gozerat—on arriving at this place, they disputed about the division of property—a part of the gang, about nineteen in number, went toward Baroda, and the rest took the road to Ahmedabad.

5. The latter party reached Ahmedabad and there halted two days, and then took the road to Baroda, with a Byragee, whom they had prevailed upon to join them, and on the road at the village of Burtooa, five coss from Ahmedabad, they were joined by another Byragee—they rested for the night under a Banyan tree near a well

outside the village, where they were both strangled, and their bodies buried under the tree. They got from them ten rupees in money and some brass pots, and the next morning proceeded on towards Baroda.

6. About five coss from this place they were joined by three travellers, two Paun-dealers and one Rajpoot, who halted with them at the bank of a tank, where they were both strangled at night and the bodies buried close by. They found on them about ten rupees and two swords—the next day they proceeded on towards Baroda, but fell in with no travellers.

7. The following day they fell in with three men from Sind, servants of the Rajah of Baroda, and old friends of Rambuksh, one of the gang, who pretended to be glad to see them, and gave them a dinner—but at night they were all three strangled and their bodies buried on the spot. The property found on them consisted of sixty rupees worth of silver, two guns, a dagger and a poney.

8. The next morning they reached Baroda and halted in that city one day. They found three Rajpoot Sipahees on their way from Surat to their homes on the Ganges, and were persuaded to proceed with the gang next morning. They halted in a grove about five coss from Baroda on the road to Dubohee, and there the three Rajpoots were strangled at night, and their bodies buried in the grove, where they have been pointed out by one of the party, Durreeaw, to the local authorities. They found on them about sixty rupees in money, two guns, one shield and one pistol.

9. The next morning they continued their journey towards Dubohee and were joined by two Sipahees from the Bombay army, 12th Regiment N. I., on their way to their homes on the Ganges. They halted with them at a Fuqueer's shrine outside the town of Dubohee, and at

night while the Fuqueer was absent, they were strangled, and their bodies buried near the spot—where they have been taken up and shewn to the local authorities by Durreaw, one of the gang. They got from them twenty-four gold coins, and the next morning entered the town. They found there some men from Bhopawur selling opium, and one heard them say that they suspected them to be Thugs—they became alarmed and left the place at night and proceeded towards Bhuroch—on the fourth day they reached the village of Neeagow, leaving Bhuroch to the left—they halted there one night and went on the next day to the village of Eckawul, five coss towards Baroda, where they took up quarters in a kind of serae, which they call Dhurum Suleh (alms house.)

10. Two travellers had taken up their abode at a well outside, but were prevailed upon by Rambuksh to join the gang in the serae, and to start with them about 3 o'clock next morning towards Baroda. They soon overtook three hackerries, and the greater part of the gang remained behind to detain these hackerries on some pretence, while six only went on with the two travellers and soon after strangled them on the road. The party having detained these Hackerries a sufficient time overtook their comrades. The bodies were taken to a water-course some hundred yards from the place and buried. The man sent to Baroda to point out the other bodies did not see these buried, and they were not in consequence pointed out to the local authorities. These two men were carrying treasure from Myaram, Himmutram and other merchants of Surat to Baroda, and had left Surat on the 18th February 1831. They found on them treasure amounting to 1,460 Spanish dollars, and seventeen gold reals or doubloons, and some pearls, each man had a share of 32 dollars, half a doubloon, and about 12 pearls.

11. The next day, they returned on the road to Dubohee, entered the town, but passed on without halting to a place one coss north, where they passed the night. The next day they were joined on the road, by a pundit, on his way from Baroda to Jhansee, and he rested with them at a grove near a village called Makunee about twelve coss from Dubohee, where they strangled him at night, and buried his body in the grove, where it has been pointed out by one of the gang to the local authorities. They got from him a turban and dooputta with gold laced borders, a cloak of red broad cloth, and a mare. This was the last murder perpetrated by this branch of the gang, which now returned home to their villages in Bundelcund, where many of them were seized by my parties stationed for the purpose of intercepting them.

A total of twenty-five men murdered in this expedition.

Proceedings of the main body of the gang under Munneeram and Budeloo continued.

1. After the great gang under Budaloo, Munneeram Heera Mussulman, Rambuksh and other leaders had reached Bissengur in Gozerat, a part of them, consisting of nineteen Thugs, separated direct to Baroda, leaving the main body to go by way of Ahmedabad. Moolooa, who was sick when they separated, soon after died on the road, the rest came on to Baroda, and there rested some days and were joined by four men of the Jat caste, who were on their way from Rajkote to their homes on the Ganges, and a Brahmin on his way from Baroda. They came with the party to Bheelpore, where they halted for the night, and immediately after dark sent the Brahmin to the village to procure some milk—

during his absence they strangled the four Jats, bound their bodies up in cloth, and sent Chiddee to the village to bring back the Brahmin—as soon as he returned he sat down by the fire, and said he could get no milk—they said it was of no consequence, and immediately he was strangled. The five bodies were buried on the spot. They found upon them two hundred rupees, which they divided and returned towards their homes in Bundelcund.

2. On reaching Shajawulpore in Bhopaul, they met a gang of twenty-two Thugs under Lall Khan Jemadar, on their way from Bundelcund to Baroda, and eleven of the party agreed to join them, but the other seven returned to their homes. The above parties left Shajawulpore for Baroda, and on passing the grove at Shahjehanpore saw three of their party, who had gone on in advance, Purumsookh Lodhee, Hoolase and Mooloo, in close conversation with two Company's Sepahees, and knowing their object, left a party of ten behind to assist them, while the main body went on and halted at a village three coss further on the road to Oojein. The party left in the grove, set out with the Sepahees about three o'clock in the morning, and having strangled them, and buried their bodies on the main road, joined the main body in the forenoon. They had found fifty rupees on them, which was divided among the whole.

3. The gang now passed through the cantonment of Mhow, and near Amjura they met a Byragee, whom they prevailed on to turn back with them to their ground of encampment at the village of Ringnode, on promise of a reward for a certain medicine he boasted the knowledge of. At night he was strangled, and his body buried close by.

4. About seven coss west of Chotee Oodeypore they fell in with two barbers, whom they invited to their ground

to shave them. They shaved half of the gang and were paid for the labor, but being suspected of having money or jewels in their shaving boxes were both strangled at night, and their bodies buried on the bank of a nullah under some large prickly bushes.

5. The gang now went on to the city of Baroda where they halted a few days, and then came on to the village of Bheelpore. On the road they fell in with four men, wearing jackets of a light blue color with thread lace on the breasts, on their way from Rajkote to their homes via Jubulpoor. They went with them to their halting ground and at night they were all strangled and their bodies buried under a mangoe tree. They got 50 rupees in silver, five sequins, two swords and other articles, in all to the amount of about 300 Rupees.

6. The next morning they were joined by Moorobah, a writer of English, and brother of Buchoba, a writer in the service of Lieut. Tapp of Asseergur, who had gone to Bombay to seek employment, and, not having succeeded, was now on his way to Mhow by Baroda, to seek employment among the English gentlemen in that Cantonment which he mentioned in a letter to his brother from Baroda. He had with him a servant named Hurree, and two Byragees, who had joined him on the road. All four rested under the same tree with the gang, and were all strangled at night and their bodies buried on the spot. They got 20 gold coins, and 25 rupees in silver. The writer had a red book with him, in which he recorded the circumstances of his journey, and this is said to have been buried with him. These bodies were taken up by a party from Saugor.

7. The next morning the gang went on towards Dubohee and fell in with two men on horseback from Rajkote

on their way home through Shajawulpore. They came on with them to Bahaderpore, five coss this side of Dubohee, and not finding it convenient to murder them there, came on with them to the village Makunee where they encamped on the bank of a tank outside the village. They were soon after joined by three other men on horseback, with a Bheestie and an old woman, on their way from Baroda to Indore. They were Dhokul Sing, Sillahdar in a Regiment of horse, commanded by a Mr. Rylee, in the Kutch and Bhooj country, his relation, and another horseman, the mother of his wife and a bheestie his servant. He was on his way home for the purpose of being present at the marriage of his brother at Indore, and had written to his wife to that effect fifteen days before he set out on his journey. The leader of the gang endeavoured to prevail on him and his party to partake of the feast prepared for the two first horsemen, but they declined. At night they were all seven strangled on the bank of a tank and their bodies buried on the spot. The gang got from them six horses, one camel, one bullock, one gold bracelet, twenty gold mohurs, and about four hundred small coin. The bodies were all taken up by a party from Saugor. After this the gang returned to their homes.

A total of twenty-four men and one woman murdered in this expedition.

Proceedings of the Bundelcund Gangs, under Bhoola Buneea, and Zulfakar, in the early part of 1831, *on the roads between Calpee and Saugor.*

In February, 1831, a gang of twelve Thugs under Zoolfakar, Bhola, and others, took the auspices, as usual, on the bank of the Dusan river, near Guteearee, and finding the auspices favourable, ate the bread, fish and curds that they brought with them, and came on to Hindora near Raht, where they fell in with Dibba, Khulak and Khooshal with another gang of thirty Thugs. The gangs united and spent the day and night together on the bank of a tank. They came on to Kutora, on the road from Saugor to Calpee, where they fell in with two Brahmins and a shop-keeper on their way from Saugor to Cawnpore. Going back with them the next day, they strangled them at night in a grove as they sat listening to some vocal and instrumental music which the gang got up. The bodies were buried in a dry well.

Going into the Bejawar Rajah's territory, in five days they reached Chouka, where they fell in with a Brahmin, and a Rajpoot on their way from Baroda to Oude. Going on with them through Chatterpore, they put them to death in a water-course in the Jhalone Rajah's territory. They were challenged by some cultivators, who were watching their fields, while they were burying the bodies, and made off as fast as they could to Banda.

Near Banda, they overtook three men on their way from Malwa to the Dooab, and passing through Banda with them they went on to the village of Ojreyta, where they lodged with the travellers in the garden of a Brahmin. Going on with them before daylight next morning, they strangled them at a place selected the evening before, and buried their bodies in a ditch. These bodies were pointed out by one of the gang in October, 1832, and taken up by the Magistrate of Banda.

Coming back to the village of Kubarae, on the great Calpee road from Saugor, they heard from some Bombay Sepahees, that a great many Thugs had been seized on that road, and made off to a less frequented one in the Humeerpore district. They were resting themselves in a small grove near the village of Gurowlee, when the native Officer of Police came up in his rounds, and seeing part of the gang run off in alarm, he seized seven and sent them to Humeerpore. Two made their escape on the road; and the other five were sent to Jubulpore. The rest of the gang returned to their homes—a total of eight men murdered in this expedition.

A total of fifty-seven men and one woman murdered during the different expeditions this season.

Names of the Principal Leaders of the Gangs engaged in the foregoing Expeditions for 1830-31.

No.	Names of Leaders.	Cast.	Resident.	Remarks.	No. of Thugs.
1	Budaloo Jemadar, ...	Lodhee,.........	Jhansee, ...	Hung at Saugor in 1832, ...	
	Munneram, ...	Ditto, ...	Ditto, ...	Ditto ditto, ...	
	Rambuksh, ...	Brahmin, ...	Gwalior, ...	At large, ...	
	Heera, ...	Moslem, ...	Jhansee, ...	Approver, ...	
5	Lall Khan Jemadar, ...	Ditto, ...	Ditto, ...	Hung at Saugor in 1832, ...	
	Purumsookh, ...	Brahmin, ...	Gwalior, ...	Approver, ...	
	Hoolasee, ...	Ditto, ...	Dooab, ...	Ditto, ...	
	Mooloo, ...	Ditto, ...	Jhansee, ...	Ditto, ...	
	Zoolfakar, ...	Moslem, ...	Ditto, ...	Ditto, ...	
0	Bhola, ...	Buneea, ...	Jhalone, ...	Ditto, ...	
	Dibba, ...	Ditto, ...	Furuckabad,...	Ditto, ...	
	Khuluk, ...	Ditto, ...	Cawnpore, ...	Hung at Saugor in 1833, ...	
13	Khooshal, ...	Moslem, ...	Jhansee, ...	Transported from Saugor in 1832, ...	

EXPEDITION

OF THE

RAJPOOTANA AND GUZERAT GANGS,

IN 1830-31-32.

Narrative by Mr. McLeod of a Thug Expedition through Rajpootana and Guzerat in the years 1830-31 *and* 32, *under Dhurum Khan, Bhimmee, Kunhye, Roopjee Sooseea, and Kadur, during which Dhurum Khan Jemadar died at Sirohee.*

1. This gang of forty Thugs under Dhurm Khan, Bhimmee, Kunhye and Budaloo Jemadars, assembled at a Bowlee in Jyepore in the end of 1830, and went to Sambhur, proceeding from thence they met a Mussulman near Kishenghur, whom they murdered.

2. At Kishenghur, they inveigled a female, her two female attendants, two Guzeratee Brahmins and another man, and murdered them at Dhoodhas.

3. The gang went on to Thana, where they were joined by a Mussulman and a Hindoo, whom they murdered about a coss from the town. The party under Budaloo left them in consequence of a quarrel with Dhurm Khan.

4. One coss from Natorah, they murdered a Mussulman and a Jat.

5. Going northwards, they fell in with a man carrying a gun and murdered him going along. They

then turned eastward, but meeting Aman of Khunchumpore and his party, and hearing of the seizure of the Madhoorajpore gang, they turned back. At Sheker Somp, Aman left them, and made for the north-west provinces.

6. At a village three coss north of Jyepore, Dhurm Khan, singly strangled a Rajpoot.

7. Proceeding they inveigled a man near Uchrol, of the Aheer caste, and murdered him.

8. Two stages south of Delhi, they murdered a shopkeeper.

9. Returning south, through Hansee and Hissar, they murdered a groom.

10. Going on they reached Mirtha and murdered a shepherd.

11. Two stages beyond Mirtha, they met and murdered a byragee.

12. At Palee, Dhurm Khan inveigled two Bombay Sepahees, and murdered them on the road to Ajmere.

13. One stage south of Palee, they murdered a Mussulman and a Guzeratee Brahmin, and then proceeded to Sirohee, where Dhurm Khan fell ill and died. He was buried with some pomp, by the assistance of Major Speirs' servants. The circumstance is known to Major Speirs—and one of his servants recognized Bhimmee Jemadar on meeting him in the Ajmere Bazar, after he had become an approver with Mr. McLeod.

14. The gang continued southward ; near the village of Beesaungur they murdered four bearers. After this continued their journey towards Baroda.

15. On reaching Baroda they murdered three Mussulmen and a Faqueer proceeding to Indore.

16. Having collected a great deal of property the gang went to Oodeepore and sold it; then proceeded southward;

taking with them two Mahrattas, whom they murdered near Jeygurh.

17. At a village further on, named Jhubboogaon, they were joined by a Sipahee proceeding to Mhow, whom they murdered at Makunnee.

18. Having been joined by a party of forty Sooseeas under Nathoo, they went through Dubohee to Meagow, near Baroach, where they murdered a Byragee.

19. At Etaudha, five coss west of Baroda, they murdered a Byragee.

20. Going from Etaudha to Bheeloogaon, they murdered a Bohra, after which they retraced their steps.

21. At Bheeloogaon they were joined by Deeraj alias Kindher Benguna and his party, after which they murdered a Rajpoot near the grove of a Bhora. After this they sent Bussunt Rae and Khundue home. They went to Kateeawar, but returned without success, to Baroda, and proceeded to Dar Koorjie where Bussunt Rae died.

22. From Darkoorjee, they took on two Brahmins, two stages on the road to Kuppergunge, where they murdered them—going on to Kheera, Alum and Chuddee caught fever and were prescribed for by the European Medical Officer of the station, but they died. From Kheera the gang went to Pittallawad, where a part separated and went to Baroda. Ten were seized by a guard from Saugor under Hurnauth Sing Tomandar.

23. The main body proceeded through Darkoorjee and Curree, Neembury, Burrwah to Doorkha, where they murdered a Byragee.

24. Proceeding through Palunpoor, on the road to Serohee, they murdered three Hoossainee Brahmins and a Rajpoot in the jungle near Dautewarrah.

25. The gang proceeded through Palee and Mirtha to Purbutsur, whence they returned southward through Palee

and Jooseeah. At a tank near Jeypore, they murdered three Mussulmen on their pilgrimage to Mecca.

26. Returning to Mirtha, they fell in with a Brahmin, his father and a Kaet, whom they murdered near Bhelaondha.

27. At Mirtha, they met a Rajpoot from Joudhpore, whom they took on to Rungowun and murdered him.

28. Proceeding to Palee, southwards, they met and murdered three Byragees.

29. Returning towards Mirtha, they murdered a cook of the Peshwa's and seven men, inhabitants of Kateawar.

30. Proceeding to Bheelwar, they murdered a man who had been to Ajmere with shields for sale.

31. Purusram, Chuddee, Gunesha, Bazkhan and Peerbuksh returned home, and the gang went through Bheelwarah, and between Jooreah and Jeytpoor they murdered a Rajpoot from Jesselmere.

32. Proceeding south the gang wandered about Guzeerat for several months: they had passed one rainy season in that country afraid to return home, as guards were out for their apprehension, and had secured the greater part of their associates—another rainy season had now set in, and they met few travellers. Returning homewards near Panteewarah, they murdered a Chuprassie, and two men armed with bows and arrows. Khinder, Purusram, Gunesha, Bazkhan, &c. rejoined them from home, and went through Palee to Burhondha, whence Kindhur and his party returned home. Bhimmee and the rest continued on the road to Sambhur, and at Peepur the Sooseeas left him, and he and his party returned home also. There were above one hundred Thugs engaged in this expedition, the greater part of whom were seized.

A total of sixty-five men and three women murdered in this expedition.

Narrative of an Expedition through Jeypore under the following Leaders with one hundred and nine Thugs. Ajabee Jemadar, Bichooa alias Pahar Sing, Mandhata, Kesuree, Bukut Rajpoot, Bukut Brahman, in 1831-32.

1. Ujubee Jemadar's party of twenty-two Thugs, before they joined the rest at Charsoo in Jeypore, fell in with three shopkeepers from Gwalior, and murdered them. They proceeded through Bamonder to Charsoo in two stages, and joined the other gangs.

2. They soon after met with seven travellers, one a Kawruttee or carrier of Ganges water, two Rajpoot Sepahees and three other men—they proceeded on their journey at midnight, and a party of fifty Thugs were appointed to accompany them—they were murdered at a spot previously selected at the Bunas Nuddee—but had not time to bury the bodies properly before daylight appeared; and covered them with stones and straw and rejoined the main body at Charsoo.

3. Their next stage was to a village called Gurrawas, where they were joined by three Khuchwah Rajpoots from Joudpore. In the evening Khomana was sent to select a spot for the murder — next morning they accompanied the travellers, and murdered them at the appointed place.

4. They returned to the city of Jeypore, remained there two days, and then took the Bhurtpore road in company with five travellers, four Sepahees and one Shop-keeper. They came to the Kale Ghat, or pass, near Jeypore, where the travellers were searched by the Custom House people —twenty-five rupees in coin were found upon them and returned. The gang halted with them next day, but in consequence of a guard being stationed there they were unable to put them to death. The following day they

proceeded to a village two coss from Doosa, where they killed two goats—and the travellers, after having partaken of the feast, were murdered and buried under a Bur-tree.

5. They continued their journey, and shortly after met two men from Jeypore, whom they murdered and threw their bodies into a Bowlee.

6. They then proceeded to a village and halted in a Serae, where they met four travellers whom they prevailed upon to accompany them. They set out in company with them next morning, and murdered them at a water-course, a coss from the village, and buried them in the bed of the stream.

7. They then proceeded to the vicinity of Bhurtpore having previously detached one of the gang to see if the bodies were secure, but found that the villagers had discovered them. The gang on hearing of this entered the Fort of Bhurtpore, and remained there two or three days. Here Lala Jemadar, with twenty-five men, left the gang to operate on the roads between Agra and Delhi; while the main body proceeded to Lalsont, and thence to the village of Garawas, two coss to the west. They met a writer from Ajmere with his two attendants and groom. The usual artifices were practised upon them, and, all travelling together, halted at a Faqueer's shrine. In the evening having sent the owner of the shrine to the bazar, they murdered the travellers during his absence, and covered the bodies with a white cloth. The owner of the temple on his return took them for travellers sleeping, and when he fell asleep the bodies were carried to some distance from the shrine and buried. They turned loose the poney and buffaloe belonging to the writer to avoid suspicion.

8. Continuing their journey they fell in with and murdered three men near Lalsont, and afterward proceeded to

Madhoorajpore, where they encamped in a mangoe grove and divided the spoils of the last affair.

At night Chutanoo, a follower of Chotee Jemadar Brahmin, was so dissatisfied with his share that he went to the Fort and told the Governor, Dhatta Ram, that they were all Thugs, and had just murdered four people, upon which they were all surrounded at midnight and sixty apprehended, the remainder having effected their escape. They were all taken before the Governor of the Fort, but denied the accusation, and requested that the accuser might be made to point out the bodies of the persons said to have been murdered. This he was unable to do as he had not seen them buried, and the Governor therefore released all but eighteen, whom he forwarded to his Chief at Jeypore. They were kept a short time in confinement, but released on the day a letter arrived from Mr. Cavendish, British authority at Ajmere, calling on the Jeypore authorities to aid in the pursuit of the gang, of whose operations he had received information from Saugor.

9. During the expedition of this gang, Bukut, one of its members, was with a gang of sixteen men, operating on the road that intersects the line of operations of the main gang, and at the village of Bowlee, about eight coss from Tonk, on the Jeypore road, they met four men and one woman and strangled them. They obtained from them a silk vest, which they afterwards gave to Jewanlall Thakoor of Burguroo, where they were arrested and detained a few days. The four murdered men were servants of a Moonshee of Kotah, who was in the service of some one in Oodeypore—the perpetrators of the murder remained only a few days with the large gang. They were all soon after apprehended and brought to Saugor.

A total of thirty-five men and one woman murdered in this expedition.

Proceedings of the Gangs under Bichoo, Bhimmee, Phoolsa, Golab Khan, Saadut and other Leaders through Rajpootana and the Dehli Territories, during an Expedition in which Saadut and his party were seized in the City of Dehli by a guard from Jubulpore.

1. In November 1831, a guard from Saugor with some troops from the Chief of Dholepore, seized in the town of Kunchunpore, in the territory of that Chief, Sipahdar, afterwards transported, Shere Khan, hung in 1832, Rustum Khan approver and other Thugs of note. Khyratee, Saadut, Khoda Buksh, Teyz Khan, Ramzanee and Man Khan, made off and concealed themselves in the jungles of Keroulee for two months. After this they went to Bhurtpore, near which place they met a man on his way from the Dooab to Kutch. They set out with him the next morning, and proceeded to Sodapore, and leaving that place the following morning put him to death, as he sat down to rest himself. They buried the body in a ditch.

2. After this affair they went to Beeanee, where they met Achul Jemadar, Dhunooa, Dhunooa the 2d, with forty Thugs from the Dooab, on their return from an expedition into Rajpootana. They mentioned that they had murdered four treasure bearers, who had deposited their treasure beforehand and yielded nothing. They joined them and went to Juberah in Bhurtpore, where they fell in with Khuluk and Purusram Jemadar, with a gang of thirty-five Thugs. They had with them a Hindoo on his way from Ajmere to Furruckabad. They set out with him before day-break, and at a chosen place, half a coss distant, put him to death among some salt pits, got fifty rupees and clothes.

3. Went on to Mirakoo, in the Agra district, and lodged in the Surae, where they met a traveller on his

way from Ajmere to Cawnpore, and going on with him the next morning before day-light put him to death.

4. After this affair Saadut's party of five took the road to Bhurtpore, and the rest all went off to the Dooab, but Dhunooa, the son of Madaree, promised to persuade part of the gang to return and join them. On reaching Achlere, in Agra, they were joined by a party of twenty-five under the two Dhunooas and Achal Jemadar. They went on together to Charsana, in Bhurtpore, where they met three travellers on their way from Alwur to Furukabad; going on with them the next morning before day-break they put them to death, and buried their bodies. They got from them one hundred rupees in money.

5. After this affair they passed through Bhurtpore, to a village under the Balahuree pass, on the road to Jeypore. Here they met a Bheestie belonging to the Governor General, whose camp was then at Dhoosa, on his way to his home on leave. Going on with him the next morning they put him to death, at a place half a coss distant, and buried his body in the sand. Got from him eighty rupees in money.

6. Went to Jutwara in Jeypore, where they fell in with three persons on their way from Agra to Jeypore; and going on with them the next morning before daylight put them to death, and buried their bodies in some deep ravines. Got from them six pieces of green silk, with two seers of gold lace. All worth six hundred rupees.

7. At this place they were joined by Johuree, who went on with them to Chaksoo, where they fell in with three men going to Lucknow; lodged with them that night, and going on with them next morning, reached Ramsur in two days. Leaving that place before daylight, put them to death on the bank of a water-course a coss distant, buried their bodies in the bed of the stream, and got from them property to the value of one hundred and fifty rupees.

8. Went thence to Indore, where they met a man on his way from Indore to Furukabad. The next day they went on with him to Birmabad in Bhurtpore; and going with him to a water-course, the next morning before day-light, put him to death. Got from him sixty or seventy rupees worth of property.

9. The Dooab men here left them, and Saadut and his friends came to Neroulee in Bhurtpore, where they met Bichoo, Purusram and Persaud with nine other Thugs, who all joined them. A Hindoo traveller on his way from Nusseerabad, came up as they were talking, and going on with him before day-light put him to death in a water-course.

10. After this affair Saadut, Khyratee and Mankhan went to their houses, promising to rejoin the gang at Secundera in Jeypore. They did so after spending eight days with their families, and in their absence two travellers had been killed at Hilleyna, and one at Mhowa on the same road, and their share of the booty had been set aside for them.

11. They now went on to Ghurta, five coss from Jeypore, where they fell in with Bukut, Thukoree, Nungooa, and five other Thugs on their way back to Jeypore; and joining parties they came back to Kagle ka Bagh, where they were overtaken by two travellers on their way from Jeypore to Dholepore. Coming on with them to Lalgur, they fell in with Bhimmee and Kunhye Jemadars, with a gang of forty Thugs, and among them Dureeaw, the run-away approver. They all joined gangs and one half went to a village four coss distant with the travellers, while the other half went to Jytwara. The travellers were killed the next morning and their bodies were buried in the sand.

12. The parties re-united at Jytwara and went to Mahesur where Nunhoo, Dibba and Sunkur ran off, lest

Satar Khan should importune them for the money they owed him. The gang went on to Jogneer where they met three Hindoos on their way from Joudpore to Lucknow. Fifteen of the gang joined them and went on with them next morning, and the following morning put them to death and buried them in the usual manner.

Here the gangs were joined by a small party of nine Thugs under Ghoolab Jemadar, whose father Aman was hung at Saugor about this time. This party left their home at Bohmunpoora, in the Gwalior territory, and set out on their expedition at three o'clock in the morning, without taking the auspices, on the alarm of the approach of one of the Saugor guards. Going on together to Sambher, they fell in with a Moonshee and four attendants on their way from Nusseerabad to their homes at Furukabad. They passed through Jogneer, Bujroo, and Doodhoo to Koondee, without finding in five days a favorable opportunity to put these travellers to death; at Koondee, they encamped with them in the court yard of the temple dedicated to Mahadeo, under a Bur-tree, on the bank of a tank. Setting out from this place a little after midnight, they reached a well on the open plain, about two coss distant long before the day broke, and here they proposed to the Moonshee and his companions to sit down, and rest themselves; and they had no sooner done so, than they were seized and strangled. Their bodies were thrown into the well. They got from them more than one thousand rupees in money and other property.

After this affair they went to Jeypore, and there it was determined to take the road to Delhi. Going on upon that road to Seetul, in the Jeypore territory, they fell in with six Mussulmen and three Hindoos on their way from Neemuch to Delhi. The Mussulmans were prevailed upon to lodge with Saadut and his Mahomedan party of

Koheleeas, and the Hindoos were persuaded to take up their quarters with Kunhye and his Hindoo gang. About the middle of the third watch Kunhye and a party of twenty-five Thugs set out with the three Hindoos, and on the open plain, about three coss distant, they prevailed upon them to sit down and wait for the main body. As they did so they were seized and strangled, and their bodies were buried in the bed of a water-course some half a mile further on. The Mussulmans of their gang set out soon after them with the Mahomedans, and on reaching the spot where the three Hindoos had been murdered, they requested them to sit down and rest themselves. Four out of the six did so, but the other two declined and stood aloof as if they had some suspicions of the gang's intentions towards them. Fearing that these two men might escape, the gang went on after resting a little to the water-course, where the first party had just completed the burial of the three Hindoos, and here again they tried in vain to persuade the two Mussulmans to sit down and rest, and were obliged to go on half a mile to another water-course. Day had now begun to appear and in despair of getting the wary men to sit down they rushed in upon them as they descended into the bed of the water-course, and strangled them. They buried their bodies in the bed of the stream, and got from the whole nine property to the value of six hundred rupees, with a fine mare, which was afterwards given as a present to one of the principal landholders in the Jhansee territory.

The gang now went to Sambhur, where Bhimmee and his gang left the rest and went down towards Joudhpore, but they were soon after joined by the party under Bechoo and Purusram. They came on to a place near Chaksoo, where they fell in with a party of four travellers on their way from the Bombay Presidency to Lucknow; and going on with them the next morning, they put them all to death.

Coming on to Debach, they fell in with two Hindoos on their way from Joudhpore to the Dooab. They travelled with them, and on the morning of the second day put them to death, and buried their bodies in the open plain.

Going on to Aree in Jeypore, they fell in with a traveller on his way from Nusseerabad to the Dooab, and going on with him the next morning they put him to death, as he sat down to smoke his hookah.

Going again to Koondee, they fell in with five travellers on their way from Nusseerabad cantonments to Lucknow. Going on with them the next morning, before day light, they strangled them in the open plain as they sat down to smoke, and buried their bodies in the long grass jungle.

Coming through Madhoorajpore, after this affair to Charsoo, they heard that the Saugor guards were after them, and Gholab and his party returned to Bahmanpoora, where they arrived in May 1832, and remained undisturbed seven months. At last being traced by the Saugor guards, the Gwalior Regent, the Beyza Bae, was induced at the suggestion of the British Resident, to send out a detachment of two companies of Infantry, with a six-pounder, to secure them. The head man of the village was determined to protect them in consideration of the share of the booty they had always given him. An action took place in which several lives were lost, while the Camp of the Governor General of India, Lord William Bentinck, and that of the Beyza Bae, were within hearing of the guns. The Thugs all made their escape in disguise with the women, but were soon after taken, brought to the Resident and by him sent to Saugor.

Phoolsa and Purusram soon after returned to their homes in the Dooab, leaving Saadut with only seven companions. These eight men went to Gosaea, in Jeypore, where they fell in with three Hindoo travellers, on their way from Bhurtpore to Boondee. Soon after, Buksha, a Sooseea Thug, came up with a gang of eight Thugs, and joining parties, they went off the next morning with the travellers and put them to death on the plain.

After this affair Saadut, Khyratee and Makhun returned to their homes and promised to rejoin the rest at Naea Shehur in six weeks. They rejoined them at the time and place appointed, and all thence went towards Delhi. On reaching Palwal they fell in with two troopers of some local corps, and went on with them the next day to Furreedabad. Leaving that place with them next morning before day break they put them to death.

Passing through Delhi the gang went to Paneeput, where they met Runnooa Moonshee and Buksheea with their gang of twenty-five Hindoo Thugs from the Dooab. They told them that they had the day before killed two travellers with eight copper pots tinned, which being of no use to Hindoos, they had buried with the bodies; Saadut and his party said they would be useful to Mussulmen and sent Makhan and Sookha Kular, with one of Runnooa's gang, to take up these utensils which were brought to them next day.

Both gangs joined and came through Delhi to Bindrabun where Runnooa expected to meet another party from the Dooab, but being disappointed they all came to Hansee where they fell in with a man going to Lucknow. The next morning Runnooa and ten of his party went on with him and put him to death and rejoined the rest at Mohein.

They all now went to Kurnaul, thence to Bedoulee. Here they fell in with four travellers on their way from Kurnaul to Meerut, and went on with them to Jhinjana. Leaving this place with them the next morning before day light they put them all to death and buried their bodies in the plain.

They went on towards Borhana, and were sitting by the side of the road when four travellers came up on their way from Lahore to Oude. They were persuaded to lodge with them that night; and going on with them the next morning before day light they were killed within a coss of Borhana.

Going on to Borhana they fell in with a traveller on his way from Lodheana to Oude. He was in the service of Soojah-ol-Molk. Two mornings after this man was put to death as he travelled with the gang.

After this affair the gang went on to Sardhuna, whence four of the party, Khoda Buksh, Sookha, Makhan and Chunderhuns, went to their homes, and six of the Dooab party did the same. The rest went to Mozuffernugur, where Runnooa and all his party insisted upon going north to Hurdwar; Saadut, Johuree, Badam, Khyratee, Ramjanee and Feyzkhan refused to join them and proceeded west. These six men passed through Saharunpore to Kurnaul, where they found an old friend Junooa, who had turned beggar and became the disciple at that place. He came to the party in the Serae and weeping with joy, resolved to return to his old trade. Here they fell in with a Mussulman and his wife, who had with them a mare and a foal. They were going from Lahore to Sardhuna. They crossed the Jumna, and went on with them to Biroree; and leaving that place with them, the next morning before day light put them to death near a well, and buried them under some Babool trees.

After this affair they searched about for service for two months, alarmed at the arrests that were every where taking place. Not finding any, they went to Bahadergur near Delhi, but Junooa lost the road, and entered the city alone, and lodged in the Serae of Ikram Mirdha. Here he found a guard of Nujeebs from Jubulpore, with Bhooree and Bukut approvers, under command of Poorun Sing Duffadar. He was recognized by Bhooree, though still in disguise, seized and taken to the Magistrate, and in his alarm he mentioned that he expected Saadut and his other friends from Bahadergur, with four ponies, and a mare and her foal.

The guard consisting of Poorun Sing, five Nujeebs, one trooper and Bhooree, set out in search of them on that road. On leaving Bahadergur, the Thugs that morning heard the *Putora*, a bad omen, and dreaded evil. Saadut proposed returning, and avoiding the city, but Badam opposed it, and he was over-ruled. On reaching the Serae of Chetaram, they saw the guard coming towards them, in blue uniforms, and mistook it for one of the Begum Sombre's; Feyz Khan was in advance, mounted upon one of the ponies, and he was seized by Maherban Sing, a Nujeeb, while Bhooree held the bridle; he got off, and unable to shake off the Nujeeb, drew his dagger and stabbed him to the heart. The Nujeeb fell dead; but Bhooree, the approver, seized his sword as he fell, and with one cut severed Feyz Khan's head from his shoulders, it hung merely by the skin; and he fell dead upon the body of the Nujeeb. Each of the other Nujeebs seized his man, while the trooper gallopped off for assistance from the police, and the whole were secured. Five of the six were mounted, four upon ponies and the other upon the mare when the guard came up; and it is probable that some of them would have escaped had they not been deterred from attempting it by the sight of the trooper. They were all taken to the Magistrate of the City, before whom they confessed their crimes and were sent to Saugor.

Names of the Principal Leaders of the Gangs engaged in the foregoing Expeditions for 1831-32.

No.	Names of Leaders.	Cast.	Resident.	Remarks.	No. of Thugs.
1	Dhurum Khan,	Moslem,	Gwalior,	Died at Serohe in 1832,	
	Bhimmee,	Lodhee,	Ditto,	Approver,	
	Kunhye,	Aheer,	Ditto,	Killed in the Gwalior Ilaka in 1833,	
	Roopjee,	Naek,	Jeypore,	At large,	
5	Kulleean,	Ditto,	Ditto,	Ditto,	
	Budaloo Jemadar,	Lodhee,	Gwalior,	Hung at Saugor in 1832,	
	Kadir,	Moslem,	Ditto,	Approver,	
	Desraj,	Brahmin,	Ditto,	Ditto,	
	Futteh,	Moslem,	Ditto,	Died at his home in 1831-32,	
10	Seolall,	Naek,	Jeypore,	Approver, in Jubulpore Jail,	
	Nuthoo,	Ditto,	Ditto,	Transported from Jubulpore in 1837,	
	Nahur Sing,	Ditto,	Soopur,	Approver,	
	Aman,	Moslem,	Dholepore,	Hung at Saugor in 1832,	
	Ajubee Jemadar,	Brahmin,	Indore,	Ditto,	22
15	Bukut,	Ditto,	Jhansee,	Ditto,	7
	Bichoo,	Lodhee,	Cawnpore,	Approver,	17
	Mandhata,	Ditto,	Etawa,	Ditto,	10
	Bukut,	Rajpoot,	Indore,	Ditto,	12
	Kesuree Soobadar,	Lodhee,	Lucknow,	Hung at Jubulpore in 1835,	20
20	Khyratee,	Moslem,	Jhalone,	Ditto,	
	Saadut,	Ditto,	Koel,	Approver,	
	Khoda Buksh,	Ditto,	Ditto,	Died in Jubulpore Jail in 1835,	
	Feyz Khan,	Ditto,	Agra,	Killed by a Nujeeb in arresting him 1832-33,	
	Ramjanee,	Ditto,	Ditto,	Approver,	

No.	Names of Leaders.	Cast.	Resident.	Remarks.	No. of Thugs.
25	Man Khan,	Moslem,	Jhansee,	Transported,	
	Achul Jemadar,	Lodhee,	Cawnpore,	Hung at Jubulpore in 1835,	
	Dhunooa,	Ditto,	Ditto,	Ditto in 1836,	
	Dhunooa second,	Ditto,	Ditto,	Approver,	
	Khuluk Jemadar,	Ditto,	Ditto,	Hung at Saugor in 1833,	
30	Purusram ditto,	Buneea,	Gwalior,	Approver,	
	Johuree,	Moslem,	Ditto,	Ditto,	
	Persaud,	Lodhee,	Furukabad,	Ditto,	
	Thakooree,	Brahmin,	Gwalior,	At large,	
	Nungooa,	Barber,	Ditto,	Ditto,	
35	Durreaw,	Lodhee,	Ditto,	Transported from Saugor in 1833,	
	Phoolsa,	Brahmin,	Ditto,	Approver,	
	Gholab Khan,	Moslem,	Ditto,	Ditto,	
	Buksha,	Ditto,	Seronje,	Died at his home in 1832,	
	Runnooa Moonshee,	Lodhee,	Dooab,	Hung at Jubulpore in 1835,	
40	Buksheea,	Ditto,	Boorhanpore,	Approver,	
41	Badam,	Moslem,	Agra,	Died in Saugor Jail in 1834,	

Narrative by Mr. McLeod of a Thug Expedition, in the latter end of 1832, *and early part of* 1833, *under Bhimmee, Kunhye, and other leaders.*

1. About two months after Bhimmee Jemadar returned from the expedition, with Dhurmkhan to the westward, he again set out in October 1832, in the same direction with six followers, in company with Kunhye alias Bijee Sing with nine followers. This party of seventeen proceeded via Antree to Kurowlee, in the Gwalior territory. Here they met a Rajpoot whom they murdered in the jungles, one coss from the town, and then proceeded westward.

2. While on the road they persuaded a Mussulman to join them, and having dined together on the bank of a river, they murdered him, and then proceeded westward.

3. At Kooryawan they were joined by Doorjun Lodhee, Kulloo Kutchwaha; shortly after they met a Brahmin, near Lalsont, whom they murdered.

4. Near Bussahee the gang fell in with Bukut Jemadar and twelve followers, and Saadut Koeleeah Jemadar with fourteen; they joined company, having enveigled two Jats, they sent a party with them. About one coss east of Tonga they were murdered.

5. On leaving Jeytwara, the Dooab Thugs left them with Nunooa Koree, Doorjun Brahmin and Tiginah, the rest went on to Jeypore, and at a pass three coss from the city, they met two Mussulmen, whom they murdered between Bussahee and Kyreen; shortly after they met a large gang under Phoolsah, Beechoo and others, with whom they operated for some time. Leaving this gang, they proceeded southward, and passing through Jeypore on the road to Kishengurh, they murdered a Rajpoot at a nuddee, a few coss from Jeypore; after this they pro-

ceeded to Sambhur and Kishengurh, where Saadut and his Koeleeas left them.

6. From Kishengurh they proceeded to Pokhur, Palee and Poonah; three coss beyond the latter, they murdered Ramchund Brahmin, a Byragee and a Jat.

7. Going on to a village named Joorya, on the road from Palee to Joudpore, they murdered four Rajpoots.

8. The gang proceeded through Dhorajee, Durar and Peepur, to a village, seven coss on the Palee road, where they murdered a Brahmin, his servant and a Jat.

9. Proceeding through Rungowan and Baroda, they murdered a Mussulman one coss west of Baroda.

10. Coming back through Baroda, a coss to the east, they murdered a Brahmin, and proceeded to Mirtha.

11. Going on towards Serohee, they murdered five Rajpoots, at a village with a large sheet of water close by it.

12. The gang now returned towards home, and passing through Rean at a water-course, one coss from Rean, they murdered three travellers.

13. At Aluneeabas they were joined by four Masons, whom they took on to Kyr, and murdered; (their bodies were exhumed by Mr. McLeod). While here they were joined by twenty Thugs of the Khoorarea clan from the Dooab, under Makun and Persaud Jemadars, who soon after left them and proceeded to Pokhur.

14. Bhimmee's gang came on through Kishengurh to Sunderee Bundree, where they murdered two Brahmins, and buried them in a small temple, where they were exhumed by Mr. McLeod.

15. Coming on to a village, four coss east of Sunderee Bundree, they murdered a Rajpoot and a Barber, and then proceeded through Saugor.

16. At Saugor ten of the gang returned home, the rest went to Lallgurh, where they met three Rajpoots and a

Barber, on their way from Jeypore to Gwalior, in search of service. They came on with them to Tunga, where they met Imam Khan and Khoda Buksh, Koeleeahs, who came on with them to Kaloobass. Leaving that place early next morning, before day-light, mistook the shout of a village watchman for the signal for murder, and strangled the four men, whose screams were heard by the watchmen. The gang immediately dispersed, but being closely pursued by orders of the Amil of Lalsont, Bhimmee, Purusram, Aman and Hussunoo were seized at Luckunpoor, and taken to Jeypore, where they were given up to the guard from Saugor under Hernauth Sing, Tomandar. Eight of the gang were soon after intercepted on their way home, by the same guard, at Beanah, and sent to Saugor.

A total of forty-one men murdered during the expedition this season.

Names of the Principal Leaders of the Gangs engaged in the foregoing Expeditions for 1832-33.

No.	Names of Leaders.	Caste.	Resident.	Remarks.	No. of Thugs.
1	Bhimmee Jemadar,	Lodhee,	Gwalior,	Approver,	
	Kunhye alias Bijee Sing,	Aheer,	Ditto,	Killed in arresting him by the Zemindar in the Gwalior Territory in 1833,	
	Doorjun,	Lodhee,	Ditto,	Hung at Saugor in 1832,	
	Kulloo Kutchwaha,	Rajpoot,	Ditto,	Killed by a Zemindar, in arresting him in the Gwalior Territory in 1835,	
5	Bukut Jemadar,	Moslem,	Ditto,	Approver,	
	Saadut Koeleea,	Ditto,	Koel,	Ditto,	
	Doorjun,	Brahmin,	Gwalior,	Hung at Saugor in 1832,	
	Nunooa,	Koree,	Ditto,	Approver,	
	Teginah,	Brahmin,	Ditto,	Hung at Saugor in 1832,	
10	Makun Jemadar,	Lodhee,	Cawnpore,	Approver,	
	Persaud ditto,	Ditto,	Ditto,	Ditto,	
	Imam Khan,	Moslem,	Gwalior,	Ditto,	
13	Khodabuksh,	Ditto,	Ditto,	Died in Jubulpore Jail in 1835,	

EXPEDITIONS

OF THE

KANTHAL GANGS.

IN 1822-23.

Narrative of an Expedition to Guzerat, made by the Thugs of Kanthal, in the end of 1822 *and beginning of* 1823, *commonly called by the Thugs the "Leep" affair.*

By Lieutenant Briggs.

1. Bhowan and Rama, Jemadars, and about forty Thugs, started from Umba Rama to Eord Sewra, near Budnawur, thence to Deshae Rajghur, near Bhopawur Cantonments, where they met a Mahratta and his wife, whom they brought on as far as Bheelpore, four or five coss east of Barodah, and murdered in their encampment; the bodies were buried in the nullah, and they proceeded to Barodah, remaining there a few days.

2. From Barodah they started to Kumach, and after leaving that place fell in with a traveller. Rambuksh Jemadar pretended he would give him service, and induced him to proceed in their company to a village further on, where he was murdered in camp at night.

3. After this affair they proceeded to Kurroo, where there is a Faqueer's Tukeea (or shrine,) and divided into two gangs. One under Sheolal Jemadar, went in the direction of Bhawnugur, and the other under Bhawun Jemadar, went towards Bunkaneer. Rama was with Sheolal's party, and proceeding about a coss, fell in with a traveller,

and took him on to Peepree. Set out with him next morning and murdered him, and buried his body in a ruin.

4. Went on to Chumaree, and at a well near the village, fell in with a traveller, whom they murdered about mid-day as they went along, and proceeded to Score, from thence through Joonagurh to Sultanpore; on the road Punnoo, brother of Chuttur, died.

5. Encamped on the banks of a nullah, at Sultanpore, where they met a traveller, whom they murdered the next morning, about one coss distant, and threw the body into a well. After this they went to Jeytpore, where Dewa and Bujja joined them. Returned to Joonagur, where Rutna and Rutta met them, and at Doorajee they were met by two others of Bhowan's party, who recommended them to return to Joonagur for fear of exciting suspicions. Stopped three or four days at Joonagur in the Dhurumsala (almshouse,) where Roopa came from Bhowan with a horse as an offering for Jumeed Shah Datah, with orders for the gang to proceed to Doorajee, where, on their arrival, they met Bhowan and his party. They learnt from him that the first affair of his party had been perpetrated at Pukarreea.

6. At Pukarreea they fell in with a man with a cart laden with cloth, he was brought into camp, and Rambuksh Jemadar persuaded him to dismiss the cart and put his property on a horse the party had with them, and in the morning they murdered him.

7. After the above affair they went to Than—fell in with two men, whom they took on to a village between Than and Bunkaneer, and at night murdered them in camp.

8. Arriving at Bunkaneer, they met a Shop-keeper, whom they killed about mid-day. After this they proceeded to Nuggur and remained there four or five days.

9. The gang proceeded towards Bhowungur, where they fell in with two men. They accompanied the gang to a village, where they were strangled in camp. The property was divided in a scramble, and they proceeded to Doorajee, where the gangs united. Started in company and settled accounts on the road; upon reaching Deree, Ujeet Khan and twenty or twenty-five followers separated and went back, the others proceeded to Bheemnauth.

10. At a small village between Bheemnauth and Neemree, while they were eating their dinner, three men came up with a camel and were inveigled, but the omens being unfavourable, they deferred murdering them, and took them on to a village, where there is a well and some Babool trees, where they put them to death at night in camp. Proceeded to Choora, from thence to Neemree Burwar, and thence to Ahmedabad, where they again divided the party. One gang under Sheolal, went to Barodah; and the other party, composed of all the useless part of the gang, were sent to Peetapore with Ruma. At Peetapore they fell in with Hussen and Doondea, alias Khoda Buksh, who had been sent with the camel, obtained in the Leep affair for sale, he realized for the same 40 rupees. The Katies obtained in the Leep affair, were left with Boadhun Lohar of Peetapore, and given to Rama on his arrival there. He put them on the camel obtained in the Segàl of Chooran affair, and went to Barodah again.

11. Here they met Bhowan, who told them he had an affair at Anunt, in which two men were strangled by the gang about two coss from Anunt, and the bodies buried in the sand. The gang joined the parties at Barodah, and went to Jumosee, from thence to Baroach, crossed the Nerbudda and went to Surat, where Dewa, brother of Futteh, died. Proceeded to Thunna, where they were stopped by the Police guards, turned back and went to Gunderee and

Nasarae, from thence to Barokolabe, where they made offerings to the shrine of Dhunnee Peer to propitiate the spirit of the deceased Dewa. They then divided the gang into two parties. Bhowan was the Jemadar of one, and the other, consisting of the refuse under Omeed and Ujeet Khan, was sent to Dubahee to await Bhowan's arrival. Rama was in charge of Bhowan's property, and went towards Dubohee.

12. At a village about eight coss from Dubohe Rama again fell in with Bhowan's party, and learnt that at Meagow they had fallen in with two treasure-bearers whom they had instantly fallen upon and put to death. They joined parties and started in the morning to Dubohee, and at a village, a short distance from it, remained to settle accounts; a share being eight rupees weight of gold, fourteen annas of silver, and fourteen or fifteen Spanish dollars. They then went on to Dubohee and put up at a Fuqeer's shrine.

13. Oomeid inveigled a man and brought him to the shrine at night, he was murdered by Khooshal in Camp. After this they agreed to go home and started for Dhar.

14. At Rajgurh they fell in with six men who had with them two horses and took them to Desahee—stopped that night there, and next morning took them on to a grove about one and a half coss off, where they strangled them. Rambuksh Jemadar took one of the horses and Bhyroom, son of Sudoo, the other. They then returned to their homes.

A total of twenty-five men and one woman murdered in this expedition.

Narrative of an Expedition into Guzerat, made by the Kanthal Thugs, in the end of 1823 *and beginning of* 1824, *commonly called by the Thugs the "Sona" affair.*

By Lieutenant Briggs.

1. Bhawun, Nathoo, Nahur Singh and Ajeet Khan Jemadars, with Rama and forty Thugs, proceeded from Umba Rama, via Banswara, Dakoorjie and Khaira to Kumach, where they divided the party into two gangs. Nathoo Jemadar set out with one party towards Dhorka, and Bhawun Jemadar with the other towards Bheemnauth. Rama was with Bhawun's party, and they started from Kumach to Bheemnauth and thence through Bata Pariawar to Bheecheea, where they met two men who would not join them—they followed them up, and about nine coss distant, strangled them in a Runn.

2. After this affair they proceeded to Sooltanpore, and were preparing to set out, when a man came up and accompanied them as far as Gondull, where they strangled him. They then went through Jytpore to Joonagurh, where they sold two pieces of silk (which they robbed from this man) for fifty rupees, and after halting one day went through Doorajie to Kundora and Kalabur—at this place they quarrelled.

3. They set out early next morning, and about one coss distant fell in with a treasure bearer at a Bowlee. A few of the gang followed him about a quarter of a mile and strangled him, then returned to their gang at a village close to the Bowlee.

4. After the last affair they went on to a nullah close to the village, and were sitting down, when another treasure bearer came up, they let him pass, and sent a party in pursuit who murdered him about one coss off. On the

road next morning they fell in with Dewa, Fouzkban, Nathoo, Jemadars, and twenty-five Thugs. Stopped one night with them, and then went on to Nuggur; the other party went to Joonagurh.

5. They halted four or five days at Joonagurh, and then went to Durrote, and from thence to Dhurrongdra. From Dhurrote they sent two of the gang with fifty Spanish dollars to Nathoo Jemadar, with directions to meet them at Dhurrongdra, which they did, and told of their having murdered four men at Doorajee.

They also related another affair, but nothing of any value was obtained. The gangs settled accounts at Dhurrongdra, and got four dollars each, the rest was carried to account of road expenses. Then proceeded to Kurree, where they halted ten or fifteen days, it being the Dusserah, went to Kullote and halted one day to divide the gang again; Bhawun and Nathoo, Jemadars, went to Ahmedabad and rested a day or two, and went to Butwan, thence to Mehmoodabad, thence to Nuryabad.

6. At Nuryabad, they fell in with a Shop-keeper, who accompanied them four coss on the Baroda road, where they put up for the night. He was strangled and the body buried at the well of a temple to Mahadeo and can be found. After this they went to Munoo Mogree, thence to Baroda, three coss from the Mhye river.

7. Proceeded to Basam. Half the gang had crossed the river Mhye with Bhawun; Nathoo and the remainder were waiting to be ferried over, when three treasure bearers came up. The bearers stopped at Basam; likewise Nathoo and his party who were at the Faqueer's shrine. When the bearers set out in the morning, they were followed by Nathoo and his party and strangled. One of the bearers remained at Basam, having a swelled leg. The gang turned off the roads, and went to Ometa, where they were

joined by Bhawun and his party; and Nuhur Sing's party likewise. They settled accounts. The share amounted to seven rupees weight of gold, a rupee weight of gold beads, twenty-five or twenty-six rupees. After this affair the gang returned home.

A total of twelve men murdered in this expedition.

Narrative of the Murders committed by part of the Thugs concerned in the "Ghora" affair.

By Lieutenant Briggs.

1. After leaving Justun Berawara, and reaching Becheea, which is about three coss from it, Rama, Bhyrow, Ooma, Hussun Chotee, Deola, Boola, Natheea, Futteh Khan, Khooshal and Bucksha, separated from Bhowan's party and went towards Rajcote, about four miles from Rampoora, and fell in with a Hindoo, whom they took on to a village, took a meal, and proceeded a quarter of a coss, when they strangled him.

2. After this they went to Goondur, where they rested two days, Seolal, Khooshal, Rambuksh, Kesera, Seolal Bhut, Chummunea and Bucksha, separated from Bhowan's gang, and met them here, having killed a Byragee in the neighbourhood of Goondur. Rambuksh brought a Hindoo into camp, whom they took on, a little before midnight, one and a half coss, and strangled at a place chosen before hand.

3. The gang returned to Rajcote, and between Pariawar and Beehora, when amusing themselves with fishing in a nullah, a Trooper on leave came up, Rambuksh inveigled him to a Fakeer's shrine, at Pariawar, where they were joined by two other persons. The gang went

to Pariawar, and about midnight took the three victims on about three coss, when they put them to death as they went along, and buried them on the spot.

4. After this affair they proceeded to Dhundooka, and put up at a village, three and half coss distant, where they met three men and a female, whom they brought on to Hudaeeleea; about three in the afternoon they took them on about one and half coss, where they strangled them in the plain. The bodies were securely buried in a cotton field. Bhyroo and his friends went to their homes after this affair, and left Seolal and his party at Baroda.

A total of eight men and one woman murdered in this expedition.

Narrative of an Expedition made by Thugs into Guzerat in the end of 1827 *and beginning of* 1828, *commonly called the "Ghora" affair.*

By Lieutenant Briggs.

1. Rama and Bhowan with about thirty followers left Rengrua, and went to Fouj Khan's, Jemadar, at Enura Sewurd. He had about twenty followers and joined the gang. They went to Kathee Baroda, thence to Deeshae and crossed the Paraghat, where they met two Brahmins, whom they took on to Baroda cantonment, where they rested the night at a tank, where there is a Pilgrims' alms-house; soon after dark, they were put to death in camp.

2. After the last affair they halted one day, and early next morning, four treasure bearers came up and passed them. They instantly set out after them, but lost sight of them—and went to Katyawar, thence to Dhorajie and

thence to Kandara, where they met two Goosaens and two women whom they inveigled, took on in the afternoon, and put them to death on the banks of the Bhadur river. After this they went to Nuggur and halted eight or ten days.

3. At Nuggur, they sent out scouts for victims, and Kanlah reported two treasure bearers were on their way to Jouria Bundur. Fouj Khan and others went in pursuit of them, but at a Bowlee two coss from Nuggur, two Sepahees of the Rajah's joined the treasure bearers, which led the Thugs to think that suspicion had been excited. They nevertheless went on to Jooria and put up at an almshouse. In the evening, three servants of an European officer, a fourth with a double barrelled gun, and a groom came up. Towards midnight they took them on one and a half coss and murdered them, and having buried the bodies returned to the almshouse unobserved.

4. At the almshouse a traveller came up and told them the bodies of three murdered travellers had been found, which induced them to set out, about four in the afternoon, for Durrole where they rested the night. In the morning one coss on the other side they fell in with a Goosaen whom they strangled. After this they went to Purduree and rested the night.

5. In the morning they arrived at Rajcote and found some horse dealers at the Fackeer's shrine near the cantonments. They encamped in a grove on the same side of the Agie river, under pretence of Bhowan Sing, a native chief, being in their camp and wishing to purchase their horses. They persuaded the men to proceed to a village five or six coss off where the horses were purchased by Bhowan Jumadar (who acted as the chief) for one thousand nine hundred rupees. At night they murdered the horse dealers in camp and buried their bodies.

6. After the last affair Rama and others went with the horses to Baroda where they soon after met Nathoo Jemadar with twenty-five or thirty followers. Fourteen or fifteen days after they were joined by Fouj Khan with fifteen followers. Rama went on to Baroda; after his departure the rest were divided into two parties. One under Bhowan went to Kumach, the other under Fouj Khan towards Darkoorjee. On reaching Loctullah they met three men from the Ganges, who were inveigled and murdered next morning.

7. Bhowan and his party rejoined Rama and the others at Baroda without having perpetrated any affair. After halting together three or four days, Bhowan with ten or fifteen followers went on towards Surat, but returned the same night with three treasure bearers, whom they met at Esolah. They strangled them near the Dhandur river and came back to Baroda that night. They set out next morning for Darkoorjee, where they hired a house and left a party to take care of Bhowan, who was sick. The remainder under Nathoo went to Kirra and thence to Pirawa, where they divided into two gangs. One under Fouj Khan went to Deesa; the other under Nathoo towards Dholka; and finally to Ahmedabad, where they remained several days and sent for Bhowan and his party who rejoined them. All set out together for Kumach where the other gang under Fouj Khan joined them, and they went to Katyawar.

8. At Peeprawlee they fell in with a traveller whom they murdered at mid-day, and buried the body in a ravine. After this they went to Bhimnauth, and settled accounts; thence to Gudawlee, where the gang was again divided. A party under Nathoo, went to Ahmedabad, another under Bhowan in the direction of Joonagurh towards Doorajie; and at a small village Bhyroom, son of Sadoo, with ten

followers separated from the rest and went on an expedition on their own account. Upon reaching Doorajie, Rambuksh and others left the main body in consequence of a mare throwing a foal, which is so bad an omen that few venture to remain out with the gang in which it occurs.

9. There remained only Bhowan, Fouj Khan and Rama Jemadars with twenty followers, who went to Jytpore and thence to Bhimnauth, where they slept at a Byragee's hut on the bank of a river. Here they fell in with a man whom Herita brought into camp, and they put him to death at night.

10. From Bhimnauth, they took on four travellers and murdered them towards evening between Dhundooka and Huddowlee, and afterwards returned to the village and slept. After this they went to Dholka, where they halted a day, thence proceeded through Soorujjeetra and Pillode to Baroda, and thence they returned to their homes.

A total of twenty-five men and two women murdered in this expedition.

A Narrative of an Expedition by the Kanthal Thugs, in the same year as the "Jurao" affair, commonly called the "Baroda Bigar."

By Lieutenant Briggs.

1. Bhyroom, Nuhur Sing and Seolal Jemadars with others, in all about seventeen Thugs, set out from Sajtullee, and went through Rajgurh to Choundpore, where they fell in with five Byragees whom they took on to Dubohee where they rested at night—thence from Chota Odeypore to Tajgurh, where they again halted at night. About

midnight they took the travellers on a quarter of a coss off the high road and strangled them.

2. After this affair they went to Baroda, where they rested five days. Went through Ahmedabad to Memedabad, where they fell in with five Byragees whom they took on five coss and put to death and buried their bodies in a field to the south of the road. They returned to Baroda and on the way fell in with Rama, Bhowan and their gangs who had just perpetrated the Jurao affair, and went onwards to Dubohee. Bhimme, Bijee Sing, Purusram and their gang of Bundelcund Thugs were at Baroda, they joined them and accompanied them to Dubohee.

3. From Dubohee, they inveigled a carpenter and brought him on to Saonkeira, and murdered him after dark in camp. In the morning reached Makunee, where they met Bhowan's gang with Nuhur Sing Jemadar, Lelleea and others accompanied. Bhowan's party returned homewards. Bhyroon's gang with Seolall and others went to Baroda, where they fell in with Bhooree Khan, Khyratee Khan and Tujja—Thugs from Koel, and Modee Khan, Ramzanee and Ulleeah—Thugs from Soopur, who were halting at Baroda.

4. In the cantonment of Baroda, they met two Rajpoots, whom they induced to lodge with them near an almshouse, where they were strangled and the bodies buried under a Neem tree.

5. After the last affair they proceeded towards Noonuggurh, and about four coss from thence fell in with a shopkeeper, whom they put to death about midday and buried.

6. After this affair they went towards Joonuggurh, and on the high road fell in with two grooms looking out for service. There was a dry well near the road, and after they strangled them, they buried their bodies in this well.

After this affair the gang returned to Baroda. On reaching a well between the cantonment and the town, Bhyroo and Dhulla went on to select lodgings for the party. They chose a Fukeer's shrine and returned to the gang, who went with them towards the place chosen. On reaching the town Bhyroo left them to purchase provisions for the party. On reaching the shrine, the gang found there one of the Saugor guards, with two approvers, Moklall and Paharee, who instantly recognized them and they were all immediately secured, with the exception of Khoshal Mahratta his son, Rambuksh, and Dulla, the adopted son of Hunmunt, who had by mistake gone to another shrine. Bhyroo returned to the shrine with the provisions and not being known to the approvers remained there three days; and was not taken till the middle of 1835, when he was arrested by Lieutenant Briggs.

Names of People Arrested.

Name	Caste	Name	Caste
Bhooree Khan, ...	Koeleeas.	Ramjanee, ...	Soopureeas.
Khyratee, ...		Alleea, ...	
Mudda Khan, ...		Dulla, son of Oomra,	
Tujja, ...		Futteeah, ...	

A total of sixteen men murdered in this expedition.

Narrative of an Expedition to Marwar and Guzerat in the end of 1828 *and beginning of* 1829, *commonly called the "Jurao" affair.*

By Lieutenant Briggs.

1. Bhowan, with about twenty-five or thirty followers, set out from a village near Umba Rama, came to

Banswarra, and thence to Sajtullee, thence via Chittore to Bhelwarra, where they fell in with two Mussulmen, whom they induced to accompany them to Shahpoora, on this side of which there is a tank where they were strangled. After this they went to Ajmere and rested one day, thence through Pokur and Reean to Meerta.

2. The gang proceeded from Meerta to Roophan's, where they were sitting on the bank of a tank sacrificing two goats, when four Brahmins came up. Bhowan taking half the gang persuaded them to accompany him in the direction of Meerta, through a bye-path; and after accompanying them two coss, put them to death, and rejoined the rest at Roophan's.

3. After this they all set out together for Palee, where they rested three days, and then proceeded to Bhumnauth, where they fell in with five men who had been in service at Joudepore, and were proceeding to their homes. Took them to Jhalore, thence to a village, where they put up for the night: proceeding a short distance next morning they were all put to death. The gang then returned to Deesa and put up at an almshouse.

4. There they fell in with two Goosaens and took them on in the direction of Palhempoor, and put up in a village for the night, next morning proceeding on to the appointed spot they were put to death, and the gang went to a village between Palhempoor and Seedhpoor.

5. Going on next morning towards Seedhpore they fell in with a traveller. Ten or twelve of the Thugs followed him and put him to death at a village, where they had put up for the night.

6. The remainder of the gang proceeded through Seedhpore, and on the high road fell in with four treasure bearers. Bhowan inveigled these men on his joining the gang from the last affair, and they remained in company with them for

eight days, when near Ahmedabad Bhowan persuaded them not to enter the town on account of the heavy duties they would have to pay, and they passed outside the town to the west. They went through Dakoorjee to a small village called Oomrait on the Baroda side. In the morning they went on with the bearers to the place that had been chosen previously for the murder and strangled them. The jewellery obtained was sold to the merchants of Ruttam Jewra, Pertabgurh and Peeplonda, and on Rama's seizure some of it was recovered by Major Borthwick.

They returned to Baroda, halted a day, and fell in with Bejee Sing, Bhimmee and their gangs, who were encamped at the Ram Talao. They then went through Dubahee to Makhunee, where Bhimmee and Seolall, with their gangs, joined them. At this place Laleea, Muna, Ajoo, Nuhur Singh and others left Seolall's party and joined Bhowan's. They then went home and had been there about two months when they were seized.

Captain Borthwick having received intelligence of the residence of these gangs arranged for their apprehension, as soon as a party of them returned from one of their excursions.

He proceeded with Captain Macmahan and about two hundred of the Jhowrah Cavalry, and came upon their villages before daylight, and so completely surrounded them, that the capture of the whole gang was effected, without the escape of a single individual, in all fifty-three Thugs—four of whom were made approvers, twenty-two executed, eleven transported, three sentenced to limited imprisonment and thirteen released for want of evidence.

A total of eighteen men murdered in this expedition.

A total of eighty-eight men and four women murdered during the different expeditions this season.

Names of the Principal Leaders of the Gangs engaged in the foregoing Expeditions from 1822 *to* 1830.

No.	Names of Leaders.	Cast.	Resident.	Remarks.	No. of Thugs.
1	Bhowan Jemadar,	Naek,		Hung at Jowra in 1832,	
	Rama ditto,	Ditto,		Approver,	
	Rambuksh ditto,	Brahmin,		At large,	
	Sheolal ditto,	Naek,		Ditto,	
5	Dewa,	Ditto,		Hung at Jowra in 1832,	
	Bhujja,	Moslem,		Hung 1836,	
	Ujeet Khan Jemadar,	Ditto,		Transported from Jowra in 1832,	
	Hussun,	Ditto,		A prisoner in the Jail at Jowra,	
	Doondee alias Khoda Buksh,	Ditto,		Dead,	
10	Omeed,	Naek,		Died at Jowra in 1834,	
	Khooshal,	Ditto,		Hung at Jowra in 1832,	
	Bhijrow,	Ditto,		Ditto ditto,	
	Nathoo Jemadar,	Moslem,		Ditto ditto,	
	Nahur Sing,	Naek,		Approver,	
15	Chotee,	Moslem,		Transported from Jowra in 1S32,	
	Deola,	Naek,		Ditto ditto,	
	Boola,	Moslem,		Ditto ditto,	
	Futteh Khan,	Ditto,		Transported from Saugor in 1832,	
	Buksha,	Ditto,		Ditto Jowra ditto,	
20	Keseree,	Lodhee,		Hung at Jubulpore in 1832,	
	Seolal Bhat,	Naek,		At large. A reward of five hundred rupees for his apprehension,	
	Chumuneea,	Ditto,		At large,	
	Fouj Khan Jemadar,	Moslem,		Hung at Jowra in 1832,	

	Bijee Sing,	Aheer,		Killed by the Chief of Aluneeabas in Rajpootana after his arrest in 1833,
25	Purusram,	Ditto,		Approver,
	Bhooree Khan,	Moslem,		At large,
	Khyratee Khan,	Ditto,		Transported from Jubulpore in 1832,
	Tujja,	Naek,		Dead,
	Modee Khan alias Motee Khan,	Moslem,		Absconded after being made approver by Major Borthwick,
30	Ramzanee,	Ditto,		Transported from Jubulpore in 1836,
	Ulleeah,	Ditto,		Doubtful whether alive or not,
	Bhimmee,	Lodhee,		Approver,
33	Ajoo,	Moslem,		Transported from Jubulpore in 1836,

EXPEDITION

OF THE

OUDE GANGS.

Narrative of an Expedition of twenty-one Thugs, under Futteh Khan, Dhoosoo, and Ruhman Jemadar, as related by Rumzan Approver.

I, with a gang of thirteen or fourteen Thugs, started from our village of Gudapore in Oude, for the purpose of Thuggee (murder and plunder!) We proceeded to the house of Futteh Khan Jemadar, in the village of distant about five miles, where we found a gang of about twelve Thugs ready to join us. We forthwith commenced the worship of Bhowanee in Futteh Khan's house. He produced the goat for the sacrifice, proceeded to slay it with a sword, but the blow fell upon the cheek bone and failed. Another sacrifice was brought, but that also failed. So we started without offering any further sacrifice. Nevertheless it was a successful journey, the gang as now assembled consisted of the following Thugs, from my village of Gudapore:

1. Jafur, son of Shakir, convicted at Lucknow.
2. Roshun, son of Eesoophe, convicted at Lucknow.
3. Kurkut, son of Sherishta Khan, convicted at Lucknow.
4. Rhuman, son of Chand Khan, convicted at Lucknow.

5. Jubber, whose head shakes, convicted at Lucknow. Dead.

6. Imambux, approver, at Lucknow.

7. Maigul, son of Peer Khan, convicted at Lucknow.

8. Madara, runaway approver.

9. Madara, son of Nihal, at large.

10. Sadee Khan, sala, or brother-in-law of Imambux, at large.

11. Ramzan, approver, (deponent.)

12. Rujub, runaway approver, besides three or four Thugs, since dead.

The above joined, at Futteh Khan's, the following Thugs:

13. Futteh Khan, Jemadar, approver, Lucknow.

14. Ramzan Pogla, convicted at Lucknow.

15. Rumzan, son of Peer Khan, convicted at Lucknow.

16. Khoosheal, son of Sidhai, convicted at Lucknow.

17. Chaidee, son of Torab, died in Lucknow Jail.

18. Dhoosoo, Jemadar, approver, Lucknow.

19. Kalee Monshee, dead at Lucknow.

20. Ameer, son of Sidhai, Lucknow Jail.

21. Jean, wounded in the arm, convicted at Lucknow.

And others whose names I do not remember.

We proceeded via Behta, Ruhmutgunge, Onao, to the Ganges, at the ghat opposite Cawnpore, (being ninety miles in a direct line.) At the ghat we fell in with Kaisree Soobadar, at the head of another large gang of twenty-six Thugs, under their respective leaders, namely, Ramdeen, approver, and Pershaud, approver. From the Cawnpore ghat the united gangs, amounting to about sixty or seventy Thugs, returned, and the next day following Sidhai fell in with and inveigled one traveller, and Dhoosoo, Futteh Khan, Ramdeen and Persaud inveigled four more travellers—the five intended victims lodged at Onao on the great Lucknow road, and the Thugs distributed themselves in small parties about the village. The single traveller rose early and was followed by six Thugs, who strangled him three miles from the village in the direction of Lucknow. The other four travellers,* viz. a Carpenter, two Kulwars, or Distillers of Spirits, and a Bearer, proceeded in the morning from Onao towards Ruhmutgunge. When they had gone about three miles, all four were strangled by Ramzan, deponent, Imambux,† approver, Lucknow, (who admits having strangled him, as he walked along! having first shoved from the traveller's head a bundle which he carried, Mukdoomee, approver, seized the legs of the traveller) and two Lode Thugs,—their bodies were instantly flung into a well.

The gang then broke into two parties,—the Lods and Jumaldies. I accompanied Futteh Khan, Dhoosoo and others, in all about eighteen Jemaldie Thugs, towards Jounpore; the Lode Thugs amounting to twenty-six or twenty-eight, proceeded under Ramdeen and others towards Bangermow. The gang which I accompanied followed the high roads for about fourteen days, until we reached Jounpore, (at least one hundred and fifty miles from Onao, the scene of the former murder) from whence we returned, and on our way back, Dhoosoo, Futteh Khan and Ramzan, inveigled a traveller, who was a Soldier, and at Hussunpore Bundwa,

* Futteh Khan, and Imambux, runaway approver, declare that there were altogether six travellers instead of five.

† Imambux, runaway approver, tells me that this is correct—that he did strangle him as above related. Mukdoomee, approver, tells me that he pulled the legs of the man, whom Imambux strangled! Kunjun, approver, tells me that he attempted to strangle one of these men as he stood, but that he mismanaged it, the victim being tall, and he, the strangler, short—that the traveller seized him and got him down, when Khan Mahomed (a prisoner in jail here) came to his aid and strangled the man. Futteh Khan tells me, he saw the struggle, and that Kunjun was covered with dust in consequence.

we had every arrangement made for murdering him, but at night, as he was approaching the intended spot where he was to be put to death, he suddenly threw down his knapsack amongst us and fled. He must have discovered that he was amongst Thugs! Our gang them broke up and we returned to our homes after a journey of seven weeks.*

It is proper to mention here as showing the diabolical feelings of Thugs, that six of that infamous gang, now sitting in the room before me, viz. Futteh Khan Jemadar, Dhoosoo Jemadar, Imambux, Ramzan, Mukdoomee, and Kunjun—all freely confessing the shares they took in the murder, and relating with evident relish, and smiles on their faces the shocking particulars, especially of the struggle between Kunjun and the victim before he was murdered! indeed so far from Thugs experiencing the least remorse, they appear to enjoy the relation of their former murders

A total of five men murdered in this expedition.

Narrative of a short Journey in Oude by two Thugs, Ramzan and Hyder, before Captain Paton, July 17, 1837.

1. I (Ramzan) and Madara set out on Thuggee from Guddopore, and unaided by others, thugged for four months. Madara is a young man, my brother-in-law, a Thug of note, a staunch man! We proceeded via Tanda and Maharajgunge—beyond which we fell in with a traveller, a khidmutgar. I won his confidence and returned with him in one day to Tuckeea, where he lodged during

* This Thug journey could not have been less than two hundred and fifty miles.

the night—next morning before day-light, we set out with him, and, about three miles from the village, Madara strangled him. He was an old man and it was not necessary for me to hold his hands. We flung his body into the river Gogra,—Madara having first stabbed him under the arm-pit with a knife. We got forty rupees and two pieces of camlet.

2. We followed the highway via Lucknow and Futtehgunge, and at Assewakgaon (having already travelled at least fifteen miles) we fell in with a large gang of Thugs, Jumaldie's and Lodie's joined, in all about thirty or thirty-five under Kaisree Jemadar, Ruhman Jemadar, Dhoosoo approver and others ; but we did not go with them, and remained only one day in their company. It happened, however, that a traveller fell in my way whilst I was with that gang, and the whole of them saw him in my snare. This traveller, Madara and myself proceeded with and lodged in Hussungunge. Next morning we accompanied him and at the distance of about five miles I strangled him, Madara held his hands. We flung him into a very deep well. Madara went home with our spoils. I awaited his arrival at Goosaengunge, forty miles to the eastward, and after ten days he returned to me.

3. We set out for Bainswarrah, and at Behta we inveigled a traveller, a grass-cutter from Hissar—he halted at Daondapoor, from whence next morning we followed him and engaged him with friendly conversation, and at the distance of three miles Madara strangled him as he sat on the ground—when dead, Madara stabbed him as usual, and we flung his body into a small tank.

5. We proceeded to Muchlee Shuhur, thence to Jounpore. We then returned through Tanda, Bungla to Mutlumnagur where we decoyed a traveller who was a weaver, and proceeding with him at the distance of five miles

Madara strangled him. We then returned to our homes having been out four months and murdered four men.

A total of four men murdered in this expedition.

Short Narrative of another Journey by two Thugs Ramzan and Hyder, taken before Captain Paton, July 17, 1837.

I (Ramzan) and Hyder approver set out, for the purpose of strangling travellers, from Guddopore, in the beginning of the rains and proceeded via Gosaengunge, the Fort of Julalabad, Newulgunge, Tukeea, Baugermow, on the banks of the Ganges (upwards of one hundred miles) from whence we returned by another route. Still no travellers ! till we reached Bowaneegunge, where we fell in with a traveller, a boatman —we inveigled him and about two miles east of Bowaneegunge Hyder strangled him as he stood,* for he would not sit.

We then made a long journey (about one hundred and thirty miles,) via Kutora, Sunbursa and Bheelhaghat, where the English troops were, thence next day we reached Hussunpore Bundwa, where at the tank we fell in with a traveller—he slept there that night; next morning we followed him and having won his confidence, at the distance of two miles, we endeavoured to induce him to sit down—but he would not, having become aware of us! I attempted to strangle him,† as he walked along, but I did not succeed —both of us then fell upon him, he made a great outcry, "they are murdering me!" at length we strangled him—we then stabbed him and flung his body into a well.

* Hyder approver confirms this, that he thugged the boatman as he stood.

† Hyder on being called in, says he attempted to strangle him but failed, and that both of them fell upon him. Hyder confirms Ramzan's statement that the poor traveller called out for help.

After this we returned to our homes, having been out a month, (they must have travelled about two hundred and sixty miles.) My companion Hyder approver was a staunch man! fearing nothing, but he is not a good inveigler—to inveigle a man is no easy matter—to answer all his questions and act a part.

A total of two men murdered in this expedition.

Narrative of an Expedition by a gang of Jemaldies Thugs in Oude, taken by Captain Paton, July 18, 1837.

Madara, son of Nihal (at large,) and Ramzan approver, (deponent,) set out from Kotdee in the cold weather and proceeded via Jugdespore, Hydergurh, &c. We followed the high road for about twenty days, in search of travellers until we reached Selempore, where we met a very old man going to the east. We won his confidence in this manner (villains!)—he carried a load which was too fatiguing for his old age. I said to him, after some other conversation, "you are an old man, I will aid you in carrying your load, as you are from my part of the country"—he said, "very well, take me with you." So we took him with us to Selempore where we slept at night. We woke him next morning before dawn and set out, and at the distance of three miles, we seated him to rest as it was very dark, Madara was ready behind him and strangled him. He was about sixty or seventy years of age—he never spoke a word. We flung his remains into a well having first stabbed his corse.

We continued our journey to Jugdespore, from whence Madara returned home—I went on for seven days alone, had I met any suitable traveller, I would have strangled him single handed, as I did on a former occasion, but I had no opportunity. On reaching the village of Kotera, I fell in with a gang of five Thugs, namely,

1. Buhram, the leader, approver, Lucknow.
2. Ouseree, approver.
3. Sirdar, approver, Lucknow.
4. Alpee, died in Lucknow jail.
5. Hathim, son of Jaree, at large, an Oude Thug.
6. Ramzan, approver, (deponent.)

The day following, I joined and returned with them; Ouseree and Hathim inveigled a Hindoo traveller—he lodged during the night at Budeyan, from whence we led him to his death, and Buhram,* approver, strangled him before my eyes—all the gang were on the spot; we flung his dead body into a well. On that very day we all lodged in Hussunpore Bundwa, where we found another gang of about fifteen or sixteen Thugs, who had come from Papamow near Allahabad, namely,

1. Imam,† run away, approver, now at Lucknow.

* Buhram, approver, declares that Ramzan himself strangled him, and these two approvers on being confronted to reconcile this difference in their statement had a warm altercation, each declaring that the other strangled! Buhram is much more worthy of belief than Ramzan, approver.

† Immediately after taking the deposition of Ramzan as above, I called in by another door, this Imambux run away, approver, with the view to corroborate Ramzan's story (the two being kept apart)—Imambux, though stating it to be twelve or thirteen years ago, told the same story about their having come from Allahabad, the dispersion of the gangs by Hinga Fakeer—the meeting of the two gangs at Hussunpore Bundwa, and from thence the flight—and of his own accord he mentioned the following names, as being in his own gang, namely, corresponding with the above:

2. Dost Alee, Lucknow jail.
3. Roshun.
4. Muckdoomee.
5. Maigul.
10. Jafir.
11. Rujub.
12. Kurkut, son of Shirista Khan.

2. Dost Alee, son of   , Lucknow jail.
3 Roshun, son of Eesooph, convieted at Lucknow.
4. Mukdoomee, son of Khoshial, convicted at Lucknow.
5. Maigul, son of Peer Khan, ditto ditto.
6. Ruhman, father of Hyder, approver, ditto ditto.
7. Ramzan, son of Peer Khan, convicted at Lucknow.
8. Kalee Khan Moonshee, died in Lucknow jail,
9. Jubbur, whose head shook, ditto ditto.
10. Jafir, son of Shakir, convicted at Lucknow.
11. Rujub, run away approver.
12. Hinga Fakeer, Saugor jail.

Besides others whom I forget. Hinga Fakeer, there, threatened, as was his custom, to give information against us if we did not purchase his silence, and began to seize Thugs. We were alarmed and fled to our homes ! thus these two gangs were for the time broken up.

A total of two men murdered in this expedition.

Narrative of an Expedition by a Gang of eight Jemaldie Thugs in Oude, taken by Captain Paton, July 19, 1837.

I, with the following gang of Thugs, started from our village of Kotdee, for the purpose of murdering travellers by Thuggee, viz.

1. Imambux, approver, (deponent.)
2. Dost Alee, son of   , Lucknow jail.
3. Roshun, son of Eesooph, convicted at Lucknow.
4. Mukdomee, son of Khoshial, ditto,

Now the mention of Dost Alee's name by both of these approvers examined apart, is strong proof against him and against all so mentioned by both. Buhram, approver, who was with Rumzan, says he does not remember the junction with this other gang, indeed he denies the junction.

5. Maigul, son of Peer Khan, convicted at Lucknow.
6. Jafir, son of Shakir, ditto.
7. Rujub, run away approver.
8. Kurkut, son of Shirishta Khan, convicted at Lucknow.

We followed the high road and proceeded via Inhona, Jugdespore, Hussunpore, Bundwa, Gondah, to Mhow—from whence we returned. At Gondha, we lodged with a decoyed traveller, who had been inveigled by myself—in the morning, we set out towards Hussunpore Bundwa, and at the distance of two miles Roshun strangled him. All the gang were present at the death—the noose fell on the man's chin, so that he had time to call out, but he was immediately afterwards strangled—fearing that his cries might have been heard, we hastened on four miles. We lodged at Peeperpore, and next day reached Hussunpore Bundwa,* where we met another gang of Thugs, viz.

1. Buhram Jemadar, approver, Lucknow.
2. Ouseree, approver.
3. Hathim, father of Ramzan, approver, dead.
4. Ramzan, approver, Lucknow.
5. Hinga Fakeer.

Fearing the latter, that he would inform against us we fled to our homes.

A total of one man murdered in this expedition.

Narrative of an Expedition by six Jemaldie Thugs in Oude, taken by Captain Paton, July 19, 1837.

After the breaking up of our last gang at Hussenpore Bundwa, in consequence of our fear that Hinga Fakeer

* The meeting and dispersion of the two gangs at Hussunpore Bundwa corresponds with the narrative of Ramzan, approver, of the 18th July, 1837.

would inform against us, I remained at my house at Kotdee for eight or nine months, when six of us resolved upon an expedition and started—we were as follows:

1. Ramzan, approver, deponent.
2. Chaidee alias Khan Mahomed, son of Buktawar, convicted at Lucknow.
3. Sirdar, approver, Lucknow.
4. Madaree, died at Saugor Jail.
5. Jaen, blind of an eye (prisoner at Saugor).
6. Budloo, dead.

It was in the rainy season we proceeded via Soneekutra to Newulgunge (not less than seventy-five miles) where I inveigled a traveller. He was a Nujeeb, a Soldier of the Jeypore Rajah, at night I awoke him, and made an excuse for starting—we proceeded with him in the direction of the next village, Entagow—when about midway between these two villages, I endeavoured to persuade him to sit down—my object being to strangle him, as the place was convenient for the murder—but he said "I will not sit down"! and took his sword in his hand—so I strangled him as he walked along—he instantly fell, and was quickly a dead man. Budloo and Madaree Thugs aided me by pulling his legs when I seized his neck in the noose. Madaree stabbed him and we buried him there. If you wish, I will dig up his bones from the spot where we deposited him. After this we all broke up and went home. I remained at home for about forty days and started again with another gang of about eleven Thugs. (See the separate narrative annexed.)

A total of one man murdered in this expedition.

Narrative of an expedition in Oude, by nine Jemaldie Thugs, taken by Captain Paton, July 19, 1837.

After the murder of the Jeypore Sepahee, near Newulgunge, I remained about forty days at home, and then started with a Thug gang of the following strength, viz.

1. Ramzan, approver, (deponent.)
2. Adhar, approver, Lucknow.
3. Mukdomee, son of Khoshial, committed at Lucknow.
4. Salarbux, approver, Lucknow.
5. Madaree, son of Nihal, at large.
6. Alpee, died in Lucknow jail.
7. Mahabut, slain by a sword, on Thuggee, by Madar.
8. Budloo, dead.
9. Madaree, son of Misree, Saugor jail.

In the rains we commenced our journey from Kotdee in search of travellers via Nawubgunge, Lucknow, Newulgunge, Tukeea to Baugurmow, about one hundred and fifty miles, which we reached in nine or ten days, from whence we returned, and that day two Thugs, Adhar and Salar, the latter of whom is an expert inveigler, won a traveller's confidence. He was a Rajpoot from Lahore going to his home, he was lodged by the decoyers in the house of a Bunya in Tukeea. They awoke him during the night and set out with him, but on the way he said to his two decoyers, "You are two suspicious persons! you look like Thugs, do not come near me!" Seeing that he had become suspicious, I said to the party in my secret Thug language, "go aside, he suspects you!" They returned. The traveller then addressed me expressing his doubts, and suggested that we two should keep together—I agreed with him and expressed my doubts of these two men—so we walked on together, and I took an opportunity of strangling him as he walked! Mukdoomee Thug was close at hand to aid: we flung the body into a spot, where there was no water and left it to be devoured by jackalls.

After this we broke into two parties, Madara and myself keeping together and alone. We proceeded in search of travellers and the same day I inveigled a traveller, a young man, a grass-cutter, and decoyed him into the village of Oouchgaon—from whence we set out with him next morning, and about midday, between that village and Goosaengunge—as he rode on a poney, and in order to get him to alight, Madara feigned illness and pretended to vomit. I induced the traveller to alight and to wait till Madara was a little better—he alighted and sat down, and I getting behind him strangled him, Madara pulled his feet. We stabbed him with a sword under the arm-pit and flung his body into a well—from whence can be had his bones and the bones of some fifteen or sixteen other travellers, which I myself flung into that well! We then went home having been out about a month, and obtained by two murders about fifty rupees as my own share. He who strangles and he who inveigles always gets the greatest share.

I always after my journey was obliged to give the Zumeendar Rugonauth Sing of my village, some present, for the whole village knew that I was a Thug, and the Zumeendar would have had me put in irons, but for these presents. All Thugs thus propitiate their Zumeendars. I never told my wife of these murders, or of my being a Thug; we do not tell our wives lest they discover the secret to others.

A total of two men murdered in this expedition.

Narrative of an expedition by three Jumaldie Thugs in Oude, taken by Captain Paton, July 20, 1837.

After the murder of the grass-cutter at Oouchgaon, I remained at my house for a year and a half, when the following gang of three, viz. Ramzan, approver, deponent, Buhram, approver, Lucknow, and Madara runaway approver, set out from Kotdee for the purpose of thugging, and proceeding via Jalondee Gunge, reached Niagunge in six days, from whence we returned without meeting a single traveller. Near Begumgunge, we found a traveller—I inveigled him, he was a boatman taking Saonee gifts to Lucknow, from the son-in-law of a Bunya at Tanda. The traveller slept with us at Begumgunge, from whence we started before day-light next morning, and about four miles towards Jalondee Gunge, I strangled him as he walked along,* he would not sit down. We flung his body into the Gogra (river)—and sent Madara home with the spoils. I ultimately went home from Seochitta Gunge, leaving Buhram approver there. It was in the midst of the rains. I was and am now the fourth shareholder of the village of Aiter, which pays one hundred Rupees a year to Government as revenue. The other shareholders are relations of mine, but not Thugs, they manage the village affairs.

A total of one man murdered in this expedition.

* P. S. August 17, on calling in Buhram, approver, to check or corroborate the above statement, I asked him who strangled the traveller? He, (Buhram) whose conscience appears seared! immediately seized the assassin and deponent Ramzan by the throat, exclaiming "This was the man!" Question to Buhram. "What share did you get of the spoils?" Answer. "This man Ramzan is a great (dugabaz) deceiver! he took the things. I got a lota and brass vessel—I ate some of the sweetmeats the traveller had, there were three of us Thugs—myself, Madara and Ramzan."

Narrative of an expedition by twelve Jumaldie Thugs in Oude, taken by Captain Paton, July 20, 1837.

After the Begumgunge affair, I remained at home for three months, when a gang assembled for Thuggee, namely,

1. Ramzan, approver, deponent.
2. Mukdoomee, son of Khoshial Khan, convicted at Lucknow.
3. Jubber, (palsied,) died at Lucknow.
4. Madara, son of Nihal, at large.
5. Jean, the wounded, convicted at Lucknow.
6. Khoshial, son of Sidhee, ditto.
7. Roshun, son of Eesooph, ditto.
8. Muckdoomee, approver, Lucknow.
9. Sadee Jemadar, brother-in-law of Imambux, late approver.
10. Ameer, son of Madara, at large.
11. Peer Khan, at large, son of Ruhman Khan.
12. Dhoosoo, approver, Lucknow.

We proceeded in the hot weather from Kotdee, through Keela, Julalabad, Ramgunge to Siraigunge, opposite to Cawnpore, on the Ganges—about ninety miles in a direct line. We then turned off and next day halted at Utchulgunge, where we fell in with a Hindoo traveller, whom Khoshial murdered next morning, about three miles from the village—all the Thugs were present, some acting as scouts—I could now produce the travellers' bones from the well where we threw the body—and in that well I since threw two other bodies—the well was used by Thugs for that purpose.

We proceeded onwards, about eighty miles, for ten days, halting at Goosaengunge, Chinhut, Nowabgunge and Pertaubgunge. In the division of the last spoil Dhoosoo and I quarrelled, and in consequence the gang had resolved to disperse fearing a disclosure, but it happened after all were ready to break up, that Jean and Ramzan, son of Peer Khan and Dhoosoo brought a decoyed traveller, who lodged during the day at Alleeabad, and this kept us all together. We set out with him and about four miles towards Sewan Bajidpore, I strangled him as he sat on the ground—Jean held his hands, we buried him under a tree, where I can dig up the bones. After this the gang broke up and we all went to our homes. We had been out about six weeks.

A total of one man murdered in this expedition.

Circumstances of a Murder by three Thugs in Oude, taken by Captain Paton, July 20, 1837.

After the Alleeabad affair, I went home to my village of Gudopore, which I left and took my family to Rudolee where I lived three years, still following from thence my trade of murder; about six months after the last affair, I started again on thuggee with the following party of three namely, Ramzan (deponent,) Salar, approver, Lucknow, Ghons, brother of Salar, approver, Lucknow. On the very day of starting we fell in with a well dressed Mahomedan traveller, apparently a Khidmutgar—we entered into conversation with him. I accompanied him to the village of Chumroulee, where all of us, including the traveller, got drunk, but three Thugs retained steadiness for business (murder! "Kaum-kurna-mafik.") At sunset we induced him to start, and at the distance of about two miles Salarbux, (still a little drunk) strangled the traveller as he walked, he (the traveller) was still a little intoxicated—we concealed the body under some manure.

Next morning, I sent three rupees to my house by Salar, who rejoined us next day, and two days afterwards in Begumgunge, we fell in with a Barber who was going to Sahole. Salar inveigled him, and at night we induced him to continue his journey and between the villages Sunahaj and Atmaram Kutra, Salar came behind him as he walked and strangled him—he fell instantly and never spoke. This was within two hundred paces of a guard station—we did not bury the body, and it was discovered in the morning and a great noise made about it. We however had started for home; from which we were only twelve miles distant. The spoil was not divided, for Salar and Ghons were my guests and I got the whole.

A total of two men murdered in this expedition.

Narrative of an expedition by five Thugs in Oude, taken by Captain Paton, July 20, 1837.

1. After the murder of the Barber, I remained in my house for a long time, about four or five months, when I again started in the rainy season with the following gang from Mohond, viz.

1. Ramzan, approver, deponent.
2. Buhram,* approver, Lucknow.
3. Ghons,† approver, Lucknow.

* Buhram allows that he was with that gang, but that being unwell he was not present at the murder; he says he urgently attempted, but in vain, to dissuade them from murdering the man with a cow, as it was a thing strictly forbidden among Thugs, but Ramzan and Salar were great rascals, thugging when no others thugged—no good ever comes of doing such things.

† Ghons being called in separately, corroborated Ramzan's statement, naming the same Thugs as present. He says, "I saw Ramzan strangle

4. Salar, approver, Lucknow.
5. Bustee alias Hussainbux, at large.

We proceeded, and on the second day fell in with a Hindoo traveller near Doadpore, where we all lodged — I inveigled him. He had with him a cow and a calf. In Thuggee to murder a man with a cow is strictly forbidden, as an act from which no good can come! We had a consultation upon this head—the elder Thugs and the rest determined to thug in this case notwithstanding the cow, for we supposed there was much money to be obtained. We set out with the traveller during the night and went three miles towards Raoneea, and at a place, where I have formerly seen many men murdered, I strangled the traveller. We flung the body into the jungle, where the jackalls will have devoured it. Salar got the cow, which was a large Nagouree, a fine animal, and when the Amil (the local authority) seized Salar on account of the Ruhmut Gunge murder, the Amil Allee Bux took the cow, and probably it may be with him till this day. We all went home, and I fell sick of a fever, which confined me for ten months—the Thugs said it was on account of thugging the man with the cow, that I was so afflicted, but I did not entertain this opinion—though I do believe that evil will follow the murder of a man with a cow! If there be no cow it does not signify!

After the murder of the man with the cow, and as soon as I recovered from my illness, through the influence of my friends, I was taken into the service of Molvee Tahawur Allee, a Zumeendar, who made me "Zillahdar," and gave

the traveller as he sat, I held his feet, and my brother Salar, (now present) held his hands and made him "ghafil," that is, put him off his guard. I advised against thugging the man because he had a cow; but we wanted money for our expenses, and the bad fortune of such a deed is upon the strangler, and not upon the assistants, if there should be one hundred of them."

me a salary of four rupees per month, and entrusted to me the collections of the Revenue of five villages, amounting to three thousand rupees a year, and containing a population of about three thousand souls. My authority extended over these people to summons them to my presence, to make them stand or sit, but merely as the deputy of the Molvee, who settled disputes himself,—I dressed well, rode my poney, and had too Sipahees to attend me—a Putwaree or scribe, and a Gorait or village guard. This was a good service for me for three years, the Molvee was well pleased with me, and so were the villagers. I used to pay each village a monthly visit, no one suspected that I was a Thug! The chief men used to wait on me to transact business, and I was supplied with fowls, mangoes, (when they were in season,) fresh milk, &c. and as I passed along old and young made their salam to me.*

During this service, I went once on Thuggee with a gang of six Thugs—leaving my duties as a Zillahdar to a friend of mine, Bucktawur, during my absence; I told the Molvee that I was going for one month on account of a marriage, and obtained leave. We followed the highway in vain in search of travellers for fifteen days, via Futteypore, Selempore to Hussungunge, from whence we returned, and near Keela Jalalabad, we fell in with two travellers—they were inveigled by myself and Imambux, they passed the day and night at Eesregunge, and during the night we

* These circumstances of Ramzan's service as a superintendant of villages, have been related as shewing the diabolical nature of a Thug's mind, and feelings, in leading him to abandon for a time a comfortable situation, for the purpose of murder and plunder, without having the excuse of penury, for it is reasonable to suppose he could have made more money in the exercise of his authority over those villages than he could have anticipated by Thuggee. Yet as will be seen, he not only left for a time this situation, and joined a gang of murderers, but himself strangled one of the victims as he walked along the road.

induced them to resume their journey—they did so—Imambux and myself were told off to strangle them, when they had gone about two miles, as they would not sit down we strangled them in walking; we flung them into a well, where I could now point out their bones—in other wells also in that neighbourhood, there are many bones of other travellers. After this I left the gang and returned to my service as Zillahdar, and remained in my situation for three months. When in fear of being seized as a Thug, for I had heard that the pursuit was going on through approvers Bhimmee, Sumboa, &c. I resigned my situation with the Molvee in due form and fled to Dunowlee, where my uncle, named Phoonda, is zumeendar of a very large village.

Through my uncle's interest, I obtained from the Raja Surat Sing of Dunowlee, a charge of collecting the revenue of a tract of country some ten miles in circumference. I was led into the presence of the Raja by my cousin Jean. The Raja is a mighty man, having five or six elephants, and four hundred soldiers, and a Fort, mounted with one or two pieces of cannons. He holds light the officers of the Oude Government, on no account allowing them to enter his Fort. I made my "salam" to the Raja, and he appointed me to collect the revenue of Sapore and Dunowlee upon a salary of three rupees a month, his people placing under my orders for this duty fifteen armed men. In these villages thus entrusted to me there were more than two thousand men, whom I could at any time call to my presence for purposes of collection. I continued in this service for six months, when the English guard in pursuit of Thugs got trace of me! the order from you to the Raja had been shewn him for my seizure. Ungoo approver, and two Nujeeb Sipahees sent from this were actually lodged at the village close to the Fort. The Raja called me and advised me to give myself up—I did so; the first approver I met at the village was Ungoo, an old associate in Thuggee. I was fully armed—a sword, shield, pistols, a matchlock and a flint gun; for I was fond of being thus arrayed, and when so armed feared not though forty men stood before me.* Ungoo said to the two Nujeebs, Patuck and Seetul, "this is Ramzan"—they laid hands on me. I said "lay not hands on me, I deliver myself up!" I stripped off my arms, and confessed myself a Thug! I was taken to Subahdar Rustum Khan, (a meritorious Native Officer of the 71st Regiment N. I.) and confessed to him also. He asked me if I could point out Buhram Jemadar, a notorious leader of Thugs, now here, an approver, for whose seizure a reward of one hundred rupees had been offered by the British Government. I said, yes,—and that very night led forth the whole English guard of eight Sepahees, to a distance of ten miles to the village of Sohanee—I went to the house, where Buhram Jemadar slept, (often has he led our gangs!) I woke him, he knew me well, and came outside to me. It was a cold night, so under pretence of warming myself, but in reality to have light for his seizure by the guards, I lighted some straw and made a blaze. Buhram and I were warming ourselves, the guards drew round us. I said to them "this is Buhram," and he was seized, (just as a cat seizes a mouse.)

Buhram was no sooner a prisoner than he confessed himself a Thug, saying "I am a Thug!" my father and grandfather were Thugs, and I have thugged with many, let the Government employ me, and I will do its work.† After this (continues Rumzan,) I went and pointed out

* This noted Thug has many wounds and is represented by his fellow Thugs, as a desperate quarrelsome character.

† This notorious leader of assassins, Buhram, is now at Lucknow, one of the best approvers. A man who for his old age, sixty or seventy, and energy of character is looked up to by all the other Thugs.

Binda Thug, the son of Buktawur, Sande, (convicted at Lucknow,) and then I was taken to Lucknow, when I was immediately sent out by you to point out other Thug associates—I pointed out the following :

1. Dhoosoo, approver.
2. Lall, (lame) his brother.
3. Ameer, son of Sudhaee, &c.

A total of three men murdered in this expedition.

Narrative of an Expedition in Oude, by a gang of Jemaldie Thugs, taken by Captain Paton, July 21, 1837.

1. About ten years ago, I, Dhoosoo, with a gang of about seventeen Jemaldie Thugs started for Meerut from Futteh Khan Jemadar's house, in Patuck ka Poorwa near Gutoulee in Oude, and proceeded via Moradabad, and Bareilly to Meerut, whence we returned homewards via Hauper and Malagurh, near which place we murdered two Mussulmen grooms. Eight or nine days journey after which we met another gang of twelve or thirteen Lod Thugs under Kusla and Umrah Jemadars—they all returned with us, and joined in the share of plunder obtained from a traveller we had that day inveigled and whom we murdered next morning, near the little village of Bakotee. After sharing the spoils thus obtained with the other gang of Lods, they separated from us in progress to Meerut. After we had inveigled the above traveller, and were accompanying him, the camp of the "Lord Sahib," (Governor General, or Commander in Chief,*) in progress to Sabatho, passed us

* This circumstance is noted here in order to fix the year of the journey, as it is extremely difficult to come within a year or two of any murder, as Thugs have no records.

on the road, and one of the camels of the Lord Sahib's, had sat down on the way and could not rise, three or four Sepahees that were with it, seeing fifteen or sixteen of us Thugs pass, stopped us, saying "unless you assist this camel to rise, you shall not be allowed to pass but be detained here,"—all of us quickly assisted and got the camel up and then proceeded on our journey. We reached the Ganges at Nanamow Ghat, and I with some others returned home, where we remained for about two months. The Thugs in the Meerut expedition were as follows:

1. Dhoosoo, approver, deponent, Lucknow.
2. Saddee Khan, still at large.
3. Futteh Khan, approver, Lucknow,
4. Alaliyar, approver, Lucknow.
5. Hyder, approver, Lucknow.
6. Adhar, approver, Lucknow.
7. Sher Khan, son of Jhaoo Khan, convicted Lucknow.
8. Johan, son of Sherishta Khan, Lucknow.
9. Jewan Khan, son of Bahadur Khan, convicted Lucknow.
10. Kalee Khan Monshee, (dead.)
11. Omaid, son of Ghons, (Lucknow, convicted.)
12. Rumzan, son of Peer Khan, ditto.
13. Sudhai, son of ditto, ditto.
14. Meherban, son of Daine, ditto.
15. Rumzan Pogha, ditto.
16. Chadee, son of Torab, Lucknow.
17. Khan Mahomed, son of Bucktawur, convicted.
18. Jubber, (dead.)

A total of three men murdered in this expedition.

Narrative of an Expedition in Oude, by a gang of thirteen Jumaldie Thugs under Dhoosoo, taken by Captain Paton, July 21, 1837.

After the Meerut expedition, I started again in two months from the house of Sidhie, father of Khoshial, in the village of Goosaen-ka-Poorwa, and performed a journey of two months, during which time we murdered three travellers—our gang was composed of, viz.

1. Dhoosoo Jemadar, deponent.
2. Bucktawur, approver, Lucknow.
3. Adhar, approver, Lucknow.
4. Mugdoomee, approver, Lucknow.
5. Muhobut, (murdered by Madara Thug.)
6. Kalee Khan Moonshee, died in Lucknow jail.
7. Khan Mahomed alias Chadee, convicted at Lucknow.
8. Sidhai, father of Khoshial, convicted at Lucknow.
9. Khoshial, son of Sidhai, ditto.
10. Alpie, brother of Mahabut, died in Lucknow jail.
11. Jubber, (palsied) ditto ditto.
12. Rujub, runaway, approver.
13. Dienallee, at large, adopted son of Mooradun.

We followed the high way for about ten or eleven days via Doodpore, Nowab Gunge, to within ten miles of Allahabad—we returned, and, passing through the village of Sewait, in the British territories, came to Nowab Gunge Serai, where I saw a traveller whom I inveigled thus.—He was a Sowar, or horseman, rode a very large horse, and was armed with two swords, a shield and pistols, &c. While he sat cooking his dinner in the Serai, I was in search of some spices for my food and was asking the Bhuttearee, or keeper of the Serai, if she could supply me—she said no. The horseman hearing this said he would give me some, and immediately supplied me, this led to a friendly conversation, before which, I had no thought of murdering him. I asked him whence he came, and whither he was going—He said he was going to Fyzabad. I said I was also going there—then let us go together said he. I agreed, and we proposed starting in the morning. I then went and communicated to all the Thugs, that there was a traveller from a great distance, upon whom we would find much money—they all agreed he would be a good man to thug. I proposed we should take him on a day's journey to Ashruf Gunge, and in advance of that to murder him—(the villain Dhoosoo relates all this with a smile upon his face as if he had been doing a kindness to the traveller, whom in return for an act of kindness and confidence, he was thus deliberately planning to murder in cold blood ! !) In the morning we set out and reached Ashruf Gunge, where we halted during the day. I sent from thence the old man Sidhai to look for a good place for the perpetration of the murder, he returned and told us he had selected a good place. As the traveller was a powerful, armed man, I selected two staunch stranglers, Adhar, approver, and Rujub. We started in the morning and when we reached the appointed spot, I and others of the gang induced him to dismount and wait for us —he did so. Khan Mahomed had a small carpet spread, and invited the traveller to sit with him—he did so, and in an instant both stranglers seized and strangled him—(here the wretch Dhoosoo smiled in describing this diabolical act of treachery and assassination; such are Thugs !)—the body was speedily thrown into a well.

After this we proceeded for about ten days and reached Surujkond, whence we went, in two days, to Jaloodee-Gunge, where we fell in with two travellers, and, going on three miles from that village, murdered them. Jubber and Alpee strangled them. We flung their bodies into the river

Gogra. We then returned to our homes. This was an unprofitable expedition, ("Hulka Suffer.")

A total of three men murdered in this expedition.

Narrative of an Expedition in Oude by a gang of seventeen Jumaldie Thugs under Dhoosoo, taken by Captain Paton, July 22, 1837.

After the last murder near Jaloodee Gunge, where we threw the bodies into the Gogra, I remained at home for about three months, and again set out on Thuggee, leading the following gang :

1. Dhoosoo, approver, Jemadar, (deponent.)
2. Rujub, runaway approver.
3. Khan Mahomed alias Chadee, convicted at Lucknow.
4. Jafir, son of Shakir, convicted at Lucknow.
5. Kalee, died in Lucknow jail.
6. Jean, with the wounded arm, convicted at Lucknow.
7. Sidhai, father of Khooshial, ditto.

We proceeded from my village Undopore, near Gutoulee, via Jumtalee Muchlee to Benares, where we fell in with another gang of eighteen or nineteen Thugs, as follows :

1. Rujub Sing Thakoor, } Brothers, Jemadars, at large.
2. Mohun Sing, }
3. Shumshere Jemadar, apprehended.
4. Dilawur, at large.
5. Kurreembux Jemadar, at large.
6. Niamut Jemadar, at large.
7. Buxee, ditto.
8. Bikahree Behna, ditto.
9. Incha Kurmee, ditto.

10. Nunkoo, apprehended at Ghazeepore, and others whose names I forget. Both gangs united and perpetrated the following murders together, viz.

One traveller at the banks of the Ganges near Nowab-Gunge.

Two travellers near Chowba, four miles from Benares.

One traveller at a Ghat on the Ganges—about six miles from Chouba Sundee.

One traveller between Saidpore and Dukulee, on the banks of the Ganges.

One traveller near Money Baba.

We all returned from Nund-Gunge towards Benares,* and at a village about sixteen miles from Benares the whole of our gang was apprehended by the Thanadar's people. We gave the Chuprassee twenty rupees and so escaped. We reached Benares, and near Gulzar-Gunge, at Bulbudur-ka-pool, we murdered two travellers. After this the gang left us, as they would not enter Oude—our gang followed the high road through Jounpore, Muchlee Shaher, and returned home without any other murder.

After the Benares affair I remained at home for about five months, after which I joined a gang led by Futteh Khan and myself. We proceeded from Futteh Khan's house and passing through Tanda, reached Jounpore in the Company's provinces, from whence we returned by another road. Near Jumtalée, we murdered two travellers. Between Goorbux Gunge and Rampore, we murdered one traveller—these were the only three men we murdered in this journey, we then broke up and went home.

A total of five men murdered in this expedition.

* These murders not having been in Oude, but in the Company's provinces, have not been detailed here, as in all probability they will be related in the Benares and Chupra Division of the Thug Department.

Narrative of an Expedition in Oude, by six Jumaldie Thugs under Dhoosoo, taken by Captain Paton, July 24, 1837.

After the murder of one man near Goorbux Gunge on the banks of the Saee Nuddee, I returned home in ten or twelve days, and remained at home three or four months cultivating my fields, as a blind, to conceal my being a Thug. A gang, as follows, again started on Thuggee, which I accompanied; we were only out for about a month and followed the highway through Tana to Moobarick Gunge, from whence we returned home by the same road without meeting a single traveller—Thuggee is a "Shikar" (a hunt,) sometimes successful, sometimes not. The gang was composed of—

1. Dhoosoo, approver, the leader (deponent.)
2. Khooshial, son of Sidhai.
3. Sidhai, father of Khooshial.
4. Jafir, son of Shakir.
5. Sirdar, son of Zorawur.
6. Jean (with the wounded arm.)
7. Alif Khan, (died at home.)

After the unsuccessful journey to Mobarick Gunge, and remaining at home for about three months, I started again on Thuggee with a gang, and murdered, during the journey, four travellers; we set out from a house I had hired at Fyzabad—(see the relation of this journey by Futteh Khan, his last journey*.)

After this journey I returned to my home, but ventured not to remain there, for the pursuit after Thugs had

* This journey is not detailed here, as it has been already related by Futteh Khan Jemadar—7th July.

become hot! The following gang was formed, and we proceeded on Thuggee, viz.

1. Dhoosoo Jemadar, approver, (deponent.)
2. Ruhman, son of Chand Khan.
3. Kurkut, son of Sherishta Khan.
4. Hingun, (Jumaldee) at large, resides in Oude.
5. Khodabux, (Jumaldee) at large, resides in Oude.
6. Sheik Bachum,* brother of Lall Mahomed Baboo, whose arm is amputated.
7. Madar, runaway approver.

We set out from Fyzabad and proceeded towards Lucknow—near Nowab Gunge we fell in with a traveller bathing in a tank near the village. Kurkut and I inveigled him, we accompanied him to Bunsa Busutee, slept there, and proceeding next morning, about two miles from the village, on the banks of the nullah, we murdered him.

This was my last murder; after a life of assassination for thirty years, I now fled from fear of the close pursuit of the British guards, until at the expiration of a flight (as a bird flies) of about three months, I surrendered myself to my pursuers, confessing myself a Thug, and was sent into Lucknow, where I immediately became an approver, and was sent out by you in pursuit of my Thug associates.

A total of five men murdered in this expedition.

A total of forty-one men murdered during the different expeditions this season.

* Sheik Bachum, if there be proof enough available, may be committed in this case.

Narrative of a Thug Expedition under Futty Khan Jumadar, or Leader, with nine Thugs, as related by himself. Lucknow Residency, June 5, 1837.

The gang consisted of the following:

1. Rumzan, (son of Peer Khan,) in Lucknow Jail, convicted by the Resident in Case 32.
2. Meherban, (No. 10.) son of Daim Ally.
3. Mirza Gons Beg, approver, died at Lucknow.
4. Khosial, (son of Tulsum,) died in Lucknow Thug Jail.
5. Bowanee, ditto ditto ditto.
6. Rumzan Pugla, Lucknow Jail, convicted by the Resident.
7. Alpee, died in Lucknow Thug Jail.
8. Muckooa, dead.
9. Madar Bux murdered by Thugs in a quarrel, all of whom are either dead or in custody.

Before starting, we all assembled in my house, and worshipped the goddess Bhowannee, that she would supply us with many victims and abundant spoil, and protect us. We sacrificed a goat as an offering to her. Khosial officiated as priest. We started from my house in the village of Guntoulee Oude—I was leader, and we proceeded to the Ghat, on the Ganges, opposite to Cawnpore, a traveller landed, from the ferry boat. Khosial inveigled him and accompanied him to Utchulgunj, two and a half miles from the Ganges, on the Runjeet Purwa road. Next morning we led him forth and about three miles from Utchulgunj towards Runjeet Purwa, where there is a tank and garden, Ulpee strangled him—we threw his body into a well,—a receptacle much used by Thugs for the concealment of the bodies; we worshipped Bhowannee, by the ceremony of Supouee, and proceeded on our expedition.

2. We reached Dalamow, on the Ganges, in about five or six days; there, at the landing place, on the river, we fell in with four travellers, whom we ultimately murdered—one was a Havildar of the Madras Army, and his three companions. I, (Futty Khan,) Jumadar, inveigled them, and accompanied them to Ray Barrailee, distant about twenty miles, which we reached on the following day—the gang all brought up the rear, but out of the sight of the travellers. For three days we marched with them towards Sultanpore finding no suitable place to assassinate them. At the small village of Peree we rested, and Bhowannee Thug having been sent out to select the ground, the travellers started in the evening and we accompanied them; for by this time, all the Thugs had, under various deceits, got acquainted, as fellow travellers without victims; between the two villages of Tiloye and Mohungunge, at a place where there is a great excavation made by the Ranee, we fell on the travellers and murdered them—the four stranglers were—Khosial, Ulpee, Mirza Ghonsbeg, and Meherban. I gave the signal—we flung their bodies into a well: next morning we worshipped Bhowannee, divided the spoil, and proceeded on our journey towards Sultanpore.* At Bundwa on the day of the Mohurrum, two koss west of Sultanpore, we accidently fell in with another gang of ten or twelve Thugs under—

Buctower, approver, Lucknow.
Dhoosoo, approver, Lucknow.

* Buctower was called in and asked—If ten years ago on the Mohurrum, his Gang and Futty Khan's gang had ever met—he at once answered, "yes! at Bundwa, where we murdered two men on the day following,"—this is strong corroboration of the truth of both stories, as they could not possibly have communicated with each other, or known that a case of ten years was to be enquired into.

Buctower approver says that Sadoola was with one of the gang on this occasion, viz. with that of Futty Khan.

Roshun in Lucknow Jail, convicted by the Resident.

Sadoola, (No. 1.) son of Alpee, Lucknow Jail.

Madara, runaway approver, Lucknow.

Peroo, son of Ruhman, at large.

Jubber, (palsied,) died in Lucknow Jail, besides others.

These Thugs had two travellers in hand (villains!) and during the night they accompanied them towards Korawun and murdered them—two of my gang accompanied them, and got a share—the other gang proceeded separately towards Allahabad and my gang returned home.

A total of five men murdered in this expedition.

Narrative of a Thug Expedition in the year 1827 *or* 26, *about twelve Thugs, as related by Buctowur approver. Lucknow, July* 1837.

Our gang was thus composed:

1. Bukram, leader, approver, Lucknow.
2. Madara, runaway approver.
3. Kooshal (son of Sirdar,) Lucknow Jail, convicted by the Resident.
4. Jafur (son of Shakir,) Lucknow Jail (convicted.)
5. Roshun (son of Yousuf,) Lucknow Jail (convicted.)
6. Imaumbux, approver, Lucknow.
7. Imaumbux (son of Mirza Ghonsbeg,) at large.
8. Uluhyar, approver, Lucknow.
9. Meherban, son of , Lucknow Jail.
10. Ruhman, son of Chand Khan, Lucknow Jail.

We started from our village of Koddeeh, and proceeded towards Jugdeespore, passing which we went on until within eight miles of Joanpore, when we all turned about and came to Singramow, on the borders of the

English territory, where we fell in with a Hindoo Bearer, and about three miles from that place, Imaumbux approver, strangled him.

4. We proceeded to Kaleepore in the Company's territory, and from thence to Lumbooa in Oude, and in the morning found two travellers going to Bainswara, we accompanied them, and at Bundwa we found another gang of Thugs under Futty Khan Jumadar, (who corroborates this statement,*) the day was the Mohurrum, the 10th of the month; the day following we strangled the two travellers about three miles from Bundwa—Futty Khan's gang got a share of the spoil, and both gangs then separated—our party diminished—but several of the gang proceeded towards Purtaub Gurh. I and five or six others kept together in search of travellers, but finding none we all went home—I did not go on Thuggee for about four months after that. Buctower having had his deposition read, confirmed it as correct.

At the expiration of this period I started on another journey with the following gang:

1. Omaid, (son of Ghons Beg,) convicted in Lucknow Jail.
2. Jean, wounded in the arm, ditto ditto.
3. Madara, who was murdered by Thugs.
4. Khooshal, (son of Sirdar,) convicted at Lucknow Jail.
5. Buctower, (deponent.)

* The meeting of the two gangs at Bundwa on the occasion of the Mohurrum and the subsequent murder of two men on the day following, is singularly well proved by the full and prompt recollection of these events by four approvers, Futty Khan, Buctower and Imaumbux, and Ullubyar, all for many months kept apart and unexpectedly required after ten or twelve years to state merely if they ever recollected meeting anywhere another gang on the Mohurrum ten years ago? "at Bundwa" was the immediate answer! Ullubyar, approver, also at once mentioned the meeting of the gang at Bundwa, but had forgotten the murder.

We started from Guntoulee, and via Jugdeespore, Simronta, Mouranwan, Runjeetpurwa and Utchulgunj, went straight to the Ganges opposite to Cawnpore to pick up travellers at the landing place. It was in the rainy season, we got no travellers at the Ghat, so we turned about to follow the same road back again—but we suffered much trouble from the rains, and on finding no travellers we all returned to our homes without a single victim—the road was stopped for travellers, we had been out in vain about sixteen days. If we were ill off for food, we would murder a man for a share of four or five rupees each, but not less. In our next journey we had great success. Buctower's deposition being read over to him, he confirms it.

A total of three men murdered in this expedition.

Continuation of the Thug Expeditions of the Leader Futty Khan Jemadar, supposed to be in the year 1826 *or* 27, (*the exact year forgotten,*) *as related by Futty Khan.*

I, Futty Khan, (Jemadar) after the last expedition (No.) in which four men were murdered between Tiloye and Makagunj—I remained in my own house for about a year and a half at Guntoulee, working upon my fields as a cultivator, for I rented one hundred begas of land, and employed labourers—the villagers knew that I was a man who went from home occasionally, but they knew not that I was a murderer!

A small gang of five Thugs was organized in the village, consisting of—

1. Futty Khan Jemadar, (deponent.)
2. Rumzan, approver, Lucknow.
3. Madara, runaway approver, Lucknow.

4. Rumzan, (son of Peer Khan,) convicted at Lucknow.

5. Rumzan Pugla, ditto ditto.

An invitation had been sent to us from a gang already on the roads fifteen days before, to go and join them, promising to give us a share of the spoil obtained in these fifteen days, so we started—after worshipping the Goddess Bhowannee in my house by the sacrifice of a goat, and imploring her aid and protection, that she would supply us with victims and spoil and guard us from evil.

We started and joined the other gang at Mouranuan, in Baiswara, we found their gang to consist of—

1. Khan Mahomud, Lucknow Jail, convicted. He was a leader.

2. * Dhoosoo, approver, Lucknow.

3. Jean (with wounded arm,) convicted at Lucknow.

4. Suddae alias Sirdar (father of Khushsaul,) convicted at Lucknow.

5. Sadee at large, brother-in-law of Imaumbux, approver.

6. Jafur (son of Shakir,) convicted at Lucknow.

The gang refused to fulfil their promise of sharing the spoil of their fifteen days' previous operations, namely, the plunder of two men whom they had murdered at Utchulgunj—so after travelling four days with them in search of travellers to slay, and finding none and getting no share of the Utchulgunj murder, I and my associates parted from them in displeasure at Roy Barraily—they followed the high road to Jugdeespore—we proceeded towards Solon, both gangs examining and re-examining ("purruckta") each traveller we met.

5. That very day we fell in with two Hindoo travellers, I and Rumzan approver inveigled them and accompanied

* See the attached narration by Dhoosoo No. 1, of the operations of that gang.

them to Solon, which we reached in the evening; next day we accompanied them to Sahebgunj, where we lodged. I dispatched Rumzan to select the place of execution and burial; at night we started, and about three miles in advance on the banks of the Saye Nuddee, (a small stream) Rumzan told me that this was the spot! I had previously appointed the two stranglers, the two Rumzans: we could not induce the two travellers to sit down—so I gave the signal and the Rumzans promptly strangled them standing! we buried their bodies in a place from whence Konkar had been dug—Madara stabbed both—we as usual worshipped Bhowannee and proceeded.

Passing through Purtaubgurh we went in the direction of Sultanpore. Near Nowabgunj, we were joined by three Thugs, namely

1. Jean, (with wounded arm) Lucknow Jail, convicted.

2. Mahabut who was murdered by Madara—who was himself afterwards murdered.

3. Ghons, approver, Lucknow.

6. We proceeded by three days' journey to Bundwa, from whence we proceeded towards Lucknow. On leaving Bundwa we fell in with a Hindoo traveller following his journey. I gained his confidence and accompanied him to Daudpore, from whence we led him forth, and at the distance of about a koss Jean strangled him—we deposited his corpse in a well—we shared about five or six rupees each.

We now skirted Lucknow, and via Keella, Julallabad, Nowabgunj, Oonao, we reached the Ganges at Siroaiya Ghat, opposite to Cawnpore, still no traveller—so we returned towards Runjeet Purwa, by the highway—and four miles from the Ganges at Bunteer, unexpectedly we fell in with another gang of Thugs, under

1. Kadir, (the leader) approver, Jubulpore.

2. Mooradun, leader, approver, Jubulpore.
3. Ukbur, dead.
4. Jummun, dead, father of the above three.
5. Imaumbux, (Poochna,) earless.
6. Odhar approver, Lucknow.
7. Torab,* (the lame,) Lucknow Jail.
8. Jubber, died in Lucknow Jail.
9. Usmut, (brother-in-law of Mooradun,) Saugor Jail.
10. Bux, (brother-in-law of Kadir.)

I and my gang joined the above gang—we next morning took the high road towards Sultanpore bent upon murdering any man we met, who might have one hundred rupees—provided we could gain his confidence.

Kadir, our leader, on our first day's march, fell in with a Hindoo traveller at Behtar, from whence we led him out to destruction to a lonely spot about three miles from the village, he was murdered, but I was not upon the spot at the time.

We proceeded next day to Baiswarah, about two miles from which place Kadir and I fell in with a horseman and his servant whom we murdered. It happened that I, and Kadir, were seated on the ground smoking—the horseman of his own accord joined us, and entered, into conversation about the road—we perceived that he would do for our purpose so we won his confidence, and speedily we accompanied him! sending intelligence to the gang that here was prize—we reached the village of Khanpoor Mawaeea, where we all slept, and in the morning we started again, the horseman and his servant with a bangy with us—we appointed a staunch strangler, Jubber,

* If needful this man Torab can be committed in this case, as Adhar his relative, includes him amongst the Thugs there assembled, without communication with Futty Khan who here mentions him. Kadir and Mooradun can be asked about the Khanpore Mawaee case.

(who died in Lucknow Jail,) to murder the horseman, and Rumzan, son of Peer Khan, to thug the servant—we crossed the Saye Nuddee, and about a mile ahead got him to dismount and seated him on my carpet, gave him tobacco and pawn, and in the act of giving these to him, Jubber twisted the roomal about his neck and strangled him! he was instantly rifled and at the same instant the servant was also murdered by Rumzan. The season of cutting my crops had arrived, so I left the gang accompanied by Ghons, approver, Rumzan Pugla, Mahabut, Jubber, Rumzan, son of Peer Khan and Torab—I remained at home for about six or twelve months, and then started again on another expedition.

I never used to have any apprehension of being discovered as a Thug, neither had I any compunction of conscience for the murders—Was it I who murdered? It was God's will! had I power to murder of myself? and as for a thought for the children of the murdered, what good would thinking of them do? (" khial kurke kea kuray.")

The above deposition was taken by me in English from the mouth of Futty Khan, whose statements regarding his murders, are generally to be relied upon.

A total of five men murdered in this expedition.

DHOOSOO'S NARRATIVE No. 1.

Narrative of a Thug expedition by Dhoosoo Jemadar, Approver. Lucknow, July 6th, 1837, *taken by Captain Paton.*

Our gang on the following Thug expedition consisted of—

1. Dhoosoo, approver, (deponent.)

2. Sudhai (son of Peer Khan,) Lucknow Jail, convicted.
3. Khushal, son of Sudhai, ditto ditto.
4. Jafur, son of Shakir, ditto ditto.
5. Alif Khan, dead.
6. Maigul, son of Peer Khan, Lucknow Jail, convicted.
7. Khan Mahomud, son of Bucktower, ditto.
8. Chheddee, brother of Dhoosoo, approver, (dead.)
9. Buctower, approver, Lucknow.

We assembled in my house, in the village of Undoopoor, close to Gutoulee, and started under my orders in the direction of Cawnpoor, on the Ganges—after four days journey we fell in with three other Thugs, namely—

1. Bindha, (son of Jowahir,) at large—a strangler whose wife is here, (since caught.)
2. Bukhtower, (Khushal-ka-Paluck,) dead.
3. Khushaul, (son of Tursum,) died in Lucknow Jail.

These three had been thugging by themselves but joined us.

Six miles from Utchulgunj, a village six miles from the Ganges, we fell in with a Hindoo traveller with a pony, he slept at Utchulgunj—Khan Mahomed was his decoyer—and two miles from the village Buctower (dead) strangled him. I saw him die, we threw his body into a well—we did not reach the Ganges opposite Cawnpore, though we often go there expecting to pick up travellers at the landing place—for those coming from the Company's provinces often make money and we watch them returning —murder them, and take their money—we left the river on our right four miles, and proceeded towards Roy Barreilly: on our progress we were joined by another gang composed of—

1. Futteh Khan, Jumadar, with the following Thugs.
2. Rumzan, Pugla.
3. Rumzan, approver, Lucknow.

4. Rumzan, brother of Peer Khan.
5. Madara, runaway approver.

(This corroborates the statement given by Futty Khan. See his second journey.)—These quarrelled with us, because we would not give them a share of the spoils of the Utchulgunj murder and they separated from us, and went after a traveller to murder him in the direction of Solon.

We proceeded to Bundwa Hussumpoor which we reached in eight days, where we met a sepoy in the king of Oude's service, who said he knew us all and frightened us, so making us pay him something for concealment, that we all proceeded to our homes to avoid detection, having been out for about a month and a half.

I remained in my own house for two months after this, cultivating in my fields, for I rented three or four bighas of land, chiefly however, as a blind to conceal that I was a Thug, and to make a show that I was a cultivator. I started again on thuggee. We only thug from necessity, not from pleasure, it is fearful business—at home we have no fear of detection, but on the road we are in anxiety. I have been a Thug for about twenty years—myself latterly leading gangs from Meerutt to Ghazeepore and upon the great roads in Oude.

The above deposition was taken by me in English from the mouth of Dhoosoo.

A total of one man murdered in this expedition.

Narrative of an expedition of sixteen Thugs as related by Futty Khan Jumadar, supposed to be in the year 1826 *or* 1827, *taken by Captain Paton.*

A Thug, Koshun, arrived at my village of Gutoulee from a "Bous" or gang at work on the road, and informed me where the gang would be, at Roy Barreilly.

1. Futty Khan, approver, deponent.
2. Rumzan, Pugla.
3. Madara, murdered.

Left our houses to join the "Bous," we found them all assembled at Roy Barreilly, they consisted of—

1. Rumzan, (son of Chand Khan, leader,) in Lucknow Jail, convicted.
2. Madara, runaway approver.
3. Peeroo, at large, son of Ruhman.
4. Madara, murdered.
5. Mugdomee, (son of Khushal,) Lucknow Jail, convicted.

We proceeded towards Cawnpore Ghat on the Ganges, we then turned towards Meangunj, where we fell in with another gang of eight Thugs, as follows, under—

1. Kairee, (Soobadar,) supposed to have been hanged, (at Saugor.)
2. Bhimma, approver.
3. Bukwa, approver.
4. Manunda, Saugor Jail.
5. Puchwa, Saugor Jail.
6. Ousairee Uheer.
7. Runna, Saugor Jail.
8. Chaidabeg, (son of Boodoo,) Lucknow.

We left Meangunj, and that day fell in with a lonely old man, a Hindoo traveller—Bhimma won his confidence—he lodged during the night (the last of his existence !) at Hussungunj, and in the morning about three miles to the east Manunda strangled him on the banks of the Saye Nuddee—the body was deposited in the sand.

We progressed next day and outside of Newulgunj we fell in with three travellers, two of them old men—they were inveigled by myself, Ousairee approver and Kessree approver—there was besides a fourth traveller (unconnected with the other three) who had a bullock with him and had come from Gwalior—we managed to inveigle him also, through Madara and Bhimma; all four travellers slept at Sonara—in the morning all went forth, each accompanied closely by an appointed strangler, viz.

1. Madara, runaway approver.
2. Madara, (murdered,) strangled the man with the bullock.
3. Ousairee.
4. Bhimma.

All four were murdered by those four and aided by other Thugs—this was in the winter.

It happened that the bullock a richly laden prize escaped, and ran off returning to the last halting place Soonara, where it was tied up until its owner could be traced—Chaida, son of Boodoobeg, went to claim it, saying "it belongs to a Soobadar who has sent me for it," but the villagers said, "if it be your's tell us what its load contains?" he could not—or, said they, "bring us a note from the Soobadar." Chaidabeg came and told this to all of us, and we all feared to try the experiment of claiming it! at length Rajah Durshun Ghalib Jung* had it brought to Lucknow and it was found to be laden with one hundred

* This case may yield proof against Chaida, who went for the bullock. The circumstance of the bullock to be enquired of from the Jubulpore approvers; if they corroborate it, no name being given to them, Chaida's guilt will be established.

rupees cash and other valuables—after this I and Madara went home.

The above was written by me from the mouth of Futty Khan.

A total of five men murdered in this expedition.

Narrative of an expedition of thirteen Thugs as related by Futty Khan Jumadar. Lucknow Residency, 7th July, 1837.

The following gang of us started on our excursion from our village of Gutoulee, on a journey of about a month and half—we were—

1. Futty Khan Jumadar, leader.
2. Dhoosoo, approver, Lucknow.
3. Khan Mohumud, (son of Buctower,) Lucknow Jail, convicted.
4. Sadhai, (son of Peer Khan,) convicted at Lucknow.
5. Khoshial, son of Sudhai, ditto ditto.
6. Jafir, (son of Shakir,) ditto ditto.
7. Kalee Khan Moonshee, died in Lucknow Jail.
8. Omed, (son of Ghons,) convicted at Lucknow.
9. Rumzan, (son of Peer Khan,) ditto ditto.
10. Chaidee, died in Lucknow Jail.
11. Rumzan, Pugla, convicted at Lucknow.
12. Jean with the wounded arm, ditto.
13. Binda, (son of Buctower,) Lucknow Jail.

We proceeded towards the east of the great Fyzabad road via Fyzabad Fanda, straight on to Jounpore, in search of travellers without success.

At Jounpore we first got tidings that a pursuit had been commenced in the Company's Provinces against Thugs, which alarmed us—we turned our faces by the Muchlee Shahur road towards Cawnpore to scour that road.

We had not got more than two miles from Jounpore when we fell in with two travellers, Hindoos, they seemed to me just suited for us, so we set ourselves to inveigle them—one was a young man of twenty-five years, the other of fifty, their confidence was won by Khan Mahomud and myself, they lodged in Muchlee Shahur, from whence we accompanied them on another day's journey to Jamtolee, from whence we accompanied them to the place of their death; I told off one strangler and one holder of hands to attend each, they were

1. Khooshall, } Stranglers.
2. Khan Mahomud, }

At two miles from the village the ground had been previously found favorable—scouts were on the look-out—I gave the signal and they were quickly strangled (A), rifled and flung into a well.

We moved along the high road for fifteen days via Roy Barreilly, and arrived near to the village of Ayhasa, a traveller came in amongst us—Omeid had said to us, "a traveller is coming, see if he will do." I addressed him in a friendly manner and gained his confidence; he was an unsuspicious old man, about fifty or sixty years of age; I found that he would do, so I and four or five of the gang returned and followed him, the rest of the gang went the other way; he remained all night on the banks of the Saye Nuddee, at the little village of Kanpore; the old man rose early and we led him into a bye path, and about two miles from Kanpore he was strangled (B), I think by Chaida; we flung the corpse into the Saye Nuddee, and we then returned to the gang which we rejoined at Morawun, giving them a share; we went on five or six days to Bansakaira, from whence we returned homewards, keeping all together but without success; we reached our village and dispersed each to his dwelling close in the vicinity of Gutoulee.

We had been out for about a month and a half, had travelled at a rough guess over two hundred and ninety miles over the high roads—murdered three travellers, and my share was only about twenty rupees. It was an unsuccessful journey—("Kooch rosgar neheen")—there were other gangs out on other roads, but we did not meet them. After this I remained in my house for nearly two years cultivating. The rumours were now becoming more frequent that Thugs were being hunted by order of the British Government!—and that numbers of our gang had become King's evidences! and were divulging our secrets!—that Daveedeen, Feringeea and others had turned against us as approvers! Four years after this I myself was caught by the approvers Salar Bux and Rumzan, now here, or rather I gave myself up on the seizure of my family.

A total of three men murdered in this expedition.

Narrative of an expedition by four Thugs, as related by Futty Khan Jumadar. Lucknow Residency, 7th July, 1837.

After the last, (the fourth expedition,) I remained at home for about a year and a half, when Sirdar, (son of Zorawur,) came to me, and urged our leaving home, to avoid the search after Thugs carrying on by the British Government, four of us started on an expedition, namely—

1. Futty Khan, (deponent.)
2. Sirdar, (son of Zorawur,) convicted at Lucknow.
3. Rumzan, Pugla, ditto ditto.
4. Rumzan, (son of Munsoor Khan,) ditto ditto.

We took the Fyzabad high road, and via Jugdespore, Roy Barreilly and Kutgur, we reached in about fifteen days the Ganges opposite to Cawnpore, expecting to fall in with some travellers crossing the river from the English territories, but we met none, and returned home via Bainswara, Roy Barreilly, &c. the same road we came, having been out about fifty days, and travelled over two hundred miles.

Q. In all this journey, did you fall in with no traveller?

A. No, because it was not God's will that we should.

Q. What! is it ever God's will that you murder people?

A. Could men be murdered if it were not God's will? men declare it sinful to murder—I think it sinful now, but then I thought it no sin! If it had not been God's will, how could men have been murdered.—Thugs then prospered —being neither troubled by ghosts nor evil spirits.

Q. You say, you have a son and a daughter, were any one to murder them, would not you say the murderers were guilty of great sin?

A. What is a greater crime than taking life? I used to lament that God had created me in the house of a Thug to commit Thuggee, my father before me was a Thug—on returning after this last journey, I remained there for three months and went on Thuggee again.

Narrative of an expedition by four Thugs under Futty Khan Jumadar as related by him. Lucknow Residency, 7th July 1837.

Hyder, approver, and Khoshal, dead, (son of Sursum,) came to my house and said—let us go on service; (Thuggee) we started as follows :

1. Futty Khan, approver, (deponent.)
2. Hyder, approver, Lucknow Jail.
3. Khoshal, dead, Lucknow Jail.
4. Rumzan, Pugla, convicted at Lucknow.

We travelled for about forty-five days a distance of about two hundred miles in search of victims along the high-way via Jugdeespore, Roy Barreilly, Mustufabad, Noubustaghat, on the Ganges, Rampoor, Salon, Sahibgunj, Purtaubghur, Nowabgunj, Gondee, Hussunpore, Bundwa, from which point we returned by the route of Davadpoor, from whence we came by a bye road, in all a distance at a guess of two hundred miles, during which journey we had only one murder of one man, which happened in this manner.

To the east of Noubustaghat, about four miles, we fell in with a traveller, a "boodha," or old man; I, Khoshal, and Hyder, inveigled him and accompanied him that day within two or three miles of Rampoor, where, after dark, in a lonely place, we got him to sit down and rest, and, as I kept him in talk, seated before him, Khoshal or Hyder behind strangled him, he made no resistance—Khoshal stabbed him under the arms and in the throat—we flung the body into a running stream—we shared about four or five rupees each—we proceeded homewards, and after this journey, I was only out on one more expedition when I gave myself up to the British guard. Thugs had now began to fear the arrival of Thug approvers for their seizure, and were on the look-out for goindas! (spies.)

A total of one man murdered in this expedition.

Narrative of an expedition of seven Thugs under Futty Khan Jemadar, as related by himself. Lucknow, July 7th, 1837.

I, and my constant attendant Rumzan Pugla, proceeded in the cold weather to Fyzabad in search of service (chakuree,) that is, plunder by murder; there I found in the house of Dhoosoo Thug, (approver) which he had hired, the following Thugs, who composed the present gang:

1. Futty Khan Jemadar, (leader,) deponent.
2. Dhoosoo, approver, Lucknow.
3. Chaidee, (died,) Lucknow Jail.
4. Ruhman, son of Chand Khan, convicted in Lucknow Jail.
5. Madara, (son of the above Ruhman,) runaway approver.
6. Kurkut,* (son of Serishta Khan,) Lucknow Jail.
7. Rumzan Pugla, convicted at Lucknow Jail.

Dhoosoo and Chaidee to avoid the hot pursuit now going on after Thugs by the British Government, had taken their families and hired lodgings in the city of Fyzabad, hoping amongst the multitude of a large city to escape detection the rest of the gang with the other Thugs had assembled around them in Dhoosoo's house (deponent remarks that this gang so assembled in one spot would have been a prize for an approver and guard in pursuit of them !)

We all started on our journey, which proved to be one of about a month's duration, through the following route,—namely, to Juladee Gunge—Begum Gunge—Kefaut Gunge

* If necessary Kurkut can be committed for trial in his gang.

On comparing the narrative of the deponent as given to-day, with that of the same journey as related on the 19th and 20th October 1836, that is, eight and a half months ago, there are the following contradictions : there, he does not at all mention the murder at Sadulgunj, but gives the Bansabusoulee murder as the first in his journey; and details a murder near Turkana as the last in the expedition, whereas to-day he does not mention Turkana at all.

—Tanda—Mobarakgunge—Sukra—from which we returned by the same route to Fyzabad; on leaving Fyzabad at the distance of six miles we fell in with one traveller (A,) I inveigled him, he lodged at Saadutgunge, from whence we accompanied him next morning and at the distance of four miles from the village, Madara strangled him, thence we proceeded towards Lucknow by the high way via Dureabad to near Nowabgunj,—one mile from which we fell in with two travellers (C) bound for Purtaubgurh, I gained their confidence and the same day we managed to misdirect them and led them to Bansabasoulee where they slept. Early the next morning they rose, and we with them, and about three miles in advance we strangled them—Madara and I think Kurkut and Dhoosoo were appointed to strangle them—Madara mismanaged the murder of his victim who rose upon his feet, when we fell upon him and dispatched him; we buried their bodies in a ready-made grave, a hole dug for holding and moistening grain—Madara got the sword by casting lots.

After this I heard that my wife and three children had been seized by the guards of the British Government—so I returned home, and in about a month after this my last murder, I delivered myself up to Rustum Khan Soobadar, sent to seize Thugs, confessing my crimes, and I at once turned King's evidence, and within three days, I pointed out to the guard the following Thugs who were seized, namely, Maigal and Ameer, now in the Jail here; when I went to catch Maigal, he was in his own house, and readily came at my call, but when he saw irons on my legs great was his consternation! he knew that I had come as a goindah to seize him! the lamentations which he and his wife made soon filled the whole village with the news of his capture. He is a well known Thug! he confessed on reaching Lucknow: besides him I have led to the capture of the following Thugs, by tracing them to their haunts, namely,

1. Khooshal, (son of Sursum,) died in Lucknow Jail. He was committed in four cases.

2. Chunchul Bhaut, committed for trial as No. 1 of Calendar 33.

3. Nehaul Khan, son of Torab.

4. Peer Khan, son of

5. Mahomed Ally, son of

6. Doanday Khan, son of Asalut.

7. Hussun Khan, son of

8. Bhowannee Brahmin.

9. Newaz Pasee.

A total of three men murdered in this expedition.

Narrative of an expedition of eleven Thugs as related by Teja approver. Lucknow Residency, 24th July, 1837.

In the same year that the fortress of Bhurtpore was taken (1825,) I was one of a gang of one hundred and one Thugs, of whom about forty-four were apprehended at Sirsagunj, taken before the Magistrate of Mynporee, and all, after three years, were let off—I had previously gone to my home in Oude. I remained at home after this without once going on Thuggee.

When Kaisree Soobadar was let out of the Mynporee jail he came into Oude, and after six months, assembled a gang of fifteen or twenty Thugs and commenced operations on the road—I was one of the gang which was thus composed :—

1. Kaisree, Soobadar, hanged at Jubulpore.
2. Runna Moonshee, ditto ditto.

3. Bhimma, approver.
4. Bukha, approver.
5. Munsa, (dead,) sala of Runna Moonshee.
6. Kaim, banished beyond seas.
7. Khushallee, (Lod,) banished beyond seas or hanged.
8. Ummur, hanged at Jubulpore.
9. Putcha, banished.
10. Deena, approver.
11. Teja, approver (deponent.)

Of the above however Nos. 7, 8, 9, and 10, went home after the first day's journey—seven of us started from Baispurwa, and proceeded to Nanamoughat, on the Ganges; thence to Bangurmow—then to Tukeea, where we decoyed a traveller, and next morning murdered (a) him about two miles from thence between Tukeea and Meangunj—Bhimma strangled him—we threw the body into a well there, in which we were always in the habit of throwing bodies—there may have been one thousand bodies thrown in that well—for all the travellers murdered near Tukeea were deposited there. Mr. Wilson personally went and saw the bones dug up from thence.

We then in two days reached Hussungunj, where Kaisree Soobadar, (hanged) and Runna Moonshee, (hanged) inveigled two travellers; next morning we strangled them between Hussungunj, and Mohan.

It happened that in strangling one of the travellers it was mismanaged, and he made a noise, and a horseman coming past at that time saw the gang, we were fearful of further discovery and broke up! I went home and returned in six days and rejoined three of the Thugs in Tukeea, and there the gang re-assembled.

We reached Bheta in three days, and there found a traveller whom we strangled next day between Bheta and Sonara—he was strangled by Kaim, (banished.)

We returned to Hussungunj, and between Sonara and Bheta we fell in with two travellers, and the same night in the evening between Sonara and Kela Julalabad, we murdered them—after this the gang broke up.

Deposition of Teja continued on the 25th July, 1837.

I erred yesterday in saying the gang broke up after the last murder near Sonara—on recollection I remember now that the gang proceeded to the Ganges opposite to Cawnpore, having previously met at Oondon, (ten miles from the Ganges,) another gang of Thugs under Dhoosoo,* approver, and Futty approver—both gangs joined and reached the Ganges—then after two or three marches to Roy Barreilly, near which we met five travellers, with whom we returned to Solone, from whence we accompanied them about two miles, where we strangled all (E) the five at one signal given by Runna Moonshee, (hanged); the stranglers were—

1. Sudhai, father of Khushal, convicted in Lucknow Jail.
2. Rumzan, (son of Peer Khan,) ditto ditto.
3. Mirza Ghonsbeg, approver, (dead.)
4. Kaim, (Lod,) banished beyond seas; and the rest of the gang were as follows:
5. Futty Khan, Jemadar, approver, Lucknow.
6. Dhoosoo, approver, Lucknow.
7. Sirdar, approver, Lucknow.
8. Sadee, at large, Buhnoee of Imaumbux, the Talee.
9. Imaumbux, at large, son of Mirza Ghonsbeg.
10. Rumzan, Pugla, convicted in Lucknow Jail.

* Dhoosoo Jemadar and Futty Khan Jemadar acknowledged to me that they were in the above expedition, leading a gang of sixteen or seventeen Thugs, and that two of the travellers were strangled by their men, namely—by Rumzan (2) and Mirza Ghonsbeg—and that the five travellers were inveigled by Runna Moonshee, (hanged) whom they represent as a most skilful inveigler, able to throw ten men off their guard by his ready conversation.

11. Khan Mahomud, alias Chaida, convicted, Lucknow.

12. Khoshial, (son of Sudhai,) convicted, in Lucknow Jail.

After this we went to Paimsah ka Poorwa, where we fell in with two men from Calcutta, they slept at Paimsah ka Poorwa—we accompanied them on the great road to Lucknow for two miles and murdered them—after this the gang broke up and I returned home—but in addition to the above murder there were some others which after so many years has escaped my memory.

A total of thirteen men murdered in this expedition.

Narrative of a Thug expedition of forty-five Thugs as related by Teja.

After the murder at Paimsa ka Poorwa, I remained at home for about five months then I started again on Thuggee with the following gang—

1. Kaisree, Soobadar, (hanged,) he was our leader.
2. Runna Moonshee, (hanged.)
3. Munsa, (dead), the brother-in-law of Runna Moonshee.
4. Shewdeen, approver, Lucknow.
5. Bhimma, approver.
6. Deena, approver.
7. Kaim, (Lod,) banished.
8. Umur, (Lod,) banished.
9. Khooshalee, (Lod,) banished.
10. Puncha, brother of Porun, (banished.)
11. Porun, brother of Puncha, (banished.)
12. Madaree, brother of Kaim, (banished.)
13. Mehelol, (banished,) brother-in-law of Goopee.

14. Sanair, (banished,) brother of Gajee.

15. Teja, approver, deponent.

The gang assembled at the adjoining houses of Kaisree Soobadar and Runna Moonshee in the village of Bais Poorwa, Oude.

We proceeded via Naubutgunj to Bangurmow—where we met another gang of about twenty-five Thugs: both gangs united—the latter was as follows:

16. Meherban, son of Daim Ally, convicted in Lucknow Jail.

17. Ruhman, son of Chand Khan, convicted in Lucknow Jail.

18. Mahabut Jumadar, father of Salar, approver, (killed by another Thug.)

19. Souban, (son of Danial,) Lucknow Jail, convicted.

20. Kurkut, (son of Sarishta Khan,) Lucknow Jail, convicted—committed for trial in many cases.

21. Mirza Ghonsbeg, (dead.)

22. Imaumbux, (son of Mirza Ghonsbeg,) at large.

23. Peer Khan, (son of Ruhman,) at large.

24. Ghons, brother of Salar, approver, a confessed Thug at Lucknow.

25. Salar, approver, at Lucknow—and many others, in all about thirty Thugs. We proceeded to Tukia, from whence we accompanied five travellers and between Tukia and Meangunj, we murdered the whole five (A) at one signal.

Two days previously to this murder near Tukia the gang was joined by—

1. Ulahyar, approver, Lucknow.
2. Shair Khan, (son of Jao Khan.)
3. Ghazie, (son of Danial,) Lucknow Jail.
4. Sobhan, (son of Danial,) ditto.
5. Alpee, (dead.)

One of the victims was awkwardly strangled and had time to make a noise! which caused all the Thugs to run off and in two days we reached the Ganges opposite to Bithoor.

We then came to Oonao, and from thence we went via Utchulgunj in ten or twelve days to Joha, where we found four travellers; we accompanied them, and the same day after dark murdered all four (B) between Joha and Bulla.

We slept at Bulla, and about ten days afterwards at about six miles on the Davindapoor side of Roy Barreilly we fell in with three travellers, with three bullocks, (there may have been five travellers,) they lodged at Davindapoor, and from thence we accompanied them about two miles —before daybreak towards the north, we murdered them all three (C) at one signal, given by Maherban and Runna Moonshee. After this we returned to our homes.

In this journey there were some more murdered, but I forget them at this distance of time.

After the murder of three or five men near Davindapoor, I remained at home for a long time, that is, three or four months, and I started again on Thuggee, but I forget who were my associates, I forget where we went—should I recollect any other murder between this and those I am about to relate, I will mention them.

The following gang assembled at the village of Baispurwa, in the house of Kaisree Soobadar, on the banks of the Ganges, opposite Menhdee ghaut, namely,

1. Kaisree Soobadar, (hanged.)
2. Runna Moonshee, (ditto.)
3. Bhimma, approver.
4. Deena, approver.
5. Shewdeen, approver, Lucknow.
6. Bukha, approver.
7. Kaim, (banished.)

8. Ummur, (banished.)
9. Khooshal, (banished.)
10. Puncha, (banished.)
11. Poorun, brother of Puncha, (banished.)
12. Munsa, (dead.)
13. Mirza Ghonsbeg, died in Saugor jail.
14. Imaumbux, at large, (son of Mirza Ghonsbeg.)
15. Futty Khan, approver.
16. Rumzan, Pugla, convicted, in Lucknow jail.
17. Mukwa, (dead,) nephew of Futty Khan.
18. Rumzan, (son of Peer Khan,) convicted, in Lucknow jail.
19. Bindha, at large, not the son of Buctower.
20. Dhoosoo Jemadar, approver, Lucknow.
21. Kurkut, (son of Sarishta Khan,) committed for trial in many cases at Lucknow.

In all about thirty or forty Thugs—I forget many of their names—we came via Bheta, and to the west of that village about thirteen miles, we fell in with five travellers; they were inveigled by Kurkut, Futty Khan, approver, and Kaisree Soobadar—we accompanied them to Kelajulalabad where they slept, and before daybreak they all arose, and accompanied by all the Thugs, they advanced about two miles in the direction of Gosaengunj, where we strangled four of them! (D) the fifth escaped and fled! Ousairee, approver, had been appointed to strangle the fifth man, but the man seeing his four companions strangled ran off before Ousairee applied the cloth to his neck. The man who thus ran off was a Sepoy in the Company's service—he alarmed the village people of Kelajulalabad, the Thugs all ran away, leaving the four dead bodies on the spot, I heard afterwards that the bodies were brought into Lucknow, we got about three hundred and fifty rupees on the bodies, but the distribution of the money was irregular, some keeping the money they had got without dividing it. The stranglers were

Ummur, (banished.)

Rumzan, (son of Peer Khan,) convicted, in Lucknow jail.

The other I forget.* I was present at the strangulation—as we fled, we agreed among ourselves to re-assemble at Behta, about twenty koss (forty miles) distant, and the gang accordingly did assemble there; from Behta we moved upon Oonao, thence to Tukia and Meangunj, in which place three travellers were lodged—they had been inveigled by my brother Kaisree, (hanged) and were accompanied by us to Hussungunj where they slept, and next morning before day, we strangled the whole three (E) between Mohan and Hussungunj,—we deceived them and led them out of the highway to the bye path where they met their death.

Gunga Bunya, at large, of Newulgunj, joined us on this occasion and remained three days with the gang. He has been in many murders.

The gang then went, for about fifteen days in pursuit of men to thug, to Newulgunj, Bangurmow, Tukia and Meangunj, whence we returned by the same route and returned home.

A total of nineteen men murdered in this expedition.

* This murder has been fully established. The traveller who happily escaped was Doulut Sing Havildar of the 37th Regiment, who attended at the Lucknow Residency and gave his deposition—all the Thugs of that gang who have yet been apprehended have either been or will be convicted.

Narrative of an Expedition of Thugs from Oude to near Loodianah, as related by Teja, approver. 3d August, 1837.

After the Julalabad and Hussungunj murders, I remained at my own house for two years cultivating; for my brother Kaisree, a Jemadar of Thugs, told me to remain to look after the fields, &c.

After this a gang of about twenty-five of us, detailed below, started on Thuggee and travelled to Loodianah! We were led by my brother Kaisree, (hanged) and Meherban Jemadar in the Jail here—and by Utchul Jemadar—after our gang had all assembled we murdered five travellers in this manner, two (a) we murdered between Behta, and Eentgawun, and the same night three (b) more between Behta and Soonara—after this we murdered two (c) men between Bangurmow and Mooradhabad—we then crossed the Ganges, and followed the highway all the way to Loodianah via Meerutt, Kurnaul, Umbalah,—we had determined in our minds to go to Loodianah, hoping to fall in with rich travellers from Lahore, such as merchants, soldiers, &c, but in consequence, I suppose of bad omens, we turned round when within fourteen miles of Loodianah, and followed the same road back—in going there we had only one murder of one man, and in returning we had eight murders* of one and two men.

I then returned home, and shortly after this, I and other Thugs were quietly sleeping in our village of Baispoora on the banks of the Ganges, when Mr. Wilson's approvers, and Sepoys suddenly seized the whole of us! I, and five others, stoutly denied that we were Thugs! Sibba alone confessed—we and others, to the number of forty-two prisoners, were sent to Saugor, where I confessed to Captain Sleeman, and became an approver,—there were

* These murders not being in Oude, are not detailed here, they will be probably related by others.

then at Saugor about nine hundred charged with Thuggee, including approvers—forty Thugs were hung, when I was at Saugor—the Jemadars or leaders were hung.

The following were the Thugs in our Loodianah excursion:

1. Teja, approver, deponent.

2. Kaisree Soobadar, (hung,) son of Budun and brother of deponent.

3. Utchul Jemadar, brother of Diaram, escaped from Jubulpore jail.

4. Bhimma, approver.

5. Bukha, approver.

6. Putcha, brother of Mahanunda, (banished.)

7. Mahanunda, brother of Putcha, (banished.)

8. Nehal Uheer, (banished,) son of Purshaud.

9. Rambux, (Lod,) banished.

10. Meherbañ, (son of Dain Ally,) convicted, Lucknow.

11. Kurkut, (son of Sarishta Khan,) Lucknow jail, convicted.

12. Kaly Khan Moonshee, died in Lucknow jail.

13. Omad, in Lucknow jail, convicted.

14. Shair Khan, (son of Jao,) Lucknow jail.

16. Mirza Ghonsbeg, died in the Saugor jail.

17. Shaik Madara, nephew of Buhram, at large.

18. Madara, runaway approver.

19. Uluhyar, approver, Lucknow.

20. Bukhut, approver.

21. Imaumbux, approver, Lucknow.

22. Futty Khan, approver, Lucknow—left us at Soonara after the first murder.

23. Rumzan, Pugla, left us also with Futty Khan.

A total of seven men murdered in this expedition.

A total of sixty-five men murdered during the different expeditions this season.

REPORT

OF A

THUG EXPEDITION

BY THE DOOAB GANGS.

1827.

Report of a Thug expedition in the year 1827, *under the*

No. of List.	Names of jurisdiction of the place where the Murder was perpetrated.	No. and Sex of the Murder.		Date of the Murder.	Intended destination of the Murdered.		Supposed value of the property robbed.
		Men.	Women.		From	To	
1	Near Pokraya, in the Cawnpore Zillah,	2	0	That season of 1827,	Saugor,	Oude,	225 rupees in ready money, Clothes and Cooking Uttensils.
2	Bewur, in the Mynpooree District,	1	0	Ditto,	Meerut,	.. ..	Valued at 50 rupees.
3	Malagurh, in the Boolund Shuhur District,	2	0	Ditto,	Kurnal,	Oude,	100 rupees.
4	Near Koorja, in the Allygurh District,	1	0	Ditto,	Meerut,	Cawnpore,	50 rupees.
5	Near Secundra, in the Furruckabad District,	2	0	Ditto,	Kurnal,	Lucknow,	150 rupees.

following leaders: Bukshee Jemadar and Runnooa Moonshee.

REMARKS.

In the month of Cheyt, in the year 1827, Girdharee Thug, now an approver at Jubulpore, joined a gang of seven Thugs under Bukshee Jemadar at Kujooah, in the Furrukhabad zillah, and set forth on an expedition. The party proceeded to Barha, pergunnah Akberpoor, zillah Cawnpore, where they were joined by Runnooa moonshee with nine Thug followers, so that the gang amounted to eighteen Thugs, who all went on to Pokraya. At this place they fell in with two travellers by caste Burboonjas, going from Saugor to the Oude territory, who were decoyed by Runnooa moonshee. and the next morning having been escorted about a couple of miles towards Cawnpore, were strangled by Oomeid and Davee Deen Thugs, and the bodies were buried in the bed of a stream.

After this the gang proceeded on the road leading to Mynpooree, as far as Bewur, where they found a Kayet on his way from Meerut to the eastward, who was decoyed by Uchul jemadar into the company of the Thugs, and after passing the night together, the traveller was taken to a garden a short distance from the village, where he was induced to sit down, and was strangled by Oomeid Thug. The body was thrown into a well.

They went onwards to Sultanpoor, zillah Mynpoore, where the number of the gang was increased to twenty-one by the junction of three more Thugs. The gang advanced on the same road as far as Kurkoodda, in the Meerut district, but meeting with no success in their search for victims, they turned back towards Malagurh, in the Boolund Shuhur District, and arriving there they sent Uchul jemadar as a scout into the town, and he discovered two travellers, a Brahmin and a Kuhar, proceeding from Kurnal to the Oude territory, whom he persuaded to join the Thug gang. They passed the night together and early in the morning the Thugs escorted the travellers about two miles beyond the village, where they were strangled by Davee Deen and Pershad. The bodies were securely buried.

After this affair the gang passed thro' Boolund Shuhur and sat down to rest themselves at a police station two miles beyond the town, soon afterwards a Chuprassee from Meerut came up to them on his way to Cawnpore. Pershad, approver, addressed him and induced him to keep company with the Thugs, and they all went to Koorja in the Allygurh district, where they rested for the night in a caravansera. Long before day-light the gang, accompanied by the traveller, proceeded on the road to Muttra, and having gone two miles Pershad Thug availed himself of an opportunity to strangle the traveller, whose body was securely buried in a field.

The Thugs next went to Secundra, in the Furrukhabad district, and while resting there decoyed two Brahmins travelling from Kurnaul towards Lucknow. Runnooa moonshee took them under his own protection, and next morning they were escorted in an easterly direction, when they were strangled by Oomeid and Pershad. The bodies were thrown into a dry well, and earth was heaped over them.

Report of a Thug expedition in the year 1827, *under the*

No. of List.	Names of jurisdiction of the place where the Murder was perpetrated.	No. and Sex of the Murder.		Date of the Murder.	Intended destination of the Murder.		Supposed value of the property robbed.
		Men.	Women.		From	To	
6	Near Jullalabad, in the Furruckabad District,	2	0	That season of 1827,	Kurnal,	Jounpore,	225 rupees.
7	Nubbeegunge, in the Furruckabad District,	3	0	Ditto,	Kurnal,	Sooltanpore,	60 rupees.
8	Bohgaon,	2	0	Ditto,	Agra,	Byswara,	100 rupees.
9	Gokool,	3	0	Ditto,	Bithoor,	Muttra,	60 rupees.

following leaders : Bukshee Jemadar and Runnooa Moonshee.

REMARKS.

After perpetrating this murder the gang went to Jullalabad in the Furruckabad district, where they rested in the caravansera; and finding that two travellers, a Brahmin and a Rajpoot, on their way from Kurnaul to Jounpore, had previously put up in the same place, Bukshee jemadar was deputed to decoy them. They agreed to accompany the Thugs, and early in the morning proceeded on their journey about a couple of miles, when they were induced on some pretence to sit down and were put to death in the usual manner by Bukhut and Oomeid. The bodies were buried in the bed of a stream.

Subsequent to this murder, Uchul jemadar, Runnooa moonshee and other Thugs, to the number of eleven, went home, and the remainder of the gang, amounting to ten men, under Oomeid jemadar, agreed to meet them again at Hurrone in the Mynpooree district. Six days afterwards Oomeid jemadar and his gang arrived at Hurrone, and were soon joined by twenty-two Thugs, namely, nine of the former gang, and thirteen others, led by Bukshee and Rambuksh jemadar. According to their previous engagement another gang, consisting of thirty-one Thugs, under Runnooa moonshee, Uchul jemadar, and Cheyne Lodhee jemadar, arrived at the place of rendezvous.

When Uchul jemadar and Runnooa moonshee left the main gang, they went directly home, without perpetrating any murders on the road. Remaining at home a few days then two leaders set out again with Cheyne Lodhee jemadar and a party of Thugs, amounting to 31 persons, and proceeded from Behareepore, in the Furruckabad district, to Nubbeegunge, where they fell in with three Hindoos travelling from Kurnaul to Sooltanpoor. Uchul jemadar decoyed them, and they rested with him in the market place during the day, and next morning early the gang took them a mile out of the town, where they strangled them in a grove of mango trees. The bodies were buried in a streamlet.

They then went on to Bohgaon, where the gang rested in a caravansera, and found two Sepahees, who were going from Agra to Byswara. They were decoyed by Runnooa moonshee, and next morning were taken two miles out of the road, and strangled by Dhunnooa and Runjeet. The bodies were buried in a marshy spot of ground. This gang went directly to Hurrone, in the Mynpooree district, the place of rendezvous, and joined the gang waiting there in expectation of their arrival.

The gang now amounted to sixty-three Thugs, who set out and proceeded westward for five days, when they arrived at a stream about two miles from Buldeojee, and sat down to rest themselves. They were soon joined by three pundits, who came from Bithoor on a visit to Muttra. The Thugs endeavoured in vain to persude the pundits to remain at Buldeojee, but they proceeded onwards accordingly—accordingly fifteen or sixteen Thugs from the main gang went after the travellers, and joining them rested for the night at Gokul. In the morning they set out again, and having gone a mile they all sat down,

Report of a Thug expedition in the year 1827, *under the*

No. of List.	Names of jurisdiction of the place where the Murder was perpetrated.	No. and Sex of the Murder.		Date of the Murder.	Intended destination of the Murdered.		Supposed value of the property robbed.
		Men.	Women.		From	To	
10	Near Gokool,	3	0	That Season of 1827,	Agra,	Byswara.	50 rupees.
11	Near Dewakee, in the Agra district,	6	0	Ditto,	Guzerat,	Ditto,	1100 rupees.
12	Near Oodbedpore, in the Agra district,	6	0	Ditto,	Bhurtpore,	Allahabad,	900 rupees.

following leaders : Bukshee Jemadar and Runnooa Moonshee.

REMARKS.

when the travellers were strangled by Runjeet, Chidda and Dhunna. The bodies were thrown into the Jumna.

The main gang rested outside of the town, at a Hindoo shrine, where they were joined by three Sepahees from Agra going to Byswarra. The travellers were decoyed as usual, and taken next morning about a mile on their road, and then put to death by Rambuksh, Dhunna and Heera. The bodies were thrown into a well.

After this murder the gang turned back towards the east, and went to Dewahee in the Agra district. There they met and decoyed five Hindoos (from Guzerat, going towards Byswarra,) and Uchal jemadar found a sixth traveller by caste a Mussulman, going the same way, whom he brought to the resting place of the gang. The six travellers were taken next morning about two miles from the village and put to death in the usual manner. The stranglers were Rambuksh, Dhumma, Runjeet, Chidda, Lalsa and Bukhut. The bodies were cast into a dry well and covered with earth.

After the murder the gang went to Oodbedpoor, in the Agra district, passed the night there, and in the morning proceeded onwards about two miles, when Bukshee jemadar overtook two travellers by caste Mussulmans. Newul jemadar who, as usual, proceeded apart from the main gang, fell in with three travellers, one a Mussulman and the other two Hindoos ; while Pershad jemadar decoyed out of the village three Hindoos who were resting there, and brought them along with him. All these travellers came from the direction of Bhurtpore and intended to go to Allahabad. The Thugs and travellers rested that day in a caravansera at Rajah Ka Talab. Next morning very early Neuzel jemadar with twenty Thugs set off in advance and going two miles sat down on the road side. A short time afterwards some others of the main gang escorted out the three travellers decoyed by Newul, and arriving at the spot where the party was resting, the travellers were strangled by Dhunna, Newul, and Layuk. The bodies were thrown into a well. Pershad jemadar next left the surae with three travellers, who were in like manner put to death by the party in waiting, and their bodies were thrown into the same well. Bukshee jemadar was the last to set out with the two travellers in his custody, but they were not destined to meet their deaths on that occasion, for some hurkarrahs came up from the eastward, and disturbed the gang, who permitted their intended victims to proceed unmolested.

The gang took their booty to a garden near Ferozabad, and were engaged in making a division of it when another party of seventeen Thugs, under Keseree soubedar, arrived at the same place. This last named party had committed no murders since they left home, and they agreed to try their luck in company with the others, whose numbers were thus increased to eighty men. They all went and rested in the town of Ferozabad.

Report of a Thug expedition in the year 1827, *under the*

No. of List.	Names of jurisdiction of the place where the Murder was perpetrated.	No. and Sex of the Murder.		Date of the Murder.	Intended destination of the Murdered.		Supposed value of the property robbed.
		Men.	Women.		From	To	
13	Near Cawnpore,	2	0	That Season of 1827,	Calpee,	Bithoor,	50 rupees.
14	Barha, in the Cawnpore district,	4	0	Ditto,	DeKhan,	Lucknow,	225 rupees.
15	Moorutgunge, in the Cawnpore district,	3	0	Ditto,	Calcutta,	To the Westward,	100 rupees.
16	Shajadpore,	3	0	Ditto,	East,	Westward,	About 1700 rupees.
17	Between Belonda and Futtehpore.	4	0	Ditto,	Allahabad,	Futtehpore,	200 rupees

following leaders: Bukshee Jemadar and Runnooa Moonshee.

REMARKS.

Next day Uchul and Runjeet jemadar, and party, consisting of nineteen Thugs, separated from the main gang, agreeing to rejoin them at Rooma in the Cawnpore district, in the space of twenty-two days. The rest of the gang divided themselves into two parties, but proceeded one before the other on the same road. The front party was led by Keseree soubedar and Bukshee jemadar, and consisted of fifteen Thugs, who in ten days arrived at Akberpore in the Cawnpore district. They had not had time to undress themselves after the third day's journey, when two travellers from Calpee, on their way to Bithoor, came up and were decoyed by Keseree soubedar. The gang proceeded on with them to Bumahin where they rested for the night, and early in the morning took the travellers two miles further towards Cawnpore, where they strangled them while seated on the bank of a stream.

The rear party, which was led by Runnooa moonshee, in the mean time came to Barha, where they decoyed four Hindoos who came from the Dakhan and were going to Lucknow. Next morning early the travellers were taken a mile on the road to Cawnpore, and strangled by Bukhat, Bijjooa, Dhunnooa and Soomaira. The bodies were thrown into a well.

After this murder the rear party came on to Sirsole, where they overtook and rejoined the first party and proceeded to Rooma, the place previously agreed on as a rendezvous. The nineteen Thugs who left the gang at Ferozabad joined again at this place but they had committed no murders during their absence. All went to Moorutgunge where three Hindoo travellers from Calcutta, going westward, were decoyed by Makhun, (approver) These were taken next morning, a short distance from the village, and put to death, on the bank of a rivulet, in the usual manner, by Runjeet, Rambuksh and Doojja.

The gang again separated into two parties, half went to Allahabad under Keseree soubedar, and the remainder headed by Runnooa moonshee, proceeded to Shajadpore. The last mentioned party met at that place three Hindoo travellers from the east, travelling westward, who were resting in the caravansera. Runnooa moonshee addressed them insinuatingly and endeavored to persuade them to rise during the night and accompany the Thugs on their journey, but without success. They did not start until broad day, and the gang consequently put off their departure till the same time. Having all proceeded a mile on their way, the Thugs represented to the travellers that as they were about to quit the banks of the sacred stream, (the Ganges,) it was proper that all should perform their ablutions in it before doing so. The travellers acquiesced in the propriety of the proposal, and the whole party went to the bank of the river to bathe, and while engaged in their ablutions, the travellers were strangled by Deveedeen, Newul and Chidda; and the dead bodies cast into the stream. This party then went to Allahabad, and rejoined their companions, who had gone direct to that place.

The entire gang now turned back, and in four days afterwards arrived between Belonda and Futtehpore, where they sat down to recreate themselves by smoking. During this interval four Sepahees came up from Allahabad, and they were persuaded by Keseree soubedar to join the party, and were conducted

Report of a Thug expedition in the year 1827, *under the*

No. of List.	Names of jurisdiction of the place where the Murder was perpetrated.	No. and Sex of the Murder.		Date of the Murder.	Intended destination of the Murdered.		Supposed value of the property robbed.
		Men.	Women.		From	To	
18	Meetapore,	4	0	That Season of 1827.	Jubbulpore,	Agra,	125 rupees.

following leaders : Bukshee Jemadar and Runnooa Moonshee.

REMARKS.

to Futtehpore where all rested in a grove of tamarind trees. There the Thugs received a visit from a man named Fukeera, who knew them, and obtained a present of a rupee, a blanket and a sheet. Early next morning the gang set off again and the travellers having been taken a mile, were put to death by Bukhat, Doojooa, Dhunna and Laek; the bodies and muskets, turbans, &c. were thrown into a well.

After proceeding onwards for three or four days, the gang reached Rooma, in the Cawnpore district, where they were joined by three Thugs who had just come from their homes. They travelled for seven or eight days more, and arrived at Khandee, in the Cawnpore district, without committing any murders. At this place twenty-seven Thugs quitted the gang and proceeded home; the remainder went to Meetapore, and when about to enter the door of the caravansera they met two travellers, one named Cheytram; one of them came from Jubbulpore, the other from Mirzapore, and both were on their way to Agra. Bukshee jemadar decoyed them, and conducted them into the seraee where they took up their quarters near him. The travellers were desirous of hiring carriage, and a friend of the Thugs named Nunha, who kept a cook-shop in the seraee, hired out a pony to them. Uchul jemadar, Newul, and fifteen Thugs had in the mean time encamped outside of the seraee, and they managed to persuade two travellers to join their party. Besides these four travellers, whom the Thugs had decoyed, there were also two persons of property resting in the seraee and they hired carriage from some other parties residing in the town. The Thugs were desirous of inducing these persons to decline the offers of the travellers to take their carriage; but they refused, in consequence of which the Thugs themselves offered to supply the rich travellers with ponies at a cheaper rate than those they would engage at Meetapore. On hearing this, the owners of the cattle threatened the Thugs that they would cause their arrest if they interfered with their arrangements. The Thugs became alarmed, and, through the intervention of their friend Nunha, came to an understanding with the other parties. In the morning Uchul jemadar and his party took the two travellers in their company, eastward, and strangled them a mile from the town. The bodies were thrown into a well. At the same time Bukshee jemadar set off with the other two travellers, in an opposite direction, and put them to death a short distance from Meetapore.

The united parties went to Sirsagunge in the Mynpooree district, the Thanadar at the place named Devedeen, knew the Thugs, and, in concert with a man who kept a cook-shop there, caused the arrest of the gang who had resisted their attempts to escort money. Hereon it was agreed that the gang should pay a fine of 125 rupees to the jemadar of the thana, but a number of the Thugs having made their escape, before the money was collected, the remainder, being forty-four in number, were forwarded to Mynpooree, where they were lodged in jail by order of the district magistrate. After a detention of fifteen months Heera, (approver) Makhun, (approver) Dijjooa, Lalchund, and others,

Report of a Thug expedition in the year 1827, *under the*

No. of List.	Names of jurisdiction of the place where the Murder was perpetrated.	No. and Sex of the Murder.		Date of the Murder.	Intended destination of the Murdered.		Supposed value of the property robbed.
		Men.	Women.		From	To	

JUBULPORE, *Supt.'s Office, the 28th January,* 1840.

List of Thugs who were engaged

No.	Name.	Parentage.	Caste.
1	Oomeid Jemadar Pathurea, ...	Son of Bhowanee, ...	Lodhee,......
	Bukshee Jemadar, ...	Ramlal,......................	Brahmin, ...
	Layk Jemadar, ...	Kishnoo, ...	Lodhee,......
	Uchul Jemadar, ...	Gunsham, ...	Ditto, ...
5	Runnooa Moonshee, ...	Sobha, ...	Ditto, ...
	Daveedeen Jemadar, ...	Son of Runna, ...	Ditto, ...
	Subsookh, ...	,, (Unknown.)......	Ditto, ...
	Bukhut, ...	,, (Unknown,)......	Rajpoot, ...
	Girdharee, ...	,, Ramlal,............	Brahmin, ...
10	Purshad, ...	,, Runna, ...	Lodhee,......
	Busawun,............................	,, (Unknown.)......	Ditto, ...
	Bhowanee, ...	,, (Ditto,)	Ditto, ...
	Gujjola, ...	,, (Ditto,)	Ditto, ...
	Bhugga, ...	,, (Ditto,)	Ditto, ...
15	Ram Buksh, ...	,, Ramkissen, ...	Ditto, ...
	Rummooa, ...	,, (Unknown,)......	Ditto, ...
	Cheyne Jemadar, ...	,, Rekha, ...	Ditto, ...
	Bukshee, ...	,, Rutta, ...	Ditto, ...
	Dhunna, ...	,, Madaree, ...	Ditto, ...
20	Eseree,...............................	,, Rutta, ...	Ditto, ...
	Shewdeen, ...	,, Assa, ...	Ditto, ...

following leaders: Bukshee Jemadar and Runnooa Moonshee.

REMARKS.

ten in number, were set at liberty; but Keseree soubedar, Devedeen and four others were retained in confinement for three months longer; but the remainder were kept in jail for three years.

N. B. The fact of the arrest of these Thugs at Mynpooree has been established by a reference to the district authorities; and one of the number, named Dijjooa, the brother of Meherban, approver, was made over to the officers of the Thuggee department.

P. A. REYNOLDS, *Superintendent for the Suppression of Thuggee.*

in the Murders detailed above.

REMARKS.

Died in Jail at Mynpooree.
Died at home at Oomree.
Hanged at Jubbulpore Sessions of 1834.
Ditto ditto Sessions of 1834-35.
Ditto ditto in 1836.
Admitted as an approver and died at Jubbulpore.
Transported Sessions of 1833.
Ditto ditto.
Approver.
Ditto.
Transported Sessions of 1834.
Died in Jail at Mynpooree.
Transported Sessions of 1833.
Ditto ditto.
Still at large.
Ditto ditto.
Died while out on Thuggee.
Approver.
Ditto.
Ditto.
Ditto.

List of Thugs who were engaged

No.	Name.	Parentage.	Caste.
	Shumma,	Son of Heera,	Lodhee, ...
	Dhunna,	,, Hurree,	Ditto,
	Dhunnooa Burmoocha,	,, Chidda,	Ditto,
25	Heera,	,, Dhya,	Ditto,
	Dhunna,	,, Kashee,	Ditto,
	Chidda,	,, Ramkissen,	Ditto,
	Lalsa,	,, (Unknown,)	Ditto,
	Newul Jemadar,	,, Punchum,	Ditto,
30	Atmaram,	,, Dhya,	Ditto,
	Sookhee,	,, (Unknown,)	Ditto,
	Desraj,	,, (Unknown,)	Ditto,
	Khoosheal,	,, Nunhee,	Ditto,
	Gungoo,	,, Kugga,	Ditto,
35	Ruttooa,	,, (Unknown,)	Ditto,
	Kunhya,	,, Nundee,	Ditto,
	Kunhya, 2d,	,, Shitabee,	Ditto,
	Kunhya, 3d,	,, Paharee,	Ditto,
	Bhimma,	,, Pirthee,	Ditto,
40	Doorgooa,	,, Chutta,	Ditto,
	Bhikna,	,, (Unknown,)	Ditto,
	Chintee,	,, Byree,	Ditto,
	Dhurma,	,, (Unknown,)	Ditto,
	Bhumma,	,, (Ditto,)	Ditto,
45	Keseree Soubedar,	,, Budda,	Ditto,
	Heera,	,, Oomeid,	Ditto,
	Bhimma,	,, Chunda,	Ditto,
	Dheena,	,, Kugga,	Ditto,
	Makhun,	,, Kissen,	Ditto,
50	Sibba,	,, Bhugwant,	Ditto,
	Madaree,	,, (Unknown,)	Ditto,
	Ximma,	,, (Ditto,)	Ditto,
	Umra,	,, Madaree,	Ditto,
	Oomeid,	,, Ditto,	Ditto,
55	Chubba,	,, Budda,	Ditto,
	Bhowanee,	,, (Unknown,)	Ditto,
	Dujjooa,	,, Munsa,	Ditto,
	Kussea,	,, Munsa,	Ditto,
59	Lalchund,	,, (Unknown,)	Ditto,

in the Murders detailed above.

REMARKS.
Approver.
Ditto.
Hanged at Jubulpore in 1836.
Ditto ditto.
Transported Sessions of 1836.
Ditto ditto.
Died in Jail at Saugor.
Hanged at Jubbulpore Sessions of 1836.
Transported from Jubbulpore Sessions of 1834.
Transported from Saugor Sessions of 1833.
Ditto ditto ditto.
Ditto from Jubulpore Sessions of 1834.
Ditto from Saugor Sessions of 1833.
Ditto ditto ditto.
Ditto ditto ditto.
Ditto ditto ditto.
Ditto ditto ditto.
Died in Jail at Saugor.
Transported from Saugor Sessions of 1833.
Ditto ditto ditto.
Approver.
Transported from Saugor Sessions of 1833.
Ditto ditto ditto.
Hanged at Jubbulpore Sessions of 1834.
Approver.
Ditto.
Ditto.
Ditto.
Ditto.
Transported Sessions of 1834.
Ditto ditto.
Ditto ditto.
Ditto ditto.
Died in Jail at Mynpooree.
Ditto Ditto.
Hanged at Jubulpore Sessions of 1836.
Transported from Jubulpore Sessions of 1835.
Ditto ditto ditto.

P. A. REYNOLDS, *Superintendent for the Suppression of Thuggee.*

Report of a Thug Expedition in the years of 1827, *Dhowkul Jemadar, Bhowanee and Lalla Lochun,*

No. of List.	Names of jurisdiction of the place where the Murder was perpetrated.	No. and Sex of the Murdered.		Date of the Murder.	Intended destination of the Murdered.		Supposed value of the property robbed.
		Men.	Women.		From	To	
1	Chupra Mhow, in the Furrukhabad district,	1	0	That season of 1827,	Muttra,	Cawnpore,	10 rupees.
2	Hurrone, in the Mynpooree district,	1	0	Ditto,	Agra,	Lucknow,	50 rupees.
3	Mukhun, in the same district,	1	0	Ditto,	Ditto,	Oude,	20 rupees.
4	Ferozabad,	3	0	Ditto,	Ajmere,	Ditto,	150 rupees,
5	Rajah ka tulab,	2	0	Ditto,	Muttra.	Lucknow,	50 rupees,
6	Kundolee,	2	0	Ditto,	Ditto,	Benares	70 rupees,
7	Buldeojee,	1	0	Ditto,	Ditto,	Eastward,	20 rupees.

1828 and 1829, under the following leaders: with Thirty-two Thugs, and other Leaders.

REMARKS.

In the month of March 1827, Dhowkul jemadar, Bhowanee, Lalla Lochun, and other leaders, having a gang of thirty-two Thugs, assembled at Chowdee ka Poorwa, in the Furruckhabad district, and determined to proceed in search of adventures. They first visited Chupra Mhow, where they rested in the bazaar and decoying a Brahmin, who was travelling from Muttra to Cawnpore, they took him next morning about a mile on his way, and then put him to death. The body was thrown into a well.

The gang next proceeded to Hurrone in the Mynpooree district, and took up their quarters in the caravanserai, where they found a Sepahee who intended to go from Agra to Lucknow. Him they addressed as usual; and took him next morning a couple of miles out of the village, and strangled him on the bank of a rivulet, where they also buried his body.

After this they went on to Mukhun, where they rested in the seraee. Lalla Lochun jemadar having gone into the bazar met a Brahmin on his way from Agra to Oude, whom he decoyed and brought to the encampment of the Thugs. Early next morning the traveller was taken to a tank some distance beyond the town, and being induced to sit down, was put to death in the usual manner. The body was thrown into a well.

The gang next went to Ferozabad, where they rested in the seraee. Shewdeen jemadar having visited the bazar brought back with him three travellers by caste Kahars, who came from Ajmere to Oude, they passed the night together and next morning having gone a couple of miles on their way, the travellers were strangled, and the bodies buried in a dry well.

After this affair the gang went to Raja ka tulab, where Bhowanee jemadar inviegled two Hindoos travelling from Muttra to Lucknow, who were taken next morning to a grave of Bubool trees and put to death.

They next proceeded to Kundolee, where they fell in with two Hindoos travelling from Muttra to Benares, who were decoyed and accommodated with a resting place near the Thugs. Next morning they all proceeded on their journey, and coming to a garden on the way side the travellers were induced to sit down and were put to death as usual.

The gang now went to Buldeojee, where Lalla Lochun, and Dhokul jemadars went to a grog shop to drink, and in the way fell in with a traveller by caste a Brahmin, who came from Muttra and intended to go to the eastward. It being in the evening they went on with the travellers, having been joined by the gang, they put the man to death under some Bubool trees two or three miles off. His body was thrown into a well.

Report of a Thug Expedition in the years 1827, *Dhowkul Jemadar, Bhowanee and Lalla Lochun,*

No. of List.	Names of jurisdiction of the place where the Murder was perpetrated.	No. and Sex of the Murdered.		Date of the Murder.	Intended destination of the Murdered.		Supposed value of the property robbed.
		Men.	Women.		From	To	
8	Mhyo,	1	0	That Season of 1827,	Muttra,	Cawnpore,	30 rupees.
9	Near Achnaira, in the Bhurtpoor district,	1	0	Ditto,	Bhurutpoor,	Agra,	About 40 rupees.
10	Near Oodbedpoor, in the Agra district,	1	0	Ditto,	....	....	10 rupees.
11	Raja ka Tulab,	5	0	Ditto,	....	Eastward,	200 rupees.
12	Mukhun,	2	0	Ditto,	Agra,	Ditto,	60 rupees.
13	Near Meatpoor,	2	0	Ditto,	Muttra,	....	50 rupees.
14	Etawah,	2	0	Ditto,	Gwalior,	Bhyswara,	40 rupees.

1828 and 1829, under the following leaders; with Thirty-two Thugs, and other Leaders.

REMARKS.

Having completed the murder the Thugs went at once to Mhyo, and rested. Bhowanee jemadar here decoyed a Mussulman going from Muttra to Cawnpore, and accommodated him with quarters near himself. He was taken next morning a short distance on his way, and was strangled.

Going onwards, the gang reached Achnaira in the Bhurtpoor district, in the course of five or six days, without perpetrating any murders on the way. They then turned back and took the direction of Agra—while sitting at the brink of a well, four miles from Achnaira, and engaged in smoking, a Hindoo traveller came up from Bhurtpoor intending to go to Agra. Lalla Lochun jemadar invited him to smoke. The pipe being placed in his hands, he was put to death while in the act of inhaling the smoke. The body was thrown into the well. The former were cast into the well.

The gang now went to Agra, and crossing the Jumna arrived at Oodbedpoor, where they rested in the seraee, a traveller came into the seraee, and having entered into conversation with Lalla Lochun, was easily persuaded by him to join the gang. Early next morning he was taken two miles out of the village and strangled by Dhokul. The body was thrown into a well.

The same day while the gang was proceeding onwards, two travellers were overtaken and addressed by Bukhtawur, while Bhowanee jemadar decoyed three others, in all five Hindoos, going eastward, who were taken to Rajah ka Tulab, and accommodated with quarters for the night in the seraee at that place. Next morning early Bhowanee set out with a portion of the gang, and the three travellers who were strangled at the distance of a mile from the town. Soon afterwards Bukhtawur and the travellers in his custody came up to the same place and the victims were forthwith put to death. The bodies were all cast into a well.

After this affair the gang went and rested in the seraee at Mukhun, where Bhowanee jemadar decoyed two Hindoos travelling from Agra to the eastward, who were taken out a couple of miles next morning on their way, and put to death. The bodies were thrown into a well.

The gang next went towards Etawah, and on the way overtook two Brahmins from Muttra, whom they decoyed and took with them to a village where there is a temple to Bhowanee near Mealapoor, where they rested. In the morning the travellers were taken to a stream, two miles from the village, and strangled.

Having arrived within four miles of Etawah the gang fell in with two Hindoos travelling from Gwalior to Byswara, who were taken to the seraee

Report of a Thug Expedition in the years 1827, *Dhowkul Jemadar, Bhowanee and Lalla Lochun,*

No. of List.	Names of jurisdiction of the place where the Murder was perpetrated.	No. and Sex of the Murdered.		Date of the Murder.	Intended destination of the Murdered.		Supposed value of the property robbed.
		Men.	Women.		From	To	
15	Pinghee, in the Cawnpoor district,	1	0	That Season of 1827,	Dekhan,	Lucknow.	9 rupees.
16	Near Maharajgunge,	1	0	Ditto,	....	Meerut.	10 rupees.
17	Near Oung,	1	0	Ditto,	Furukhabad.	Jounpoor.	30 rupees.
18	Mulwah,	1	0	Ditto,	....	....	24½ rupees.
19	Taranugur,	2	0	Ditto,	....	....	45 rupees.

1828 and 1829, under the following leaders: with Thirty-two Thugs, and other Leaders.

REMARKS.

at Etawah. They passed the night there and next morning went to a well some distance from the town, where the travellers were, as usual, strangled and their bodies thrown into the well.

They afterwards went as far as Roodroo, and there the gang broke up. Lalla Lochun jemadar, Dhowkul jemadar, and four others remained, and the others went to their homes. These six Thugs went to Pinghee in the Cawnpoor district, where they were joined by Gopaul (approver) Lalla Lochun jemadar having gone to a distiller's shop to take a dram, fell in with a Chupprassee from the Dekhan about to visit his home in the Lucknow states, whom he brought to the encampment of the gang, and having accommodated him for the night, took him next morning a couple of miles out on his way and strangled him. The body and the belt's badge which he wore, were thrown into a well.

The next day while they were going to Maharaj Gunjh, and about a mile distant from it, they fell in with a Lodhee on his way to Meerut. Lalla Lochun decoyed him and they all rested for the night in a Fuqueer's garden. In the morning the traveller was strangled about a mile off and his body thrown into a well.

After this affair, the Thugs went to Oung and passed the day in the seraee. There they found a shopkeeper bunniah, with a poney, on his way from Furruckhabad to Jounpore, whom they induced next morning to accompany them, and strangled him a couple of miles from the town.

They went onwards to Mulwah, and a short time before reaching that place they fell in with a Kuhar whom Lalla Lochun decoyed and took to the seraee, they slept there, and in the morning the traveller was strangled about a mile from the seraee, his body being thrown into a well.

At length they reached Belinda, which had been fixed upon as a place of rendezvous for the Thugs who had separated at Roodroo. All who had visited their homes, and in addition to them, Dibba (approver) and three other Thugs joined here, so that the gang now amounted to 36. Bhowanee jemadar had previously decoyed and brought with him two Rajhpoot travellers, whom they induced to remain a day at Belinda and then took them to Ahmedgunge, where they met the gang of eighty Thugs under Keseree subadar, whose proceedings have been already detailed. After interchanging enquiries the two gangs proceeded on their way, Lalla Lochun's gang went to Jaranugger and rested, next morning they took the Rajhpoots a couple of miles out off the town and strangled them.

Report of a Thug Expedition in the years 1827,
Dhowkul Jemadar, Bhowanee and Lalla Lochun,

No. of List.	Names of jurisdiction of the place where the Murder was perpetrated.	No. and Sex of the Murdered		Date of the Murder.	Intended destination of the Murdered.		Supposed value of the property robbed.
		Men.	Women.		From	To	
20	Near Kurha,	1	0	That season of 1827,	....	Benares,	35 rupees.
21	Ditto,	2	0	Ditto,	Rewah,	Lucknow,	400 rupees.
22	Ahmedgunge,	2	0	Ditto,	Benares,	Furrukhabad,	50 rupees.
23	Near Oung,	1	0	Ditto,	Mirzapoor,	Ditto,	45 rupees.
24	Chickuttea,	1	0	Ditto,	....	Westward,	5 rupees.

1828 *and* 1829, *under the following leaders: with Thirty-two Thugs, and other Leaders.*

REMARKS.

They next went to Kurha where Buktawur brought a Hindoo on his way to Benares, who passed the night with the Thugs, and was strangled next morning on the banks of the Ganges into which his body was thrown.

The gang now turned back to Kurha where they passed the day in the seraee. They found a Brahmin and a Kuhar there, who came from Rewah, and intended to go to Lucknow, and Bhowanee decoyed them. In the morning they were taken to the bank of a river, on pretence of bathing, and after there being strangled their bodies were committed to the stream.

After the murder they went to Ahmudgunge, and resting in the seraee found two travellers by caste Rajhpoots from Benares to Furrukhabad, whom they decoyed, and took next morning with them about a mile when they put them to death.

They continued their journey westward, and in the evening fell in with a Hindoo travelling from Mirzapore to Furrukhabad, whom Bhowanee decoyed and took to Oung, where they slept, and next morning taking the traveller to a garden two miles off strangled him there.

The next stage was Chickuttea, and at the distance of a mile or two from thence they fell in with a Mussulman traveller going westward, whom they took to the seraee at that place, and there they found three travellers by caste Burboonjas, whom they decoyed and early next morning Bhowanee jemadar, and others having taken the Mussulman with them strangled him and buried his body in a dry well. The other three travellers were taken eastward, by the rest of the gang, to the bank of the river, where they intended to despatch them; when the signal was given, the stranglers threw their roomals over the heads of their victims, two of the travellers were brought to the ground, but the intended strangler of the third missed his mark. Just at this moment some people were driving carts loaden with grain from the direction of Kujjooa Bindkee, and hearing the screams of the travellers, called out in threatening terms that they were coming. The Thugs taking the alarm, abandoned their victims and their booty, and fled for their lives: some of them gave intelligence of the disaster to the gang who had taken out the Mussulman in an opposite direction, and all went to their homes as speedily as possible, arriving there they heard the unwelcome news of the capture and imprisonment of Kaseree subadar's gang at Sirsagunge. The Thugs depose that the three travellers whom they abandoned, were seized by the Thanadar of Police, who, in consequence of the suspicious circumstances attendant in their capture, sent them prisoners to Cawnpore, where they were detained for three years.

Report of a Thug Expedition in the years of 1827, *Dhowkul Jemadar, Bhowanee and Lalla Lochun,*

No. of List.	Names of jurisdiction of the place where the Murder was perpetrated.	No. and Sex of the Murdered.		Date of the Murder.	Intended destination of the Murdered.		Supposed value of the property robbed.
		Men.	Women.		From	To	
25	Gopeegunge,	1	0	That season of 1827,	Agra,	Cawnpoor,	15 rupees.
26	Bhind,	2	0	Ditto,	Gwalior,	Barreilly,	62 rupees.
27	Near Gobind,	1	0	Ditto,	Sindeah's Camp,	Lucknow,	About 7 rupees.
28	Bhowra Ghattee,	6	0	Ditto,	....	....	About 300 rupees.
29	Gwalior,	5	0	Ditto,	Dekhan,	Delhie,	115 rupees.

1828 and 1829, under the following leaders: with Thirty-two Thugs, and other Leaders.

REMARKS.

About the commencement of the year 1827, Mehrban and Lalla Lochun jemadars, with a gang of eighteen Thugs, left their homes in Juddee ka Purwa, in Furruckabad, and set off on an expedition into the Dooab. They proceeded to Gopeagunge where they fell in with a traveller by caste a Kachee, on his way from Agra to Cawnpore, who was decoyed by Lalla Lochun, and being taken next morning two miles from the village, was strangled and buried in a dry well.

The gang after this affair crossed the Jumna, and went to Bhind, where they met a Brahmin, and a bunneah, going from Gwalior to Bareilly, whom they accommodated near them for the night, and next morning early put them to death about three miles off. The bodies were thrown into a well.

Proceeding onwards for two days the Thugs reached Gobind, and there fell in with a Koormee, travelling from Scindeah's camp to Lucknow, who was decoyed by Uchul jemadar, and strangled next morning a short distance from the village.

Two days more brought the gang to Gwalior, which place they passed through, and in ten days arrived at Bhowra Ghatee, where they came upon Moorlee (approver) with thirty or thirty-two Thug followers, and six travellers in their company—Lalla Lochun jemadar and five or six Thugs were deputed from Mehrban's gang, to assist at the murder of these travellers and receive their share of the booty. The gang under Mehrban remained at their quarters in expectation of their return. They took the six travellers a short distance up the mountain pass and put them to death. Lalla Lochun having received a share returned to Bhowra Ghattee, and rejoined his companions. This affair has formed the subject of trial in the Agent's Court at Jubulpore, and the remains of the murdered travellers have been found.

The gang turned back towards Gwalior where they arrived in ten or twelve days. There they found Koshial Khan Guzratee jemadar, with six or seven Thugs and five travellers, Munnears, from the Dekhan going to Delhie, resting there in a garden for the day. As this number was insufficient to overpower the travellers, Lalla Lochun's gang was invited to assist, and taking up their quarters in the same place, the Thugs commenced to sing and beat the drum, when the time for the murder arrived they let loose their ponies, and during the scuffle that ensued, the five travellers were put to death and the bodies were securely buried in the garden.

The whole of the Thugs then left Gwalior for Dholepoor, and on the way fell in with a gang of Oothaigeers, who being acquainted with Lalla Lochun jemadar laid hold of him. His followers taking the alarm fled to their homes,

Report of a Thug Expedition in the years of 1827,
Dhowkul Jemadar, Bhowanee and Lalla Lochun,

No. of List.	Names of jurisdiction of the place where the Murder was perpetrated.	No. and Sex of the Murdered.		Date of the Murder.	Intended destination of the Murdered.		Supposed value of the property robbed.
		Men.	Women.		From	To	
30	Chowbepore, in zillah Cawnpoor,	2	0	That Season of 1827,	....	Rampore,	200 rupees.
31	Berha,	3	0	Ditto,	Khyaat,	Cawnpore,	250 rupees.
32	Pokaroya,	2	0	Ditto,	Bundelkhund,	Oude,	200 rupees.
33	Berha,	2	0	Ditto,	Nagpore,	Lucknow,	200 rupees.
34	Kooheerpore, in Futtehpore,	1	0	Ditto,	....	....	100 rupees.
35	Kurreh,	4	0	Ditto,	Meerut,	Mirzapore,	125 rupees.
36	Near Sirsole, in zillah Cawnpore,	2	0	Ditto,	....	....	50 rupees.
37	Ditto,	3	0	Ditto,	....	Bithoor,	500 rupees.

REMARKS.

and the jemadar purchased his own release by the payment of ten rupees, and then returned homewards.

About the month of April 1827, Bhowanee Pershad and Dhowkul jemadars led out a gang of thirty-five Thugs from Chowleeka Poorwa in Furrukhabad and went to Chowleepore in zillah Cawnpore. There they met two travellers, Mussulmans, going to Rampoor, who were decoyed and next morning taken to a garden two miles off, when they were put to death and their bodies thrown in a well.

The gang then went on to Barha, where they decoyed three travellers, namely, a Kayet, a Brahmin and a Kuhar, who were going from Kyta to Cawnpore, next morning early they were taken out and put to death as usual, the bodies were thrown into a well.

After this affair the Thugs went to Pokrya and rested in the bazar. There they met and decoyed two travellers, Aheers, from Bundelkhund, going to Oude, who were taken next morning to the banks of a tank two miles off and strangled. The bodies were, as usual, thrown into a well.

They then returned to Barha, and went into the bazar, where two Sepoys from Nagpoor, going to Lucknow, were resting. They were decoyed by Shunker and taken next morning two miles on their way and then put to death.

They next proceeded to Kooherpoor in Futtehpoor, where they rested in a seraee and found a Bunneah there, who was decoyed, and taken next morning some distance out of the village and put to death. The body was thrown into a well.

The Thugs then went to Kurreh and met four Bunneahs from Meerut on their way to Mirzapoor, resting in a plain, they encamped there also for the day. Bhowanee decoyed them, and next morning they were conducted to the bank of the river, where they were put to death and the bodies committed to the stream.

Having gone to the seraee at Minda they met Runnooa moonshee, Runjeet and Bukshee jemadars, and a gang of 30 Thugs, who had a few days before set out from Behareepoor, and having put to death two travellers (Hindoos) near Sirsole, in the Cawnpore district, they came to Minda ka seraee.

The gang now amounted to sixty five Thugs, and they found in the caravansera three Hindoos proceeding to Bithoor, whom they decoyed and took out next morning two miles, and then strangled under some Mowha trees. The bodies were thrown into a well.

Report of a Thug Expedition in the years of 1827,
Dhowkul Jemadar, Bhowanee and Lalla Lochun,

No. of List.	Names of jurisdiction of the place where the Murder was perpetrated.	No. and Sex of the Murdered.		Date of the Murder.	Intended destination of the Murdered.		Supposed value of the property robbed.
		Men.	Women.		From	To	
38	Pingee,	1	0	That Season of 1827,	Gwalior,	Lucknow,	30 rupees.
39	Near Kujwah, in Furrukhabad,	2	0	Ditto,	Mirzapore,	Meerut,	405 rupees.
40	Shewrajpoor, in Cawnpore,	2	0	Ditto,	....	....	36 rupees.
41	Mudna,	3	0	Ditto,	Patna,	Samlee,	700 rupees.
42	Sirdhanah Jageer,	2	0	Ditto,	....	Bhyswarah,	100 rupees.
43	Shamlee,	2	0	Ditto,	Lodheanah,	Ditto,	50 rupees.
44	Purwah, in Cawnpore,	4	0	Ditto,	Eastward,	....	150 rupees.

1828 and 1829, under the following leaders: with Thirty-two Thugs, and other Leaders.

REMARKS.

After this affair the two parties again separated. Dhowkul and Bhowanee jemadars led their gang of thirty-five Thugs to Pingee, where they found a Hindoo from Gwalior going to Lucknow resting in the bazar. Him they decoyed and murdered next morning a short distance off. The body was thrown into a well. The gang then went homewards without committing any other murder.

When Runnooa moonshee's gang left Minda, they went to Futtehpoor, where they observed an unfavorable omen, in a fight between two cats, and went home without further prosecution of their adventures.

During the hot weather of 1827, Lalla Lochun, Mehrban, Rambuksh, and Pershadee jemadars and fifteen Thugs, set out on a second expedition from Rujjee Mhow in Furruckhabad, and in the space of three days arrived at Bindkee. There they discovered two travellers from Mirzapoor going to Meerut, carrying boxes on their heads. They decoyed and escorted them near to Kujwa, a distance of five miles, where they put them to death and threw the bodies into a well.

After this affair eight of the Thugs returned home, and the remaining seven, under Lalla Lochun jemadar, proceeded to Shewrajpoor in the Cawnpore district, where they met two travellers, bheesties, or water carriers by caste, whom they took a short distance out next morning, and put to death, throwing the bodies into a well.

They then went to Mudna, where they fell in with and decoyed three Brahmins from Patna to Shamlee in the Meerut district, whom they conducted next morning to a grove of mango trees, and having strangled them, threw their bodies into a well. The gang after this returned home.

After remaining at home a few days Ramdeen and Mehrban jemadars led out a gang of ten Thugs from Rujjee Mhow in Furruckhabad and proceeded by the usual stages to Kerrooa in the Sirdhana Jageer, where they fell in with a Rajpoot and a barber proceeding towards Bhyswara, who were decoyed and taken next morning a couple of miles and put to death as usual. The bodies were thrown into a well. They then determined on returning home.

They next went to Shamlee where two sepahees, by caste Brahmins, from Lodheana, going to Bhyswara were inveigled by them. The travellers were taken out next morning and put to death as usual. The bodies were thrown into a well.

In the month of October 1827, Dhowkul and Bhowanee jemadars assembled a gang of 35 Thugs at Chowde ka Poorwa in Furruckhabad, and proceeded

Report of a Thug Expedition in the years of 1827, *Dhowkul Jemadar, Bhowanee and Lalla Lachun,*

No. of List.	Names of jurisdiction of the place where the Murder was perpetrated.	No. and Sex of the Murdered.		Date of the Murder.	Intended destination of the Murdered.		Supposed value of the property robbed.
		Men.	Women.		From	To	
45	Near Mulwa,	1	0	That Season of 1827,	Cawnpore,	Futtehpore,	190 rupees.
46	Ditto,	1	0	Ditto,	Meerut,	Allahabad,	25 rupees.
47	Ahmedgunge,	2	0	Ditto,	Ditto,	Benares,	100 rupees.
48	Moorutgunge,	3	0	Ditto,	Benares,	Furruckhabad,	100 rupees.
49	Koonherpoor,	3	0	Ditto,	Mirzapoor,	Muttra,	25 rupees.
50	Echun Nuddee,	2	0	Ditto,	Benares,	Myanpooree,	20 rupees.
51	Zillah Mynpooree, at Sooltangunge,	1	0	Ditto,	Calcutta,	Delhie,	20 rupees.

1828 and 1829, under the following leaders: with Thirty-two Thugs, and other Leaders.

REMARKS.

to Purwa in Cawnpore. Next morning they set out again and fell in with four Hindoos proceeding eastward, whom they took with them to Joohee, ate their bread there, and then set out again in the evening. Having gone a few miles, they put the travellers to death in a plain and threw the bodies into a well. They returned to Joohee and slept there.

In the morning they went on their way and fell in with a Hindoo from Cawnpore going to Futtehpore, with a poney laden with copper coin. Him they took to Sirsolee, passed the night there, and next morning proceeded towards Mulwa, arriving at a tank two miles from Mulwa they sat down and strangled the traveller about midday. The body was buried in the mud of the tank.

On the same day some of the Thugs lagged behind on the road, and falling in with a traveller from Meerut going to Allahabad they conducted him to the same tank, where the preceding murder was committed, and put him to death in the evening. The body was buried on the brink of the tank.

The whole gang passed the night at Mulwa and the day after slept at Futtehpoor. In the morning they went to the bridge over the river Susser Kudheelee, where they sat down. A havildar from Meerut going to Benares, with his son, came up to the same place. They were decoyed and taken to Ahmedgunge where they passed the night, and in the morning were put to death two miles off, at a well into which the bodies were thrown.

After this affair the Thugs went and rested in the seraee at Moorutgunge. There they found three barbers from Benares going to Furruckhabad whom they decoyed and turned back with next morning and murdered a short distance from the village. The bodies were thrown into a well.

After this the gang went to Koonherpoor where they rested in the bazar, and fell in with three travellers from Mirzapoor on their way to Muttra, and decoyed them, and next morning early strangled them a short distance from the town. The bodies were thrown into a well.

Going on, they arrived in a few days at Poorra in the Cawnpore district, and there they met two travellers by caste Kuhars, from Benares, going to Mynpooree, whom they decoyed along with them next day, and in the evening reaching Echun Nuddee, they sat down and put their victims to death after dark. The bodies were thrown into the stream.

They reached Bhogaon in Mynpooree three days afterwards, and there fell in with a traveller from Calcutta to Delhie, whom they took with them, went

Report of a Thug Expedition in the years of 1827, *Dhowkul Jemadar, Bhowanee and Lalla Lochun,*

No. of List.	Names of jurisdiction of the place where the Murder was perpetrated.	No. and Sex of the Murdered.		Date of the Murder.	Intended destination of the Murdered.		Supposed value of the property robbed.
		Men.	Women.		From	To	
52	Mullawun,	3	0	That season of 1827,	....	....	100 rupees.
53	Secundra, in Coel,	2	0	Ditto,	Kurnool,	Jounpoor,	100 rupees.
54	Boolund Shuhur,	2	0	Ditto,	Lahore,	Eastward,	100 rupees.
55	Haupper,	2	0	Ditto,	Ditto,	Ditto,	50 rupees.
56	Humeerpore,	4	0	Ditto,	Ditto,	Cawnpoor,	300 rupees.
57	Tirwah,	3	0	Ditto,	Kurnal,	Mirzapoor,	40 rupees.
58	Boykoontapoor, in Mulwa,	3	0	Ditto,	Shujahanpoor,	Chupra,	500 rupees.

1828 and 1829, under the following leaders: with Thirty-two Thugs, and other Leaders.

REMARKS.

next morning to a tank near Sooltangunge, and strangled him. The body was thrown into the tank. The body having been discovered by the inhabitants, a chowkee was established in consequence at the tank.

They next went to Mullawun when the Thugs met two sepahees and a chuprasee, all Hindoos, whom they took with them next morning to a garden two miles off, and put to death as usual. The bodies were carelessly buried in a ravine.

After this they proceeded to Secundra in Koel, when they met two Kuhars from Kurnal travelling to Jounpoor, whom they decoyed and murdered next morning at a sheet of water two miles off. The bodies were concealed in the mud.

They next arrived at Boolundshuhur and met two sepahees from Lahore travelling eastward, who were next morning taken to a well some distance off, and put to death. The bodies were deposited in a ravine and covered with stones.

The same day they went to a stream near Haupper and sat down. Two Hindoo travellers from Lahore came up to the same place. They were invited to try the hooqqa, and while smoking were put to death. The bodies were thrown into the stream.

After this affair nineteen of the Thugs, led by Dibba Bunneah, left the gang and proceeded homewards. The remainder promised to follow them in a short time, and going in the first place to Koorja, turned back and travelled by stages to Humeerpoor in the Cawnpoor district. Near that place they sat down on the road side and were joined by four Rajpoots from Lahore proceeding to Cawnpoor. They all went together to Humeerpore, cooked and ate their dinners, and in the evening proceeded onwards a distance of four miles, when the travellers were put to death, and their bodies thrown into a well.

The gang then turned off the road and went to Chupra Mhow, where they fell in with three shepherds from Kurnal on their way to Mirzapoor, who accompanied them next day and continued their journey till evening after dark till they reached a stream two miles from Tirwa, where they strangled the travellers and threw their bodies into the water. The next morning the gang dispersed and went to their respective homes.

At the same time that the preceding expedition was on foot, Cheyne jemadar, Runjut alias Devedeen, with a gang of twenty-five Thugs, set out from Behareepoor in Cawnpoor, and proceeded to Bykoontapoor, where they fell in

Report of a Thug Expedition in the years of 1827, *Dhowkul Jemadar, Bhowanee and Lalla Lochun,*

No. of List.	Names of jurisdiction of the place where the Murder was perpetrated.	No. and Sex of the Murdered.		Date of the Murder.	Intended destination of the Murdered.		Supposed value of the property robbed.
		Men.	Women.		From	To	
59	Shajadpore, in Futtehpore,	1	0	That season of 1827,	....	....	15 rupees.
60	Moorutgunge,	5	0	Ditto,	Achmul,	Bhyswarah.	300 rupees.
61	Chowleepore, in Cawnpore,	1	0	Ditto,	....	Westward,	40 rupees.
62	Rohun,	2	0	Ditto,	Mukhanpore,	....	300 rupees.
63	Shujadpore,	1	0	Ditto,	Cawnpore,	Mirzapore,	100 rupees.
64	Near Mohun ka Serae,	1	0	Ditto,	Ditto,	Benares,	400 rupees.

1828 *and* 1829, *under the following leaders: with Thirty-two Thugs, and other Leaders.*

REMARKS.

with a jemadar and two sepahees, all Hindoos, from Shajihanpore, on their way to Chupra, whom they decoyed and took with them to Mulwa, where they passed the night, early next morning they were put to death a few miles from the village and their bodies thrown into a well.

They proceeded onwards and in course of a few days arrived at Shahajadpore in Futtehpore. At midday they came to the banks of the Ganges, where they found a traveller by caste a Hindoo, engaged in performing his ablutions. The Thugs instantly followed his example and while doing so took an opportunity of strangling the traveller in the water, and allowed his body to float away with the stream.

They next went to Moorutgunge and advanced the same afternoon to the eastward, but meeting five Hindoo travellers from Achanuck going to Bhyswara, they turned back with them and put them to death on the road. The bodies they carried to a well and had precipitated three of them into the water when they were perceived by some cultivators in an adjacent field, who ran towards them. The Thugs taking the booty along with them fled homewards, and arriving there divided the spoil obtained at the last murder.

In the year 1827, about the month of November, Lalla Lochun and Bhowanee jemadars, assembled fifty-two Thugs at Chowlee ka Poorwa in Furruckhabad and set out on an expedition. They went to Chowleepore in Cawnpore and decoyed a Hindoo (with three bullocks in his possession,) travelling westward, whom they took next morning and strangled about two miles off.

The gang then went to Rohun and fell in with two Brinjarahs from Mukhunpore, whom they decoyed, and took next morning some distance on their way and strangled. The bodies were thrown into a well.

Proceeding eastward, they arrived at Shahazadpore, and fell in with a Bunneah on his way from Cawnpore to Mirzapore. With the characteristic caution of his tribe, the Bunneah refused to travel during the night. The Thugs therefore accompanied him in broad day, and when they reached the Ganges induced him to stop to bathe. Their victim was put to death, while performing his ablution, and the body floated away in the stream.

The gang crossed the river and went to Furruckhabad; while sitting on the road side, a Mussulman traveller from Cawnpore, on his way to Benares, came up to the spot, he was decoyed and taken to Mohun ka Serae in the Benares district. They slept there and next morning completed the murder of the traveller a couple of miles off. The body was thrown into a well.

Report of a Thug Expedition in the years of 1827, *Dhowkul Jemadar, Bhowanee and Lalla Lochun,*

No. of List.	Names of jurisdiction of the place where the Murder was perpetrated.	No. and Sex of the Murdered.		Date of the Murder.	Intended destination of the Murdered.		Supposed value of the property robbed.
		Men.	Women.		From	To	
65	Bindachul, near Mirzapore,	2	0	That Season of 1827,	Benares,	Nagpore,	250 rupees.
66	Durawungunge,	2	0	Ditto,	Ditto,	Ditto,	100 rupees.
67	Hunmunna,	2	0	Ditto,	Nagpore,	Jounpore,	300 rupees.
68	Between Rewah and Amurputtum,	3	0	Ditto,	Poona,	Ajoodhea,	200 rupees.
69	Mulgowhan,	5	0	Ditto,	Hydrabad,	Cawnpore,	600 rupees.
70	Barha, in the Cawnpore district,	3	0	Ditto,	....	....	700 rupees.

1828 and 1829, under the following leaders: with Thirty-two Thugs, and other Leaders.

REMARKS.

After the murder the gang went to the ghat on the Ganges opposite to Mirzapore, and entered the ferry boat intending to cross the river. Two Gossaeens from Benares on their way to Nagpore came and entered the same boat. They were forthwith decoyed and on disembarking from the boat, the Thugs took them to Bindachul near Mirzapore, the site of a temple to Bhowanee, where they rested for the day. Next morning early the Gossaeens were taken two miles on the road to Nagpore, and being put to death. Their bodies were securely buried.

After this affair the gang went to Durawungunge, where they fell in with two Hindoos travellers on their way from Benares to Nagpore, whom they took out to a stream two miles off and put to death. The bodies were buried in a ravine.

The gang immediately ascended the ghat and went to Hunmunna, where they discovered two travellers from Nagpore, on their way to Jounpore, whom they decoyed, and taking out a mile on the Mirzapore road, they strangled and buried the bodies.

They turned back after the murder and went to Rewah, and thence to a village midway between that town and Amerputum, where they found three travellers by caste shepherds from Poona on their way to Ajoodheah, whom they decoyed and accompanied next morning a mile towards Rewah, when they put them to death. The bodies were buried.

After completing the murder the Thugs went to Amerpatum, and thence determined on returning towards Allahabad. When they had retraced their steps a few miles they overtook five travellers, by caste Hindoos, going from Hyderabad to Jounpore, whom they inveigled and passed that night in their company at Raepore, next day they rested at Mulgowan, and on the succeeding morning strangled their victims two miles from the village. The bodies were buried in a ravine.

They then went to Ghatee Sohawul, from whence ten Thugs separated from the gang and went homewards. The remainder proceeded to Budleepore in Allahabad where they crossed the Jumna, and rested at a seraee in a village, name of which is unknown. In the evening the Thugs went to the Police station to register their names and distinction, when they fell under the suspicion of the thanadar. During the night the gang was visited by the thanadar and his attendants, who demanded their weapons, which they gave up, and afterwards fled homewards without waiting to recover them.

When they arrived at Barha, in the Cawnpore district, they fell in with three Hindoo travellers, whom they inveigled into their company, and taking

Report of a Thug Expedition in the years of 1827, *Dhowkul Jemadar, Bhowanee and Lalla Lochun,*

No. of List.	Names of jurisdiction of the place where the Murder was perpetrated.	No. and Sex of the Murdered.		Date of the Murder.	Intended destination of the Murdered.		Supposed value of the property robbed.
		Men.	Women.		From	To	
71	Muchunda, in Ambulla,	6	0	That Season of 1827,	Lodhe-ana,	Oude,	100 rupees.
72	Budwus, in Coel,	1	0	Ditto,	Meerut,	Cawn-pore,	13 rupees.
73	Secundra,	2	0	Ditto,	Delhie,	East-ward,	40 rupees.
74	Akerabad, in Coel,	1	0	Ditto,	Ditto,	Cawn-pore,	10 rupees.
75	Maunagurh,	2	0	Ditto,	Calcutta,	Meerut,	2 or 3 rupees.

1828 *and* 1829, *under the following leaders: with Thirty-two Thugs, and other Leaders.*

REMARKS.

them out next morning, put them to death at a well, into which the bodies were thrown, after which they divided the booty and forthwith went to their homes.

During the year 1827, about the month of September, Runnooa moonshee and Uchul jemadars proceeded with a gang of thirty Thugs from Behareepoor in Furruckhabad towards the west, in search of adventures. They advanced as far as Hunjarah ka seraee, in the Putteala state, without committing any murder. At that place they fell in with six Hindoo travellers from Loodheana on their way to the Oude territory, whom they decoyed and took next day to Muchunda in Umballee where they slept. In the morning the travellers were put to death at a stream two miles off and their bodies buried there.

After this affair they went and sat down on the bank of the river at Shahabad where they were joined by Heera Singh subadar, in the service of the Ruler of the Punjab, with nine attendants, all on their way from Lahore to Chutterkote. They ingratiated themselves with the subadar, whom they escorted to Goolchutr and Kurnal. At the latter place the party rested for three days, and during that time four of the subadar's followers separated and went towards Delhi. The remainder of the travellers, six in number, accompanied the Thugs to Jhinjana and Kurrah in Sirdhana Jageer. At Kurrah, Runnooa moonshee's party fell in with another gang of Thugs, thirty in number, led by Rambuksh and Mukhun jemadars, who had set out a short time previously from Dulputnugger in the Furruckhabad district, and committed the following murders on the way.

The first went to Budwas in Coel, where they decoyed a traveller by caste a Choomar, going from Meerut to Cawnpore, and took him out next morning a short distance and put him to death. The body was thrown into a well.

After this affair they proceeded to Secundra and rested in the Bazar. They found two chupprassees going from Delhi to the eastward, whom they put to death next morning at a tank a mile off, and threw the bodies into the water.

They next went to Coel, and in the bazar where they passed the night they found a Hindoo traveller from Delhi going to Cawnpore, whom they sent off next morning in charge of seven Thugs towards the eastward, while the rest of the gang proceeded to Sobna and rested. The seven Thugs took the traveller to Akerabad in Coel, where they passed the night, and having strangled him next morning and thrown his body into a well.

They proceeded onwards to Boolundshuhur, where Pershad Thug decoyed two travellers, Hindoos, from Calcutta, going to Meerut, and took them to

Report of a Thug Expedition in the years of 1827,
Dhowkul Jemadar, Bhowanee and Lalla Lochun,

No. of List.	Names of jurisdiction of the place where the Murder was perpetrated.	No. and Sex of the Murdered		Date of the Murder.	Intended destination of the Murdered.		Supposed value of the property robbed.
		Men.	Women.		From	To	
			0				
76	Boorhana,	2	0	That season of 1827,	Kurnool,	Lucknow,	150 rupees.
77	Hurreer, in Oude,	1	0	Ditto,	Lahore,	Bazar Mhow,	235 rupees.
78	Budowlee,	1	0	Ditto,	Kurnal,	Lucknow,	60 rupees.
79	Kurreer,	10	0	Ditto,	Lahore,	Bhyswara,	1600 rupees.
80	Goolowtee, in Happur,	3	0	Ditto,	....	....	100 rupees.
81	Akerabad,	8	0	Ditto,	Delhie,	Salone, in Oude,	700 rupees.

1828 and 1829, under the following leaders: with Thirty-two Thugs, and other Leaders.

REMARKS.

Manaugurh, slept there, and next morning put them to death at a stream two miles from the village. The bodies were buried. Two boxes were found in possession of the travellers one containing musical instruments, and the other cigars, which were buried with the bodies.

After this affair they went on to Boorhana, where they fell in with two shroffs from Kurnal on their way to Lucknow, whom they decoyed and strangled next morning at a stream. Throwing the bodies into the water.

They proceeded into Shamlee and found there a Rajpoot traveller from Lahore going to Bâgur Mhow, in Oude, whom they took with them to Kurreer and having slept there strangled him next morning a short distance from the village. The body was thrown into a well.

The gang then turned towards the west, and went to Budolee where they fell in with a Hindoo, travelling from Kurnal to Lucknow, whom they decoyed and took next morning a mile on his way, when they strangled him and threw his body into a well.

Having completed the murder they turned back again and went to Shamlee, and proceeded onwards next day—on the road they overtook four Hindoos from Lahore on their way to Byswara, whom they decoyed with them to Kurreer. At the last named place they met Runnooa moonshee, and his gang as before mentioned, and having united their forces they amounted in number to sixty Thugs.

Having slept at Kurreer, Debdeen's gang took the four travellers about two miles on their way next morning and put them to death. The bodies were thrown into a well. They were followed by Runnooa moonshee, with the six travellers before mentioned, who were strangled at the same spot, and their bodies thrown into the same well. The gang went to Boorhana and proceeded to divide the spoil, when it was discovered that a gold armlet had been stolen. This produced a quarrel between Pershad and Runnooa moonshee, the consequence of which was the separation of the two gangs.

Pershad and Rambuksh, with thirty Thugs, went to Goolowtee, Pergunnah Haupper, where they fell in with three Ganges water-carriers, whom they decoyed and took next morning to a well two miles off, where they put them to death and threw the bodies into it.

The gang then went to Coel, and found in the seraee there eight Sepahees from Delhi going to Salone in Oude, whom they induced to accompany them to Akerabad where they passed the night. In the morning, the travellers were

Report of a Thug Expedition in the years of 1827, *Dhowkul Jemadar, Bhowanee and Lalla Lochun,*

No. of List.	Names of jurisdiction of the place where the Murder was perpetrated.	No. and Sex of the Murdered.		Date of the Murder.	Intended destination of the Murdered.		Supposed value of the property robbed.
		Men.	Women.		From	To	
82	Near Akerabad,	3	0	That Season of 1827,	Lahore,	Jehanabad,	600 rupees.
83	Boorhana,	4	0	Ditto,	Punjub,	Sooltanpore,	300 rupees.
84	Hunsegunge,	2	0	Ditto,	Coel,	Muttra,	550 rupees.
85	Tukkeah, in the Oude State,	2	0	That Season of 1828,	Westward,	Oude,	50 rupees.
86	Hussungunge,	2	0	Ditto,	Ditto,	....	80 rupees.
87	Bunter, in Bhyswara,	2	0	Ditto,	Cawnpore,	Bhyswara,	100 rupees.

1828 and 1829, under the following leaders: with Thirty-two Thugs, and other Leaders.

REMARKS.

put to death a short distance from the town and their bodies thrown into a well. The bodies were subsequently discovered by the Police, and the fact has been substantiated by the enquiries instituted by Lieut. E. Robinson.

When the gang had gone a short distance from the scene of the last murder they were overtaken by three travellers, a Brahmin, a Rajpoot, and a Kuhar, who came from Lahore and intended to go to Jehanabad. As it was still dark, the Thugs put the three travellers forthwith to death and threw their bodies into a well. After this affair the gang went home.

In the meantime the gang under Runnooa moonshee left Boorhana, and went to a village six miles off, the name of which is not remembered. There they found four Hindoo travellers from the Punjab on their way to Sultanpore, whom they decoyed, and next morning strangled at a well a short distance off, into which the bodies were thrown.

The gang went onwards for several days and at last arrived at Akrabad where Pershad and Rambuksh's gang had a few days previously strangled the eight Sepahees whose bodies had subsequently been discovered. In consequence all passengers from the westward were stopped and examined by the Police authorities. The Thugs hearing this circumstance turned back and went to Coel where they passed the night, and next morning proceeded towards Muttra. At a distance of four miles, they were overtaken by two Hindoos from Coel, proceeding also to Muttra, who joined them, and they proceeded together to Hunseagunge, near which place the travellers were strangled and their bodies thrown into a well.

As the recent murders had created a great sensation in the country the gang became fearful of detection, and therefore proceeded homewards by way of Hatrass.

In the month of January, 1828, Nawul jemadar with sixteen Thugs in his train left Behareepore, and proceeded on an expedition into Oude, they first went to Tukkeeah in the Oude state, where they fell in with two Hindoos from the west travelling in the same direction with themselves, whom they decoyed and put to death at a well, into which the bodies were thrown.

They next went to Meeahgunge, where they decoyed two Hindoos from the west, whom they took with them next day to Hussungunge and slept there. Next morning early the travellers were put to death, and their bodies thrown into a well.

After this affair the gang went to Bunter, in Bhyswara, where they fell in with two travellers by caste Hindoos, on their way from Cawnpore to

Report of a Thug Expedition in the years of 1827, *Dhowkul Jemadar, Bhowanee and Lalla Lochun,*

No. of List.	Names of jurisdiction of the place where the Murder was perpetrated.	No. and Sex of the Murdered.		Date of the Murder.	Intended destination of the Murdered.		Supposed value of the property robbed.
		Men.	Women.		From	To	
88	Kutgurh, in Rae Bareilly,	2	0	That season of 1828,	Dekhan,	Hydergurh,	50 rupees.
89	Bubotee, in Cawnpore Zillah,	1	0	Ditto,	Etawah.	Lucknow,	80 rupees.
90	Chowbe Seraee, in Futtehpore,	1	0	Ditto,	East,	Furruckhabad,	7 Gold Mohurs and 10 rupees.
91	Daranuggur,	2	0	Ditto,	....	....	Gold and Cash to the value of 1000 rupees.
92	Chukutea, in Cawnpore,	2	0	Ditto,	....	....	50 rupees.
93	Emamgunge,	4	0	Ditto,	....	Benares,	400 rupees.

1828 and 1829, under the following leaders: with Thirty-two Thugs, and other Leaders.

REMARKS.

Bhyswara, whom they put to death next morning, and threw their bodies into a well two miles off.

They then went to Kutgurh in Rae Bareilly, where they met two Hindoos from the Dekhan going to Hydergurh, whom they decoyed and took next morning two miles on their way, when they were strangled and their bodies thrown into a well. After this affair the gang returned home.

In the month of March 1828, Khuluk, Bhowanee, and Dhowkul jemadars set out from Metapoor in Furruckhabad, with a gang of thirty Thugs and proceeded to Bubootee in Cawnpore zillah. There they were joined by a chupprassee from Etawah on his way to Lucknow, who was decoyed by Bhowanee, and accommodated for the night. Next morning he was taken to a stream two miles off and strangled. The body was thrown into the water.

Proceeding onwards the gang arrived at Chowbee seraee in Futtehpore, and there they met a Brahmin from the east going to Furruckhabad, whom Khuluk decoyed and took him next morning to a well some distance off, and put him to death. The body was thrown into the well.

After this affair the Thugs went to the Chowkee at Appoohee, where they sat down on the road, they were soon after joined by two Hindoos, whom they invited to accompany them, and took to Deranugur where they passed the night. In the morning the travellers were taken to a rivulet and strangled. The bodies were thrown into a well.

Having completed this murder the gang returned to the Chowkee of Appoohee, where they rested, and were joined by another gang of thirty Thugs led by Lalla Lochun, Hurlall, Devedeen, and Mehrban jemadars, who had left Duleepnuggur in Etawah on an expedition to the eastward. They had perpetrated the following murders on the way.

They first went to Chikkutteah in Cawnpore, and on the bank of the tank there they found two Brahmins travelling the same way with themselves, whom they decoyed and took next morning to a stream, when they put them to death and threw the bodies into the water.

After this they proceeded to Ahmedgunge in Futtehpore, where they found four Hindoos travelling to Benares, whom they decoyed and took with them next morning to Appoohee, where, as above stated, they found Kulluk jemadar and party resting themselves. The two parties having united went with the travellers in company to Emamgunge, and put up in the caravansera. Next morning the travellers were strangled a short distance from the village and their bodies thrown into a well.

Report of a Thug Expedition in the years of 1827,
Dhowkul Jemadar, Bhowanee and Lalla Lochun,

No. of List.	Names of jurisdiction of the place where the Murder was perpetrated.	No. and Sex of the Murdered.		Date of the Murder.	Intended destination of the Murdered.		Supposed value of the property robbed.
		Men.	Women.		From	To	
94	Chukowtea,	2	0	That Season of 1828,	....	....	150 rupees.
95	Chowleepore,	2	0	Ditto,	Mirzapore,	Furruckhabad,	Valued at 1000 rupees.
96	Muckrundnuggur,	1	0	Ditto,	Cawnpore,	Agra,	32 rupees.
97	Meergaon,	3	0	Ditto,	Furruckhabad,	Bolundshuhur,	32 rupees.

1828 *and* 1829, *under the following leaders: with Thirty-two Thugs, and other Leaders.*

REMARKS.

The united gang went on by stages as far as Allahabad, but meeting with no success they in disgust turned back and came as far as Chikkutteah without committing another murder. At this place they found two Hindoo travellers, whom they decoyed and took next morning a short distance to the westward and put them to death. The bodies were thrown into a well.

The Thugs next went to Chickeeree, and sat down in a garden. A chupprasee came to the spot—and remarked that they looked like the inhabitants of Futteh and Tirwa notorious for dacoits whereon they took alarm and the gangs separated—Khuluk jemadar's party took the road to Chowbeepore, and Lalla Lochun jemadar's party that towards Furruckhabad.

When Khuluk jemadar and gang arrived at Chowbeepore, they rested and found two travellers by caste Koormees, who had with them two bullocks laden with Mirzapore chintz which they were taking to Furruckhabad. These men were decoyed and taken by the Thugs to Gungooapore where they passed the night and next morning were put to death a mile off, and their bodies thrown into a well. The gang after this affair returned to their homes.

Lalla Lochun jemadar and his party when they left Checheeree, proceeded to Mukrundgunge, where they rested and decoyed a Hindoo travelling from Cawnpore to Agra and next morning strangled him two miles off. The body was thrown into a well.

They then went to Furruckhabad and passed the night there. In the morning, when they were about to depart, Makhun (approver) came out of the town with three Hindoo travellers, who were conveying idols from that place to Boolundshuhur, they all went together to Meergaon, where they slept, and put the travellers to death next morning near a sheet of water, into which the bodies and idols were thrown.

After this they proceeded to Apapore, where they fell under the suspicion of the jemadar of Police. During the day the Thugs had been drinking at a spirit seller's, and many of them were intoxicated when they went in the evening to register themselves at the Police Office. Their style and language having assured the jemadar of the fact of their being suspicious characters, he surrounded their camp during the night and seized Makhun and fifteen Thugs, the rest managing to effect their escape. The arrested Thugs were sent to the Magistrate of Furruckhabad and put into prison, several of the Thugs having produced security for their good behaviour were set at liberty, the remainder were detained in confinement till the year 1834, when they were made over to the Officers of this department on a requisition from Major Sleeman.

Report of a Thug Expedition in the years of 1827, *Dhowkul Jemadar, Bhowanee and Lalla Lochun,*

No. of List.	Names of jurisdiction of the place where the Murder was perpetrated.	No. and Sex of the Murdered.		Date of the Murder.	Intended destination of the Murdered.		Supposed value of the property robbed.
		Men.	Women.		From	To	
98	Bilhore, in the Cawnpore district,	1	0	That Season of 1828,	Hurdwar,	Allahabad,	20 rupees.
99	Poorwa,	2	0	Ditto,	....	Eastward,	50 rupees.
100	Near Kurra,	2	0	Ditto,	....	....	50 rupees.
101	Near Ahmedgunge at Menda,	2	0	Ditto,	Mirzapore,	Banda,	Clothes, valued at 500 rupees, and a pony.
102	Shewrajpore,	1	0	Ditto,	Furruckhabad,	Cawnpore,	Copper coin, valued 100 rupees.
103	Kunnooa Khaira, in the Humeerpore district,	1	0	Ditto,	Mhow,	Lucknow,	50 rupees cash, and 10 rupees worth of other property.

1828 and 1829, under the following leaders: with Thirty-two Thugs, and other Leaders.

REMARKS.

In the month of June, 1828, Pershad and Mehrban jemadars, with a gang of thirty Thugs, set out from Seetapore in Furruckhabad, on an expedition, and proceeded to Belhore in the Cawnpore district. There they found a Ganges water-carrier going from Hurdwar to Allahabad, whom they decoyed and strangled next morning at a well, into which they threw the body.

They next went to Poorwa, where they fell in with two Hindoos travelling to the eastward, whom they decoyed and took next morning, two miles out of the village, and put to death. The bodies were thrown into a well.

After this affair they proceeded to Kurrah, and there they met two Hindoos, whom they decoyed, and took with them next morning to the Ganges, where, having stopped to bathe, they seized the opportunity to put the travellers to death and committed the bodies to the stream.

They then went and rested for the day in the seraee at Ahmedgunge. There they found two travellers, one a Brahmin and the other a Bunneah, on their way from Mirzapore to Banda, whom they decoyed and took next day to Menda, where they passed the night in the seraee. Next morning early the travellers were conducted a short distance on their way and strangled, the bodies were thrown into a well.

The gang proceeded to Shewrajpore, and rested in the bazar. During the day a nephew of Khooshalee mahajun of Futteea in Furruckhabad, came to the same place with a pony laden with copper coin, which he was conveying to Cawnpore, he was persuaded to join some of the party, who pretended to be travelling in the same direction, and next morning was strangled a short distance from the village, and his body thrown into a well.

After this affair the gang returned to their homes. It has since been ascertained by a reference to the Magistrate of Cawnpore, that the body of the murdered Bunneah was discovered by the thannadars of Shewrajpore, who threw it into the Ganges—and that a fine of twenty-five rupees was imposed upon the thannadars, in consequence of their endeavoring to keep the circumstance a secret.

About the month of April, 1828, a gang of Thugs, fifty-seven in number, assembled under Khuluk jemadar at Cherkaira in Cawnpore, and set out on an expedition. They proceeded to the river Jumna which they crossed near Calpee, and entering Bundelkhund went to Kunnooakaira in the Hameerpore district. They fell in with a Hindoo, travelling from Mhow to Lucknow, whom they decoyed and next morning put to death at a stream two miles off, and buried the body on the bank.

Report of a Thug Expedition in the years of 1827, *Dhowkul Jemadar, Bhowanee and Lalla Lochun,*

No. of List.	Names of jurisdiction of the place where the Murder was perpetrated.	No. and Sex of the Murdered		Date of the Murder.	Intended destination of the Murdered.		Supposed value of the property robbed.
		Men.	Women.		From	To	
104	Oojra, in the Jhalone State,	2	0	That season of 1828,	Saugor,	Oude,	200 rupees.
105	Kaleepaharee,	4	0	Ditto,	Ditto,	Lucknow,	150 rupees.
106	Besaynee, in the Punna State,	3	0	Ditto,	Nagpore,	Banda,	200 rupees worth of gold and 2 ponies, worth 25 rupees.
107	Shahgurh,	1	0	Ditto,	Ditto,	Byswara,	100 rupees.
108	Besaynee,	5	0	Ditto,	Dekhan,	Byswara,	14 gold mohurs and other property, 700 rupees worth.
109	Near Suttassee,	3	0	Ditto,	Nagpore,	Leonee, in the Cawnpore district,	400 rupees.

1828 *and* 1829, *under the following leaders: with Thirty-two Thugs, and other Leaders.*

REMARKS.

The gang then went to Chutterpore, where they found two spirit distillers from Saugor on their way to Oude, who were decoyed as usual, and next day conducted to Oojra in the Jhalone state where they passed the night. In the morning the travellers were taken a mile out of the village and strangled. The bodies were buried in a ravine.

They next went to Muhoba, where they decoyed four Bunneahs, travelling from Saugor to Lucknow. They set out with them next day and continued their journey till night, when they arrived near Kaleepaharee and strangled them. The bodies were buried in a field.

After this affair the Thugs went to Besaynee in the Panna state, where they found three Brinjarees from Nagpore on their way to Banda, whom they persuaded to travel in their company, and next morning put to death in the usual manner. The bodies were buried in a ravine.

The gang then went and rested at Shahgur. The next day a Brahmin traveller on his way from Nagpore to Byswara, arrived at the same place, but continued his journey onwards. Seven Thugs were immediately sent in pursuit of him, and they managed to put him to death at a thickly wooded stream only two or three miles off. The body was thrown into the water, and the murdering party returned to Shahgurh by midday.

The next morning the gang took the road to Saugor, and on the way fell in with a Havildar and four Sepahees, Hindoos by caste, who had come from the Dekhan intending to go to Byswara. The Thugs decoyed them, and turned back in their company, taking them to Besaynee, where they slept, and next morning the travellers were strangled and their bodies buried in a water course a couple of miles off.

After this they went to Chutterpore, where Khuluk jemadar discovered and decoyed three Brahmins from Nagpore, who were travelling to Seonee, in the Cawnpore district. At the same time Bhowanee jemadar fell in with seven other travellers, a Havildar and six Sepahees from Baitool, who intended to proceed to Boicoonta in Cawnpore, who were persuaded to join the gang. Next morning Khuluk jemadar and eight Thugs, set out with the three Brahmin travellers in company, and having previously made arrangements for seven more Thugs to overtake him on the way, they went to Mujhgaon and rested for the night, but the seven Thugs having missed the way, did not join. Accordingly Khuluk jemadar carried the travellers to Suttasee, where the seven men overtook him. In the morning the three Brahmins were put to death at a streamlet, a mile from the village, and their bodies buried in the bank.

Report of a Thug Expedition in the years of 1827, *Dhowkul Jemadar, Bhowanee and Lalla Lochun,*

No. of List.	Names of jurisdiction of the place where the Murder was perpetrated.	No. and Sex of the Murdered.		Date of the Murder.	Intended destination of the Murdered.		Supposed value of the property robbed.
		Men.	Women.		From	To	
110	Jaitpore,	7	0	That Season of 1828,	Chutter-pore,	Towards Jaitpore,	500 rupees.
111	Babawallah, near Keitah,	4	0	Ditto,	Nagpore,	Delhie,	400 rupees.
112	Suttassee, in Jaitpore,	2	1	Ditto,	Saugor,	Cawn-pore,	100 rupees.
113	Momina,	4	0	Ditto,	Baroda,	Ditto,	500 rupees.

1828 and 1829, under the following leaders: with Thirty-two Thugs, and other Leaders.

REMARKS.

The remainder of the Thugs who has the seven travellers with them, left Chutterpore the same morning, and proceeded towards Jaitpore, when they were within a couple of miles of that town, the gang was joined by Peer Mahomed (Approver) with eight Thugs, who had recently left their homes; they all went together to Jaitpore and passed the night there. In the morning early the travellers were taken out about three miles and strangled. The bodies were concealed in a ravine, but were subsequently discovered by the inhabitants and burnt by order of the Rajah of Jaitpore. Evidence of the fact of murder has been procured in the two last cases, and the Thugs concerned have been tried in the Agent's Court at Jubulpore.

After this affair the gang went to Keitah, and rejoined Khuluk jemadar and the fifteen Thugs, who murdered the three Brahmins. At that place Peer Mahomed and his eight followers again left the party and proceeded home. At Keitah the Thugs found four Khuttrees travelling from Nagpore to Delhi, whom they induced to join their company and took to the village of Babawalla, where they slept, and next morning the travellers were put to death at a stream two miles off. The bodies were buried in the stream.

The gang then went to Rât, where they found a gang under Dibba Bukhal jemadar, and other leaders, sixty-seven in number, who were going towards the Dekhan on an expedition. After an interchange of enquiries, Khuluk jemadar and his gang went homewards and arrived there without perpetrating any other murders.

Dibba Bukhal jemadar, above alluded to, left his home in Jhalone, and assembled a gang of seven Thugs at Kunnoa Kaira in Humeerpore, in the month of April 1828 at the latter place they found Bichoo, Mandhata, and Nowul jemadars with a gang of sixty Thugs, whom they joined and proceeded to Rât, where they met Khuluk jemadar's gang—and after parting with them, went on to Chutterpore—meeting with no success on their route, they took a different direction, and visited Jaitpore, where they fell in with three travellers, namely, a sepahee, a tailor, and his wife, all Hindoos, on their way from Saugor to Cawnpore. They decoyed them as usual, and conducted them to Suttasee, where they passed the night, and next morning early the travellers were put to death, some distance from the village, and their bodies buried in a water course.

They next went to Burwara, where they met four travellers, a subadar and three sepahees, going on leave from Boroda to Cawnpore, whom they persuaded to join their party and took on to Kelinga and slept there. Next day they all went to Momina, passed the night there, and early next morning the travellers were strangled a mile or two from the village, and their bodies

Report of a Thug Expedition in the years of 1827, *Dhowkul Jemadar, Bhowanee and Lalla Lochun,*

No. of List.	Names of jurisdiction of the place where the Murder was perpetrated.	No. and Sex of the Murdered.		Date of the Murder.	Intended destination of the Murdered.		Supposed value of the property robbed.
		Men.	Women.		From	To	
114	Tukkeah, in Oude state,	1	0	That Season of 1828,	Westward,	Jounpore,	100 rupees.
115	Near Hussungunge,	2	0	Ditto,	....	....	90 rupees.
116	Summaira,	2	0	Ditto,	Dekhan,	Gorukpore,	50 rupees and a poney.
117	Baita,	1	0	Ditto,	Meerut,	Sooltanpore,	50 rupees.
118	Kurrya,	1	0	Ditto,	Dekhan,	....	35 rupees.

1828 *and* 1829, *under the following leaders: with Thirty-two Thugs, and other Leaders.*

REMARKS.

carried to a ravine for the purpose of being buried, when the Thugs were scared a way by the approach of a party travelling that way.

They all fled to Gooroo ka Etaway in Calpee, where they made a division of their body, and then went to their homes. The bodies murdered in the last case were discovered by the passengers, who pointed them out to the police authorities, and authentic information of the facts detailed by the approvers, having been obtained from the Magistrate of Humeerpore, a number of the Thugs engaged in the murder were committed to trial at Saugor in 1834.

In the month of April or May 1828, Kuseree subadar, having obtained his release from jail at Mynpooree, (where it has before been related that he was confined on suspicion of being concerned in the Sersagunge murder,) joined Runnooa moonshee, and four other Thugs at the village of Bhynska Poorwa in Oude, and set out on an expedition. They went to Tukkeah in the Oude state, and fell in with a Hindoo traveller from the westward going to Jounpore, whom they decoyed and next morning put to death a couple of miles from the village, throwing his body into a well.

They then proceeded onwards to Hussungunge, where they found two Hindoos travelling in the same direction with themselves, whom they took next morning to a stream two miles off and strangled. The bodies were thrown into the water.

After this affair the gang went to Summaira, where they fell in with two travellers by caste Hindoos, who came from the Dekhan intending to go to Gorukpore. They had a pony with them. As usual the travellers were decoyed and next morning put to death at a sheet of water two miles off, and the bodies thrown into it.

The gang next proceeded to Baita, where they decoyed a Hindoo travelling from Meerut to Sultanpore, who set out with them next morning and was put to death at a well some distance off, and threw his body into it.

The next day's stage was Kutgurh, on arriving at which place the Thugs met another gang of Jumaldhees, consisting of twenty men under Futteh and Kooshal jemadars. The proceedings of these men will be found in the Narratives of the Oude gangs, compiled by Captain Paton.

The united gangs went to Kurrea, where they passed the night. They found there a Hindoo who had come from the Dekhan, whom they decoyed, and took next morning a mile out of the village and strangled. The body was thrown into a well.

Report of a Thug Expedition in the years of 1827, *Dhowkul Jemadar, Bhowanee and Lalla Lochun,*

No. of List.	Names of jurisdiction of the place where the Murder was perpetrated.	No. and Sex of the Murdered.		Date of the Murder.	Intended destination of the Murdered.		Supposed value of the property robbed.
		Men.	Women.		From	To	
119	Salone,	5	0	That season of 1828,	Meerut,	Eastward,	140 rupees in cash and property.
120	Bullagaon,	4	0	Ditto,	....	....	130 rupees.
121	Tukkeah, in the Oude state,	5	0	Ditto,	Muttra,	Lucknow,	100 rupees.
122	Bheestee,	2	0	Ditto,	Gwalior,	Sooltanpore,	100 rupees.
123	Bholla and Bulla,	4	0	Ditto,	....	....	270 rupees.
124	Dhoondapore, in Bareilly,	5	0	Ditto,	Dekhan,	Northward,	300 rupees.

1828 and 1829, under the following leaders: with Thirty-two Thugs, and other Leaders.

REMARKS.

They proceeded to Salone and fell in with five Hindoos, travelling from Meerut to the eastward, whom they inveigled and put to death next morning a short distance from the village. The body was thrown into a well.

After this affair the gang went to Bullagaon, and there Runnooa moonshee decoyed four travellers, by caste Hindoos, who were taken out next morning and strangled in a plain two miles off. The bodies were thrown into a well. After this the gang broke up, and the Thugs proceeded to their respective homes.

In the month of October, 1828, Keseree subadar, Runnooa moonshee, and sixteen Thugs assembled at Bhyska Poorwa, and looked out for the usual omens taken previous to setting out on an expedition. The result was that Keseeree determined on remaining at home for ten days, and then following the gang, who at once set out and went to Bhanger Mhow in Oude, where they joined another gang of sixteen Jumaldhee Thugs, under Mehrban jemadar, and other leaders. The party amounted altogether to thirty-one Thugs, and they went to Tukkea where they fell in with five Hindoos travelling from Muttra to Lucknow, who were decoyed by Runnooa moonshee, and accommodated near the gang during the night. Next morning early they were put to death, a short distance on the road to Lucknow, and their bodies thrown into a well.

After this affair the gang went to Bheestee, where they encamped in a grove of Tamarind trees. Two Hindoos from Gwalior, on their way to Sultanpore, came up and were invited by the Thugs to take up their quarters there. They consented, and having continued their journey next morning in company with the gang, were put to death at a garden two miles off. The bodies were thrown into a well.

They proceeded onwards, and arriving between the two villages of Bhala and Bulla, they overtook four travellers by caste Kuhars, who were decoyed and taken onwards to the last named village. Night coming on, the Thugs took advantage of the darkness to strangle the travellers, and threw their bodies into a well.

The Thugs slept at Bhullagaon, where they were overtaken and joined by Keseeree subadar. Next morning they proceeded towards Jehanabad near Bareilly, near which about midday they fell in with five Hindoos from the Dekhan travelling northward, whom they persuaded to accompany them to Dhondapore, where they all passed the night. Next morning the travellers were put to death a mile or two from the village, and their bodies thrown into a well.

Report of a Thug Expedition in the years of 1827,
Dhowkul Jemadar, Bhowanee and Lalla Lochun,

No. of List.	Names of jurisdiction of the place where the Murder was perpetrated.	No. and Sex of the Murdered.		Date of the Murder.	Intended destination of the Murdered.		Supposed value of the property robbed.
		Men.	Women.		From	To	
125	Surrufraznugger,	2	0	That Season of 1828,	....	Jounpore,	25 rupees.
126	Futtehgunge,	1	0	Ditto,	Cawnpore,	Lucknow,	80 rupees.
127	Tukkeah, in Oude,	2	0	Ditto,	....	Furruckhabad,	55 rupees.
128	Moorutgunge,	2	0	Ditto,	Eastward,	Meerut,	12 rupees in cash, kinkhabs, satin, chintz, &c. worth 3,000 rupees.
129	Rooma, in Cawnpore,	1	0	Ditto,	Kurnal,	Benares,	25 rupees.
130	Near Chekutea,	2	0	Ditto,	Cawnpore,	Chuktea,	50 rupees.

1828 *and* 1829,* *under the following leaders: with Thirty-two Thugs, and other Leaders.*

REMARKS.

After this affair the gang of Jumaldhee Thugs separated from the others and took another direction. The party led by Keseeree subadar proceeded to Surufraznuggur, where they decoyed two travellers, by caste Hindoos, on their way to Jounpore, and slept there. In the morning the travellers were strangled as usual a short distance off, and their bodies thrown into a well.

They then went to Futtehgunge and found in the bazar a Hindoo who had come from Cawnpore intending to go to Lucknow. He was decoyed and taken out next morning two miles on his way and strangled. His body was thrown into a well.

The gang then turned back and went to Tukkeah, where they fell in with two Hindoo travellers on their way to Furruckhabad, who were decoyed by Keseeree subadar and accommodated near him in the bazar. Next morning they were put to death near a well outside the village, into which their remains were thrown. After this affair the Thugs returned to their respective homes.

In the month of October 1828, Ramdeen and Rambuksh jemadars, with a gang of twelve Thugs, left the village of Dhoorjunapore in Furruckhabad, on an expedition, and proceeded to Huthgaon. They were joined by Lalla Lochun jemadar and twelve more Thugs. They proceeded onwards as far as Mookhtee-ka-Poorwa in Allahabad, but without meeting with any success in their search after victims. They therfore turned back and went to Bohgaon, four miles from the last named place. While resting in a garden they heard two boys singing and at that moment two men carrying boxes on their heads came up from an easterly direction. They addressed them and found they were on their way to Meerut and were induced to accompany the Thugs to Mooradgunge, where they all rested in the seraee, and next morning the travellers were strangled outside of the village and their bodies thrown into a well. Having obtained a rich booty, the gang forthwith proceeded homewards where they arrived without committing any other murder.

About a month or six weeks afterwards in the year 1828 Deveedeen, Purshad and other leaders set out from Doorjunapore with nineteen Thugs and went to Rooma in the Cawnpore zillah. At that place they decoyed a Hindoo traveller from Kurnal on his way to Benares and put him to death next morning in a mangoe grove outside of the village. The body was thrown into a well.

They then proceeded onwards to Chekutea and were joined by Lalla Lochun jemadar and five Thugs who increased their numbers to twenty-four. Soon afterwards two travellers, by caste Hindoos, from Cawnpore, arrived at the same place and rested for the day in the bazar near the Thugs. They were

Report of a Thug Expedition in the years of 1827, *Dhowkul Jemadar, Bhowanee and Lalla Lochun,*

No. of List.	Names of jurisdiction of the place where the Murder was perpetrated.	No. and Sex of the Murdered.		Date of the Murder.	Intended destination of the Murdered.		Supposed value of the property robbed.
		Men.	Women.		From	To	
131	Mullwah, in Futtehpore,	2	0	That Season of 1828,	....	....	40 rupees.
132	Mainda-ka-seraee, in Futtehpore,	1	0	Ditto,	Benares,	Agra,	30 rupees.
133	Kurrah,	3	0	Ditto,	....	Benares,	175 rupees.
134	Chipolah, in Futtehpore,	1	0	Ditto,	....	Bhyswara,	400 rupees.
135	Huthgaon,	3	0	Ditto,	....	Meerut,	3 boxes containing books and pistols.

1828 and 1829, under the following leaders: with Thirty-two Thugs, and other Leaders.

REMARKS.

decoyed and put to death next morning a short distance from the village. The bodies were thrown into a well.

After the murder the gang went to Mallooa in Futtehpore, and there they fell in with two travellers, by caste Hindoos, who were decoyed by Lalla Lochun jemadar, and next morning were strangled at a well on the road side, into which the bodies were thrown.

They continued their journey and reached Mainda-ka-seraee in Futtehpore.

They found at that place a Musulman who had come from Benares intending to go to Agra. He was decoyed, and early the next morning was taken out and put to death as usual. The body was thrown into a well.

The gang next reached Kurrah where they rested in the seraee. They there fell in with three Hindoos travelling to Benares who were decoyed, and next morning were escorted to the banks of the Jumna, where they were strangled and their bodies thrown into the stream.

They then went to Ahmedgunge and accommodated themselves in the seraee. During the day a gang of fifteen Thugs under Cheyne, Newul and Dhunna jemadars came to the same place, having only just set out on an expedition in which they had as yet met with no success. The gangs initiated them and agreed to proceed onwards together. Soon afterwards a subadar mounted on a large horse arrived at the seraee, and having represented himself to be on the way to Bhyswarah, he was invited by Deveedeen jemadar to take up his quarters near him. He consented, and next morning pursued his journey accompanied by Deveedeen and ten Thugs, who went with him to Chipola in Futtehpore. They passed the night there, and next morning the subadar was strangled outside the village. The body was thrown into a well.

The rest of the gang having left Ahmedgunge, went to the Chowkee at Appohee were they sat down. Soon afterwards three porters carrying boxes on their heads came up to the spot. The Thugs enquired who they were, and ascertained that they were going to Meerut. They proposed that they should travel together and all went the same day to Huthgaon, where they passed the night. Next morning the three travellers were conducted to a tank some distance off, where they were strangled and the bodies thrown into the water. On opening the packages they were found to contain articles entirely of European consumption and from the dread of detection, were thrown by the Thugs into a well not far off. A portion of this property was found and recovered by the exertions of Mr. Wilson in the year 1833.

Report of a Thug Expedition in the years of 1827, *Dhowkul Jemadar, Bhowanee and Lalla Lochun,*

No. of List.	Names of jurisdiction of the place where the Murder was perpetrated.	No. and Sex of the Murdered.		Date of the Murder.	Intended destination of the Murdered.		Supposed value of the property robbed.
		Men.	Women.		From	To	
136	Echun River, near Bilhoree,	1	0	That Season of 1828,	....	....	30 rupees.
137	Near Huthgaon,	4	0	Ditto,	....	....	80 gold mohurs cash and ornaments 400 rupees; other articles worth 100 rupees, a horse valued 200 rupees.
138	Hussungunge,	2	0	That Season of 1829,	....	Lucknow,	60 rupees cash, 40 rupees worth of property.
139	Near Jullalabad,	4	0	Ditto,	Nusseerabad,	Sultanpore,	400 rupees.

1828 and 1829, under the following leaders: with Thirty-two Thugs, and other Leaders.

REMARKS.

After this murder the gang went to Belunda, where they were joined by the Thugs, who had put the subadar to death, as before described. They all proceeded to the town Bilhore, and met a Hindoo traveller, whom they decoyed and took with them to pass the day in the caravansera. Next morning he was conducted to the banks of the Echun river and strangled. The body was thrown into the stream. They then went to the chowkee at Bugotee, and sat down to smoke. The Dâk runners stationed there seeing them, remarked that the Thugs looked like persons who committed murder, in consequence of which the gang determined to separate and proceeded to their respective homes.

In the month of December 1828, Rambuksh and Makhun jemadars assembled eleven Thugs at Rujahee Mhow in the Furruckhabad district, and set out on an expedition. They proceeded as far as the chowkee at Apohee in Futtehpore in search of victims, but failed to discover a single one. They accordingly determined to turn back, and having retraced their steps for the distance of two miles they halted, and Rambuksh jemadar spread a carpet for the purpose of reposing on it. At this moment a traveller, Hindoo by caste, and a spirit distiller by trade, came up to the spot, mounted on horseback, and attended by three other persons: namely, a Mahomedan, a saece of low caste, and a Brahmin, and without stopping passed on towards Cawnpore. Heera, one of the Thugs, immediately proposed that the party should be put to death, but Rambuksh jemadar remarked that mounted as the head man of the party was this would be a difficult matter. After some discussion it was determined that the gang should follow on the track of the travellers and see what could be done. They therefore bound up their loins and hastened on to Chowbee-ka-seraee, where the travellers halted for the night. Tho Thugs ingratiated themselves with the mounted traveller, and he and his companions were induced to prosecute their journey in company with the gang. They all went to Huthgaon and slept there, and early next morning having proceeded a couple of miles out of the village the travellers were strangled, and their bodies thrown into a well. Having obtained valuable booty the gang returned home without committing any other murder.

In the beginning of the year 1829, Keseeree subadar and Runnooa moonshee assembled a gang of sixteen Thugs at Bhyska Poonoa in Oude, and determined upon an expedition. They first proceeded to Hussungunge, and there they fell in with two Hindoos travelling to Lucknow, who were decoyed, and put to death next morning at a stream, into which the bodies were thrown.

They then went to Baita and there met Futteh and Ruhman jemadars and a gang of fifteen Thugs, whom they joined and entered into conversation with, while thus engaged five Sepahees, by caste Hindoos, who had come from Nusserabad, intending to go to Sultanpore, arrived at the same place. They were

Report of a Thug Expedition in the years of 1827, *Dhowkul Jemadar, Bhowanee and Lalla Lochun,*

No. of List.	Names of jurisdiction of the place where the Murder was perpetrated.	No. and Sex of the Murdered.		Date of the Murder.	Intended destination of the Murdered.		Supposed value of the property robbed.
		Men.	Women.		From	To	
140	Near Bunter,	1	0	That Season of 1829,	South,	Sooltanpore,	20 rupees.
141	Mullaira,	4	0	Ditto,	Saugor,	Bithoor,	100 rupees.

1828 and 1829, under the following leaders: with Thirty-two Thugs, and other Leaders.

REMARKS.

addressed by Keseeree subadar and induced to join the Thugs, who forthwith arose and pursued the road which the travellers intended to travel. They all went and slept at Jullalabad, and next morning getting up very early, they travelled a couple of miles and then sat down. Five Thugs had previously been appointed to perform the office of stranglers, and the signal for executing their purpose was given by one of the jemadars. It so happened that one of the travellers had at the very moment stepped aside to answer the calls of nature, unobserved by the jemadar, so that only four of the number were strangled. The intended strangler of the fifth unaccountably held his tongue, and did not give notice to the gang that his victim had got out of the way. The fortunate individual who thus escaped death, was a witness of the fate of his companions and having concealed himself in the underwood, crept stealthily away: when the bodies were taken up as usual by the Thugs for the purpose of disposing of them, they were found to be only four in number. Alarmed at this the Thugs threw two of them into a well. The third, which showed some remains of life, was cut to pieces with their swords;—but being terrified at the sound of approaching cart wheels, the fourth body was abandoned by the way side. The gang decamped with 400 rupees in ready money found on the persons of the travellers, but did not carry away their other property. The sepahee who escaped proceeded to the nearest authorities of the Oude Government, and made a statement of the circumstances that had occurred. The bodies were discovered by them and proceedings instituted against the zumeendars of the village, where the murder had been perpetrated—but without success. Several years afterwards, (in 1835,) the particulars of the case were deposed to by approvers before Captain Paton at Lucknow, and search was made for the sepahee, who had escaped from the hands of the Thugs. He was discovered to be a havildar in the —— Regiment, and having repaired to Lucknow, corroborated by his evidence the statements of the approvers, and recognized several articles that had been plundered by them on that occasion referred to.

After this murder the gang of Jumaldhee left Keseeree subadar's party and proceeded to their homes. The Lodhee Thugs fled to Bunter, and rested there. A Hindoo traveller from the south on his way to Sultanpore, came to the same place and was decoyed by the Thugs, who put him to death next morning two miles from the village, and threw his body into a well. Having completed this murder the gang returned home.

About the end of the month of February 1829, Cheyne jemadar and Bukshee jemadar, with twenty Thugs, set out from Behareepore in Bela upon an expedition in search of adventures. They proceeded by Calpee, where they crossed the Jumna, to Chitterkote in Bundelkhund; while resting there they discovered two Maharattas travelling from Saugor to Bittoor, whom they

Report of a Thug Expedition in the years of 1827, *Dhowkul Jemadar, Bhowanee and Lalla Lochun,*

No. of List.	Names of jurisdiction of the place where the Murder was perpetrated.	No. and Sex of the Murdered		Date of the Murder.	Intended destination of the Murdered.		Supposed value of the property robbed.
		Men.	Women.		From	To	
142	Oojra,	2	0	That season of 1829,	Sreenuggur,	Chuttepore,	2000 rupees.
143	Kukrettee, in the Punna Principality,	2	0	Ditto,	Jubulpore,	Cawnpore,	150 rupees.
144	Punna,	3	0	Ditto,	Jubulpore,	Cawnpore,	300 rupees.
145	Logassee,	1	0	Ditto,	Saugor,	Oude,	20 rupees.
146	Near Jaitpore,	3	0	Ditto,	Mhow,	Dooab,	30 tolas of gold, 125 rupees.

1828 *and* 1829, *under the following leaders: with Thirty-two Thugs, and other Leaders.*

REMARKS.

decoyed and accompanied to Mallaira. They slept there and next morning strangled the travellers at a stream a mile from the village, and buried their bodies.

They then went to Mohoba, and sleeping there, returned to Chutturpore, and thence proceeded to Oojra and sat down to rest themselves. It was mid-day when two treasure carriers, by caste Hindoos, who came from Sreenagger, and were on their way to Chutterpore, passed by. The Thugs followed quickly after them and, arriving at a thickly wooded spot about two miles off, they fell on them and put them to death. The bodies were thrown into a ravine in the jungle.

The gang then went towards Jaitpore, and when they arrived within a few miles of that place, they met Bhowanee, Khulluk and Dhowkul jemadars with a gang of Thugs, who had recently set out on an expedition, and having treated them to a refreshment of sweetmeats, they took leave of them and proceeded to their homes.

About the end of the month of March 1829, Khulluk jemadar and Dhowkul jemadar led out a gang of thirty-two Thugs from Maika-ka-Poorwa in Furruckhabad, and took the road to the South They crossed the Jumna river at Calpee, and reached Kukrettee in the Punna principality, without perpetrating any murder. There they found two Hindoo chuprassees, who had come from Jubulpore on their way to Cawnpore, whom they decoyed and taking with them next morning, put to death a mile or two from the village and buried the bodies.

The gang then proceeded to Punna. At that place they discovered three travellers, by caste Hindoos, who had come from Jubulpore, intending to go to Cawnpore, whom they decoyed, next morning early the Thugs accompanied the travellers a distance of two miles on their way, and, having strangled them, buried the bodies in a ravine.

Having completed the murder they went towards Logassee near Jaitpore, and fell in with Cheyne and Bukshee jemadars, (whose proceedings have been already detailed) who treated them to sweetmeats, and taking leave of them proceeded to their homes. The gang proceeded to Logassee and passed the night there. A Hindoo traveller from Saugor, on his way to the Oude territory, was resting there. He was decoyed by the Thugs, who put him to death next morning a short distance from the village and buried his body.

They next proceeded to Jaitpore, and found there a gang of fifty Sindouse Thugs under Bhola bunneeah, and Sheikh Enayut jemadars. This gang had

Report of a Thug Expedition in the years of 1827, *Dhowkul Jemadar, Bhowanee and Lalla Lochun,*

No. of List.	Names of jurisdiction of the place where the Murder was perpetrated.	No. and Sex of the Murdered.		Date of the Murder.	Intended destination of the Murdered.		Supposed value of the property robbed.
		Men.	Women.		From	To	
147	Suttassee,	3	0	That Season of 1829,	Seronge,	Cawnpore,	500 rupees.
148	Tukeeah,	5	0	13th March, 1829.	....	....	250 rupees.
149	Jehanabad,	2	0	March, 1829.	Bhurtpore,	Benares,	50 rupees.

1828 *and* 1829, *under the following leaders: with Thirty-two Thugs, and other Leaders.*

REMARKS.

in their company three sepahees from Mhow, going to the Dooab, who had been invited to join the Thugs and partake of some refreshment that had been prepared for them. Khuluk jemadar's gang joined the party, and next morning the sepahees were taken out and strangled a short distance from the village. The bodies were buried.

The entire gangs then went to Suttassee, and fell in with three sepahees who had come from Seronge on their way to Cawnpore, whom they decoyed, and took next morning to a water-course about three miles off, and strangled. The bodies were buried, and were afterwards discovered by the local authorities, a copy of whose proceedings in the case has been forwarded to Jubulpore. After this affair the gang broke up and proceeded homewards.

N. B. The Sindouse Thugs have in their narratives stated that the Lodhees assisted at the murder of a moonshee and four followers at Jhoojar Ghat, but the Lodhees say, though they knew of the affair and joined the Sindousees immediately afterwards, they did not participate.

About the same time that the above mentioned party set out, Rambuksh jemadar assembled a gang of twenty-five Thugs at Rujaee Mhow in Furruckhabad, and set out on an expedition. They first proceeded to the Ganges, and crossing it at Nana Mhow, arrived at Bhanger Mhow. They next went towards Tukeeah, and on the way overtook two travellers by caste Hindoos, whom they decoyed and took with them to that village. On arriving there they found a party of ten Jumaldehee Thugs resting at that place, who were invited to join them. Soon afterwards Lalla Lochun jemadar, with a gang of twenty-five Thugs, came up with three Hindoo travellers in their company, and also rested at Tukeeah. It was determined that all should unite together, and next morning the five travellers were put to death a short distance from the village, and their bodies thrown into a well. This affair has been investigated by Capt. Paton, and satisfactory proof sent to Jubulpore of the discovery of the murdered remains.

The united gangs proceeded to Meeahgunge—and after that returned home without committing any murders on the way.

In the month of March, 1829, Sumadhan jemadar and Cheyne jemadar, with a gang of eight Thugs, left Amolee in the Cawnpore zillah, and set out on an expedition. They first proceeded to Ghatumpore, and having slept there set out again next morning, when they had gone about six miles they overtook two travellers by caste Kuhars, who had come from Bhurt ore intending to go to Benares. They entered into conversation with them, and persuaded them to accompany them to Jehanabad, where they passed the night, and next morning put them to death at a stream not far from the town, and buried the bodies.

Report of a Thug Expedition in the years of 1827,
Dhowkul Jemadar, Bhowanee and Lalla Lochun,

No. of List.	Names of jurisdiction of the place where the Murder was perpetrated.	No. and Sex of the Murdered.		Date of the Murder.	Intended destination of the Murdered.		Supposed value of the property robbed.
		Men.	Women.		From	To	
150	Near Belunda,	1	0	March, 1829,	Lahore,	Benares,	80 rupees.
151	Kurree,	2	0	Ditto,	Delhi,	Buxar,	100 rupees.
152	Chikuttea, in Cawnpore,	1	0	Ditto,	....	Lucknow,	40 rupees.
153	Near Jhinjana,	3	0	June, 1829,	Kurnal,	Oude,	50 rupees and a pony.
154	Muchunda,	5	0	Ditto,	Lahore,	Eastward,	200 rupees, 25 rupees of property.
155	Koolchutr,	2	0	1829,	....	....	50 rupees in cash, a pony, a silver armlet worth 25 rupees, a

1828 *and* 1829, *under the following leaders: with Thirty-two Thugs, and other Leaders.*

REMARKS.

The gang then went to Futtehpore, and there fell in with a Hindoo from Lahore, going on a pilgrimage to Benares, whom they decoyed, and next morning conducted half way towards Belunda, where they put him to death at a stream. The body was buried.

They next proceeded to Kurree, and decoyed two Hindoo travellers from Delhi on their way to Buxar; and having passed the night there, they strangled their victims next morning on the banks of the Ganges, and threw their bodies into the water.

After this affair the gang went to Shahzadpore, and falling under the suspicion of the Police thanadar, who showed a disposition to search them, they fled from thence, and did not stop till they arrived at Chikuttea in Cawnpore. They rested on the bank of the tank, and were shortly afterwards joined by a Kuhar, who represented himself to be on the way to Lucknow, and agreed to travel in their company. He was strangled next morning a mile from the village, and his body thrown into a well. The gang now determined on returning home, and arrived there without committing any other murder.

In the month of June 1829, Runnooa moonshee, Achul and Bukshee jemadars, with a gang of thirty Thugs, left Behareepore on an expedition—and proceeded by stages to Jhinjana. Having left that place behind them a distance of two miles towards Bedolee, they lay down at a well on the way side. Soon afterwards three Hindoo travellers from Kurnal, on their way to Oude, came up to the same spot. They were addressed by one of the jemadars, and having agreed to accompany him, the gang turned back and passing through Jhinjana went to a village four miles beyond it, where they all rested for the night, next morning early the travellers were taken out a distance of one mile and put to death at a well into which their bodies were thrown. The remains of the bodies have since been discovered at the spot denoted by the approvers.

The gang then passed through Bidole and Kurnal, and arrived at Umbala, where they rested on the bank of the tank close to a well. They there decoyed five Hindoos travelling from Lahore to the eastward, whom they took next day to Muchunda. They slept there, and next morning strangled the travellers four miles on their way and buried the bodies in a ravine.

The Thugs then proceeded to Shahabad, and having passed the night there went to a village about ten miles off where they rested in a building. In the evening two travellers, by caste Mussulmans, arrived at the same place. They had with them a camel with a young one, and a pony. They were decoyed and next morning accompanied the Thugs two miles towards Koolchutr, where they were induced to sit down and were strangled. The bodies were

Report of a Thug Expedition in the years of 1827, *Dhowkul Jemadar, Bhowanee and Lalla Lochun,*

No. of List.	Names of jurisdiction of the place where the Murder was perpetrated.	No. and Sex of the Murdered.		Date of the Murder.	Intended destination of the Murdered.		Supposed value of the property robbed.
		Men.	Women.		From	To	
							camel and a young one, all worth 500 rupees.
156	Near Chanta,	1	0	That Season of 1829,	Delhi,	....	20 rupees.
157	Bulupgurh,	3	0	Ditto,	Lahore,	Bundelkhund,	50 rupees and a sword.
158	Furrukhnuggur,	2	0	Ditto,	Dekhan,	Punjab,	12 rupees.
159	Near Paniput,	2	0	Ditto,	Benares,	Goolchutr,	Gold and ornaments worth 600 rupees.
160	Poorwah, in Cawnpore,	1	0	July, 1829,	Delhi,	Allahabad,	60 rupees.

1828 and 1829, under the following leaders: with Thirty-two Thugs, and other Leaders.

REMARKS.

thrown into a tank. The camel and young one were taken to the residence of the Thugs by Dhunna and Manahata (approvers) with ten Thugs, and the rest of the gang pursued their way to Delhi, and thence took the road to Hansi. Meeting with no success they turned back from Hansi, and revisited Delhi. They then went to Muttra and Bindrabun at which place the gang rested for six days having met with no travellers.

Leaving Bindrabun, they again took the road towards Delhi. Soon afterwards they fell in with a traveller by caste a shepherd, also proceeding to the same place, and they took him to Chanta to pass the night, next morning early the shepherd was strangled about four miles from the village, and his body buried in a plain.

After this they went successively to Bhurtpore, Goverdhun, and Bullumgurh, where they rested in a seraee. Three travellers, by caste Hindoos, on their way from Lahore to Bundelkhund, had taken up their quarters in the same place, and were decoyed by Bukshee. The Thugs by cunning speeches persuaded the travellers to leave the seraee, and encamp with them at a well outside of the village. Early next morning they were taken about a mile along the road, and then put to death. The bodies were buried in a field of grain.

They proceeded on to Furrukhnuggur, where Runnooa moonshee decoyed two Gosaens from the Dekhan on their way to a shrine in the Punjab, and induced them to rest in the Bazar. Next morning they were put to death two miles from the village, and their bodies were buried.

The gang next went to Delhi, and from thence to a small village on the way to Paniput, where they rested. They there decoyed two Hindoos travelling from Benares to Goolchutr, and having conducted them out of the village, early next morning put them to death in the usual manner. The bodies were buried.

After this they all proceeded to their respective homes.

During the same year about the month of July, Hurlal and Dhowkul jemadars assembled eleven Thugs, at Ghaze-ka-Poorwa in Furruckhabad and proceeded on an expedition. They first went to Poorra in the Cawnpore district, and there they met a traveller by caste Hindoo, on his way from Delhi to Allahabad, whom they decoyed and conducted to Shewrajpore. Having slept there the traveller was next morning strangled a short distance from the village, and the body thrown into well.

Report of a Thug Expedition in the years of 1827, *Dhowkul Jemadar, Bhowanee and Lalla Lochun,*

No. of List.	Names of jurisdiction of the place where the Murder was perpetrated.	No. and Sex of the Murdered.		Date of the Murder.	Intended destination of the Murdered.		Supposed value of the property robbed.
		Men.	Women.		From	To	
161	Rooma, in the Cawnpore district,	2	0	July, 1829,	....	....	200 rupees.
162	Ahmedgunge,	2	0	Ditto,	Furruckhabad,	Byswara,	250 rupees.
163	Mhow, in Oude,	1	0	Ditto,	Benares,	Lucknow,	120 rupees.
164	Budlapore,	1	0	Ditto,	Dekhan,	Ditto,	125 rupees and a pony.
165	Gujerreea,	2	0	Ditto,	Lucknow,	Benares,	300 rupees.
166	Chowbepore, in Cawnpore,	2	0	August, 1829,	Kurnal,	Ditto,	500 rupees and a pony.
167	Chikutteea,	3	0	Ditto,	Loodhiana,	Benares,	300 rupees.

1828 and 1829, under the following leaders: with Thirty-two Thugs, and other Leaders.

REMARKS.

The gang then proceeded onwards, and on the road fell in with two Hindoo travellers, milk-men by caste, whom they persuaded to join their party and took to Rooma where they all slept. Next morning early the travellers were put to death at a well outside of the village, into which the bodies were thrown.

They next arrived at Ahmedgunge and rested in the seraee. They found there two Hindoo travellers, by caste Kayuts, from Furruckhabad on their way to Byswara, whom they decoyed, and proceeding in company with next morning they strangled them on the banks of the Ganges, and committed the bodies to the stream.

After this the gang crossed the Ganges and went to Mhow in Oude. They there succeeded in decoying a Hindoo travelling from Benares to Lucknow. He was taken out by them next morning and strangled at a well, into which the body was thrown.

Proceeding onwards the Thugs reached Budlapore, and accommodated themselves for the day in the seraee. They found there a sepahee, by caste a Mussulman, from the Dekhan on his way to Lucknow, and having decoyed him, put him to death next morning about two miles from the village. The body was thrown into a well.

They next arrived at Gujureea, and met at that place two Kuhars who were travelling from Lucknow to Benares, they engaged themselves to travel in company with these men, but put them to death next morning outside of the village. The bodies were thrown into a well.

The gang after this affair pursued their course to the westward and arrived at home without committing any other murder.

In August 1829, the same gang whose proceedings have been above described again assembled at Ghazie-ka-poorwa, and set out on an expedition. They first visited Chowbepore in Cawnpore, and then fell in with two travellers, one a Brahmin and the other a Rajpoot, the former being a havildar and the latter a sipahee in the regular service, who came from Kurnal intending to proceed to Benares. The travellers were as usual decoyed, and put to death next morning at a well, into which their bodies were thrown.

The gang then went on to Chikutteea, and fell in with two Hindoos (Burboonjas,) who came from Loodiana on their way to Benares, whom they persuaded to join them, and conducted next morning to a stream two miles off, where they strangled them, and threw their bodies into the water.

Report of a Thug Expedition in the years of 1827, *Dhowkul Jemadar, Bhowanee and Lalla Lochun,*

No. of List.	Names of jurisdiction of the place where the Murder was perpetrated.	No. and Sex of the Murdered.		Date of the Murder.	Intended destination of the Murdered.		Supposed value of the property robbed.
		Men.	Women.		From	To	
168	Shahzadpore, in Allahabad,	2	0	That Season of 1829,	Muttra,	Jounpore,	200 rupees cash, 50 rupees property.
169	Ahmedgunge,	2	0	Ditto,	Calcutta,	Muttra,	300 rupees cash, 50 rupees of property.
170	Belunda, in Futtehpore,	1	0	Ditto,	Mirzapore,	Etawah,	100 rupees.
171	Bazar Mhow,	2	0	October, 1829,	....	Bareilly,	100 rupees.
172	Tukeea,	4	0	Ditto,	....	Sultanpore,	100 rupees.
173	Meeahgunge,	2	0	Ditto,	....	....	100 rupees.
174	Hussungunge,	3	0	Ditto,	....	Lucknow,	150 rupees.

1828 and 1829, under the following leaders: with Thirty-two Thugs, and other Leaders.

REMARKS.

They proceeded onwards and arrived at Ahmedgunge in Futtehpore. They were sitting at the chowkee there at midday, when two Hindoo travellers from Muttra on their way to Jooupore came up; and having been addressed by the Thugs, were persuaded to pursue their journey in their company. They went that afternoon to Shazadpore in Allahabad, and slept there, and next morning early the travellers were put to death on the banks of the Ganges. The bodies were thrown into the river.

The gang then turned back and went to Ahmedgunge again. There they found two Brahmins, who had come from Calcutta on their way to Muttra, who were decoyed by Hurlal jemadar, and having been taken out next morning a distance of two miles, were strangled as usual, and their bodies thrown into a well.

They next proceeded as far as Belunda in Futtehpore, and there decoyed a Hindoo traveller on his way from Mirzapore to Etawah. Having passed the night together at that place, the traveller was next morning put to death at a well some distance from the village, and his body was thrown into the water. Having completed this murder, the Thugs returned to their respective homes.

In the month of October 1829, Keseeree subadar collected together fifteen Thugs at Bhyske Poorwa in Oude, and set out on an expedition. They first proceeded to Bagur Mhow, where their numbers were increased to twenty-five by the junction of another gang under Futteh jemadar. During the day that they remained at the last named place, the Thugs discovered two travellers by caste Mussulmans, who were proceeding to Bareilly, whom they invited to join them, they consented, and having set out next morning early, the travellers were put to death a few miles from the village, and their bodies thrown into a well.

The gang went on to Tukeeah, where they found four Hindoo travellers, who intended to go to Sooltanpore. Runnooa moonshee decoyed them, and the Thugs having taken them a short distance out of the village next morning, strangled them, and threw their bodies into a well.

Proceeding onwards they arrived at Meahgunge, where they decoyed two travellers by caste Hindoos, and having taken them on next morning to a garden outside of the village, strangled them, and threw their bodies into a well.

The gang next went to Hussunge. At that place they found three Hindoos, horse keepers, who were on their way to Lucknow, and had rested there for the day. They were decoyed as usual, and escorted next morning to a stream, a few miles on their way, and having been strangled, their bodies were thrown into the water.

Report of a Thug Expedition in the years of 1827, *Dhowkul Jemadar, Bhowanee and Lalla Lochun,*

No. of List.	Names of jurisdiction of the place where the Murder was perpetrated.	No. and Sex of the Murdered.		Date of the Murder.	Intended destination of the Murdered.		Supposed value of the property robbed.
		Men.	Women.		From	To	
175	Baita,	1	0	October, 1829,	....	Sooltanpore,	25 rupees.
176	Nowguzza Peer,	2	0	That Season of 1829,	....	Meerut,	100 rupees.
177	Nuwabgunge,	2	0	Ditto,	Saugor,	Northward,	100 rupees.
178	Meeahgunge,	2	0	Ditto,	Jounpore,	Mynpoorie,	125 rupees.
179	Munna, in Hameerpore,	1	0	Ditto,	Dekhan,	Byswara,	100 rupees.
180	Oureya, in Bundelkhund,	1	0	Ditto,	Chutterpore,	Muttra,	50 rupees.
181	Umbaree, in Bhopal,	1	0	Ditto,	Indore,	Oude State,	150 rupees.

1828 and 1829, under the following leaders: with Thirty-two Thugs, and other Leaders.

REMARKS.

After this affair the Thugs went on to Baita, and fell in with a Hindoo on his way to Sooltanpore. who was persuaded to join the party, and being taken a mile out of the village next morning, was put to death and his body thrown into a well.

They went on to Gosaengunge where Keseeree subadar decoyed two travellers, by caste Hindoos, on their way to Meerut. They all slept at Gosaengunge, and morning went on to Nowguzza Peer, a couple of miles off, where the travellers were strangled and their bodies thrown into a well.

They proceeded onwards and reached Nowabgunge—at that place they found two Hindoos who had come from Saugor and were travelling northward. These men were induced to join the gang, and next morning having been taken to a well, a couple of miles out of the town, were strangled, and their bodies thrown into it.

Having completed this murder, the gang turned back and retraced their steps to Meeahgunge. There they fell in with two Hindoo travellers from Jounpore on their way to Mynpoorie, whom they decoyed and took out next morning early to a well, two miles from the village, where they induced them to sit down and then strangled them. The bodies were thrown into a well. After this murder, the gangs broke up and returned to their respective homes.

During the same month (October 1829) a gang of thirty Thugs, led by Bhowanee, Dowkul and Khuluk jemadars, assembled at Maita-ka-Poorwa in Furruckhabad, and set out in search of adventures. They proceeded to the Jumna river, which they crossed at Culpee, and arrived at Munna in Humeerpore, where resting there, they decoyed a Hindoo traveller from the Dekhun on his way to Byswara. He was taken out next morning and strangled at a distance of two miles from the village, the body was buried.

After the murder the Thugs took the road to the south again and reached Oureya in Bundelkhund. There they found a Brahmin who had come from Chutterpore, intending to go to Muttra. He was decoyed and taken next morning to a tank some distance from the village and put to death. The body was buried on the bank.

The gang proceeded onwards without perpetrating any murder, till they arrived at Bhopal. From thence they turned back, and having come to a small tank about six miles from the city, they sat down. They were soon after joined by a Hindoo who came from Indore, on his way to the Oude States, who was induced to join the party, and proceeded onwards with them all day, when it was dark, they were about two miles distant from Umbaree in Bhopal and

Report of a Thug Expedition in the years of 1827, *Dhowkul Jemadar, Bhowanee and Lalla Lochun,*

No. of List.	Names of jurisdiction of the place where the Murder was perpetrated.	No. and Sex of the Murdered.		Date of the Murder.	Intended destination of the Murdered.		Supposed value of the property robbed.
		Men.	Women.		From	To	
182	Muholee, in the Saugor district,	3	0	That Season of 1829,	Dekhan,	Toward North,	100 rupees and a mare.
183	Dulputpore, in the Saugor district,	3	0	Ditto,	Saugor,	Cawnpore,	300 rupees in cash, 50 rupees property.
184	Goolgunge,	6	0	Ditto,	Baroda,	Oude,	45 tolas of gold and 500 rupees, &c. worth 1300 rupees.

1828 *and* 1829, *under the following leaders: with Thirty-two Thugs, and other Leaders.*

REMARKS.

took advantage of the opportunity and put the traveller to death. His body was buried in a ravine.

Having passed the night at Umbarie, the gang travelled as far as Maholee in the Saugor district, where they rested for the day. Three Hindoos from the Dekhun who were going towards the north, were at the same place, and having been decoyed, were taken next morning to a water course two miles out of the village and put to death. The bodies were buried in the bed of the stream.

They next preceeded to Dulputpore in the Saugor district, and fell in with three other travellers, by cast Hindoos, on their way from Saugor to Cawnpore. They were decoyed by Khuluk jemadar, and next morniug early were strangled about two miles off to the north of the village, and their bodies concealed under a heap of stones.

After this affair the Thugs went to Soonnooa where they found six Hindoos from Baroda on their way to the Oude state. They were persuaded to join the gang, and taken successively to Soorwa and Goolgunge, at each of which places they passed a day. At the latter village another gaug of thirty-seven Sindouse Thugs under Noor Khan and Bhola Bukhal, were encamped for the day; and it was agreed by the gangs that they should prosecute the expedition in company with each other.

N. B. The nature of this affair is not among the Sindouse Expeditions.

Next morning early the travellers were aroused from sleep, and conducted to a tank about two miles off, where they were induced to sit down. They were forthwith put to death in the usual manner, and their bodies thrust into the mud of the tank.

After this murder the Sindouse Thugs quitted the party and went homewards, while the Lodhees took the road to the Dooab. The latter arrived at home without perpetrating any other murder on the way.

It has since been ascertained that the very day on which the last mentioned murder was committed, an elephant belonging to the Rajah of Cherkaree in Bundelkhund, was taken to the tank to drink. The attendant being engaged in washing the animal disturbed the dead bodies which had been thrown into the tank by the Thugs. The village anthorities having been apprized of the circumstances, caused search to be made and discovered the six corpses which were burnt by them; authentic information of the fact having been procured from the Rajah, a number of the Thugs engaged on that occasion, were brought to trial at Saugor in the year 1833.

Report of a Thug Expedition in the years of 1827, *Dhowkul Jemadar, Bhowanee and Lalla Lochun,*

No. of List.	Names of jurisdiction of the place where the Murder was perpetrated.	No. and Sex of the Murdered		Date of the Murder.	Intended destination of the Murdered.		Supposed value of the property robbed.
		Men.	Women.		From	To	
185	Near Chikutteea, in Cawnpore,	2	0	December, 1829,	Muttra,	Benares,	125 rupees.
186	Kuleanpore,	1	0	Ditto,	Agra,	Allahabad,	40 rupees, and a pony worth 10 rupees.
187	Mullooa, in Futtehpore,	2	0	Ditto,	Furruckhabad,	Mirzapore,	200 rupees.
188	Moosanuggur,	1	0	Ditto,	Eastward,	Agra,	130 rupees.
189	Chutterpore,	1	0	That season of 1829,	Saugor,	Muhaba,	15 rupees.
190	Near Punna,	1	0	Ditto,	....	Jubulpore,	60 rupees.
191	Besaynee,	5	0	Ditto,	Jubulpore,	....	600 rupees cash, 100 rupees property.

1828 *and* 1829, *under the following leaders: with Thirty-two Thugs, and other Leaders.*

REMARKS.

In the month of December 1829, Rambuksh and Pershad jemadars, with forty Thugs, assembled at Sehapore in Furruckhabad, and set out on an expedition. They reached Chikkutteah in Cawnpore, and there met two Hindoo travellers from Muttra to Benares, whom they decoyed and took with them next morning early to a well a few miles off, and strangled them. The bodies were thrown into the well.

They next proceeded to Kuleeanpore and rested in the caravansera—a Hindoo from Agra on his way to Allahabad, came there also and was decoyed by the Thugs, who took him next morning along with them, and put him to death, throwing his body into a well.

The gang went onwards and arrived at Mullooa in Futtehpore, where they fell in with two travellers, by caste Kuhars, on their way from Furruckhabad to Mirzapore. They decoyed them, and next morning put them to death at a well some distance from the village, and threw their bodies into it.

The Thugs turned back after this, and proceeded to Moosanugur, and there they found a Brahmin from the eastward on his way to Agra, him they persuaded as usual to join the gang, and taking him out next morning put him to death, and threw his body into a well.

Proceeding onwards after this murder, the gang crossed the Jumna at the Bullooa Boodha Ghat near Calpee, and reached the town of Punna, where they were joined by another party of Lodhee Thugs, thirteen in number, under Hurlal and Cheyne jemadars.

The last mentioned gang had left their homes at Behareepore in Furruckhabad, only a few days before, and having crossed the Jumna at Calpee had gone to Chutterpore. There they had been joined by a Hindoo traveller from Saugor, who intended to go to Muhaba in Jhalone, and requested permission to travel with the Thugs in that direction. The traveller was put to death next morning a short distance from Chutterpore, and his body buried in the bed of a stream, after which the Thugs went to Punna and joined the other gang.

Having united the gangs, they now amounted to seventy men, who all took the road to Jubulpore, and at the distance of a couple of miles from Punna they overtook a traveller proceeding the same way, whom they put to death on the road, and buried his body under some stones in a ravine.

They went on to Kompa, and there met Sheikh Enayut and Bhola Bukhal jemadars, with forty Sindouse Thugs, whose proceedings will be found in the

Report of a Thug Expedition in the years of 1827, *Dhowkul Jemadar, Bhowanee and Lalla Lochun,*

No. of List.	Names of jurisdiction of the place where the Murder was perpetrated.	No. and Sex of the Murdered.		Date of the Murder.	Intended destination of the Murdered.		Supposed value of the property robbed.
		Men.	Women.		From	To	
192	Pukkar, in the Punna principality,	3	0	That season of 1829,	Dekhan,	North,	200 rupees, and 2 bullocks worth 30 rupees.
193	Amood, in Humeerpore,	2	0	Ditto,	Nagpore,	Byswara,	100 rupees cash, 25 rupees of property.
194	Kunnooa Kaira,	3	0	Ditto,	Mhow,	Jounpore,	50 rupees cash, 50 rupees property.
195	Near Amerpatun,	6	0	Ditto,	Hydrabad,	Benares,	500 or 600 rupees was obtained, but much property was abandoned by the Thugs.

1828 *and* 1829, *under the following leaders: with Thirty-two Thugs, and other Leaders.*

REMARKS.

narratives of the gangs of that class. The whole agreed to prosecute their journey together, and went to Pereunea. There they decoyed five travellers, namely, one a Mahomedan horseman, and four Kullals, who came from Jubulpore and were travelling northwards, and turned back with them to Besayuee, where they all passed the night. In the morning the travellers resumed their journey, and were escorted by the Thugs to a stream thickly wooded, and about six miles off, where they were strangled by the Thugs. Their bodies were concealed under heaps of stones.

N. B. These bodies have since been disinterred, and the perpetrators of the murder brought to trial at Saugor in 1833.

After this affair the gangs went to Pukkar in the Punna principality, and found three travellers, by caste Brahmins, who came from the Dekhan and were proceeding to the north. They were decoyed, and as usual taken out next morning early to a water course, and strangled. The bodies were buried.

After the murder Hurlal jemadar and ten Thugs left the main gang and determined to return home. They went first to Amoond in Humeerpore and decoyed two Hindoos travelling from Nagpore to Byswara. They took them out next morning and strangled them at a nullah, and buried their bodies.

They next proceeded to Kunnooa Kaira, and found three travellers, by caste shepherds, on their way from Mhow to Jounpore, whom they persuaded to join them, and next morning put them to death, and buried the bodies in a ravine two miles off. After this affair they proceeded to their homes without committing any murder on the way.

The main gang left Pukkar, and in the course of two or three days arrived at Subbhagunge in Myher, where they were joined by Bheekhun Khan jemadar (now an approver) with twelve Thugs from Sindouse. In the morning the gangs were preparing to proceed onwards towards Mirzapore, and some of the Thugs had already set off, when they fell in with four travellers from Jubulpore on their way to Mirzapore. It had already been determined to put these men to death, when a guard of infantry with some suwars in the pay of the Rajah of Myher came up to the spot. This circumstance sorely perplexed the Thugs, who feared lest they should fall under the suspicion of the military party and they were moreover confounded to find their fears realized by the almost immediate arrest of Sheikh Innaeut jemadar (now an approver) by some approvers who were proceeding from Mirzapore to Jubulpore in the train of Lieutenant James Sleeman. This proved the signal for every Thug who was in the vicinity to seek safety in flight. The Sindouse Thugs, whose leader had been captured, proceeded to their homes, and the Lodhees fled to Amer-

Report of a Thug Expedition in the years of 1827, *Dhowkul Jemadar, Bhowanee and Lalla Lochun,*

No. of List.	Names of jurisdiction of the place where the Murder was perpetrated.	No. and Sex of the Murdered.		Date of the Murder.	Intended destination of the Murdered.		Supposed value of the property robbed.
		Men.	Women.		From	To	
196	Bhowungaon,	1	0	That season of 1829,	East,	Dekhan,	10 rupees.
197	Bhag Puragaon,	3	0	Ditto,	Meerut,	....	100 rupees.
198	Tiggber,	2	0	Ditto,	Rampore,	Meerut,	80 rupees cash, a mare worth 80 rupees, 36 rupees worth of ornaments.
199	Near Shahabad,	3	0	Ditto,	Loodhiana,	Eastward,	200 rupees and a horse.

1828 and 1829, under the following leaders: with Thirty-two Thugs, and other Leaders.

REMARKS.

patun, where they rested on the brink of a tank. While there they decoyed six travellers, by caste Gosaens, from Hydrabad, on their way to Benares, whom they accommodated for the night, and next morning conducted towards Myher, strangling them two miles from Amerpatun. While engaged in carrying the bodies to the place of burial it turned out that life remained in the body of one of the travellers, who managed to effect his escape from the hands of the men, who were carrying him and ran off calling out loudly for assistance. Two Thugs, Pershad and Doojjooa, pursued him, but at the moment a band of travellers were advancing from the direction of Rewah, who replied to the screaming fugitive not to be afraid, as they were coming to his assistance. The two Thugs however caught the poor wretch and despatched him before he could be rescued, and abandoning the body, escaped with the rest of the gang, who took the way home, and arrived there without perpetrating any murder on the road.

N. B. The particulars above detailed have been fully established by subsequent investigation, and the perpetrators of the murder have been brought to trial in the Agent's Court at Jubulpore.

About the time that the gang set out, whose proceedings are above detailed, that is, in the end of November, 1829, another gang of thirty-five Thugs under Runnooa moonshee, left Behareepore, and crossing the Ganges at the ghat at Nunna Mhow, proceeded to Bhanger Mhow in the Oude State. There they found seven Jumaldhee Thugs under Futteh jemadar. They all took the road to Bareilly and arrived at Bhowungaon, where they decoyed a Hindoo traveller, who came from the east and was going to Delhi. He passed the night with them, and was put to death next morning some distance from the village. The body was buried.

After this affair they proceeded onwards, and in the course of some days arrived at Bhag Puragaon in the Moradabad zillah. They fell in with three travellers, by caste Hindoos, who came from Meerut, whom they persuaded to join them. Early next morning the travellers were roused from sleep and being taken to the banks of a stream, were strangled, and their bodies buried on the bank.

They next went to Tiggher on the banks of the Ganges, and decoyed two travellers, by caste Hindoos, on their way from Rampore to Meerut, whom they took with them next day across the river to Deotye. They slept there, and next morning the travellers were put to death a mile from the village. The bodies were buried.

Having passed through Meerut and Kurnal, without meeting with any adventures, the gang arrived at Shahabad in the Putteeala principality, they

Report of a Thug Expedition in the years of 1827, *Dhowkul Jemadar, Bhowanee and Lalla Lochun,*

No. of List.	Names of jurisdiction of the place where the Murder was perpetrated.	No. and Sex of the Murdered.		Date of the Murder.	Intended destination of the Murdered.		Supposed value of the property robbed.
		Men.	Women.		From	To	
200	Sirhind,	1	0	That Season of 1829,	Kurnal,	Loodhiana,	125 rupees.
201	Near Sirhind,	2	0	Ditto,	Lucknow,	Loodhiana,	100 rupees and a pony, &c.
202	Ditto,	3	0	Ditto,	Loodhiana,	Eastward,	100 rupees.
203	Between Shahabad and Amballa,	3	0	Ditto,	Lahore,	....	132 rupees.
204	Between Goolchutter and Kurnal,	3	0	Ditto,	Lahore,	Byswara,	100 rupees, and weapons and clothes.

1828 *and* 1829, *under the following leaders: with Thirty-two Thugs, and other Leaders.*

REMARKS.

passed the night there, and in the morning went six miles towards Loodhiana, and sat down at a well. Just then a havildar and two sepahees came up from the direction of Loodhiana on their way to the eastward, and being addressed by one of the leaders, it was agreed that they should be accompanied by fifteen Thugs under the decoyer, who conducted them to Shahabad. They slept there, and next morning the travellers were strangled two miles out of the village. The bodies were buried.

After this affair the murdering party proceeded to Muchunda, where they found their companions who had engaged to meet them there. From thence they all went to Sirhind, and managed to decoy a Mahomedan camel man by profession, who came from Kurnal on his way to Loodhiana. He was taken out next morning a short distance from the town and strangled at a nullah, in which the body was buried.

The gang advanced about eight miles after the murder and sat down to rest at a well, where they were joined by two Fucqueers who came from Lucknow and were going to Loodhiana. Attracted by the beauty of a pony which the Fucqueers had in their possession, the Thugs determined on their destruction, although it was contrary to their practice to put religious men of this description to death. Dhunna Burmoocha, one of the Thugs, however desirous of possessing the pony talked over the scruples of the rest of the gang, and the Fucqueers were decoyed, and conducted to a village some miles further from Sirhind, where they passed the night, and next morning the travellers were strangled some distance from the village. The bodies were buried on the bank of a tank.

They advanced to Loodhiana, and then turned back and revisited Sirhind; next day they went on, and having gone four miles sat down at a Chowkee on the road side. There they were joined by three travellers, by caste gardeners, who came from Loodhiana, on their way eastward, who were decoyed, and taken to a village four miles further on. They slept there, and in the morning the travellers were put to death at a tank two miles off, and their bodies buried.

After this affair they went to Dawood Mangira, between Shahabad and Umballa. As they were going along they fell in with three Hindoos who came from Lahore, who were decoyed by Uchul jemadar and taken to the above named place. Next morning early the travellers were put to death two miles from the village, and their bodies buried.

The gang next proceeded to Goolchutter, and thence set out again next morning. When they had gone two miles, they overtook three travellers on their way to Byswara from Lahore. Runnooa moonshee addressed them and

Report of a Thug Expedition in the years of 1827, *Dhowkul Jemadar, Bhowanee and Lalla Lochun,*

No. of List.	Names of jurisdiction of the place where the Murder was perpetrated.	No. and Sex of the Murdered.		Date of the Murder.	Intended destination of the Murdered.		Supposed value of the property robbed.
		Men.	Women.		From	To	
205	Kumrora,	3	0	That Season of 1829,	Loodhiana,	Byswara,	A bullock worth 30 rupees, and other property 150 ——— 180
206	Near Koel,	4	0	Ditto,	Meerut,	Oude,	200 rupees, a horse, and other property worth 100 rupees.
207	Sooltangunge, in Mynpooree,	3	0	Ditto,	Kurnal,	Eastward,	100 rupees.
208	Sekunderpore, in Furruckhabad,	3	0	Ditto,	Ajmere,	Kurnal,	150 rupees.
209	Hussungunge, in the Oude territory,	3	0	Ditto,	Lahore,	....	150 rupees.
210	Chewdagaon,	2	0	Ditto,	Neemuch,	Sooltanpore,	100 Rs. cash, and 50 rupees property.

REMARKS.

persuaded them to join his party; they were taken to a village between Goolchutter and Kurnal, where they passed the night, and next morning the travellers were strangled about two miles from the village. Their bodies were buried.

They went on to Kurnal and reached the river Jumna, where they fell in with three travellers, Burboonjas from Loodhiana, on their way to Byswara, who were decoyed and taken across the river to Kumrora, where they all rested. In the morning the travellers were taken to a small tributary stream of the Jumna about a mile off, and put to death. The bodies were buried.

Proceeding onwards the gang reached the vicinity of Coel by several stages. On the road they fell in with four travellers, by caste Mussulman, one of them a khansaman in the service of an European, who were going to the Oude state from Meerut. The travellers were conducted through Coel to a village four miles to the eastward of it, where they slept and in the morning the murder was completed in the usual manner, and the bodies thrown into a well a mile or two off.

After the affair the gang went to Sooltangunge in Mynpoorie, and there they decoyed three travellers from Kurnal on their way eastward. They were Hindoos by caste. Next morning the travellers were taken a mile out of the village, and being strangled, their bodies were thrown into a well.

They next proceeded to Bewar in Mynpoorie. Three travellers from Ajmere on their way to Kurnal, by caste Hindoos, were decoyed and conducted to Secundrapore in Furruckhabad. At that place a quarrel took place between Runnooa moonshee and the Police chokydars, in consequence of which he and the gang who followed him, in number twenty-eight, left the place and sought safety in flight. There thus remained seven Lodhees and seven Jumaldhees, who, returning, escorted the travellers out of town as usual, and strangled them at a well a couple of miles off, into which the bodies were thrown.

After this they proceeded as far as the Ganges, which they crossed at the Nana Mhow ghat, and arrived at Meeangunge in the Oude territory—next morning they set out again on their journey, and having advanced four miles they overtook three Hindoos from Lahore, travelling in the same direction with themselves, who were decoyed and taken to Hussungunge, where they slept, and in the morning the travellers were conducted out a couple of miles and strangled. The bodies were thrown into a well.

The gang next went to Chewdagoan, where they fell in with two Hindoo travellers from Neemuch, on their way to Sooltanpore. Uchul jemadar decoyed

Report of a Thug Expedition in the years of 1827, *Dhowkul Jemadar, Bhowanee and Lalla Lochun,*

No. of List.	Names of jurisdiction of the place where the Murder was perpetrated.	No. and Sex of the Murdered: Men.	No. and Sex of the Murdered: Women.	Date of the Murder.	Intended destination of the Murdered: From	Intended destination of the Murdered: To	Supposed value of the property robbed.
211	Mhow,	1	0	That Season of 1829,	West-ward,	....	50 rupees.
212	Khanpore, in Oude,	2	0	Ditto,	Cawn-pore,	....	100 rupees.

JUBULPORE, SUPERINTENDENT'S OFFICE,
The 24th February, 1840.

1828 ***and*** **1829,** ***under the following leaders:***
with Thirty-two Thugs, and other Leaders.

REMARKS.

them, and next morning they were taken out a mile from the village and put to death. The bodies were thrown into a well.

Their next march was to Mohur, and there they decoyed a Hindoo from the westward, whom they accommodated near them for the night, and next morning strangled at a well a mile off, and threw his body into it.

They proceeded on to Khanpore in Oude, and there they decoyed two Hindoos from Cawnpore, who passed the night with them, and next morning they were put to death at a tank a couple of miles off. The bodies were thrown into the water.

After this affair the gang broke up, and each individual proceeded to his respective home. The gang under Runnooa moonshee, who ran away from Sekunderpore, reached home without perpetrating any other murder.

P. A. REYNOLDS,
Superintendent for the
Suppression of Thuggee.

List of Thugs engaged in the Murders during the Expeditions of 1830.

No.	Name.	Parentage.	Caste.	Remarks.
1	Cheyne Jemadar, ...	Son of Rukka, ...	Lodhee, ...	Died while out on Thuggee.
	Bukshee Jemadar, ...	,, Rutta, ...	Ditto, ...	Approver.
	Dhunna, ...	,, Mudaree, ...	Ditto, ...	Ditto.
	Dhunna, 2d,....................	,, Hurree, ...	Ditto, ...	Ditto.
5	Dhunna Burmoocha, ...	,, Chidah, ...	Ditto, ...	Hanged at Jubulpore Sessions of 1836.
	Soomair, ...	,, Muthoulee,...........	Ditto, ...	Approver, (dead.)
	Dhunna, ...	,, Kashee, ...	Ditto, ...	Transported from Saugor.
	Seetla, ...	,, Chidda, ...	Ditto, ...	Died while out on Thuggee.
	Nihalooa, ...	Brother-in-law of Dhunna,..	Ditto, ...	Transported from Jubulpore.
10	Boodhooa, ...	Ditto, ...	Ditto, ...	Ditto ditto.
	Budlaw, ...	Ditto, ...	Ditto, ...	Ditto ditto.
	Khoosheeal,....................	Son of Nunha, ...	Ditto, ...	Ditto ditto.
	Bhola, ...	,, Mukka, ...	Buneah, ...	Approver.
	Desraj,.........................	....	Rachee, ...	Transported from Saugor.
15	Jowihur, ...	....	Rajpoot, ...	Ditto Jubulpore.
	Shewla, ...	Son of Jeykissen, ...	Choomar,......	Ditto Saugor.
	Bukshee, ...	....	Lodhee, ...	Hanged at Saugor Sessions of 1833.
	Himma, ...	....	Brahmin, ...	Ditto ditto ditto.
	Khulluck Jemadar,............	Son of Rutta, ...	Lodhee, ...	Ditto ditto ditto.
20	Budlee,.........................	,, Suntoke,...............	Ditto, ...	Approver.
	Gopal, ...	,, Dyah, ...	Ditto, ...	Ditto.
	Khoodye,......................	,, Mukka, ...	Ditto, ...	Ditto.
	Dibbah, ...	,, Dyaram, ...	Buneah, ...	Ditto.
	Shunker, ...	,, Ditto, ...	Ditto, ...	Hanged at Jubulpore in 1836.
25	Dhowkul........................	,, Chutta, ...	Lodhee, ...	Ditto Saugor in 1833.
	Kesseeree Subadar,...........	,, Buddha, ...	Ditto, ...	Ditto Jubulpore 1835.

	Runnooah Moonshee, ...	Son of Jeysookh, ...	Lodhee,.........	Hanged at Jubulpore, 1835.
	Shewdeen, ...	,, Assa, ...	Ditto, ...	Approver.
	Dhunna, ...	....	Ditto, ...	Ditto.
30	Dhumma,.........................	....	Ditto, ...	Ditto.
	Tijja, ...	Son of Buddha, ...	Ditto, ...	Ditto.
	Ummer, ...	,, Madaree,...............	Ditto, ...	Transported.
	Khoosheealee, ...	....	Ditto, ...	Ditto.
	Mirhahee, ...	....	Ditto, ...	Ditto.
35	Rumzan, ...	....	Musulman, ...	Approver at Lucknow.
	Ouseyree,.........................	....	Aheer, ...	Approver.
	Futteh Jemadar,...............	....	Musulman, ...	Ditto.
	Koorkut, ...	....	Ditto, ...	A prisoner at Lucknow.
	Jubbur,............................	....	Ditto, ...	Approver.
40	Noor Khan.	Son of Dhowkul, ...	Ditto, ...	Hanged at Jubulpore, 1835.
	Bhowanee Jemadar, ...	,, Mukka, ...	Lodhee,.........	Died at home.
	Deorae Jemadar,...............	....	Ditto, ...	Ditto ditto.
	Mulla, ...	Son of Sookhtee, ...	Ditto, ...	Approver.
	Teeka, ...	,, Nundee, ...	Ditto, ...	Ditto.
45	Anward, ...	,, Deorae, ...	Ditto, ...	Transported from Jubulpore, 1836.
	Tijna, ...	,, Gungaram,............	Ditto, ...	Ditto ditto ditto.
	Gunesh, ...	....	Ditto, ...	Died in Jail at Saugor.
	Budlee,...........................	Son of Dya,.....................	Ditto, ...	Died while out on Thuggee.
	Gopaul, ...	,, Mukka, ...	Ditto, ...	Transported from Saugor.
50	Bhukka, ...	,, Ditto, ...	Ditto, ...	Hanged at Jubulpore, 1835.
	Hurlal Jemadar, ...	,, Sookha, ...	Ditto, ...	Ditto Saugor, 1833.
	Nowul, ...	....	Ditto, ...	Ditto ditto.
	Burka, ...	....	Ditto, ...	Transported.
	Ram Buksh Jemadar,.........	Son of Runna,..................	Ditto, ...	Approver.
55	Pershad, ...	,, Ditto, ...	Ditto, ...	Ditto.
	Mehrban, ...	,, Bijjaeen, ...	Ditto, ...	Ditto.
	Bijjooa Jemadar,...............	,, Munna, ...	Ditto, ...	Transported from Jubulpore.
	Heera, ...	,, Oomeid, ...	Ditto, ...	Approver.
	Sumbher,..........................	,, Bhugwant, ...	Ditto, ...	Ditto.

No.	Name.	Parentage.	Caste.	Remarks.
60	Summa,	....	Lodhee,	Approver.
	Essooree,	Son of Rutta,	Ditto,	Ditto.
	Hurlal,	....	Ditto,	Hanged at Jubulpore, 1835-36.
	Mohna,	Son of Bujja,	Ditto,	Approver.
	Uchull Jemadar,	,, Gunsam,	Ditto,	Hanged at Jubulpore, 1835.
65	Mandhata,	,, Dulput,	Ditto,	Approver.
	Heera,	,, Sumadhun,	Ditto,	Ditto.
	Nowul,	,, Punchum,	Ditto,	Hanged at Jubulpore, 1835-36.
	Chidda,	,, Ramkissen,	Ditto,	Transported from Jubulpore.
	Dhumma,	,, Oodah,	Ditto,	Ditto ditto.
70	Cheyne,	,, Gungaram,	Brahmin,	Approver.
	Sumadhan Jemadar,	....	Ditto,	Dead.
	Gunesh,	Son of Sumadhan,	Ditto,	Still at large.
	Jowkee,	,, Ditto,	Ditto,	Ditto ditto.
	Cheyne,	,, Gunga,	Lodhee,	Died at home.
75	Bhimmee,	....	Ditto,	Transported.
	Chidda,	....	Ditto,	Ditto.
	Deveedeen,	Son of Runna	Ditto,	Approver, since died.
	Heera,	,, Ramdeen,	Ditto,	Approver.
	Lalla Lochun Jemadar,	,, Koonjmull,	Ditto,	Hanged at Jubulpore, 1835.
80	Allahyar,	....	Musulman,	Approver at Lucknow.
	Bijjooa,	Son of Munsa	Lodhee,	Transported from Jubulpore, 1836.
	Ajeet,	....	Ditto,	Ditto ditto.
	Runjeet, alias Deveedeen Jemadar,	Son of Kurhoree,	Ditto,	Died in Jail at Saugor.
	Mudaree,	,, Misseeree,	Ditto,	Approver.
85	Hummunchulla,	,, Runnooa moonshee,	Ditto,	Ditto.
	Atmaram,	,, Dya,	Ditto,	Transported from Jubulpore, 1836.

No.	Name	Parentage	Caste	Fate
	Doosoo, ...	....	Mussulman, ...	Approver at Lucknow.
	Heera, ...	Son of Tijja, ...	Lodhee,........	Hanged at Cawnpore.
	Lalsa, ...	....	Ditto, ...	Transported from Saugor, 1835.
90	Myngooa,........................	Son of Chidda, ...	Ditto, ...	Approver.
	Lalsa, ...	....	Ditto, ...	At large.
	Cheyne, ...	....	Ditto, ...	Ditto.
	Anoop,........................	Son of Cheyne, ...	Ditto, ...	Transported.
	Bhola, ...	,, Mudaree, ...	Ditto, ...	Ditto.
95	Bukkha, ...	,, Muthoulee,...........	Ditto, ...	Approver, since dead.
	Beehareelal,........................	,, Mudden,...........	Kaet,...........	Escaped from Jail at Jubulpore (still at large.)
	Dhummee, ...	....	Bukhal,.........	Transported from Saugor, 1833.
	Pershad, ...	....	Ditto, ...	Died at home.
	Pershad, 2d, ...	Son of Dhya, ...	Ditto, ...	Transported from Saugor.
100	Pershad, 3d, ...	....	Lodhee,........	Ditto Ditto.
	Bujja, ...	Son of Oomeid Jemadar, ...	Ditto, ...	Ditto from Jubulpore.
	Layuk,........................	,, Kisshun, ...	Ditto, ...	Hanged at Saugor, 1833.
	Hurreah, ...	Adopted of Lalla Lochun,...	Ditto, ...	Died at home.
	Dhowkulla, ...	Son-in-law of Hurreah,......	Ditto, ...	Still at large.
105	Ram Buksh, ...	,, Ramkissen,...	Ditto, ...	Ditto ditto.
	Letchmunna, ...	,, Ditto, ...	Ditto, ...	Ditto ditto.
	Ramkissen, ...	....	Ditto, ...	Ditto ditto.
	Jowihur, ...	Son of Ramsingh, ...	Ditto, ...	Ditto ditto.
	Nowla, ...	,, Oomeid, ...	Ditto, ...	Transported from Saugor.
110	Chiddooa,........................	,, Ditto, ...	Ditto, ...	Hanged at Cawnpore.
	Bukshea, ...	,, Ditto, ...	Ditto, ...	Transported.
	Ramdeen Jemadar,...........	,, Runna, ...	Ditto, ...	Hanged at Cawnpore.
	Dhunna, ...	,, Rutta, ...	Ditto, ...	Approver.
	Gholabee,........................	,, Bukhtawer,...........	Ditto, ...	Hanged at Bareilly.
115	Shewdeen, ...	,, Bukhtawer,...........	Ditto, ...	Transported from Jubulpore.
	Bukhtaver, ...	,, Koonj,..............	Ditto, ...	Died at home.
	Ghazee, ...	,, Bhugwant, ...	Ditto, ...	Transported from Saugor.
	Ramdeen,........................	,, Heera,..............	Ditto, ...	Approver.
	Myheen Laul, ...	,, Dya, ...	Ditto, ...	Transported from Saugor.

No	Name.	Parentage.	Caste.	REMARKS.
120	Gopaul,	Son of Muheen Laul,	Lodhee,	Transported from Saugor.
	Shewdeen,	,, Munsa,	Ditto,	Ditto ditto.
	Ram Buksh,	,, Pirthee,	Ditto,	Hanged at Cawnpore.
	Mudaree,	,, Suntake,	Ditto,	Ditto ditto.
	Hoolassee,	,, Munsookh,	Ditto,	Ditto ditto.
125	Bhumma,	,, Budlee,	Ditto,	Ditto ditto.
	Dhunna,	,, Bissa,	Ditto,	Ditto ditto.
	Munglee,	,, Suntoke,	Ditto.	Transported from Saugor.
	Permesseree,	....	Brahmin,	In Jail at Jubulpore.
129	Makhun Jemadar,	Son of Kissen,	Lodhee,	Approver.

P. A. REYNOLDS,
Superintendent for the Suppression of Thuggee.

JUBULPORE, SUPERINTENDENT'S OFFICE,
The 24th February, 1840.

REPORT

OF A

THUG EXPEDITION

IN THE

YEARS 1829 AND 1830.

Report of a Thug Expedition in the years of 1829 *and*
Uchul Jemadar, Cheyne Jemadar, Runjeet Jemadar,

No. of List.	Names and jurisdiction of the place where the Murder was perpetrated.	No. and Sex of the Murdered.		Date of the Murder.	Intended destination of the Murdered.		Supposed value of the property robbed.
		Men.	Women.		From	To	
213	Near Nobutgunge,	1	0	That Season of 1829,	Westward,	Lucknow,	25 rupees.
214	Bhâgur Mhow,	2	0	Ditto,	Dhampore Nugeena,	....	100 rupees.
215	Meahgunge,	4	0	Ditto,	Meerut,	Lucknow,	300 rupees.
216	Hussungunge,	1	0	Ditto,	....	Sooltanpore,	20 rupees.
217	Nowulgunge,	2	0	Ditto,	Gwalior,	Ditto,	250 rupees.
218	Near Choontgaon,	3	0	Ditto,	Meerut,	Lucknow,	200 rupees.
219	Nuwabgunge,	2	0	Ditto,	....	Sekroda,	100 rupees.

1830, *under the following leaders: Keseeree Subadar, Rambuksh Jemadar, and other Leaders.*

REMARKS.

In the month of November, 1829, a gang of Lodhees under Keseeree Subadar was assembled at Bhynska Poorwa in Oude, their numbers amounted to fourteen men, and having made the usual offerings to Bhowanee, they set out and reached Nobutgunge, there they discovered a traveller resting in the Bazar, a Hindoo, from the westward, on his way to Lucknow, whom they decoyed, and next morning conducted to a garden, where they put him to death and buried his body.

Having gone on to Bhâgur Mhow, they decoyed two Hindoos from Dhampore Nugeena, and took them next morning to a grove of mangoe trees, a mile from the village, where they strangled them and threw their bodies into a well.

They next arrived at Tukkeah, and found a gang of twenty Jumaldhee Thugs resting there, under Futteh Danyal and Khan Mahomed jemadars. The parties united and set out together next morning. On the road they overtook four travellers, by caste Hindoos, from Meerut, on their way to Lucknow, who were induced to accompany the Thugs to a garden near Meahgunge, where they passed the night. In the morning the travellers were put to death at a well a short distance off, and their bodies are thrown into it.

They then went to Hussungunge, where Rumzan jemadar discovered and decoyed a Hindoo traveller on his way to Sooltanpore, he passed the night with the Thugs, who strangled him next morning in a field a short distance off, and threw his body into a well.

Having divided the booty they went on to Nowulgunge, where Futteh decoyed two Hindoos who came from Gwalior, intending to go to Sooltanpore, and brought them to the encampment of the Thugs. Next morning the travellers were taken to a well a mile off and strangled. Their bodies were thrown into the well.

After the murder the Thugs went on to Futtehgunge, where three travellers, by caste Hindoos, were resting in the Bazar. They came from Meerut and were going to the neighbourhood of Lucknow, and having been persuaded by the gang to join them, were taken next day across the Goomtee river; travelling all day, they arrived at dark near Choontgaon, and the murder was completed under favor of the night. The bodies were thrown into the river.

Their next stage was Nuwabgunge, and there Keseeree subadar inveigled two Hindoo travellers on their way to Sekroda, who passed the night in company with the Thugs, and were strangled next morning at a well two miles off, and their bodies thrown into it.

Report of a Thug Expedition in the years of 1829 *and*
Uchul Jemadar, Cheyne Jemadar, Runjeet Jemadar,

No. of List.	Names and jurisdiction of the place where the Murder was perpetrated.	No. and Sex of the Murdered.		Date of the Murder.	Intended destination of the Murdered.		Supposed value of the property robbed.
		Men.	Women.		From	To	
220	Near Gosein-gunge,	1	0	That Season of 1829,	Luck-now,	Joun-pore,	25 rupees.
221	Near Oonnow,	4	0	Ditto,	Dekhan,	....	200 rupees.
222	Near Choont-gaon,	2	0	Ditto,	Bundel-khund.	Luck-now,	100 rupees.
223	Mullaoon-ka-Poorwa, in the Oude State,	2	0	Ditto,	Gwalior,	Ditto,	125 rupees.
224	Bunter,	2	0	Ditto,	Dekhan,	Sooltan-pore,	125 rupees.
225	Bhankaira,	2	0	Ditto,	Meerut,	Ditto,	100 rupees.
226	Cazeegunge, in the Cawnpore district,	2	0	Ditto,	Ditto,	Allaha-bad,	125 rupees.

1830, ***under the following leaders: Keseeree Subadar, Rambuksh Jemadar, and other Leaders.***

REMARKS.

After the murder the gang turned back and took a southerly direction. They proceeded across the Goomtee and arrived at Gosaingunge, where they fell in with a traveller, by caste a Hindoo, on his way from Lucknow to Jounpore. He was decoyed, and next morning taken by the gang to a well two miles off, where he was strangled and his body thrown into the water.

They went to Oonnow and resting there fell in with four travellers from the Dekhan, by caste Hindoos, whom they decoyed and taking them out next morning to a garden two miles from the village. They induced them to sit down and strangled them. The bodies were thrown into a well.

The gang again reached Choontgaon, which they had previously passed through. Two Hindoo travellers from Bundelkhund, on their way to Lucknow, were resting there, and having been discovered by the Thugs were persuaded to join the party of one of the jemadars, and being taken next morning to a well two miles off, they were strangled and their bodies thrown into it.

Having completed the affair the Thugs went to Mullaoon-ka-Poorwa, Pergunnah Hurra, in the Oude State, where they rested. Two Hindoo travellers from Gwalior, on their way to Lucknow, were at the same place, and were invited by the Thugs to travel in their company. They consented and next morning were put to death at a well half a mile off, and their bodies thrown into it.

They then proceeded to Bunter and decoyed two Hindoos who came from the Dekhan on their way to Sooltanpore. Next morning they conducted the travellers to a well half a mile off, strangled them and threw their bodies into the water.

After this affair the Thugs went to Bhankaira and rested there. They inveigled two travellers by caste Bunneahs, who had come to the same place on their way from Meerut to Sooltanpore, and took them out next morning a short distance from the village, and strangled them—their bodies were thrown into a well.

The Jumaldhee Thugs after this murder, separated from the Lodhees and proceeded homewards. Keseeree Subadar's gang crossed the Ganges and went to Cazeegunge, in the Cawnpore district. There the leader of the party discovered two Hindoo travellers from Meerut on their way to Allahabad, whom he decoyed and brought to the encampment of the Thugs. Next morning they were conducted about a mile along the bank of the river, and having been put to death in the usual manner their bodies were committed to the stream.

Report of a Thug Expedition in the years of 1829 *and*
Uchul Jemadar, Cheyne Jemadar, Runjeet Jemadar,

No. of List.	Names and jurisdiction of the place where the Murder was perpetrated.	No. and Sex of the Murdered.		Date of the Murder.	Intended destination of the Murdered.		Supposed value of the property robbed.
		Men.	Women.		From	To	
227	Aroun,	4	0	That Season of 1829,	Lodhiana,	Sooltanpore,	300 rupees.
228	Mukrundnugger,	2	0	Ditto,	....	Eastward,	125 rupees.
229	Near Chowbepore,	1	0	Ditto,	Kurnal,	Benares,	40 rupees cash, 2 bullocks worth 30 rupees.
230	Near Mulwah, in Futtehpore,	5	0	Ditto,	Ditto,	Ditto,	350 rupees.
231	Near Kurrah,	1	0	Ditto,	Dekhan,	Bithoor,	200 rupees, 50 rupees a shawl, and 50 rupees of ornaments.
232	Kankerabad, in Allahabad,	1	0	Ditto,	Kotah,	Benares,	150 rupees.
233	Emamgunge,	1	0	Ditto,	....	Furruckhabad,	50 rupees.

1830, ***under the following leaders: Keseeree Subadar, Rambuksh Jemadar, and other Leaders.***

REMARKS.

They went onwards and arrived the same day at Aroun and were joined at that place by a gang of twenty-one Lodhee Thugs led by Lalla Lochun Khuluck and Dhowkul jemadars. Four Hindoo travellers, on their way from Loodhiana to Sooltanpore, were resting there for the day and were decoyed by Keseeree subadar. They were taken out a mile from the village next morning, and strangled, the bodies being thrown into a well.

Proceeding on they reached Mukrundnuggur, and there two travellers were decoyed by Khuluk jemadar. They were Hindoos by caste and travelling eastward. They were put to death next morning in a water-course a short distance from the town, and their bodies thrown into a well.

Their next stage was Chowbepore, where Keseeree subadar fell in with a Hindoo traveller from Kurnal, intending to go to Benares, whom he decoyed, and next morning put to death a couple of miles from the village. The body was thrown into a well.

They had scarcely completed this murder when another gang of Lodhee Thugs, nineteen in number, under Bhowanee and Budlee (Approvers) jemadars, came up to this spot, and all agreed to prosecute the expedition in company; accordingly they travelled on to Kulleanpore, and there discovered five gram-parchers travelling from Kurnal to Benares, whom they inveigled and escorted next day to Mulwa, in the Futtehpore district: having passed the night there the travellers were put to death next morning at a well two miles from the village, and their bodies thrown into the water.

The gangs went on to Ahmedgunge and rested in the seraee; a traveller, by caste a Muhratta, mounted on a horse and on his way from the Dekhan to Bithoor, had taken up his quarters for the day in the same place, he was persuaded to join the Thugs, who took him next morning to the vicinity of Kurrah on the Ganges, and having put him to death threw his body into the stream. The horse was let loose in the jungle.

After this the Thugs proceeded onwards for several days, without falling in with any traveller, and reaching Kankerabad in the Allahabad district, rested there. Khuluk jemadar decoyed a Hindoo who was travelling from Kotah to Benares and brought him to his encampment. He was put to death next morning a short distance from the town, and his body thrown into a well.

Having arrived at Allahabad, the Thugs performed their ablutions in the sacred stream with the usual ceremonies, and then turned back and went to Emamgunge. There they found resting in the seraee, a Hindoo travelling towards Furruckhabad, whom they decoyed, and next morning strangled at a well two miles off, throwing the body into the water.

Report of a Thug Expedition in the years of 1829 *and*
Uchul Jemadar, Cheyne Jemadar, Runjeet Jemadar,

No. of List.	Names and jurisdiction of the place where the Murder was perpetrated.	No. and Sex of the Murdered.		Date of the Murder.	Intended destination of the Murdered.		Supposed value of the property robbed.
		Men.	Women.		From	To	
234	Chickutteah, in Cawnpore,	3	0	That Season of 1829,	....	....	200 rupees.
235	Ramyepore,	4	0	Ditto,	....	Benares,	200 rupees.
236	Chutterpore,	3	0	Ditto,	Dekhan,	Cawnpore,	200 rupees.
237	Muchgaon,	2	0	January, 1830,	Ellichpore,	Mhow,	150 rupees.
238	Amoond,	3	0	Ditto,	Dekhan,	Oude,	132 rupees.

1830, under the following leaders: Keseeree Subadar, Rambuksh Jemadar, and other Leaders.

REMARKS.

They proceeded slowly onwards and arrived in the course of several days at Chickuttea, in the Cawnpore district, where they inveigled three Hindoo travellers, who were going in the same direction with themselves. They were put to death in the usual manner next morning, and their bodies thrown into a well two miles from the village.

After this murder the Thugs went to Ramyepore and fell in with four travellers, by caste Hindoos, on their way to Benares, whom they decoyed, and accompanied a short distance next morning and having strangled them threw their bodies into a well.

They next went to Pinkhee, in the Cawnpore district, and from thence Bhowanee, Khuluk and Lalla Lochun jemadars, with their followers, proceeded to their respective homes. The remaining fourteen Thugs under Keseeree subadar crossed the Jumna at Calpee and advanced into Bundelkhund as far as Chutterpore. There they found three Hindoos on their way from the Dekhan to Cawnpore, who became victims to the persuasions of the Thug leaders, who induced them to rest for the night in a place of religious worship outside the town. The travellers were put to death next morning at the distance of a mile from the town, and their bodies were buried.

Turning back from the place of murder the Thugs again went to Chutterpore and were joined by Zoolfukar, Bhooree, and Noor Khan leaders from Sindouse,* with a gang of thirty-two Thugs of that class. They all took the road next day towards Calpee, and reached Cullianee, where they found two Mahomedan sowars from Ellichpore on their way to Mhow, who were decoyed by Keseeree subadar and joined the party. They were escorted to Muchgewan and the succeeding morning were strangled some distance from the village, their bodies being buried.

* This meeting is not noticed in the Sindouse narratives, but the approvers of that class deposed to the fact before me.

(Sd.) P. A. Reynolds,
Supt.

N. B. The remains of the bodies have since been disinterred by the approvers. The murder took place in January, 1830.

They proceeded onwards, and between the villages of Rath and Amoond, on the road to Calpee, they fell in with three travellers, one a Mahomedan and the other two Hindoos from the Dekhan, on their way to the Oude State, who were decoyed and conducted the same day to Amoond. Next morning early the travellers were put to death a short distance from the village, and their bodies buried in a water-course.

Report of a Thug Expedition in the years of 1829 and
Uchul Jemadar, Cheyne Jemadar, Runjeet Jemadar,

No. of List.	Names and jurisdiction of the place where the Murder was perpetrated.	No. and Sex of the Murdered.		Date of the Murder.	Intended destination of the Murdered.		Supposed value of the property robbed.
		Men.	Women.		From	To	
239	Muhoba, in Jhalone,	1	0	That Season of 1830,	Mhow,	Cawnpore,	2 gold mohurs, 2 rupees and clothes.
240	Chutterpore,	2	0	Ditto,	Poona,	Bithoor,	100 rupees.
241	Arown,	1	0	Ditto,	Muttra,	Cawnpore,	15 rupees.
242	Kunnooa Khaira,	3	0	Ditto,	Saugor,	Cawnpore,	200 rupees.
243	Nyagaon,	3	0	Ditto,	Buroda,	Oude territory,	200 rupees.

1830, *under the following leaders : Keseeree Subadar, Rambuksh Jemadar, and other Leaders.*

REMARKS.

N. B. The remains of these bodies have been disinterred by the approvers, and the case committed to trial in the Court of the Agent Governor General. The murdered persons were Girdharee, the nephew of Bhowanee and Buldee distillers of Mhow, and Soyboo Chuprasee, of Durriabad, the name of the third has not been ascertained.

The gangs again changed their direction and proceeded to Muhoba in Jalone, where they found a Hindoo travelling from Mhow to Cawnpore, whom they decoyed and accommodated in their encampment outside of the village. He was strangled in his bed during the night, and his body buried on the spot.

The Sindouse Thugs, after this murder, separated from the Lodhees and took another direction, while the latter, under Keseeree subadar, proceeded to Chutterpore. There they rested at the Meeta Kooa, outside the town, and found there two Mahrattas from Poona on their way to Bithoor, whom they persuaded to accompany them next morning and put to death a couple of miles off, burying their bodies.

After the affair was completed the gang went to Sereenuggur, and there met Mehrban and Shunker jemadars, with fourteen Lodhee Thugs.

Mehrban's gang had assembled at Seetaka-Poorwa, and, after taking the auspices, went to Arown, where they decoyed a Brahmin on his way from Muttra to Cawnpore, and, having induced him to set out with them next morning, they strangled him at a well a mile from the village. The body was thrown into the water.

The expeditions having commenced thus auspiciously, (Saudka, in the slang language,) the Thugs went, in the course of three days, to Bindwa in Jhalone, which was the residence of Bhola jemadar, who joined them with another Thug follower, and next morning all went on to Kunnooa Kaira, where they passed the day in a Gosaeen's house. Three travellers, by caste Hindoos, from Saugor, on their way to Cawnpore, were resting in the same place, and they were decoyed by the Thugs; next morning early, having taken the travellers out to a stream two miles from the village, they put them to death in the usual manner, and threw the bodies into the Behur river.

After this affair Bhola and his companions (above alluded to) left the main gang and returned home. The remainder went on by the regular stages to Sereenuggur, where they joined Keseeree subadar's party, as before related.

Soon after the union of the two gangs, three travellers, sepoys, on their way from Boroda to the Oude territory, were met by them, and were decoyed

Report of a Thug Expedition in the years of 1829 *and*
Uchul Jemadar, Cheyne Jemadar, Runjeet Jemadar,

No. of List.	Names and jurisdiction of the place where the Murder was perpetrated.	No. and Sex of the Murdered.		Date of the Murder.	Intended destination of the Murdered.		Supposed value of the property robbed.
		Men.	Women.		From	To	
244	Komp Newaree, in the Punna Principality,	1	0	That Season of 1830,	Banda,	Bhopal,	3 gold mohurs, 20 rupees.
245	Jheenjun,	3	0	Ditto,	Indore,	Lucknow,	300 rupees.
246	Near Punna,	1	0	Ditto,	Nagpore,	Chutkaree,	250 rupees, in gold and cash.
247	Beseynee,	2	0	Ditto,	Ditto,	Byswara,	250 rupees.
248	Ditto,	3	0	Ditto,	Northward,	Nagpore,	300 rupees.

1830, *under the following leaders: Keseeree Subadar, Rambuksh Jemadar, and other Leaders.*

REMARKS.

and conducted to Myagaon, where they all slept; next morning early the travellers were strangled about two miles from the village, and their bodies securely buried.

They then went on some distance to a garden on the way side, where they sat down to divide the booty. While engaged in this business a Hindoo traveller from Banda on his way to Bhopal came up to the spot, and was decoyed by one of the Thug leaders. He was taken to Komp Newaree, in the Punna principality, where they all passed the day and succeeding night. In the morning the traveller was strangled some distance from the village, and his body was buried.

Having divided the booty of the last affair, Dibba and Merban's gang separated from Keseeree subadar's, and went to Jheenjim, where they fell in with three travellers, by caste a Rajhpoot, a Brahmin and a Kullul, who had come from Indore on their way to Lucknow. They were decoyed, and next morning were put to death some distance from the village, and their bodies buried. The gang then proceeded homewards and arrived there without committing any other murder on the road.

Keseeree subadar's gang left Komp Newaree, and proceeded to Punna, where they rested upon the bank of the tank. Soon afterwards a traveller, by caste shop-keeper, came to the same place. He was on his way from Nagpore to Chutkaree. He had the appearance of being a religious mendicant, in consequence of which the Thugs entertained scruples as to putting him to death. Next morning the Thugs did not show any disposition to move, in the hopes that the traveller would proceed on his way alone, and after waiting several hours, and endeavouring to persuade him to be off, they were under the necessity of making a shew of departure by starting the traveller with seven Thugs in his company. He was conducted a distance of three miles into the jungle and then strangled. The body was buried, and afterwards the murdering party rejoined the main gang.

The Thugs proceeded onwards and reached Beseynee, where they found two Hindoos from Nagpore, on their way to Byswara, who were decoyed and put to death next morning a mile or two from the village. The bodies were concealed under heaps of stones.

They next went to Shahgurh, and decoyed three travellers on their way northward from Nagpore. They turned back with them and returned to Besaynee, where they passed the night. Next morning the travellers were strangled two miles from the town, and their bodies covered with heaps of stones.

Report of a Thug Expedition in the years of 1829 *and*
Uchul Jemadar, Cheyne Jemadar, Runjeet Jemadar,

No. of List.	Names and jurisdiction of the place where the Murder was perpetrated.	No. and Sex of the Murdered.		Date of the Murder.	Intended destination of the Murdered.		Supposed value of the property robbed.
		Men.	Women.		From	To	
249	Culleanee,	1	0	That Season of 1830,	Bombay, Presidency,	Byswara,	A hookah, and a brass drinking cup, 2 or 3 copper coins.
250	Mirgayan,	5	0	Ditto,	Mhow,	Lucknow,	1400 rupees.
251	Pokarayan, in the Cawnpore district.	2	0	Ditto,	Saugor,	Ajoodhea,	100 rupees.
252	Secundra, in the Coel district,	2	0	February 1830,	....	Delhi,	100 rupees, 20 rupees property.

1830, under the following leaders: Keseeree Subadar, Rambuksh Jemadar, and other Leaders.

REMARKS.

Proceeding onwards for five or six days, the gang again reached Chutterpore, where they were joined by Zoolfukar and Noor Khan jemadars, with twenty-five Thugs, and Chand Khan jemadar, with twenty-two Thugs. The united parties took the road next morning towards Calpee, and having proceeded a couple of miles, they overtook a sepahee from the Bombay Presidency going to Byswara, whom they decoyed and took to Culleanee. Having encamped there, the Thugs strangled the traveller on his bed during the night and buried his body in a water-course. Though the Thugs had been induced by their victim's respectable appearance to put him to death, they were disappointed in their hopes of a rich booty, for he proved to be almost destitute.

The gang next went to Burwara, and there fell in with three Hindoo travellers (two Kullals and one Chupprassee,) from Mhow, on their way to Lucknow, whom they decoyed and took out next morning intending to put them to death. When they arrived at Oundeyra, a most unlucky omen was observed, in a crow calling out while perched on the back of a buffaloe. The Thugs of Sindouse, under Zoolfukar and other leaders, being particularly influenced by this prestige of evil, turned back and left the travellers in charge of the Lodhees and seven Sindousee Thugs under Hyat approver. These went onwards with the travellers, and near Rath met with two more travellers, Hindoos, from the Dekhan, proceeding in a northerly direction, whom they took on with them to Momna in Humeerpore. About midnight the five travellers were roused from sleep and taken a few miles onwards towards Mirgayan, where they were strangled. The bodies were buried.

N. B. These bodies have been disinterred upon the evidence of an approver, and it has otherwise been ascertained that the murder was perpetrated on the 5th February, 1830. The case has been made the subject of trial in the Court of the Agent Governor General, and several of the Thugs have suffered the penalty of the laws in consequence.

After the affair Hyat and his companions from Sindouse, received their shares of the booty and went home. The Lodhee Thugs advanced to the Jumna, and having crossed it at Calpee, they arrived at Pokarayan in the Cawnpore district. There they found two Hindoo travellers on their way from Saugor to Ajoodhea, whom they decoyed and next morning put to death, a mile or two out of the village, throwing the dead bodies into a well. The gang then went home without committing any other murder.

In the month of February, 1830, Uchul jemadar, Cheyne jemadar, and Runjeet jemadar, assembled their respective parties of Thugs at Behareepore, and set out on an expedition with thirty-five followers. In the usual course of travelling, they arrived at Secundra in the Coel district, and fell in with

Report of a Thug Expedition in the years of 1829 *and*
Uchul Jemadar, Cheyne Jemadar, Runjeet Jemadar,

No. of List.	Names and jurisdiction of the place where the Murder was perpetrated.	No. and Sex of the Murdered.		Date of the Murder.	Intended destination of the Murdered.		Supposed value of the property robbed.
		Men.	Women.		From	To	
253	Secundra,	4	0	February 1830,	Delhi,	Cawnpore,	100 rupees.
254	Purputgunge,	1	0	Ditto,	Benares,	Delhi,	10 gold mohurs, 60 rupees in cash, 125 rupees other property.
255	Khoorja,	2	0	Ditto,	Lahore,	Byswara,	100 rupees.
256	Boorhana,	3	0	Ditto,	Loodhiana,	Ditto,	100 rupees.
257	Kimrora,	3	0	Ditto,	Lahore,	Eastward,	150 rupees.
258	Soomka,	3	0	Ditto,	Loodhiana,	Byswara,	100 rupees cash, a horse worth 50 rupees.

1830, ***under the following leaders: Keseeree Subadar, Rambuksh Jemadar, and other Leaders.***

REMARKS.

two Hindoos travelling to Delhie, whom they decoyed, and having taken with them next morning, strangled them about two miles from the village, and threw the bodies into the water.

After the murder the gang returned to Secundra and passed the day there. Four travellers, by caste Hindoos, on their way from Delhi to Cawnpore, arrived at the same place, and having been decoyed by the Thugs agreed to pursue their journey in their company; next morning early the travellers were conducted to a tank a mile from the town and put to death. The bodies were buried.

They proceeded immediately to Purputgunge, where Uchul jemadar met with a native horseman (a Mahomedan) on his way from Benares to Delhi, whom he induced to rest for the day in the same seraee with the Thugs. The Thugs exerted all their eloquence to persuade the traveller, whose death they had determined on, to set out on his journey in the dark, but he resisted their persuasions, and deferred his departure till the sun was up. Hereon the Thugs determined to divide the gang into two parties, one of which was sent on before daylight to a tank on the road to Delhi, while the other accompanied the traveller. When the rear party reached the tank with the horseman in their company, they proposed to him to dismount and smoke a pipe. He fell into the snare and sat down to smoke, when he was instantly strangled, and his body thrown into the water.

Having completed the murder the Thugs went to Khoorja, and decoyed two travellers, by caste Hindoos, on their way from Lahore to Byswara, whom they strangled next morning at a well two miles from the village, the body was thrown into the water.

Their next day's journey brought them to Boorhana, and there they found three Hindoos going from Loodhiana to Byswara, whom they persuaded to join their party, and taking them next morning to the bank of a river put them to death and committed the bodies to the stream.

Proceeding onwards the Thugs arrived at Kimrora, where they found three Hindoo travellers, from Lahore, on their way eastward, whom they decoyed and conducted next morning to a stream running into the Jumna, where they strangled them, and buried the bodies in a field.

They then passed through Kurnal, and went to the village of Soomka, ten miles west of it. Three spirit dealers travelling from Loodhiana to Byswara rested for the day at the same place, and having been decoyed by the Thugs, were taken out before day-break next morning a distance of two miles and strangled. The bodies were buried in the bed of a tank.

Report of a Thug Expedition in the years of 1829 *and*
Uchul Jemadar, Cheyne Jemadar, Runjeet Jemadar,

No. of List.	Names and jurisdiction of the place where the Murder was perpetrated.	No. and Sex of the Murdered.		Date of the Murder.	Intended destination of the Murdered.		Supposed value of the property robbed.
		Men.	Women.		From	To	
259	Shahabad,	4	0	February 1830,	Lahore,	Byswara,	250 rupees.
260	Khunna,	4	0	Ditto,	Ditto,	Benares,	25 rupees.
261	Sirhind,	2	0	Ditto,	....	Benares,	150 rupees.
262	Muchunda,	2	0	Ditto,	Loodhiana,	Cawnpore,	60 rupees.
263	Turowlee,	2	0	Ditto,	Moultan,	Muttra,	120 tolahs of gold with 2500, rupees and 500 rupees of other property.

1830, *under the following leaders : Keseeree Subadar, Rambuksh Jemadar, and other Leaders.*

REMARKS.

After the murder they went to Goolchutter, and thence to Shahabad. They were engaged in cooking their bread on the banks of a stream at the last named place, when four travellers came up on their way from Lahore to Byswara, they were addressed by the Thugs, who scraped an acquaintance with them and induced them to join their party, next morning early they were put to death two miles from the village. The bodies were buried.

The Thugs then proceeded to Loodhiana and rested in the seraee. They were soon after joined by four travellers, by caste Hindoos, who sought accommodation in the seraee for the day. Being very cleanly dressed the Thugs thought they must be wealthy, ingratiated themselves in their favor, and found that they were on their way from Lahore to Benares. An agreement was made to travel together, and the intended victims were taken next day to Khunna, where the whole party passed the day in the seraee, next morning the travellers were put to death, a short distance from the village, and their bodies securely buried. Enraged at having been deluded into an opinion of the travellers being possessed of wealth, the Thugs treated the dead bodies with every indignity, when they found they were possessed of little more than the white clothes they wore.

The gang proceeded on to Sirhind, and inveigled two Hindoos travelling the same way. They all rested in the seraee, and next morning the travellers were strangled a mile from the town, and their bodies buried in a field.

They next went to Umballa, and succeeded in decoying two Mahomedans on their way from Loodhiana to Cawnpore, whom they took with them next day to Muchunda. Having slept there the Thugs put the travellers to death next morning, and buried the bodies in a field two miles from the town.

They revisited Goolchutter, where they accommodated themselves in the house of Lekhraj Pundit which is frequented by travellers. The Thugs there performed their ablutions in the sacred tank, and after resting three days set out again on their journey. Having proceeded two miles towards Kurnal, they overtook two travellers from Moultan, on their way to Muttra, mounted on ponies. They were in appearance very poor, for excepting their ponies they had nothing about them to tempt cupidity. The Thugs consulted whether it would be worth while to put them to death. Some said that as they had been taken in with the fine clothes of the men they strangled at Khunna, what were they to expect from travellers apparelled in rags ; but Bukshee (approver,) advocated the measure of strangling them, and offered to pay the gang 100 rupees for the booty which might be obtained. Their death was accordingly determined on, and they were conducted by the Thugs to Turowlee where they rested in the seraee, and Cheyne jemadar invited the poor wretches to partake

Report of a Thug Expedition in the years of 1829 *and*
Uchul Jemadar, Cheyne Jemadar, Runjeet Jemadar,

No. of List.	Names and jurisdiction of the place where the Murder was perpetrated.	No. and Sex of the Murdered.		Date of the Murder.	Intended destination of the Murdered.		Supposed value of the property robbed.
		Men.	Women.		From	To	
264	Malown,	2	0	February 1830,	Kurnal,	Oude Territory,	40 rupees.
265	Poorwaha,	2	0	Ditto,	Ditto,	Benares,	100 rupees.

1830, ***under the following leaders: Keseeree Subadar, Rambuksh Jemadar, and other Leaders.***

REMARKS.

---

of a repast. The travellers, who it seems had visited all parts of India as religious mendicants, enlivened the evening by relating their adventures. Next morning they were taken out a distance of a mile from the village, and strangled. The bodies were taken to the place of burial, and some of the Thugs were engaged in digging a grave when the neighing of horses was heard at a distance, and as day was breaking, the gang perceived some mounted travellers approaching the spot. In great alarm they concealed themselves behind a mound of earth at some distance, leaving the bodies on the ground. The horsemen passed by, the approvers say, without stopping, but when the Thugs returned to the grave, they found that the dead bodies had disappeared! The approvers who have been questioned on the subject of the disappearance of the bodies, are unable, or pretend to be so, to account for the circumstance. They admit that the Goddess Bhowany has long since left off disposing of the bodies of their murdered victims, but still desire it to be supposed that as the travellers were religious mendicants, the deity to whom they were devoted had probably removed the bodies adding; that though this interference on the part of the deity would argue a dereliction of duty on their parts, in having put such holy persons to death. yet as they had unlimited authority from Bhowanee herself to commit murder, and the mendicants had through their means obtained a speedy passage to paradise, no sin can possibly attach to them from the commission of the act. The gang, setting aside the fears they had been subjected to, was delighted at their good fortune in meeting with such a booty, and proceeded on to Coel.

At Coel, two Hindoo travellers from Kurnal, on their way to the Oude territory, came and joined their party, but the Thugs having their purses tolerably well filled with money, did not care to put them to death, and they accordingly travelled with them for three days although they endeavoured to get rid of their company. Having arrived at Malown, the Thugs determined, as they could not otherwise get rid of the travellers, to put them to death, and accordingly they were strangled next morning a couple of miles from the village. The bodies were buried. After this affair the gang proceeded home without any other adventure.

In the month of February 1830, the gang of Thugs under Girdaree and Bukshee jemadars, who had been arrested at Mynpooree in the year 1827, as before related, were set at liberty. Soon afterwards Girdharee proceeded to Seeahpore, in Furruckhabad, and told Rambuksh jemadar that his brother Bukshee refused to go again on Thuggee, and as a gang of nineteen Thugs was ready to start as soon as they could get a leader, invited him (Rambuksh) to take command of the party. He agreed, and they set out, proceeding to Meeran-ka-seraee in Cawnpore, where they decoyed two travellers, a Brahmin and a Kuhar, on their way from Kurnal to Benares, and took them to Poor-

Report of a Thug Expedition in the years of 1829 *and*
Uchul Jemadar, Cheyne Jemadar, Runjeet Jemadar,

No. of List.	Names and jurisdiction of the place where the Murder was perpetrated.	No. and Sex of the Murdered.		Date of the Murder.	Intended destination of the Murdered.		Supposed value of the property robbed.
		Men.	Women.		From	To	
266	Apohee,	2	0	February, 1830,	Muttra,	Bojhpore,	Carpets worth 20 rupees, 7 rupees cash, a bullock and pony.
267	Mooftee-ka-Poorwaha,	1	0	Ditto,	Mirzapore,	Bareilly,	50 rupees.
268	Hudgaon,	2	0	Ditto,	Barrackpore,	Dulmhow,	100 rupees.
269	Futtehgunge, in Bareilly,	2	0	Ditto,	Kurnal,	Lucknow,	100 rupees.
270	Near Shamlee,	2	0	Ditto,	Loodhiana,	Cawnpore,	250 rupees.
271	Kurreer, in the Sirdhana Jageer,	2	0	Ditto,	Kurnal,	Meerut,	25 Rs. cash, 2 ponies worth 30 rupees.

1830, ***under the following leaders: Keseeree Subadar, Rambuksh Jemadar, and other Leaders.***

REMARKS.

waha, where they passed the day. Next morning the travellers were strangled at a well about two miles off and their bodies thrown into the water.

The gang went on to Apohee, where they met two travellers, a Choomar and the other a Barber, with the pony and a bullock laden with carpets, the property of a subadar named "Mirhaee," in a Regiment of Native Infantry, which they were conveying from Muttra to Bojhpore. The travellers were decoyed, and next morning strangled some way out of the village. The bodies were thrown into a well.

They then proceeded on to Mooftee-ka-Poorwa, and decoyed a Brahmin travelling from Mirzapore to Bareilly, whom they took out next morning and strangled two miles from the village. The body was thrown into a well.

The gang then went to Hudgaon, and fell in with two travellers, one a sepahee, by caste Rajpoot, and the other a Brahmin, who were proceeding from Barrackpore to Dulmhow in the Oude State. They were inveigled as usual and next morning put to death, and their bodies thrown into a well outside the village.

Proceeding onwards for several days the Thugs reached Banska Kuttra, in Oude, without meeting with any victims. Their numbers were however reinforced by the arrival of Lalla Lochun and Mehrban jemadars, with eight Thugs in their train, who had just left home on an expedition. The gang amounting to nineteen Thugs, proceeded to Futtehgunge, in Bareilly, where they met two Hindoos in the bazar, who had come from Kurnal with the intention of visiting Lucknow. They were decoyed and having been conducted out of the village, next morning were strangled in the denk near a well, into which their bodies were thrown.

The gang travelled on by Bareilly to Mooradabad, and crossed the Ganges at Goormuktasir, and went to Shormlee without meeting with any success in their search after victims. But when they had advanced near Jhinjana, they perceived four Hindoos on their way from Loodhiana to Cawnpore, coming towards them. The advanced members of the Thug gang immediately gave notice to those in the rear, who lost no time in turning back and retracing their steps very leisurely, so that the travellers very soon overtook them. They addressed and pursuaded the travellers to prosecute their journey in their company, and took them to a village near Shamlee, where they passed the night, and next morning early the travellers were put to death and their bodies thrown into a well.

The Thugs went next to Kurreer in the Sirdhana Jageer, where they were joined by two shopkeepers, Bunneahs, from Kurnal, on their way to Meerut,

Report of a Thug Expedition in the years of 1829 *and*
Uchul Jemadar, Cheyne Jemadar, Runjeet Jemadar,

No. of List.	Names and jurisdiction of the place where the Murder was perpetrated.	No. and Sex of the Murdered.		Date of the Murder.	Intended destination of the Murdered.		Supposed value of the property robbed.
		Men.	Women.		From	To	
272	Pootee seraee, in the Boolund-shuher district,	4	0	That Season of 1830,	Shaja-hanabad,	Baroda,	200 rupees.
273	Bhakree,	2	0	Ditto,	Delhi,	Calpee,	60 rupees.
274	Mehendeeghat,	3	0	Ditto,	Ajmere,	Luck-now,	100 rupees, a horse was let loose in the jungle.
275	Hussungunge,	2	0	Ditto,	Loodhi-ana,	Salone,	50 rupees cash, 30 rupees property.
276	Baita,	3	0	Ditto,	Luck-now,	Bareilly,	150 rupees.

1830, under the following leaders: Keseeree Subadar, Rambuksh Jemadar, and other Leaders.

REMARKS.

whom they decoyed and accommodated for the day near themselves. They were strangled a couple of miles out of the village next morning and their bodies thrown into a well.

Having completed the murder they went by Bhagput Barode Purputgunge. When they had left the last named place and advanced two or three miles they fell in with four travellers, by caste Hindoos, on their way from Shajahnabad to Beroda. They were decoyed as usual, and conducted to Pootee seraee in the Boolundshuher district, where all rested in a garden outside; next morning early the travellers were strangled a couple of miles from the village, and their bodies buried in the bed of a stream.

They passed through Soorujgurh and reached Soobhna, where they rested to smoke; two travellers, by caste Hindoos, from Delhi, going to Calpee, came up from behind, and were addressed and decoyed by Rambuksh jemadar. On the same day they all went to Bakra, and encamped at the brink of a well under a Peepul tree. Next morning early the travellers were strangled some distance from the village, and their bodies buried in a swamp.

After this the gang went to Sultangunge in Mynpooree, where a burkundaz came to them and made a very low salam to Daveedeen jemadar, who immediately deposited five rupees in his hands. When he was gone the Thugs began to entertain apprehensions of being arrested, so they packed up their baggage and set off home at once, arriving there without committing any other murder on the way.

In the month of April, 1830, Uchul jemadar, Bukshee jemadar, and thirty Thugs assembled at Behareepore, and having set out on an expedition reached Bhângur Mhow; after crossing the Ganges at Mehendee Ghat, Uchul jemadar having gone into the village decoyed and brought out with him, three Hindoo travellers from Ajmere, on their way to Lucknow, who were accommodated for the day near the Thugs. They were strangled near a nullah next morning and their bodies thrown into a well.

They proceeded on and arrived at Hussungunge, there they met two travellers one a sepahee and the other his servant, both Hindoos, who were on their way from Loodhiana to Salone, whom they decoyed, and next morning put to death in a field outside of the village, throwing their bodies into a well.

After this the gang went to Baita, and fell in with three palkee bearers proceeding from Lucknow to Bareilly, who were decoyed and next morning put to death near some trees in a plain, and their bodies were buried.

Report of a Thug Expedition in the years of 1829 *and*
Uchul Jemadar, Cheyne Jemadar, Runjeet Jemadar,

No. of List.	Names and jurisdiction of the place where the Murder was perpetrated.	No. and Sex of the Murdered.		Date of the Murder.	Intended destination of the Murdered.		Supposed value of the property robbed.
		Men.	Women.		From	To	
277	Near Oonnow,	1	0	That Season of 1830,	Hydrabad,	Lucknow,	250 Rs. worth gold, 50 Rs. other property.
278	Athooa Bunther,	2	0	Ditto,	Cawnpore,	Bynswara,	50 rupees.
279	Near Baidurka,	4	0	Ditto,	Ditto,	Ditto,	100 rupees.
280	Near Runjeet-ka-Poorwah,	3	0	Ditto,	Agra,	Salone,	150 rupees.
281	Morown,	3	0	Ditto,	Meerut,	Jugdespore,	300 rupees.
282	Kutkur,	3	0	Ditto,	Banda,	Lucknow,	500 rupees.
283	Near Rooma,	2	0	Ditto,	Mirzapore,	Furruckhabad,	100 rupees.
284	Poorwah,	3	0	Ditto,	Ditto,	Ditto,	50 rupees and other trifling articles.
285	Bewurgaon,	1	0	Ditto,	Benares,	Delhi,	20 rupees.

1830, *under the following leaders: Keseeree Subadar, Rambuksh Jemadar, and other Leaders.*

REMARKS.

The gang then went to Oonnow and found there a Rajpoot from Hydera-bad on his way to Lucknow, who was decoyed and next morning strangled at a well a mile from the village, into which his body was thrown.

The next day's journey brought the gang to Athooa Bunther, where Bukshee jemadar decoyed two Hindoos on their way from Cawnpore to Bynswara, who were strangled next morning, and their bodies thrown into a pit.

After the murder the gang went to Baidurka, where they decoyed four travellers, by caste Hindoos, on their way from Cawnpore to Bynswara. They were strangled next morning a couple of miles from the village, and their bodies thrown into a well.

They next arrived at Bans-ka Krippeara, and found three Hindoo sepahees travelling from Agra to Salone, who were decoyed and put to death next morning six miles off near Runjeet-ka-Poorwa. The bodies were thrown into a well.

Having proceeded to Morown the Thugs fell in with three Hindoo travellers, bound to Jugdespore from Meerut, whom they decoyed and strangled next morning two miles from the village, leaving the bodies exposed on the plain.

They then went to Kutkur and rested. Three Hindoos travelling from Banda to Lucknow came to the same place, and being decoyed by the Thugs, were taken out and strangled next morning at a well a short distance off, into which the bodies were thrown.

The gang recrossed the Ganges at Dalla Mhow and proceeded by Futteh-pore to Sirsole in the Cawnpore District. There they inveigled two travellers, by caste Bearers, on their way from Mirzapore to Furruckhabad, whom they conducted next day to Rooma and rested in the seraee, next morning early the travellers were put to death, and their bodies were thrown into a well outside the town.

The gang after this proceeded to Nuwabgunge, and there fell in with three Hindoo travellers from Mirzapore on their way to Furruckhabad, who were decoyed and taken next day to Poorwa, where they all passed the night; next morning early the travellers were put to death about two miles from the village, and their bodies buried. After this affair the gang returned home without committing any other murders.

In the month of June 1830, Lalla Lochun jemadar, with eighteen Thugs, assembled at Chowdee-ka-Poorwa, and set out on a Thuggee expedition,

Report of a Thug Expedition in the years of 1829 *and*
Uchul Jemadar, Cheyne Jemadar, Runjeet Jemadar,

No. of List.	Names and jurisdiction of the place where the Murder was perpetrated.	No. and Sex of the Murdered.		Date of the Murder.	Intended destination of the Murdered.		Supposed value of the property robbed.
		Men.	Women.		From	To	
286	Secundra,	3	0	That Season of 1830,	Benares,	Byswara,	150 rupees, and 2 ponies.
287	Near Khoorjah,	9	0	Ditto,	Hansi,	Bojhpore	1200 rupees.
288	Achnair,	3	0	Ditto,	Neemuch,	Byswara,	150 rupees cash, 100 rupees property.
289	Buldeojee,	2	0	Ditto,	Muttra,	Ditto,	300 rupees cash, a pony, worth 100 rupees.
290	Dhyee Mutana,	1	0	Ditto,	Ditto,	Cawnpore,	150 rupees worth of gold, 100 Rs. cash.
291	Malagurh,	1	0	Ditto,	Neemuch,	Saharunpore,	100 rupees, a horse, and a gun.

1830, under the following leaders: Keseeree Subadar, Rambuksh Jemadar, and other Leaders.

REMARKS.

They first went to Chuppree-ka-Mhow, and there fell in with a traveller, by caste a Byragee, on his way from Benares to Delhi, who was decoyed and conducted next day to Bewurgaon, where they all passed the night. There they were joined by Uchul jemadar, Purusram jemadar and twenty Thugs, who had just left Behareepore in search of adventures, all went out next morning with the travellers, who were put to death about two miles from the village, and their bodies thrown into a well.

They proceeded onwards to Secundra, where Lalla Lochun jemadar dcoyed three Rajpoots travelling from Benares to Byswara. They were taken to a tank near the village early next morning and put to death. The bodies were buried.

After this they arrived at Soorujpore, and found nine sepahees, all Hindoos, from Hansi, on their way to Bojhpore, whom they decoyed and took to Khoorjah, and rested for the night; early next morning the travellers were conducted out of the village, and having been persuaded to sit down on the road, were put to death in the usual manner. The bodies were buried.

The Thugs all went on to Mahagurgh, where Dhunna (approver) with fifteen Thugs, left the party and returned home, promising to rejoin the gang at Buldeojee, near Muttra. The rest of the gang having visited Bhurtpore turned back and came to Achnair, where they inveigled three shop-keepers travelling from Neemuch to Bhyswara, and took them out next morning and strangled them a couple of miles from the village. The bodies were thrown into a well.

The gang roamed about that part of the country for some time without meeting with any success in their search for victims, and at length reached Buldeojee, where they fell in with two Rajpoots on their way from Muttra to Bynswara, who were decoyed and induced to take up their quarters near the Thugs. The party under Dhunna, which had gone home returned and joined the main gang. Next morning early the travellers were taken to a grove of Mangoe trees outside of the town and put to death. The bodies were thrown into a well.

They next went to Dhyee Mutana. There Uchul jemadar decoyed a traveller, by caste Hindoo, on his way from Muttra to Cawnpore. He was put to death early next morning as usual, and his body thrown into a well.

Proceeding onwards they reached Hatrass, where they fell in with Mean Khan Thug (now an approver) who laid hold of Uchul jemadar with the view of extorting money. The jemadar gave him a present of five rupees, and then

Report of a Thug Expedition in the years of 1829 *and*
Uchul Jemadar, Cheyne Jemadar, Runjeet Jemadar,

No. of List.	Names and jurisdiction of the place where the Murder was perpetrated.	No. and Sex of the Murdered.		Date of the Murder.	Intended destination of the Murdered.		Supposed value of the property robbed.
		Men.	Women.		From	To	
292	Near Boorhana,	1	0	That Season of 1830,	....	Sirdhana,	50 rupees, a horse, and a matchlock.
293	Kurreer,	4	0	Ditto,	Simlah,	Eastward,	150 rupees, 3 fishing nets.
294	Kurkoodda,	6	0	Ditto,	Kurnal,	Byswara,	300 rupees cash, a horse worth 250 rupees, 2 matchlocks.
295	Soorujhpore,	2	0	Ditto,	Delhi,	Cawnpore,	100 rupees.
296	Koorjah,	2	0	Ditto,	Hansi,	Lucknow,	50 rupees cash, 20 rupees property.

1830, ***under the following leaders: Keseeree Subadar, Rambuksh Jemadar, and other Leaders.***

REMARKS.

decamped accompanied by the gang. They did not rest till they reached Malagurh and there they fell in with and decoyed a trooper on his way from Neemuch to Saharunpore. He was conducted by the Thugs next morning a distance of a mile or two on his way, and then strangled on the bank of a small stream. His body was buried in the sandy bed of the river.

The gang next went by Meerut and Sirdhana to Boorhana which place they reached late in the afternoon, and before they had time even to divest themselves of their travelling dresses, a traveller, by caste a Brahmin, mounted on horseback, arrived at the same place on his way to Sirdhana. The gang turned back in the direction in which the Brahmin was proceeding, entered into conversation with him, and when they reached a stream between Sirdhana and Boorhana, they took advantage of the opportunity to strangle him, and threw the body into the stream.

They passed the night at Kurreer, and found four palkee bearers from Simla on their way eastward, who were resting at the same place, they were decoyed, and next morning were put to death outside of the village. The bodies were buried.

After this affair the gang went to Bidolee on the Jumna. There two of the gang of Thugs took leave and proceeded home. The remainder took the road to Meerut, where they arrived in the usual number of stages. When they had left that place they overtook six Hindoos travelling from Kurnal to Byswara, who were addressed and decoyed, and taken to pass the night at Kurkoodda; next morning early the travellers were strangled at a short distance from the village, and their bodies thrown into a well.

They next went to Soorujhpore and inveigled two Mahomedan travellers, one the servant of an European and the other a butcher by trade, who were proceeding from Delhi to Cawnpore. They were strangled early next morning, after leaving the village, and their bodies were buried.

After this affair they came to Secundra, rested there, and proceeded towards Khoorjah. On the road Lalla Lochun decoyed three travellers and Dhunna two travellers. The former came from Delhi and the latter from Hansi, and all intended to go to Lucknow, and were all Hindoos. All rested for the night in the seraee at Khoorjah, and next morning the two travellers decoyed by Dhunna were first taken out and strangled. After this Lalla Lochun endeavored to persuade the three travellers, who had joined him to set out, but from some cause or other, they had imbibed suspicions of their companions, and refused to leave their present quarters. The jemadar and his followers therefore abandoned their intended victims in despair.

Report of a Thug Expedition in the years of 1829 *and*
Uchul Jemadar, Cheyne Jemadar, Runjeet Jemadar,

No. of List.	Names and jurisdiction of the place where the Murder was perpetrated.	No. and Sex of the Murdered.		Date of the Murder.	Intended destination of the Murdered.		Supposed value of the property robbed.
		Men.	Women.		From	To	
297	Secundra,	3	0	That Season of 1830,	Delhi,	Byswara,	200 rupees.
298	Mullwa, in Mynpooree,	4	0	October, 1830,	Meerut,	Lucknow,	200 Rs. cash, and clothes.
299	Near Jhinjana,	4	0	That Season of 1830,	Loodhiana,	Furruckhabad,	100 rupees.
300	Bidolee,	3	0	Ditto,	Ditto,	....	150 rupees.
301	Koorja,	2	0	Ditto,	....	....	40 rupees.
302	Gosaeengunge,	3	0	Ditto,	Muttra,	Oude,	400 rupees.

1830, under the following leaders: Keseeree Subadar, Rambuksh Jemadar, and other Leaders.

REMARKS.

All the Thugs went to Akerabad and rested there. They fell in with three travellers with three ponies, on their way from Delhi to Byswara, who were decoyed by Lalla Lochun. Next day they all rested at Secundra, and early the succeeding morning the travellers were put to death as usual, and their bodies secreted in a marsh.

After this affair the gang broke up, and the Thugs proceeded to their respective homes.

In the month of October, 1830, Khulluk and Dhowkul jemadars, collected a gang of twenty-five Thugs at Maitee-ka-Poorwa in Furruckhabad, and set out on an expedition. They first went to Chupra Mhow and then to Mullwa in Mynpooree, where they found four shepherds on their way from Meerut to Lucknow, whom they decoyed and next morning put to death about two miles from the village. Being scared away by the approach of some wayfarers, the Thugs were unable to bury the bodies, which were abandoned in a field.

They fled from the place of murder and went to Jhinjara, where they rested in a Fuqueer's garden. Four Hindoo travellers from Loodhiana, on their way to Furruckhabad, came to the same place, and having been decoyed by one of the Thugs, were taken to pass the day in the Bazar. Next morning early they were strangled at a well, two miles off, and their bodies thrown into it.

The gang crossed the Jumna and went to Kurnal, where they fell in with three Burboonjas (gram-parchers) who came from Loodhiana. They were decoyed and passing the day in the Bazar, proceeded the succeeding morning to Bidolee. The travellers were strangled as usual the morning afterwards, at a distance of a couple of miles from the village, and their bodies were thrown into a well.

After this affair the gang went to Koorjah, where Khulluk jemadar decoyed two Hindoo travellers going the same way, who were taken to a well next morning and put to death. The dead bodies were thrown into the water.

They proceeded on to Goorsahagunge, and fell in with three Hindoos on their way from Muttra to the Oude territory. They were decoyed, and having passed the night with the Thugs were taken out and strangled next morning at a well two miles off, and their bodies thrown into it.

Having come near their homes, the Thugs determined to proceed there, without prosecuting their expedition further.

Report of a Thug Expedition in the years of 1829 *and*
Uchul Jemadar, Cheyne Jemadar, Runjeet Jemadar,

No. of List.	Names and jurisdiction of the place where the Murder was perpetrated.	No. and Sex of the Murdered.		Date of the Murder.	Intended destination of the Murdered.		Supposed value of the property robbed.
		Men.	Women.		From	To	
303	Poorwa, in Cawnpore,	2	0	November, 1830,	Loodhiana,	Benares,	250 rupees.
304	Near Minda seraee,	1	0	Ditto,	Delhi,	Ditto,	60 rupees, a pony.
305	Chikuttea, in Cawnpore,	2	0	Ditto,	Muttra,	Benares,	50 rupees.
306	Mulwa, in Futtehpore,	1	0	That Season of 1830,	Agra,	Ditto,	20 rupees.
307	In the vicinity of Allahabad,	3	0	Ditto,	Barrackpore,	....	250 rupees.

1830, *under the following leaders: Keseeree Subadar, Rambuksh Jemadar, and other Leaders.*

REMARKS.

In November 1830, Khulluk, Dhowkul and Bhowanee jemadars, with thirty Thugs, assembled at Maitee-ka-Poorwa in Furruckhabad, and then proceeded to Poorwa in Cawnpore. There they inveigled two travellers, a Rajpoot and a Koormee, from Loodhiana, on their way to Benares, who were passing the day in the bazar. They were strangled next morning early at a well two miles from the village, and their bodies thrown into the water.

They next proceeded to Cawnpore, and rested at the subadar's tank, there they found a Kayut on his way from Delhi to Benares, whom they decoyed and took with them next day to Roomah, and then to Kulleanpore. The succeeding morning they set out again and went all day long with the traveller in company. After night-fall they arrived within two miles of Mainda seraee, and took the opportunity to strangle the traveller, whose body they threw into a well.

Proceeding onwards, the gang reached Moghul-ka-seraee in the Allahabad district, and while passing the building they were perceived by Purshad jemadar, (now an approver,) who was resting there with a gang of about twenty-two Thugs, he called out to the passers by, who, on his invitation, joined this gang, and agreed to prosecute their expedition together.

The prior proceedings of this gang were as follows:

Mehrban and Lalla Lochun jemadars assembled seven Thugs at Judaee-ka-Poorwa in Furruckhabad, and set out on an expedition. They first went to Chikuttea in Cawnpore, where they decoyed two travellers, Hindoos by caste, on their way from Muttra to Benares: they took them to pass the day with them on the bank of the tank, and next morning having strangled them about two miles from the village, buried their bodies in a water-course.

They then went to Mulwa in Futtehpore, where they inveigled a Brahmin, travelling from Agra to Benares. He was put to death next morning a mile from the village, and his body thrown into a well.

The gang travelled on by regular stages to the vicinity of Allahabad without committing any other murder, and rested in the Moghul-ka-seraee. In the seraee Mehrban and Lalla Lochun were joined by Purshad jemadar and fifteen more Thugs, who had a short time previously left Dullepungger in Furruckhabad, and had come thus far without committing any murders on the way. Their numbers were still further augmented by the arrival of Ummer jemadar and five Thugs from Bhyns-ka-Poorwa in Oude, all remained in the seraee for several days, when one day Lalla Lochun jemadar having got drunk, created a great disturbance, and from dread of the results Ummer jemadar and

Report of a Thug Expedition in the years of 1829 *and* *Uchul Jemadar, Cheyne Jemadar, Runjeet Jemadar,*

No. of List.	Names and jurisdiction of the place where the Murder was perpetrated.	No. and Sex of the Murdered.		Date of the Murder.	Intended destination of the Murdered.		Supposed value of the property robbed.
		Men.	Women.		From	To	
308	Kakerabad,	1	0	That Season of 1830,	Kakerabad,	....	200 rupees, 2 gold mohurs.
309	Bindkee,	2	0	Ditto,	Agra,	Benares,	100 rupees.
310	Byana,	2	0	November, 1830,	Indore,	Jahanabad,	100 rupees.

1830, ***under the following leaders: Keseeree Subadar, Rambuksh Jemadar, and other Leaders.***

REMARKS.

his five followers instantly packed up their baggage and proceeded on their way. The remainder stopped at the seraee. The next day three travellers from Barrackpore, a Mahomedan and two Hindoos, with a pony laden with baggage, came to the caravansera, Rambuksh decoyed them and accommodated them near himself. Soon afterwards Khulluck jemadar's party, as before narrated, arrived at the same place. Next morning all set out very early and having gone a mile, the three travellers were put to death, and their bodies thrown into a well.

While the gang was proceeding onwards after the murder, a Thug came up with intelligence that Ummer jemadar had fallen in with a traveller and wanted assistance. It appears that after quitting the seraee Ummer jemadar and his five followers went to Emaungunge, where they fell in with a Hindoo traveller from Calcutta, whom they decoyed and proceeded onwards next morning towards Kakerabad. When near that place they were overtaken by Mehrban and others, in all seven Thugs, from the gang whom they had left at the seraee, and whose assistance they had solicited: the river Ganges flows near Kakerabad, and the Thugs persuaded their victim to accompany them to the river to bathe, and while performing his ablutions he fell an easy prey to them, and his dead body was permitted to float away in the stream.

The murdering party went to Shujadpore, where they were soon afterwards joined by the main gang. During the day the Thugs learnt from the report of some travellers, that three dead bodies had that morning been discovered in a well near Mughul-ka-seraee, and hearing this Khulluk, Dhowkul, Bhowanee and Ummer jemadars, with their followers, took their departure homewards immediately. The remainder of the gang, twenty-two in number, under Lalla Lochun and Ram Buksh proceeded to Bindkee. There they decoyed two Hindoo travellers. They passed the night together in the seraee, and next morning the travellers were put to death about a mile from it, and their bodies thrown into a well.

After this affair the gang determined to return home, and arrived there without any further adventure.

In the same month, (November 1830,) Samadhan and Cheyne jemadars, with nine Thugs, assembled at Macha in Cawnpore. They set out on an expedition and proceeded through Bhurtpore to Byana, where they fell in with two travellers, by caste Rajpoots, on their way from Indore to Jehanabad, whom they decoyed and next morning put to death in a field of grain about a mile from the village. The bodies were buried in a dry water-course.

Report of a Thug Expedition in the years of 1829 *and Uchul Jemadar, Cheyne Jemadar, Runjeet Jemadar,*

No. of List.	Names and jurisdiction of the place where the Murder was perpetrated.	No. and Sex of the Murdered.		Date of the Murder.	Intended destination of the Murdered.		Supposed value of the property robbed.
		Men.	Women.		From	To	
311	Keroulee,	2	0	That Season of 1830,	Indore,	Allahabad,	150 rupees.
312	Khoodbedpore,	2	0	Ditto,	Bhurtpore,	Benares,	25 rupees.
313	Khaira, in Sirdhana,	3	0	December, 1830,	Kurnal,	Oude,	60 rupees.
314	Near Haita,	2	0	Ditto,	Loodhiana,	Ditto,	90 rupees.

JUBULPORE, SUPERINTENDENT'S OFFICE,
The 18*th March*, 1840.

1830, ***under the following leaders: Keseeree Subadar, Rambuksh Jemadar, and other Leaders.***

REMARKS.

They continued their course to Hindown and thence went to Keroulee, where they rested in the seraee. Two Mahomedans from Indore, on their way to Allahabad, were resting there, and were decoyed by the Thugs. Next morning they all set out together on the road, where the travellers were strangled and their bodies buried in a water-course.

Having completed the murder, the Thugs turned back and went to Khoodbedpore. There they found two Brahmins, on their way from Bhurtpore to Benares, who were decoyed and next morning taken out two miles from the village and strangled as usual. The bodies were thrown into a well.

This was the last murder perpetrated during this expedition, and the Thugs proceeded home afterwards.

During the month of December, 1830, Bichoo jemadar and fifteen Thugs agreed to go out in search of adventures. They left Maitee-ka-Poorwa in Furruckhabad, and went to Khaira in Sirdhana, where they fell in with three Hindoo travellers from Kurnal on their way to the Oude territory, whom they decoyed, and next morning, having conducted them two miles out of the village, put them to death, and buried the bodies in a swamp.

The gang proceeded onwards to Haita, where they decoyed two Hindoos, who were travelling from Loodhiana to Oude, and induced them to rest near the Thugs; about midnight they all set out together, and the travellers were put to death before day-break, and their bodies thrown into a well.

Having completed the murder, the gang returned home again.

P. A. REYNOLDS,

Superintendent for the

Suppression of Thuggee.

1830.

List of Thugs engaged in the foregoing Murders.

No.	Name.	Parentage.	Caste.	Remarks.
1	Uchul Jemadar,	Son of Gunsham,	Lodhee,	Hanged at Jubulpore, 1835
	Cheyne Jemadar,	Rukah,	Ditto,	Died while out on an expedition.
	Runjeet, alias Deveedeen Jemadar,	Kurhora,	Ditto,	Died in Jail at Saugor.
	Dhunna Burmoocha,	Chidda,	Ditto,	Hanged at Jubulpore, 1836.
5	Nowul Jemadar,	Punchum,	Ditto,	Ditto at Saugor, 1833.
	Dhunna,	Mudaree,	Ditto,	Approver.
	Bukshee Jemadar,	Rutta,	Ditto,	Ditto.
	Eseree,	Ditto,	Ditto,	Ditto.
	Heera,	Sumadhan,	Ditto,	Ditto.
10	Shewdeen,	Asa,	Ditto,	Ditto.
	Dhunna,	Kashee,	Ditto,	Transported from Saugor.
	Chidda,	Ramkissen,	Ditto,	Ditto Jubulpore.
	Heera,	Tijja,	Ditto,	Hanged at Cawnpore.
	Lalshah,	....	Ditto,	Still at large.
15	Soomair,	Muthoulee,	Ditto,	Approver, since dead.
	Keseeree Subadar,	Budda,	Ditto,	Hanged at Jubulpore, 1835.
	Tijja,	Ditto,	Ditto,	Approver.
	Khooshalee,	....	Ditto,	Transported.
	Rumma,	Munna,	Ditto,	Ditto.
20	Bulla,	Ditto,	Ditto,	Ditto.
	Futtee Jemadar,	....	Mussulman,	Approver, at Lucknow.

	Danyal Jemadar,		Mussulman,	Approver, at Lucknow.
	Khan Mahomed,	Torab,	Ditto,	Ditto ditto.
	Rumzan Jemadar,		Ditto,	Ditto ditto.
25	Mudar,		Ditto,	Ditto ditto.
	Soller,		Ditto,	A prisoner at Lucknow.
	Sadee,		Ditto,	Ditto ditto.
	Koorkoot,		Ditto,	Ditto ditto.
	Mehrban,		Ditto,	Ditto ditto.
30	Bukhtawer,	Koonj,	Lodhee,	Died at home.
	Khulluk Jemadar,	Rutta,	Ditto,	Hanged at Saugor in 1833.
	Dhowkul Jemadar,	Chutta,	Ditto,	Ditto ditto.
	Lalla Lochun,	Koonj,	Ditto,	Hanged at Jubulpore, 1835.
	Gunna,	Huns,	Ditto,	Transported.
35	Bhikka,	Heera,	Ditto,	Ditto.
	Anward,	Mudaree,	Ditto,	Ditto from Jubulpore.
	Budlee,	Dyah,	Ditto,	Died while on an expedition.
	Zoolfukar Jemadar,	Kumal,	Ditto,	Approver.
	Bhoorge,		Ditto,	Ditto.
40	Noor Khan Jemadar,	Dhowkul,	Ditto,	Hanged at Jubulpore, 1835.
	Shunker Jemadar,	Dhyaram,	Bukhal,	Ditto ditto.
	Dibba,	Ditto,	Ditto,	Approver.
	Dhummee,		Ditto,	Transported.
	Oomeid Koobra,		Lodhee,	At large.
45	Ram Buksh Jemadar,	Runna,	Ditto,	Approver.
	Deveedeen Jemadar,	Ditto,	Ditto,	Ditto (dead.)
	Girdharee,	Ramlal,	Brahmin,	Approver.
	Sumbha,	Bhugwant,	Lodhee,	Ditto.
	Suma,	Ghassee,	Ditto,	Ditto.
50	Doojjooa,	Munsa,	Ditto,	Hanged.
	Nowlah,	Oomeid,	Ditto,	Transported.
	Hummunchulla,	Runnooa Moonshee,	Ditto,	Approver.
	Dhunnooa,		Ditto,	Ditto.

No.	Name.	Parentage.	Caste.	Remarks.
	Purusram Jemadar,	Oodey,	Lodhee,	Died at Jubulpore, under sentence of death.
55	Surrawan,	Ditto,	Ditto,	At large.
	Hurlal,	Sookka,	Ditto,	Hanged at Saugor in 1833.
	Dhumma,		Ditto,	Approver.
	Binda,		Ditto,	Transported from Jubulpore.
	Atmaram,	Dhya,	Ditto,	Ditto ditto.
60	Oodeye,	Bukha,	Ditto,	Approver.
	Gopal,	Dhya,	Ditto,	Ditto.
	Moollooa,	Sookhtee,	Ditto,	Ditto.
	Bhowanee Jemadar,	Mukha,	Ditto,	Died at home.
	Purshad Jemadar,	Runna,	Ditto,	Approver.
65	Ummer Jemadar,	Madaree,	Ditto,	Transported.
	Mukkooa,		Ditto,	Ditto.
	Gunesh,	Mukhun,	Ditto,	Died in Jail at Saugor.
	Bichoo Jemadar,	Puttee,	Ditto,	Approver.
	Suroop,	Gunesh,	Ditto,	Transported from Jubulpore.
70	Durrear,	Ditto,	Ditto,	Ditto ditto.
	Sibbooa,		Ditto,	Approver.
	Mohun,		Ditto,	Ditto.
	Mandhata,	Dulput,	Ditto,	Ditto.
	Runnooa Moonshee,	Jeysookh,	Ditto,	Hanged at Jubulpore, 1835.
75	Gumbhooa,		Bukhal,	At large.
	Dhunna,	Hurree,	Lodhee,	Approver.
	Seetulla,	Chidda,	Ditto,	Died while out on Thuggee.
	Neehullooa,		Ditto,	Transported from Jubulpore.
	Boodhooa,		Ditto,	Ditto.
80	Budla,		Ditto,	Ditto.

No.				
	Bhola,	Mukeh,	Bunesh,	Approver.
	Khoosheeal,	Nutha,	Lodhee,	Transported from Jubulpore.
	Desraj,		Kachee,	Ditto Saugor.
	Jowihur,		Rajpoot,	Ditto ditto.
85	Bukshee,		Kullal,	Hanged at Saugor.
	Himma,		Brahmin,	Ditto ditto.
	Budlee,	Suntoke,	Lodhee,	Approver.
	Deoraee Jemadar,		Ditto,	Died at home.
	Teeka,	Nundee,	Ditto,	Approver.
90	Cheyne,	Gungaram,	Brahmin,	Ditto.
	Sumadhun Jemadar,		Ditto,	Died at home.
	Gunesh,	Sumadhan,	Ditto,	At large.
	Jowkee,	Ditto,	Ditto,	Ditto.
	Cheree,	Gunga,	Lodhee,	Died at home.
95	Heera,	Ramdeen,	Ditto,	Approver.
	Muhbooa,	Chedda,	Ditto,	Ditto.
	Cheyne,		Ditto,	At large.
	Anoop,	Cheyne,	Ditto,	Transported.
	Bhola,	Mudaree,	Ditto,	Ditto.
100	Bhikka,	Ditto,	Ditto,	Approver, since dead.
	Peareelal,	Mudden,	Kayut,	At large.
	Purshad,	Dya,	Bukhal,	Transported.
	Bhujja,	Oomeid Jemadar,	Lodhee,	Ditto.
	Layuk,	Kishnoo,	Ditto,	Hanged at Saugor.
105	Purshad, 2d,		Ditto,	Transported.
	Hurrea,	Adopted by Lalla Lochun,	Ditto,	Died at home.
	Dhowkulla,	Son-in-law of Harea,	Ditto,	At large.
	Ram Buksh,	Ram Kissen,	Ditto,	Ditto.
	Letchmuna,	Ditto,	Ditto,	Ditto.
110	Ram Kishen,		Ditto,	Ditto.
	Chittooa,	Oomeid,	Ditto,	Hanged at Cawnpore.
	Buksheea,	Ditto,	Ditto,	Transported.

No.	Name.	Parentage.	Caste.	Remarks.
	Ramdeen,	Runna,	Lodhee,	Hanged at Cawnpore.
	Gholabee,	Bukhtawer,	Ditto,	Ditto at Bareilly.
115	Shewdeen,	Ditto,	Ditto,	Transported.
	Ghazee,	Bhugwant,	Ditto,	Ditto.
	Muheenlal,	Dhya,	Ditto,	Ditto.
	Shewdeen,	Munsa,	Ditto,	Ditto.
	Rambuksh,	Pitthee,	Ditto,	Hanged at Cawnpore.
120	Mudaree,	Suntoke,	Ditto,	Ditto ditto.
	Hoolassee,	Munsookh,	Ditto,	Ditto ditto.
	Bhimma,	Ditto,	Ditto,	Ditto ditto.
	Dhunna,	Hussa,	Ditto,	Ditto ditto.
	Munglee,	Santoke,	Ditto,	Transported.
125	Makhun Jemadar,	Kissen,	Ditto,	Approver.
	Khooshaleea,	Uchul Jemadar,	Ditto,	Transported from Jubulpore.
	Nowal,	Oomeid,	Ditto,	Ditto.
	Ramnath,	Nynsookh,	Jossee,	A prisoner at Jubulpore.
	Gunesh,	Koondun,	Ditto,	At large.
130	Sibba,		Carpenter,	Died in Jail at Jubulpore.
	Hulbulla,	Ditto,	Ditto,	Ditto ditto.
	Asa,	Munnee,	Lodhee,	Transported.
	Mohun,	Dhya,	Ditto,	Ditto.
	Budlee,	Ditto,	Ditto,	Transported.
135	Lalla,		Barber,	Died in Jail at Jubulpore.
	Mudaree,	Nuthee,	Lodhee,	Ditto ditto.
	Doorgooa,	Bhujja,	Ditto,	Transported.
	Jowihur,	Dhowkul,	Ditto,	At large.
	Rumma,	Munsa,	Ditto,	Approver, since dead.

140	Goorooa,	Dhya,	Ditto,	At large.
	Munnooa,	Oomeid,	Ditto,	Ditto.
	Pemmooa,	....	Bearer,	Ditto.
	Dooberea,	Kooshal,	Lodhee,	Ditto.
	Gungooa,	....	Ditto,	Ditto.
145	Hurlal,	Pemma,	Ditto,	Hanged at Saugor.
	Dhowkul Jemadar.	Ditto,	Ditto,	Ditto ditto.
	Mehrban Jemadar,	Bijjaeen,	Ditto,	Approver.
148	Heera,	Oomeid,	Ditto,	Ditto.

P. A. REYNOLDS,

Superintendent for the

Suppression of Thuggee.

JUBBULPORE, SUPERINTENDENT'S OFFICE,
The 18th March, 1840.

REPORT

OF A

THUG EXPEDITION

In the Year 1831.

Report of a Thug Expedition in the year 1831, *Rambuksh, Deveedeen, with Twenty-five*

No. of List.	Names and jurisdiction of the place where the Murder was perpetrated.	No and Sex of the Murdered.		Date of the Murder.	Intended destination of the Murdered.		Supposed value of the property robbed.
		Men.	Women.		From	To	
315	Poorwa, in Cawnpore,	1	0	January, 1831,	Benares,	Mynpooree,	50 rupees.
316	Sooltangunge, in Mynpooree,	1	0	Ditto,	Kurnal,	Cawnpore,	100 rupees.
317	Mallawa,	2	0	Ditto,	Loodhiana,	Ditto,	150 rupees.
318	Somp, in the Coel district,	2	0	Ditto,	Ditto,	Eastward,	200 rupees.
319	Khoorjah, in Anoopshuhur,	2	0	Ditto,	Ditto,	Mirzapore,	100 rupees.
320	Boorhana,	2	0	Ditto,	Kurnal,	Cawnpore,	200 rupees, a sword and musket.

under the following leaders: Mehrban, Thugs, and other Leaders.

REMARKS.

In January 1831, Mehrban, Rambuksh, Daveedeen and other leaders with twenty-five Thugs, assembled at Rajee Mhow in Furruckhabad, and set out on an expedition. In the course of three or four days they arrived at Bithoor, and when next morning they were about to set out towards the east, a bird chirped, without repeating its cry—alarmed at this monitary omen, the Thugs agreed among themselves, that it would be dangerous to pursue the proposed route, and they accordingly took the road to the west. They went and rested at Poorwa in Cawnpore, where they fell in with a Hindoo from Benares on his way to Mynpooree, mounted on a pony, whom they decoyed, and next morning having taken him a mile out of the village, put him to death. His body was thrown into a well.

After the murder, they proceeded on towards Secundra, which place they reached in two days—on the road onwards next day they were joined by another gang of fifteen Lodhee Thugs under Budlee, Hurlall and Lallah Lochun jemadars.

This gang had, a short time previously, set out from Chouda-ka-Poorwa in Cawnpore, and proceeded in the first instance to Sooltangunge in Mynpooree. There they had decoyed a Brahmin from Kurnal on his way to Cawnpore, whom they strangled next morning, and threw his body into a well a mile or so distant from the village.

They then went to Mallawa and inveigled two travellers, by caste shepherds who had come from Loodhiana, intending to go to Cawnpore. The travellers were taken out next morning and strangled at a well two miles off, and their bodies thrown into it.

Having proceeded onwards they reached Somp, in the Coel district, where Lalla Lochun decoyed two troopers, by caste Mahomedans, from Loodhiana, travelling eastward. They were strangled next morning on the road two miles from the village, and their bodies buried.

Their next stage was to Koorjah in Anoopshuhur; and there they fell in with and decoyed two travellers, shop-keepers by trade, who came from Loodhiana, on their way to Mirzapore. They were put to death next morning as usual, and their bodies buried.

After this the gang reached Boorhana. There they found two Hindoos from Kurnal on their way to Cawnpore, whom they induced to take up their quarters with them. Next morning the travellers were taken to a river which runs near the town, and having been put to death, their bodies were thrown into the stream.

Report of a Thug Expedition in the year of 1831,
Rambuksh, Deveedeen, with Twenty-five

No. of List.	Names and jurisdiction of the place where the Murder was perpetrated.	No. and Sex of the Murdered.		Date of the Murder.	Intended destination of the Murdered.		Supposed value of the property robbed.
		Men.	Women.		From	To	
321	Jhinjana,	1	0	That Season of 1831,	Loodhiana,	Oude,	100 rupees.
322	Bidolee, near Kurnal,	1	0	Ditto,	Lahore,	Allahabad,	50 rupees.
323	Kerooa,	2	0	Ditto,	Ditto,	Lucknow,	300 rupees.
324	Haupper,	1	0	Ditto,	Kurnal	Cawnpore,	150 rupees.
325	Near Secundra,	3	0	Ditto,	Meerut,	Ditto,	5 copper coins, and some old clothes.
326	Ditto,	2	0	Ditto,	Hurdwar,	Allahabad,	300 rupees.
327	Near Buldeojee.	2	0	Ditto,	Baroda,	Byswara,	50 rupees.

under the following leaders: Mehrban, Thugs, and other Leaders.

REMARKS.

The gang next proceeded to Jhinjana, and met a traveller, by caste a Hindoo, who came from Loodhiana on his way to the Oude State, whom they decoyed; and taking him out next morning a mile from the town, they strangled him, and threw his body into a well.

The Thugs proceeded in the same direction as far as Bidolee near Kurnal, whence having turned back they came to a village ten miles distant. They found a traveller, by caste herdsman, who was going from Lahore to Allahabad. He was decoyed and next morning put to death on the way-side, where his body was also buried.

Passing through Sirdhana, the capital of the Begum Sumroo, they went to Kerooa, where they fell in with two travellers from Lahore, who were proceeding to Lucknow. They were Hindoos by caste, and were persuaded to join the gang, who put them to death next morning as usual, and buried their bodies about two miles from the village.

Having visited Meerut, the Thugs went to Happur and decoyed a traveller, by caste Hindoo, who was going from Kurnal to Cawnpore, who was conducted out next morning and strangled two miles off. The body was buried.

After this they arrived by easy stages at Coel, from whence they again took the road to Secundra. Before reaching the latter place they overtook three Hindoos, by caste Kuhars, who were travelling from Meerut to Cawnpore. These men were decoyed and the gang had not proceeded many paces when they fell in with Deveedeen jemadar, Mehrban and others, who had murdered the Hindoo as already described. This party of Thugs had two Ganges water-carriers with them, whom they had also just decoyed, and who were on their way from Hurdwar to Allahabad. It was agreed that Deveedeen and ten Thugs should join Lalla Lochun's party, and that the rest of his gang should rendezvous at Shamlee. The five travellers passed the night at Secundra, whither they were accompanied by the murdering party. Next morning early the Ganges water-carriers were taken out first, and put to death two miles from the town. The bodies were buried. Next the Kuhars were led out to their fate, and having been conducted to a tank four miles off, they were strangled and their bodies buried on the brink.

After completing the murders they went to Buldeojee, and fell in with two travellers, a Rajpoot and a Cow-keeper, on their way from Barodah to Byswara, who were decoyed, and next morning having been taken to a well two miles from the village, they were strangled, and their bodies thrown into the water.

Report of a Thug Expedition in the year 1831, *Rambuksh, Deveedeen, with Twenty-five*

No. of List.	Names and jurisdiction of the place where the Murder was perpetrated.	No. and Sex of the Murdered.		Date of the Murder.	Intended destination of the Murdered.		Supposed value of the property robbed.
		Men.	Women.		From	To	
328	Bohgaon, in the Mynpooree district,	2	0	That Season of 1831,	Baroda,	Byswara,	50 rupees.
329	Near Kurreer,	3	0	Ditto,	Kurnal,	Cawnpore,	50 rupees.
330	Mukhun-ka-seraee, in Mynpooree,	1	0	Ditto,	Muttra,	Ditto,	25 rupees.
331	Ajeetgunge, in the Mynpooree zillah,	2	0	Ditto,	....	Benares,	6 Gold mohurs, and other property, all worth 150 rupees.

under the following leaders: Mehrban, Thugs, and other Leaders.

REMARKS.

Lalla Lochun jemadar's gang of fifteen Thugs separated at this place from Deveedeen's party, and took the road homewards; while the latter proceeded to keep their appointment with their companies at Shamlee.

Lalla Lochun's party travelled on towards Bohgaon in the Mynpooree district, which place they reached in the course of some days. They fell in with two Brahmins from Benares on their way to Byswara, whom they decoyed, and having passed the night with them at Bohgaon, they put them to death next morning, and threw their bodies into a well two miles off. After the murder this gang reached home without any other adventure.

Part of Deveedeen's gang under Mehrban Sing left Secundra, and proceeded at once to Shamlee, where they remained in expectation of Deveedeen's arrival. After the murder at Bohgaon, Deveedeen and his companions went directly to Shamlee, and were welcomed with great delight by the rest of the gang, who had begun to entertain apprehensions for their safety.

Next day, they all set out again, and proceeded as far as Bidolee, without meeting with any success in their search after victims. They therefore turned back and came to Kurreer, where they fell in with three shoe-makers travelling from Kurnal to Cawnpore, whom they decoyed, and next morning escorted a couple of miles on their way, and then put to death. The bodies were thrown into a well.

Marching onwards by regular stages, the Thugs, in the course of some days, arrived at Mukhun-ka-seraee, in Mynpooree, and inveigled a Hindoo traveller on his way from Muttra to Cawnpore. He passed the night in their company, and next morning was strangled a mile out of the town, and his body thrown into a well.

They went on to Shukoorabad, slept there, and next day proceeded onwards. About eight o'clock in the morning, they reached a tank near Arown in the Mynpooree zillah, and fell in with two travellers, by caste Lodhees, on their way to Benares. They were decoyed, conducted to Ajeetgunge, where they passed the night, and next morning were put to death outside the town, and their bodies thrown into a well.

After the murder, they went to Mudpore, and there Deveedeen and Mehrban were recognized by a Brahmin, who knew them to be Thugs. The Brahmin gave information in the town, and a number of people came out, seized Rambuksh, Deveedeen, Bhowanee and Mohun, and made them over to the thanadar of the Police, who forwarded them to the magistrate at Mynpooree. These four men were detained on suspicion for six months, after

Report of a Thug Expedition in the year 1831, *Rambuksh, Deveedeen, with Twenty-five*

No. of List.	Names and jurisdiction of the place where the Murder was perpetrated.	No. and Sex of the Murdered.		Date of the Murder.	Intended destination of the Murdered.		Supposed value of the property robbed.
		Men.	Women.		From	To	
332	Barha, in Cawnpore,	1	0	That Season of 1831,	Bundelkhund,	Benares,	20 rupees, a pony.
333	Baba Wallagaon,	2	0	Ditto,	Oude,	Mhow,	100 rupees.
334	Near Burwara,	2	0	Ditto,	Lucknow,	Saugor,	80 rupees.
335	Near Muhoba,	2	0	Ditto,	Mhow,	....	150 rupees.
336	Near Oomree,	2	0	Ditto,	Dekhan,	Northward,	40 Rs. cash, 36 rupees worth a silver armlet.

under the following leaders : Mehrban, Thugs, and other Leaders.

REMARKS.

which intelligence having intermediately been conveyed to Saugor of their imprisonment, they were made over to a party sent from that place to receive them. Of the number three were admitted approvers at Saugor, and the fourth, Mohun, was tried and sentenced.

The remainder of the gang, on perceiving that their leaders were captured, dispersed and returned home.

At the same time that the above proceedings were being carried on, (in January, 1831,) another gang of thirty Thugs, under Bhowanee, Dhowkul, and Shunkur jemadars assembled at Motee-ka-Poorwa in Furruckabad, and set out on an expedition; they went as far as Barha in Cawnpore, and there fell in with their first victim, a Hindoo, on his way from Bundelkhund to Benares, who was decoyed; and having passed the night with the Thugs, was put to death next morning in a field, and his body securely buried.

The gang crossed the Jumna at Calpee, and were joined while in the boat by a sepahee and another man, both Hindoos, on their way from Oude to Mhow in Malwa. They agreed to travel with the Thugs, and went and slept at Baba Wallagaon. Next morning they were strangled, and their bodies buried in a water-course.

After this affair they went on to Keitah in Bundelkhund. There they managed to decoy two travellers, a Brahmin and a Kuhar, who were going from Lucknow to Saugor, and conducted them to Killowa. Having slept there, the travellers were taken near to Burwara next morning, and then put to death. The bodies were buried.

The gang went on to Chutterpore, and rested near the well called Meetah Kooa. They fell in with two shepherds, who were going from Mhow to their homes in the Dooab, and took them to a hamlet near Muhoaba, where they passed the night. Next morning the travellers were put death, two miles from the village.

They next arrived at Rahut, and rested in a garden. There they were joined by Bhikka, son of Sunnum jemadar, with nine Thugs from Sindouse, and soon afterwards, two Hindoos from the Dekhan, on their way northward, came to the same place and were decoyed. They were taken to Oomreea, and the next morning setting out again the Thugs put them to death at a nullah two miles off, and buried their bodies. The remains have been disinterred, and the case tried by the Agent to the Governor General S. and N. T.

Report of a Thug Expedition in the year 1831, *Rambuksh, Deveedeen, with Twenty-five*

No. of List.	Names and jurisdiction of the place where the Murder was perpetrated.	No. and Sex of the Murdered.		Date of the Murder.	Intended destination of the Murdered.		Supposed value of the property robbed.
		Men.	Women.		From	To	
337	Kunnooa Khairah and Baba Wallagaon,	4	0	That Season of 1831,	Keitah,	Cawnpore,	180 rupees.
338	Oude State,	2	0	Ditto,	Saugor,	Beyrajh,	100 rupees.
339	Near Futtehgunge,	2	0	Ditto,	....	Sultanpore,	60 rupees.
340	Bulla,	2	0	Ditto,	Gwalior,	Bulla,	125 rupees, and a pony.
341	Moraya,	1	0	Ditto,	....	Sultanpore,	50 rupees.

under the following leaders: Mehrban, Thugs, and other Leaders.

REMARKS.

The Sindouse Thugs now took their leave of the Loodhees of the Dooab, who proceeded to Jullalpore, and at the river near it they met and decoyed two Hindoos travelling from Keitah to Cawnpore. The party had scarcely got clear of the bed of the river, when two Bhisties (water-carriers) from Keitah, also proceeding to Cawnpore, came up, and being addressed were persuaded to join the gang. The Thugs divided themselves into two parties. One took the two water-carriers to Kunnooa Khairah, and the other the two Hindoos to Baba Wallagaon. Next morning all four were put to death in the usual manner. The bodies were buried in both instances.

Having visited Calpee the gang returned home, without any further adventures.

In the month of March, 1831, Khuluk, Dhowkul, and Bhowanee jemadars, with six Thugs collected together, and went to Maita-ka-Poorwa, in the Furruckhabad district. They arrived at Sirsaya Ghat on the Ganges, where their numbers were increased by the junction of Shewdeen, Runna, and others, seven Thugs, all crossed the river Ganges and entered the Oude State. They soon afterwards decoyed two travellers, Hindoos by caste, from Saugor, on their way to Bhurach who passed the night in their company, and next morning were put to death as usual. The bodies were thrown into a well.

They then went on to Futtehgunge, there they fell in with two Hindoos, who were going to Sultanpore, who were decoyed, and next morning put to death two miles from the village. The bodies were thrown into a well.

After the murder they proceeded slowly onwards and were joined by Gunga Buneea, a Thug, who had come out in search of them, and continued their journey unsuccessfully as regarded victims till they reached Runjeet-ka-Poorwa. There they decoyed two cowherds from Gwalior, on their way to Bulla, and took them to Bassa Peepeerea and rested. Soon afterwards a gang of twenty Jumaldee Thugs of Oude, under Mehrban, Ruhman, and others came to the same place. All the Thugs set out next day with the travellers—they proceeded onwards till nightfall, when they arrived within a mile of Bulla. The travellers already imagined themselves safe at home and had even invited their murderers to partake of their evening meal at their own houses, when the fatal signal was given and they were put to death in the usual manner. The bodies were buried in a dry water-course.

The gangs went and slept at Moraya: there they met a barber on his way to Sultanpore, whom they decoyed, and next morning strangled a mile or two from the village, burying his body in the sand.

Report of a Thug Expedition in the year 1831, *Rambuksh, Deveedeen, with Twenty-five*

No. of List.	Names and jurisdiction of the place where the Murder was perpetrated.	No. and Sex of the Murdered.		Date of the Murder.	Intended destination of the Murdered.		Supposed value of the property robbed.
		Men.	Women.		From	To	
342	Hydergurh,	4	0	That Season of 1831,	....	Jounpore,	300 rupees.
343	Supowlee, in the Gwalior State,	2	0	Ditto,	Gwalior,	Jhalone,	50 rupees.
	Meeting of Sindouse Thugs.						
344	Near Nowr,	2	0	1831,	Gwalior,	Oude territory,	100 rupees.
345	Sobhana, in the Coel district,	2	0	Ditto,	Mynpooree,	Subathoo,	100 rupees.

under the following leaders: Mehrban, Thugs, and other Leaders.

REMARKS.

Hydurgurh was their next day's journey; and while there four travellers, by caste Hindoos, fell into their hands. These men were proceeding to Jounpore. Next morning the travellers were conducted out of the village, and strangled at a well two miles off, into which their bodies were thrown.

After this murder, the two gangs of Jumaldhees and Lodhees separated, and went to their respective homes without perpetrating any other murder.

In the month of March 1831, a gang of twenty-two Thugs was collected by Shunker and Hurlal jemadars at Kurrooa in Furruckhabad. They determined to proceed into Bundelkhund, and crossed the Jumna at Shergurh. Here they were joined by Bhola Buneea, and two other Thugs, and all went to Supowlee in the Gwalior State. A Brahmin and a Kuhar, on their way from Gwalior to the neighbourhood of Jhalone, were decoyed at that place, and next morning were taken out and strangled in a field in which their bodies were buried.

The gang then proceeded to Rampooree. There they decoyed two travellers, a Brahmin and a Buneea, who were going from Gwalior to the Oude territory, and took them with them next day to Nowr, where they passed the night in the bazar. A gang of twenty-seven Thugs from Sindouse under Bukbut Mooreah, Thukoree, Zalim and other leaders happened to be at the same place, and were invited to assist at the murder of the travellers, who were taken out a short distance next morning and put to death. The bodies were thrown into a well.

N. B. These remains of bodies have been pointed out by Bhola Buneea approver, and exhumed—the case was tried by the Agent to the Governor General at Jubulpore. The murder has been ascertained to have been committed on the 24th March 1831. Having completed this murder, the gang returned home.

In the month of May, 1831, Uchul, Bukshel and twenty-five Thugs met Bahareepore, and agreed to try their fortune together on an expedition. It was determined that ten Thugs of the number should set out at once, and the remaining fifteen should join them at Sirhind twenty days afterwards The ten Thugs first went to Sobhna, in the Coel district, where they fell in with two Hindoo travellers of the Kaet caste, on their way from Mynpooree to Subathoo, who were decoyed and induced to join the party. The same day twenty Thugs under Lalla Lochun jemadar came to Sobhna, and rested for the day outside of the village. The two gangs interchanged enquiries, but those inside of the village did not reveal to their friends outside, that they had any travellers in their train. Next morning early, the travellers

Report of a Thug Expedition in the year 1831, *Rambuksh, Deveedeen, with Twenty-five*

No. of List.	Names and jurisdiction of the place where the Murder was perpetrated.	No. and Sex of the Murdered.		Date of the Murder.	Intended destination of the Murdered.		Supposed value of the property robbed.
		Men.	Women.		From	To	
346	Near Goorsahee-gunge,	2	0	That Season of 1831,	Muttra,	Byswara.	200 rupees, and a pony.
347	Koorjah,	2	0	Ditto,	Delhi,	Ditto,	200 rupees.
348	Jhinjanah,	3	0	Ditto,	Loodhi-ana,	Cawn-pore,	150 rupees.
349	Semgurh,	3	0	Ditto,	Loodhi-ana,	Cawn-pore,	300 rupees.
350	Bunjara-ka-seraee,	2	0	Ditto,	Lahore.	Gya,	500 Rs. cash, 2 horses, &c.

under the following leaders: Mehrban, Thugs, and other Leaders.

REMARKS.

were inveigled out and put to death, a couple of miles from the village. The bodies were buried. Having completed the murder, the gang returned and joined the other party under Lalla Lochun jemadar.

It appears that Lalla Lochun jemadar with his twenty Thugs, having set out from Jiddee-ka-Poorwa in the Furruckhabad district, went to Goorsahee Gunge, where they decoyed two Brahmin sepahees on their way from Muttra to Byswara, and put them to death next morning a mile from the village, and threw their bodies into a well.

After this they went at once to Sobhna and joined Uchul jemadar's party, as has been above related.

The two parties having united went to Koorja There they met with two travellers, by caste Brahmins, on their way from Delhi to Byswara, whom they inveigled into their company, and having conducted them out next morning to a well two miles off, they strangled them and threw their bodies into the water.

Proceeding onwards, the gangs passed through Boolundshuhur, Meerut and Sirdhana to Bidolee. They had not even undressed themselves after three days' journey at the last places, when three sepahees, Hindoos by caste, arrived there from Loodhiana, on their way to Cawnpore. They were decoyed by Uchul jemadar, and the gang proceeded onwards with them to Jhinjana, where they all halted to sleep. Early next morning the travellers were taken two miles from the village, and having been strangled, their bodies were thrown into a well.

After the murder the gang went on to Kurnal, and thence to Semgurh, where they decoyed three travellers, by caste Hulwahees, or confectioners, on their way from Loodhiana to Cawnpore, and induced them to pass the night in their company. The travellers were strangled next morning some distance from the village, and their bodies buried.

The gang went on by the usual stages to Dooraha seraee near Loodhiana, without meeting with any further success. and therefore turned back; and having travelled eight miles sat down at a well by the way side to rest themselves. Two horsemen, Sheikhs, from Lahore, on their road to the sacred shrine at Gya, came up to the same place, and were easily persuaded by the Thugs to prosecute the journey in their company. They were conducted on the same day to Bunjara-ka-seraee, where they all slept, and next morning setting out again, the travellers were put to death a couple miles off, and their bodies buried.

Report of a Thug Expedition in the year 1831, *Rambuksh, Deveedeen, with Twenty-five*

No. of List.	Names and jurisdiction of the place where the Murder was perpetrated.	No. and Sex of the Murdered. Men.	Women.	Date of the Murder.	Intended destination of the Murdered. From	To	Supposed value of the property robbed.
351	Kurreer,	6	0	That Season of 1831,	Loodhiana,	Byswara,	450 rupees.
352	Buxar,	2	0	Ditto,	Delhi,	Lucknow,	150 rupees.
353	Tiggur,	5	0	Ditto,	Meerut,	Ditto,	500 rupees.
354	Kumorah Dumora,	4	0	Ditto,	Ditto,	Lucknow,	250 rupees.
355	Banska Ruttra,	3	0	Ditto,	Bareilly,	Shajahanpore,	4000 rupees.

under the following leaders: Mehrban, Thugs, and other Leaders.

REMARKS.

They had proceeded but a short distance onwards after completing this murder, when the fifteen Thugs alluded to above, of Uchul jemadar's gang, arrived and joined the gang. All agreed to turn back and try their luck to the eastward, and having passed through Kurnal, they arrived at Shamlee, where they fell in with six travellers, by caste Bhurbhoojas, on their way from Loodhiana to Byswara, who fell an easy prey to the Thugs. They were taken to the village of Kurreer, where they passed the night, and next morning were strangled a short distance from the village. The bodies were buried.

The gang then went on to Hauper, from whence twenty Thugs of their number took leave and went home, with a promise to rejoin in the course of fifteen or twenty days at a shrine in the Oude State. The next day the remainder of the gang set out in the direction of Boolundshuhur, and in the way fell in with two Kuhars proceeding from Delhi to Lucknow, who were decoyed and conducted to Buxar. Next morning early the travellers were strangled some distance from the village, and their bodies thrown into a well.

They all went on to Goormuktessir, on the Ganges, and embarked on the ferry-boat to cross the Ganges. Five travellers, Kuhars by caste, on their way from Meerut to Lucknow, had taken advantage of the same opportunity of crossing the river, and being addressed by some of the Thugs were easily persuaded to join their party. They all went to Tiggera, where they slept, and next morning the travellers were put to death on the bank of the river. Four of the bodies were buried in a ravine on the bank, but as it began to rain the fifth was thrown into the stream.

They proceeded next through Moradabad to Kumora Dhumora on the road to Bareilly, overtook and succeeded in decoying four travellers, by caste Hindoos, on their way from Meerut to Lucknow. The next morning the travellers were put to death outside of the village, and their bodies buried.

Having completed this murder the gang went to Bareilly, and taking the road to Shujahanpore, arrived at Futtehgunge. Next day they proceeded six miles further on and sat down at a well near a tank to refresh themselves, when three treasure carriers from Bareilly, on their way to Shujehanpore, came up to the well and commenced to bathe themselves. They consisted of a Musulman and two Hindoos, and their names have since been ascertained to have been Bhooree Khan, Myaram and Saligram. The circumstance of their being the conveyers of specie could not for a moment be concealed from the Thugs, whose cupidity led them instantly to discover the fact They were addressed and decoyed, and beguiling the road with their insinuating discourse, the Thugs conducted the treasure-carriers to Bans-ka-Kuttra, where they all slept. Next morning the travellers were strangled about a mile from that place, and

Report of a Thug Expedition in the year 1831,
Rambuksh, Deveedeen, with Twenty-five

No. of List.	Names and jurisdiction of the place where the Murder was perpetrated.	No. and Sex of the Murdered.		Date of the Murder.	Intended destination of the Murdered.		Supposed value of the property robbed.
		Men.	Women.		From	To	
356	Koorowlee, in the Mynpooree district,	1	0	That Season of 1831,	Meerut,	Cawnpore,	15 rupees.
357	Moghul-ka-saraee,	3	0	Ditto,	Muttra,	Lahore,	100 rupees.
358	Near Sirhind,	6	0	Ditto,	....	....	300 rupees.

under the following leaders: Mehrban, Thugs, and other Leaders.

REMARKS.

the dead bodies were thrown two into one well, and the third into another. They then pursued their way. The traveller whose body was thrown singly into the well, by name Myaram, was not quite dead, and the cold water acting upon his frame, recovered him from the state of suffocation in which he had been left by the Thugs. He managed to scramble out of the well after the departure of the Thugs, and running into the village gave instant information to the Police authorities. The thanadar mounted his horse and attended by his Police runners followed in pursuit of the gang. The majority of the Thugs had got safe to Shahabad, but twelve of the number, as follows, having lagged behind, fell into the thanadar's hands:

Lalla Lochun jemadar—Buldee—Bukshee jemadar—Himunchula—Seetla—Heerooa—Hurrea—Sukkoo—Mooradea—Dhya Lodhee—Purshadooa—Uchul jemadar.

These were overtaken, and eleven of them were secured. The twelfth, Uchul jemadar, eluded the Police, and fled to Shahabad, where he gave information to the main gang, who immediately set off homewards. These eleven men had a bag of 600 rupees in their possession, which they threw away as soon as they were seized, and on being searched nothing was found in their possession. The thanadar put them all into confinement. It so happened that a man soon after went to the spot, where the money had been thrown away, to cut grass, and found the bag of rupees, which the Thugs now say he appropriated, without their daring to point out the fact to their captors. These eleven men were detained in confinement for six months and then released.

In the month of September or October, 1831, Runnooa moonshee, Uchul and Hurlal jemadars, with a gang of thirty Thugs, assembled at Behareepore, in the Furruckhabad district, and set out on an expedition. They went first to Koorowlee in Mynpooree, where they decoyed a traveller. Hindoo by caste, on his way from Meerut to Cawnpore, whom they kept near them all day, and next morning put to death at a well a mile from the village, throwing his body into the water.

The gang went onwards and reached Moghul-ka-seraee by regular stages. There they fell in with three travellers, by caste Sheiks, on their way from Muttra to Lahore, whom they inveigled and induced to join the gang. They were put to death next morning about two miles from the village, and their bodies buried.

After this the Thugs went to Loodhiana, and met six travellers, about to leave that place for the Oude territory, Runnooa moonshee decoyed them and agreed to travel in their company. The whole gang accordingly turned back

Report of a Thug Expedition in the year 1831, *Rambuksh, Deveedeen, with Twenty-five*

No. of List.	Names and jurisdiction of the place where the Murder was perpetrated.	No. and Sex of the Murdered.		Date of the Murder.	Intended destination of the Murdered.		Supposed value of the property robbed.
		Men.	Women.		From	To	
359	Near Kurnal,	3	0	That Season of 1831,	Lahore,	Hurdwar,	400 rupees.
360	Near Goolchutter,	4	0	Ditto,	West,	Banda,	500 rupees, a horse worth 50 rupees, 2 dogs.
361	Near Boorhana,	2	0	Ditto,	Lahore,	Benares,	100 rupees.
362	Tukkeah,	2	0	Ditto,	Meerut,	Sultanpore,	100 rupees.
363	Near Hussungunge,	6	0	Ditto,	Ditto,	Jugdespore,	500 rupees.

under the following leaders: Mehrban, Thugs, and other Leaders.

REMARKS.

and accompanied the travellers to a village, a little to the west of Sirhind, where they slept. Early next morning the travellers were strangled a mile or two off, and their bodies buried in a tank.

They again turned back and proceeded for two or three stages to the vicinity of Umballa, where they were sitting on the bank of a stream—when three travellers on their way from Lahore to Hurdwar, came up and were decoyed and taken to Umballa. They slept there, and next morning went towards Kurnal, passing the next night in a village, name unknown. Next morning the travellers were as usual strangled, and their bodies buried on the bank of a stream some distance off.

The gang next proceeded to Goolchutter, where they managed to inveigle four Hindoos travelling on their way from the west to Banda. They had two dogs with them which they were taking to the Chief of Banda. They took them to a village ten miles off, where they slept, and next morning the travellers were put to death in the usual manner two miles from the village, and their bodies buried.

Having crossed the Jumna, the Thugs arrived at Boorhana in the Begum Sumroo's territory, where they decoyed two Brahmins travelling from Lahore to Benares, and took them to a village four miles off to sleep. Next morning they were escorted two miles on their way and then strangled. The bodies were buried in the bed of a stream.

After this affair the gang returned home without any further adventure.

About the same time that the before-mentioned gang was out Keseeree subadar and Shewdeen jemadar with a gang of thirteen Lodhee Thugs left Byns-ka-Poorwa in Oude, and set out on an expedition. They first went to Tukkeah, where they fell in with two travellers, by caste Hindoos, on their way from Meerut to Sooltanpore, whom they decoyed. Soon after a gang of sixteen Jumaldhee Thugs from Oude under Sirdar jemadar arrived at the same place, and joined the Lodhees. Next morning early the travellers were conducted to a garden a mile off and strangled. The bodies were thrown into a well.

Having gone on to Hussungunge, the gang was joined by another party of six Thugs under Dhambul jemadar and Ouseeree, (approver.) Soon after six Mahomedans from Meerut on their way to Jugdespore in Oude, came to the same place, and being addressed by Keseeree subadar, were easily drawn into his snare. Next morning the travellers were strangled only a mile from the village, and their bodies thrown into a well.

Report of a Thug Expedition in the year 1831, *Rambuksh, Deveedeen, with Twenty-five*

No. of List.	Names and jurisdiction of the place where the Murder was perpetrated.	No. and Sex of the Murdered.		Date of the Murder.	Intended destination of the Murdered.		Supposed value of the property robbed.
		Men.	Women.		From	To	
364	Etawah,	2	0	That Season of 1831,	Saugor,	Koonda,	100 rupees.
365	Near Bhunter,	1	0	Ditto,	Dekhan,	Sultan-pore,	30 rupees.
366	Bhaukaira,	2	0	Ditto,	Ditto,	....	100 rupees.
367	Ruhmutgunge,	1	0	Ditto,	Cawn-pore,	Jugdes-pore,	40 rupees.
368	Futtehgunge,	2	0	Ditto,	Meerut,	Sultan-pore,	50 rupees.
369	Nuwabgunge,	1	0	Ditto,	Nussee-rabad,	Goruck-pore,	30 rupees, 2 bullocks.
370	Subdhulgunge	1	0	Ditto,	Luck-now,	Ajoo-dhea,	12 rupees.
371	Gossaingunge,	2	0	Ditto,	West,	Sultan-pore,	60 rupees.
372	Bhicknapore,	4	0	Ditto,	Muttra,	Byswara,	300 rupees.

under the following leaders: Mehrban, Thugs, and other Leaders.

REMARKS.

The gang now crossed the Ganges, and proceeded to Etawah, where they found two Hindoos travelling from Saugor to Koonda, who were decoyed and next morning put to death as usual some distance off. The bodies were thrown into a well.

They then went to Bhunter, and decoyed a Hindoo travelling from the Dekhan to Sooltanpore. Having passed the night there, the traveller was strangled next morning two miles from the village, and his body thrown into a well.

They next went to Bhaukhaira, were they fell in with two travellers from the Dekhan, whom they decoyed and took out next morning a distance of two miles, and then strangled them. The bodies were thrown into a well.

After this affair the gang went to Ruhmutgunge, where they decoyed a traveller, by caste Mussulman, on his way from Cawnpore to Jugdespore. During the day twenty-five more Jumaldhee Thugs from Oude under Futhee, Hyder and Dhossoo jemadars came and joined the gang. The Thugs next morning conducted their victim to a tank two miles off, and then put him to death. His body was buried.

They then went on to Futtehgunge, where they fell in with two travellers, by caste Chumars, who were employed as grooms, and were on their way from Meerut to Sooltanpore. They were decoyed and next morning put to death a mile from the village. The bodies were buried.

Having proceeded to Nuwabgunge, they fell in with a Hindoo on his way from Nusseerabad to Goruckpore, whom they decoyed, and next morning strangled, as usual, outside of the village. The body was thrown into a well.

The Thugs then proceeded to Subdhulgunge and decoyed a traveller, by caste a gardener, on his way from Lucknow to Ajoodhea. He was decoyed and next morning despatched a mile outside of the village, in the usual manner. His body was thrown into a well.

They next went to Gosaeengunge, where they met two travellers from the west on their way to Sooltanpore, whom they decoyed, and next morning took out a mile from the village, where they were strangled at a well, into which the bodies were thrown.

After this, Futteh jemadar and his gang took another direction, and the rest of the Thugs went to Bhicknapore, where they decoyed four Hindoos

Report of a Thug Expedition in the year 1831, *Rambuksh, Deveedeen, with Twenty-five*

No. of List.	Names and jurisdiction of the place where the Murder was perpetrated.	No. and Sex of the Murdered.		Date of the Murder.	Intended destination of the Murdered.		Supposed value of the property robbed.
		Men.	Women.		From	To	
373	Chupra,	2	0	That Season of 1831,	Delhie,	Oude Provinces,	50 rupees, and a pony.
374	Juhangeerabad,	4	0	Ditto,	Loodhiana,	Futtehpore,	250 rupees.
375	Malagurh,	3	0	Ditto,	....	Kurnal,	100 rupees.
376	Rajhpore, in the Putteeala State,	3	0	Ditto,	Loodhiana,	Eastward,	300 rupees.
377	Kunheyah,	3	0	Ditto,	Amritsir,	Furruckhabad,	100 rupees.
378	Doorhaha,	3	0	Ditto,	Lahore,	Ditto,	150 rupees.

under the following leaders: Mehrban, Thugs, and other Leaders.

REMARKS.

travelling from Muttra to Byswara. Next morning they were conducted a mile out of the village and strangled. The bodies were thrown into a well.

Having completed this murder the Thugs returned to their respective homes.

In the month of October, 1831, Runnooa moonshee, Bukshee jemadar and others, assembled a gang of thirty-five Thugs at Behareepore in the Furruckhabad district, and determined on trying their fortune again on the roads. They went first to Chupra, where the moonshee decoyed two Hindoos from Delhi on their way to the Oude Provinces, whom the Thugs took out next morning to a tank a mile from the village and strangled. The bodies were thrown into a well.

They then proceeded to Juhangeerabad, where they fell in with four Hindoos travelling from Loodhiana to Futtehpore, who were decoyed and accommodated with a resting place near one of the Thug jemadars. Next morning before daylight, they went on their way again and the travellers were put to death at the distance of a couple of miles. The bodies were thrown into a well.

The gang went on to Boolundshuhur, and there they decoyed three Hindoo travellers on their way to Kurnal, whom they took with them to Malagurh. They slept there and next morning the travellers were put to death at a stream about two miles off, and the bodies thrown into a well.

Proceeding onwards the Thugs passed through Kurnal, and arrived at Rajhpore in the Putteeala State. They there fell in with three travellers, by caste Brahmins, from Loodhiana, going eastwards, who were decoyed and next morning being conducted a mile on their way were put to death, and their bodies buried on the bank of a stream.

After this the Thugs went to the seraee at Kunheya, where they found three travellers resting, who had come from Amritsir on their way to Furruckhabad. They were decoyed, and taken out next morning a mile or two on the road, and then put to death. The bodies were buried.

The gang went on to Doorada and put up in the seraee. Three travellers, one a Pundit and two Kuhars, were resting there. They had come from Lahore intending to go to Furruckhabad, and were persuaded to join the Thugs. Next morning they were strangled about a mile from the village, and their bodies buried in a field.

Report of a Thug Expedition in the year 1831,
Rambuksh, Deveedeen, with Twenty-five

No. of List.	Names and jurisdiction of the place where the Murder was perpetrated.	No. and Sex of the Murdered.		Date of the Murder.	Intended destination of the Murdered.		Supposed value of the property robbed.
		Men.	Women.		From	To	
379	Near Sirhind,	6	0	That Season of 1831,	Lahore,	Dhoondea,	900 rupees.
380	Bunjara-ka-seraee,	2	0	Ditto,	Loodhiana,	Cawnpore,	50 rupees cash, and clothes, &c.
381	Umballa,	2	0	Ditto,	Ditto,	Furruckhabad,	100 rupees.
382	Dahoo Manjarah,	4	0	Ditto,	....	....	500 rupees.
383	Kurreeakhaira,	3	0	Ditto,	Lahore,	Byswara,	250 rupees.
384	Near Goolchutter,	2	0	Ditto,	Loodhiana,	Furruckhabad,	100 rupees.

under the following leaders : Mehrban, Thugs, and other Leaders.

REMARKS.

Having arrived at Loodhiana, the gang rested at the house of Bhageeah Bhuteeara for two days. On the third day they turned back to the eastward, and had scarcely got out of the town, when they were joined by six travellers, by caste Hindoos, from Lahore, on their way to Dhoondea. Runnooa moonshee entered into conversation with and decoyed them. They went on together for two days, and on the third day took them to a village, a short distance from Sirhind, where they slept, and next morning the murder was completed about three miles from that place. The bodies were buried.

After that the gang went to Bunjara-ka-seraee and fell in with two Kuhars from Loodhiana on their way to Cawnpore, who were decoyed and next morning put to death as usual a short distance from the village. The bodies were buried.

They next went to Umballa, and met two water-carriers on their way from Loodhiana to Furruckhabad, who were persuaded to continue their journey in company with the Thugs. Early next morning the travellers were taken out two miles from the town and strangled. The bodies were buried, and have since been disinterred on the showing of Heera approver.

The gang then went to Muchunda where they found four travellers, one a Mewatee named Makhun, and three Koormees (Hindoos,) whom Uchul jemadar managed to inveigle out of the village, and next day they were conducted to Dahoo Manjira, where they all passed the night, and early on the ensuing morning the travellers were put to death about two miles off, and their bodies buried. These four bodies have since been pointed out and exhumed.

After the murder the gang went on to Shahabad, where three Hindoos, on their way from Lahore to Byswara, fell into the snares of the Thugs and next day accompanied them to Kurreeakhaira. The succeeding morning the travellers were strangled about two miles from the village, and their bodies buried.

After this murder seven Thugs left the gang, went home with money for their families, agreeing to rejoin at the ford of the Jumna at Kurnal. The remainder went to Goolchutter. They then decoyed two Hindoos from Loodhiana, on their way to Furruckhabad, whom they took next morning to a village ten miles off, and rested there. Early next morning the travellers were escorted a mile out of the village and strangled. Their bodies were buried.

Report of a Thug Expedition in the year 1831, *Rambuksh, Deveedeen, with Twenty-five*

No. of List.	Names and jurisdiction of the place where the Murder was perpetrated.	No. and Sex of the Murdered.		Date of the Murder.	Intended destination of the Murdered.		Supposed value of the property robbed.
		Men.	Women.		From	To	
385	Near Bugroor,	4	0	That Season of 1831,	Amritsir,	....	500 rs cash, 2 horses worth 120 rupees, a matchlock.
386	Bidolee,	2	0	Ditto,	Loodhiana,	Furruckhabad,	50 rupees cash, 10 rupees property.
387	Gurheya,	3	0	Ditto,	Kurnal,	Byswara,	150 rupees.
388	Mallawah, in Mynpooree,	2	0	Ditto,	Mynpooree,	Coel,	40 rupees.
389	Near Khoorjah, in the Boolundshuhur zillah,	2	0	Ditto,	Loodhiana,	Byswara,	100 rupees.

under the following leaders: Mehrban, Thugs, and other Leaders.

REMARKS.

The gang arrived at Kurnal and halted there. Then they went to the ford at Sneikhpoora on the Jumna, where they fell in with four travellers, Hindoos, from Amritsir, whom they decoyed, and having taken a coss on the river, they were met by the Thugs, who had been to their homes and returned. All went to Bugroor and rested there, and before daylight next morning, the travellers were strangled about a mile from the village, and their bodies thrown into a well. They have since been discovered in the place indicated by Heera approver.

They next went to Bidolee, where they found two shoe-makers on their way from Loodhiana to Furruckhabad, whom they decoyed and next morning early put to death two miles from the village. The bodies were buried in a tank.

Proceeding onwards the Thugs passed through Jhinjana to Shamlee, at which place three cowherds from Kurnal, intending to go to Byswara, were resting and bathing themselves. The Thugs seeing they were travellers also engaged in their ablutions at the same spot, and then accompanied the cowherds to Gurheya, where they passed the night. Before daylight next morning the travellers were escorted out a distance of a couple of miles from the village in the Begum Sumroo's territory and strangled. The bodies were thrown into a well.

N. B The remains of these bodies have been pointed out by Eseree approver, and the case committed to trial in the Court of the Agent Governor General.

After this affair the gang returned home without any further adventure.

While the proceedings beforementioned were going on, another gang of thirty Thugs under Shunker, Hurlal, and Shewdeen jemadars, set out during the month of October, 1831, from Sooltangunge, and proceeded to Mullawah, in the Mynpooree district. At the last named place they found two Bunneahs, who were going from the town of Mynpooree to Coel, whom they persuaded to travel with them and next morning put to death a mile from the village, throwing their bodies into a well.

After quitting the scene of murder, the gang met another party of nineteen Thugs under Budlee and Mandhata, who agreed to pursue their journey in company with them. This gang had set out a short time before from Jodeeka-Poorwa, and having passed through Coel, had gone to Koorja, in the Boolundshuhur district. They found resting in the caravansera two travellers,

Report of a Thug Expedition in the year 1831, *Rambuksh, Deveedeen, with Twenty-five*

No. of List.	Names and jurisdiction of the place where the Murder was perpetrated.	No. and Sex of the Murdered.		Date of the Murder.	Intended destination of the Murdered.		Supposed value of the property robbed.
		Men.	Women.		From	To	
390	Goolowtee,	1	0	That Season of 1831,	Lahore,	Oude,	100 rupees.
391	Boorhana,	3	0	Ditto,	Kurnal	Cawnpore,	150 rupees.
392	Near Coel,	2	0	Ditto,	Ditto,	Benares,	100 rupees cash, 50 rupees property.
393	Soorujpore, in Boolundshuhur,	2	0	Ditto,	Hansi,	Cawnpore,	80 rupees.
394	Goolowtee,	2	0	Ditto,	Kurnal,	Ditto,	40 rupees.
395	Near Goolchutter,	4	0	Ditto,	Loodhiana,	Ditto,	22 rupees.

under the following leaders: Mehrban, Thugs, and other Leaders.

REMARKS.

a Brahmin and a Rajpoot, who had come from Loodhiana on their way to Byswara. They agreed to travel with the Thugs, who took them out next morning, and strangled them two miles from the seraee. The bodies were buried. They then went to Goolowtee and put up in the seraee—where a traveller, by caste a Rajpoot, on his way from Lahore to Oude, came and joined them. He was decoyed, and next morning strangled two miles from the village. The body was buried.

After this murder they went on to Boorhana, and took up their quarters in the seraee. Three travellers, Kuhars, on their way from Kurnal to Cawnpore, were resting there, whom the Thugs inveigled, and taking with them next morning strangled a mile out of the village. The bodies were buried.

They turned back again after this affair, and re-visited Coel, where they fell in with two travellers, on their way from Kurnal to Benares. They came and joined the Thugs of their own accord, and were invited to travel with them. They were taken the same day to a small village near a Police thana, six miles from Coel, where they passed the night, and next morning were put to death two miles on their way. The bodies were buried.

While the gang was going eastward after completing this murder, they fell in with the party under Shunker and other jemadars as above described.

After mutual enquiries had passed between the two gangs, it was agreed that their entire numbers should be divided into two parties, who should conduct their proceedings independently of each other, though for the common benefit of both.

Budlee jemadar's party went to Soorujpore in Boolundshuhur, and having rested in the seraee found there two travellers, on their way from Hansi to Cawnpore, whom they decoyed, and next morning strangled outside of the village at the distance of two miles. The bodies were buried.

They then went to Shamlee, where they again fell in with Shunker jemadar's gang, who on parting had gone to Goolowtee, where they decoyed two Hindoo travellers, on their way from Kurnal to Cawnpore. Next morning early the travellers were put to death, as usual, a mile from the village. The bodies were thrown into a well.

The united gangs proceeded to Kurnal, and thence came to a village near Goolchutter, where they sat down in a garden. One of the Thugs had fallen in with two travellers, by caste barbers, whom he decoyed and brought to join the Thugs—and Hurlal jemadar inveigled two cow-herds, who, all four, were

Report of a Thug Expedition in the year **1831,**
Rambuksh, Deveedeen, with Twenty-five

No. of List.	Names and jurisdiction of the place where the Murder was perpetrated.	No. and Sex of the Murdered.		Date of the Murder.	Intended destination of the Murdered.		Supposed value of the property robbed.
		Men.	Women.		From	To	
396	Near Secundra,	2	0	That Season of 1831,	Kurnal,	Cawnpore,	150 rupees.
397	Jhinjana,	2	0	Ditto,	Loodhiana,	Byswara,	250 rupees.
398	Khoorjah, zillah Booluudshuhur,	2	0	Ditto,	Kurnal,	Ditto,	300 rupees.
399	Horagaon,	2	0	Ditto,	Lucknow,	Kurnal.	200 rupees,

under the following leaders : Mehrban, Thugs, and other Leaders.

REMARKS.

on their way from Loodhiana to Cawnpore. It was determined to pass the night in the garden, where all made themselves comfortable under the trees. During the night the four travellers were strangled on their beds, and their bodies were buried in the garden.

Next day the gang went to the seraee at Kunhya, where they discovered two treasure carriers; and having placed spies to watch their movements, they followed them till on the second day they arrived at Umballa. There, one of the Thugs named Shewdeen, managed to introduce himself to one of the treasure carriers, and made him a present of a new pair of shoes. While the present was making, another Thug incautiously lifted up the bundle, belonging to the treasure carriers to discover its weight, on which the owner, (proverbially careful from the nature of this employment,) took the alarm, and told his Thug friends that he intended to proceed no further than Umballa—leaving the gang in despair at the loss both of their new pair of shoes and the anticipated booty.

The gang went on to Kurnal, where they again separated into two parties. Dibba jemadar with half the Thugs went towards Muttra, and the remainder, under Budlee jemadar, took the road to Cawnpore.

The party under Budlee having arrived within four miles of Secundra, fell in with two travellers, by caste Kayuts or scribes, on their way from Kurnal to Cawnpore, whom they engaged in conversation, and took with them to Secundra, where all passed the night. Early next morning the travellers were roused and conducted out of the village, and at the distance of two miles from it they were put to death, and their bodies buried in a marsh. After this affair Budlee's gang proceeded home without perpetrating any other murder.

The party of Thugs under Gopal and Baichoo jemadars, which parted from the main gang at Kurnal, first proceeded to Jhinjana, where they fell in with two travellers, on their way from Loodhiana to Byswara, who were induced to join the Thugs, who took them out about two miles, and then strangled them. The bodies were thrown into a well.

They next went to Khoorjah, zillah Boolundshuhur, and soon after their arrival two travellers, Hindoos, from Kurnal, intending to go to Byswara, came and took up their quarters in the seraee. They were decoyed and next morning put to death some distance from the town. The bodies were buried. This gang then returned home without further adventure.

In the mean time Mehrban, Hurlal, Bhola Bunneah and other Thugs, who had separated from the main gang at Kurnal, proceeded by way of Panniput to a village called Horagaon, where they rested in a Faqueer's garden. They

Report of a Thug Expedition in the year 1831, *Rambuksh, Deveedeen, with Twenty-five*

No. of List.	Names and jurisdiction of the place where the Murder was perpetrated.	No. and Sex of the Murdered.		Date of the Murder.	Intended destination of the Murdered.		Supposed value of the property robbed.
		Men.	Women.		From	To	
400	Cheretta,	2	0	That Season of 1831,	Gwalior,	Cawnpore,	50 rupees.
401	Rajee Mhow,	2	0	Ditto,	Benares,	Westward,	50 rupees.
402	Kureagaon,	3	0	Ditto,	....	Eastward,	100 rupees in cash, 50 rupees property, and a fighting ram.

Jubulpore, Superintendent's Office,
The 31*st March*, 1840.

under the following leaders: Mehrban, Thugs, and other Leaders.

REMARKS.

---

found there two Hindoo Brinjaras from Lucknow, on their way to Kurnal, whom they decoyed, and next morning escorted about two miles on their way, and then strangled them. The bodies were thrown in a well.

After this affair, all the Thugs, with the exception of six, returned to their homes. Bhola Bunneeah led this small band, which took the road to Gwalior, where they arrived in fifteen days. They thence proceeded to the village of Cheratta, where they were soon afterwards joined by two travellers, both from Gwalior, on their way to the vicinity of Cawnpore. One of these men was a Mahomedan mendicant, and the other a Brahmin named Gunesh. They were decoyed and next morning early, having been taken to a field two miles off, on the road side—they were put to death, and their bodies buried.

The six Thugs then returned home again.

N. B. The above affair was established by the proceedings of Mr. J. C. Wilson, of the Civil Service, while engaged in the arrest of these gangs in the Dooab.

In the month of December, 1831, Mehrban jemadar accompanied by four followers, set out in search of adventures. They went, in the first instance, to Kora Jehanabad, but as they were going thence in an easterly direction, a wolf crossed their path; which being looked upon by Thugs as an exceedingly unfavorable omen, they turned back, and proceeded to Poorra in the Cawnpore district. There they were joined by Pershad jemadar (approver) with ten Thugs, who had just left Rajee Mhow, intending to go on an expedition. Soon afterwards Khulluck and Bhowanee. jemadars of Thugs, with nine followers, came to the same place from Metee-ka-Poorwa, so that the party was increased to twenty-six Thugs. During the day two Hindoo travellers from Benares, intending to go to westward, arrived at the village and were inveigled; and early next morning were put to death at a well a mile off, and their bodies thrown into it.

The gang went on to Kureagaon and Soowrujpore, where they fell in with three travellers, by caste Hindoos, who were going to the eastward. They were decoyed, and next morning early were conducted some distance to the banks of the Ganges, where theywere strangled and their bodies committed to the stream.

The Thugs then turned back and went home again.

After this expedition, it has been ascertained that Bhowanee jemadar, who was the greatest leader of Thugs in his time, died at home.

P. A. REYNOLDS,
Superintendent for the Suppression of Thuggee.

List of Thugs who were concerned in the above Murders.

No.	Name of Thugs.	Parentage.	Caste.	Remarks.
1	Uchall Jemadar,	Son of Gunsham,	Lodhee,	Hanged at Jubulpore, in 1835.
	Cheyne Jemadar,	Bukha,	Ditto,	Died while out on Thuggee.
	Runjeet alias Daveedeen,	Kurhoree,	Ditto,	Died in Jail at Saugor.
	Dhunna, the whiskered Jemadar,	Chidda,	Ditto,	Hanged at Jubulpore, 1836.
5	Nowul Jemadar,	Punchum,	Ditto,	Ditto Saugor, 1833.
	Dhunna,	Madaree,	Ditto,	Approver.
	Bukshee Jemadar,	Rutta,	Ditto,	Ditto.
	Esseeree,	Ditto.	Ditto,	Ditto.
	Heera,	Sumadhan,	Ditto,	Ditto.
10	Shewdeen,	Assa,	Ditto,	Ditto.
	Dhunna,	Kashee,	Ditto,	Transported from Saugor.
	Chidda,	Ramkissen,	Ditto,	Ditto Jubulpore.
	Heera,	Tijja,	Ditto,	Hanged at Cawnpore.
	Lalsa,		Ditto,	At large.
15	Soomair,	Muthoulee,	Ditto,	Approver (dead.)
	Keseeree Subadar,	Buddo,	Ditto,	Hanged at Jubulpore, 1835.
	Tijja,	Ditto,	Ditto,	Approver.
	Khooshallee,		Ditto,	Ditto.
	Rumma,	Munna,	Ditto,	Ditto.
20	Bulla,	Ditto,	Ditto,	Ditto.
	Bukhtawer,	Koonj,	Ditto,	Died at home.
	Khulluck Jemadar,	Rutta,	Ditto,	Hanged at Saugor, 1833.
	Dhowkul Jemadar,	Chutta,	Ditto,	Ditto.
	Lalla Lochun,	Koonj,	Ditto,	Hanged at Jubulpore, 1835.

No.	Name	Father	Caste	Fate
25	Gunna,	Huns,	Lodhee,	Transported.
	Bukka,	Heera,	Ditto,	Ditto.
	Anward,	Mudaree,	Ditto,	Ditto.
	Budlee,	Dya,...	Ditto,	Died while on an expedition.
	Shunker Jemadar,	Dyaram,	Buneah,	Hanged at Jubulpore, 1835.
30	Dibba,	Ditto,	Ditto,	Approver.
	Dummee,		Ditto,	Transported.
	Oomeid Kobra,		Lodhee,	At large.
	Ram Buksh Jemadar,	Runna,	Ditto,	Approver.
	Daveedeen Jemadar,	Ditto,	Ditto,	Approver (died.)
35	Girdharee,	Ramlal,	Brahmin,	Approver.
	Summa,	Bhugwant,	Lodhee,	Ditto.
	Sumbha,	Ghassee,	Ditto,	Ditto.
	Dijja,	Mansa,	Ditto,	Hanged at Jubulpore, 1836.
	Nowla,	Oomeid,	Ditto,	Transported.
40	Himmunchula,	Runnooa Moonshee,	Ditto,	Approver.
	Dhunna,		Ditto,	Ditto.
	Purusram Jemadar,	Oodey,	Ditto,	Died at Jubulpore.
	Surawan,	Ditto,	Ditto,	At large.
	Hurlal Jemadar,	Sookha,	Ditto,	Hanged at Saugor, 1833.
45	Dhumma,		Ditto,	Approver.
	Binda,		Ditto.	Transported from Jubulpore.
	Atmaram,	Son of Dhya,	Ditto,	Ditto.
	Oodey,	Mukka,	Ditto,	Approver.
	Gopal,	Dhya,	Ditto,	Ditto.
50	Moollooa,	Sookhtee,	Ditto,	Ditto.
	Bhowanee Jemadar,	Mukka,	Ditto,	Died at home.
	Pershaud Jemadar,	Runna,	Ditto,	Approver.
	Ummer Jemadar,	Madaree,	Ditto,	Transported.
	Mukkooa,		Ditto,	Ditto.
55	Gunesh,	Mukhan,	Ditto,	Died at Saugor.
	Bichoo Jemadar,	Ruttee,	Ditto,	Approver.
	Suroop,	Gunesh,	Ditto,	Transported from Jubulpore.

No	Name of Thugs.	Parentage.	Caste.	Remarks.
	Dureawo,	Gunesh,	Lodhee,	Transported from Jubulpore.
	Shewa,		Ditto,	Approver.
60	Mohun,		Ditto,	Ditto.
	Mandhata,	Dulput,	Ditto,	Ditto.
	Mandhata, 2d,		Ditto,	Ditto.
	Runnooa Moonshee Jemadar,	Jeysook,	Ditto,	Hanged at Jubulpore, 1835.
	Gumbhooa,		Bunneah,	At large.
65	Dhunna,	Hurree,	Lodhee,	Approver.
	Seetla,	Chidda,	Ditto,	Died while out on Thuggee.
	Neehalooa,		Ditto,	Transported from Jubulpore.
	Boodhooa,		Ditto,	Ditto ditto.
	Budla,		Ditto,	Ditto ditto.
70	Bhola,	Son of Mukka,	Ditto,	Approver.
	Khoosheal,	Mutta,	Ditto,	Transported from Jubulpore.
	Desraj,		Kachee,	Ditto from Saugor.
	Jowihur,		Rajpoot,	Ditto ditto.
	Bukshee,		Abkar,	Hanged at Saugor, 1833.
75	Himma,		Brahmin,	Ditto ditto.
	Budlee Jemadar,	Suntoke,	Lodhee,	Approver.
	Deorae Jemadar,		Ditto,	Died at home.
	Teeka,	Nundee,	Ditto,	Approver.
	Heera,	Ramdeen Jemadar,	Ditto,	Ditto.
80	Magooa,	Chidda,	Ditto,	Ditto.
	Cheyne,		Ditto,	At large.
	Anoop,	Cheyne,	Ditto,	Transported.
	Bhola,	Mudaree,	Ditto,	Ditto.
	Bikka,	Ditto,	Ditto,	Approver (dead.)
85	Peareelal,	Mudden,	Kayet,	At large.

No.	Name	Father	Caste	Fate
	Pershaud,	Dya,	Bukhal,	Transported.
	Pershaud, 2d,		Lodhee,	Ditto.
	Bujja.	Oomeid Jemadar,	Ditto,	Ditto.
	Layuk,	Kishen,	Ditto,	Hanged at Saugor, 1833.
90	Hurrea,	Adopted of Lalla Lochun,	Ditto,	Died at home.
	Dhowkula.		Ditto,	At large.
	Ram Buksh,	Ramkissen,	Ditto,	Ditto.
	Letchmuna,	Ditto,	Ditto,	Ditto.
	Ramkissen,		Ditto,	Ditto.
95	Jowihur,	Ram Singh.	Ditto,	Ditto.
	Chittooa,	Oomeid.	Ditto,	Hanged at Cawnpore.
	Bukshea.	Ditto,	Ditto,	Transported.
	Ramdeen Jemadar,	Runna.	Ditto,	Hanged at Cawnpore.
	Goolabee,	Bukhtawer,	Ditto,	Ditto Barielly.
100	Shewdeen Jemadar,	Ditto.	Ditto,	Transported.
	Ghazee.	Bhugwant.	Ditto,	Ditto.
	Maheen Lal,	Dhya,	Ditto,	Ditto.
	Shewdeen,	Munsa,	Ditto,	Ditto.
	Rambuksh,	Pirthee,	Ditto,	Hanged at Saugor.
105	Mudaree,	Suntoke.	Ditto,	Ditto.
	Hoolassee,	Munsookh.	Ditto,	Ditto.
	Bhimma,	Ditto,	Ditto,	Ditto.
	Dhunna,	Hissa,	Ditto,	Ditto.
	Mungle,	Suntoke,	Ditto,	Transported.
110	Makhun Jemadar,	Kishen,	Ditto.	Approver.
	Khooshallea.	Uchul Jemadar.	Ditto,	Transported from Jubulpore.
	Asa.	Benee,	Ditto,	Ditto ditto.
	Mohun,	Dhya,	Ditto,	Ditto ditto.
	Budlee,	Ditto.	Ditto,	Ditto ditto.
115	Mudaree,	Mutta,	Ditto,	Died at Jubulpore.
	Doorgooa,	Ducha,	Ditto,	Transported.
	Jowihur,	Dhowkul,	Ditto,	At large.
	Chittooa,	Oomeid,	Ditto,	Hanged at Cawnpore.

No.	Name of Thugs.	Parentage.	Caste.	Remarks.
	Rumma,	Hunsa,	Lodhee,	Approver (dead.)
120	Gurrooa.	Dhya,	Ditto,	At large.
	Munnooa,	Oomeid,	Ditto,	Ditto.
	Pemmooa,		Kuhar,	Ditto.
	Dooburrea,	Koosal,	Lodhee,	Ditto.
	Gumbhooa,		Ditto,	Ditto.
125	Mehrban,	Bijjaeen,	Ditto,	Approver.
	Heera,	Oomeid,	Ditto,	Ditto.

P. A. REYNOLDS,
Superintendent for the
Suppression of Thuggee.

JUBULPORE, SUPERINTENDENT'S OFFICE,
The 31*st March*, 1840.

REPORT

OF A

THUG EXPEDITION

In the Year 1832.

Report of a Thug Expedition in the year
Lalla Lochun, Budlee, and Mukhun

No. of List.	Names and jurisdiction of the place where the Murder was perpetrated.	No. and Sex of the Murdered.		Date of the Murder.	Intended destination of the Murdered.		Supposed value of the property robbed.
		Men.	Women.		From	To	
403	Near Charsoo,	7	0	January 1832,	Ajmere,	Upper Provinces,	500 rupees cash, 200 rupees property.
404	Near Dhoosa,	5	0	Ditto,	Jodhpore,	Dooab,	700 rupees.
405	Kaleekah,	2	0	Ditto,	Jeypore,	....	4 or 5 rupees.

1832, under the following leaders:
Jemadars, and other Leaders.

REMARKS.

In the month of January, 1832, Lalla Lochun and Budlee jemadars collected a gang of sixteen Thugs at Chowdee-ka-Poorwa in Furruckhabad and went to Goolsahagunge, intending to proceed on an expedition in a westerly direction. At the latter place their numbers were increased by the junction of Khuluk jemadar with sixteen more Thugs, who had recently left their homes at Maitee-ka-Poorwa. All went together to Shukoorabad, where they met Bichoo jemadar and twenty-six followers, who had also just set out from Gurhea, in zillah Etawah, in search of adventures.

The entire gang now amounting to nearly sixty Thugs, took the road leading to Jeypore, and arrived at Ramsur in that principality. At that place Budlee Lodhee, brother of Gopaul approver, died, and the latter left the party and returned home as required by the rules of the fraternity. The remainder proceeded to the town of Charsoo, where another gang of ninety Thugs from Sindouse, led by Chotee jemadar, was encamped on the bank of the tank. The prior proceedings of the Sindouse Thugs will be found in the narratives of expeditions of that class.

The Lodhee gang took up their quarters at the same place with the Sindousees, and the leaders of the two parties interchanged enquiries. It appears that the Lodhee gang had been so unfortunate, that they had not fallen in with a single victim, since they had left their homes, and were in consequence nearly reduced to a state of starvation. A wary Thug (Khuluk jemadar) was therefore instantly despatched into the bazar in search of travellers, and he succeeded in discovering seven sepahees, Hindoos by caste, who were on their way from Ajmere to their homes in the Upper Provinces. These he decoyed, and brought with him to the tank, where they were accommodated with a resting place, and having been induced to set out before daylight, the travellers were put to death at a distance of two miles, and their bodies were buried.

They then proceeded by regular stages to Jeypore, and turned back again from thence having came two miles to a small Ghât, they fell in with five Hindoos from Jhodpore, travelling to the Dooab, whom they decoyed and took with them to Huttea, and next day to a village near Dhoosa (name unknown) where they encamped in a garden outside of the place. During the night the travellers were put to death on their beds, and their bodies were securely buried.

In the morning went on towards Kaleekah, and on the road fell in with a Hindoo moonshee and his servant who had come from Jeypore, and were travelling in the same direction with themselves. They were decoyed and taken to Kaleekah, where they slept, and early in the morning the travellers were strangled some distance from the town and their bodies buried.

Report of a Thug Expedition in the year
Lalla Lochun, Budlee, and Mukhun

No. of List.	Names and jurisdiction of the place where the Murder was perpetrated.	No. and Sex of the Murdered.		Date of the Murder.	Intended destination of the Murdered.		Supposed value of the property robbed.
		Men.	Women.		From	To	
406	Near Mowah,	2	0	That Season of 1832,	Jodhpore,	Upper Provinces,	150 rupees cash, 1 bullock and a cow.
407	Between Bhurtpore and Muttra,	1	0	Ditto,	Ajmere,	Byswara,	100 rupees.
408	Ferozabad,	2	0	Ditto,	....	....	250 rupees.
409	Ramsir,	4	0	Ditto,	....	....	125 rupees, 3 gold mohurs.

1832, *under the following leaders:*
Jemadars, and other Leaders.

REMARKS.

They next arrived at Bhanpore, where they discovered and decoyed two travellers, by caste Hindoos, on their way to the Upper Provinces from Jodhpore. They set out together next morning, and travelled all day. It was eight o'clock at night when they came to the vicinity of Mowah when the travellers were put to death as usual, and their bodies buried in the bed of a stream.

The gang then proceeded to Hulena where Lalla Lochun jemadar separated with sixteen Thugs and took the road homewards. When this small party had arrived at a village between Bhurtpore and Muttra, they fell in with a Hindoo travelling from Ajmere to Byswara, whom they accommodated near themselves and next morning put them to death at a well two miles from the village. The bodies were thrown into the water.

The Thugs then went on to Muttra and rested in the seraee. A religious mendicant had taken up his quarters in the seraee who recognized the Thugs and went and gave information of their arrival to the Police. The jemadar of the thanna came with a body of burkundazes to make enquiries, which the Thugs managed to answer to his satisfaction. The thannadar therefore did not molest them. In the morning when the Thugs had gone on and reached the ferry of the Jumna, near Muttra, the same jemadar was met by them. He had come to see his brother set out on a journey, and it so happened that the Thugs, this jemadar's brother, and an attendant, all embarked on the same boat, and having crossed the stream went to Buldeojee, where they passed the night. Next morning the two travellers were conducted by the gang to Ferozabad where they slept, and the following morning early the murder was completed about two miles from the town. The bodies were thrown into a well. After completing this murder the gang went home without any other adventure.

The main gang of Thugs which was left at Hulena left that place and proceeded by easy stages to Muhbeer, where Khuluk jemadar took leave of his companions and went home accompanied by sixteen Thugs. They perpetrated no murders on the road.

The relict of the gang now consisted of Bichoo jemadar's party of twenty-six Lodees and ninety Sindousees. They all went to Ramsir where they decoyed four travellers, by caste Hindoos, of the tribe of Kayuts, and induced them to rest in a garden outside the town, where the Thugs had accommodated themselves: soon after dark the travellers were strangled on their beds and their bodies were buried in the garden.

N. B. The remains of these bodies have been disinterred upon the shewing of an approver and the case has formed the subject of trial in the Agent's Court.

Report of a Thug Expedition in the year
Lalla Lochun, Budlee, and Mukhun

No. of List.	Names and jurisdiction of the place where the Murder was perpetrated.	No. and Sex of the Murdered.		Date of the Murder.	Intended destination of the Murdered.		Supposed value of the property robbed.
		Men.	Women.		From	To	
410	Chowbepore,	1	0	That Season of 1832,	Westward,	Allahabad,	125 rupees cash, 25 rupees of property.
411	Mullooa,	2	0	Ditto,	Kurnal,	Ditto,	70 rupees.
412	Chickutteah,	1	0	Ditto,	Bundelkhund,	Cawnpore,	11 rupees, and a bullock.
413	Poorwa, in the Cawnpore zillah,	2	0	Ditto,	Calcutta,	Furruckhabad,	50 rupees.
414	Tukkeah,	1	0	February 1832,	....	Lucknow,	30 rupees.

1832, *under the following leaders :*
Jemadars, and other Leaders.

REMARKS.

Proceeding onwards the gang reached Madhoorajpore, where they were recognized by a Rajpoot jemadar of the thanna by name Mahtah Singh, who came with a force of armed men to arrest the Thugs. Bichoo jemadar, Mandhata (approver) Kurhoree, Chotee jemadar, Hurrea, Nunhooa-koree (approver) and Bijjaeen and others, to the number of nineteen Thugs, were seized by the thannadar. The remainder of the gang sought refuge in flight and reached their homes without further molestation.

In the month of January, 1832, Mukhun jemadar, with sixteen Thugs, set out from Rujaee Mhow in the Furruckhabad district, intending to proceed on an expedition to the eastward. They first went to Poorra in Cawnpore, and there they fell in with a Hindoo travelling from the westward to Allahabad, whom they decoyed and took on with them at once towards Chowbepore. It was dark before they got there so they strangled the traveller on the road and threw his body into a well.

After the murder the gang went to Mullooa, and met two travellers, by caste Brahmins, having two bullocks with them, on their way from Kurnaul to Allahabad. They were decoyed and brought to the seraee at Mullooa to the shop of Fuqueera Bhuteearee, next morning early the travellers were strangled about two miles from the village and their bodies were thrown into a well.

Having completed the murder the Thugs returned to Mullooa, made the Bhuteearee a present of a rupee, and then continued their journey to Chickuttea. There they inveigled a Hindoo traveller from Bundelkhund on his way to Cawnpore, and having kept him near themselves all day, took him out next morning a distance of a couple of miles and strangled him. The body was thrown into a well.

N. B. The bullock obtained at this murder was recovered by Mr. J. C. Wilson.

Proceeding on, the gang arrived at Poorwa in the Cawnpore zillah, where they discovered two Hindoos, tailors by trade, who were from their way from Calcutta to Furruckhabad, whom they decoyed and conducted next morning early to a tank a mile from the village, where they were strangled and the bodies thrown into a well. After this affair the Thugs returned to their respective homes.

During the month of February, 1832, Keseree subadar, with eight Thugs, left Bys-ka-Poorwah in Oude, and set out in the direction of Lucknow. They first arrived at Tukkeah, where they were joined by a Hindoo, travelling in the

Report of a Thug Expedition in the year
Lalla Lochun, Budlee, and Mukhun.

No. of List.	Names and jurisdiction of the place where the Murder was perpetrated.	No. and Sex of the Murdered.		Date of the Murder.	Intended destination of the Murdered.		Supposed value of the property robbed.
		Men.	Women.		From	To	
415	Nowulgunge,	2	0	That Season of 1832,	Gwalior,	Sultanpore,	100 rupees.
416	Chickuttea,	2	0	Ditto,	....	Benares,	125 rupees.
417	Futtehpore,	2	0	Ditto,	....	....	200 rupees.
418	Belinda,	1	0	Ditto,	Lahore,	Gya,	225 rupees.
419	Ahmedgunge,	3	0	Ditto,	....	Ditto,	60 rupees.
420	Kakerabad,	1	0	Ditto,	....	Eastward,	25 rupees.
421	Futtehpore,	1	0	Ditto,	Eastward,	Bithoor,	100 rupees.

1832, under the following leaders:
Jemadars, and other Leaders.

REMARKS.

same direction with themselves, whom they decoyed, and next morning strangled at a well two miles off and threw his body into the water.

They then proceeded on to Nowulgunge, where they managed to decoy two travellers, by caste Hindoos, on their way from Gwalior to Sultanpore. After they had made themselves comfortable for the day, the Thugs were joined by another gang of Jumaldhees, sixteen in number, from Oude, under Futteh and Rhuman jemadars. They all conducted the travellers out of the village early next morning and strangled them about a mile off from it. The bodies were thrown into a well.

After this they proceeded southward to Sindhora, where a yearly fair was just then taking place, and their numbers were further increased by the junction of Mukhun jemadar with eight Lodhee Thugs. They had just left home, and had not perpetrated any murders. From Sindhora the united gangs went to Chickuttea, where two travellers, on their way to Benares, were discovered and decoyed, next morning early they were taken out and put to death at a well a mile from the village. The bodies were thrown into a well.

After this they went to Futtehpore and fell in with two Mussulmans travelling in the same direction with themselves, whom they decoyed and next morning early put to death some distance from the village. The bodies were thrown into a well.

Their next stage was Belinda, where they found a Hindoo traveller from Lahore, on his way to Gya, whom they decoyed, and took out next morning to the place of murder two miles off, where he was strangled and his body thrown into a well.

The Thugs proceeded to Ahmedgunge where they decoyed three Hindoos on their way to Gya. In the morning the travellers were conducted to the bank of the Ganges on pretence of bathing, and while performing their ablutions they were strangled and their bodies thrown into the stream.

They went on to Kakerabad and rested for the day—a traveller, by caste a Hindoo, came to the same place on his way eastward, and was decoyed by Keseeree subadar. He was put to death as usual next morning about a mile from the village. The body was thrown into a well.

The gang then turned back and proceeded to Futtehpore where they fell in with a traveller, by caste a Rajhpoot, on his way from the eastward to Bithoor. He was decoyed, and next morning accompanied the gang to the

Report of a Thug Expedition in the year
Lalla Lochun, Budlee, and Mukhun

No. of List.	Names and jurisdiction of the place where the Murder was perpetrated.	No. and Sex of the Murdered.		Date of the Murder.	Intended destination of the Murdered.		Supposed value of the property robbed.
		Men.	Women.		From	To	
422	Pinghee, in the Cawnpore district,	1	0	That Season of 1832,	Gwalior,	Benares,	50 rupees.
423	Bilhore,	1	0	Ditto,	Subathoo,	Byswara,	70 rupees.
424	Ditto,	1	0	Ditto,	Ditto,	Ditto,	100 rupees, a pony.
425	Futtehpore,	3	0	Ditto,	....	Benares,	300 rupees.
426	Kuttra, in the Oude state,	2	0	Ditto,	Lahore,	Ditto,	100 rupees.
427	Bela,	1	0	Ditto,	Dekhan,	Northward,	150 rupees.
428	Daoodpoorah,	1	0	Ditto,	....	Furruckhabad,	30 rupees.

1832, under the following leaders:
Jemadars, and other Leaders.

REMARKS.

banks of the Ganges where he was strangled while bathing. The body was abandoned to the stream.

After this they all went to Rooma, where the Jumaldhee Thugs, sixteen in number, and two of the Lodhees, took leave of their companions and proceeded to their homes. The remainder went to Pinghee, in the Cawnpore district, where they fell in with a Hindoo on his way from Gwalior to Benares, who was decoyed and next morning strangled in the usual manner about a mile from the village. The body was thrown into a well.

It was next determined that Mukhun jemadar, with seven Thugs, should proceed home with money for their families with a promise of rejoining the gang at Bilhore in the course of five days, Keseeree subadar who had now only sixteen Thugs left with him proceeded by regular stages to Bilhore, and there fell in with a Hindoo traveller on his way from Subathoo to Byswara, who was decoyed, and next morning early, having been taken out half a mile from the village, he was strangled and his body thrown into a well.

They then returned to Bilhore where they succeeded in decoying another Hindoo, also from Subathoo, on his way to Byswara; soon afterwards the eight Thugs who had proceeded home rejoined the gang, accompanied by another Thug named Ramnath Josee, next morning early they set out and having taken the traveller to a well a mile from the village they strangled and threw him into it.

N. B. The pony was subsequently recovered by Mr. J. C. Wilson.

The gang arrived at Futtehpore and decoyed three travellers on their way to Benares, whom they brought to pass the day with them at the seraee. They were strangled early next morning at a well a mile from the town and their bodies thrown into the water.

They then went to the ferry across the Ganges at Raychoora, and entered the boat, in which they found two travellers, Hindoos by caste, on their way from Lahore to Benares, whom they decoyed and took with them to Kuttra in the Oude state; next morning early the travellers were taken out to a stream two miles off, where they were strangled and their bodies buried.

The gang went and passed the night at Bela: they found at that place a Hindoo from the Dekhan, travelling northward, whom they decoyed and took out next morning and strangled, the body was thrown into a well.

After this they proceeded to Daoodpoora and were soon afterwards joined by a Hindoo traveller on his way to Furruckhabad, who was decoyed and

Report of a Thug Expedition in the year
Lalla Lochun, Budlee, and Mukhun

No. of List.	Names and jurisdiction of the place where the Murder was perpetrated.	No. and Sex of the Murdered.		Date of the Murder.	Intended destination of the Murdered.		Supposed value of the property robbed.
		Men.	Women.		From	To	
429	Oomrea, in the Jhalone,	3	0	March, 1832,	Gwalior,	Oude,	200 rupees.
430	Pergunna,	1	0	Ditto,	Ditto,	Ditto,	50 rupees, and some cooking utensils.
431	Ditto,	2	0	Ditto,	Ditto,	Cawnpore,	125 rs., 1 bullock, 1 matchlock, & other

1832, *under the following leaders:*
Jemadars, and other Leaders.

REMARKS.

strangled next morning soon after leaving the village. The body was thrown into a well. The gang after this murder returned home.

In the month of March 1832, Shunkur, Bukhal, Dibba and other Thugs, amounting in number to ten persons, assembled at Tilwa, in the Furruckhabad district, and set out on an expedition to Bundelkhund. They first proceeded to Oomrea where they were joined by Bholah Bukhal with eleven Thugs, and all went on to Bussuntpore, in the Gwalior state. There eleven more Thugs from Sindouse led by Bukhut Mooreah jemadar joined the gang, which was now increased to thirty-six persons, who all went and rested on the bank of the tank at Rown. Three travellers, one a gardner, and the other two Brahmins, on their way from Gwalior to Oude, came and rested near the Thugs. They were decoyed and taken next day to Oomrea in Jhalone where all slept, and before daylight the succeeding morning were conducted to a thickly wooded spot, two miles from the village, where they were strangled while sitting by the road side. The bodies were buried in a field.

They had not proceeded far after completing this murder when they heard an ass bray, which being considered a most inauspicious omen, the Thugs turned back and went home.

N. B. It appears that soon after the perpetration of the murder, a person of the name of Nowul, the zemeendar, who owned the field in which the bodies had been insecurely buried, went to look at his crop: beasts of prey had already dug up the bodies, and were devouring them. The fact was witnessed by many persons and the remains were collected and burnt. These circumstances were ascertained by Mr. J. C. Wilson, who has fixed the date of the murder to have been the 13th March 1832.

During the same month of March 1832, Bholah Bukhal, Girdharee and Phoolsa, who then resided at Rewah, in the Jhalone state, abandoned their homes in consequence of hearing of the numerous arrests of Thugs that was then going forward. They came to Burragaon in Gwalior, where they found sixteen Thugs from Sindouse, led by Bhikka and Heera jemadars, whom they joined. The last mentioned gang had only just left their homes and they all went to Dhyegaon, where they fell in with a traveller, by caste a Khuttree, from Gwalior, on his way to Oude, whom they decoyed and took next day to Pergunna. They slept there and next morning the traveller was put to death about a mile from the village. The body was buried in a water-course.

They returned to Dhyegaon as soon as the murder was completed and encamped in a garden. Girdharee and Bhola went into the bazar and found two travellers, by caste Hindoos, who had come from Gwalior intending to go

Report of a Thug Expedition in the year
Lalla Lochun, Budlee, and Mukhun

No. of List.	Names and jurisdiction of the place where the Murder was perpetrated.	No. and Sex of the Murdered.		Date of the Murder.	Intended destination of the Murdered.		Supposed value of the property robbed.
		Men.	Women.		From	To	
							property worth 25 rupees.
432	Suppowlee,	1	0	March, 1832,	Cawnpore,	Gwalior,	40 rupees.

1832, *under the following leaders:*
Jemadars, and other Leaders.

REMARKS.

towards Cawnpore, whom they decoyed and brought to the garden; next day they took the travellers with them to Pergunna and rested in the bazar, and early next morning they put them to death about two miles from the village, and buried their bodies.

The Thugs then went on to Indoorkee, where they halted. There Phoolsa jemadar was recognized by an inhabitant of the place, who induced the native authorities to detain him. During the night Phoolsa effected his escape, in consequence of which the villagers came and surrounded the members of the gang, who were sleeping in the bazar. Only one of the number, Bhola approver, was able to decamp, and he abandoned his property and sought safety in flight. The remainder were kept in durance for four and twenty hours and then set at liberty. The property abandoned by the runaway Bhola, was detained by the villagers. The Thugs, in despair at the inauspicious circumstance, returned to their homes.

The gang whose proceedings have just been detailed did not think it safe to remain at home more than a day or two, for guards from the department for the suppression of Thuggee were out in all directions in search of them. So Girdharee and Eseree jemadars assembled twenty-five Thugs at Maitee-ka-Poorwa in Furruckhabad, during the month of March, and took to the roads again. They crossed the Jumna, and reached Nowdha in the Gwalior state, where they met Bhola Bukhal and Bukhul Moorea jemadars, with a gang of fifteen Thugs, who joined them and they all went to Suppowlee. A traveller, by caste a Rajpoot, named Zubber Singh, who was on his way from Gwalior to the vicinity of Jhalone, came to the same place to rest for the day, and being decoyed by one of the Thugs was brought to the encampment of the gang. Soon afterwards Dibba Bunneah discovered a traveller, by caste a Brahmin, on his way from Cawnpore to Gwalior, whom he decoyed and accommodated for the day near himself. Early next morning Dibba, with a few followers, set out with the Brahmin traveller in his train, and having put him to death at a short distance from the village, threw his body into a water-course, and returned to the main gang bringing his property with them. Soon afterwards Bhola Bunneah and Girdharee set out with the Rajpoot in an opposite direction. Bhikka jemadar was previously fixed upon as the strangler of the traveller. Having gone a mile from the village, a pretext was framed for inducing the traveller to sit down, but the intended victim, perhaps taking alarm at some suspicious circumstance or other, instead of consenting, threw down the bundle which he was carrying and fled for his life. Five or six of the most active among the Thugs went in pursuit of him; but fear giving wings to the traveller's speed, they were unable to overtake him; and returned back in despair. From dread of the result of this unfortunate incident, the gang proceeded with all despatch to the village of Amayin, and thence to Nowta

Report of a Thug Expedition in the year
Lalla Lochun, Budlee, and Mukhun

No. of List.	Names and jurisdiction of the place where the Murder was perpetrated.	No. and Sex of the Murdered.		Date of the Murder.	Intended destination of the Murdered.		Supposed value of the property robbed.
		Men.	Women.		From	To	
433	Wowlee,	4	0	20th March, 1832,	Gwalior,	Cawnpore,	800 rupees.
434	Gokul, in the Muttra zillah,	1	0	April, 1832,	Bhurtpore,	Ditto,	30 rupees.
435	Near Agra,	2	0	Ditto,	Jeypore,	Oude,	50 rupees.

1832, under the following leaders: Jemadars, and other Leaders.

REMARKS.

where they rested. At the latter place they found four travellers, one a subadar, by caste a Brahmin, the second a palankeen bearer, the third a Rajpoot named Murdan Singh, and the fourth a cultivator, who had come from Gwalior on their way to Cawnpore, and managed to decoy them. They took the travellers next day to Wowlee, where they passed the night, and before daylight in the morning put the travellers to death about two miles from the village, and threw their bodies into a well.

After this affair the gang went home again.

N. B. About the close of the year, 1832, when Mr J. C. Wilson proceeded from Saugor on deputation to the Dooab, the facts above detailed were elicited by his enquiries. Zubber Singh, a Rajpoot, appeared before that gentleman and detailed the circumstances of his escape from a violent death, and the bodies of the subadar and his companions were disinterred on the showing of Bhola approver. When this approver, Bhola Bunneah, arrived at home, he found that his wife and child had during his absence been arrested and carried away prisoners by a guard sent by Major Sleeman from Saugor. Being cast down at this event he refrained from proceeding on another expedition, and a guard again visiting his village, he fell into their hands, was made prisoner, and brought to Saugor, where he confessed his crimes and was admitted an approver in the month of May, 1832.

In the month of April, 1832, Mehrban jemadar, and Heera, son of Oomeid jemadar, with seven other Thugs, met together at Seetul-ka-Poorwa, in Furruckhabad, and being in distress for want of money determined to try their fortune on the roads. They proceeded towards the west by regular stages till they reached Gokul in the Muttra zillah, where they fell in with a Hindoo, travelling from Bhurtpore to Cawnpore, whom they decoyed, and next morning put to death at the distance of three miles from the village, and buried his body in the bed of a water-course. They then turned back after the murder and proceeded homewards, arriving there without any other adventure.

About the same time Dhunna approver and fourteen Thugs had assembled at Behareepore, and had taken the auspices preparatory to setting out on an expedition, when intelligence reached them that a guard had set out for the purpose of arresting some Thugs, who had been pointed out by Rambuksh and Daveedeen, who has recently been seized and admitted approvers at Saugor. They therefore travelled with all speed westward till they arrived at a village twelve miles from Agra, on the road to Bhurtpore. There they fell in with two Brahmins on their way from Jeypore to the Oude provinces, whom they decoyed and conducted next morning some distance on the way to Agra, when they strangled them and buried their bodies in a cotton field.

Report of a Thug Expedition in the year
Lalla Lochun, Budlee, and Mukhun

No. of List.	Names and jurisdiction of the place where the Murder was perpetrated.	No. and Sex of the Murdered.		Date of the Murder.	Intended destination of the Murdered.		Supposed value of the property robbed.
		Men.	Women.		From	To	
436	Mahabeer,	3	0	That Season of 1832,	Tonk,	Koree-Jehana-bad,	100 rupees, and 20 shields.
437	Sheekooabad, in the Mynpooree district,	2	0	Ditto,	....	Agra,	100 rupees.
438	Mahabeer, in the Jeypore State,	3	0	Ditto,	Jeypore,	Oude,	100 rupees.
439	Doostpoora,	3	0	Ditto,	Bundel-khund,	Marwar,	40 pieces of coloured cloths, 10 pieces of chintz, 10

1832, under the following leaders:
Jemadars, and other Leaders.

REMARKS.

After the murder, they proceeded south, till in the course of a few days, they arrived at Mahabeer in the Jeypore state, where they found three travellers, by caste Hindoos, on their way from Tonk to Koree Jehanabad, whom they persuaded to join their party. Next morning they were put to death about two miles from the village, and their bodies buried in the bed of a water-course.

They then went Birmabad in Bhurtpore, where they met Saadut jemadar with a gang of eight Thugs, who told them that they had been wandering about in dread of arrest, as Roostumkhan and Kadirkhan, had been seized and became approvers, and were scouring the country in charge of a guard with the avowed purpose of capturing them, that whatever seraee they rested in they obtained information from the Bhutearees, that arresting parties were in the vicinity. The two parties determined to try their luck in company, and then went on to Neebhaira, where they found Khulluk jemadar with forty-three Thugs encamped.

Khulluk and his party had, about the beginning of April, collected thirty Thugs at Meytee-ka-Poorwa in Furruckhabad, and set out on an expedition. He first led his gang to Sheekooabad in Mynpooree, and when he had arrived at the gate of the seraee intending to enter it, two travellers, by caste Hindoos, came up on their way to Agra. He immediately addressed them, and managed by his insinuating manners to gain their confidence so far that they took up their quarters for the night in the same chamber with him. During the afternoon Bichoo jemadar with eight Thug followers, arrived at the seraee, having just left their homes in search of adventures. It was agreed that they should join Khulluk's party, and all set out early next morning, and put the travellers to death, about a mile from the village, and threw the bodies into a well.

Proceeding onwards they arrived at Mahabeer, in the Jeypore State, and there decoyed three Hindoos, travelling from the city of Jeypore to Oude, whom they took to a garden outside of the village intending to pass the night there. When the travellers were gone to rest it was determined at once to despatch them: the stranglers were warned to perform their office, and a cry of a snake was suddenly raised by the leader of the gang. The travellers attempting to escape the apprehended danger, fell an easy prey to their destroyers, who having strangled them, buried their bodies in a water-course not far off.

As soon as the murder was completed the gang packed up their baggage and set off again, and when they had proceeded a few miles, they met four Sindousee Thugs among whom was Hussunnooa (now an approver), who also gave them alarming accounts of the proceedings of parties sent out to arrest the fraternity. They went on to Bawurbhas, and while resting there were joined by three

Report of a Thug Expedition in the year
Lalla Lochun, Budlee, and Mukhun

No. of List.	Names and jurisdiction of the place where the Murder was perpetrated.	No. and Sex of the Murdered.		Date of the Murder.	Intended destination of the Murdered.		Supposed value of the property robbed.
		Men.	Women.		From	To	
							pieces calico, 100 rupees, and a camel.
440	Pokur,	1	0	That Season of 1832,	Dekhan	Gangetee provinces.	40 rupees worth of gold, and 2 rupees cash.
441	Nuggur, in the Jeypore State,	7	0	Ditto,	Ditto,	Byswara,	400 rupees, 1 camel, 1 horse, and 2 ponies.
442	Nubhaira, in the Bhurtpore State,	2	0	Ditto,	Ditto,	Oude,	50 rupees.
443	Neebhaira,	1	0	Ditto,	Ditto,	Dooab,	30 rupees.
444	Boorakur, in the Agra district,	1	0	Ditto,	Neemutch,	Furruckhabad,	35 rupees.

1832, under the following leaders:
Jemadars, and other Leaders.

REMARKS.

Marwarees on their way from Bundelkhund to their own country with a laden camel, who were persuaded to prosecute their journey in their company. They took them next day to Dostpoora, and having slept there set out again next morning. Soon after sunrise they reached the bank of a stream that crossed the road, where it was proposed by the Thugs that they should stop to perform their ablutions. Two of the travellers consented to this proposal, but the third refused to remain, and said he would pursue his way alone. However Dhowkul jemadar was sent with him to watch his movements,—and obtaining a favorable opportunity he sprung upon him, before he had proceeded far from the stream, and strangled him without assistance. He instantly called out to his companions in the slang language informing them what he had done, whereon the other two Marwarees were forthwith put to death. The bodies of all three were buried on the bank of a river.

The gang then went to Pokur, where they fell in with a Hindoo, who had come from the Dekhan on his way to the Gangetee provinces, whom they decoyed, and taking out early next morning put him to death about a mile from the town. The body was buried.

After this affair they proceeded to Nugger, in the Jeypore State, where they found seven Hindoo travellers, from the Dekhan, who intended to go to Byswara. Khulluk jemadar decoyed them, and next morning they were conducted to a tank about three miles from the village, and having been strangled their bodies were buried close by.

They then went to Nubhaira, in the Bhurtpore State, and managed to inveigle two travellers, by caste Hindoos, from the Dekhan, on their way to the Oude provinces, and took them to pass the night on the bank of a tank. After dark they were invited to smoke and converse with the leader of the Thugs, and were put to death in the usual manner. The bodies were buried.

Next day the gang moved on to Birmabad, and on the road Khulluk fell in with and decoyed a Hindoo who was travelling from the Dekhan to the Dooab, and took him to Neebhaira, where they found Saadut and Dhunna jemadars encamped with twenty-four Thugs as before mentioned. The two parties united their forces and next morning put the traveller to death about two miles from the village and buried his body.

Proceeding onwards they arrived in the course of two or three days at Borakur in the Agra district, and took up their quarters in the seraee; a traveller, by caste a Hindoo, from Neemutch, on his way to Furruckhabad, was resting there, and having been decoyed, he was taken out next morning about a mile from the village and put to death. The body was buried.

Report of a Thug Expedition in the year
Lolla Lochun, Budlee, and Mukhun

No. of List.	Names and jurisdiction of the place where the Murder was perpetrated.	No. and Sex of the Murdered.		Date of the Murder.	Intended destination of the Murdered.		Supposed value of the property robbed.
		Men.	Women.		From	To	
445	Chiksana,	4	0	That Season of 1832,	Ulwer,	Furruckhabad,	70 rupees.
446	Bhala Hurree, in the Jeypore State,	1	0	Ditto,	Ajmere,	Dooab,	80 rupees.
447	Jytwara,	3	0	Ditto,	Agra,	Jeypore,	1300 rupees.

1832, *under the following leaders :*
Jemadars, and other Leaders.

REMARKS.

After this Khulluk jemadar, with his party of thirty Thugs, determined to proceed home. The other Thugs vehemently exhorted him not to attempt so dangerous a proceeding stated that a guard was out in pursuit of him and his followers, and that he would certainly have cause to regret that he had resisted their persuasions : he was however firm in his purpose and separated from the rest of the party. As soon as they arrived at home they learnt that guards were searching for them in the Etawah and Furruckhabad districts, they therefore determined to loose no time but to take to the roads again ; accordingly they offered up a goat as a sacrifice to Bhowanee, and were assembled to ook for an omen preparatory to setting out, when Badulkhan Duffadar, with a guard of Nujeebs and some approvers, came suddenly upon them, and arrested Khulluk and Dhowkul jemadars with eighteen other Thugs, and carried them prisoners to the thanna at Phupoond. The thannadar demanded from the Duffadar a list of the Thugs at large whom he was authorized to arrest, and upon examining it he found that the name only of Khulluk jemadar was inserted in it. He therefore detained the jemadar and set the other Thugs at liberty, saying that they were to appear when called for. Fifteen or sixteen days afterwards the Magistrate of the district demanded the production of these people, and they were sent to his Court, where they were recognized by the approvers, and carried prisoners to Saugor ; at that early stage of proceedings there were not approvers at Saugor capable of substantiating murders against the whole of these men, and five of the number were released upon security.

The remainder of the gang whom Khulluk jemadar left at Boorakar, led by Uchal jemadar, also took the road homewards. When they arrived at Chiksana in Bhurtpore, they again met Saadut jemadar, who advised them not to go in the vicinity of their homes as they would assuredly get into trouble. They therefore took his advice and rested at Chiksana ; soon afterwards four Hindoo travellers from Ulwer, on their way to Furruckhabad, arrived at the same place, and were decoyed by the Thugs, who took them out next morning and put them to death two miles from the village. The bodies were buried.

They then went to Bhurtpore, and in the course of eight days more they reached Bhala Hurree in Jeypore, where they inveigled a Mahomedan who was travelling from Ajmeer to the Dooab. He was put to death early next morning soon after quitting the village. The body was buried.

The gang proceeded to Jeytwara, and fell in with three Hindoo travellers, from Agra, on their way to Jeypore, who were decoyed and induced to remain near the Thugs : they were put to death next morning immediately after leaving the village, and their bodies buried.

Report of a Thug Expedition in the year
Lalla Lochun, Budlee, and Mukhun

No of List.	Names and jurisdiction of the place where the Murder was perpetrated.	No. and Sex of the Murdered.		Date of the Murder.	Intended destination of the Murdered.		Supposed value of the property robbed.
		Men.	Women.		From	To	
448	Ramsir,	3	0	That Season of 1832,	Bombay.	Furruckhabad,	100 rupees cash, 25 rupees property.
449	Birmabad,	1	0	Ditto,	Neemutch,	Ditto,	80 rupees.
450	Purteeagaon, in the Mynpooree district,	1	0	Ditto,	Ajmere,	Byswara,	50 rupees, 1 bullock.
451	Belhore, in the Cawnpore State,	1	0	May 1832,	Furruckhabad,	Mirzapore,	25 rupees.
442	Kakerabad, in the Allahabad district,	2	0	Ditto,	Muttra.	Jounpore,	50 rupees.
453	Kosea, in the Benares district,	3	0	Ditto,	Calcutta,	Etawah,	1000 rupees.

1832, under the following leaders:
Jemadars, and other Leaders.

REMARKS.

After this they arrived at Chaksoo, at which they were joined by three travellers, by caste Lodhees, on their way from Bombay to Furruckhabad. They were decoyed and taken to Lalsout and the day after to Ramsir. The next morning the travellers were put to death, and their bodies abandoned in the jungle.

Having completed the murder they went on to Hindown in Jeypore. There they met a Hindoo on his way from Neemutch to Furruckhabad, whom they persuaded to travel along with them. They slept the next night at Birmabad, and early in the morning strangled the traveller on the road side, and buried his body there.

The gang then determined that as arresting had even reached the part of the country in which they were then roaming, and they daily heard intelligence of them from the Bhutearas at the seraees, they might as well return home, as brave the danger of arrest at a distance. Accordingly Uchul jemadar, and his fifteen followers, set off for their homes in the Dooab, while Saadut jemadar and his Thugs took the road to Dholepore.

Uchul jemadar and his gang proceeded by way of Agra to Purteagaon, in the Mynpooree zillah, where they fell in with a Brahmin who was travelling from Ajmere to Byswara, whom they decoyed, and next morning strangled at a well a mile from the village, throwing his body into it. After this affair Uchul jemadar's gang reached home without further adventure.

In the month of May, 1832, Budlee jemadar's party of eleven Thugs assembled at Ghazee-ka-Poorwa, in Furruckhabad, and set out on an expedition. They first went to Bithore in Cawnpore, and in the evening fell in with a Brahmin, who had just come from Furruckhabad on his way to Mirzapore, they decoyed him and before daylight next morning put him to death at a well a mile from the village, and threw his body into the water.

They proceeded onwards till they arrived at Kakerabad in the Allahabad district, where they discovered two cow-keepers, on their way from Muttra to Jounpore, whom they decoyed and put to death early in the morning. The bodies were thrown into the well two miles from the village.

They next arrived at Koseea in the Benares district, where they fell in with three Hindoo travellers, on their way from Calcutta to Etawah, two were Brahmins and another a Kayut. They took them out early next morning and strangled them. The bodies were thrown in a tank.

After this affair the Thugs returned home without further adventure.

Report of a Thug Expedition in the year
Lalla Lochun, Budlee, and Mukhun

No. of List.	Names and jurisdiction of the place where the Murder was perpetrated.	No. and Sex of the Murdered.		Date of the Murder.	Intended destination of the Murdered.		Supposed value of the property robbed.
		Men.	Women.		From	To	
454	Chowbe-ka-seraee, in Cawnpore,	2	0	That Season of 1832,	Kurnal,	Cawnpore,	50 rupees.
455	Akberpore,	1	0	Ditto,	Dekhan,	Byswara,	150 rupees cash, and 50 rupees of property.
456	Kazeegunge,	2	0	Ditto,	....	Eastward,	50 rupees.
457	Mooshkabad,	2	0	Ditto,	Dekhan,	Sultanpore,	3 gold mohurs, 1 horse, and 25 rupees.
458	Hussungunge,	2	0	Ditto,	Loodhiana,	Ditto,	50 rupees.

1832, *under the following leaders:*
Jemadars, and other Leaders.

REMARKS.

When Budlee and his companions arrived at home, they found it unsafe to remain there long, as guards had constantly visited their dwellings during their absence in the hopes of arresting. They accordingly determined to take to the roads again, and seventeen Thugs, led by Budlee and Ramdeen jemadars, set out from Chowdeeka Poorwa, and arrived at Mukrundnuggur. There they found Phoolsa jemadar and two followers, who had fled from Sindouse, where guards were also engaged in arresting Thugs. They joined the Lodhees, and all went to Chowbe-ka-seraee in Cawnpore, where they fell in with a Musulman and a Brahmin on their way from Kurnal to Cawnpore, whom they decoyed and put to death as usual next morning. The bodies were thrown into a well.

They then took the direction of Calpee, and having passed through Chichindee were sitting at the bank of a stream when they heard from some passengers that an arresting party had reached Calpee and would presently come up in that direction. In great alarm they set off from thence and travelled with the utmost despatch to Akberpore. There they decoyed a Rajpoot sepahee from the Dekhan on his way to Byswara, and having taken him out next morning to a well two miles from the village they strangled him and threw his body into the water.

After the affair Budlee left the party intending to go home, and promised to rejoin at Hurole. The rest of the gang went to Kazeegunge, where their numbers were increased by the arrival of a party of Lodhee Thugs amounting to twenty-one persons, led by Mukhun, Surrawan and other jemadars. Ramdeen jemadar fell in with two Hindoo travellers on their way eastward, whom he decoyed and brought to the encampment of the Thugs. They were taken out next morning to a dry water-course two miles off and strangled. The bodies were thrown into a well.

While the Thugs were engaged in settling accounts after the murder in a garden at Hurole, Budlee jemadar came up and rejoined them. From thence the gang went on and crossed the Ganges, entering the Oude territory at the village of Gujdhurrun. They were sitting on the bank of a tank when two travellers, by caste Hindoos, came up from the Dekhan on their way to Sultanpore They were persuaded to prosecute their journey with the gang, who took them on that day to Mooshkabad, where they slept, and the next morning were put to death in the usual manner, the distance of two miles from the village. The bodies were thrown into a well.

They then proceeded to Hussungunge. Two Hindoo travellers from Loodhiana on their way to Sultanpore, were decoyed at this place, and being taken out next morning were put to death at a well, into which the bodies were thrown.

Report of a Thug Expedition in the year
Lalla Lochun, Budlee, and Mukhun

No. of List.	Names and jurisdiction of the place where the Murder was perpetrated.	No. and Sex of the Murdered.		Date of the Murder.	Intended destination of the Murdered.		Supposed value of the property robbed.
		Men.	Women.		From	To	
459	Gosaeengunge,	3	0	That Season of 1832,	Lahore,	Byswara,	1000 rupees, a horse.
460	Nuwabgunge,	2	0	Ditto,	....	Lucknow,	125 rupees, 2 shields.
461	Maharajpore, in Cawnpore,	2	0	Ditto,	Calcutta,	Agra,	150 rupees, 50 rupees property.
462	Rooma,	2	0	Ditto,	....	Southward,	80 rupees.

1832, *under the following leaders:*
Jemadars, and other Leaders.

REMARKS.

After this the gang arrived at the bridge over the river Mohawn, and were soon afterwards overtaken by three travellers, Brahmins and Rajpoots by caste, who came from Lahore intending to go to Byswara They had just left one of their companions, who had died at Tukkeah, and the remaining three expressed to the Thugs their great grief at the bereavement. They all went together to Gosaeengunge, where five Jumaldhee Thugs under Ouseree (approver) joined the party. In the morning the travellers were strangled soon after they had set out, and their bodies were buried in a water-course.

N. B. The horse obtained at this affair was subsequently recovered by Mr. Wilson.

After this affair the Jumaldhee Thugs received their share of the booty, and proceeded in a different direction. The Lodhees went to Nuwabgunge, where they decoyed two Hindoos, who were travelling to Lucknow. Next morning they were put to death, and their bodies thrown into a well.

As soon as the murder was completed, Budlee and Ramdeen jemadars, with twenty Thugs, separated from the main gang, which now consisted of Mukhun and Phoolsa jemadars of twenty-one Thugs.

Budlee and Ramdeen proceeded by regular stages till they arrived at Maharajpore in Cawnpore. where they fell in with a Hindoo havildar with his son, who had come from Calcutta on their way to Agra, Budlee decoyed them, and next morning they were strangled, and their bodies thrown into a well.

They then went home without committing any other murders.

In the mean time Mukhun and Phoolsa led the twenty-one Thugs, across the Ganges to Shazadpore, in the Allahabad zillah, and having halted there, some of them got intoxicated. In this state they excited the suspicion of the thanadar, who arrested the whole party. When the Thugs came to their senses, they with characteristic cunning overcame the suspicions of the Police and through the intervention of a Bhuteara managed to effect their release. They went to Rooma, where they fell in with two travellers, by caste Hindoos, on their way south, whom they decoyed, and next morning put to death at a well two miles from the village, throwing the bodies into the water.

The gang then went home again.

N. B. Heera, son of Oomeid, one of the leaders of this party, states that after arriving at home, he remained there for four months, when a guard came from Saugor and arrested him and four other Thugs, who were carried away

Report of a Thug Expedition in the year
Lalla Lochun, Budlee, and Mukhun

No. of List.	Names and jurisdiction of the place where the Murder was perpetrated.	No. and Sex of the Murdered.		Date of the Murder.	Intended destination of the Murdered.		Supposed value of the property robbed.
		Men.	Women.		From	To	
463	Burrye, in the Coel district,	2	0	July, 1832,	....	Oude State,	100 rupees.
464	Boorhana,	2	0	Ditto,	Loodhiana,	Byswara,	150 rupees.
465	Kutteah,	3	0	Ditto,	Lahore,	Ditto,	100 rupees, 2 shawls, 1 horse.
466	Mulwa thana,	1	0	Ditto,	Cawnpore,	Kurnal,	15 rupees.
467	Secundra,	2	0	Ditto,	Kurnal,	Byswara,	50 rupees.
468	Sobhna,	1	0	Ditto,	Loodhiana,	Benares,	25 rupees.
469	Malagurh,	2	0	Ditto,	Calcutta,	Kurnal,	100 rupees.

1832, under the following leaders :
Jemadars, and other Leaders.

REMARKS.

prisoners. At Saugor when Heera found that denial was useless he became an approver.

In the month of July, 1832, Uchul and Hurlal jemadars led out twelve Thugs from Maitee-ka-Poorwa, and went to Burrye in the Coel zillah. They first met two Hindoos on their way to the Oude State, whom they decoyed, and put to death next morning a short distance from the village. The bodies were thrown into a well.

They turned back and proceeded by stages to Boorhana, where they met two travellers in the bazar, who had come from Loodhiana, and were going to Byswara. They were decoyed, and next morning strangled on the bank of the river, into which the dead bodies were thrown.

After the murder the Thugs were sitting in a garden a mile from Boorhana, when three Hindoos from Lahore on their way to Byswara, came there. The Thugs addressed and entered into an engagement to travel with them, so they turned back and proceeded to Kurkoodda. They escorted them successively to Haupper and Kutteah, without being able to effect their object, but next morning put them to death soon after they had set out, and threw the bodies into a well.

They then went to Sultangunge in Mynpooree, where they met Mehrban and Lalla Lochun jemadars, with a gang of fifteen Thugs, who had just set out on an expedition from Satul-ka-Poorwa. Oodey and Gopal were sent home from hence in charge of the shawls obtained at the last affair, with instructions to rejoin at Coel. The rest of the Thugs went to Mulwa thana, where they met a Hindoo, on his way from Cawnpore to Kurnal, whom Lalla Lochun decoyed, and next morning he was put to death as usual. The body was thrown into a well.

They next arrived at Secundra, and inveigled two travellers, a Brahmin and a Rajpoot, on their way from Kurnal to Byswara. These men were strangled next morning as usual, and their bodies thrown into a well.

Reaching Kakerabad they passed on to Coel, where Gopal and Oodey were waiting for their arrival. Next day went to Sobhna, and decoyed a traveller of the gardener caste, on his way from Loodhiana to Benares. He was taken to a tank a mile off the next morning, and having been strangled, his body was thrown into a well.

The gang then proceeded to Malagurh. Two travellers from Calcutta, one a Musulman and the other a Hindoo, on their way to Kurnal, were

Report of a Thug Expedition in the year
Lalla Lochun, Budlee, and Mukhun

No. of List.	Names and jurisdiction of the place where the Murder was perpetrated.	No. and Sex of the Murdered.		Date of the Murder.	Intended destination of the Murdered.		Supposed value of the property robbed.
		Men.	Women.		From	To	
470	Boorhana,	2	0	That Season of 1832,	Kurnal,	Lucknow,	100 rupees.
471	Shamlee,	4	0	Ditto,	Lahore,	Oude Provinces,	150 rupees.
472	Kirrooa,	4	0	Ditto,	Ditto,	Sultanpore,	200 rupees cash, 2 matchlocks, 500 rupees worth of silver. 800 Total.
473	Bhakree,	4	0	Ditto,	Kurnal,	Lucknow,	150 rupees.
474	Kakerabad,	1	0	Ditto,	Ditto,	Oude,	25 rupees.
475	Boorhea-ka-Poorwa,	5	0	Ditto,	Ditto,	Gungotree,	100 rupees.

1832, under the following leaders:
Jemadars, and other Leaders.

REMARKS.

resting at the same place. They were decoyed and put to death next morning at a water-course, in the bed of which the bodies were buried.

The Thugs passed through Hauper and Kirrooa, and arrived at Boorhana. They then met two Hindoo travellers from Kurnal, on their way to Lucknow, whom they decoyed, and next morning strangled at a river into which the bodies were thrown.

After this they went to Shamlee and falling in with four travellers, (two Rajpoots and two Aheers,) on their way from Lahore to the Oude provinces, they persuaded them to join the party, and next morning put them to death. The bodies were thrown into a well.

They then turned back and came to Boorhana, where they rested in the seraee. In the morning when they had proceeded a mile from the village, they were overtaken by four travellers, by caste Rajpoots from Lahore, intending to go to Sultanpore, whom they addressed and conducted to Kirrooa, where they all passed the night. Early next morning the travellers were strangled a mile from the village, and their bodies were buried.

Proceeding onwards they arrived at Bhakree and met 25 Thugs under Bichoo, Phoolsa, Mukhan and Mandhata jemadars. These people had only a short time previously set out from Rajee Mhow, and had not yet perpetrated any murder. Next morning all set out together, and were accompanied by four travellers who had joined them in the evening, consisting of two Bhurbhoojas, a Pathan and a Bunneah, who had come from Kurnal on their way to Lucknow. They were put to death about two miles from the village, and their bodies were buried.

After dividing the booty the gangs separated again. Lalla Lochun's party took the direction of Coel and Phoolsa, and Bichoo went to the westward.

Lalla Lochun's gang passed through Coel, and arrived at Kakerabad where they decoyed a Hindoo, who was travelling from Kurnal to Oude, and taking him out next morning, strangled him at a well three miles from the village. The body was thrown into the well.

Having completed the murder the Thugs went and sat down on the bank of the tank at Bailwagaon, and soon afterwards Gopal and Oodey came up with five Hindoo travellers from Kurnal on their way to Oude, whom they had decoyed. They took them the same day to Boorhea-ka-Poorwa, where they passed the night and next morning strangled them two miles from the village and buried their bodies.

Report of a Thug Expedition in the year
Lalla Lochun, Budlee, and Mukhun

No. of List.	Names and jurisdiction of the place where the Murder was perpetrated.	No. and Sex of the Murdered.		Date of the Murder.	Intended destination of the Murdered.		Supposed value of the property robbed.
		Men.	Women.		From	To	
476	Sobhna, in the Coel district,	3	0	That Season of 1832,	Cawnpore,	Meerut,	1,700 rupees worth of English chintz.
477	Hindown,	3	0	Ditto,	Tonk,	Oude,	50 rupees cash, 3 gold mohurs.
478	Burakar, in zillah Agra,	2	0	Ditto,	Nusseerabad,	Dooab,	150 rupees.
479	Koseegaon, in the Muttra zillah,	1	0	Ditto,	Jeypore,	Bareilly,	2 rupees, a camel.
480	Mhendee Ghât,	1	0	August, 1832,	....	....	No property.

1832, ***under the following leaders:***
Jemadars, and other Leaders.

REMARKS.

After this they returned home again.

When Bichoo and Phoolsa separated from this gang, they went and rested at Sobhna in the Coel district. There Mukhun decoyed a Kuhar, and two coolies, on their way from Cawnpore to Meerut, whom they put to death next morning, and secreted in a field about two miles from the village. Having gone to Koorja they despatched a party of Thugs, to look after the bodies which they had abandoned, with instructions to bury them; on arriving there the Thugs found that a cowherd had discovered the corpses and was in the act of looking at them. They turned back in great alarm, and rejoining their companions, related what they had observed, on which it was determined to break up the gang. Bichoo and Phoolsa took fourteen Thugs and went to Hindown, where they fell in with three travellers, by caste Rajpoots, from Tonk, on their way to the Oude State, whom they decoyed and took into the bazar. Setting out next morning before daylight the Thugs strangled the travellers two miles from the village, and buried their bodies.

After the murder they went to Burakar, in the Agra zillah. There they decoyed two travellers, who came from Nusseerabad intending to go to their homes in the Dooab, and having taken them next morning to a field a mile from the village, they put them to death, and buried their bodies.

They then went home without further adventure.

Mukhun jemadar and his eleven companions went from Koorja to Koseegaon in the Muttra zillah. A Marwaree with a camel, on his way from Jeypore to Bareilly, arrived at the same place, and was persuaded by the Thugs to travel in their company. He was put to death next morning, and his body buried in a water-course.

They then went home.

In the month of August, 1832, Bukshee, Dhunna and other leaders assembled fifteen Thugs at Unmee-ka-Nowada and set out on an expedition into the Oude State. Bukshee took seven Thugs with him, and crossed the Ganges at Mhendee Ghât. He had scarcely got to the opposite side of the river, when a man of the name of Doorgooa came up to him and enquired where Keseeree subadar was to be found, declaring that if he did not point out his hiding place he would arrest him, (Bukshee.) The jemadar replied, come along and I will show you. The man was conducted along the bank of the river till a convenient place was found when he was strangled, and his body thrown into the stream. After this they went to Nawabgunge, where Dhunna and his eight followers had arrived before them.

Report of a Thug Expedition in the year
Lalla Lochun, Budlee, and Mukhun

No. of List.	Names and jurisdiction of the place where the Murder was perpetrated.	No. and Sex of the Murdered.		Date of the Murder.	Intended destination of the Murdered.		Supposed value of the property robbed.
		Men.	Women.		From	To	
481	Hussungunge,	2	0	That Season of 1832,	Lahore,	Sultanpore,	200 rupees, 20 rupees property.
482	Futtehgunge,	2	0	Ditto,	Meerut,	Gogra,	125 rupees.
483	Moonsheegunge,	2	0	Ditto,	Ditto,	Eastward,	125 rupees.
484	Dawoodpore,	2	0	Ditto,	....	Jounpore,	150 rupees.

1832, *under the following leaders:*
Jemadars, and other Leaders.

REMARKS.

At the last named place the gang fell in with three Hindoo travellers, on their way from Lahore to Sultanpore, in Oude, whom they decoyed and took to Hussungunge. From that place they sent a messenger to call Keseeree subadar, who lived close by, and soon afterwards joined them with seven followers. A Jumaldhee Thug named Emaum Buksh, also arrived and joined the party. It appears that one of the three travellers lived very near that place, and without saying a word to the Thugs he packed up his baggage and went home. However the gang took the remaining two with them next morning, and strangled them on the bank of the river, into which their bodies were thrown.

They then proceeded to Futtehgunge, there they met two Hindoo travellers from Meerut, who were going to their homes across the Gogra, whom they decoyed, and next morning strangled. The bodies were thrown into a well.

After this they went and rested in the bazar at Moonsheegunge, where they found two Hindoos, travelling from Meerut to eastward. They decoyed them and took them out next morning to a well two miles off, where they were strangled, and their bodies thrown into the water.

Sookha and Bhimmee, two Thugs, left the gang after this murder, and went home. The remainder proceeded to Dawoodpore, where they decoyed two travellers, by caste Hindoos, who were on their way to Jounpore and took them to pass the night in the seraee. Next morning the travellers were strangled on the road, and their bodies thrown into a well.

They arrived next at Hunnoomangunge, and in the morning when they had gone four miles further, they fell in with a treasure carrier, a Brahmin, from Sultanpore, on his way to Benares, whom they decoyed and took through Chanapertabpore to a tank, a gunshot on the other side, and a squall of wind and rain coming opportunely on, the Thugs put their victim to death. It however so happened that a villager who was close at hand witnessed the murder, and he proceeded forthwith to the village and gave intelligence of what he had seen.

The inhabitants came out in a mass to seize the perpetrators of the deed, but the Thugs fled on observing their approach, Shewdeen, (now an approver,) seized the bag of 1,000 rupees which the treasure carrier had on his person and ran off with it. The villagers pursuing the Thugs, overtook and captured five of them, namely, Runjeet alias Deveedeen jemadar, Shewdeen (approver) Rummee, Chimmun and Cheyne.

Report of a Thug Expedition in the year
Lalla Lochun, Budlee, and Mukhun

No. of List.	Names and jurisdiction of the place where the Murder was perpetrated.	No. and Sex of the Murdered.		Date of the Murder.	Intended destination of the Murdered.		Supposed value of the property robbed.
		Men.	Women.		From	To	
485	Baita,	5	0	November, 1832,	Meerut,	Sultanpore,	350 rupees.
486	Eetgaon,	2	0	Ditto,	Ditto,	Sultanpore,	150 rupees, 50 gold venetins.
487	Sereyagaon,	1	0	Ditto,	....	Ditto,	50 rupees.
488	Bhangee Mhow,	2	0	Ditto,	Lucknow,	Rampoor,	1 pony, 1 sword, 1 pistol, 50 rupees.
489	Ajeetpore,	1	0	Ditto,	Ditto,	Meerut,	30 rupees, cash, a pony (which was let loose.)

1832, *under the following leaders:*
Jemadars, and other Leaders.

REMARKS.

N. B. By the statements of the approvers it appears that a Thug named Mooradee, who was of the party has been lost sight of since that day, and it is unknown what has become of him.

The remainder of the Thugs returned to their homes as quickly as possible.

N. B. The approvers state that the bag of rupees which was captured on the person of Shewdeen approver was taken by Govind Buksh zemindar of the village. The Thugs were sent prisoners to Rajah Dursun Sing, who transmitted them to Lucknow. After a detention of eighteen months Mr. Wilson obtained intelligence of the circumstance, and four of the prisoners were made over to him, the fifth having died—of this number Shewdeen became an approver, and the other three suffered the punishment due to their crimes.

In the month of November, 1832, Keseree subadar set out from Bhys-ka-Poorwa with six followers, and proceeded to Meeahgunge in search of Thuggee adventures, there he fell in with Futteh jemadar, Mehrban and Rumzan, altogether sixteen Jumaldhee Thugs, and two Lodhees, one of whom was Uchul jemadar. They united their forces, and the same day decoyed five travellers, (two Mussulmans and three Hindoos,) who had come from Meerut on their way to Sultanpore. The Thugs divided into two parties, one of which took the Mussulmans to Baita and the other the Hindoos to Eetgaon. Both villages being close to each other. In the morning the three Hindoos were put to death a mile from Baita, and their bodies thrown into a well. About the same time the Mahomedans were conducted out of Eetgaon, and were strangled before day break not far from the village, and their bodies thrown into a well.

The two gangs re-united and went to Sereyagaon, where they fell in with a Hindoo Koormee, on his way to Sultanpore, whom they decoyed and next morning put to death at a nullah about a mile from the village. The body was buried.

After this affair they proceeded to Bhangee Mhow, where two Rohillahs, on their way from Lucknow to Rampore, were resting; Uchul jemadar decoyed them, and they were conducted next morning a distance of one mile, and then put to death. The bodies were thrown into a well.

As soon as the booty had been divided Futteh jemadar, with three Jumaldhee Thugs, took leave of the gang and proceeded home. The remainder proceeded onwards by stages till they reached Ajeetpore, a couple of miles from

Report of a Thug Expedition in the year
Lalla Lochun, Budlee, and Mukhun

No. of List.	Names and jurisdiction of the place where the Murder was perpetrated.	No. and Sex of the Murdered.		Date of the Murder.	Intended destination of the Murdered.		Supposed value of the property robbed.
		Men.	Women.		From	To	
490	Doorhaha, in the Putteeala State,	2	0	That Season of 1832,	Lahore,	Cawnpore,	80 rupees.
491	Near Doorhaha,	1	0	Ditto,	Umritsir,	Lucknow,	25 rupees.
492	Near Doorhaha,	2	0	Ditto,	Lahore,	Cawnpore,	100 rupees, 1 pony.
493	Khunna,	2	0	Ditto,	Ditto,	Lucknow,	80 rupees.
494	Mukoowa,	2	0	Ditto,	Ditto,	Oureya,	250 rupees cash, 2 matchlocks, 2 pistols, 2 swords.
495	Shamlee,	2	0	Ditto,	Ditto,	Lucknow,	100 rupees cash, 60 rupees gold.

1832, under the following leaders :
Jemadars, and other Leaders.

REMARKS.

Rampore. There they met and decoyed a Hindoo from Lucknow, who intended to go to Meerut, and next morning they took him a distance of one mile and strangled him. The body was thrown into a well.

Passing through Mooradabad, Meerut and Kurnal without falling in with any travellers, the Thugs arrived in the course of twenty days at Doorbaha, in the Putteeala state, where they rested in the seraee. In the morning when they were about to set out again, they met two Hindoo travellers, from Lahore, on their way to Cawnpore, whom they addressed and conducted to a village, (name unknown,) about eight miles off. Next morning early the travellers were put to death half a mile from the village, and their bodies were buried.

After this affair they proceeded eight miles further and rested in a small village, the name of which is not remembered, where they found an empty Fakeer's hut in which they accommodated themselves for the night. A Mussulman traveller on his way from Umritsir to Lucknow, came there in the course of the day, and was invited by the Thugs to join their party. Early next morning before daylight, they strangled the traveller while he slept in the hut, and buried his body not far off.

Leaving the place of murder they went onwards and overtook two Hindoos travelling from Lahore to Cawnpore. Keseeree subadar addressed them, and by his insinuating address, inveigled them to a village three miles off, where they were persuaded to rest for the night. Next morning early the travellers were put to death in a field two miles off from the village and their bodies buried on the spot.

They then went to the seraee at Khunna, where they found two Hindoos from Lahore on their way to Lucknow, whom the Thugs decoyed and took next morning to a stream two miles off, where they put them to death and buried their bodies.

Turning back after this affair, the gang passed through Kurnal, crossed the Jumna and took the road to Meerut. On the way they fell in with two Hindoo travellers from Lahore who intended to go to Oureya, who were decoyed and taken to Mukoowa to pass the night. In the morning the travellers were conducted a couple of miles to the banks of the Jumna, where they were strangled and their bodies thrown into the stream.

They next arrived at Shamlee, where they met two Hindoo travellers, who had come from Lahore on their way to Lucknow, whom they decoyed to a village some miles from Shamlee, and passed the night there; next morning

Report of a Thug Expedition in the year
Lalla Lochun, Budlee, and Mukhun

No. of List.	Names and jurisdiction of the place where the Murder was perpetrated.	No. and Sex of the Murdered.		Date of the Murder.	Intended destination of the Murdered.		Supposed value of the property robbed.
		Men.	Women.		From	To	
496	Sooltangunge, zillah Mynpooree,	1	0	That Season of 1832,	Meerut,	Cawnpore,	60 rupees.
497	Secundra, in Furruckhabad,	2	0	Ditto,	Ditto,	Ditto,	125 rupees.

JUBULPORE, SUPERINTENDENT'S OFFICE,
The 9th April, 1840.

1832, *under the following leaders:*
Jemadars, and other Leaders.

REMARKS.

early the travellers were put to death at a nullah half a mile off, and their bodies were buried.

After this they went to Sooltangunge zillah Mynpooree. Mehrban jemadar had fallen in with a Hindoo, who was going from Meerut to Cawnpore, whom he decoyed and brought to join the Thugs. He was put to death next morning a mile from the village and his body thrown into a well.

They next went to Secundra in Furruckhabad and fell in with two Mahomedans, who were travelling from Meerut to Cawnpore, whom they decoyed and put to death next morning at the distance of two miles from the village. The bodies were thrown into a well.

Soon afterwards they heard from some travellers that a guard was in the vicinity in search of Thugs, and the gang taking the alarm, separated and proceeded to their respective homes.

P. A. REYNOLDS,

Superintendent for the

Suppression of Thuggee.

List of Thugs engaged in the affairs of 1832.

No.	Name.	Parentage.	Caste.	Remarks.
1	Budlee,	Son of Suntokh,	Lodhee,	Approver.
	Lalla Lochun Jemadar,	Koonj,	Ditto,	Hanged at Jubulpore, 1835.
	Bukhtawer,	Ditto,	Ditto,	Died in Jail.
	Hurlal Jemadar,	Sookha,	Ditto,	Hanged at Saugor, 1833.
5	Khulluk Jemadar,	Rutta,	Ditto,	Ditto ditto.
	Gopal,	Dya,	Ditto,	Approver.
	Behar Jemadar,	Puttee,	Ditto,	Ditto.
	Mandhata,	Dulput,	Ditto,	Ditto.
	Suroop,		Ditto,	Transported.
10	Purusram,	Laljoo,	Ditto,	At large.
	Girdharee,	Ramlal	Brahmin,	Approver.
	Dibba,	Dyaram,	Bukhal,	Ditto.
	Shunker Jemadar,	Ditto,	Ditto,	Hanged at Jubulpore, 1835.
	Bhola,	Mukka,	Ditto,	Approver.
15	Heera,	Oomeid,	Lodhee,	Ditto.
	Mukhun Jemadar,	Kishen,	Ditto,	Ditto.
	Sumbha,	Ghassee,	Ditto,	Ditto.
	Deena.	Kugga,	Ditto,	Ditto.
	Summa,	Heera,	Ditto,	Ditto.
20	Deena alias Moolla,	Sookha,	Ditto,	Ditto.
	Keseeree Subadar,	Budda.	Ditto,	Hanged at Jubulpore, 1835.
	Bhimma,		Ditto,	Approver.
	Shewdeen,	Assa,	Ditto,	Ditto.
	Chinta,		Ditto,	Ditto.
25	Futteh Khan Jemadar,		Mussulman,	Ditto.

No.	Name	Father	Caste	Fate
	Ruhman Jemadar,		Mussulman,	Approver.
	Zuber Jemadar,		Ditto,	Ditto.
	Ram Buksh,		Lodhee,	Ditto.
	Muhbooa,		Ditto,	Ditto.
30	Mehrban Jemadar,	Son of Bijjaeen,	Ditto,	Ditto.
	Moollooa,		Ditto,	Ditto.
	Phoolsa Jemadar,	Dhyaram	Brahmin,	Ditto.
	Mokhum,		Lodhee,	Transported.
	Bhikka,		Ditto,	Approver.
35	Eseree,	Rutta,	Ditto,	Ditto.
	Bukhut Moorea,	Kandhee,	Brahmin,	At large.
	Muhbooa,	Dhun Singh,	Mussulman,	Ditto.
	Purchum,	Kalee,	Ditto,	Fate unknown.
	Bhikka Jemadar,	Sunnum,	Ditto,	At large.
40	Dhunna,	Madaree,	Lodhee,	Approver.
	Nowul,	Punchum,	Ditto,	Hanged at Jubulpore, 1836.
	Dhunna Burmoocha,	Chidda,	Ditto,	Ditto ditto.
	Dhowkul Jemadar,	Chitta,	Ditto,	Ditto at Saugor, 1833.
	Sadut Jemadar,	Khundee,	Mussulman,	Approver.
45	Tej Khan,		Ditto,	Killed by a Nujeeb at Delhi.
	Khyrattee,		Ditto,	Transported.
	Bhikka,		Lodhee,	Hanged at Cawnpore.
	Munna,		Ditto,	Transported.
	Dhunna,	Hurree,	Ditto,	Approver.
50	Ramdeen Jemadar,	Runna,	Ditto,	Hanged at Cawnpore.
	Bhikka,	Muthoulee,	Ditto,	Approver.
	Madaree,		Ditto,	Transported.
	Purusram,	Oodey,	Ditto,	Died in Jail at Jubulpore.
	Surawun,	Ditto,	Ditto,	Ditto ditto.
55	Purshad Jemadar,	Runna,	Ditto,	Approver.
	Bijjooa,	Munsa,	Ditto,	Hanged at Jubulpore, 1836.
	Oodhye,	Mukka,	Ditto,	Approver.
	Uchul Jemadar,	Gunsham,	Ditto,	Hanged at Jubulpore, 1835.

No.	Name of Thugs.	Parentage.	Caste.	Remarks.
	Dhumma,		Lodhee,	Transported.
60	Cheyne Jemadar		Ditto,	Died in Jail at Saugor.
	Shewdeen Jemadar,	Bukhtawer,	Ditto,	Transported, 1836.
	Himunchella,	Runnooa Moonshee,	Ditto,	Approver.
	Bukshee,	Rutta,	Ditto,	Ditto.
	Tijja,	Budda,	Ditto,	Ditto.
65	Bhimma,		Ditto,	Ditto.
	Emaum Bux,	Ghous Beg,	Mussulman,	Ditto.
	Runjeet alias Deveedeen,	Kurhora,	Lodhee,	Died in Jail at Saugor.
	Rumma,		Ditto,	Ditto ditto.
	Mooradee,		Ditto,	Fate unknown.
70	Nowla,		Ditto,	Transported.
	Chidda,	Ramkissen,	Ditto,	Ditto.
	Chimun,		Ditto,	Died in Jail at Saugor.
	Rumma,	Heera,	Ditto,	Ditto.
	Heera,	Kugga,	Ditto,	Hanged at Cawnpore.
75	Runnooa Moonshee,	Jeysookh,	Ditto,	Hanged at Jubulpore, 1835.

P. A. REYNOLDS,
Superintendent for the Suppression of Thuggee.

JUBULPORE, SUPERINTENDENT'S OFFICE,
The 9th April, 1840.

REPORT

OF A

THUG EXPEDITION

IN THE YEARS 1833 AND 1834.

Report of a Thug Expedition by the Dooab
the following leaders : Girdharee,

No. of List.	Names and jurisdiction of the place where the Murder was perpetrated.	No. and Sex of the Murdered.		Date of the Murder.	Intended destination of the Murdered.		Supposed value of the property robbed.
		Men.	Women.		From	To	
498	Near Gwalior,	1	0	That Season of 1833,	Rampore,	Gwalior,	5 rupees, 1 sword and pistol.
499	Bhalahurree,	2	0	Ditto,	Bithoor,	Jeypore,	250 rupees.
500	Bhanpore,	2	0	Ditto,	Jeypore,	Cawnpore,	40 rupees.
501	Dhoosa,	2	0	Ditto,	Ditto,	Oude State,	60 rupees.
502	Lamba, near Nusseerabad,	3	0	Ditto,	Nusseerabad,	Lucknow,	80 rupees.

Gangs, in the years 1833 *and* 1834, *under Dibba, Shunker, and other Jemadars.*

REMARKS.

About the commencement of the year 1833, Girdharee (approver) who resided at Oomree in Jhalone, hearing of the arrest of Bholah Bunneah, left his home and proceeded to Cherayta in Gwalior, where he met Dibba and Shunker jemadar. They left the place and determined to try their fortunes together and soon afterwards fell in with Bukhut Moorea jemadar, with eleven Thugs from Sindhouse, whom they joined and accompanied to Gwalior—passing through that place they arrived at a small village, two miles to the west of it, where they rested. They found there a Pathan, who had come from Rampore, on his way to Gwalior, whom they invited to join them, and next morning they put him to death immediately after leaving the village.

After the murder they fell in with some passengers who gave them information of the approach of an arresting party, which caused the Thugs to mend their pace and proceed with all expedition to Mhow, in the Jeypore State, where they arrived in the course of some days. There they managed to decoy two Mahrattas who were on their way from Bithoor to Jeypore, and were conducted next day by the Thugs to Bhalahurree, where they rested. Before daylight next morning the travellers were conducted to a small mountain pass a mile distant, where they were strangled and their bodies buried.

After this they proceeded to Bhanpore. There they decoyed two travellers, by caste Hindoos, on their way from Jeypore to Cawnpore, and took them to pass the night at a Fuqueer's garden, next morning the travellers were taken to the bank of a water-course, near the village, and having been strangled their bodies were buried on the spot.

The gang arrived next at Dhoosa and discovered two hurkarahs on their way from Jeypore to the Oude State whom they decoyed and accommodated near themselves during the night. In the morning the travellers were strangled a mile from the village and their bodies buried in a nullah.

After this affair the Thugs proceeded as far as Lamba near Nusseerabad, where Bukhut jemadar decoyed a Bramin and two Kuhars who were travelling from Nusseerabad to Lucknow—they were strangled next morning at a tank about two miles from the village, and while the Thugs were engaged in burying the bodies a hurkaru was observed coming from the direction of Nusseerabad, so they left their work and decamped.

Hearing soon afterwards that several guards had arrived in that vicinity and were searching for Thugs, the members of the gang determined to separate and each man took his own road in hopes of escaping arrest. Girdharee having roamed about for some time, visited his home, and was soon afterwards arrested by two approvers who arrived there with a guard.

Report of a Thug Expedition by the Dooab the following leaders: Girdharee,

No. of List.	Names and jurisdiction of the place where the Murder was perpetrated.	No. and Sex of the Murdered.		Date of the Murder.	Intended destination of the Murdered.		Supposed value of the property robbed.
		Men.	Women.		From	To	
503	Chowbe-ka-seraee,	1	0	February 1833,	....	....	50 rupees.
504	Mulwa, in Futtehpore,	2	0	Ditto,	Agra,	Jounpore,	125 rupees.
505	Mahraj Gunge, in the Benares district,	3	0	Ditto,	Cawnpore,	Patna,	150 rupees.
506	Raja-ka-Tulub,	1	0	Ditto,	Kurnal,	Monghyr,	15 rupees.
507	Soane Budder river,	2	0	Ditto,	Allahabad,	Gya,	20 rupees.
508	Kaymranuggur, in the Arrah district,	2	0	Ditto,	Calcutta,	Byswara,	100 rupees.

Gangs, in the years 1833 *and* 1834, *under Dibba, Shunker, and other Jemadars.*

REMARKS.

In the month of February, 1833, Lalla Lochun, Mherban, and Hurlal jemadars, with a gang of twenty-two Thugs, set out from Maitee-ka-Poorwa and proceeded to Chowbe ka-seraee. A goldsmith was resting there and being addressed by Lalla Lochun was persuaded to join the gang. Next morning early he was strangled at a well, a mile distant from the village, and his body thrown into it.

They passed through Cawnpore and reached Mulwa in Futtehpore, where they found two Hindoos travelling from Agra to Jounpore, whom they inveigled and put to death next morning soon after leaving the village. The bodies were thrown into a well.

They went on to Allahabad and crossing the Ganges arrived at Mahraj Gunge in the Benares district. They fell in with and decoyed three travellers, a Brahmin, a Bunneah and a Hindoo, who came from Cawnpore and were going to Patna. Next morning early the travellers were strangled and their bodies thrown into a well, about a mile from the village.

The gang then proceeded to Raja-ka-Tulub, on the way Lalla Lochun decoyed a traveller, by caste a cowherd, who was going from Kurnaul to Monghyr. He passed the night with the Thugs, and in the morning was strangled outside of the village and his body thrown into a well.

Having crossed the Ganges at Benares the Thugs took the road to Gya, and reached the Soane river, where they entered the ferry boat for the purpose of crossing the stream. They were joined by two Ganges water-carriers, who were on their way from Allahabad to Gya; and being overcome by the insinuating address of Lalla Lochun jemadar agreed to prosecute their journey in his company. The stream only filled a small portion of the bed of the river, and there was a wide expanse of loose sand beyond, very difficult to pass on foot. Before they got across the Ganges the water-carriers were overcome with fatigue and all agreed to sit down and rest themselves. Some amused themselves by throwing sand at each other while others dug a hole in the sand intended as a grave for the unfortunate men whom they had thus early determined to destroy. It was now about 3 o'clock in the afternoon, and the Thugs observing that no other persons were within view fell on their victims, and strangled them. Their bodies were instantly thrown into the grave and covered up.

In the course of three or four days the Thugs reached Sherpore and then turned back to the westward and arrived at Rewagaon, where they decoyed two Brahmins from Calcutta on their way to Byswara, whom they took with them to Kaymranuggur in the Arrah district. Next morning the travellers

Report of a Thug Expedition by the Dooab
the following leaders: Girdharee,

No. of List.	Names and jurisdiction of the place where the Murder was perpetrated.	No. and Sex of the Murdered.		Date of the Murder.	Intended destination of the Murdered.		Supposed value of the property robbed.
		Men.	Women.		From	To	
509	Mahomedabad, in Ghazeepore,	2	0	That Season of 1833,	....	Muttra	80 rupees, a pony.
510	Nowsherah,	3	0	Ditto,	....	....	200 rupees.
511	Peyntee Burone, in the Allahabad district,	2	0	Ditto,	....	....	5 rupees, a piece of green broad cloth.
512	Purla, in the Allahabad zillah,	2	0	Ditto,	....	Russoolabad,	125 rupees, a mare.
513	Huleena, in the Bhurtpore principality,	3	0	February 26, 1833.	Benares,	Samber,	4 gold mohurs, 1 seer weight of silver, 20

Gangs, in the years 1833 *and* 1834, *under Dibba, Shunker, and other Jemadars.*

REMARKS.

were put to death at the distance of a mile from the village. The bodies were buried.

They next went to Mahomedabad in Ghazeepore, and fell in with two travellers on their way to Muttra, whom they decoyed and next morning put to death in a field a mile distant from the village.

Their next stage was Ghazeepore; and next day they went to a tank about a mile off and sat down. Three travellers, (a Brahmin and two Bunneahs,) came up and joined them. They were decoyed and taken to Nowshera, where they passed the night, and early next morning the travellers were strangled and their bodies thrown into a well.

N. B. The remains of these bodies were pointed out to the local authorities by approvers sent for the purpose.

Having passed the night at Mohin-ka-seraee, they set out again next morning, and at the distance of a mile or so overtook Kader jemadar and three other Thugs, who joined them, and they all went on to Peyntee Burone, in the district of Allahabad. They found there two Hindoo travellers, bound the same way with themselves, whom they decoyed and strangled early next morning a mile from the village.

They went on after the murder, and overtook a Brahmin and a Rajpoot on their way to Russoolabad, whom they decoyed and took to Purla, in the Allahabad district. Having slept there they put the travellers to death before daylight next morning a short distance from the village. The bodies were thrown into a well.

The gang visited Allahabad, and then went to Futtehpore, where a Bhutteara named Fuqueera recognized Lalla Lochun and Mehrban jemadars, and demanded a present of ten rupees and a pony. They took the alarm and decamped with their ten followers. Gopal and other Lodhee Thugs made the Bhutteara a present of a few rupees, and were not molested.

This gang also went home without further adventures, and soon after arriving there, an arresting party visited the place from Cawnpore, who seized Lalla Lochun, and carried him a prisoner to Mr. Wilson, who forwarded him to Saugor.

In the month of April, 1833, Mukhun jemadar led out a gang of twenty-two Thugs from Mouzumpore, in Cawnpore, and proceeded by stages to Huleena in the Bhurtpore principality. There they fell in with three travel-

Report of a Thug Expedition by the Dooab the following leaders: Girdharee,

No. of List.	Names and jurisdiction of the place where the Murder was perpetrated.	No. and Sex of the Murdered.		Date of the Murder.	Intended destination of the Murdered.		Supposed value of the property robbed.
		Men.	Women.		From	To	
							rupees, and a pony.
514	Bhowlegaon,	3	0	That Season of 1833,	Delhi,	Oujein.	Two quarter rupees, and a pony laden with wooden beads.
515	Kosee, zillah Muttra,	1	0	Ditto,	Oujein,	Bareilly.	20 gold mohurs, 40 rupees, 20 rupees worth gold.
516	Chickutteah, in Cawnpore,	3	0	Ditto,	Bareilly,	Benares,	200 rupees.
517	Kaseea, in the Benares district,	2	0	Ditto,	....	Gya,	100 rupees, a pony.
518	South of Mirzapore, in the Rewah principality,	2	0	Ditto,	Jubulpore,	Mirzapore,	100 rupees.

Gangs, in the years 1833 *and* 1834, *under Dibba, Shunker, and other Jemadars.*

REMARKS.

lers, by caste Brahmins, who came from Benares on their way to Sambur in Rajpootana, whom they decoyed, and next morning put to death a short distance from the village.

After this affair the gang went as far as Pokur, without meeting with any travellers. From Pokur they turned back and came three stages to a village, name unknown, where they met three Brahmins, who came from Delhi and intended to go to Oujein. The Thugs addressed and persuaded them to travel with the gang, whom they accompanied next day towards Bhowlegaon. Night setting in before they reached it, an opportunity was taken to put the travellers to death. The bodies were buried.

Turning back again the Thugs arrived at Kosee, in the Muttra district. There they decoyed a Bunneah from Oujein, travelling to Bareilly, whom they conducted next morning a couple of miles out of the village and put to death. The body was buried.

After this affair the gang broke up and went homewards Mukhun jemadar proceeded to Dukkerea to the house of Ramnath Josee, where he was soon afterwards arrested by a guard sent for the purpose, and immediately offered his services as an approver The guard acting upon the information which he gave, soon arrested Pershad jemadar and fourteen followers.

About the same time in the month of April, 1833, Ramdeen jemadar and Budlee jemadar (approver) assembled a gang of fourteen Thugs at Chobee-ka-Poorwa, in Furruckhabad, and proceed to Chickutteah in Cawnpore. There they fell in with three travellers, (Hindoos,) two spirit distillers and a Koormee, who came from Bareilly on their way to Benares, and having decoyed them they took them out next morning and put them to death about two miles from the village. The bodies were thrown into well, from which the remains have since been taken out by persons sent for the purpose.

The gang passed through Allahabad and arrived at Kaseea, in the Benares district. Two travellers, by caste Hindoos, on their way to Gya, came to the same place and were decoyed by the Thugs, who strangled them next morning, and threw their bodies into a well outside of the village.

After this the Thugs crossed the Ganges and went to a village, (name unknown) south of Mirzapore, in the Rewah principality They there met two Mussulmen servants of Europeans, who were travelling from Jubulpore to Mirzapore, whom they decoyed, and put to death next morning a short distance from the village. The bodies were buried.

Report of a Thug Expedition by the Dooab the following leaders : Girdharee,

No. of List.	Names and jurisdiction of the place where the Murder was perpetrated.	No. and Sex of the Murdered.		Date of the Murder.	Intended destination of the Murdered.		Supposed value of the property robbed.
		Men.	Women.		From	To	
519	Mulgaon,	3	0	That Season of 1833,	Nagpore,	Benares,	250 rupees.
520	Kakerabad,	1	0	Ditto,	Calcutta,	Etawah,	200 rupees.
521	Chickutteah,	3	0	Ditto,	....	....	12 rupees cash, a pony laden with shawls valued at rupees 10,525-4, 700 rupees worth of satin, 2 necklaces.

Gangs, in the years 1833 *and* 1834, *under Dibba, Shunker, and other Jemadars.*

REMARKS.

The gang proceeded towards the south as far as Amerpatun, and then turned back towards Mirzapore. They reached Mulgaon, and fell in with three Brahmins, who had come from Nagpore on their way to Benares, whom they decoyed and next morning put to death a short distance from the village, burying their bodies.

They then took the road to Allahabad; and arriving there they found in the bazar a Rajpoot with a child who was on his way from Calcutta to Etawah, whom they persuaded to go with them to Kakerabad. They passed the night there, and early next morning the Rajpoot was put to death soon after leaving the village; but the child's life was saved. Budlee jemadar took the boy intending to adopt him.

N. B. When this leader was arrested, the child was taken to Etawah to Mr. Wilson, and afterwards died there.

After this affair the gang went to Mulwa and rested under the Banyan trees outside the village. Three travellers, by caste Hindoo Mahajuns, soon afterwards passed by and entering the village, took up their quarters in the serae. Ramdeen jemadar went to them and being of the same tribe, soon ingratiated himself in their good opinion. They agreed to travel in company with him, and set out next day after sunrise. The Thugs followed after them to Chickuttea. On the road Budlee jemadar fell into conversation with them and induced them to rest for the night in a confectioner's shop, and to set out early in the morning. When they had gone a short distance from the village the Thugs put them to death and threw their bodies into a well.

N. B. The remains of these bodies have since been discovered, as well as the owners of the property, by the exertions of Mr. Wilson, and a considerable portion of the Goods restored to them. Several of the Thugs suffered the extreme penalty of the law agreeably to the sentence passed upon them by the Special Commissioner, Mr. Stockwell, by whom they were tried for the murder at Cawnpore.

Ramdeen Jemadar, Mudaree, brother of Budlee Jemadar, Bhikka, Kunhya, Hoolassee, Rambuksh, Dhunna, Bhumma, Heera,	Hanged.

Report of a Thug Expedition by the Dooab the following leaders: Girdharee,

No. of List.	Names and jurisdiction of the place where the Murder was perpetrated.	No. and Sex of the Murdered.		Date of the Murder.	Intended destination of the Murdered.		Supposed value of the property robbed.
		Men.	Women.		From	To	
522	Minda, in the Futtehpore district,	1	0	June, 1833,	Muttra,	Benares,	7 rupees.
523	Wahidnuggur, in the Mirzapore zillah,	1	0	Ditto,	Kurnal,	Furreedpore,	50 rupees, a bullock.
524	Burwan,	3	0	Ditto,	Eastward,	Byswara,	200 rupees.
525	Koonda, in the Oude State,	3	0	Ditto,	Jamulpore,	Byswara,	7 Gold mohurs, 200 rupees cash, 1 pony.
526	Raja-ka-Tulab,	1	0	Ditto,	Patna,	....	14 rupees.

Gangs, in the years 1833 *and* 1834, *under Dibba, Shunker, and other Jemadars.*

REMARKS.

Sooktee, }
Bichooa, } Imprisoned for life.

This was the last affair during this expedition.

In the month of June 1833, the Lodhee Thugs found it so dangerous to remain at home, although the rains had set in, that they took to the roads as a last resort. Gopal jemadar with eight followers, left Meytee-ka-Poorwa in Furruckhabad, and proceeded through Cawnpore to Futtehpore. The next day, soon after setting out, they overtook a traveller, by caste Hindoo, on his way from Muttra to Benares, whom they decoyed and took to pass the night in the serae at Minda. Next morning he was strangled a mile distant from the village, and his body was thrown into a well.

Having arrived at Allahabad the gang crossed the Ganges and reached Burote, where they met eight Thugs from the eastward under Kadir and Moradeen, who joined them, and all rested in a garden; a traveller, by caste Hindoo, from Kurnaul, on his way to Furreedpore, arrived at the same place and was decoyed by Rambuksh Jemadar, and taken to Wahidnugger, in zillah Mirzapore, where they passed the night. In the morning early he was put to death two miles from the village, and his body thrown into a well.

They next went to Benares, and fell in with Mohun Singh jemadar, and eight or nine Thugs from the eastward, who joined the party. All took the western road and having gone a mile, sat down under some Toddy trees and commenced drinking Toddy. Just then three travellers, by caste Hindoos, came up from the eastward on their way to Byswara. The Thugs addressed and took them to Burwan where they passed the night. Early next morning they were strangled a short distance from the village, and their bodies thrown into a well, from which they have since been taken out.

They then went to Kazee-ka-serae, where they found three Rajpoots on their way from Jumalpore to Byswara: they were decoyed and taken to Koonda, in the Oude state, where they passed the night, and next morning were put to death a short distance from the village, and their bodies thrown into a well.

After this affair the gang went to Gosseegunge, and then to Raja-ka-Tulab, where they took up their quarters in a religious mendicant's dwelling. A Hindoo from Patna came and took up his quarters at the same place. They decoyed him, and next morning he was put to death a mile from the village, and his body thrown into a well.

Report of a Thug Expedition by the Dooab the following leaders: Girdharee,

No. of List.	Names and jurisdiction of the place where the Murder was perpetrated.	No. and Sex of the Murdered.		Date of the Murder.	Intended destination of the Murdered.		Supposed value of the property robbed.
		Men.	Women.		From	To	
527	Between Kuppuldhar and Ghazeepore,	2	0	July 6, 1833,	....	....	3 bullocks, 25 rupees.
528	Bhanger Mhow,	2	0	Ditto,	....	Lucknow,	100 rupees, a pony.
529	Near Tukkeah,	3	0	Ditto,	....	Eastward,	150 rupees.
530	Baita,	2	0	Ditto,	....	Jounpore,	125 rupees.

Gangs, in the years 1833 *and* 1834, *under Dibba, Shunker, and other Jemadars.*

REMARKS.

N. B. This body was found by the villagers, who took it out of the well and buried it. The remains were disinterred by the inhabitants, when Gopal approver went to search for it.

The gang went to Benares, and rested in the Mohun-ka-serae, where they found two travellers, by caste Hindoos, who were decoyed by Mohun Singh jemadar. They were taken to Kuppuldhar, where they slept, and next morning proceeding on the road to Ghazeepore, the travellers were put to death, and their bodies thrown into the stream close by.

After this murder the Thugs from the eastward, under Kader and Moradun, took leave of the Lodhees and went homewards. The Lodhees proceeded to the westward, and on the second day reached Madhoopore, zillah Mirzapore, and rested in the serae. It so happened that a guard of regular sepahees and nujeebs under Akram Allee Toomundar, with Sheikh Enayut, Ram Buksh, Mukka, and Madaree approvers, were resting in the same serae, having been sent in that direction from Saugor by Major Sleeman in pursuit of the gang. The gang was recognized and the whole nine were arrested on the spot. On the 6th of July, two of them, Gopal and Kashee, having confessed, were admitted approvers ; and on the 24th August, they effected the arrest of Kadir and Mooradun, two leaders of great note in the Shahabad district, who were also admitted approvers, and they pointed out the bodies of numerous travellers they had lately murdered to the Magistrates of the Mirzapore and Benares districts.

In the month of January, 1833, Esuree jemadar and seven Thugs, left their homes at Annee-ka-Nowada, from fear of arrest, and proceeding to Nanna Mhow, crossed the Ganges and went to Bhanger Mhow. There they were joined by five more Thugs led by Mehrban and Uchul jemadars. They went to Madarpore, where they found Keseeree subadar and seven followers. They united their forces and returned to Bhanger Mhow, where they found two Hindoo travellers on their way to Lucknow, whom they decoyed, and put to death next morning a mile from the village. The bodies were thrown into a well.

They then went on to Utterdhunnee, where they found three Mussulmans going eastward, whom they decoyed and next day took to Tukkeah. Having slept there they set out next morning early, and the murder of the travellers was completed a mile from the village, and their bodies were thrown into a well.

After the affair the Thugs went on to Baita, two travellers, by caste Hindoos, on their way to Jounpore, came and rested at the same place. They

Report of a Thug Expedition by the Dooab the following leaders : Girdharee,

No. of List.	Names and jurisdiction of the place where the Murder was perpetrated.	No. and Sex of the Murdered.		Date of the Murder.	Intended destination of the Murdered.		Supposed value of the property robbed.
		Men.	Women.		From	To	
531	Sampla, in the Hansi district,	1	0	That Season of 1833,	....	Oude,	30 rupees, a horse.
532	Jhinjana,	4	0	Ditto,	Loodhiana,	Furruckhabad,	100 rupees.
533	Near Sirdhana,	4	0	Ditto,	Lahore,	Cawnpore,	150 rupees, a pony.
534	Near Boorhana,	1	0	Ditto,	Loodhiana,	Lucknow,	80 rupees, 20 rupees property, a pony.
535	Between Hurdwar and Dhounpoor Nugeena,	1	0	Ditto,	Lahore,	Gya,	12 rupees.

REMARKS.

were induced to pass the night in the bazar and to set out next morning in company with the Thugs who put them to death at a tank a couple of miles distant, and thrust their bodies into the mud.

They then went to Sytoo, and on arriving there were joined by Runnooa moonshee, Bukshee jemadar and ten other Thugs, who had set out from Behareepoor a short time before in search of adventures.

They first advanced to Somp in the Jeypore state, and fell in with Saadut jemadar and six Thugs from Coel—all proceeded together to Sampla in the Hansi district, where they fell in with a Hindoo sepahee on his way to the Oude territory, whom they decoyed and strangled next morning a short distance from the village. The body was buried.

The Thugs then went to Kurnal, and passing through Bilole, they overtook a few miles beyond it four Hindoo travellers who had come from Loodhiana on their way to Furruckhabad. They entered into discourse with the travellers and decoyed them to Jhinjana where they passed the night, and next morning put them to death soon after leaving the village. The bodies were thrown into a well.

After the murder the gang went eight miles towards Sirdhana, and on the way overtook four Hindoos from Lahore who were proceeding to Cawnpore. They decoyed them to a small village two miles further on where they slept, and next morning the travellers were put to death in a plain four miles distant from the village and their bodies buried on the spot.

Passing through Boorhana the Thugs fell in with a Hindoo traveller who was going from Loodhiana to Lucknow, whom they decoyed and took to a village, name unknown, where they passed the night—next morning the traveller was taken to a stream two miles further on, and put to death. The body was buried.

They arrived at Sirdhana, and then at Mozuffernugger, where Saadut and the Coel Thugs separated from the Loodhees; Ruttoo and two Lodhee followers also went home. The remainder pursued their journey towards Hurdwar.

Having visited the fair at Hurdwar, they went to a village, name unknown; between that place and Nugeena in Rohilcund where they fell in with a Punjabee from Lahore, on his way to Gya, whom they decoyed and took to a water-course next morning and put him to death. The body was buried.

Report of a Thug Expedition by the Dooab the following leaders : Girdharee,

No. of List.	Names and jurisdiction of the place where the Murder was perpetrated.	No. and Sex of the Murdered.		Date of the Murder.	Intended destination of the Murdered.		Supposed value of the property robbed.
		Men.	Women.		From	To	
536	Near Sytoo,	2	0	February 7, 1833,	Agra,	Lucknow,	60 rupees, 2 bullocks.
537	Baita,	2	0	Ditto,	....	....	100 rupees.
538	Futtehgunge,	1	0	Ditto,	Cawnpore,	Northward,	50 rupees.
539	Nuwabgunge,	2	0	Ditto,	Meerut,	Ajoodhea,	100 rupees.
540	Hussungunge,	1	0	Ditto,	Lucknow,	Furruckhabad,	50 rupees.
541	Near Bhagur Mhow,	3	0	Ditto,	....	Eastward,	100 rupees.

Gangs, in the years 1833 *and* 1834, *under Dibba, Shunker, and other Jemadars.*

REMARKS.

From Nugeena the gang went on by Moradabad and Bareilly to Bhanger Mhow in the Oude state. Leaving that place they went and sat down in a garden, where they were joined by two Hindoo sepahees with two bullocks, who came from Agra on their way to Lucknow. Runnooa moonshee decoyed them, and they were taken to Sytoo to pass the night. At Sytoo the gang found the party of Thugs under Keseeree subadar, whose proceedings have already been detailed.

The two parties having united, the travellers were conducted out the next morning the distance of two miles, and having been strangled, their bodies were thrown into a well.

N. B. These bodies have since been discovered upon the testimony of Heera and Pershaud approvers.

They then went to Etagaon, where they found two travellers, by caste Hindoos, whom they decoyed and carried to Baita and passed the night in the bazar. Early next morning the travellers were strangled at a tank a mile from the village and their bodies thrust into the mud.

After this affair Keseeree subadar and his party went to the westward, and Dhunna and Runnooa moonshee's gang proceeded to the eastward.

Keseeree subadar and party reaching Futtehgunge decoyed a traveller, by caste a Kayut, who came from Cawnpore, and intended to proceed north, and next morning put him to death a short distance from the village, and threw the body into a well.

The gang then crossed the Goomtee river, and went to Nuwabgunge. There they discovered two Hindoo travellers from Meerut on their way to Ajoodhea, whom they decoyed and strangled next morning at a well, a mile from the village. The bodies were thrown into the well.

They then proceeded to Hussungunge, and were joined by Ramdeen jemadar with seventeen Thugs, who had just left their homes and set out on the expedition. The parties having united decoyed a Hindoo traveller who came to the same place from Lucknow, on his way to Furruckabad. He was taken out to a nullah early next morning and put to death. The body was buried in the sand.

Three Thugs were sent home from hence to go in search of intelligence of the arresting parties, which it was feared might have come there, and the rest of the gang went to Bhagur Mhow. Three travellers, by caste Hindoos, came to the

Report of a Thug Expedition by the Dooab the following leaders: Girdharee,

No. of List.	Names and jurisdiction of the place where the Murder was perpetrated.	No. and Sex of the Murdered.		Date of the Murder.	Intended destination of the Murdered.		Supposed value of the property robbed.
		Men.	Women.		From	To	
542	Utterdhunnee, near Tukkeah,	2	0	That Season of 1833,	Meerut,	Sultanpore,	100 rupees.
543	Near Bhunter,	2	0	Ditto,	....	....	125 rupees.
544	Mahone, in the Oude State,	1	0	Ditto,	Jeypore,	Kakerabad,	60 rupees.
545	Bhunter,	3	0	Ditto,	Meerut,	Jounpore,	150 rupees cash, 50 rupees property, a mare.
546	Mahomed Shah's Tukkeah,	2	0	Ditto,	Saugor,	Towards Gogra river.	50 rupees.

Gangs, in the years 1833 *and* 1834, *under Dibba, Shunker, and other Jemadars.*

REMARKS.

same place on their way eastward, and having been decoyed, were taken out a distance of two miles next morning and put to death. The bodies were thrown into a well.

Turning back the gang proceeded to Utterdhunnee, near Tukkeah, and decoyed two Hindoo travellers, from Meerut, on their way to Sultanpore, whom they strangled next morning at the distance of a mile from the village, and threw their bodies into a well.

After this affair four Thugs left the gang and returned home, the rest went to Bhunter, where they found two sepahees of the Artillery, one a Hindoo and the other a Mussulman, who were decoyed and taken into the bazar to pass the night. Early next morning they were strangled some distance from the village, and their bodies thrown into a well.

They then reached Uchulgunge, where the three scouts who had been sent to their homes rejoined the gang, accompanied by four other Thugs. The accounts brought by these people of the state of affairs in the Dooab, were most alarming to the Thugs, who despaired of ever finding a place of rest in that Province, and determined on taking up their quarters in the Oude territory.

The gang then went to Mahone in Oude, and fell in with a Hindoo from Jeypore, on his way to Kakerabad, whom they decoyed, and taking out next morning put him to death, and threw his body into a well, a mile from the village.

They then went to Bhalagaon in Byswara, where they fell in with Futteh Dhoosoo and Khan Mahomed, and fifteen or sixteen Jumaldhee Thugs, who joined them, and they all went to Bhunter. There they decoyed three Hindoo travellers, from Meerut, on their way to Jounpore, whom they took into the bazar to pass the night, next morning they were put to death, and their bodies thrown into a well.

The gang next arrived at Rae Bareilly, and found two Burboonjas, Hindoos, from Saugor, on their way home across the Gogra river, whom they decoyed and took the same day to Mahomed Shah's Tukkeah to sleep, next morning the travellers were conducted to a water-course about two miles off and strangled. Their bodies were thrown into the stream.

After this affair nine of the Thugs went home with an agreement to return in a few days. It so happened that while these men were at their homes Mr. Wilson proceeded personally with an arresting party to Bys-ka-Poorwa,

Report of a Thug Expedition by the Dooab the following leaders: Girdharee,

No. of List.	Names and jurisdiction of the place where the Murder was perpetrated.	No. and Sex of the Murdered.		Date of the Murder.	Intended destination of the Murdered.		Supposed value of the property robbed.
		Men.	Women.		From	To	
547	Sonee-ka-kuttra, in the Oude State,	1	0	That Season of 1833,	....	Sultanpore,	40 rupees, a pony.
548	Near Jounpore,	3	0	Ditto,	Barrackpore and Benares,	Lucknow and Ajoodhea,	80 rupees, 1 mare.
549	Near Mohungunge,	3	0	Ditto,	Lahore,	Benares,	100 rupees, a pony.

Gangs, in the years 1833 *and* 1834, *under Dibba, Shunker, and other Jemadars.*

REMARKS.

and seized the whole number. Bichoo, and Tejja, the brother of Keseeree subadar, were admitted approvers—when these people were arrested, a cowherd of the place gave intelligence to Keseeree subadar of the arrest of his brother, whereon Keşeeree himself and the Thugs of his party determined to abandon further proceedings for the present and go home. They accordingly went at once to Bys-ka-Poorwa.

In the mean time Runnooa moonshee and his gang, who were left at Baita, proceeded to Sonee-ka-kuttra, in the Oude state, where they decoyed a traveller, by caste a Hindoo, who was on his way to Sultanpore, and induced him to rest with them in the bazar. Next morning early he was strangled some short distance from the village and his body thrown into a well.

They then all went to Jounpore, and taking the road to Ajoodheea they sat down to rest themselves in a garden by the road side. A sepahee, by caste a Rajpoot, who came from Barrackpore intending to visit Lucknow, arrived at the same place, and being decoyed by the Thugs was taken to a village about fifteen miles further on (name unknown) where they all passed the night in the bazar. There Bhola jemadar discovered two Hindoo travellers, on their way from Benares to Ajoodheea, whom he persuaded to proceed in company with the Thugs. Next morning the three travellers were conducted out of the village to a sheet of water two miles distant, where they were put to death, and their bodies were buried.

Proceeding onwards the gang reached Mohungunge on the Gogra river, and found there three Hindoos from Lahore, who intended to go to Benares, who were decoyed and next morning taken along the bank of the river and strangled at the distance of a mile from the village. The bodies were thrown into the stream.

After this affair they turned back to Hussungunge, a hurkara, by caste a Hindoo, who was travelling from Gwalior to Lucknow was resting there, and was persuaded by the Thugs to join their party. He was taken out next morning a distance of two miles from the village, and one of the Thugs named Chidda, had got the roomal round his neck with the intent of putting him to death, when a party of Nujeebs in the service of the King of Oude, suddenly came up and called out to "Beware." The Thugs taking the alarm abandoned their victim and decamped as quickly as possible. They proceeded home at once without any further adventure.

The traveller whose life had thus been providentially saved, returned to Hussungunge, and told the kotwal all that had occurred.

Report of a Thug Expedition by the Dooab the following leaders: Girdharee,

No. of List.	Names and jurisdiction of the place where the Murder was perpetrated.	No. and Sex of the Murdered.		Date of the Murder.	Intended destination of the Murdered.		Supposed value of the property robbed.
		Men.	Women.		From	To	
550	Near Bithoor,	4	0	That Season of 1833,	Lahore,	Patna,	150 rupees.
551	Burrail,	1	0	Ditto,	Etawah,	Lucknow,	4 rupees.
552	Jullalabad,	1	0	Ditto,	....	Jounpore,	30 rupees.

Gangs, in the years 1833 *and* 1834, *under Dibba, Shunker, and other Jemadars.*

REMARKS.

N. B. Soon after the Thugs reached home, a guard from the Thuggee Suppression Department visited their villages, Bhola, Heera, Atmaram, and Kashee Thugs, of the gang whose proceedings are above detailed, were arrested, and Runnooa moonshee, and Nowul and Bukshee jemadars, and Humunchella and Chinta escaped to Ruttungurh, in the Umballa principality, where they took up their abode. Dhunna jemadar who also fled, after roaming about for some time, was arrested by the zemindar of Howna, in the Cawnpore zillah. Dhunna confessed before Mr. Wilson and became an approver, and effected the arrest of Uchul jemadar and six other Thugs.

At the beginning of 1833, another gang of Thugs, consisting of Mehrban, Lall Chund, Ghazeea, and Newazie, left Bithoor and crossed the Ganges into the Oude territory. There they met Cheyne jemadar with seven Thugs and Keseeree subadar with twelve Thugs, whom they joined, and soon afterwards four travellers, two Brahmins and two Rajpoots, one of whom was Pylwan Singh subadar, arrived at the same place from Lahore, on their way to Patna and were addressed and decoyed by Keseeree subadar—next morning early the travellers were conducted three miles out of the village and were put to death at a nullah, where their bodies were also buried.

After this affair, intelligence was received of the arrest of Tijja, brother of Keseeree subadar, who recommended that the gang should break up in consequence. The Lodhee Thugs thereon went to their respective homes, and Keseeree subadar proceeded into Oude, where he attached himself to the Jumaldhee Thugs for the space of six or seven months, when he was arrested by a party under the orders of Mr. Wilson in person.

In the month of February the same year, Mehrban jemadar, Ramdeen, Mukhun, and Heera fled from Setul-ka-Poorwa and proceeded to Bithoor, where they were joined by Dhunna (approver.) They agreed to proceed together upon Thuggee, but as fewer arresting parties were engaged in the Oude territory, they determined to try their fortune in that country. After they had started their numbers were increased by the junction of Sumbhoo (approver,) and eleven followers, so that the gang then amounted to seventeen. They proceeded to Burrail and decoyed a cowherd from Etawah on his way to Lucknow; and having taken him next morning to a tank about a mile from the village, they strangled him, and sunk the dead body in the water.

After this affair they went to Jullalabad, where they were joined by a Rajpoot, who was going to Jounpore, whom they decoyed, and next morning put to death as usual. The body was thrown into a well.

Report of a Thug Expedition by the Dooab
the following leaders: Girdharee,

No. of List.	Names and jurisdiction of the place where the Murder was perpetrated.	No. and Sex of the Murdered.		Date of the Murder.	Intended destination of the Murdered.		Supposed value of the property robbed.
		Men.	Women.		From	To	
553	Baita,	2	0	That Season of 1833,	Kurnal,	....	18 rupees, a mare.
554	Tukkeah,	2	0	Ditto,	Jounpore,	Furruckhabad,	50 rupees.
555	Near Rampore,	2	0	Ditto,	Meerut,	Lucknow,	10 rupees.
556	Rooderpore,	2	0	Ditto,	Ditto,	Almorah,	10 rupees.

Gangs, in the years 1833 *and* 1834, *under Dibba, Shunker, and other Jemadars.*

REMARKS.

They next arrived at Baita, and fell in with a Mussulman and a Brahmin, who had come from Kurnal, whom they decoyed and took into the bazar to pass the night. Early next morning they were strangled and their bodies buried.

N. B. These bodies have since been disinterred by Dhunna approver and the case made the subject of trial at Jubulpore.

They took the road to Tukkeah, and down about two miles from that place on the way side, when a Brahmin and a Byragee came up from Jounpore on their way to Furruckhabad, who were decoyed and taken to pass the night at Tukkeah, next morning before day-break the travellers were strangled at a water-course two miles distant, and their bodies thrown into a well.

N. B. These bodies have been discovered.

After this affair four of the Thugs left the gang and went to Bithoor, promising to return in three days. The remainder proceeded to Hussungunge, and rested in the bazar. Intelligence of the arrival of the four Thugs above-mentioned reached an arresting party in that vicinity, who proceeded to Bithoor with Mukhun and Pershad approvers, and effected the seizure of Dhunna, (now an approver) the rest making their escape. Dhunna was at once sent to Mr. Wilson who admitted him an approver, and obtained information from him that Ramdeen and Mehrban jemadars were expecting his arrival at Hussungunge. Thereon Mr. Wilson himself proceeded in pursuit of the gang mounted on a camel, with Dhunna approver behind him: he made a forced march during the night from Cawnpore to Hussungunge, where he effected the arrest of Ramdeen jemadar and twelve other Thugs, and returned to Cawnpore, bringing in his prisoners with him.

About the same time that the above proceedings were going on, Dhoojjooa jemadar and nine Thugs set out from Jepora in the Oude territory, and dreading that they might fall in with an arresting party, proceeded with all haste by Bareilly to Rampore. Turning back from Rampore they fell in with two Hindoo travellers, on their way from Meerut to Lucknow, whom they decoyed and were taking them along the road when they met Heera, son of Ramdeen, and three other Thugs who had escaped from Bithoor. These men joined the party, and all went to a village (name unknown) to pass the night. In the morning the travellers were put to death, and their bodies buried by the side of a tank.

Soon afterwards they learnt that an arresting party, with Sewa approver, was in the neighbourhood, so they turned off and proceeded towards Moradabad. At Rooderpore they fell in with two Hindoo travellers, from Meerut on

Report of a Thug Expedition by the Dooab the following leaders: Girdharee,

No. of List.	Names and jurisdiction of the place where the Murder was perpetrated.	No. and Sex of the Murdered.		Date of the Murder.	Intended destination of the Murdered.		Supposed value of the property robbed.
		Men.	Women.		From	To	
557	Near Almorah,	1	0	That Season of 1833,	....	....	5 or 6 rupees.
558	Shahjehanpore,	2	0	Ditto,	Meerut,	Lucknow,	30 rupees.
559	Hussungunge, in the Bareilly district,	1	0	Ditto,	Lucknow,	Bareilly,	60 rupees.
560	Bunjaree-ka-serae,	2	0	January, 1834,	....	....	50 rupees.

Gangs, in the years 1833 *and* 1834, *under Dibba, Shunker, and other Jemadars.*

REMARKS.

their way to Almorah, whom they decoyed and strangled early next morning at a tank a mile distant, on the bank of which the bodies were buried.

After this affair they ascended the hills to Almorah, and having passed two or three days at that place, they descended into the plains again. On their way they were joined by a traveller, by caste a tailor, whom they conducted a short distance, and having strangled him threw his body into a ravine.

They then went with all speed to Shahjehanpore where they decoyed two Hindoo travellers, who came from Meerut on their way to Lucknow, and took them to a village four miles from that place: next morning early the travellers were put to death, and their bodies buried.

N. B. The remains of these bodies have since been disinterred. The gang then went to Bawun and met three other Thugs, who were roaming about in fear of arrest. They gave them a share of the booty obtained at the last murder, and took leave of them. The three Thugs went to Bareilly, and the Lodhee gang proceeded to their homes, where a guard also arrived immediately afterwards. Heera, son of Ramdeen, Bussawun and three other Thugs were first arrested. The next morning Bhimma (approver) fell into their hands and in the course of a month the whole of this gang of fourteen Thugs were captured, with the exception of two, who eluded the search of the party.

The three Thugs above mentioned, having arrived at Bareilly, Gunesh, one of them, fell sick and died; the other two named Dibba and Shunker left that place, and came to their homes. A day or two afterwards they proceeded to Hussungunge, where they met Phoolsa jemadar and two followers. They all went to Hussungunge, in the Bareilly district, where they found a moonshee, by caste a Kayut, who had come from Lucknow on his way to Bareilly, whom they decoyed and next morning put to death at a well about a mile distant. The body was thrown into the well. After the murder the Thugs returned home again. There they remained in great alarm, passing the day time out in the jungles and fields, and only returning to their houses in the dead of the night. In this manner they passed several months, till the commencement of the year 1834, when they were discovered and arrested by a party under the orders of Mr. Wilson.

Runnooa moonshee and four Thugs, it has already been stated, fled from Bithoor to Ruttungurh, where they built houses and took up their abode—sometime afterwards three other Thugs, Dhunna, Gunnooa and Oomeid, came and also took up their abode there, and were followed by Seetulla, Dhunna, Burmoocha and Muhbooa. They all set out in the month of January, 1834, to try their fortune on the roads, and proceeded to Bunjaree-ka-serae, where they

Report of a Thug Expedition by the Dooab the following leaders : Girdharee,

No. of List.	Names and jurisdiction of the place where the Murder was perpetrated.	No. and Sex of the Murdered.		Date of the Murder.	Intended destination of the Murdered.		Supposed value of the property robbed.
		Men.	Women.		From	To	
561	Kunna,	2	0	That Season of 1834,	Lahore,	Cawnpore,	2 gold mohurs, 50 rupees.
562	Sunnoo-ka-serae, in the Loodhiana district,	1	0	Ditto,	Lahore,	Byswara,	50 rupees cash, 50 rupees property, a silk shawl.
563	Suwana,	1	0	Ditto,	Loodhiana,	Kurnal,	60 rupees cash, 6 rupees property.
564	Near Kurnal,	2	0	Ditto,	Lahore,	Byswara,	350 rupees cash, 100 rupees property.
565	Kukker-ka-serae,	1	0	March, 1834,	....	....	14 rupees silver ornaments, 12 rs. gold ditto, 12 rs. cash.
566	Kunna-ka-serae,	1	0	Ditto,	....	....	40 rupees, cash, 10 rupees property.

Gangs, in the years 1833 and 1834, under Dibba, Shunker, and other Jemadars.

REMARKS.

fell in with two shoe-makers who were decoyed, and next morning put to death at a distance of two miles, and their bodies buried.

N. B. These bodies have since been disinterred.

They then went to Kunna and rested in the serae. They there decoyed two travellers, one a Brahmin and the other a Lodhee, who came from Lahore on their way to Cawnpore, next morning they took them out a distance of a mile and strangled them, the bodies were buried.

N. B. These bodies have also been discovered.

The Thugs then went to Loodhiana and rested for a day. Next they went to Sunnoo-ka-serae and halted there. A Rajpoot arrived there from Lahore on his way to Byswara, and was decoyed. In the morning he was put to death as usual some distance from the village. The body was buried, and the remains have since been disinterred.

Passing through Gooлchutter the Thugs took the road eastward. They decoyed a shoemaker who was travelling from Loodhiana to Kurnal, and took him to Suwana to sleep. In the morning he was strangled as usual and his body buried. The remains have since been disinterred.

Having reached Kurnal the gang continued their course to the eastward. On the way they overtook two sepahees (a Brahmin and a Rajpoot) who were going from Lahore to Byswara. They were decoyed and taken across the Jumna to a village (name unknown). In the morning the travellers were strangled and their bodies thrown into the river.

After this Runnooa moonshee and his gang returned home again, first despatching Dhunna and Oomeida to Cawnpore to invite all the fugitive Thugs in that quarter to come and take up their abode in Ruttungurh. At Razoo, in the Furruckhabad zillah, they fell in with Eseree and a boy named Chundana, whom they conducted to Ruttungurh.

In the month of March, 1834, these Thugs again set out on an expedition. They went to Umballa, where they decoyed a Hindoo Goojur and took him to Kukker-ka-serae. The next morning they strangled him a short distance from the serae and buried the body. The remains have since been disinterred.

They next went to Kunna-ka-serae, where they fell in with a cowherd travelling in the same direction, whom they decoyed, and next morning put to death two miles from the village and buried the body.

Report of a Thug Expedition by the Dooäb the following leaders : Girdharee,

No. of List.	Names and jurisdiction of the place where the Murder was perpetrated.	No. and Sex of the Murdered.		Date of the Murder.	Intended destination of the Murdered.		Supposed value of the property robbed.
		Men.	Women.		From	To	
567	Pupoorthala,	2	0	That Season of 1834,	Lahore,	....	100 rupees, 20 gold mohurs, 50 rupees property.
568	In the vicinity of Lahore,	1	0	Ditto,	....	Eastward,	50 rupees.
569	In the Seikh State,	1	0	Ditto,	Lahore,	Oude,	200 rupees.
570	Bawun, in the Bareilly district,	2	0	Ditto,	Lucknow,	Bareilly,	25 rupees.

Gangs, in the years 1833 *and* 1834, *under Dibba, Shunker, and other Jemadars.*

REMARKS.

The gang then crossed the Sutledge at Loodhiana and advanced as far as Amritsir without any adventure. They turned back from thence, and reached Pupoorthala, where they decoyed two travellers from Lahore, and taking them out next morning a distance of two miles, strangled them and buried their bodies.

They then went to a village (name unknown) in Lahore, where they decoyed a traveller who was proceeding to the eastward and strangled him next morning about two miles from the village. The body was buried.

From thence they went to another village in the Seikh states, and rested in a Fukeer's garden. There they decoyed a Brahmin who was travelling from Lahore to Oude, and next morning put him to death two miles from the village. The body was buried.

After this affair the Thugs returned to their homes, when they arrived there they sent two Thugs (Chinta and Dhunna) towards Cawnpore for intelligence respecting arresting parties. These two men went to their former homes in the Dooab. It so happened that a guard accompanied by Makhun and Pershad approvers, had set a man to watch at Chinta's house, and as soon as he arrived he was arrested. He forthwith confessed. Dhunna hearing this, fled with all speed to Ruttungurh, where he gave intelligence to Runnooa moonshee and his companions, who immediately abandoned their houses, and proceeded to Dhurmkote in the Punjab, where they took up their abode. Mr. Wilson into whose hands Chinta approver had fallen, sent him with an arresting party to Ruttungurh, and from thence he traced the fugitives to Dhurmkote, at which place Runnooa moonshee, Eseree and Chundana were first arrested. The others decamped, but next day Dhunna was taken. Bukshee and Newal, two leaders, who were of the party, escaped to Ulwer; and Dhunna, Burmocha, Nihullooa, and Omeida went to Meerut. They had not however an opportunity of going out on another expedition, and were all arrested during the year 1835.

About the end of the year 1834, a number of the arrested Thugs who had been sent from Saugor to Jubulpore effected their escape from the jail at the latter place. This they managed by cutting through their irons and the bars of the jail windows with thread smeared with oil and powdered stone. The fugitives consisted of Keseree subadar, Lalla Lochun and Balkishen jemadars and other Thugs, to the number of twenty-seven. Keseeree subadar was immediately arrested and two Thugs were killed by the pursuing Nujeebs. Several others were seized in the course of a few days. Showdeen jemadar and his brother Heera got clear off, and proceeding to Komoyea Pergunah Sandie in the Oude state, they built houses to live in. A short time afterwards

Report of a Thug Expedition by the Dooab
the following leaders: Girdharee,

No. of List.	Names and jurisdiction of the place where the Murder was perpetrated.	No. and Sex of the Murdered.		Date of the Murder.	Intended destination of the Murdered.		Supposed value of the property robbed.
		Men.	Women.		From	To	

JUBULPORE, SUPERINTENDENT'S OFFICE,
The 20th April, 1840.

Gangs, in the years 1833 *and* 1834, *unaer Dibba, Shunker, and other Jemadars.*

REMARKS.

this leader assembled a small gang of six Thugs, and set out on an expedition. They first proceeded to Bawun in the Bareilly zillah, where they fell in with two Hindoo travellers, one a Brahmin and the other a goldsmith, who had come from Lucknow on their way to Bareilly; they decoyed them, and taking them out next morning a distance of a mile, they put them to death in the usual manner, and threw their bodies into a sugar-cane field.

After this affair the gang returned home without further adventures. They had not been there many days when an arresting party with Makhun and Budlee approvers were sent out by Mr. Wilson, and visiting the village of Kumoyea, seized six Thugs, viz. Gunga, Mukka, Bukhtawur, Heera, Goolabee and Shewdeen. From among this party Heera became an approver and related the particulars of the abovementioned murder. The bodies were discovered and the relations of the murdered men produced to substantiate the facts of the case on trial—Goolabee and Gunga were hanged and Mukka was transported—Buktawur died in jail. Shewdeen was forwarded to Jubulpore, where sentence of transportation was passed upon him and carried into effect.

P. A. REYNOLDS,
Superintendent for the Suppression of Thuggee.

List of Thugs concerned in the affairs of 1833.

No.	Name.	Parentage.	Caste.	Remarks.
1	Girdharee,	Ramlal	Brahmin,	Approver.
	Dibba,	Dhyaram,	Bunneah,	Ditto.
	Shunker Jemadar,	Ditto,	Ditto,	Hanged at Jubulpore, 1835.
	Budlee,	Suntoke,	Lodhee,	Approver.
5	Lalla Lochun Jemadar,	Koonj,	Ditto,	Hanged at Jubulpore, 1835.
	Buktawur,	Ditto,	Ditto,	Died in Jail.
	Gopaul,	Dhya,	Ditto,	Approver.
	Bichoo,	Puttee,	Ditto,	Ditto.
	Suroop,	....	Ditto,	Transported.
10	Mukhun Jemadar,	Kishun,	Ditto,	Approver.
	Summa,	Ghasee,	Ditto,	Ditto.
	Sumbha,	Heera,	Ditto,	Ditto.
	Deena,	Kugga,	Lodhee,	Ditto.
	Deena alias Moolla,	Suktee,	Ditto,	Ditto.
15	Keseeree Subadar,	Budda,	Ditto,	Hanged at Jubulpore, 1835.
	Bumma,	....	Ditto,	Approver.
	Chinta,	....	Ditto,	Ditto.
	Muhbooa,	....	Ditto,	Ditto.
	Mehrban,	Bijjaeen.	Ditto,	Ditto.
20	Moollooa,	....	Ditto,	Ditto.
	Phoolsa,	Duryar,	Brahmin,	Ditto.
	Mukhun,	....	Lodhee,	Transported.
	Bhikka,	....	Ditto,	Approver.
	Esuree,	Rutta,	Ditto,	Ditto.
25	Bukhut Moorya,	Khanda,	Brahmin,	At large.
	Bhikka,	Sunnum,	Lodhee,	Ditto.

	Dhunna,	Mudaree,	Lodhee,	Approver.
	Nowul,	Punchum,	Ditto,	Hanged at Jubulpore, 1836.
	Dhunna Burmoocha,	Chidda,	Ditto,	Ditto ditto.
30	Seetulla,	Ditto,	Ditto,	Died at home.
	Sadut Jemadar,	Kunjee,	Ditto,	Approver.
	Dhunna,	Hurree,	Ditto,	Ditto.
	Ramdeen Jemadar,	Runna,	Ditto,	Hanged at Cawnpore.
	Pershad Jemadar,	Ditto,	Ditto,	Approver.
35	Dijjooa,	Munsa,	Ditto,	Ditto.
	Oodhye,	Mukka,	Ditto,	Ditto.
	Uchul Jemadar,	Gunsham,	Ditto,	Hanged at Jubulpore, 1835.
	Dhumma,		Ditto,	Transported.
	Shewdeen Jemadar,	Buktawur,	Ditto,	Transported from Jubulpore.
40	Humunchulla,	Runnooa Moonshee,	Ditto,	Approver.
	Bukshee Jemadar,	Rutta,	Ditto,	Ditto.
	Tijja,	Budda,	Ditto,	Ditto.
	Bumma,		Ditto,	Ditto.
	Emam Buksh,	Ghousbeg,	Mussulman,	Ditto.
45	Chidda,	Ramkishun,	Lodhee,	Transported, 1836.
	Rumma,	Heera,	Ditto,	Transported.
	Heera,	Kugga,	Ditto,	Hanged at Cawnpore.
	Runnooa Moonshee,	Jeysookh,	Ditto,	Hanged at Jubulpore, 1835.
	Nunnooa,	Adopted of Subsookh,	Kolee,	Approver.
50	Hussunnooa,	Kolee,	Mussulman,	Ditto.
	Booddooa,	Dhun Singh,	Ditto,	In Jail at Jubulpore.
	Bukhut,	Bhagwan,	Brahmin,	At large.
	Doorjunna,	Ditto,	Ditto,	Ditto.
	Mudaree,		Lodhee,	Hanged at Cawnpore.
55	Bhikka,		Ditto,	Ditto ditto.
	Kunyha,		Ditto,	Ditto ditto.
	Hoolasee,		Ditto,	Ditto ditto.
	Rambuksh,		Ditto,	Ditto ditto.

No.	Name.	Parentage.	Caste.	Remarks.
	Dhunna, ...	....	Lodhee, ...	Hanged at Cawnpore.
60	Bumma, ...	....	Ditto, ...	Ditto ditto.
	Sookhee, ...	....	Ditto, ...	Imprisonment for life at Cawnpore.
	Bichooa, ...	....	Ditto, ...	Ditto ditto.
	Kader, ...	Joomun, ...	Mussulman, ...	Approver.
	Mooradun, ...	Ditto, ...	Ditto, ...	Ditto.
65	Mohr Singh, ...	....	Rajhpoot, ...	Hanged at Moozufferpore.
	Kashee, ...	....	Loodhee, ...	Transported.
	Unwurd, ...	....	Ditto, ...	Ditto.

P. A. REYNOLDS,
Superintendent for the
Suppression of Thuggee.

JUBULPORE, SUPERINTENDENT'S OFFICE,
The 20th April, 1840.

List of Thugs concerned in the affairs of 1834.

No.	Name.	Parentage.	Caste.	Remarks.
1	Heera,	Son of Bukhtawur,	Lodhee,	Approver.
	Gunga,		Ditto,	Hanged at Bareilly.
	Goolabee alias Oodeyt,	Bukhtawur,	Ditto,	Ditto ditto.
	Shewdeen Jemadar,	Ditto,	Ditto,	Transported from Jubulpore, 1836.
5	Bukhtawur,		Ditto,	Dead.
	Mukka,		Ditto,	Transported from Bareilly.
	Dibba,	Dhyaram,	Bukhal,	Approver.
	Shunker Jemadar,	Ditto,	Ditto,	Hanged at Jubulpore, 1835.
	Phoolsa,	Duryan,	Brahmin,	Approver.
10	Runnooa Moonshee,	Jeysookh,	Lodhee,	Hanged at Jubulpore, 1835.
	Nowul Jemadar,	Punchum,	Ditto,	Ditto ditto 1836.
	Bukshee Jemadar,	Rutta,	Ditto,	Approver.
	Chinta,		Ditto,	Ditto.
	Himunchella,	Runnooa Moonshee,	Ditto,	Ditto.
15	Dhunna,	Hurree,	Ditto,	Ditto.
	Gunnooa,		Ditto,	Transported, 1836.
	Oomeida,		Ditto,	Ditto.
	Seetulla,	Chitta,	Ditto,	Died while on an Expedition.
	Dhunna Burmoocha,	Chidda,	Ditto,	Hanged at Jubulpore, 1836.
20	Esuree,	Rutta,	Ditto,	Approver.
	Chundana,		Ditto,	Ditto
	Nehallooa,		Ditto,	Transported, 1836.

P. A. REYNOLDS,
Superintendent for the Suppression of Thuggee.

JUBULPORE, SUPERINTENDENT'S OFFICE,
The 20th April, 1840.

Alphabetical list of Thugs at large, or unaccounted for, in all parts of India, up to the 1st of January, 1840.

No. in Genl. Register.	Names.	Age	Caste.	Birth.	Place of Residence. Village.	Pergunna.	District.
	A.						
65	Aman alias Amna, ...	24	Lodhee, ...	Son of Hirdee, ...	Dutmunpore,..	....	Cawnpore.
71	Anunt alias Punooa Jemadar,	35	Brahmin, ...	,, Bhowaneepersaud,	....	....	Ditto.
194	Anoopa, ...	32	Lodhee, ...	,, Khurgee, ...	Nowgaon,......	....	Ditto.
446	Anwur Sheikh, ...	30	Moslem, ...	,, Zareeb Khan,......	Munohur,......	Kotah, ...	Kotah.
536	Ashruf,..........................	30	Ditto, ...	,, Ikteear, ...	Shajehanpore,.	Jhalone, ...	Bundelkhund.
643	Ameerah,........................	35	Ditto, ...	Adopted of Ruheem Khan, son of Sheikh Roshun, ...	Myahpore, ...	Jhansee, ...	Ditto.
712	Ajub Sing Jemadar, ...	36	Sooseea, ...	Brother of Hurry Sing,...	Lutchurra, ...	Nara Sehur,...	Jeypore.
786	Allayar, ...	45	Moslem, ...	....	Pansee	Ellichpore, ...	Hydrabad.
816	Ameer Khan Jemadar, ...	40	Ditto, ...	....	Amgow, ...	Umroutee, ...	Ditto.
847	Anwur Khan, ...	35	Ditto, ...	Son of Rajee Khan,.........	Kuluffur, ...	....	Ditto.
927	Alum, brother of Chutter, approver, ...	50	Chumar, ...	Adopted of Ghasee Subadar,	Behetgaon, ...	Sohagpore, ...	Nursingpore.
940	Aman Sing,......................	30	Rajpoot, ...	Son of Makhun, ...	Heerapore, ...	Deoree,.........	Saugor.
1148	Ashruf,..........................	40	Moslem, ...	,, Ruheem, ...	Buhmunpore,	....	Gwalior.
1168	Ajeet Sing, ...	45	Naek Sooseea,	,, Ram Sing, ...	Soorbar, ...	....	Jeypore.
1217	Akbur Khan alias Pungureea,	25	Moslem, ...	,, Noor Khan Gomanee alias Gunesh, ...	Khylagaon or Banpore,	Chunderee, ...	Gwalior.
1343	Ajub Sing, ...	20	Rajpoot, ...	....	Kuchwabadhar,	....	Ditto.

1348	Ameera, ...	20	Moslem, ...	Son of Madar alias Sirdar,	Gudhoopore, ..	Rudowlee, ...	Lucknow.
1363	Ahmuda, ...	30	Ditto, ...	,, Shuffee, ...	Sreenagur, ...	Koel,............	Koel.
1810	Ajura, brother of Ruheem Khan, ...	50	Ditto, ...	....	....	....	Tonk.
1954	Ahmud,........................	30	Ditto, ...	Son of Bolakee, ...	Esagur,.........	....	Gwalior.
1963	Allabuksh, ...	45	Ditto, ...	Brother of Peerbuksh, approver, ...	....	....	Ditto.
1974	Allabuksh, ...	30	Ditto, ...	,, Peerbuksh, ...	Thana Munohur, ...	....	Kotah.
2106	Ahmeed Sheikh, ...	50	Ditto, ...	,, Taj Mahomud,	Papal, ...	....	Hydrabad.
2138	Ameer alias Ameen, ...	35	Ditto, ...	....	Keemee, ...	Booegow, ...	Ditto.
2231	Amura,........................	...	Naek Sooseea,	Son of Khoshal, ...	Khasras, ...	Dataramgur,...	Jeypore.
2236	Ameera, ...	32	Moslem, ...	,, Bhoodha,...........	Oonapa, ...	....	Cawnpore.
2829	Assea, ...	...	....	Nephew of Bhyroon Jemr.,	Oneara,.........	Oneara,.........	Jeypore.
2994	Azim, ...	40	Moslem, ...	....	Julhureea, ...	Thana Chutna,	Bancoorah.
3124	Alum Dass Byragee, ...	50	Byragee, ...	....	Sahibgunge,...	Mungulkote,...	Burdwan.
3308	Anoopoodeen Sheikh,.........	60	Moslem, ...	....	Sopoor,.........	....	Beerbhoom.
3425	Ameer Khan, ...	...	Ditto, ...	....	Jailgee,.........	Sorapore, ...	Hydrabad.
3469	Allabux alias Abash, ...	30	Ditto, ...	Adopted of Aup Khan Emam Sahib Jemadar, ...	*Residence not known.*		
3559	Abbass Sha, No. 2............	40	Ditto, ...	Son of Fuqueer Sha Jemadar, ...	Cowatcotah,...	Masulipatam, .	Masulipatam.
3755	Asa (Bowree,).................	...	Naek, ...	....	Rujowlee,......	....	Jodhpore.
3789	Amanuth,......................	40	Durgee, ...	....	Choorkokur,...	Busdee,.........	Ghazeepore.
3820	Abass Allee,...................	18	Moslem, ...	Son of Torawala Madar Sahib,...............	Billolee, ...	Sufrar Khan's Jageer,	Hydrabad.
3831	Appah, ...	20	Ditto, ...	,, Kalee Sha, ...	Hypergaon, ...	Sholapore, ...	Bombay.
3866	Ahmud,........................	43	Ditto, ...	....	Ellore, ...	....	Masulipatam.
3913	Ameen Sahib, ...	35	Ditto, ...	Adopted of Sahib Khan,	Mobarpullee,..	Gudree,.........	Cuddapah.
4028	Achumbeet alias Ajeet, ...	30	Aheer, ...	Brother of Nejhoot,.........	Mutteea, ...	Chowbar, ...	Sarun.
4279	Anwur Khan, ...	60	Moslem, ...	....	Tanda, ...	....	Oude.

No. in Genl Register.	Names.	Age	Caste.	Birth.	Place of Residence.		
					Village.	Pergunna.	District.
4280	Ashruf Khan, ...	32	Pathan,......	Son of Oree Khan, ...	Ghinawan, ...	....	Jugdeespore.
4286	Alleebuksh Khan, ...	40	Ditto, ...	Brother of Imambuksh,...	Mudeapoora, ..	Fyzabad, ...	Lucknow.
4329	Allee Sahib,.....................	55	Moslem, ...	Brother-in-law of Hussun Khan, (prisoner,)	Narhutpulee,..	Hoteenpore,...	Nuggur.
4403	Aluf Khan alias Alpee, ...	50	Ditto, ...	....	Bhalkhana, ...	Norahee, ...	Oude.
4462	Answur Bhae,..................	50	Ditto, ...	Adopted of Bowleewala Noor Khan, ...	Wurnul, ...	Aloor, ...	Hydrabad.
4478	Alee Shah, ...	15	Ditto, ...	Son of Meean Shah, ...	Hujgeera,......	....	Ditto.
4549	Aradhun Sein,..................	40	Kaet,.........	,, Nursing Sein,......	Meragonah, ...	Atteeah, ...	Mymunsing.
4550	Aradhun Deo, ...	40	Ditto, ...	Nephew of Bydenath Sircar, ...	Woolile, ...	Ditto, ...	Ditto.
4551	Aradhun Sircar, ...	35 or 40	Ditto, ...	....	Deonie,.........	Muthora, ...	Pubna.
4553	Azim Khan,......................	50	Moslem, ...	....	Umra, ...	Ditto, ...	Ditto.
4623	Arjuna,..........................	...	Koree, ...	Brother of Balmakund, ...	Hureeowree,...	....	Bhurtpore.
4840	Azim Khan,......................	55	Moslem, ...	Son of Burreh Khan, ...	Kuladgee,......	Kuladgee,......	Belgaum.
4967	Arnundodoto, ...	50	Golah, ...	....	Beterosimgo, ..	Gooesekor, ...	Pooree or S. Cuttack.
	B.						
64	Bahadoor, (said to be dead,)	25	Lodhee,......	Son of Hirdee, who was married to the sister of Misree approver, ...	Duthumpore,..	Deirapore, ...	Cawnpore.
307	Bukhut Mondea,..............	40	Brahmin, ...	Son of Kundee approver,..	Bughae, ...	Omree, ...	Gwalior.

361	Budha,	30	Moslem,	Son of Noora,	Puchpahar,	Eesagur,	Gwalior.
365	Bahadoor,	36	Ditto,	,, Gazee,	Omree,	Ditto,	Ditto.
367	Bhowanee alias Humeela,	...	Kular,	Adopted of Rughobar Aheer Jemadar's brother, son of Sokunpal approver,	Ghora,	Ditto,	Ditto.
400	Bhugwan,	35	Moslem,	Son of Ruheem Khan, the son of Roshun Kunja Jemadar,	Akajeree,	Nurwar,	Ditto.
425	Bhorah,	20	Ditto,	Son of Furzund,	Juttukpore,	Chundelee,	Ditto.
556	Bukta alias Buktawur Jemr.	30	Ditto,	,, Jannoo,	Nawlee,	Ojein,	Ditto.
631	Bheekum Khan,	35	Ditto,	,, Bhujjoo,	Sikree,	Jhalone,	Bundelcund.
632	Bhika alias Nayeksaiyah,	36	Ditto,	Adopted of Dhurm Khan,	Nadeekagaon,	Datrah,	Ditto.
707	Bahdoor, (one eyed,)	28	Sooseea,	Son of Khoman,	Bujorah,	....	Jeypore.
709	Bishun Sing,	26	Ditto,	,, Zalim,	Ditto,	....	Ditto.
995	Bhujjoo,	30	Brahmun,	,, Ramchund alias Purmsookh,	Amowlee,	Rusdahan,	Cawnpore.
1050	Bhikaree alias Bhika Jemr.	40	Moslem,	,, Sunum,	Nowratta,	....	Gwalior.
1085	Bhorah,	30	Ditto,	,, Ruheem Khan,	Jignee,	Jhansee,	Bundelcund.
1170	Bhowanee Jemadar, 2d,	40	Sooseea,	,, Kumaul Sing,	Jhalae,	Purnecara,	Jeypore.
1171	Bhiroo,	35	Naek or Sooseea,	,, Dullah, brother of Kishen Sing,	Deoree,	Onearee,	Ditto.
1173	Bhiroo Jemadar,	40	Ditto,	Brother of Dongur Sing, brother-in-law of Hurlal approver,	Surwar,	Kishungur,	Ditto.
1194	Bhugwunt,	40	Brahmun,	Adopted of Pasheeram Jemadar,	Byakapoorwa,	Patun,	Jubulpore.
1215	Bahadur Chabooksuwar,	40	Moslem,	....	....	....	Nursingpore.
1229	Bukhta,	35	Koree,	....	Narainpore,	Jhalone,	Bundelcund.
1236	Bussawun,	30	Moslem,	Brother-in-law of Inaeut, who was the father-in-law of Dulele, the brother of Sheikh Inaeut approver,	Toree,	Tehree,	Ditto.

No. in Genl. Register.	Names.	Age.	Cast.	Birth.	Place of Residence.		
					Village.	Pergunna.	District.
1238	Bahadur alias Rusooleea, ...	...	Moslem, ...	Adopted of Junguleea, ...	Toree, ...	Tehree,.........	Bundelcund.
1372	Budda Jemadar, ...	40	Ditto, ...	Son of Khobun, brother of Chundun,............	Khandpore, ...	Ouria, ...	Cawnpore.
1373	Bhikka Jemadar, ...	45	Mewatee, ...	Brother of Chunda, adopted son of Jowahir,.........................	Aiyah, ...	....	Allygurh.
1375	Ballah Jemadar, ...	50	Brahmun,...	....	Pahurgurh, ...	....	Gwalior.
1378	Buda or Byda, (nose cut off,)	60	Moslem, ...	Son of Rahmut, ...	Baree, ...	....	Dholepore.
1403	Bahadur Sing alias Munbode,	26	Rajpoot, ...	....	Kuttesur, ...	....	Azemabad.
1416	Bhujja, ...	...	Moslem, ...	Son of Zoolfakar, ...	Agra, ...	Khass, ...	
1417	Birja alias Birjban or Burda,	40	Sooseea, ...	,, Pearjee, ...	Jhilae, ...	....	Jeypore.
1419	Buksha Jemadar, ...	...	Ditto, ...	,, Omed Sing,.........	Omard, ...	....	Ditto.
1420	Bhugooa, ...	50	Ditto, ...	,, Geeanjee, ...	Omairee, ...	Oneeara, ...	Ditto.
1421	Bahadur alias Jonda, ...	50	Moslem, ...	,, Emamee and brother of Jadoola,	Gopalpore, ...	Seiriss, ...	Ditto.
1422	Boodhooa alias Bhoonoo, ...	35	Sooseea, ...	,, Sewaram, relation of Gyaneea Jemadar,........	Gopalpore, Pepuleea, ..	Jhilae, ...	Ditto.
1425	Bohara,...........................	45	Ditto, ...	The maternal uncle of Gyaneea Jemadar, ...	Bawlee,.........	....	Ditto.
1432	Bahadoora, ...	30	Aheer, ...	Son of Bussunt, ...	Baleepooree,...	....	Mynpooree.
1715	Bulloo alias Bulum or Molooa,	50	Moslem, ...	....	Burkhera,......	Arone, ...	Gwalior.
1853	Buria alias Harbaree Shah, .	30	Ditto, ...	Son of Fuqueer Mahomud,	Momenpeth or Uchulgaon, ...	Koheer or Dighoor, ..	Hydrabad.

1904	Bhooree Khan, ...	22	Moslem, ...	Son of Hossein Khan,......	....	....	Gwalior.
1927	Bhunjun Sing, ...	55	Lodhee, ...	Adopted of Chuttur Rajpoot, and brother of Rutteram, hung at Indore, ...	Phurtolee, ...	....	Humeerpore.
1944	Bhoree alias Nurputtee,......	32	Moslem, ...	Son of Doorghar, son of Muddee, ...	Chandpore, ...	....	Gwalior.
1966	Boodhoo, ...	60	Ditto, ...	,, Lokman,...........	Onka, ...	Seolee, ...	Cawnpore.
2001	Bhujjooa, ...	40	Lodhee, ...	,, Chiddee,...........	Ashteapoorwa,	Bela,...........	Furruckabad.
2005	Bhoree,..........................	32	Moslem, ...	Adopted of Noor Khan Jemadar, ...	Boorowlee, ...	Chunderee, ...	Gwalior.
2065	Buhadoor, ...	20	Munehar, ..	Son of Roshun, ...	Jumeek, ...	Omree,.........	Ditto.
2092	Bhinsayn, ...	...	Koormee,...	....	Peepulgaon,...	Sanour, ...	Hydrabad.
2109	Burun Syud, ...	55	Moslem, ...	Son of Nubee Khan, brother of Syud Emam,	Higgeerah or Maholee,	Nadgaon, ...	Ditto.
2123	Bheekun Khan, ...	35	Ditto, ...	,, Baukur Khan Jemadar, ...	Kurragaon, ...	Akola, ...	Ditto.
2153	Baboo Sheikh,..................	50	Ditto, ...	,, Sheikh Peerun,	Tillee, ...	Nugrole, ...	Ditto.
2159	Birahim, ...	35	Ditto, ...	,, Anwur, ...	Ellichpore, ...	....	Ditto.
2162	Bahadur, ...	40	Ditto, ...	....	Dehgow, ...	Ellichpore, ...	Ditto.
2165	Bheekun Khan, ...	30	Ditto, ...	Son of Saadut alias Saadul,	Arobee,.........	....	Ditto.
2184	Buldeo Jemadar,..............	40	Jat, ...	Brother of Motee, ...	....	....	Nagpore.
2214	Bukta alias Barasha Jemadar, ...	...	Sooseea, ...	,, Goolab Sing Jemadar, ...	Durreawal, ...	Jhilae, ...	Jeypore.
2246	Behrah, ...	50	Moslem, ...	Son of Hutholee,...........	Habrae, ...	Jhalone, ...	Bundlecund.
2248	Bhirova, ...	...	Sooseea, ...	....	Pholeyta, ...	....	Jeypore.
2280	Behar alias Pahar Sing,......	55	Rajpoot, ...	....	Poona, ...	....	Poona.
2353	Baboo Ram, ...	50	Weaver, ...	Brother of Sehena Jemadar, No. 2351,......	Bhugwangola,	....	Moorshedabad.
2354	Boodha Khansuma Jemadar,	40	Moslem, ...	....	Serampore, opposite Barrackpore.		
2405	Boorah, ...	30	Brahmun,...	Son of Subsookh Purasoor,..................	....	....	Nagpore.
2550	Baba Khan, ...	35	Moslem, ...	....	Augur, ...	Sorapore Bedur,	Hydrabad.

No. in Genl. Register.	Names.	Age.	Cast.	Birth.	Place of Residence. Village.	Pergunna.	District.
2704	Buksha Hobra Jemadar, ...	50	Naek, ...	Brother of Kuja, ...	Nowha, ...	Tonk, ...	Tonk.
2727	Bhyroon, ...	35	Ditto, ...	Son of Bhowanee Jemadar, ...	Bumangaon, ..	Boondee, ...	Boondee.
2777	Bhowanee Sing, ...	30	Charaw, ...	Brother of Pirthee Sing,..	Boondee, ...	Boondee, ...	Huroutee.
2786	Bhyroon Chiruchera, ...	...	Naek, ...	Son of Bulloo, ...	Eugurh, ...	Oneara, ...	Jeypore.
2796	Bhyroon, ...	...	Ditto, ...	,, Goolaba, ...	Paondera, ...	....	Ditto.
2809	Bhalleah Ghuttoo, ...	35	Ditto, ...	,, Seogee, ...	Rajwas, ...	Newaee, ...	Ditto.
2816	Bhyroon Sirgea, ...	45	Sooseea, ...	....	Khoteadha, ...	....	Ditto.
2841	Bhageerut, ...	40	Ditto, ...	....	Burwara, ...	Newaee, ...	Ditto.
2846	Bhageerut Burr, ...	40	Ditto, ...	Son of Oodda, ...	Buntullee, ...	Ditto, ...	Ditto.
2866	Bhyroon Alsia, ...	...	Soosea Alsee,	Nephew of Gyanea Jemadar, ...	Aorna, ...	Madhapoor, ..	Ditto.
2902	Bhowanee Dugras, ...	...	Naek, ...	Son of Chumuneea, ...	....	....	Ditto.
2918	Burreh Khan, ...	35	Moslem, ...	Brother of Judagona Jee,	....	Dawul Kharee,	Mysore.
2926	Bhowanna, ...	...	Naek, ...	Son of Ramkishun, ...	Sopur, ...	Sopur, ...	Gwalior.
2929	Boonda, ...	...	Sooseea, ...	....	Peepuldee, ...	Jullonee, ...	Jeypore.
2953	Binda alias Torab, ...	25	Pathan, ...	Son of Jowahir, ...	Jaes or Ashrafpore, ...	Jaes, ...	Oude.
3004	Bhurut, ...	30	Kaet, ...	,, Kuntee Mooseeb (hung), ...	Suppoor, ...	....	Bankoora.
3005	Bhola, ...	30	Bowlee, ...	....	Budua, ...	Geurundee, ...	Ditto.
3006	Binda, ...	40	Dome, ...	....	Ramkistpoor, .	Sakoolee, ...	Seoree.
3007	Bhola, ...	35	Bagtee, ...	Brother of Sunkur, ...	Raegaon, ...	....	Burdwan.
3011	Bhurut, ...	40	Kaet, ...	Son of Teekaram Mooseeb (dead), ...	Kherobaska, ...	....	Ditto.
3012	Bhola, ...	55	....	....	Sooltangunge,	Koourgunge, .	Bhagulpore.

3169	Baba Sahib, ...	40	Moslem, ...	Cousin of Sirkanee Jemr.,	Kheroor Khora,	Chottee, ...	Mysore.
3170	Burree Sahib, ...	20	Ditto, ...	Brother-in-law of Kurnal,	Chitnullee, ...	Ditto, ...	Ditto.
3229	Beelas Khan, ...	30	Ditto, ...	Son of Meean Khan,......	Seootee, ...	Tirhoot, ...	Mozufferpore.
3249	Bhosee Khan alias Bhimma,	50	Ditto, ...	,, Jumaet Khan, ...	Dhurmpore,...	....	Purneeah.
3257	Bukshoe, ...	35	Ditto, ...	....	Ditto, ...	....	Ditto.
3268	Bucktawar, ...	30 or 40	Sheikh, ...	Son of Sheik Kaleb, ...	....	....	Bengal.
3269	Bucktawur Takooa, ...	60	Pathan,......	....	....	Adjoodeah, ...	Oude.
3278	Bishunpersaud,..............	40 or 50	Bengalee, .	....	....	Ditto, ...	Ditto.
3293	Buhram alias Buhramdee or Bhowul, ...	50	Moslem, ...	Brother of Kalee Churn,.	Seoree, ...	Beerbhoom, ..	Bengal.
3300	Bindanarain, ...	60	Bhowree, ...	....	Gyjapore,......	Ditto, ...	Ditto.
3305	Burree Sirkar,..................	65	Kaet, ...	Son of Punder Doss, ...	Sewurgow, ...	Ditto, ...	Ditto.
3306	Bhala, ...	...	Ditto, ...	....	Ditto, ...	Ditto, ...	Ditto.
3323	Bukwar Jemadar, ...	50	Moslem, ...	Adopted of Kadir Khan alias Hyderjee,.........	Near Bangalore, ...	....	Mysore.
3351	Burra Goodoo Bhae, ...	35	Ditto, ...	Son of Meean Sahib,......	....	....	Hydrabad.
3420	Bhowun Khan, ...	40	Ditto, ...	....	Tirhoot, ...	Mozufferpore,.	Behar.
3430	Baba, ...	50	Ditto, ...	Brother of Futteeah,......	Bunderdoodee,	....	Mysore.
3476	Busma Buree Khan Jemr.,	70	Ditto, ...	....	....	....	Hydrabad.
3565	Baben Khan, (arrested and released, why ?) ...	41	Ditto, ...	....	Hurrepollem,..	....	Vizagapatam.
3572	Bheekaree Khan alias Sunasee Sahib or Soona Khan, (arrested and released, why ?)...........	35	Ditto, ...	Brother of Hoosaen Khan,	Carcarapillee,.	....	Ditto.
3573	Bejah, ...	18	Dome, ...	Son-in-law of Soobal Dome, ...	Surgreea, ...	Ujmutsae thana Mungulkote,	Burdwan.
3574	Bejah Dome, ...	32	Ditto, ...	Son of Gobind Dome, ...	Ditto, ...	Ditto,...........	Ditto.

No. in Genl. Register.	Names.	Age.	Cast.	Birth.	Place of Residence.		
					Village.	Pergunna.	District.
3617	Bundhoo Haldar, ...	...	Mullah, ...	....	....	....	Bhagulpore.
3637	Bhugwan Paudey, ...	50	Pandey, ...	....	Teerla or Munsa, ...	....	Ganjam.
3690	Boodhoo Sheikh, ...	33	Moslem, ...	Son of Sheikh Hyder alias Hurradhun,......	Seebpore,......	Berhampore thana Mutkoorah,	Pubna.
3691	Bahae Chung,..................	50	Chundal, ...	....	Sootanooree,...	Thana Newulgunge,	Fureedpore.
3734	Bishnath alias Beesoo, ...	32	Moslem, ...	....	Bagurgole, ...	Jaffergunge,...	Ditto.
3757	Buddun Thakoor, ...	25	Brahmun,...	....	Putalee bazar near Dum-Dum and		Moorshedabad.
3814	Baba, ...	30	Moslem, ...	....	Banapore,......	Gaudharee, ...	Hydrabad.
3815	Boodheea, ...	17	Ditto, ...	Son of Lala Faqueer Mahomud, ...	Gaoor, ...	Afzulpore,......	Ditto.
3819	Burra Sahib, ...	17	Ditto, ...	,, Emam Sahib Bucheewalla. brother-in-law of Mundaka Nasir.	Ungurgah, ...	Bodhun,.........	Ditto.
3847	Babah, ...	52	Ditto, ...	Son of Noor Khan, ...	Umulgah,......	Nelingah, ...	Ditto.
3864	Burrey Khan alias Burrey Sha, ...	28	Ditto, ...	,, Hoosaen Sha,......	Merchella, ...	....	Masulipatam.
3910	Bapjee Jemadar, ...	60	Ditto, ...	....	Moroo, ...	Suradhown. ...	Hydrabad.
3933	Bura Khan Daerawalla,......	60	Ditto, ...	....	Asseepullee, ...	Bhegeepullee,	Bangalore.
3935	Bura Sahib alias Poosul Bureea, ...	40	Ditto, ...	Son of Faheem Bhae,......	Yuukutpullee,	Ditto, ...	Ditto.
3977	Baboo, ...	60	Ditto, ...	....	Jhoogul, ...	....	Hydrabad.

3978	Burra Kaleea,	40	Ditto,	Adopted of Fuqueer Mahomud,	Elaredypeth,	Sattowlee,	Ditto.
3986	Bundoo, (arrested and released by Captain Malcolm),	30	Ditto,	Son of Siddhee,	Naraen Khaee,	...	Ditto.
3994	Ballaram,	50	Rajpoot,	...	Busunt,	Nadair.	Ditto.
3997	Budhoo,	25	Bhoreawalla,	Adopted of Tawukool Sha, approver,	Rajahpore,	Moodhul,	Ditto.
4011	Bundoo,	40	Moslem,	Brother of Kaloora Hussun,	Churuklee,	Ditto,	Ditto.
4029	Bhoond Khan,	40	Ditto,	...	...	...	Tirhoot.
4064	Buksha,	30	Meena,	Nephew of Hookma Jemr.,	Keora,	Kurnekote,	Tejara.
4085	Boodhoo,	40	Puthan,	Son of Gubwah,	Mudunee,	Oomree,	Gwalior.
4096	Baben Khan alias Baben Sha,	30	Moslem,	,, Hoosaen Sha,	Merchela,	...	Masulipatam.
4099	Burree Sahib,	30	Ditto,	,, Fuqueer Sahib,	Chintopullee,	Byalpullee,	Cuddapah.
4103	Bawa Sahib,	25	Ditto,	,, Goolamee Boodha,	Puruhullee,	...	Nuggur.
4105	Bajra Fuqueer,	30	Ditto,	,, Kasim.	Near Terakheru,	...	Ditto
4112	Burree Sahib alias Jotebah,	62	Ditto,	,, Boodhun Sahib,	Eltapore,	Hoolee Hunoor,	Ditto.
4126	Baboolah,	50	Syud,	Brother of Molah,	Gouroleeah,	Kooseeah,	Goruckpore,
4130	Boodhooa,	30	Kunchun,	Son of Jehanee,	Kutchwahaga,	...	Gwalior.
4131	Bhoora,	35	Lodhee,	...	Arrowlee,	...	Ditto.
4133	Bussuntur,	40	Kunchun,	...	Dabow,	Jhansee,	Bundelcund.
4135	Beechooa,	40	Bhenah,	...	Alumpore,	...	Indore.
4142	Bhoodhooa,	30	Moslem,	Son of Ramzanee,	Thoon,	Eesagur,	Gwalior.
4152	Bheekha,	40	Lodhee,	...	Futtypore,	...	Mynpooree.
4157	Badoolah,	45	Moslem,	Son of Beerum,	Muruae,	...	Gwalior.
4167	Badhee Rae,	60	Rajpoot,	Adopted of Jobha Rae,	Kola Murairah,	...	Goruckpore.
4170	Buksha Bhae alias Nungee Ankuleas Bukshee Bhaee,	70	Moslem,	,, Dowluttea Bhaee,	...	...	Hydrabad.
4238	Bridgelall,	15	Aheer,	,, Luchmun,	Bangra or Roopchupra,	Munjhawa or Ruthee,	Sarun or Tirhoot.
4258	Bucktawur,	...	Ditto,	,, Ruttu,	Raneepore,	...	Cawnpore.

No. in Genl. Register	Names.	Age.	Caste.	Birth.	Place of Residence. Village.	Pergunna.	District.
4259	Bhoora,	22	Lodhee,	Adopted of Kuman,	....	Sindouse,	Etawah.
4281	Bhagoo alias Mukhdoom-buksh,	36	Puthan,	,, Jyne,	Bhudursa,	Fyzabad,	Oude.
4282	Bukshoo,	50	Moslem,	,, Ramzanee,	Dhumoregurh,	Ahmytee,	Ditto.
4283	Bhowanee Buksh,	25	Lodhee,	Son of Odyut,	Khujooa,	Roosoolabad,	Cawnpore.
4296	Burree Sahib,	...	Moslem,	,, Dadeema Jhugnee,	....	....	Hydrabad.
4301	Bhoora,	50	Ditto,	,, Khajoo,	Sopur,	....	Gwalior.
4315	Buksha,	20	Naek,	,, Futtah,	Agnode,	....	Dewass.
4316	Badul alias Buduloo,	40	Moslem,	....	Lahur,	....	Gwalior.
4317	Bhowanee,	30	Brahmun,	Son of Omeed,	....	....	Ditto.
4338	Bhana,	50	Koormee,	Related to Mahadev Jemadar, hung,	Sungumpeth,	....	Hydrabad.
4404	Bhaee Khan,	70	Moslem,	....	Ahoree,	Tellohee,	Oude.
4430	Bheekoo Pandey,	55	Brahmun,	Brother of Birja Pandey,	Papna,	....	Papna.
4457	Bhoorhan,	60	Moslem,	Adopted of Nudeemoola Jemadar and uncle of Raja Khan appvr.,	Moodhul,	....	Boondee.
4461	Budda Kaloo,	60	Ditto,	Son of Allaya Khan,	....	Boregam,	Hydrabad.
4479	Banah Moollah,	50	Moslem,	Son of Mukdoom Sahib,	Hypurga in Hydrabad.		
4501	Bheema, (arrested and released, why ?)	30	Koree,	,, Hittooa's sister, dead.	Serole in ditto.		
4510	Baba,	60	Moslem,	,, Noor Khan,	Kulleeanee in ditto.		
4520	Baleea,	20	Ditto,	Brother of Moheoodeen,	Ousa Ilaka ditto.		
4523	Burjee, nephew of Bheehun Burra Khan,	50	Ditto,	Son of Kurroo Jemadar,	Ukulgah,	Telingana,	Hydrabad.

4538	Boodhoo,	30	Ditto,	Adopted of Tawekulohan approver,	Rajagow in Hydrabad.		
4847	Bhowangeer,	25	Gosaen		Mubaloor	Dhandashew,	Nizam.
4853	Bhola Kotal,	32	Kotal,		Shahangur,		Burdwan.
4854	Bhungsee Huldar,	50	Malloo,		Doulatabad.		Moorshedabad.
4855	Bejeeah Bowrie,	45	Bowrie,	Brother of Gungaram Bowrie,	Gopeenathpore, formerly Aimah,		Bankoora.
4874	Burria,	45	Moslem,	Son of Guroor Jemadar,	Akulga,	Telingana,	Hydrabad.
4877	Burrun,	30	Ditto,	Son-in-law of Kalameean,	Resides in the Hydrabad district.		
4881	Burreea,	50	Ditto,	Son of Nowla,	Nulwar,	Nuldroog,	Nizam.
4882	Baba Koorkoondawalla, Jemadar Einwalla,	70	Ditto,	His father's name unknown but his nickname is Deodoorga,	Koorkonda	Ditto,	Ditto.
4885	Burrun,	45	Ditto,	Adopted of Shabaz Burrey Shah,	Butnoor,	Indee,	Sholapore.
4886	Boorun,	45	Ditto,		Madwalla,	SorapoorBedar,	Nizam.
4889	Burree Khan Jhareewalla, Jemadar Einwalla,	65	Ditto,		Aphunda,	Ousa,	Ditto.
4893	Bunmalee Bagdee,	50	Bagdee,		Asooreeah,	Munteshar,	Burdwan.
4963	Basoomahantee,	32	Goalah,	Brother of Koosoamahuttee,	Bettorojungo,	Gooseekoo,	Pooree or S. Cuttack.
4965	Bhigemahantee,	52	Ditto,		Ditto,	Ditto,	Ditto.
4970	Bhobhonepote,	19	Ditto,		Goparoopoor,	Runapoor,	Ditto.
4988	Bhugwan Sowein,	...	Ditto,		Putrojugho,	Gororosugo,	Cuttack.
4991	Babun Sautra,	...	Ditto,		Buroojungoo,	Ditto,	Ditto.
4992	Boondoodah,	...	Ditto,		Ditto,	Ditto,	Ditto.
	C.						
26	Chutteh Jemadar,	50	Lodhee,	Brother of Jyrah,	Kutkah,	Rusoolabad,	Cawnpore.
63	Cheynooa,	18	Ditto,	,, Deena,	Duthanpore,	Ditto,	Ditto.
362	Cheethora alias Seetaram,	30	Goojur,	Son of Munhualall,	Koolpoolra,	Esagur,	Gwalior.
517	Choteelall alias Chotee,	40	Brahmun,	Adopted of Pertab and Salah of Eesuree,	Eklownee,	Ghatkagow,	Ditto.

No. in Genl. Register.	Names.	Age	Caste.	Birth.	Place of Residence.		
					Village.	Pergunna.	District.
543	Chinta, ...	50	Aheer, ...	Brother of Chunda and Pershad.	Tirdhoo, ...	Jhalone, ...	Bundelcund.
634	Chand Khan alias Lall Khan,	28	Moslem, ...	Son of Dowlut alias Sherah.	Purbeeara, ...	Jhansie, ...	Ditto.
789	Chotee Khan, ...	40	Ditto, ...	,, Aluf Khan, ...	Punuj, ...	Ellichpore, ...	Hydrabad.
808	Chotee Khan, ...	29	Ditto, ...	,, Aluf Khan, ...	Amgaon, ...	Amrowtee, ...	Ditto.
849	Chund alias Chundeea, ...	42	Ditto, ...	Father of Peerun, ...	Kulufgur,......	....	Ditto.
862	Chotee Khan alias Poothoo alias Nunhoo, ...	50	Ditto, ...	,, Bodhun, son of Burree Sahib.	Ditto, ...	....	Ditto.
892	Chand Khan, ...	45	Ditto, ...	,, Khan Mahomud.	Nandair, ...	....	Ditto.
1117	Chiddee Jemadar, ...	30	Brahmun,...	Related to Essuree Jemadar, cousin and son of Pertaub.	Karour-ka-Chokee....	....	Etawah.
1176	Chota Sing, ...	...	Sooseea, ...	Son of Bhyroo, ...	Yasurda, ...	....	Jeypore.
1180	Chaeth Ram, ...	...	Ditto, ...	....	Sonedee, ...	Boondee, ...	Boondee.
1181	Chintheea, ...	...	Ditto, ...	....	Ditto.	Ditto, ...	Ditto.
1182	Chand Sing, ...	45	Ditto, ...	Son of Roopa.	Soreear, ...	Ditto, ...	Jeypore.
1183	Cheyn Sing, ...	...	Ditto, ...	,, Madho Sing, ...	Ditto, ...	Kishengur, ...	Boondee.
1206	Chutterbooj, ...	50	Aheer, ...	....	Kaleepadar, ...	Saekhera, ...	Nursingpore.
1228	Chimna.	25	Koree, ...	Brother of Bukhta, ...	Naranpore, ...	Jhalone, ...	Bundelcund.
1265	Chand Khan, ...	45	Moslem, ...	Son of Lalla Hurtal, ...	Phool.	Baroda, ...	Gwalior.
1278	Chimnah, ...	35	Sooseea, ...	,, Goomanee, ...	Pertabgurh, ...	....	Ditto.
1447	Chiddoo, ...	35	Moslem, ...	,, Lall Khan, ...	Rampoora, ...	....	Ditto.
1452	Chimuneea, ...	40	Naek, ...	,, Deena, ...	Gopalpore, ...	Bowrie, ...	Jeypore.
1468	Chundooa, ...	30	Moslem, ...	,, Muddee Khan, son of Heera, ...	Jhunga, ...	....	Koel.
1771	Chotee Meean Jemadar, ...	...	Ditto, ...	....	Chenapatun, ..	Chenapatun,...	Madras.

1912	Chunda, ...	...	Ditto, ...	Son of Mulik Mahomud, .	Beladhana, ...	Katul, ...	Dhar.
2029	Chiddah, ...	35	Dhanuk, ...	Brother of Chutta Ram,...	Jugumunpore,	Jhalone, ...	Bundelcund.
2030	Chetaram, ...	32	Ditto, ...	,, Chiddah, 2029,	Ditto, ...	Ditto, ...	Ditto.
2049	Chokura, ...	...	Khungur,...	....	Kuchwadhar,..	....	Gwalior.
2059	Chuttoree, ...	50	Brahmun,...	Son of Prethee, ...	Bulokagurea,..	Sindouse, ...	Etawah.
2095	Chunda, ...	25	Moslem, ...	,, Moheeodeen, ...	Dhuroulee, ...	Amroutee, ...	Nagpore.
2163	Chunmun Sheikh Jemadar, .	60	Ditto, ...	,, Mukhdoom Sahib, Boodee Walla,	Nighora, ...	Gora, ...	Hydrabad.
2250	Chinma or Chunmee, 2d, Jemadar, ...	35	Sooseea, ...	,, Lala Omeid Jemadar, ...	Gopalpore or Phonelia,	Oneara,.........	Jeypore.
2252	Chunda Bhutteea, ...	...	Moslem, ...	....	Samp, ...	....	Ditto.
*2728	Chumuneea,.....................	26	Naek, ...	Son of Bhowanee Jemadar, Brother of Peearjee, ...	Bamangaon or Zuna,...	Boondee or Subar, ...	Ditto.
2749	Chummuneea, ...	30	Ditto, ...	,, Keshna, ...	Nativarie,......	Bowrie,.........	Ditto.
*2654	Cassim,...........................	28	Moslem, ...	Adopted by Emam Sahib, Chabriah, ...	Gaoor, ...	Afzulpore, ...	Hydrabad.
3350	Cassim,...........................	28	Ditto, ...	Son of Madar alias Boodhoo Mudar Sahib, ...	....	....	Madras.
3591	Chunder Mohunpaul,.........	30	Chassa,......	Brother-in-law of Nuffur Ghose Jemadar of Seoor,...............	Basutpore, ...	Mozufursae Thanah Boalkissen,	Burdwan.
3593	Chakur Haldar, ...	50	Buneea, ...	Son of Kishen Haldar,......	Formerly Cheergaon now Belgaon,......	Monoursae Thanah Keogaon Burooah,	Beerbhoom.
3609	Cheneebhose Chukurbutty.	35	Brahmun,...	Son of Jugmohun Chukurbutty, ...	Kurgaon, ...	Thana Sakooleepore,	Ditto.
3694	Chedam Mistree,...............	30	Chotar, ...	....	Atteeah.	Betkeeah,......	Fureedpore.
3758	Cheedhur.........................	30	Chasa, ...	....	Cheergaon, ...	....	Moorshedabad.
3860	Cassim Sha,.....................	40	Moslem, ...	Son of Malik Sha.	Bhogul,.........	....	Masulipatam.
3919	Chundeeah Emamsahib,......	30	Ditto, ...	Brother of Juggooma Jemadar, ...	....	....	....

No. in Genl. Register.	Names.	Age.	Caste.	Birth.	Place of Residence.		
					Village.	Pergunna.	District.
3979	Chota Kaleea, ...	40	Moslem, ...	Adopted of Fuqueer Mahomud, ...	Elaredypeth,...	Satowlee, ...	Hydrabad.
4008	Chuttoo, ...	30	Nadaf, ...	....	Bhoree,.........	....	....
4036	Chitroo,........................	60	Pathan,......	Son of Joomun Khan,......	Kasurreea, ...	Beteea, ...	Saurun.
4088	Chedduma, ...	38	Koolee,......	,, Bustee,..............	Rumeea, ...	Thutteea, ...	Furuckabad.
4090	Cheynah, ...	35	Lodhee,......	....	Chubranow,...	....	Ditto.
4147	Chiddah, ...	32	Koree, ...	Son of Nynsookh, ...	Bindooah,......	Sindouse, ...	Etawah.
4361	Chema..........................	...	Binjarah ...	....	....	....	Jeypore.
4849	Casheepooree, ...	55	Goshaen, ...	....	Khudgaon, ...	Umbah, ...	Gwalior.
4984	Cherrun Sowein,...............	...	Goalah, ...	....	Paturjungo, ...	Gowsoko,......	Pooree or S. Cuttack.
	D.						
189	Debee, ...	30	Lodhee,......	Son of Munsookh, ...	Doondu, ...	....	Furuckabad.
239	Dhownkkul,.....................	30	Ditto, ...	Brother-in-law of Hurreea,	Kulloo, ...	Teroa, ...	Goruckpore.
344	Deokee,..........................	40	Koormee, ...	Son of Poorun,..............	Calpee, ...	....	Humeerpore.
345	Doorjun, ...	32	Ditto, ...	,, Poorun,..............	Ditto, ...	....	Ditto.
403	Doorjuna,.......................	18	Moslem, ...	,, Dhurm Khan Jemr.,	Akajeree, ...	Murwar, ...	Gwalior.
478	Dhurmjeet alias Tabeerjeet,.	40	Ditto, ...	Adopted of Heera, ...	....	Ditto, ...	Ditto.
644	Doorjun Jemadar, ...	40	Brahmun,...	Son of Bukut Brahmun, adopted of Bhugwan Rajpoot, ...	Bumar, ...	Jhansie,.........	Bundelcund.
713	Doulut Sing.	50	Sooseea,......	Brother of Ajub Sing,......	Malpore, ...	....	Jeypore.
740	Durab Khan, ...	30	Moslem, ...	....	Kurnal,.........	....	Ditto.
757	Doulut,..........................	50	Brahmun,...	....	Kujoree, ...	....	Bhurtpore.
758	Davee, ...	40	Ditto,.........	....	Ditto, ...	....	Ditto.

845	Dhurum Khan, ...	30	Moslem, ...	...	Naudair, ...	...	Hydrabad.
944	Deokee...	50	Brahmun,...	Son of Jeswunt, ...	Koraree, ...	Saekhera,...	Bhopal.
947	Dhun Sing, ...	40	Gond, ...	Adopted of Kosal, ...	Mokhun, ...	Ditto, ...	Ditto.
980	Doorjun, ...	30	Rajpoot, ...	Son of Bhajee alias Sulsa,	Oodeypore, ...	Ooreya,...	Cawnpore.
1069	Durreaw, ...	25	Koomhar,...	,, Kemraj, ...	Gontee,...	Gorsurae,...	Jhalone.
1186	Dowlut Sing, ...	70	Sooseea, ...	Brother of Newul Sing,...	Julhur,...	Jeypore, ...	Jeypore.
1188	Dougur Sing, ...	42	Ditto, ...	...	Surwur, ...	Kishengur, ...	Ditto.
1289	Dhurmah Dhureeah, ...	30	Ditto, ...	Son of Peearjee, ...	Pertabgurh,...	...	Indore.
1504	Dhumwoa, ...	20	Lodhee, ...	,, Oola, ...	Talgow,...	...	Furuckabad.
1508	Desraj, ...	35	Ditto, ...	,, Sooklal and nephew of Persaud,	Punaree, ...	Sumther, ...	Bundelcund.
1510	Dulla, ...	30	Moslem, ...	,, Ruffee Khan, ...	Moorsan (now in service at Gwalior,)		Koel.
1513	Dowluttea, ...	40	Sooseea, ...	...	Surwa, ...	...	Jeypore.
1515	Dulla, ...	45	Ditto, ...	...	Gopaulpore,...	...	Ditto
1516	Dullooa, ...	43	Ditto, ...	...	Ditto, ...	...	Ditto.
1519	Doorjunna alias Jadoolla, ...	25	Lohar, ...	Son of Nundlal, ...	Pathereea, ...	...	Saugor.
1841	Dawul, ...	32	Moslem, ...	Brother of Gondoo Jemr.,	...	...	Hydrabad.
1880	Dulla Mustam, ...	...	Ditto, ...	Son of Futteh Khan, ...	Hirpora, ...	...	Indore.
1923	Dorjunnah, ...	30	Lodhee, ...	...	Loharee, ...	Sumtee, ...	Jeypore.
1931	Dorgha,...	40	Rajpoot, ...	Adopted of Amur Sing,...	Nagpore, ...	...	Nagpore.
1934	Durroo,...	55	Moslem, ...	,, Jummun,...	...	...	Saugor Khass.
1948	Dorgha,...	30	Rajpoot, ...	Son of Jysing,...	Awun, ...	Hoonah, ...	Gawlior.
1967	Deoleea, ...	45	Rungrez, ...	,, Kasim, ...	Dehalgaon, ...	...	Ditto.
1980	Delawur Khan Jemadar, ...	...	Moslem, ...	Son of Russut Khan, ...	...	...	Gwalior.
2006	Dulput,...	50	Chumar, ...	...	Bhojae,...	...	Ditto.
2078	Dhunsundur, ...	36	Rajpoot, ...	...	Alumpore, ...	...	Indore.
2107	Dawul Kuleea,...	35	Moslem, ...	Son of Ghotte Karmeea,...	Mansallee, ...	Lalore, ...	Hydrabad.
2114	Doolee Sheikh Jemadar, ...	50	Ditto, ...	,, Sheikh Dawul, ...	Punar, ...	...	Nagpore.
2137	Dondhee, ...	50	Basketer, ...	...	Ashtie, ...	Nachungow,...	Nagpore.
2179	Daood Sheikh Jemadar,...	50	Moslem, ...	...	Dakagaon, ...	Mungrole,...	Hydrabad or Nagpore.
2199	Dhunna, ...	...	Ditto, ...	Son of Bhoopa, ...	Deohuttee, ...	...	Indore.

No. in Genl. Register.	Names.	Age.	Cast.	Birth.	Place of Residence.		
					Village.	Pergunna.	District.
2253	Dooma,	...	Sooseea,	...	Jeypore,	...	Jeypore.
2347	Deendar Allee,	40	Syud,	...	...	...	Burdwan.
2385	Dan Sing,	50	Sheikh,	...	Berhampore,	...	Gwalior.
2439	Daood Sheikh Jemadar,	...	Ditto,	...	Bunsee,	...	Dharwar.
2494	Dan,	25	Pathan,	Son of Badoolla Khan,	Madeb,	...	Mozufferpore.
2577	Dewuljee alias Dadeh-meea Jemadar,	67	Moslem,	...	Moordee,	Ulmalla,	Bombay.
2842	Dallah,	...	Naek,	Brother of Motee,	Ruwajnee,	Madhapore,	Jeypore.
2849	Deobuksha Meena,	...	Meena,	Son of Khenga,	Gopaulpore,	...	Ditto.
2152	Deepa Meena,	...	Ditto,	...	Sadarah,	Nuwae,	Ditto.
2868	Dullah,	40	Bheel,	Son of Dulla,	Ruwajnee,	Madhapore,	Ditto.
2876	Dewa Sirgea,	40	Sooseea,	...	Peepuldee,	Jhillae,	Ditto.
2879	Dewah Torab, (doubtful if arrested or not,)	...	Ditto,	...	Jewamaree,	Tonk,	Tonk.
2883	Dhunna Dholeea,	...	Naek Mawareea,	...	Adoleea or Dowareea,	Madhapore or Dhonee,	Jeypore.
2889	Dhunna Jemadar,	50	...	...	Bowrara,	...	Ditto.
2905	Dewa Powar,	...	Naek,	Son of Suckta,	Neepoad,	Moolarna,	Ditto.
2959	Doondee,	50	Moslem,	Brother-in-law of Jubber,	Rudowlee,	Lucknow,	Oude.
3017	Dea Naraien Mozumdar,	...	Kaet,	Son of Chotear,	Laldanga,	...	Dacca.
3019	Deena Ghat Manjee,	50	Moslem,	...	Chapghatee	...	Moochreeabad.
3020	Dulleep Jemadar,	57	Ditto,	...	Bhowanegunge,	...	Kamsla.
3162	Dada Sheikh,	50	Ditto,	...	Chotee,	...	Mysore.
3212	Deena Sheikh,	60	Sheikh,	Brother of Sheik Golamee,	...	...	Goruckpore.
3245	Dowla Khan,	30	Moslem,	Son of Meer Khan,	Dhurmpore,	...	Poorneeah.

3251	Davee Khan,	20	Ditto,	„ Mustoo Khan,	Ditto,		Poorneeah.
3260	Daboo Khan,	60	Ditto,	„ Munnoo Khan,	Bukole	Otemgal,	Mozufferpore.
3340	Dawul, 2d,	30	Ditto,	„ Hajjee,	Çatapully,	Cadapa,	Madras.
3394	Dhantall, 2d,	30	Pathan,	„ Jowlee Khan, (the dark,)	Eurowa,	Jujdur,	Nepal.
3445	Dhab Khan alias Dhameen Khan,	...	Moslem,		Kunjunpore,	Kokulpulee,	Hydrabad.
3473	Daood Sheikh,	40	Ditto,	Adopted of Daood Bhai,	Jotee,		Mysore.
3550	Dadun Shah,	60	Ditto,		Cowalcottah,		Masulipatam.
3618	Donadhun,	26	Kaet,	Son of Suda Kissen,	Suppoor,	Ajuwotsahee thana Sakooleepore,	Beerbhoom.
3627	Darroo Jemadar,	50	Moslem,		Ashtee,	Nuldroog,	Hydrabad.
3650	Dookheeram Chung,	...	Chundal,		Near Gopenathpore.		Pubna.
3652	Dusserut Jowardar,	...	Kaet,	Induree Ram Jowardar,	Burkapore,	Islampore Nazirgunge	Ditto.
3685	Dawulleah,	20	Moslem,	Son of Bapoona,	Higgeerah,		Hydrabad.
3696	Dheenoo Chung,	32	Chundal,		Burdem Kandee,	Kulseenee Jafurgunge	Fureedpore.
3745	Daneea Jemadar,	45	Naek,		Raepore,		Jodhpore.
3753	Dullah Baoree,	...	Ditto,		Rujalee,	Ururka,	Ditto.
3851	Dulleah,	25	Moslem,	Son of Meean Sahib alias Goree Meean Khan,	Palgee,	Mundrar,	Sholapore.
3857	Dawood Khan,	40	Sheikh,		Banglee,		Ditto.
3952	Dawul Sahib,	20	Moslem,	Son of Bura Khan Buchewala,	Aseepullee,	Bugapullee,	Bangalore.
3953	Dewanjee,	60	Ditto,	Brother of Balheeah,	Admupullee,	Ditto,	Ditto.
3956	Dada Bhaee Syud,	50	Ditto,		Aseepullee.	Ditto,	Ditto.
4065	Dowlah,	40	Jaut,		Kurnekotee,	Kurne Kotee,	Koth.
4091	Dheena,	32			Naira,	Futteea,	Furruckabad.
4151	Doolra,	30	Rajpoot,	Son of Dhun Sing,	Timaulee,	Dumowa,	Jhansee.
4236	Deena,	25	Lodhee,	„ Gunga,	Sursae,		Cawnpore.

No. in Genl. Register.	Names.	Age	Cast.	Birth.	Place of Residence.		
					Village.	Pergunna.	District.
4248	Deojee, ...	50	Koolee,......	....	Sindhee, ...	Nandair, ...	Hydrabad.
4263	Dhareea, 2d, sister's son of Pershaud, approver, ..	25	Lodhee,......	Son of Khoman, ...	Murnae, ...	....	Gwalior.
4274	Dhurm Khan alias Fyzut Khan, ...	...	....	,, Noor Khan,.........	Nothing mentioned in the original.		
4275	Dildar Khan, ...	...	Moslem, ...	,, Jowahir, ...	....	....	....
4285	Deen Allee, ...	22	Syud, ...	Adopted of Mooradun, ...	Koelwur, ...	....	Patna.
4299	Deya, ...	60	Lodhee,......	,, ukshee, ...	Pehropore, ...	....	Cawnpore.
4331	Dada, ...	28	Moslem, ...	Brother of Meeah, ...	Teomogha, ...	Nuggur, ...	....
4332	Doong Munjoo, ...	30	Hindoo, ...	....	Arkheree,......	Holee Honoor,	Nuggur.
4339	Dhunnooa, brother of Ghazee and Shumshera, both transported,.........	30	Lodhee, ...	Son of Lodhur, ...	Residence not mentioned.		
4418	Doolal Surkar, ...	60	Kaet, ...	....	Jungeepore,...	Kunkur, ...	Moorshedabad.
4429	Deokee, ...	...	Lodhee, ...	Son of Dhurum,...........	Jumeh,.........	....	Gwalior.
4432	Doorgahchurn Holdar, ...	45	Buneea, ...	,, Buddun Holdar,...	....	....	....
4471	Daoo, ...	60	Moslem, ...	Adopted of Jenan Khan,...	Khuluk-mundgee,	Ulmulla, ...	Dharwar.
4491	Dawul Jemadar, Salla of Meean Bhae, approver, ...	40	Ditto, ...	Son of Maekha Jemadar, .	Morud,.........	Latoor, ...	Hydrabad.
4544	Deojee,.........................	60	Koree, ...	....	Ghuttoor,......	....	Dharwar.
4834	Dhookoo Meeteea, ...	40	Meeteea Bagdee,	Son of Pubun Meeteea, ...	Wuzeerpore,...	Mungulkote, ..	Burdwan.
4837	Doongra Bhae, ...	55	Moslem, ...	....	Hingoorah, ...	Bagulkota, ...	Belgaum.
4842	Daoo Gowlee, ...	50	Gosaen, ...	....	Umbaloor, ...	Dhandashew,..	Nizam.

4883	Deena alias Emam-ka-Deena,	50	Moslem, ...	Adopted of Bodewala Emam Sahib,	Seenoor, ...	Allund, ...	Ditto.
4891	Dolchee Hoosein,	50	Ditto, ...	....	Golusgaon, ...	Akulkote, ...	Satara.
4971	Deenajenna,	28	Goalah, ...	Brother of Pooreejunah, No. 2,	Mathoure, ...	Runapore, ...	Pooree or S. Cuttack.
	E.						
311	Eseree alias Esureea Jemr.,	32	Brahmun, ...	Son of Birbhan,	Sureeapoor, ...	Ahma, ...	Furruckabad.
337	Emamee,	30	Moslem, ...	Adopted of Peermahomed, approver,	Churkaree, ...	....	Bundelcund.
766	Emam Khan,	40	Ditto, ...	Son of Aluf Khan,	Akolee, ...	....	Hydrabad.
1121	Emamee,	16	Ditto, ...	,, Bhuddae,	....	....	Humeerpore.
1342	Emamee,	30	Ditto, ...	,, Misree, (adopted of Dhurm Khan,	....	....	Gwalior.
1346	Elahee Buksh alias Himmut,	30	Ditto, ...	Adopted of Bussawun, ...	Nanaree, ...	Sumthur, ...	Bundelcund.
1349	Emam Buksh,	25	Ditto, ...	Son of Bukhtawar,	Devdee Hindoo Sing,	Lucknow, ...	Oude.
1367	Emameea,	28	Ditto, ...	Brother of Bahadoor, ...	Gopalpore, ...	Seris, ...	Jeypore.
1368	Emam Khan,	40	Ditto, ...	Son of Badam,	Khidgree, ...	Rusoolabad, ...	Cawnpore.
1751	Emam Buksh,	19	Ditto, ...	,, Ghous Beg Mogul,	Selon, ...	Lucknow, ...	Oude.
1861	Emam,	40	Ditto, ...	,, Sirjee Khan, ...	Deonsurah, ...	Ranour, ...	Hydrabad.
1884	Emamee,	...	Ditto, ...	,, Munoo Kunchunee Caste, ...	Kauthal, ...	....	Muhwha.
2419	Emam Sheikh or Hamal Dandga,	40	Ditto, ...	,, Fuqueer Mahomed,	Chitmully or Bamully,	Shewmaga or Ulmalla,	Mysore.
2451	Emam Sahib,	...	Ditto, ...	,, Fuqueer Mean Sahib,	Jhoree Khoord,	Afzulpore, ...	Hydrabad.
2530	Emam,	40	Ditto, ...	,, Beeree Khan, ...	Jharee, ...	Ditto, ...	Ditto.
2670	Emam Sha,	...	Ditto, ...	,, Nubbee,	Mausingee, ...	Indee, ...	Bombay.
2675	Emam,	...	Ditto, ...	,, Kallee Khan, ...	Ditto, ...	Sorapoor Beedur,	Hydrabad.
2844	Esureea,	35	Meena, ...	,, Mheelah,	Mahpoora, ...	Esurdah, ...	Jeypore.

No. in Genl. Register	Names.	Age.	Caste.	Birth.	Place of Residence.		
					Village.	Pergunna.	District.
3164	Emam Sadee Wallah,.........	35	Moslem, ...	Son of Kassim Sahib,......	Bensee,.........	....	Dharwar.
3345	Emam Sahib alias Jotee Emam, ...	70	Ditto, ...	....	....	....	Hydrabad.
3359	Emam, ...	...	Ditto, ...	Adopted by Botcheea, ...	Kokuntee, ...	Cuddapah, ...	Madras.
3463	Emam Sahib, ...	30	Ditto, ...	Son of Seeroo Bhae Jemadar, ...	....	....	Hydrabad.
3466	Emam alias Bellary Walla, .	65	Ditto, ...	Adopted by a Thugnee named Kaleema.			
3531	Emam, ...	60	Ditto, ...	....	Near Dawnugheera,		Mysore.
3547	Emam Sha, No. 1, ...	27	Ditto, ...	Son of Casim Sha, No. 1,	Cowalcotta, ...	....	Masulipatam.
3629	Emam, ...	55	Ditto, ...	,, Hoosaen Shadara,	Sirsumbha, ...	Allund, ...	Hydrabad.
3687	Emam Sahib, ...	20	Ditto, ...	,, Buree Khan (dead.)	Nandraee,......	Sholapore, ...	Bombay.
3833	Emam Khan, ...	30	Ditto, ...	....	Mulkootah, ...	Mundroo, ...	Sholapore.
3845	Essoo Bae, ...	40	Ditto, ...	Son of Faqueer Mahomud,	Near Bedar	Sholapore,	Nizam.
3856	Emam Patail, ...	20	Ditto, ...	,, Houlgy Mean Khan,	Bauglee, ...	....	Sholapore.
3863	Emam Sha, ...	37	Ditto, ...	Adopted Son of Nasir Mahomud,...............	Masulipatam.		
3865	Ebrahim Sahib, ...	35	Ditto, ...	....	Sunumpendah,	....	Masulipatam.
3914	Emama, ...	16	Ditto, ...	Son of Roodhun Sahib,...	Mulurpullee,...	Guddree, ...	Cuddapah.
3915	Emama, 2nd, ...	30	Ditto, ...	,, Chootoo Bhaee, ...	Near Sakillah,		Bangalore.
3917	Emam Sahib, ...	30	Ditto, ...	,, Bawa Sahib, ...	Koondmar-pullee, ...	....	Masulipatam.
3919	Emam Sahib Chundeea,......	30	Ditto, ...	Brother of Sugooma, Jemadar, ...	....	....	Hydrabad.
3924	Emam Sahib, ...	40	Ditto, ...	,, Sugooma Jemadarnee,............	Aseepulee, ...	Bhugepullee,...	Bangalore.

3990	Eroo, ...	40	Koolee,......	....	Bhookee, ...	....	Hydrabad.
4095	Emam Sha, ...	24	Moslem, ...	Son of Burray Sha,.........	Cowalcottah,..	....	Masulipatam.
4132	Emam Khan, ...	45	Ditto, ...	....	Keleea, ...	Jhalone, ...	Jhalone.
4178	Emam Sahib, ...	50	Ditto, ...	Adopted Son of Hunoor Sahib, ...	....	....	Hydrabad.
4278	Emambux alias Ulleebuksh,	40 or 60	Ditto,......	Son of Mushud Allee,......	Midnapore, ...	Fyzabad, ...	Oude.
4322	Esurea,...........................	45	Brahmun,...	,, Oomeid, ...	Mehdepore, ...	Luckna,.........	Etawah.
4334	Emam, ...	50	Moslem, ...	....	Near Hurreehur,		Nuggur.
4416	Emam, follower of Aub Khan Jemadar, ...	30	Ditto, ...	Son of Julloo Bhae,......	Punbullee, ...	Horee Hunoor,	Ditto.
4490	Emam, Son-in-law of Unda Walla Meean Bhae,	35	Ditto, ...	,, Zinda Madar,......	Moorud, ...	....	Hydrabad.
4507	Emam Sahib, Nephew of Mahomud Hoosein,......	35	Ditto, ...	,, Boor Ally Fu-queer Mahomed,......	Elghandhat,...	....	Ditto.
4534	Emam, ...	18	Ditto, ...	,, Kalla Ismael,......	Gogrogon-doogee,...	....	Dharwar.
4542	Eereea,...........................	50	Koree, ...	....	Ghuttoor, ...	....	Ditto.
4546	Eedoo Sheikh,...................	33	Moslem, ...	....	Sonakaucee,...	Jhanah Dhunupore,	Pubna.
4832	Essura, ...	30	Naek, ...	Son of Bulloo, who is a Sepoy of Kirpa Jemr.,	....	....	Dholepore.
4945	Emam, ...	35	Moslem, ...	,, Sungra Nubbee Sahib, ...	Oomree, ...	Nadare,.........	Hydrabad.
	F.						
447	Fojh Khan, ...	37	Moslem, ...	Son of Jurub Khan, ...	Burwarghat,...	....	Seronge.
1232	Fyzoo, Brother of Beharee,	55	Ditto, ...	,, Talib, ...	Pokhriah,......	Thana Memgul-pore,	Cawnpore.
2004	Fouladee, ...	35	Ditto, ...	Adopted of Noor Khan Jemadar, ...	Murhore, ...	Cundelee,......	Kulonur or Gwalior.

No. in Genl. Register.	Names.	Age.	Caste.	Birth.	Place of Residence. Village.	Pergunna.	District.
2160	Fukeera alias Fukeer Mahomud, ...	35	Nadik, ...	....	Ellichpore, ...	....	Hydrabad.
2177	Futtun,..........................	55	Moslem, ...	....	Ghurjola, ...	Mungrole, ...	Ditto.
2209	Futtah,..........................	...	Sooseea Naek,	Son of Chundah,...........	Bhistrutpore,..	....	Bhurtpore.
2431	Fukeer Myan Khan Jemr.,	...	Moslem, ...	Brother of Bhuleem, ...	Josee, ...	Afzulpore, ...	Hydrabad.
2755	Futtah,..........................	30	Sooseea, ...	Son of Mulla, ...	Nubbera, ...	Toda, ...	Jeypore.
*3198	Fukroodeen, ...	30	Moslem, ...	,, Chota Hoosain Khan, ...	Chutmellee, ...	Nuggur, ...	Mysore.
3346	Fucqueera, ...	30	Ditto, ...	Adopted by Daood Khan Jemadar, dead,.........	Chunkoopa, ...	Bellary, ...	Madras.
3358	Furreed, ...	...	Ditto, ...	,, Bochera Hoosaen Sahib,	Koknee,.........	....	Arcot.
3399	Fondee,.............	25	Shaikh,......	Nephew of Roshun, ...	Geereea, ...	Near Moorshedabad.	
3455	Futteh alias Jeea Mahka Futteh Jemadar, ...	56	Moslem, ...	....	Bunder,.........	Doodee,.........	Mysore.
3494	Fukroodeen	60	Ditto, ...	Son of Mullik Bae,.........	....	....	Nizam.
3554	Fukeeroodeen,..................	30	Ditto, ...	,, Bursera Sahib Khan Thug,...	Monrapilly, ...	Cuddapah.	
*3176	Fukeera, ...	40	Ditto, ...	,, Bojepa Hoosaen,...	Chutnullee, ...	Nuggur, ...	Mysore.
3829	Futtah Khan, ...	50	Ditto, ...	....	Dewarnadgee,	Ulmulla, ...	Dharwar.
4104	Fuqueer Moondewar, ...	50	Ditto, ...	....	Near Torrekhera,		Nuggur.
4140	Fuddehla,.......................	26	Ditto, ...	Son of Jumaeut,...........	....	....	Gwalior.
4168	Fuqueer Sing, ...	40	Rajpoot, ...	....	At the Police Chokee of Jojrah, Patna.		
4176	Fuqueera alias Fuqueer Ahmed Khan, ...	...	Moslem Nadaf,	Adopted of Ahmed Khan,	....	....	Debban.

4266	Fyz alias Goohur, ...	...	Moslem, ...	Son of Jaffer, ...	Present residence not known.		
4313	Futta, ...	40	Naek, ...	....	Dewas, ...	....	Jeypore.
4333	Fuqueer, ...	50	Moslem, ...	Son of Bura Sahib Khan,	Koondmar Jukkee,	Bagapullee, ...	Bangalore.
4480	Fuqueer Shah,..................	45	Ditto, ...	„ Mookdoom Sahib,	Hipurgah,......	Sholapore, ...	Hydrabad.
	G.						
220	Gunesh, ...	30	Brahmun Joshee,	Son of Kundun alias Bustee and Brother of Mahomud, ...	Nagureea,......	....	Mynpooree.
331	Goolab Khan alias Goobeea,	35	Moslem, ...	Adopted of Alee Khan Jemadar,..................	Sindouse, ...	....	Gwalior.
423	Gilleea,..........................	20	Ditto, ...	Son of Kassim, ...	Banpore, ...	Chundelee, ...	Mynpooree.
513	Gurha alias Doorjuna,......	40	Lodhee,......	....	Ditto, ...	....	Ditto.
853	Gunesha, ...	25	Koormee, ...	....	Kulufgur,......	....	Hydrabad.
887	Gunga, a female,..............	...	Moslem, ...	....	Oomroutee, ...	....	Ditto.
1143	Goolab Khan, ...	30	Ditto, ...	Son of Bahadoor, ...	Shurree, ...	Sumthur, ...	Bundelcund.
1219	Gilly Khan,.....................	30	Ditto, ...	„ Kassim, ...	Bhanpoora, ...	Chundelee, ...	Gwalior.
1237	Goolab Khan, ...	40	Ditto, ...	Brother-in-law of Sheik Inaeut approver, ...	Jonee Futtehpore,	Tehree,.........	Bundelcund.
1277	Goteea Jemadar,..............	40	Sooseea, ...	Son of Omedea Jemadar,	Pertabgurh, ...	....	Indore.
1526	Gunesha, ...	35	Moslem, ...	„ Khoobah, ...	Sojawul, ...	Gungbasonda,	Bhopal.
1711	Gholab, ...	25	Mirdha, ...	Brother of Hubboo, brother-in-law of Jumna, transported, ...	Bygnee, ...	Seonee, ...	Tonk.
1775	Ghous Mahomud Jemadar, ...	35	Moslem, ...	Son of Mohwoodeen,......	Yargee,.........	Mirgul,.........	Hydrabad.
1826	Gunesh, ...	...	Gurerea, ...	....	....	....	Baroda.
1975	Goodeenah, ...	30	Moslem, ...	Son of Kassim, ...	Bhaupore, ...	....	Gwalior.
2010	Goolab Khan, ...	40	Ditto, ...	....	Konch, ...	Humeerpore,...	Bundelcund.
2021	Godurra, ...	50	Ditto, ...	Son of Lala Huttar,......	Baroda, ...	Pertabgurh, ...	Indore.
2032	Gunesh, ...	35	Ditto, ...	Adopted of Zalima, ...	Phool Baroda,	Sooker, ...	Gwalior.
2034	Gunesh, ...	...	Buneea, ...	Sallah of Dibba, approver,	Sumreea, ...	....	Furruckabad.

No. in Genl. Register.	Names.	Age.	Caste.	Birth.	Place of Residence.		
					Village.	Pergunna.	District.
2058	Gungolah, ...	...	Lodhee,......	Son of Purmola and Nephew of Runjeet, approver, ...	Calpee, ...	Humeerpore,..	Bundelcund.
2088	Gool Mahomud Jemadar, ...	50	Moslem, ...	....	Aujungow. ...	Omroutee, ...	Hydrabad.
2117	Ghuffoor, ...	30	Ditto, ...	Son of Muddee Mahomud,	Kulglisoor, ...	Nachangow,...	Ditto.
2121	Gholab Khan Jemadar,......	70	Ditto, ...	....	Goreegow, ...	Akola, ...	Ditto.
2169	Gholaub, ...	26	Ditto, ...	....	Gaba, ...	Nigherekeh,...	Ditto.
2186	Gunee Sahib, ...	40	Ditto, ...	....	Kosorekheree,.	Nerbera, ...	Ditto.
2240	Gunesh, ...	30	Lodhee, ...	Son of Dibun and Brother of Kuleean, approver, ...	Nichee Bunuldeo,	....	Bhopal.
2243	Ghasee, ...	50	Gurereea,...	Nephew of Hirpyah,......	Sindouse, ...	....	Etawah.
2254	Ghasee Jemadar,..............	...	Sooseea, ...	Salah of Huree Sing,......	Hurdegow, ...	Tonk, ...	Rajpootana.
2256	Godureea, ...	...	Ditto, ...	....	Gopaulpore, ...	....	Jeypore.
2258	Gopaul Jemadar................	...	Ditto, ...	....	....	....	Ditto.
2388	Ghoroo Sheik alias Kalee Khan, ...	28	Weaver, ...	Son of Moulla, ...	Mooldee, ...	Ulmulla, ...	Bombay.
2483	Ghazee Khan Jemadar, ...	35	Pathan,......	Son of Thanoo Misree, ...	Ghantee, ...	....	Chupra.
2500	Goolbea, ...	20	Moslem, ...	....	Bungureea, ...	....	Goruckpore.
2592	Ghazee,..........................	30	Ditto, ...	Son of Nubbee Khan,......	Higgerah,......	Afzalpore, ...	Hydrabad.
2761	Goolal, ...	30	Ditto, ...	....	Gorolee, ...	Boondee, ...	Hurrowtee.
2817	Goolab Dass, ...	40	Byragee, ...	Adopted of Motee Dass Byragee, ...	Is a servant of a sweetmeat seller in Muthura.		
2823	Gomanee (Dugla,)	40	Sooseea, ...	Son of Diharam,..	Kendla or Isurdah,	Sonaree or Mulpoora,	Jeypore.
2839	Gomanee (Meena,)............	40	Meena, ...	....	Malpoora,......	Isurdah, ...	Ditto.

2845	Golaba (Burasheea,)	40	Sooseea, ...	Son of Oodda, ...	Buntullee, ...	Newae, ...	Ditto.
2857	Golaba, ...	40	Ditto, ...	,, Dhunna, ...	Sedura.	Ditto, ...	Ditto.
2860	Golab (Hulanee Bhimalee,)..	55	Ditto, ...	....	Sowah.	Tonk, ...	Tonk.
2864	Gearsee Jemadar, ...	50	Ditto, ...	....	Sumea or Khohaprap Sumeer Duturmurgurh, ...		Shekawatee.
2869	Gopaul, ...	32	Ditto, ...	Nephew of Gyana Jemadar,	Rawnjuah, ...	Madhopore, ...	Jeypore.
2897	Gomanee (doubtful whether arrested or not,) ...	...	Ditto, ...	Son of Munga Jemadar,...	Burwara, ...	....	Ditto.
2898	Gyana (Alseea,)	60	Ditto, ...	....	Malarnee, ...	....	Ditto.
3023	Golam Dass Sircar Jemadar,	50	Kaet, ...	Maternal Nephew of Rampersaud Jemadar.	Thoopsara, ...	Sakoleepore,...	Seoree.
3024	Gunga Huree Mistree Jemr.,	30	Ditto, ...	....	Chanuck, ...	Seoree, ...	Ditto.
3025	Gopaul, ...	30	Ditto, ...	Son of Buddun, ...	Lupoor, ...	....	Bancoora.
3032	Golam, ...	40	Moslem, ...	,, Golabdee, ...	Narainpore, ...	....	Ditto.
3034	Gobee, ...	60	Ditto, ...	....	Chopghatee,...	....	Moorshedabad,
3035	Gunga Hurree, ...	40	Kaet, ...	Son of Goluck Mistree, (dead,)	Chanuck, ...	Mungulkote,...	Burdwan.
3194	Ghousee, ...	...	Moslem, ...	,, Sureek Jemadar,	Chitmillee, ...	Nuggur, ...	Mysore.
3278	Gooman Sircar, ...	40	Kaet, ...	....	Kulna, ...	Mucknooa, ...	Calcutta.
3376	Girdharee, ...	40	Bengalee, ...	....	....	....	Bengal.
3277	Geelamun Sircar alias Gulma Sircar, ...	35	Ditto, ...	....	....	....	Dacca.
3290	Goodree, ...	25	Koormee, ...	Son of Dhora, ...	Bhugunutpore near Furyakurantee, ...	Gooah, ...	Sarun.
3296	Guddoo, ...	40	Moslem, ...	....	Keejapoor, ...	Beerbhoom, ...	Beerbhoom.
3302	Gorachan Biswas, ...	...	Kaet, ...	....	Salkatee, ...	Kishnugur, ...	Kishnugur.
3349	Golamee, ...	32	Moslem, ...	Son of Booda Mudar Sahib.			
3367	Guffor, 2nd, ...	50	Ditto, ...	,, Mular Meesh Khan,	....	....	Mysore.
3400	Gunesh, ...	40	....	....	....	....	Bengal.
3401	Goorooa Kyebart, ...	35	Kyebart, ...	....	Near Morshedabad.		
3423	Ghulabun Sircar Jemadar,...	...	....	....	....	....	Bengal.
3444	Gungaram, ...	30	Hindoo, ...	Son of Luchmun Doss,...	Nelinghat, ...	....	Chittoor.

No. in Genl. Register.	Names.	Age.	Caste.	Birth.	Place of Residence.		
					Village.	Pergunna.	District.
3465	Guddoo Baba Jemadar,	60	Moslem,	Nephew of Fukeer Sahib (dead,)	Bangalore,	...	Mysore.
3476	Geedeea,	55	Ditto,	Dukunkee Fukeer Sahib.			
*3679	Son of Gour Doss,	...	Kaet,	...	Bukapore Thanna Islampore Nazirgunge,		Pubna.
3674	Gopee Capalee,	...	Capalee,	...	Nemteah,	Th. Jafurgunge,	Fureedpore.
3676	Gunga Gobind Capalee,	...	Ditto,	...	Teentarmarae,	Ditto,	Ditto.
3677	Gour Mohun Capalee,	...	Ditto,	...	Ditto,	Ditto,	Ditto.
*3742	Goluck (Biswas,)	...	Kaet,	Son of Gorachand (Biswas,)	Burkhapoor,	Islampore Thannah Nazirgunge,	Pubna.
3748	Goomanee (Hoobanee,)	45	Naek,	...	Jalalpore,	Nodha,	Jeypore.
3754	Gaja (Bowrie,)	...	Ditto,	...	Ururka,	...	Jodhpore.
3759	Goorooah Dome,	36	Dome,	...	...	...	Burdwan.
3968	Gooroo,	25	Moslem,	Son of Burra Khan Daera Walla,	Aseepullee,	Bhagepullee,	Mysore.
4001	Ghurroo alias Kurhae,	45	Ditto,	...	Sarygaon,	Unaygaon,	Hydrabad.
4012	Goolamee,	40	Ditto,	...	Mudnoor,	...	Ditto.
4038	Gooman alias Goomanee,	50 or 60	Bengalee,	...	...	...	Bengal.
4039	Goga,	40	Dhoonia,	...	Murkiri,	Nonpur,	Goruckpore.
4076	Gujjooa,	25	Lodhee,	Nephew of Runooa Moonshee,	Beharepore,	Belah,	...
4149	Gobura,	45	Koree,	Son of Deena,	Murnae,	Omree,	Gwalior.

4150	Gunsoondura,	30	Rajpoot,	...	Alumpoora,	Indore,	Indore.
4164	Gopaul Mookerjee,	32	Brahmun,	Son of Oochup Mokerjee,	Shunkerpore,	Buree Bara,	Moorshedabad.
4251	Gunooah,	...	Lodhee,	,, Byjah,	Mateepore,	...	Cawnpore.
4260	Gunesh,	36	Brahmun,	,, Samadhun,	Sikunpore,	...	Ditto.
4264	Goplah,	...	Lodhee,	,, Hurjee,	Residence not mentioned.		
4271	Ghurreeb alias Roshun,	...	...	,, Bichuck,	...	...	...
4287	Guzufur Khan,	26	Moslem,	,, Sherista Khan,	South of Poorwa Ghutolee,	Deoresing,	Hindoo Oude.
4288	Ghazee,	27	Koondegur,	Brother of Emambuksh Koondeegur,	Ulliabad,	Rudowlee,	Oude.
4297	Ghasee,	34	Moslem,	Damad of Goteeah,	Bhutbudah,	...	Kotah.
4298	Gomaneea,	30	Ditto,	Son of Sheikh Chand approver,	Bumorea,	Untaberaeto,	Ditto.
4352	Gunglah,	50	Naek,	,, Bhugwanoo,	Kochawun,	...	Jeypore.
4409	Ghouse,	30 or 40	Tehlee,	,, Mirhae alias Madaree,	Kesureah,	Jaes,	Oude.
4434	Gobind Kotal,	27	Kotal,	...	Kantadree Jorapore,	Thana Gungoreea,	Burdwan.
4435	Goroochurn Bagdee,	50	Bagdee,	Son of Bowanee Bagdee,	Moorgacha,	Thana Poobthal,	Ditto.
4436	Gopal Kotal,	22	Kotal,	,, Rughoonath Kotal,	Burdwan, formerly Ramkishunpore,		Ditto.
4528	Gungaram,	60	Rajpoot,	Adopted of Hunjh Rajpoot,	Ashta,	...	Hydrabad.
4564	Goluck Jung,	55	Chundal,	...	Hatklee,	Ghutapoora,	Pubna.
4565	Goluckpall,	35	Kaet,	Son of Ramsurunpaul or Damoopaul,	Malundha,	Muthora,	Ditto.
4566	Gokulmundee,	35 or 36	Ditto,	,, Oodanundee,	Bhisundee,	Etah,	Mymensing.
4567	Goluck Dee, cousin of Myndee,	25	Ditto,	,, Kaleechurn,	Pokhareea,	Jufirgunge,	Fureedpore.
4568	Gora Chund (Biswas,)	50	Ditto,	...	Delakanudy,	Neelkachy,	Ditto.
4569	Gopee (Biswas,)	35	Ditto,	...	Singasee,	Mithora,	Pubna.

No. in Genl. Register.	Names.	Age.	Cast.	Birth.	Place of Residence. Village.	Pergunna.	District.
4570	Goorjung,......................	40	Chundalee,..	Brother of Jogul Jung,...	Baghulpore,...	Kubnopara, ...	Pubna.
4571	Goorpaul, ...	25 or 30	Kaet, ...	Son of Ramsurunpaul or Damoopaul, ...	Malahmaho,...	Mithora, ...	Ditto.
4572	Goopee Jung, ...	50	Chundal, ...	....	Baghulpore,...	Kubnopara, ...	Ditto.
4573	Gokul Jung, ...	40	Ditto, ...	....	Gureebpore,...	Jafirgunge, ...	Fureedpore.
4574	Gireedhur Dutt Jemadar,...	...	Kaet,.........	....	Benalagnee,...	Mehmoodpore.	Jessore.
4835	Gooroochurn Haldar,.........	40	Malloo,......	Son of Gopee Haldar,...	Kalkapore......	Thana Cosimbazar.	Moorshedabad.
4844	Gobind Bhartee,...............	35	Gosaen, ...	....	Joepul, ...	Howsah, ...	Nizam.
4851	Gumwa, ...	...	Lodhee, ...	Son of Baja,..................	Huttepore, ...	....	Cawnpore.
4852	Gungee (a female),...........	28	Gosaen, ...	Wife of Gobind Bhartee,	Jabul.	Dhasee..........	Hydrabad.
4950	Goolam Hoosain,...............	50	Weaver, ...	....	Bhippora, ...	Nowapar, ...	Goruckpore.
4968	Gobindo Mahante, ...	19	Goalah, ...	....	Pamporah, ...	Rungpore,......	Pooree or S. Cuttack.
4973	Gopeputty, ...	50	Ditto, ...	....	Mauthore, ...	Ditto, ...	Ditto.
4982	Govindotto, ...	45	Ditto, ...	....	Aumedapore,..	Ditto, ...	Ditto.
4983	Ghunghamahante, ...	18	Ditto, ...	Younger Brother of Krisnamahante, ...	Phittoropugoo,	Goroseko,......	Ditto.
4990	Goondiejennah, ...	...	Ditto.				
	H.						
300	Heera	36	Lodhee,......	Son of Ramsing, brother of Jowahir, Son Hurra, ...	Heita Kangro,	Pransote, ...	Etawah.
317	Heerasing alias Mudlall, ...	50	Rajpoot, ...	....	Currah,.........	Currah,.........	Futtehpore.

506	Heera Khan Jemadar, ...	40	Moslem, ...	....	Deogurh Bilara,	....	Odeypore.
528	Hurrsing Rae Jemadar,......	50	Brahmun,...	Son of Pertaub, related to Esuree Jemadar, ...	Akloone, ...	Ateree, ...	Gwalior.
553	Hurreea, ...	25	Rajpoot, ...	Adopted of Feringeea approver, ...	Murnae, ...	Indore, ...	Indore.
574	Hormut Khan alias Hooseyn Khan, ...	60	Moslem, ...	Related to Ruheem Khan,	Ghisnee, ...	Jhansie, ...	Bundelcund.
631	Hingun Khan alias Bheekum,	35	Ditto, ...	Son of Ruheem, ...	Ditto, ...	Ditto, ...	Ditto.
699	Hurreea Jemadar, ...	40	Sooseea, ...	....	Bhugwuntnugur,	....	Jeypore.
738	Hurreesing Jemadar, ...	40	Rajpoot, ...	Adopted of Bukletawarsing,..................	....	....	Kurnool.
784	Hoosain Khan, ...	30	Bheestie, ...	Nephew of Hosaen Khan,..	Futteh, ...	Omrowtee, ...	Hydrabad.
886	Hoosain Khan Jemadar, ...	35	Moslem, ...	Son-in-law of Hoosain Bux Jemadar, ...	Yadapullee, ...	Gillaruck......	Ditto.
1157	Hooreesing alias Boreesing,	23	Sooseea......	Brother of Bukhtawar, ...	Nugur, ...	....	Jeypore.
1716	Huppoo, ...	30	Moslem, ...	,, Tajeea, ...	Bynguna, ...	Seronje, ...	Oude.
1772	Hoosain Sahib Jemadar, ...	40	Ditto, ...	Grand Son of Oosman Khan or Sahib Oodeen,	Sholapore, ...	Carnati Indee,	Arcot or Bombay.
1830	Heera, ...	40	Soosea Naek,	Son of Senjee, ...	Kauthul, ...	....	Jeypore.
1867	Hussun, ...	60	Moslem, ...	Son of Ullabux, ...	Dansura, ...	Arpore,.........	Hydrabad.
1896	Huttoo Kanchanee,...........	...	Ditto, ...	,, Cheynee, related to Peera approver,...	Dhar, ...	....	Gwalior.
1929	Hurlall,........................	40	Lodhee,......	,, Makun, ...	Kotah, ...	....	Kotah.
1961	Hurmook,......................	50	Rajpoot Byse,	,, Gya Daso, ...	Kuchwakhar,..	....	Gwalior.
1997	Hussuna or Daem, ...	40	Moslem, ...	....	....	....	Jeypore.
2016	Heera alias Simbhoo, ...	35	Lodhee, ...	Son of Munnoo, ...	Kaseepore, ...	....	Cawnpore.
2027	Hurpala, ...	...	Ditto, ...	Adopted of Bukut and Son of Nutha, ...	Palooadora, ...	....	Gwalior.
2079	Himmutteea, ...	40	Moslem, ...	Adopted of Ajeeta,.........	Ojein, ...	....	Ditto.
2085	Hurr Sing, ...	...	Rajpoot, ...	Son of Baljeet Subadar,...	....	....	Jeypore.

No. in Genl. Register.	Names.	Age.	Cast.	Birth.	Place of Residence.		
					Village.	Pergunna.	District.
2145	Hoseea, ...	35	Moslem, ...	Brother of Pikheea, ...	Wakoolee, ...	Nachangow,...	Nagpore.
2176	Heeramun, ...	50	Lohar Moslem,	....	Kosarkheree or Gour,	Nabeera or Afgulpore,	Hydrabad.
2188	Hashim, ...	...	Moslem, ...	Son of Motee.			
2344	Hurree Sircar Jemadar,......	65	Hindoo Brahmun	....	....	....	Burdwan.
2383	Hyder Sookteewala Jemadar,	60	Moslem, ...	Son of Bungee Sahib,......	Dour, ...	Koondulwaree or Logaon,	Hydrabad.
2384	Hyder (one eyed,)	60	Ditto, ...	Brother-in-law of Sahib Khan,..............	Gowgaon,......	Gudur, ...	Ditto
2466	Hoosaen Sahib alias Bowla,.	...	Ditto, ...	Brother of Emam Khan No. 2665, ...	Surutgee,......	Surutgee, ...	Goolburga or Masulipatam.
2565	Hoosaenee (stout.)	40	Moslem, ...	Adopted Lall Khan, ...	Purtoar, ...	Rijjapore, ...	Sattarah.
2652	Hoosaenee, ...	...	Ditto, ...	Son of Thoonta Fukeera,	Bullongee, ...	....	Hydrabad.
2821	Hurdalve, ...	30	Meena, ...	....	Cheeplie, ...	Tonk, ...	Tonk.
2825	Heera, ...	50	Naek, ...	....	Lameea, ...	....	Jeypore.
2836	Hookman Lorah,..............	55	Sooseea, ...	....	Pipanwara Hurkurra,	....	Ditto.
2907	Heera (Debareea,)	29	Ditto, ...	....	Jhoonooara, ...	Boondee, ...	Ditto.
2919	Hoonooreyah Jemadar alias Hoonooreyah Hoosain, ...	50	Moslem, ...	Brother of Chabriah Emam, ...	Tinnapully Mundgul Cuddapa,	Byzwara, ...	Masulipatam.
2928	Hurr Naraen.	...	Naek, ...	....	Tanna, ...	Sopur, ...	Boondee.
2957	Husnoo or Hoosaen Khan,...	50	Moslem, ...	....	Nemoleea, ...	Bhydrasa,......	Oude.

3039	Hurra Saen,......................	22	Kaet,.........	Son of Mohun Sing (dead),	Sewur, ...	....	Burdwan.
3042	Hurree Meeteea, 2nd,.........	40	Meeteea, ...	....	Korgaon, ...	....	Ditto.
3171	Hoosaen Khan, ...	20	Moslem, ...	Son of Noor Mahomed Bhithooreea,............	Chowtee, ...	Shikarpore, ...	Mysore.
3192	Hoonoor Sahib, ...	30	Ditto,.........	Sheikh Hoosaen Jemadar,.	Koormogha near Chutmullee, ...	....	Ditto.
3294	Hyder, ...	60	Ditto, ...	Brother-in-law of Kaleechurn, No. 3291,...	Sheopore,......	....	Beerbhoom.
3304	Hurree Doss, ...	35	Kaet,.........	Son of Burree Sircar,......	Ditto, ...	....	Ditto.
3312	Hoonoor Sahib, ...	25	Moslem, ...	,, Jugdeea Jemadar, No. 2941, ...	Cotapilly,......	Cuddapa, ...	Madras.
3376	Hoosainee Neem-walla, ...	...	Ditto, ...	....	....	Arcott, ...	Ditto.
3377	Hoosainee, ...	...	Ditto, ...	Tharanee alias Bodhun or Taradeen,............	Bulondgee, ...	Afzulpore, ...	Hydrabad.
3450	Hoosaen Khan, ...	30	Ditto, ...	....	Koonpulla, ...	....	Nizam.
3451	Hoosaen Khan Kulloowalla,	...	Ditto, ...	....	....	....	Hydrabad.
3456	Hussain Khan Jemadar alias Gungaloo, ...	55	Ditto, ...	....	Resides in a small village near Bublee,		Northern Circars.
3468	Hoosaen Sheikh alias Hoosaen Sahib, ...	31	Ditto, ...	....	Turpurtry, ...	Cuddapah.	
3478	Hoosaen Sahib (Lumba,) ...	50	Ditto, ...	Son of Dekhan ka Fukeer Sahib, ...	Paplee, ...	....	Dekhan.
3485	Hoosaen Sahib alias Gungaloo,..................	22	Ditto, ...	....	Resides in a small village near Bablee, ...	Northern Circars.	
3520	Hoosainee, ...	20	Ditto, ...	....	Davingheera,..	....	Mysore.
3524	Hyder Khan, ...	40	Ditto, ...	....	Koondalee.		
3562	Hoosaen Sahib alias Undah Hoosaen Sahib,......	45	Ditto, ...	Uncle of the late Sheikh Ahmed Jemadar's wife,	9 coss north of Chittoor,	....	Chittoor.
3599	Hemaeuth Sheik, ...	50	Ditto, ...	Son of Sheikh Turbent,...	Hurree Bukitpore,	Jhellingy,......	Moorshedabad.

No. in Genl Register.	Names.	Age	Cast.	Birth.	Place of Residence.		
					Village.	Pergunna.	District.
3606	Heera Bowree, ...	32	Bowrie,......	Son of Bowree, ...	Sabela, ...	Sakoolypore ...	Burdwan.
3631	Hoosaen, ...	60	Moslem, ...	....	Kurchela, ...	Akulkote,......	Bombay.
3634	Himmut Pandy Jemadar,...	...	Pandey, ...	....	Tulah or Munsah,	....	Ganjam.
3653	Hurree Chung, ...	...	Chundal.				
3670	Huranee, Chung's son-in-law,	...	Ditto.				
3698	Hurradhun Chung,............	80	Ditto, ...	Son of Talook Chund Chung, ...	Formerly Kulkupore now Chur Bulrampore,	Birhumpore, Thana Pubna,	Pubna.
3795	Hurruck Roy, ...	31	Rajpoot, ...	,, Ramdeal Roy,...	Koraree, ...	Tajpore, ...	Chupra.
3799	Hoosainee Jemadar, ...	25	Syud, ...	Son of Khoaja Gurmoot Kalla, ...	Hulgee, ...	Afzulpore, ...	Hydrabad.
3827	Hoosaen, ...	45	Moslem, ...	,, Peep Mahatab, ...	Kurhoor, ...	Akulkote.	
3859	Hoosain Shah,.................	32	Ditto, ...	,, Fuqueer Ahmed Jemadar alias Nacta Fuqueer,	Rajapore, ...	....	Masulipatam.
3861	Hoosain Sha, ...	23	Ditto, ...	,, Malik Sha,.........	Bhogul, ...	....	Ditto.
3940	Hoosainee Bhai, (cotton cleaner, ...	60	Ditto, ...	....	Mohaipullee, .	Cuddree, ...	Cuddapa.
3942	Hyder Sahib, ...	25	Ditto, ...	Son of Fuqueera, ...	Village near Kungoor,	Unknown, ...	Ditto.
3944	Hoosaen Meeah, ...	30	Ditto, ...	,, Sheik Hoosaen Bellary Wallah,	Morumpullee,	Bagapullee, ...	Bangalore.
3946	Hoosain Sahib,..................	25	Ditto, ...	,, Bureh Khan Buchewalla, ...	Aseepullee, ...	Ditto, ...	Ditto.

3947	Hoosaina,	25	Ditto,	Adopted son of Jumal Khan,	Koondarpullee,	Ditto,	Ditto.
3975	Hoonoor Sahib Jemadar,	40	Ditto,	Son of Putteeburra Khan,	Kundmarpullee,	Ditto,	Mysore.
3981	Hoosain Kotgeerwalla,	40	Ditto,		Aurungabad,		Hydrabad.
3989	Hoosainee,	28	Ditto,	Adopted of Benarwala Banleea,	Nuldroog,		Dharwar.
4043	Hurdial Rae Jemadar,	60	Rajpoot,	Son of Pursun Raee,	Mahooa,		Goruckpore.
*4097	Hossein,	17	Moslem,	,, Buree Sahib Kuntgoor,	Nainchero-pullee,		Cuddapa.
4063	Hookma Jemadar,	40	Meena,		Kearo,	Kuruckote,	Tejara.
*4120	Hyder Sahib,	50	Moslem,	Son of Abdoollah,	Koregera,	Holee Hunoor.	Nuggur.
4153	Heera Sing alias Nundlal,	40	Rajpoot,		Burwur,		Etawah.
4162	Hurmookh,	35	Ditto,	Son of Koosul,	Bianna,		Bhurtpore.
4171	Hyder Sahib,	50	Moslem,	,, Bukshee Bhae, No. 4170,			Vizagapatam.
4172	Hoosain alias Sheik Hoosainee,	32	Ditto,	,, Bukshee Bhae, No. 4170,			Ditto.
4180	Hoosain alias Tundoo Burree Khan's Hoosain,	50	Ditto,	Adopted of Burreh Khan,			Ditto.
4227	Hirooah 2d,	50	Lodhee,	Son of Kullee,	Behareepore,		Etawah.
4231	Hirooah, 3d,	25	Dhanuk,	,, Tijuna,	Sooreea,		Cawnpore.
4245	Hoosainee,	26	Moslem,	,, Muhetab Chabria approver, brother of Meean and cousin of Mean, son of Nubbhoo,	Nunnah,	Ihitcotah,	Hydrabad.
4293	Huttoor Khan alias Hunoo Khan,	50	Ditto,	,, Bhye Khan,	Ahoree,	Tilloe,	Oude.
4325	Heera,	40	Khunjur,		Kirthonda,		Gwalior.
4410	Hinga,	35	Moslem,		Goujah,	Gondah,	Oude.
4415	Hussun Khan,	20	Ditto,	Son of Burreh Khan,	Kurchunpullee,	Honepullee,	Nuggur.

No. in Genl. Register.	Names.	Age	Caste.	Birth.	Place of Residence.		
					Village.	Pergunna.	District.
4417	Hyder Kaleea,..................	55	Moslem, ...	....	Gorulgudra,...	Honechoonoor,	Nuggur.
4418	Hussun, ...	25	Ditto, ...	Son of Noor Khan,.........	Holee Kuttah,	Sadnoor, ...	Dharwar.
4437	Halodhur Kotal,...............	60	Kotal, ...	....	Nundye, ...	Thana Culna,	Burdwan.
4454	Hyder Sheikh alias Tekooreea, ...	42	Moslem, ...	....	Jawud, ...	Dhurmpore,...	Patna.
4475	Haderaj (ought to be Kadir),	60	Ditto, ...	Nephew of Sumboo Burrea, son of Hoosain Sahib, ...	Golkonda, ...	Cheerapore, ...	Hydrabad.
4486	Hoosainee, ...	35	Jut, ...	Sala of Kadir,..............	Hunjgee, ...	Akulkote,......	Sattarah.
4496	Hussain, ...	25	Moslem, ...	Son of Chupreea Muletab Jemr, ...	Boastee, ...	....	Hydrabad.
4500	Hittoo,...........................	40	....	,, Hilkuttee,...........	Serole, ...	....	Ditto.
4504	Hoosainee, ...	22	Moslem, ...	,, Shabaz Bura Khan,	Nagay, ...	....	Dharwar.
4511	Hoosainee, ...	50	Ditto, ...	,, Noor Khan, ...	Kuleanee,......	....	Hydrabad.
4516	Hussun Sala Teaka Buddya,	60	Ditto, ...	Adopted of Ramadjee Patail, ...	Ousa, ...	....	Ditto.
4519	Hubbea, ...	20	Ditto, ...	Brother of Moheoodeen,...	Moonga, ...	....	Ditto.
4884	Hoosainee, ...	30	Ditto, ...	Nephew of Teglia,.........	Tegol, ...	....	Nizam.
4892	Hussun, ...	40	Ditto, ...	....	Mogurga,......	Akola, ...	Ditto.
4899	Hurgobind,......................	50	Chumar, ...	....	Sekrakote, ...	Oomree, ...	Gwalior.
4901	Hurree Sing, ...	40	Dhoona, ...	Son of Ahmood,............	Modegow, ...	Omree, ...	Ditto.
4933	Heej Sheikh, ...	30	Moslem, ...	Son of Sheikh Dhingoo,...	Fukeer ka Nudda, ...	Putta Hijramee, ...	Mymensing.

	I.						
1973	Imamee,	40	Moslem, ...	Adopted by Ruhman,	Ruttaun,		Indore.
2118	Illahee Buksh,	50	Ditto,				Nagpore.
2237	Islam alias Brahmun,	30	Ditto,	Adopted of Ruheem Khan,	Hurrae,		Nursingpore.
2363	Imam Buksh Jemadar,	35	Ditto,	Son of Khoda Buksh,	Tunroog,	Mundroop, ...	Hydrabad.
2528	Ismael Jemadar,	45	Moslem, ...	,, Nassoo Khan,	Kolesha.	Akulkote,	Hydrabad.
2538	Ismael Koonjra,	55	Ditto,		Hooly Kota,...	Dharwar,	Bombay.
2597	Ismael alias Kala Ismael, ...	...	Ditto,	Son of Ismael Bambarea approver,	Sambhur,	Ulmulla,	Ditto.
2700	Ismael (Karia,)	45	Ditto.	,, Makhmool,	Seya,	Utla,	Ditto.
3869	Inkutta,	48	Weaver, ...		Metpullee, ...	Metpullee, ...	Hydrabad.
4323	Imrit Rae,	...	Koree,	Son of Ramkishun,		Khass,	Etawah.
4481	Imam,	20	Moslem, ...	,, Kala Ismael, approver, dead, ...	Hanoor,	Afzulpore, ...	Hydrabad.
4485	Ismael Nagay Ka,	45	Ditto,	Brother of Emam alias Lingra Hosein and Brother of Imam ka Hoosaen,	Nagae,	Indee,	Dharwar.
4870	Ismael alias Essoo,	40	Ditto,	Adopted of Surwur,	Wastora,	Kullanee,	Nizam.
	J.						
304	Jussa Thakoor,	45	Rajpoot, ...		Lalpore,		Etawah.
527	Jhurree,	26	Brahmun,...	Son of Gour Dada,	Bursallee,		Gwalior.
759	Jykishur,	40	Ditto,	Brother of Danee,	Khujoorea, ...		Bhurtpore.
761	Jussooa,	50	Ditto,	,, Danee,	Ditto,		Ditto.
1161	Jewunneea,	32	Moslem, ...	Son of Mohobut Jemadar,	Sopur,...		Gwalior.
1179	Jewun Sing,	40	Sooseea, ...	,, Hurnath Sing,	Julal,		Jeypore.
1227	Jangullea,	40	Moslem, ...	,, Badul,	Goorum,	Jhalone,	Bundelcund.
1439	Jhurra,	...	Brahmun,...	,, Pearun alias Gunesh,	Bhoreepore,...	Phuphond, ...	Cawnpore.
1471	Jussoo,	40	Sooseea, ...	,, Bhimma Jemadar,	Nugur Mypore,	Oneara,	Jeypore.

No. in Genl. Register.	Names.	Age.	Caste.	Birth.	Place of Residence. Village.	Pergunna.	District.
1519	Judowlee,........................	30	Lohar, ...	Son of Nundlall, ...	Boohunpore,...	....	Gwalior.
1578	Jokee, ...	35	Brahmun,...	,, Sumadhun, ...	Leirapore, ...	Mongulpore,...	Cawnpore.
1728	Juhan Khan, ...	30	Moslem, ...	,, Sherista Khan,......	Ghurtoulee,...	Rudowlee, ...	Oude.
1947	Jysing Rae, ...	50	Rajpoot, ...	....	....	Kuchwaha-dhar, ...	Gawlior.
2033	Jewumieea (Barber)	...	Barber,......	....	Somp, ...	Mekhasronde,	Jeypore.
2163	Joman Jemadar, ...	60	Moslem, ...	Son of Mukhdoom Sahib,	Soorwal, ...	Korah, ...	Hydrabad.
2765	Jyta Jemadar,..................	50	Naek, ...	Brother in law of Moi-doo Jemadar, (dead,)	Oneara or Bunearea,	Diggee, ...	Jeypore.
2896	Jouneea (Lorah), ...	45	Ditto, ...	Son of Sewa, ...	In service at,...	....	Ditto.
2956	Joomun (Guddie), ...	50	Guddie, ...	....	....	Rudowlee, ...	Khass.
3045	Juggoo alias Kala Jugoonath,	50	Chundal, ...	....	Magugaon, ...	....	Burdwan.
3046	Juggoonath,.....................	...	Ditto, ...	Brother of Leloo Jemadar,	Sidureea, ...	....	Ditto.
3047	Jugoo alias Bura Jugoonath,	60	Julleea, ...	....	Dilta Bazar,...	Dilta, ...	Moorshedabad.
3048	Juggernath,.....................	40	Kaet, ...	Nephew of Balee Kaet,...	Ima, ...	Lioree, ...	Ditto.
3050	Jhaboo Jemadar,..............	50	Moslem, ...	....	Gooptepara,...	Kishennugur,.	Bengal.
3057	Jummun, ...	34	Ditto, ...	....	Rajmahal,......	Bhagulpore,...	Bhagulpore.
3177	Jumal Khan Jemadar, ...	40	Ditto, ...	Son of Teepoo Jemal,......	Bablee,.........	....	North. Circars.
3283	Jugmohun Persaud, ...	50	Kaet, ...	....	Ayma, ...	Mungulkote,..	Burdwan.
3352	Jumal Sahib, ...	60	Moslem, ...	Son of Chutput Bura Sahib,	Bangalore, ...	....	Mysore.
3353	Jumal, ...	50	Dome, ...	,, Duleephuffer.			
3477	Julloo, ...	55	Moslem, ...	Brother of Dukun kee Fuqueer Sahib, ...	....	....	Dukhan.

3479	Jindah Khan,	55	Ditto,		Formerly resided near Chaneapilly.		
3498	Julall.	50	Ditto,	Son of Kumal Khan,			Hydrabad
3519	Jumal Khan,	20	Ditto,	,, Noor Khan,	Chotee,		Mysore.
3597	Jubaree Sheikh,	38	Ditto,	,, Sheikh Goolabdee,	Chandpore Gureeah,	Selumpore Balghata,	Moorshedabad.
3636	Jugganath Paundey,	60	Paundey,		Teerla or Munsa,		Ganjam.
3683	Jogginah,	35	Brahmun,		Nirsimpilly,		Rajamundry.
3741	Jyah Chung,	...	Chundal,		Kamarhat,	Thana Najirgunge,	Pubna.
3899	Jewun Khan,	40	Mooltanee,		Suraba,		Khytul.
3902	Jumal Khan,	40	Ditto,		Ditto,		Ditto.
3991	Jullea,	50	Koastee,		Surwar,		Hydrabad.
4098	Jummoo Row,	60	Moslem,	Son-in-law of Emam Bhai,	Yeuktepullee,	Bagapullee,	Bangalore.
4147	Jundah,	32	Kooree,	Son of Nynsookh,	Bindawul,	Sindouse,	Etawah.
4159	Jowahir,	38	Moslem,	,, Kinhur,	Pilooadanda,	Oomree,	Gwalior.
4294	Jankee Raee,	28	Rajpoot,	Cousin of Jodhee Raee approver and Brother-in-law of the late Soobuns Raee Jemadar,	Pursownee,	Muhissee,	Champarun.
4419	Jubboo Bhutiara,	23	Bhutiara,	Son of Kadie,	Bhodeaghore,	Rajmahal,	Rajmahal.
4438	Juggunath Thakoor,	60	Kotal Brahmun		Muhsurgoongree,	Thana Culna,	Burdwan.
4467	Jhussur ka Baba,	50	Moslem,		Kurtha,	Sholapore,	Hydrabad.
4577	Jana Sheikh,	25	Ditto,	Son of Manoolla,	Mugurkote.	Jafirgunge,	Fureedpore.
4578	Joogulsaen,	100	Kaet,	,, Pran Kishen Saen,	Mihmoodpore,	Shizadpore,	Pubna.
4806	Juhaneea,	50	Moslem Muliwattee,	,, Budul,	Midoulee,	Mahlebra,	Koel.
4818	Jooree Sheikh,	24	Moslem,	,, Sheikh Jyfoo.	Lukhpore,		Bancoora.
4846	Juggrah,	16	Gosaen.	,, Danoo Gowlee,	Mubuloor,	Dhandashew...	Nizam.
4898	Juggurnath Thakoor,	80	Brahmun,	Brother of Kumal Thakoor,	Surgureeah,	Culna,	Burdwan.

No. in Genl. Register.	Names.	Age.	Caste.	Birth.	Place of Residence. Village.	Pergunna.	District.
4976	Jollodorojennah, ...	40	Goalah,......	....	Nundapore, ...	Gorobaropilly,	Pooree or S. Cuttack.
	K.						
50	Kallooa alias Pirooa, ...	30	Moslem, ...	Son of Ghasee, ...	Saimramow,...	Roosoolabad,.. (Said to be at Nagpore.)	Cawnpore.
100	Koshalee Jemadar, ...	40	Lodhee, ...	,, Mokund, ...	Maharajpore,..	Roosoolabad,..	Cawnpore.
111	Kohman, ...	40	Ditto, ...	,, Mokund, ...	Ditto, ...	Ditto, ...	Ditto.
198	Khulluck,......................	...	Ditto, ...	,, Muna Lodhee and Nephew of Ghasee, ...	....	....	Gwalior.
360	Koodhyar Khan,...............	35	Behua, ...	Adopted of Ghubboo,......	Umrode, ...	Esagurh, ...	Ditto.
427	Khodabux alias Bhika, ...	40	Moslem, ...	Son of Jowahir, ...	Baugebere, ...	....	Ditto.
495	Khoshala Jemadar,............	45	Soosea Rajpoot,	....	Dutoree, ...	Boondee, ...	Jeypore.
561	Kalee Khan,.....................	30	Moslem, ...	Brother of Nasir,...........	Nagpore, ...	....	Nagpore.
608	Koodroo Bahadoor,............	50	Ditto, ...	Nephew of Kunjee Jemadar, ...	Soojee ka Nugra, ...	Ayah, ...	Koel.
627	Kullooa, ...	30	Ditto, ...	Son of Ruheem or Nawar Khan,..............	Mote (lives in Oude,)	Jhansie, ...	Bundelcund.
698	Khoosal Sing, ...	50	Sooseea, ...	....	Buragow, ...	....	Jeypore.
704	Kishun Sing Jemadar, ...	50	Ditto, ...	Son of Omrea Soosea Thug	Nineale, ...	Oneara,.........	Ditto.
719	Kaleean alias Kalgana, ...	30	Ditto, ...	....	Nugur,.........	....	Ditto.
721	Khoman, ...	60	Ditto, ...	Son of Kurnal Sing, ...	Ditto, ...	Oneara,.........	Ditto.
725	Kishan,..........................	30	Ditto, ...	,, Sawnuth Sing,......	Ditto, ...	....	Ditto.

726	Kullean, ...	60	Ditto, ...	,, Bijjey Sing, ...	Bomunkeree,..	....	Ditto.
729	Kullooa, ...	35	Ditto, ...	Brother of Nathea,.........	Labsorah,......	Naeushabar,...	Ditto.
778	Khoshallee	35	Lodhee, ...	Adopted of Rutteeram, ...	Akote, ...	....	Ellichpore.
890	Kullooa alias Kalee Khan alias Kurreem Khan, ...	40	Moslem, ...	....	Goolburga, ...	Ouchairjee, ...	Hydrabad.
919	Kuleean Sing alias Munsookh, ...	55	Rajpoot, ...	Adopted of Kishnae, ...	Naudair, ...	....	Ditto.
922	Kumode alias Kureema,......	25	Moslem, ...	Son of Mudeh Khan,......	Saunkur, ...	Naraingpore Kundailee,	Bundelcund.
957	Kullooa Jemadar, ...	...	Lohar, ...	,, Nundlall, ...	Boorhanpore,..	....	Gwalior.
997	Kinnurra,........................	30	Ditto, ...	,, Khurgah, ...	Mounsout, ...	....	Etawa.
1076	Kemraj, ...	44	Koomhar,...	,, Durha, ...	Ghoutee, ...	Jhalone, ...	Bundelcund.
1077	Kaley Khan Jemadar, ...	30	Moslem, ...	,, Ajur by adoption,. .	Gorsurae,......	Ditto, ...	Ditto.
1104	Kulwa alias Kaem Khan, ...	25	Ditto, ...	,, Ruheem Khan......	Banda, ...	Khass.	
1115	Khodabux alias Gudumma,	30	Moslem, ...	Adopted of Ruheem, ...	Pungurra, ...	Jhansie, ...	Bundelcund.
1152	Khuluk, ...	30	Khunjur, ...	....	....	Khutamda, ...	Gwalior.
1162	Khoda Buksha, ...	35	Moslem Bursote,	Son of Huttee Rae,.........	Joura, ...	Kotah, ...	Kotah.
1184	Khoshalee Sing,...............	40	Sooseea, ...	,, Hurnath Sing,......	Jular, ...	....	Jeypore.
1247	Khomanee, ...	25	Ditto, ...	,, Himmuttea, ...	Nowla, ...	....	Ditto.
1291	Kullean Sing,..................	40	Ditto, ...	....	Dutooree,......	....	Ditto.
1293	Kalajee, ...	40	Ditto, ...	Son of Nuthee Sing, ...	Ditto, ...	....	Ditto.
1294	Keseea,..........................	45	Ditto, ...	Adopted of Bhopeea, ...	....	Rutlam, ...	Gwalior.
1554	Kaloea,..........................	32	Moslem, ...	Son of Wuzeera,............	Khengode, ...	Rusoolabad,...	Cawnpore.
1611	Khoda Buksh,..................	30	Ditto, ...	,, Suboodeen, ...	Kuloaka Nugra,	....	Mynpooree.
1770	Kalameea Jemadar, ...	...	Ditto, ...	....	Kuroul, ...	....	Hydrabad.
1888	Kaloo, ...	...	Kachnee, ...	,, Nasir Jemadar Kachnee,.........	....	....	Ditto.
1895	Khoman, ...	...	Huttar, Moslem,	Adopted of China Kachnee, ...	....	....	Jeypore.
1901	Khoshal alias Kureena, ...	40	Moslem, ...	,, of Mohobut, ...	....	....	Ditto.

No. in Genl. Register.	Names.	Age.	Caste.	Birth.	Place of Residence. Village.	Pergunna.	District.
1906	Kalee Khan,......................	27	Moslem, ...	Adopted of Hussun Khan and son of Hoormut Khan,......	....	....	Gwalior.
1910	Kadir, ...	20	Ditto, ...	Son of Khyrattee, ...	....	....	Dholepore.
1924	Kullooah,......................	30	Khunjur, ...	....	Guttownda, ...	....	Gwalior.
1938	Kohman, ...	45	Brahmun,...	Son of Birjee, ...	....	....	Ditto.
1942	Khuppoor Khan,..............	50	Moslem, ...	....	Chuteroo-tehree,	Nursingpore,..	Bhopal.
1950	Khurga, ...	60	Chumar, ...	Adopted of Kunhye Jemadar, ...	Khureeah, ...	Kushwahaga,..	Gwalior.
1952	Kaem, ...	50	Moslem, ...	Brother of Sookbuttea, ...	Kunawar,......	Kuchwaka-gura, ...	Ditto.
1969	Kasim, ...	37	Ditto, ...	Son of Bajoo alias Kaem Khan Thug, ...	Kheroueka, ...	Serown, ...	Jhalone.
1970	Khunooa alias Munwur,......	50	Ditto, ...	,, Mungul and Brother of Puncha,	Chirowree, ...	Sirsagunge, ...	Mynpooree.
1987	Kumoodeen Khan,...........	30	Ditto, ...	,, Dulele Mehwatee,..	Lohar, ...	....	Gwalior.
1991	Khooshalla, ...	40	Moslem Mehwa-tee,	....	Soopur,.........	....	Ditto.
2013	Kullean Sing, ...	50	Rajpoot, ...	....	Bhind, ...	....	Ditto.
2014	Kusseea alias Kaseeram or Chidoo, ...	32	Koolee,......	....	Kunkeepore,..	Alumpore, ...	Indore.
2024	Kasee Kirar, ...	...	Rajpoot, ...	Adopted of Bhikka, ...	Dobeereea, ...	....	Hussingabad.
2025	Khodabuksh, ...	60	Moslem, ...	Phoopa of Ameer Khan,...	Owreeah, ...	....	Cawnpore.
2026	Khoman, ...	40	Dhanuk, ...	....	Jugunumpore,	Jhalone, ...	Bundelcund.
2040	Kesureea,......................	40	Moslem, ...	Adopted of Ramzanee, ...	Ditto, ...	Ditto, ...	Ditto.

2063	Kadir,	50	Ditto,	Son of Imamee,	Lulsuria,	Nursingur,	Bhopaul.
2098	Kishna Pinglia,	70	Koonbee,	...	Naudore,	Nachungow,	Hydrabad.
2197	Kulloo,	...	Bheel,	...	Gopaulpore,	...	Jeypore.
2206	Kohman,	...	Sooseea,	Salah of Bhyroo,	Jeypore,	...	Ditto.
2212	Kulean alias Mustaw Shah,	...	Moslem,	...	...	...	Ditto.
2261	Kaloo,	40	Naek,	Son of Mehrab and related to Peera approver,	Ihilae or Koriwas,	...	Ditto.
2262	Kashee, alias Kishna or Kasheea,	40	Sooseea,	,, Tara,	Ihilae,	...	Ditto.
2264	Kohman alias Komjee,	...	Ditto,	...	Malpoora,	...	Ditto.
2265	Khowjabuksh Gobindaz,	...	...	...	Somp,	...	Ditto.
2339	Kureem Alee Khan,	50	Pathan,	Son of Jhow Khan,	Mithaea,	Bullea,	Gazeepore.
2346	Khuruk Baboo Jemadar,	45	Kaet,	...	...	...	Burdwan.
2404	Kullooa, Brother of Bhoora,	40	Brahmun,	Adopted of Subsook Purasur,	...	...	Nagpore.
2456	Kalee Khan,	30	Moslem,	Uncle of Umoe-mean,	Chinchoolee or Koolee Khoor's,	Myudergee or Ulmulla,	Company's Territory Bombay.
2474	Kassim Sahib,	...	Ditto,	Son of Sheikh Emam,	Soorwal,	...	Hydrabad.
2475	Khajah,	...	Ditto,	,, Abdool Nubbee,	Dewarnadgee, or Mohur,	Sorapore Bedur,	Ditto.
2597	Kala Ismael,	35	Ditto,	Son of Ismael Bambareea approver,	Sumbhour,	Ulmulla,	Dharwar.
2654	Kassim Arcottee, Brother of Chabria alias Jubureea,	30	Ditto,	,, Emam Sahib Chabria,	Bilwar or Gour,	Afzulpore,	Hydrabad.
2657	Kalee Sha alias Kaloo,	40	Ditto,	Son of Sheikh Sahib,	Chincoolee,	Ditto,	Ditto.
2698	Kalee Khan,	40	Ditto,	,, Burra Sahib,	Hapurka,	Sholapore,	Ditto.
2703	Khooshala, (Doutful whether arrested or not)	40	Naek,	A relation of Nunda,	Majam or Sama,	Boondee,	Boondee.

No. in Genl. Register.	Names.	Age.	Caste.	Birth.	Place of Residence. Village.	Pergunna.	District.
2717	Kanajee,	60	Naek,	Brother-in-law of Goman, dead,	Majam,	......	Tonk.
2769	Kishna Jemadar,	45	Ditto,	Son of Fuqueer, Brother-in-law of Chumuneea,	Horepoora or Cashire,	Tonk or Tara,	Tonk or Jeypore.
2824	Khoshal (Gwareea.)	50	Naek,	......	Munto,	Kotah,	Kotah.
2894	Kana Jemadar, (Goodeala,)	40	Sooseea,	......	Hurreea,	Mowa,	Jeypore.
2901	Kana,	50	Ditto,	......	Lameea,	Khapras,	Shekawatee.
2925	Kirparam,	32	Naek,	......	Bhundaraj,	Dooseea,	Bhurtpore.
2958	Khoshal,	30	Lodhee,	Son of Nunha,	Behareepore,	......	Dooab.
3052	Kistoo,	32	Dome,	......	Aimah,	Mungulkote,	Bancoora.
3053	Konta,	29	Kaet,	Son of Buddun,	Luppore,	......	Ditto.
3055	Kattick,	39	Haldar,	,, Letay Haldar, transported,	Dhurmpore,	......	Moorshedabad.
3056	Kistoo,	40	Ditto,	......	Ditto,	......	Ditto.
3058	Koondee Ram,	30	Kaet,	......	Kistnagur,	......	Bancoora.
3059	Kalee Churn,	50	Byragee,	......	Ramkistpore,	Soukoleepore,	Seoree.
3060	Kattick,	30	Juleea,	Son of Letay,	Dhurmpore,	......	Moorshedabad.
3061	Khooshal Sheikh,	45	Moslem,	,, Punchoo Sheikh,	Narainpore,	......	Bancoora.
3062	Kalee Churn Jemadar,	50	Choteea,	......	Laldanga,	......	Latour.
3063	Koora,	65	Bowlee,	......	Bygaon,	......	Bancoora.
3064	Kassee Bukshee,	40	Kaet,	......	Chanuck,	Mungleepore,	Burdwan.
3065	Kishun Jemadar, Haldar,	60	Bunneea,	Nephew of Chunder, Haldar,	Kheergaon,	Ajmutsae,	Moorshedabad.
3066	Kamul Mundeel,	50	Chasa,	......	Sewur,	......	Burdwan.
3121	Keenoo Sheik,	45	Moslem,	......	Goree Maree,	......	Moorshedabad.

3143	Kaleechurn Jemadar Mozundar, ...	55	Kaet, ...	......	Laldanga, ...	......	Latour.
3267	Kharoo, ...	30 or 40	Pathan, ...	......	Lodha, ...	Durkhunga, ...	Tirhoot.
3291	Kaleechurn alias Sheik Kalae, ...	35	Moslem, ...	......	Soopur, ...	......	Beerbhoom.
3296	Koodoo, ...	40	Ditto, ...	......	Geejapore, ...	......	Ditto.
3329	Kamuleea, ...	35	Ditto, ...	Son of Chiteral Emam Sahib, ...	Near Cottapilly, ...	Cuddapah, ...	Madras.
3350	Kassim, ...	28	Ditto, ...	,, Mudar Sahib, ...	......	......	Hydrabad.
3360	Kadir Hoosainee, ...	12	Ditto, ...	,, Moosad Khan, ...	Ellore, ...	Ellore, ...	Madras.
3379	Kootbee, ...	...	Ditto, ...	,, Sahib Khan	Bunderkote, ...	Mundroop, ...	Sholapore.
3447	Kala Khan, ...	...	Ditto, ...	,, Emam Bhae, ...	......	......	Hydrabad.
3454	Kalashah, ...	35	Ditto, ...	,, Kalashah, ...	Formerly resided at the Village of Neerolagpilly near Wobadhebur Cheeroo.		Mysore.
3578	Kumaul Dome, ...	40	Dome, ...	......	Formerly Ramkistpore now Chanuck	Ujmootsae Thana Mungulkote Sakooleepore,	Beerbhoom or Burdwan.
3579	Kanchun Doss, ...	60	Byragee, ...	......	Cheergow, ...	Moonoarsae Thanah Keogaon.	Beerbhoom.
3600	Kartick Ghose, ...	25	Chassa, ...	......	Phalga Julga,	Ujmootsal Thanah Mungulkote,	Burdwan.
3602	Kunhae Kuhar, ...	65	Bagdee, ...	......	Mirzapore, ...	Umboo Thanah Umbooah,	Ditto.

No. in Genl. Regis-ter.	Names.	Age.	Caste.	Birth.	Place of Residence.		
					Village.	Perguuna.	District.
3628	Khutal, ...	45	Moslem, ...	....	Sursumbha, ...	Allnud,.........	Hydrabad.
3655	Kumul Chowdree, ...	32	Kaet, ...	Son of Jewun Kishen Chowdry, ...	Ekrah, ...	Sindry,.........	Pubna.
3699	Kissen Mistree, ...	25	Chotur, ...	,, Goroochurn Mistry,	Ghoogodah, ...	Birhampore Thanah Muthoora,	Ditto.
3703	Kokoram Doss, ...	30	Koeburt, ...	,, Kalechurn Doss, ...	Seebpore,......	Berhampore,...	Ditto.
3704	Kissen Chung,.................	25	Chundal, ...	....	....	Thanah Batkeetoo,	Fureedpore.
3752	Kaneea Dhankeea,...........	...	Naek, ...	....	....	Jhirana, ...	Tonk.
3761	Kaloo, ...	40	Sheikh, ...	....	....	....	Burdwan.
3762	Kunhye, ...	35	Dome, ...	....	....	....	Ditto.
3763	Kishun Ghose,.................	55	Kaet, ...	....	....	....	Ditto.
3802	Khan, father of Burun approver, ...	80	Moslem, ...	Son of Hawuljee, ...	Ulmulla, ...	Dharwar, ...	Dharwar.
3825	Kuttal Sha Moollah, ...	40	Ditto, ...	,, Dureakhan Mojawur,...............	Sursimbah, ...	Ulnud, ...	Hydrabad.
3860	Kassim Shah, ...	40	Ditto, ...	,, Mullick Shah, ...	Boogul,.........	....	Mucklateen.
3867	Kadir, ...	28	Ditto, ...	Adopted of Nasir, ...	Waguloara,...	Modhur, ...	Hydrabad.
3871	Khanoo, ...	30	Ditto, ...	Related to Sheikh Hoosaen approver, ...	....	....	Ditto.
3880	Kumoodbeea, ...	30	Mehwatee,..	Son of Dulele Jemadar,...	Midowlee, ...	....	Muttra.
3889	Khooseah, ...	...	Ditto, ...	Brother of Dulla, ...	Aera, ...	....	Ditto.
3964	Kassim (cotton cleaner)......	20	Moslem, ...	Son of Hoosaen Bhae, ...	Mulepullee,...	Cuddree, ...	Cuddapah.
3965	Kaissim (Bellarywalla)	40	Ditto, ...	....	Morumpullee,	Bhagapullee,...	Bangalore.
3987	Khistneeah, ...	40	Mahratta,...	Son of Thukoojee, ...	Dongergow,...	Sohgaon, ...	Hydrabad.

4000	Kullion,	40	Dhangur, ...	...	Saurygaon, ...	Umnargow, ...	Ditto.
4001	Khurroo,	45	Moslem, ...	...	Sare, ...	Bhigaon, ...	Ditto.
4020	Kooslah,	...	Meena, ...	...	Medhwass, ...	...	Tonk.
4047	Kurna,	40	Aheer, ...	...	...	Gooah, ...	Sarun.
4108	Khadir Sahib,	30	Moslem, ...	Son of Mullick Sahib Nurray Gawalla, ...	Kooroo, ...	Hoonhullee, ...	Nugur.
4122	Khyat Syud,	50	Ditto, ...	...	Lived formerly at Sakillah in Bangalore division, now at Bysingee Kolkotta, ...		Cuddapah.
4137	Kaseeram,	25	Koree, ...	Son of Ajeet, ...	Mahgaon, ...	...	Gwalior.
4149	Kobra,	45	Ditto, ...	,, Deena, ...	Murnae, ...	Omree, ...	Ditto.
4150	Khunsoondra,	30	Rajpoot, ...	...	Alumpore, ...	...	Indore.
4155	Kaem,	60	Chonhan, ...	...	Porehoree, ...	Chukurungpore,	Phapoond.
4160	Kullooa,	40	Moslem, ...	Brother of Zalim, ...	Sopur, ...	...	Gwalior.
4177	Khooshala,	45	Moslem Dhoonea,	Adopted of Hoosaen Sahib alias Moheoodeen Goorwur.			
4272	Khoda Buksh alias Sheikh Jhorun,	...	Moslem, ...	Son of Sheikh Rahmut.			
4300	Kullooa alias Kala Khan, ...	50	Ditto, ...	,, Mihrab, ...	Jeeghun, ...	Soopur, ...	Ditto.
4302	Kumla,	40	Ditto, ...	,, Hureea, adopted of Pearjee, hung at Jubulpore, ...	Nagudda, ...	Ditto, ...	Ditto.
4304	Koonjee Beharee alias Beharee,	35	Soonar, ...	,, Jorawun, ...	Prais, ...	Mumair, ...	Patna.
4406	Khoda Buksh,	36	Moslem, ...	,, Mahobut, ...	Jalalood-deen Gunge,	Fyzabad, ...	Oude.
4407	Khoda Buksh,	35	Behna, ...	...	Umdhae, ...	Gourah, ...	Ditto
4430	Kumla,	...	Rajpoot, ...	Son of Dhurmpall, ...	Boorhanpore.	...	Kandeish.
4439	Kumal Haldar,	45	Byragee, formerly Malee,	...	Makoondpore,	Thannah Douletabad,	Moorshedabad.

No. in Genl. Register.	Names.	Age.	Caste.	Birth.	Place of Residence. Village.	Pergunna.	District.
4440	Kartick Dome,	30	Dome,	......	Ramkishunpore,	Upnootsae Thana Shakooleepore,	Beerbhoom.
4441	Kamoo Jooardar,	40	Moslem,	......	Jhaodhuh,	Thana Dhurmpore,	Pubna.
4442	Kisheu Haldar,	32	Malloo,	......	Mudhubpore,	Bebureea,	Rajshaye.
4443	Kumal Thakoor,	60	Kotal Brahmun,	......	Beetra,	Thana Gungoorea,	Burdwan.
4444	Kumal Haldar,	...	Buneea.				
4445	Kalee Churn Sircar,	...	Kaet,	......	Ramchundpore,	Thana Balkishen,	Ditto.
4473	Khooshaleea,	60	Moslem,	Adopted of Butnoor Mean Khan.	Bhutnoor,	Ulmulla,	Dharwar.
4476	Kumal,	50	Ditto,	,, Mukdoom Putail,	Goorlah,	Cheetapore,	Hydrabad.
4498	Kadir, Brother of Hoosainee approver,	40	Ditto,	,, Bahadoor Mean Khan,	Bhutnoor,	Ousa,	Ditto.
4526	Kureem Uthar,	55	Ditto,	......	Hurrosay,	......	Ditto.
4537	Kishnea Sepoy of DaoodJemr.	40	Ditto,	......	Buswunt,	......	Ditto.
4559	Kashee Shah,	50	Sahoo,	Brother of Basee Sahoo,	Joka,	Jafurgunge,	Furreedpore.
4560	Kumul Chowdree Jemadar,	55	Kaet,	Son of Sadasib Chowdree.	Burkhopore,	Ulotopore.	Pubna.
4561	Kashee Sircar,	35	Ditto,	......	Dhukejora,	Jafurgunge,	Furreedpore.
4562	Kala Joogee,	...	Joogee,	......	Pookhureea,	Nichmoodpore,	Jessore.
4579	Khodba,	50 or 60	Jorlaha,	......	Pokhureea Ribrechura,	Mishoorun,	Pubna.

4580	Khodha Ram Jung,...........	40	Chundal, ...	....	Kuchhunpore,	Pugla, ...	Mymensing.
4808	Kheeman, ...	35	Brahmun,...	Son of Pame, ...	Bullore, ...	Mungulpore,..	Cawnpore.
4811	Kassim Teekaree, ...	70	Moslem, ...	....	Indrael, ...	....	Hydrabad.
4815	Kashee Dhanuck, ...	40	Dhanuck,...	....	Hargud, ...	Khilgaon,......	Bhagulpore.
4848	Khooshalgeer,.................	25	Gosaen, ...	....	Bhanee, ...	Toogapore, ...	Nizam.
4849	Kasheepooree,................	58	Ditto, ...	....	Khidgaon, ...	Numbah, ...	Gwalior.
4857	Khungal Haree, ...	35	Haree, ...	....	Kaleahutpore,.	Shahoolapore,	Beerbhoom.
4866	Khwajah,........................	20	Moslem, ...	Son of Noorkhan Bowleea,	Buddial, ...	....	Satara.
4876	Kala Khan Jemadar, ...	25	Ditto, ...	,, Jafur Khan.........	....	....	Ditto.
4887	Kala Moorad.	80	Ditto, ...	Brother to Mukmool,......	Butnoor, ...	Judee.	Sholapore.
4895	Kartick, ...	46	Dome, ...	....	Sardhureea, ...	Gungoreah, ...	Burdwan.
4897	Kumal Thakoor,..............	65	Brahmun,...	Brother of Jugurnath Thakoor Thug, ...	Choto Beatreah,	Culna, ...	Ditto.
4959	Kaliadoto, ...	26	Goalah, ...	....	Nundapore, ...	Gorobaropilly,	Pooree or S. Cuttack.
4962	Koosoomahante Sirdar, ...	40	Ditto, ...	....	Beturojungo,..	Goroseko,......	Ditto.
	L.						
52	Lall Khan alias Purteya,...	30	Moslem, ...	Adopted of Doorgah......	Kuchrond, ...	Jhansee, ...	Bundelcund.
908	Lall Khan, ...	40	Ditto, ...	....	Telingana, ...	....	Hydrabad.
1774	Loonda alias Nubbee Sahib Jemadar, ...	30	Ditto, ...	Brother of Hyder Sahib,	Mugapore, ...	....	Ditto.
2000	Luteefa, ...	40	Dharee, ...	....	....	....	Jeypore.
2001	Lalljooena, ...	42	Meena, ...	....	....	....	Ditto.
2007	Luchmun, ...	40	Chamar, ...	....	Multura, ...	....	Gwalior.
2012	Lushkureea,...................	30	Koolee,......	Son of Nunda,.............	Paharjow, ...	Jhansee, ...	Bundelcund.
2077	Lulseeah, ...	40	Koree, ...	....	Sumoule Kureow,	....	Gwalior.
2102	Luchmun,......................	40	Koormee,...	Brother of Bhaloo, ...	Esapoor, ...	Deolee, ...	Ditto.
2154	Luteef.	55	Moslem, ...	....	Debgowa,......	Ellichpore, ...	Hydrabad.
2168	Lall Sheikh,..................	25	Ditto, ...	Brother of Sheikh Manulla,	Mohjurree, ...	Koorher, ...	Ditto.
2351	Lohooa Jemadar,.............	60	Tantaon, ...	....	....	....	Moorshedabad.
2493	Lall Baboo Bengalee Jemr.,	55	Rajpoot, ...	....	....	....	Ditto.

No. in Genl. Register.	Names.	Age.	Caste.	Birth.	Place of Residence.		
					Village.	Pergunna.	District.
2647	Luteef, ...	...	Moslem, ...	Son of Madour, ...	Dewarudgee,..	Ulmulla, ...	Bombay.
2697	Ladla, ...	...	Ditto.	....	Usterar, ...	Gorapore Bedur,	Hydrabad.
2827	Lalleah, ... (Doubtful whether arrested or not.)	...	Kachee, ...	Adopted of Lala Omeid,...	Bulopa,.........	Etawah, ...	Kotah.
3069	Lethee Dutt Sircar Jemadar,	50	Kaet, ...	....	Thoosara, ...	Mungulkote, .	Burdwan.
3071	Lall, ...	30	Ditto, ...	Son of Buddun,...........	Suppore, ...	....	Bancoora.
3072	Larun, ...	40	Dome, ...	....	Ramkistpore,..	....	Seoree.
3073	Ludeea, ...	25	Kaet, ...	Son of Rampersad Jemadar.	Aihmah, ...	Mungulkot, ...	Burdwan.
3074	Laby Thakoor,..................	45	Brahmun,...	Brother of Ramkissore,...	....	....	Bengal.
3075	Leloo Jemadar, ...	40	Chundal, ...	Son of Kinnoo Mozumdar,	Sidhureea, ...	....	Burdwan.
3076	Lookoor Meeteea, ...	50	Juleea, ...	....	Berageetoolo, .	....	Ditto.
3077	Lukhee Mohaldar, ...	55	Moslem ...	....	Chopgottee, ...	....	Moorshedabad.
3078	Lakool Meeteca,..............	50	Meeteea, ...	Nephew of Seeta Meeteea,	Baraguetolah,.	Mungulkot, ...	Burdwan.
3082	Lubbeea, ...	40	Kaet, ...	Son of Teloke,...............	Kistinugur, ...	Thana Chutna,	Maunbazar.
3114	Lehoo Sheikh,..................	40	Moslem, ...	,, Bunuk Oshomee Sheik, ...	Bancoora,......	....	Bancoora.
3122	Laboo Sheikh,..................	35	Ditto, ...	....	Goree Baree,..	....	Moorshedabad.
3187	Lalla Myan,....................	26	Ditto, ...	Son of Jugduma Jemadarnee, ...	Cotapilly. ...	Cuddapa, ...	Madras.
3318	Lutcheram, ...	80	Brahmun,...	....	Kaseeral, ...	Chittoor, ...	Ditto.
3439	Lukhooram alias Sumbhooram, ...	50	Rajpoot, ...	Son of Begaram,...........	....	....	Hydrabad.
3440	Lullooram, ...	60	Brahmun,...	Son of Beejaram, ...	Kaseeral, ...	Chittoor, ...	Madras.

3442	Luchmun Dass, ...	60	Ditto, ...	....	Nelinghat, ...	Ditto, ...	Hydrabad.
3478	Lubba Hoosain Jemadar, ...	50	Ditto, ...	Son of Dukhun kee Faqueer Sahib............	Publee, ...	....	Otur Sircar.
3509	Luteef, ...	30	Ditto, ...	,, Coddawalla Dada Bhae,...........	....	....	Mysore.
3635	Luchmun Paundey, ...	35	Paundey, ...	....	Teerla or Munsa,	....	Ganjam.
3657	Lucknath Roy Jemadar, ...	...	Brahmun,...	....	Sunkurpara Pookhorrea,	....	Pubna.
3709	Luchun Sein.	40	Kaet, ...	Son of Hardhun Sein, ...	Narjee.	Thana Jafurgunge,	Fureedpore.
3764	Lall Mahomed, ...	36	Sheikh,......	....	....	....	Burdwan
3793	Leeloo, ...	50	Rungrez, ...	Son of Sunahee.	Esoopoora, ...	Mahunda.......	Ghazeepore.
3904	Luteye,..........................	40	Belochee, ...	,, Jowahir, ...	Chandooa, ...	....	Hansie.
4061	Lalsa, ...	35	Kunskur, ...	,, Ramdial.	....	....	Sarun.
4165	Lahooaram Chutoorjee, ...	40	Brahmun,...	,, Davee,...............	Putlee Narainpore,	Nownehal, ...	Burdwan.
4243	Lalooa, ...	50	Moslem, ...	Adopted of Inaeut, ...	....	Sindouse, ...	Gwalior.
4307	Lall Chund,.....................	50	Lodhee, ...	....	Rajamow. ...	Tirwa, ...	Cawnpore.
4311	Laljooa, ...	...	Ditto, ...	Son of Bhujja, ...	Jodeekaporwa,	....	Furruckabad.
4483	Latheef Nadof, ...	35	Moslem, ...	,, Madar, ...	Hymurgah, ...	....	Hydrabad.
4505	Lahreeah,........................	42	Ditto, ...	Adopted of Pathan's Mean Khan,...........	Hijgerah, ...	Afzulpore. ...	Ditto.
4581	Lojun Kurunkar, ...	40	Soonar,......	Son of Jeenoo Kurunkar,	Kopla....	Jufurgunge,...	Fureedpore.
4582	Lochun Chung, ...	20 or 25	Chundal,..	,, Kucheeram Chung,	Ghosee Bumoopore,	Ditto, ...	Ditto
4583	Lochun Soonar, ...	40	Mystree, ...	....	Komarjanee,...	Pugla, ...	Mymensing.
4836	Loharam Chatoorjeea, ...	37	Brahmun,...	,, Debbee Chatoorjee,..............	Narainpore, ...	Thana Poobthal,	Burdwan.
4878	Lalloo Jhareewalla, ...	45	Moslem, ...	Adopted of Burree Khan Jemadar Jhareewalla, ...	Jhowlee, ...	....	Nizam.

No. in Genl Register.	Names.	Age.	Caste.	Birth.	Place of Residence. Village.	Pergunna.	District.
4991	Lookoo Sowein,	...	Goalah,	...	Putturjungo,	Gorosoko,	Pooree or S. Cuttack.
	M.						
303	Moolooa,	45	Brahmun,	Son of Dan by adoption	Daleepragas,	...	Etawah.
327	Maheeput,	42	Rajpoot,	...	Goosteea, Gurheea,	Sindouse,	Ditto.
363	Monohur,	40	Moslem,	Son of Badul,	Ourae,	Esagur,	Gwalior.
519	Madhoo,	30	Brahmun,	Nephew of Esuree,	Uklownee,	Ghatgaon,	Ditto.
521	Mullah,	30	Ditto.	Adopted of Drigpaul,	Ditto,	Ditto,	Ditto.
531	Muddun,	40	Goojur,	...	Punaree,	Sunter,	Bundelcund.
555	Mukunna,	30	Moslem,	Son of Khadhureea,	Namlee,	Ojein,	Gwalior.
588	Munnoo,	65	Ditto,	,, Hussoo,	Rootherpore,	...	Koel.
591	Mudaree,	40	Ditto,	,, Heera and Brother of Eideeb,	Maenuggur,	Aipal,	Ditto.
918	Madhoo,	40	Sooseea,	...	Nugur,	...	Jeypore.
1084	Mudaree,	29	Moslem,	Adopted of Azim,	Rulree,	Jhalone,	Bundelcund.
1134	Mungul,	25	Aheer,	Son of Chuttee Jemadar	...	Gwalior.	Ditto.
1201	Mungleea,	30	Rajpoot,	...	Patun,	Jubulpore,	Ditto.
1212	Makhun,	40	Brahmun,	...	Chutterpore,	...	Chutterpore.
1213	Mugulleea,	30	Moslem,	Nephew of Bahadur Chubaksowar,	Kundalee,	Nursingpore,	Nursingpore.
1223	Meer Khan,	30	Bhistee,	...	...	Jhalone,	Bundelcund.
1266	Maunkeea,	35	Moslem,	Nephew of Bukshoo,	Phool,	Baroda,	Indore.
1280	Mothee Jemadar,	30	Sooseea,	Son of Omed Sing,	Pertabgur,	...	Ditto.

1314	Mudaree (absconded, approver,)......................	27	Moslem, ...	,, Ruhman Khan, ...	Kotehdeh, ...	Rudowlee, ...	Oude.
1559	Mudaree, ...	60	Ditto, ...	Adopted of Ajubut Khan,	Peeprah, ...	....	Rehlee in Raja Heera Sing's Daka.
1617	Mohna,............................	25	Dome Bhat,	Son of Chundeemee, alias Shah Baz,.........	Ullahpore, ...	....	Koel.
1703	Mohbuteea, ...	30	Moslem, ...	Son of Himmuteea,.........	Bhurkheera,...	Arone, ...	Gwalior.
1715	Mulloo alias Mullooa, ...	50	Ditto, ...	....	Ditto, ...	Ditto, ...	Ditto.
1718	Manick, ...	30	Sonar, ...	....	Pattun, ...	Bhilsa, ...	Gwalior.
1724	Muddeh Khan, ...	25	Moslem, ...	Son of Ruhman Khan Jemadar, ...	Kotedee, ...	Rudowlee, ...	Oude.
1759	Meean Khan Jemadar, ...	...	Ditto, ...	....	Dewarnadgee,.	Beejapore, ...	Hydrabad.
1847	Mudaree, ...	40	Ditto, ...	Son of Nehal, ...	Guddoopore,...	Rudowlee, ...	Oude.
1874	Mahmudallee, ...	50	Ditto, ...	....	Bangurkote....	Bangurkote,...	Bombay.
1906	Mohumudda Khan,...........	30	Ditto, ...	....	Bhyswara, ...	....	Gwalior.
1915	Mudaree, ...	30	Lodhee, ...	Son of Mandhata, ...	Duttumpore,...	Derapore,......	Cawnpore.
1926	Moollooa,.........................	35	Brahmun,...	,, Bhugwan Dichit,...	Bhurotote, ...	....	Humeerpore.
1974	Munohwur, ...	32	Aheer, ...	,, Hurree Sing, ...	Khurwa, ...	Jhansie, ...	Bundelcund.
1987	Mohna (an absconded approver)	30	Moslem, ...	,, Muddee and Nephew of Hussunnooa.			
1995	Motee, ...	30	Rajpoot, ...	Brother of Bhowun, ...	Kunchunpore,	....	Dholepore.
2002	Mullooah,.........................	30	Lodhee,......	....	Loharee, ...	Sumter, ...	Bundelcund.
2003	Munnooah, ...	35	Moslem, ...	Adopted of Rambuksh, who was the son of Rudowlee, ...	Guteearae, ...	Jhansie, ...	Ditto.
2020	Muchula, ...	40	Ditto, ...	,, Aman Sirjee,	Chutterpore,...	....	Ditto.
2052	Munsookh Jemadar, ...	40	Brahmun,...	....	Noorae,.........	....	Poona (said to be a Havildar. at Bombay.
2064	Mothee, ...	40	Buneea, ...	....	Lukna, ...	....	Etawah.
2070	Mungulla alias Ameera,......	26	Moslem, ...	Adopted of Lah Khan, ...	Bunchore,......	Raeseyn, ...	Bhopaul.

No. in Genl. Register.	Names.	Age	Caste.	Birth.	Place of Residence. Village.	Pergunna.	District.
2086	Mohummud Beraree,.........	40	Moslem, ...	....	Tuddewaree,...	Beejapore, ...	Bombay.
2093	Malgee, ...	45	Koormee,...	....	Peepulgow, ...	Sanour,.........	Ditto.
2096	Moheeoodeen, ...	60	Moslem, ...	Son of Burra Jemadar alias Burjee,............	Dhuroree,......	....	Nagpore.
2099	Munowur Jemadar,...........	50	Ditto, ...	....	Baundar, ...	Naehingoan,...	Ditto.
2104	Mohomud Ameen, ...	45	Ditto, ...	....	Ranee kee Omrowtee,	....	Hydrabad.
2150	Mukhdoom, ...	60	Ditto, ...	....	Buroreea, ...	Arohee, ...	Nagpore.
2157	Mahtab Khan Nadof.........	40	Ditto, ...	Son of Koorcheera,..	Ellichpore or Koocheerar	Ellichpore, ...	Hydrabad.
2158	Munnoo, ...	35	Ditto, ...	....	Dehgawa,......	Ditto, ...	Ditto.
2170	Mahtab, ...	35	Ditto, ...	Brother of Gholaub, ...	Mobjeree Kheree,	....	Ditto.
*2185	Mohun Sing, ...	30	Rajpoot, ...	Son of Puhar Sing,.........	....	....	Nagpore.
*2183	Motee, ...	40	Jat, ...	....	....	....	Ditto.
2187	Mohubbut, ...	...	Moslem, ...	Son of Khoda Buksh,......	Peela Dhana,..	Dhar, ...	Malwah.
2192	Motee, ...	...	Naek Bheel,	,, Dullah, ...	Midhorajpore,	....	Jeypore.
2219	Motee, ...	...	Moslem, ...	,, Nutha Jemadar,...	....	....	Ditto.
2242	Maundhata, ...	35	Lodhee, ...	Related to Misree, ...	....	....	Cawnpore.
2289	Moheeooddeen, ...	40	Moslem, ...	....	Kundedemee, .	Ilardepeth, ...	Hydrabad.
2290	Morad Khan Jemadar, ...	40	Ditto, ...	Son of Alnf Khan, ...	Jalgow, ...	Iamode, ...	Ditto.
2341	Momen Sheikh, ...	56	Ditto, ...	....	....	....	Burdwan.
2393	Mahomed Sahib,..............	30	Ditto, ...	Son of Meerun Sahib, ...	Golagaon, ...	Akulkote,......	Hydrabad.
2403	Matadeen alias Munsook, ...	50	Brahmun,...	,, Nudeh Brahmun,	....	....	Nagpore.
2406	Malwah alias Khyrah, ...	40	Moslem, ...	,, Badul Khan, ...	Nirmul, ...	....	Hydrabad.

2407	Munsookha,	32	Rajpoot, ...	Adopted of Kishen Doss Brahmin,	Ditto,		Ditto.
2416	Malka,	...	Moslem, ...	Son of Fucqueer Mahomed,	Mooldee,	Ulmulla,	Bombay.
2425	Moolteea,	...			Sangthan, ...	Ditto,	Ditto.
2614	Moheeoddeen,	30	Moslem, ...	Son of Buhleem Burree Khan Jemadar, ...	Chincoolee, ...	Afzulpore, ...	Hydrabad.
2617	Moheeoodeen,	40	Ditto,	,, Kasim,	Bulondgee, ...	Ditto,	Ditto.
2629	Meean alias Ismael,	...	Sheikh,	,, Sheikh Emam, ...	Nagie,	Ulmulla,	Bombay.
2637	Meean,	...	Synd,	,, Ismael Sha,	Goorgundgee,	Ditto,	Ditto.
2682	Mudar,	...	Moslem, ...		Somar,		Hydrabad.
2683	Meean, brother of Kadir, ...	...	Ditto,	Son of Bundegee,	Soorwul or Choteea,		Ditto.
2692	Mullung Sha Fucqueer, ...	...	Ditto,		Dewarudgee, .	Ulmulla,	Bombay.
2764	Motee,	40	Ditto,	Son of Bhowana,	Belatah,	Tonk,	Tonk.
2768	Mungulleea,	25	Ditto,	,, Nanga,	Kashire,	Toordul,	Jeypore.
2797	Motee Byragee,	65	Fucqueer, ...				Muttra.
2799	Mahtab Sing (Hawdunut Hudo,)	...	Naek,		Koondel,	Oneara,	Jeypore.
2843	Motee,	40	Nayk,		Nawajnush, ...	Madhopore, ...	Ditto.
2892	Motee (Utwar,)	30		Son of Hathee,	Bharingpore, .	Mowa,	Ditto.
2900	Mansa Jemadar,	50	Sooseea, ...		Sameea,	Khaprass,	Shekawattee.
2910	Mungulleea (Dherunda,) ...	...	Naek,		Jhooloondee, ..	Bowrie,	Jeypore.
2977	Mowlah,	30	Weaver, ...		Kurhuna,		Goruckpore.
2978	Mahabah,	30	Koormee, ...		Jumna,	Guya,	Behar.
3084	Mathur,	40	Kaet,	Son of Mohun (dead,) ...	Secor,	Munglekote, ..	Burdwan.
3089	Munta,	50	Moslem, ...		Jeeneeadow, ..		Natoor.
3090	Milna,	55	Ditto,		Ditto,		Ditto.
3091	Muddun Jemadar,	25	Juleea,	Father of Muddun,	Sooneea Koree,		Morshedabad.
3092	Mohun,	30	Tantee,	Brother of Sunkur,	Sewur,		Burdwan.
3093	Mungun Sircar,	21	Kaet,	Son of Seeam Sircar,	Tapeara,		Seoree.
3094	Mohun Doss,	...	Brahmun, ...		Nyagaon,	Sakoollee, ...	Ditto.
3132	Miceehoo,	60	Moslem, ...		Souwee Kaee,		Morshedabad.

No. in Genl. Register.	Names.	Age	Caste.	Birth.	Place of Residence. Village.	Pergunna.	District.
3150	Mudar, ...	30	Moslem, ...	....	Chutnullee, ...	Nuggur, ...	Mysore.
3154	Myne, ...	25	Ditto, ...	....	Ditto, ...	Ditto, ...	Ditto.
3196	Mudar Munkerewalla, ...	30	Ditto, ...	....	Kishenpullee,.	....	Arcot.
3222	Moradhun Khan, ...	50	Pathan,......	Son of Kurnoo Khan,......	Peepureea, ...	Kurhoor, ...	Tirhoot.
3259	Mouzun Sircar, ...	60	Kaet,.........	....	....	....	Moorshedabad.
3275	Motee Sircar, ...	44	Bengallee,...	....	Culna, ...	....	Calcutta.
3292	Motun Sheikh, Brother of Kallee Churn, No. 3291, ...	30	Moslem, ...	....	Sopur, ...	....	Beerbhoom.
3299	Mohun, Brother of Mohun,	40	Ditto, ...	....	Gujjapore, ...	....	Ditto.
3303	Mindoo Biswas,..............	...	Kaet,.........	....	Salkatee Kissengur,	....	Nudea.
3307	Mooree Sheikh,..............	30	Moslem, ...	....	Sopur, ...	....	Beerbhoom.
3315	Meeah,..........................	45	Ditto, ...	Son of Bitchpilly Burree Sahib, ...	Keelputtee, ...	Chittoor, ...	Madras.
3327	Mooshkil, 2d, ...	30	Ditto, ...	,, Syud Peer, ...	Cottapilly, ...	Cuddapah, ...	Ditto.
3334	Moosah Khan,.................	70	Ditto, ...	,, Dewul Pataib,...	Ditto, ...	Ditto, ...	Ditto.
3348	Mukdoom, ...	20	Ditto, ...	Adopted of Barreek Rae Hoosain Khan,	Ellore, ...	Ellore, ...	Ditto.
3364	Madar, ...	60	Ditto, ...	Adopted by Saboollah Jemadar alias Cooloonteely, ...	Chinmulla, ...	....	Hydrabad.
3366	Moheeoodeen, 4th,...........	35	Ditto, ...	Son of Surcone, ...	Chittledroog,..	Mysore, ...	Madras.
3368	Mahomed Ibrahim,...........	55	Ditto, ...	....	Bulloudgee,...	....	Hydrabad.
3416	Mohun Pershad, ...	40 or 45	Bengallee.				

3453	Moheeoodeen, ...	45	Moslem, ...	Son of Kala Sha, ...	Neeroolag-pilly,	Cuddapah, ...	Madras.
3472	Mooleearick, ...	50	Ditto, ...	Adopted by Mullaree Meeah Khan.			
3560	Mobarick or Yalekur Mosah Khan ka Mobaruck, ...	50	Ditto, ...	Adopted by Mosah, Brother of Goree Futtie Khan, ...	Dursee, ...	Nellore.	
3568	Meeun Bhaee Dukunee alias Meeah Sahib, ...	60	Ditto, ...	....	Parmullee, ...	....	Mysore.
3598	Moonsad alias Moona, ...	38	Ditto, ...	Son of Joynuddee, ...	Chandpoor Isuriah,	Seelampore, ...	Moorshedabad.
3604	Mohun, (Kotal)	70	Kotal, ...	....	Bhowanee-poor,	....	Burdwan.
3614	Mothoor Haldar, ...	60	Buneea, ...	....	Hat Saramdee.	Thannah Kushda,	Beerbhoom.
3615	Manick, ...	35	Ditto, ...	Son of Surroop, ...	Bagoordee, ...	Ujmotsae, ...	Burdwan.
3640	Mahomed Ally, ...	60	Moslem, ...	....	Vizianagram, .	....	Vizagapatam.
3642	Mahomed Khan, ...	49	Ditto, ...	....	Pettapore, ...	....	Rajamundry.
3680	Meeran Bee (arrested and released—why ?)	47	Ditto, ...	....	Unkapilly, ...	....	Vizagapatam.
3765	Monna alias Munsa, ...	28	Sheikh, ...	Son of Golaubdeen Ollah,	Chaund-pore, Guriah,	Khumra, ...	Moorshedabad.
3766	Mahoena, ...	40	Bowree, ...	....	....	....	Burdwan.
3787	Mulluk Shah, ...	...	Moslem, ...	....	Jungul Eerooa towards Budnoor,	....	Junoomee.
3797	Meean, ...	40	Ditto, ...	Son of Fucqueer, ...	Bullondgee, ...	Bullourgee, ...	Hydrabad.
3823	Meeram Bai Pinjarah, ...	60	Ditto, ...	....	Wurruttee, ...	Bhalkee, ...	Ditto.
3826	Moheeooddeen, ...	45	Ditto, ...	Son of Durreea Moojawur, ...	Sursenbeh, ...	Ullund, ...	Ditto.
3828	Meeah, ...	20	Ditto, ...	" Bambariah Ismael, approver, ...	Sabhud, ...	Ulmulla, ...	Dharwar.

No. in Genl. Register.	Names.	Age	Caste.	Birth.	Place of Residence. Village.	Pergunna.	District.
3868	Molonah, ...	45	Huthur, ...	....	Dhunoora, ...	Moodhur,......	Hydrabad.
3901	Mewashee, ...	...	Moultanee,..	....	Suraba,.........	....	Khytul.
3905	Mudaree, ...	...	Ditto, ...	Son of Jowahir, ...	Ditto, ...	....	Ditto.
3971	Mulluk Sahib, Brother of Hydur Sahib, ...	70	Moslem, ...	....	Useebullee, ...	Behugeepullee	Bangalore.
3995	Mulloo, ...	50	Koolee,......	....	Sindhee, ...	Nandair, ...	Hydrabad.
4023	Mah Sing (Goodeeala)	50	Nayk, ...	Son of Dheera, ...	Ramgurh, ...	....	Ulwur.
4039	Mohna,..........................	25	Gwala, ...	,, Dabun,..............	....	....	Sarun.
4043	Maha Sing, ...	50	Naek Goopalla	....	Ramgud, ...	....	Ulwur.
4049	Mohona, ...	25	Gwala, ...	Son of Deebun, ...	Khorometea,...	Nonowur Dhaka thana	Sarun.
4092	Munta alias Munsa, ...	...	Shepherd,...	,, Cheyna, ...	Futtia,.........	Sunareepore,...	Furruckabad.
4141	Muchla, ...	50	Moslem, ...	,, Bunseeah,............	Peeproullee,...	Etawa, ...	Etawa.
4173	Moheeuddeen Sahib, ...	60	Ditto, ...	....	....	....	Hydrabad.
4184	Mokund, ...	50	Naek, ...	....	Joda,............	....	Patun.
4221	Mungulla, ...	40	Kondee, ...	Son of Koosial, ...	Mohungunge,.	....	Moorshedabad.
4250	Maneeajee, ...	60	Koolee,......	,, Munsajee,...........	Mootulee,......	Kendhar, ...	Hydrabad.
4253	Mohna,..........................	30	Lodhee, ...	Nephew of Mangooa, ...	Bhusar,.........	Thateeah,......	Cawnpore.
4254	Mohuna, ...	25	Ditto, ...	Brother of Nowla, ...	Churkheree,...	Mungulpore,...	Ditto.
4261	Mahraj, ...	25	Ditto.	Son of Gunness, ...	Sindouse, ...	....	Gwalior.
4269	Munsaram, ...	...	Brahmun.				
4276	Mungulleea, ...	...	Weaver Nadoff,	Son of Kasim.			
4289	Morad Buksh, ...	30 or 40	Moslem,...	Brother of Hoosain Bux,...	Syudpore,......	Khundasa Jugdespore,	Oude.

4290	Muhung Fucqueer, ...	35 or 40	Moslem, Fucqueer,	....	Burwah, ...	Jugeer of Tufzul Hooseen Onowlee,	Ditto.
4291	Moullah Buksh, ...	35	Kolar, ...	Son of Sudae, ...	Gopee Sing ka Poorwa,	....	Ditto.
4310	Mukkooa, ...	25	Lodhee, ...	....	Gazeepoorwa,.	Tirwa, ...	Furruckabad.
4320	Maharaj alias Bukshis *Saugor*, ...	35	Ditto, ...	Son of Gunesh, ...	Oojoo, ...	....	Etawah.
4321	Mudaree, ...	40	Weaver, ...	....	Murnae, ...	Oomree, ...	Gwalior.
4330	Meean, ...	40	Moslem, ...	Brother of Hussun and Father of Bajra Fucqueer, ...	Juthi, ...	Shewmaghos,..	Toolookya.
4335	Meeran, ...	20	Ditto, ...	....	Hureehur, ...	Hoolee Hunoor,	Nuggur.
4413	Mungulleea, ...	...	Ditto, ...	Son of Maun, ...	....	....	Seronge.
4422	Mohun, ...	35	Koondee, ...	,, Byjnath, ...	Mohungunge,	Sumthurgunge,	Moorshedabad.
4458	Moheeooddeen, ...	40	Moslem, ...	Adopted of Ayrun walla Meean Bhai, ...	....	Telingana, ...	Hydrabad.
4463	Milkeea, ...	40	Ditto, ...	,, Bowlee walla Noor Khan,	Gosurgaon, ...	Gwalior, ...	Ditto.
4470	Mullung, ...	25	Ditto, ...	,, Boodun approver, ...	Oouchay, ...	....	Dharwar.
4472	Mukdoom, ...	50	Ditto, ...	,, Ruheem Khan	Allund, ...	....	Hydrabad.
4474	Moheeoodeen Dupalakha,...	60	Ditto, ...	Related to Noor Khan, Bowlee walla, ...	Shugurga, ...	Allund, ...	Ditto.
4477	Mukhdoom, ...	60	Ditto, ...	Son of Mudar, ...	Goorlah, ...	Cheetapore, ...	Ditto.
4484	Madar, ...	70	Ditto, ...	Father of Luteef, ...	Humurgah, ...	Afzulpore, ...	Ditto.
4487	Moheeoodeen, ...	60	Ditto, ...	Adopted of Kalay, father of Aproop Khan,	Nagthana, ...	Indore, ...	Dharwar.
4488	Mukhmool, ...	40	Ditto, ...	,, Boodun, ...	Bhutnoor, ...	....	Sattara.
4508	Moheeoodeen, ...	30	Ditto, ...	Son of Boor Allay Fucqueer Mahomed, ...	Elgandhut, ...	....	Hydrabad.

No. in Genl. Register.	Names.	Age.	Caste.	Birth.	Place of Residence.		
					Village.	Pergunna.	District.
4512	Meean, ...	45	Moslem, ...	Son of Noor Khan, ...	Kulleeanee, ...	....	Hydrabad.
4517	Moheeooddeen, ...	60	Ditto, ...	Adopted of Ramadgee Putail, son-in-law of Emam Sahib, ...	Ousa, ...	....	Ditto.
4518	Moheeooddeen 2d, ...	50	Ditto, ...	Son of Moorajee Putail,...	Mohgurga, ...	Ousa, ...	Ditto.
4522	Mudar, ...	50	Ditto, ...	....	Ditto, ...	....	Ditto.
4535	Mirza, ...	70	Ditto, ...	....	Peepulnair, Jageer of Surwar Jung,	....	Ditto.
4541	Mootooja Sheikh, ...	40	Ditto, ...	....	Afzulpore, ...	....	Ditto.
4543	Mulleeah, ...	40	Koree, ...	....	Guttoo, ...	....	Dharwar.
4547	Manick Jowardar, ...	...	Moslem, ...	....	Jhaodah, ...	Thana Dhurmpore	Pubna.
4584	Mahomud Zumma, ...	50	Ditto, ...	....	Waldale or Indevaree,	Pugla, ...	Mymensing.
4585	Mahdoo Biswass, Brother of Goora Chund Biswass,	80	Kaet, ...	....	Salkantee, ...	Balgujjee, ...	Fureedpore.
4586	Munnee Kishimta, ...	45	Sahoo, ...	....	Jhutkeea, ...	Jafurgunge, ...	Ditto.
4841	Maungeer, ...	27	Gosaen, ...	Son of Bhowangeer, ...	Umbulpore, ...	Dhandashew, ..	Nizam.
4845	Mynah Jemadarnee, ...	50	Ditto, ...	Wife of Bhowangeer, ...	Ditto, ...	Ditto, ...	Ditto.
4865	Mudareea, ...	50	Moslem, ...	Father-in-law of Budhoo,	....	....	Gwalior Khass.
4872	Meeyn, ...	20	Ditto, ...	Son of Boburia Ismail, ...	Kolsa, ...	Akulkote, ...	Sattara.
4879	Meean, ...	70	Ditto, ...	Son of Nowlah, ...	Nalwur, ...	Naldroog, ...	Nizam.
4890	Moheeoodeen, ...	55	Ditto, ...	....	Golsar, ...	Indee, ...	Sholapore.
4900	Mungul, ...	60	Brahmun, ...	Son of Dabee, ...	Khukino, ...	....	Gwalior.

4958	Manopole,	21	Goalah, ...		Manopore, ...	Godoseko, ...	Pooree or S. Cuttack.
4974	Mahdopote,	19	Ditto,		Ditto,	Runnapore, ...	Pooree or ditto.
4977	Magoondoto,	32	Ditto,	Brother of Kaliadote No. 6,	Nundapore, ...	Gorobaropilly,	Pooree.
4979	Mhodo Sowein,	19	Ditto,		Pampoora, ...	Manopore, ...	Ditto.
4983	Mhone Mahapatroo Sirdar,	67	Ditto,		Bhittorojungo,	Godoseko, ...	Ditto.
4988	Meechoojennah,	...	Ditto,		Puturjungo, ...	Ditto,	Ditto.
	N.						
520	Nynsookh,	40	Brahmun, ...	Saleh of Esuree Jemadar,	Aklonee,	Ghatka,	Gwalior.
554	Nathoo Ram Jemadar,	60	Moslem, ...	Son of Shadee Chotee, ...	Nawlee,	Ojein,	Ditto.
558	Nathee Khan Jemadar,	50	Ditto,		Hingunghat, ...		Nagpore.
562	Noor Khan Jemadar,	45	Ditto,	Son of Reheree,	Nagpore,		Ditto.
697	Newul Sing,	40	Sooseea, ...	,, Bhyroo,	Paragow,		Jeypore.
701	Nathee Khan,	40	Moslem, ...		Alumgunge, ...		Ditto.
716	Nathee Sing alias Nutheea,	40	Sooseea, ...	Cousin of Omed Sing Jemadar,	Raepore,		Ditto.
768	Noor Khan,	27	Moslem, ...	Son of Aluf Khan,	Hengow,	Akola,	Hydrabad.
1078	Nakesha alias Maun Khan, ...	25	Ditto,	Son of Sunam alias Gunesh,	Moorutta,		Gwalior.
1091	Nathoo,	25	Ditto,	Son of Kenher,	Pillna,		Ditto.
1092	Nuggooa,	28	Ditto,	Adopted son of Punchum, Brother of Dhun Sing,	Nadeekaga, ...	Duteea,	Ditto.
1158	Nunda Sing,	39	Sooseea, ...	Son of Omrae,	Yasoorda,		Jeypore.
1218	Nungoo Jemadar,	32	Barber,	,, Jyram,	Tehree,		Bundelcund.
1253	Nutha alias Nutheea,	30	Moslem, ...	,, Fouj Khan,	Rutlam,		Gwalior.
1285	Nunda,	30	Sooseea, ...	,, Taygeea,	Pertaubgur, ...		Indore.
1689	Nirputeea alias Lall Khan alias Bhoree Khan,	30	Moslem, ...	,, Dhoorga Thug,	Nurnaenow Khenjarree,	Sindouse Rosullabad,	Cawnpore.
1705	Nutha,	30	Ditto,	,, Golaub,	Mankeree, ...	Seronge,	Tonk.

No. in Genl. Register.	Names.	Age.	Caste.	Birth.	Place of Residence.		
					Village.	Pergunna.	District.
1708	Nijabut alias Monowur,......	35	Moslem, ...	Son of Mohubbut, ...	Onha, ...	Seolee, ...	Cawnpore.
1743	Naraen (father of Duseeree approver,)	50	Aheer, ...	,, Buldee,..............	Arowlee, ...	Gosaengunge,	Oude.
1834	Nundlall, ...	36	Sooseea, ...	....	Pora,............	....	Jeypore
1854	Nasir Khan Jemadar,.........	35	Moslem, ...	Son of Shah Budeen Khan,	Sergapore, ...	Narainkhet, ...	Hydrabad.
1878	Nahyojee Telinga alias Nagoo, ...	40	Marhatta,...	....	Monore, ...	Bhokur, ...	Ditto.
1886	Nahis Jee Jagjee, ...	...	Bhat,.........	....	....	....	Jeypore.
1932	Naensookh alias Munsaram,	40	Brahmun,...	....	Nagpore, ...	....	Nagpore.
1958	Naggooa, ...	35	Moslem, ...	Brother-in-law of Sheikh Mungloo Jemr.	Mynpore,......	Jhansie, ...	Bundelcund.
2023	Nooreea, ...	50	Ditto, ...	Adopted of Mohubat, ...	Baroda, ...	Sopur, ...	Gwalior.
2047	Noora, ...	30	Ditto, ...	Son of Bhyroo, ...	Soopur, ...	Ditto, ...	Ditto.
2079	Nasir Jemadar, Chandawalla, ...	...	Ditto, ...	....	....	....	Hydrabad.
2100	Nujeeb alias Sheikh Nujeeb,	60	Ditto, ...	....	Soopur, ...	Nachungow,...	Nagpore.
2129	Nathee Khan, ...	40	Ditto, ...	....	Bareegaon, ...	....	Hydrabad.
2136	Nasir Khan Jemadar alias Nuseer, ...	55	Ditto, ...	....	Hinghunghat,	....	Nagpore.
2164	Noor Mahomed Jemadar, ...	50	Ditto, ...	Son of Rajee Mahomed,...	Sindouse, ...	Nachingow, ...	Ditto.
2180	Noor Mahomed Jemadar, ...	30	Ditto, ...	,, Raz Mahomed, ...	Deheegow, ...	Mangrole, ...	Hydrabad.
2195	Nundlall, ...	...	Bheel, ...	,, Talim Bheel, ...	Gopaulpore, ..	....	Jeypore.
2266	Nursing, ...	...	Bolae, ...	....	Sabha or Jutwara,	....	Ditto.
2267	Nynia, ...	...	Sooseea, ...	Brother of Peearjee Jemr.,	Dawur,.........	....	Ditto.
2268	Nynsookh, ...	...	Ditto, ...	....	Bhopy, ...	....	Ditto.

2281	Noor Khan Jemadar, ...	40	Moslem, ...	Son of Sahib Khan, ...	Nurkonda, ...	....	Hydrabad.
2282	Nubbee Sahib (Jurreewalla.)	30	Ditto, ...	....	Goorgundgee,	Ulmulla, ...	Bombay.
2283	Nasir Jemadar alias Chunda-ka-Nasir, ...	40	Ditto, ...	Son of Shahbadeen Khan,	Makunkurga, .	Koondulwurree,	Ditto.
2285	Nawab, ...	50	Ditto, ...	Saleh of Dowlut Khan Jemadar, ...	Kousallee, ...	Nijora, ...	Hydrabad.
2361	Nowbut, ...	24	Ditto, ...	....	Cheynpore, ...	Andee, ...	Chupra.
2621	Nussib Khan, ...	25	Ditto, ...	Son of Emam Khan,......	Hoorgee Khoord or Hygerah,	Ulmulla, ...	Bombay or Hydrabad.
2622	Noor Khan.....................	25	Ditto, ...	,, Emam Ladheea,...	Howulgee, ...	Ditto.	Dharwar.
2625	Nubbee Shaw,..................	30	Ditto, ...	Chuka Muck's Jharee Meean Khan, ...	Joree the 2d,..	Afzulpore, ...	Sholapore.
2638	Noora, ...	...	Ditto, ...	Son of Sheikh Emam, ...	Holgee,.........	Ulmulla, ...	Dharwar.
2685	Noor Khan (Nandnee walla,)	60	Ditto, ...	,, Emam Sahib Bawolee walla, ...	Lutchen, ...	Satarah, ...	Bombay.
2754	Nanjee,........................	30	Nayek, ...	,, Simbhoo Mehera,	Busmangaon,..	Boondee, ...	Jeypore.
2790	Newulleea (Ghuttara.)	...	Sooseea, ...	,, Poora, ...	Torah, ...	Esurdah, ...	Ditto.
2795	Nunda,.........................	...	Ditto, ...	,, Bhopa, ...	Balapoora, ...	Oneeara, ...	Ditto.
2830	Nunda (Sorah.)	...	Ditto, ...	,, Toolseea...........	Lives in a village inhabited by fishermen.		
2886	Nunda (Noor Hote,)	...	Ditto, ...	,, Kesura, ...	Choroo, ...	Rampoor, ...	Jeypore.
2887	Nugga Jemadar (Mergut,)	...	Ditto, ...	,, Maun, ...	Nugger, ...	Oneeara, ...	Ditto.
2890	Neola Ghuttura,..............	40	Ditto, ...	,, Poora,...............	Daby, ...	Chatsoo, ...	Ditto.
2924	Nubbee, ...	35	Moslem, ...	,, Alla Buksh, ...	Lonee, ...	Ulmulla, ...	Sattara.
2931	Nunga,........................	...	Sooseea, ...	....	Rowujna, ...	Madhopore, ...	Jeypore.
2963	Nuthee Khan,.................	40	Mehwattee,.	....	Beeja, ...	Fyzabad, ...	Oude.
2981	Nurkoo, ...	30	Dome, ...	Brother of Munsa and son of Kalee Khan,...	....	....	Dacca.
2991	Nanneh Khan,.................	...	Moslem, ...	Son of Ahmed Khan Jemadar, ...	Joogwul, ...	Bynwara, ...	Masulipatam.
3095	Nuffer, ...	40	Bowrie,......	,, Seeam Bowrie,......	Ragaon, ...	....	Bancoora.
3096	Nandkour, ...	25	Kaet,.........	,, Goolam Doss Jemr.,	Tapesurra, ...	....	Seoree.
3115	Nehal Sheikh, ...	30	Moslem, ...	,, Mowen,...............	Narainpore, ...	....	Bancoora.

No. in Genl. Register.	Names.	Age.	Caste.	Birth.	Place of Residence.		
					Village.	Pergunna.	District.
3165	Nutha, ...	...	Moslem, ...	Son of Emam Sahib Hoolkee, ...	Chutnullee, ...	Nugger, ...	Mysore.
3182	Noor Khan, ...	70	Ditto, ...	,, Burree Khan, ...	Laichan, ...	...	Sattara.
3213	Noonoon Rae alias Shewuk Rae, ...	40	Rajpoot, ...	,, Jrig Rae, ...	Khurnemo Chupra,	Munjhar, ...	Goruckpore.
3215	Nehal, ...	40	Sheikh, ...	,, Ally, ...	Peeprae, ...	...	Ditto.
3218	Nowhur, ...	30	Rajpoot, ...	,, Hirra Rae, ...	Somaee, ...	Doognee, ...	Ditto.
3244	Nizzam, ...	40	Moslem, ...	,, Golam Meer Khan,	...	Dhurmpore, ...	Purnea.
3417	Niddhee Ram, ...	60	Kaeth, ...	...	...	...	Moorshedabad.
3488	Noor Khan, ...	50	Moslem, ...	,, Abdoolla Bhai, ...	Mahomedabad,	Cuddapa, ...	Madras.
3493	Nizam Sahib, ...	58	Ditto, ...	,, Lukra Kalee Khan,	Parugdolee, ...	Ditto, ...	Ditto.
3510	Neyka alias Hoosaineea, ...	25	Ditto, ...	...	...	...	Hydrabad.
3581	Nuffer Nundun Jemadar, ...	40	Buneea, ...	Son of Ropa, ...	Formerly Jagessur Giddhir,	Ujmootsal Thanna Mungulkote,	Burdwan.
3582	Nunkowree, ...	25	Dome, ...	...	Bamantabpore,	Sahakleepore,	Beerbhoom.
3608	Nuffer Kotal, ...	50	Kotal, ...	...	Narkoolbaree,	Bhurtpore, ...	Ditto.
3619	Nuffer Mullah, ...	35	Chassa, ...	Son of Gooroochurn, ...	Koorma, ...	Thana Mungulkote,	Burdwan.
3625	Nujema, ...	60	Mewattee, ..	...	Aiya, ...	Julesur, ...	Muttra.
3630	Nussoo, ...	40	Moslem, ...	Son of Hoosain Sha Dora,	Sirsumbha, ...	Allund, ...	Hydrabad.
3659	Neetae Coond, ...	...	Kaet, ...	...	...	...	Pubna.
3714	Neilmony Chung, ...	32	Chundal, ...	...	Near Kuduntalee,	Atteah, ...	Mymensing.

3715	Neobeen Toe.	...	Tellee, ...	....	....	... .	Pubna.
3737	Nukkee Sukdar, ...	40	Moslem, ...	....	Dantoo,.........	Brahimpore,...	Ditto.
3768	Nubboo Thakoor, ...	25	Brahmun,...	....	Punalee Bazar,	....	Burdwan.
3778	Nubboo Thakoor's Brother,	30	Ditto, ...	....	Ditto, ...	....	Ditto.
3821	Noor Khan, ...	70	Moslem, ...	Son of Emam Sahib Nadnee walla, ...	Ashta, ...	Nuldroog, ...	Hydrabad.
3832	Noor Khan,....................	40	Ditto, ...	Son of Baboo, ...	Sapoor,.........	Afzulpore, ...	Ditto.
3858	Noor Mahomed alias Noordee Shah,...........	33	Ditto, ...	Son of Fucqueer Homed alias Nucktee Fucqueer, ...	Yerullee, ...	....	Masulipatam.
3862	Nasir Mahomed, ...	35	Ditto, ...	,, Nasir Mahomed, ...	Agrarum,......	....	Ditto.
3973	Nunha Bhai Jemadar, ...	30	Ditto, ...	,, Puttee Burree Khan, ...	Koondmarpullee,	Bhageepillee,..	Mysore.
3974	Nunha 2nd, ...	16	Ditto, ...	Brother of Furreed, ...	....	....	Ditto.
4002	Nurseea, ...	50	Kolee, ...	....	Jharee, ...	Umnagam, ...	Hydrabad.
4052	Naraish, ...	45	Aheer, ...	Son of Tubukool, ...	Mutteea, ...	....	Sarun.
4054	Nuckchaid, ...	25	Hujam,......	....	Beeteea, ...	Mujhooa, ...	Ditto.
4158	Nunnay (approver, absconded), ...	50	Moslem, ...	....	Nungla, ...	Dholepore, ...	Dholepore.
4163	Niamut Khan,..................	50	Ditto, ...	....	Chetta, ...	Bara,...........	Sarun.
4256	Nowajee, ...	...	Lodhee, ...	Son of Moonah, ...	Onah, ...	....	Cawnpore.
4262	Nukseea, ...	25	Ditto, ...	,, Purumsookh, ...	Hutyanugra,...	Luckna, ...	Gwalior.
4270	Nuckched alias Nuthoo Khan,....................	...	Moslem, ...	....	....	....	Chupra.
4292	Nishan,..........................	40	Ditto, ...	Son of Roshim Khan, ...	Mahoobygunge,	Tandah, ...	Oude.
4299	Nutha alias Nathea alias Nathoo (a fugitive, approver, ...	45	Ditto, ...	,, Peetha, ...	Jhujjur or Modhopore.		
4412	Nathoo Rae,....................	50	Rajpoot, ...	,, Rugoonath Rae, ...	Deranjah,......	Nowareea, ...	Goruckpore.
4446	Narain Kotal.	22	Kotal, ...	....	Kafoolah, ...	Kunoe, ...	Burdwan.
4460	Nunha Kaloo, ...	40	Moslem, ...	Son of Allahay Khan, ...	Boregaon,......	....	Hydrabad.
4495	Nubbee Moorud walla, Brother of Meean Bhai,	60	Ditto, ...	Cousin of Meean Bhai, ...	Katora,.........	....	Ditto.

No. in Genl. Register.	Names.	Age.	Caste.	Birth.	Place of Residence. Village.	Pergunna.	District.
4513	Noor Khan Jemadar, ...	40	Moslem, ...	Father of Hoosain and Meean, ...	Kutteeana.		
4529	Newaz, cousin of Allahooddeen, approver, ...	30	Ditto, ...	Son of Zara, ...	Chincholee. ...	....	Sattara.
4533	Nooreeah nephew of Jumal Khan, ...	12	Ditto, ...	Son of Bootee Peer Khan, son of Jumal Khan's sister.	Hoolgee, ...	....	Dhar.
4539	Nursinga Putail Sepahee, ...	70	Mahratta,...	Sipahie Buhleem Burra Khan Ka, ...	Mookhair, ...	....	Hydrabad.
4587	Neelmun Jung, ...	60	Chundal, ...	....	Hathkoolee,...	Nazirgunge,...	Pubna.
4588	Neyn Nunda Surin,.........	40 or 45	Kaet, ...	Son of Odda Nundee,......	Bosundah, ...	Pugla, ...	Mymensing.
4590	Nundoo Joarwar, ...	30	Ditto, ...	,, Bucharam Joarwar,	Burkhapore,...	Khuthopara,...	Pubna.
4591	Nursing Dutt,..................	...	Ditto, ...	....	Banagnee, ...	Inchmoodpore,	Jessore.
4824	Narain,..........................	...	Kotal, ...	Son of Rughonath Kotal,	Gapooleeah,...	Cutwah, ...	Burdwan.
4825	Nussir,..........................	32	Dome, ...	,, Goosae Dome, ...	Mungulpore,..	Kopore, ...	Beerbhoom.
4858	Netae Haldar alias Chakur Haldar, ...	25	Buneea, ...	Son-in-law of Kishtoo Haldar, ...	Belgaon, ...	Mowleeshur,...	Ditto.
4867	Noor Khan,......................	45	Moslem, ...	Adopted of Dewgoleeah,	Munglore, ...	....	Sattara.
4880	Nubbee, ...	60	Ditto, ...	Son of Nowla,..............	Nalwur, ...	Nuldroog, ...	Nizam.
4893	Nunjalee, ...	50	Bengalee,...	....	Mooreea, ...	Binsur,.........	Goruckpore.
4903	Nuksoo alias Budloo, ...	34	Rajpoot, ...	Son of Bussunt Rajpoot,	Rannee, ...	Hono, ...	Gwalior.
4905	Nundlall, ...	30	Goojur	....	Bhandaree, ...	Tehree,.........	Bundelcund.
4949	Neyka, ...	35	Jolah, ...	Son of Goolam Hoosain,	Bhippooa,......	Naroopore, ...	Goruckpore.
4956	Nokadee Noodee, ...	33	Goalah,......	....	Manopore, ...	Godoseko, ...	Pooree or S. Cuttack.

4961	Naronodotto,	19	Ditto,		Anundapore,...	Rumapore, ...	Pooree.
4964	Netirjennah,	38	Ditto,		Bettorojungo.	Godoseko, ...	Ditto.
4973	Nhiddeepote,	22	Ditto,		Manopore, ...	Rumapore, ...	Ditto.
4975	Nunmoodah,	64	Ditto,		Nundapore, ...	Gorobaropilly,	Ditto.
	O.						
435	Omrow,	25	Brahmun,...	Son of Nowae and Brother of Mutholee,	Bhumwie, ...	Deoree or Cheynpore, Barree,	Bhopaul.
706	Oorjee,	40	Sooseea, ...	Son of Newul Sing,	Lanehowia, ...	Naeshehur, ...	Jeypore.
1157	Orsing,	23	Ditto,	" Bhareka and Brother of Buktawur Sing,	Nuggur,	Oneeara,	Ditto.
1185	Ooheyee alias Oodeea,	35	Ditto,	Brother of Buktawur	Inerda,		Ditto.
1336	Oomah,	30	Lodhee, ...		Bethoor,		Cawnpore.
1345	Oodhooah,	32	Sooseea, ...	Brother of Chimmee,	Drigeh		Jeypore.
1354	Omrow,	25	Moslem, ...	Son of Ramzan,	Deodee Hindoo Sing,	Lucknow,	Oude.
1357	Omrow Sing Thakoor,	30	Rajpoot, ...	" Aman Sing.	Dabahee,	Jhansee,	Jhansee.
1763	Oosman Khan Jemadar,	40	Moslem, ...	" Ramzan Khan,	Sanoor,		Mysore.
1811	Omeid,	...	Surwur, ...	" Gooman who was hung at Rutlam,	Rutlam,	Kanthut,	Indore.
1812	Onkar alias Oonkaria,	40	Naek,		Ditto,		Indore.
2174	Oosman Khan Kunjur,	45	Moslem, ...		Kulansy,	Hoorah,	Hydrabad.
2207	Omma 2nd,	...	Ditto,	Son of Bhoweea Jemadar,	Kanthut,		Indore.
2208	Odda,	...	Sooseea, ...				Ditto.
2235	Omrow,	29	Kunjur, ...		Kuchwahadar,		Gwalior.
*2269	Omla,	...	Sooseea, ...		Hurdigaon, ...		Tonk.
*2358	Omur Sheikh,	45	Moslem, ...		18 coss N. E	from Dhurbunga,	Mozufferpore.
2521	Ottalia,	34	Ditto,	Son of Emam Sahib.	Oorahee,	Mirgoollee, ...	Dharwar.
2758	Omeida,	70	Naek,		Oneara.	Diggee,	Jeypore.
2781	Omeida, (Kharroo)	65	Ditto,	Son of Odda,	Akoorah,	Oneeara,	Ditto.

No. in Genl. Register.	Names.	Age.	Caste.	Birth.	Place of Residence. Village.	Pergunna.	District.
3146	Omeid, ...	...	Moslem, ...	Son of Peearjee, (Pr.) ...	Datonah, ...	....	Tonk.
3717	Otoo Sheikh, ...	25	Ditto, ...	....	Narainpore, ...	Thana Jaffirgunge,	Pubna.
3718	Orjun Pramanick, ...	55	Chandal, ...	....	Kamarganee, ..	Atteeah, ...	Ditto.
3836	Oghee Moheeooddeen, ...	40	Moslem, ...	....	Dholegeer, ...	Mundroo,......	Hydrabad.
4154	Omaida, ...	40	Lodhee, ...	....	Bughie, ...	....	Gwalior.
4314	Onkaria, ...	35	Naek, ...	....	Bureear, ...	Mundsore, ...	Jeypore.
4620	Ootul Sah, ...	45	Sahoo, ...	....	Futtehpore, ...	Pugla, ...	Mymensing.
4919	Omeida Jemadar, ...	25	Naek, ...	Son of Doolla,...............	Hindawun, ...	Beeana,.........	Jeypore.
	P.						
289	Pursadooa,......................	40 or 45	Brahmun,.	Adopted of Durgpaul Subadar, ...	Bhagwuntgur,	....	Jeypore.
359	Poonooah,.......................	40	Tehwur, ...	....	Umowdah, ...	Esagurh, ...	Gwalior.
384	Punchum (some say he is dead,)	...	Moslem, ...	,, Kanray,..............	Banwara, ...	....	Ditto.
565	Peer Buksh,.....................	40	Ditto, ...	Son of Moolloa and Brother of the wife of Hyatt approver, ...	Burkhara,......	Rhagoghur, ...	Ditto.
910	Paunday alias Hinder, ...	40	Brahmun,...	,, Bhugwan, ...	Omrowtee, ...	Rajungaon, ...	Hydrabad.
932	Puharee, ...	40	Gond, ...	....	Undheeara, ...	Sheenagur, ...	Nursingpore.
1109	Puharee, ...	35	Moslem, ...	Son of Talib, ...	Khanpore, ...	....	Cawnpore.
1231	Peerooa alias Peer Buksha,	16	Ditto, ...	Adopted of Nijabut approver, ...	Naranpore, ...	Jhalone, ...	Bundelcund.

1284	Peeareea, ...	26	Sooseea, ...	Son of Tajeea, ...	Pertabgur, ...	....	Indore.
1315	Peer Khan Jemadar, ...	20	Moslem, ...	,, Ruhman, ...	Kotadeh, ...	Rudowlee, ...	Lucknow.
1426	Pumma, ...	25	Aheer, ...	....	Muderpore, ...	....	Furruckabad.
1434	Purumsookh, ...	40	Ditto, ...	Brother-in-law of Nynsookh, ...	Pholuree, ...	....	Mynpoorie.
1919	Peerooa alias Peer Mahomed,	20	Moslem, ...	Son of Fyjoo, ...	Souhsoura, ...	Ghogunee, ...	Cawnpore.
1943	Puharee, ...	...	Lodhee, ...	,, Budda Jemadar, ...	....	....	Gwalior.
1951	Poonooa Jemadar, ...	40	Chumar, ...	Adopted of Kunhye Jemr.,	Khureea, ...	Kuchwadhur,..	Ditto.
1953	Poonooa 2nd, ...	27	Brahmun,...	Son of Chottee Pattuck,...	....	Ditto, ...	Ditto.
1965	Phoolsa, ...	28	Rajpoot, ...	,, Bhooree, ...	Kheeroo, ...	Ditto, ...	Ditto.
1977	Purumsookh or Phitta, ...	35	Moslem, ...	,, Bodhoo, ...	Mhohee, ...	Jhansie, ...	Bundelcund.
1978	Peer Khan, ...	...	Ditto.				
1994	Punchum (a prison breaker from Jubulpore,)	35	Naek, Barber,	Son of Gopaul, ...	Dhurmpore,...	Secundra,......	Cawnpore.
1995	Pearee Lall (absconded from Jubulpore,)	40	Kaet, ...	,, Mudun Sing, ...	Girdhurpore,..	Bhagnee, ...	Ditto.
2004	Phooladee, ...	35	Moslem, ...	,, Noor Khan, ...	Kiroor, ...	Chundelee, ...	Gwalior.
2042	Peera, ...	40	Ditto, ...	,, Sadho, ...	Sopah, ...	....	Ditto.
2048	Peer Buksh (Hindoostan,)...	35	Ditto, ...	Adopted Son of Ramzanee,	....	....	Nagpore.
2074	Pisooa, ...	50	Ditto, ...	,, Imamee,...	....	....	Gwalior.
2082	Puckhooa, ...	30	Pearree, ...	Brother of Bhujja, ...	Jugmunpore,..	Jhalone, ...	Bundelcund.
2084	Punchum, ...	30	Lodhee, ...	....	Loharee, ...	Sumpther, ...	Ditto.
2116	Peerun, ...	25	Moslem, ...	Son of Bola Mahomed, ...	Kujlesur, ...	Nachungow,...	Nagpore.
2189	Peer Khan, ...	...	Ditto, ...	....	....	....	Jeypore.
2218	Peyma, ...	...	Naek, Sooseea,	Brother of Laloo, ...	....	....	Ditto.
2223	Peyma, ...	...	Moslem, ...	Son of Dewa, brother of Fuckeera, ...	Doogurie,......	Boondee, ...	Kotah.
2276	Peerbhooa, ...	40	Koormee, ...	....	Munday, ...	Nadair, ...	Hydrabad.
2279	Puhar Sing, ...	55	Rajpoot, ...	....	....	....	Poonah.
2352	Peko Jemadar, ...	70	Moslem, Tantooa,	....	Bhugwangolah,	....	Moorshedabad.
2453	Patail Sahib, ...	...	Moslem, ...	Son of Purtulla Emam Sahib, ...	Jhouree Koond	Afzulpore, ...	Hydrabad.

No. in Genl. Register.	Names.	Age.	Caste.	Birth.	Place of Residence. Village.	Pergunna.	District.
2458	Punnoo, ...	...	Sooseea, ...	Son of Dyaram and son-in-law of Moha Sing Jemr. ...	Duniar,.........	Newur, ...	Jeypore.
2776	Pusshee Sing, ...	35	Chamar, ...	....	Boondee, ...	Boondee, ...	Rajpootana.
2955	Puthan Bunneea,...............	35	Bunneea, ...	....	Honamangunge,	Tulloe, ...	Oude.
3099	Poodoo, ...	30	Kaet,.........	Son of Punchoo Sircar, ...	Ausgow Juddai thana,	Gope Ghoo,...	Burdwan.
3256	Poorooa, ...	35	Koebuthur,.	....	....	Dhurmpore,...	Moorshedabad.
3309	Puddoolochun,..................	59	Kaet,.........	....	Soopur,.........	....	Beerbhoom.
3452	Peer Khan, ...	35	Moslem, ...	....	Kodhee Koonda,	....	Mysore.
3483	Papunna alias Papeea,.........	50	Hindoo, ...	....	In the vicinity of Chargul and Satagaon.		
3501	Pahar Khan, ...	35	Moslem, ...	....	Gopee Koonda,	....	Mysore.
3873	Peer Khan, ...	50	Ditto, ...	Son of Eenat Khan, ...	....	Candal,.........	Hydrabad.
3907	Peer Khan, ...	25	Bhuggurreea.	....	Chandooa,......	....	Hansee.
4055	Pattehwat alias Mujjehwat,..	30	Aheer, ...	....	Muljhona, ...	....	Sarun.
4140	Puddala, ...	26	Moslem, ...	Son of Jummaet,...........	Lushkur, ...	....	Gwalior.
4145	Purshaud,.......................	30	Brahmun,...	Adopted of Drigpaul, ...	Bhugwuntgur,	....	Jeypore.
4183	Peima, ...	40	Naek, ...	Brother-in-law of Rambuksh, ...	Doorjunapore,.	....	Jhujjur.
4225	Poosooa, ...	26	Lodhee,......	Adopted of Attmaram, ...	Akberpore, ...	....	Cawnpore
4244	Paun Khan,......................	32	Moslem, ...	,, Gorya, ...	Hurdonee,......	Jhansee, ...	Burdwan.
4257	Purmoolah, ...	...	Lodhee, ...	Son of Bhuggee, ...	....	....	Cawnpore.

*4319	Peera,	36	Moslem, ...	Adopted of Bhowun,	Sindouse,		Etawah.
4391	Paroo,	25	Naek,	Son of Paroo,			Rajpootana.
4392	Poosa,	30	Ditto,				Bogur.
*4318	Phoolseya,	40	Kooree,		Rowlee,		Gwalior.
4405	Pullooa,	35	Mollee,	Son of Rooha,	Raeputhee, ...	Khundhasa, ...	Oude.
4423	Puddoo Doss,	32	Byragee, ...	,, Kobur Doss,	Kurchowlee,...	Allypore,	Beerbhoom.
4464	Padsha,	50	Puthan,	,, Makat Khan,	Gosurgaon, ...	Akulkote,	Sattara.
4465	Pinjarree-ka-Enam,	40	Moslem, ...	Brother of Sansee Bhai...	Boregaon, ...		Hydrabad.
4469	Pattaleeah Burreh Khan, Noor Khan,	40	Ditto,		Moodda Noor,		Dharwar.
4493	Peer Khan, Khaloo of Sheikh Daood, approver, and Phoopa of Meean Bhai,	50	Ditto,		Kukenmulla,..	Sorapora,	Hydrabad.
4527	Powladee, nephew of Abohund Meean Khan,	50	Ditto,	Adopted of Lungra Hoosain,	Apchunda, ...		Ditto.
4592	Pidroo Dur,	40	Kaet,		Zikwa,	Teekeea,	Furreedpore.
4593	Peetmur Chung,	40	Chundal, ...		Burreechura,..	Mehtowra, ...	Pubna.
4594	PundutChung alias Papoosah.	50	Ditto,		Near Utra, ...	Ditto,	Ditto.
4823	Pershaud alias Rampershad Sonee,	60	Souree,		Checherone,...	Konwurgunge,	Bhagulpore.
4869	Pijjoo Sheikh,	21	Moslem, ...		Ghaheegunge,	Radnadhee, ...	Moorshedabad.
4871	Pholad,	50	Mahratta,...	Adopted of Abchunda Meyn Khan,			Hydrabad.
4904	Peerbuksha,	50	Moslem, ...		Burhara,		Etawah.
4955	Pooreejenna,	36	Goalah,		Manopore, ...	Godeseko, ...	Pooree or S. Cuttack.
4269	Pinde Kopote,	60	Ditto,		Goparopore,...	Runnapore, ...	Pooree or ditto.
4978	Pooneechodotto,	26	Ditto,	Brother of Kalliadotto and Mogoondotto, ...	Nundapore, ...	Gobaropilly,...	Ditto ditto.
4980	Porosopote,	64	Ditto,		Goparopore,...	Manopore, ...	Ditto ditto.
4993	Pooreedah,	...	Ditto,		Puturjunge,...	Gorosoko, ...	Pooree or S. Cuttack.

No. in Genl. Register.	Names.	Age.	Caste.	Birth.	Place of Residence. Village.	Pergunna.	District.
	R.						
45	Roshun Khan,..................	40	Moslem, ...	Son of Khoman approver,	....	....	Jounpore.
108	Rambux, ...	30	Lodhee, ...	,, Ramkishen, ...	Katha, ...	Russolabad, ...	Cawnpore.
239	Rumma Dhawakul, ...	...	Ditto, ...	....	Bahareepore,..	....	Furruckabad.
357	Rae Sing,.......................	43	Brahmun,...	Son of Zorowur,...........	Kurmetee, ...	Esagur,.........	Gwalior.
695	Roopla,..........................	40	Nayk, Sooseea,	,, Simbhoo, ...	Pholadpore Sewah, ...	Kotah, ...	Jeypore.
706	Rodhye, ...	40	Ditto ditto,..	,, Newul, ...	Luchoora,......	Naia,...........	Ditto.
788	Ruhmut Khan, ...	60	Moslem, ...	....	Bunuj, ...	Ellichpore, ...	Hydrabad.
925	Ram Sing, ...	30	Goojur,......	....	Kurreylee, ...	....	Nursingpore.
1151	Rambux, ...	25	Kolee, ...	Adopted of Maharaj Patuck Jemadar, ...	Jugoree, ...	Kuthounda,...	Gwalior.
1157	Roree Sing alias Rogee, ...	40	Sooseea, ...	Son of Peearjee, ...	Nuggur, ...	Oneara,.........	Jeypore.
1273	Ramzaneea, ...	60	Moslem. ...	Adopted of Mohbuteea,...	Peepurda Kurwar,	Moorlee, ...	Ojein.
1701	Ramkishen, ...	50	Lodhee, ...	Father of Rambuksh,......	Khajooa, ...	Phuphond, ...	Gwalior.
1709	Ruhmut, ...	40	Moslem, ...	Uncle of Zoolfukur approver, ...	Onha, ...	Seolee, ...	Cawnpore.
1722	Roostum, ...	40	Ditto, ...	....	Achardee, ...	....	Bhopaul.
1746	Roshun Khan,..................	65	Pathan,......	Son of Poorun Khan,......	Simgora, ...	....	Oude.
1821	Ramsing, ...	...	Sooseea, ...	....	Sobargaon, ...	Juhurgaon, ...	Odeypore.
1890	Rusool Khan alias Rambux,	...	Moslem, ...	Son of Kooshal Kanchnee,	Khatulwar, ...	....	Malwa.
1972	Rahmoo, ...	44	Ditto, ...	Adopted of Sahoo, ...	....	....	Gawlior.
					In the service of Colonel Joseph Secunder.		
2022	Rateaba, ...	60	Dhare, ...	....	Khasrode, ...	Ojeyn, ...	Gwalior.

2152	Roostum,	35	Moslem,	Son of Sheikh Asruf,	Ojeytee,	Gorha,	Hydrabad.
2227	Ramzanee,	...	Ditto,	,, Godur,	....	....	Jeypore.
2580	Rajee Sahib,	50	Ditto,	....	Sourlongee,	Dharwar,	Bombay.
2731	Ramla,	25	Nayk,	Son of Dheera,	Sohelia or Poondeh-lia,	Naithur,	Jeypore.
2740	Rajoo Jemadar,	40	Ditto,	,, Futteh and Brother-in-law of Omeid Jemadar and Brother of Buksha Jemadar Thabullia,	Nyndwah,	Boondee,	Boondee.
2811	Roopla Alsea,	30	Sooseea,	....	Khumdewunt,	Newae,	Jeypore.
2863	Roopa Jemadar,	56	Ditto,	....	Laneea or Khapraso near Duk-tumnogurh,	Sumur,	Shekawattee.
2871	Rooreea,	50	Bhuteeara,	Son of Roopoo,	Serain—a great accessary of Thugs in service at Bhurtpore.		
2878	Rambuksha,	...	Sooseea,	....	Benotah,	Newae,	Jeypore.
2904	Radha Kishen,	...	Ditto,	Son of Bhyroon,	....	....	Ditto.
2930	Ram Sing,	...	Ditto,	....	Peepulda,	Jalyia,	Ditto.
2989	Rujah,	...	Moslem,	Son of Sheikh Ahmed Jemadar,	Joogul,	Byzwara,	Masulipatam.
3103	Ramkishtoo,	40	Barber,	....	He lives in a village near Moorshedabad near the Byrabbee River.		
3104	Roshun Sheikh Jemadar,	50	Moslem,	....	Girreea Chopghat-tee,	....	Moorshedabad.
3111	Ram Soondur,	...	Chasa,	Son of Tuwokool Mo-zundar,	Sewur,	Mungulkote,	Burdwan.
3253	Roshun,	50	Moslem,	Father-in-law of Noor-oodeen,	Bustee Gu-reea Chop-ghattee,	....	Moorshedabad.

No. in Genl. Regis-ter.	Names.	Age.	Caste.	Birth.	Place of Residence.		
					Village.	Pergunna.	District.
3271	Ramjewun, ...	40	Kaet,.........	....	Kulna, Banks Kuttooa, 20 coss from Bhagruttee.		
3274	Ramdial Pershaud,...........	50	Bengallee,...	....	Kulna, ...	Mukunwa, ...	Calcutta.
3279	Ram Bhunjum,...............	40 or 45	Ditto,......	....	Kutwa, ...	....	Bengal.
3281	Ramdutt, ...	50	Ditto, ...	....	....	....	Ditto.
3282	Ruheem Oodeen,...............	40	Moslem, ...	....	....	....	Ditto.
3482	Rama, ...	55	Hindoo.				
3583	Rejoo, ...	22	Dome, ...	Son-in-law of Soobul Dome, ...	Formerly Ramkishen-pore, now Aimapo-rah,	Ujmootsae, Thana Sakoolee-pore Mun-gulkote,	Burdwan.
3585	Ram Mohun Sing, ...	40	Kaet,.........	....	Coorgaon,......	Ujmootsal, Thana Sakoolee-pore,	Beerbhoom.
3592	Ram Haldar, ...	44	Euneea, ...	Son of Kasim Haldar, ...	Formerly Cheergaon now Belga-on,	Monoorsal, Thana Koegaon Burroa.	Ditto.
3662	Ramnedhee Thakoor,.........	...	Brahmun,...	....	Kajeerbagh,...	Hurrampore,	Furreedpore.
3672	Radhoo Raree,..................	...	Ditto, ...	....	Panowur, ...	Thana Batkah,	Ditto.
3678	Ram Sing, ...	28	Paundey, ...	Nephew of Luchmun Pandy, ...	....	Ganjam, ...	Ganjam.

3721	Raj Chunder Mitre, ...	32	Brahmun,...	Son of Akool Mitre, ...	Formerly Seebpore now Kapass Kandee,	Brichinpore Muthora,	Pubna.
3722	Rajnarain Mistree, ...	38	Chotur,......	Son of Gopee Mistree, ...	Ghoogooduh formerly Ockhalee,	Brehampora, Mithoura,	Ditto.
3723	Rajchunder Doss, ...	30	Kaet, ...	....	Khalkholah,...	Thana Batkeea,	Furreedpore.
3724	Ruttun Ghose Jemadar,......	53	Ditto, ...	....	Khagooteea,...	Thana Atteea,	Mymensing.
3725	Rubbee Doss Chung,.........	40	Chundal, ...	....	....	....	Furreedpore.
3770	Rampershaud the fair, alias Parshauda, ...	40 or 42	Dome, ...	....	Khurgaon, ...	....	Burdwan.
3771	Ram Mohun 1st,...............	31	Byragee, ...	Father-in-law of Gopaul,	Ditto, ...	....	Ditto.
3772	Ram Mohun 2nd, ...	35	Brahmun,...	....	Ditto, ...	....	Ditto.
3773	Ram Mohun 3rd, ...	40	Tewur, ...	....	Ditto, ...	....	Ditto.
3849	Rajah, ...	40	Moslem, ...	Son of Gooroo Bhai, ...	Unulyah, ...	Nelingah,......	Hydrabad.
3852	Rostum, ...	20	Ditto, ...	„ Hussun Khan approver,...........	Bundarkote,...	....	Sholapore.
4014	Rajeh Mahomed of Ahmed (doubtful whether arrested or not ?).........	60	Ditto, ...	„ Babun Sahib, ...	Gour, ...	Afzulpore, ...	Hydrabad.
4022	Raroo Gaeea, ...	...	Meena, ...	....	Shekawattee,..	....	Shekawattee.
4128	Runjeeta, ...	30	Khungur,...	....	Kaise, ...	Kuchwahagur,	Gwalior.
4134	Ramchund, ...	40	Koree, ...	....	Murora, ...	Sumthur, ...	Sumthur.
4175	Rusool,.........................	60	Nadof, ...	....	....	....	Mysore.
4239	Ramoo Rae, ...	19 or 20	Rajpoot,...	Son of Rambuccus Raee,	Booraha near Sooseeghat,	....	Sarun.
4277	Rujub (absconded, approver,)	24	Moslem, ...	Adopted of Bhyram, ...	Kotedeh, ...	Rudowlee, ...	Oude.

No. in Genl. Register.	Names.	Age	Caste.	Birth.	Place of Residence. Village.	Pergunna.	District.
4295	Ramzan Khan, ...	90	Moslem, ...	Son of Musund Khan Puthan....................	Daioreea, ...	Joginnee, ...	Goruckpore.
4337	Ramlall, ...	...	Aheer, ...	Son of Purusram, ...	Mynpoorie, ...	....	Mynpoorie.
4447	Roop Bagdee, ...	30	Bagdee,......	Brother Surroop Bagdee,	Nuggur, ...	Keogaon, ...	Beerbhoom.
4448	Radhanath, ...	...	Buneea, ...	....	Babladee, ...	Mungulkote,...	Burdwan.
4449	Ramjewun Thakoor, ...	25	Brahmun,...	....	....	....	Calcutta.
4595	Ramdolall, ...	25	Kaet,.........	....	Unegow, ...	Manickgunge,	Furreedpore.
4596	Rubbee Doss Chung 1st, ...	50	Chundal, ...	Nephew of Jotaram Jung,	Birwaghattee,.	Nowabgunge,.	Ditto.
4597	Rubbee Doss Chung 2nd, ...	60	Ditto, ...	....	Bureehurra. ...	Metowra, ...	Pubna.
4598	Rughoonath Jung, ...	35	Ditto, ...	Son of Teloke Jung, ...	Bunachur Kalapore,	Jafurgunge, ...	Furreedpore.
4599	Ramdhun Jung, ...	60	Ditto, ...	....	Hatkoolee, ...	Nazirgunge,...	Pubna.
4600	Ramdhun Chund, ...	40	Kaet, ...	....	Sutorael, ...	Pugla, ...	Mymensing.
4601	Ramdhun Biswas, ...	60	Ditto, ...	....	Raepore, ...	Nazirgunge,...	Pubna.
4602	Rajmohun Soom,..............	40	Ditto, ...	Son of Joorachund Soom,	Olael, ...	Pugla, ...	Mymensing.
4603	Ramdhun Joaburdar, ...	25	Ditto, ...	,, Radhun Jwarder,...	Burkhapore,...	Khetoopore,...	Pubna.
4604	Ramcoomar Mujowadar, ...	60	Ditto, ...	....	Benagnee, ...	Mihundpore, ..	Jessore.
4605	Ramcoomar Mujowadar, ...	30	Ditto, ...	Son of Kunhye Mujowadar, ...	Butkhapore,...	Kheetoopara,..	Ditto.
4606	Rungoo Bunwaree,...........	60	Brahmun,...	....	Ditto, ...	Ditto, ...	Ditto.
4607	Runjoo Sheikh, ...	40	Moslem, ...	....	Kunchunpore,	Pugla, ...	Mymensing.
4850	Rampooree, ...	40	Gosaen, ...	....	Bhorgum,......	Ambah, ...	Nizam.
4875	Rajun Mooltanee, ...	...	Moslem, ...	....	Wastora, ...	Soropore, ...	Ditto.
4894	Roop Bagdee, ...	45	Bagdee, ...	....	Majeergaon,...	Mantashur, ...	Burdwan.
4902	Ramchund, ...	30	Lohar, ...	Son of Saljee Doobey, ...	Mudnee, ...	....	Gwalior.
4943	Ruttun Sheikh, ...	35	Moslem, ...	....	Koondee, ...	Dhurmpore,...	Pubna.

4957	Rhadhapoty, ...	45	Goalah, ...	....	Mathore, ...	Goroseko,......	Pooree or S. Cuttack.
4960	Ragodah, ...	25	Ditto, ...	....	Nundapore, ...	Gorobaropilly,	Ditto.
	S.						
37	Sookha (said to be dead), ...	60	Lodhee, ...	Father of Rambuksh,......	Kutha, ...	Rusoolabad, ...	Cawnpore.
93	Sookhooa,......................	30	Ditto, ...	Adopted of Alumgur,......	Kaseepore, ...	Sewlee,.........	Ditto.
226	Seethala 2nd, alias Persaud,	30	Ditto, ...	Son of Munsookh, ...	Behareepore,...	Belah.	Furreedpore.
261	Sookah,........................	32	Rajpoot, ...	....	Kyrooah, ...	Jhansie, ...	Bundelcund.
265	Seogee,........................	40	Sooseea, ...	....	....	....	Jeypore.
288	Sirrawun,......................	32	Lodhee, ...	Son of Odey, ...	Ramugee,......	Phuphond, ...	Cawnpore.
325	Soorjun Jemadar, ...	40	Aheer, ...	,, Bhikka,...............	Sindouse, ...	....	Etawah.
343	Soomair, ...	30	Koormee, ...	,, Poonood, ...	Calpee, ...	Humeerpore, ..	Bundelcund.
433	Sirrawun,......................	50	Brahmun,...	,, Jeswunt, ...	Bumahee,......	Deoree,.........	Bhopaul.
502	Simbhoo Jemadar, ...	60	Rajpoot, ...	....	Dongerpore,...	....	Odeypore.
504	Seolall Jemadar, ...	40	Sooseea, ...	Son-in-law of Ramlas and brother of Omeid,	Ditto, ...	....	Ditto.
549	Soondur alias Sewdeen, ...	40	Brahmun,...	Son of Mohun Havildar,	Gouthee, ...	Jhalone, ...	Bundelcund.
563	Sheikh Natheea, ...	50	Moslem, ...	,, Doolgee, ...	....	....	Nagpore.
587	Sunnoo, ...	50	Ditto, ...	,, KalehKhan and brother of Munnoo,...	Bamsha, ...	Aipah, ...	Allygurh.
677	Sheikh Lall,.....................	...	....	....	Jaes.	....	Lucknow.
710	Sawun Sing,....................	40	Sooseea, ...	....	Bujjorah, ...	....	Jeypore.
717	Sooklall, ...	40	Ditto, ...	Brother of Bhyroo,.........	Nugur, ...	Saipore, ...	Ojein.
722	Sawuth Sing, ...	60	Ditto, ...	....	Sawla, ...	Charsoo, ...	Jeypore.
765	Sobhan Khan, ...	50	Moslem, ...	Son of Aluf Khan, ...	Akulkote,......	....	Hydrabad.
771	Saddee Khan Jemadar, ...	40	Bohee, ...	,, Roostum, ...	Mangrole,......	....	Ditto.
852	Sheikh Kalee, ...	42	Muneear, ...	,, Abdool Kadir, ...	Kuluckghur, ..	....	Ditto.
883	Sha Sahib Jemadar, ...	40	Moslem, ...	Son of Baba Jemadar,......	Yaidpully, ...	....	Ditto.
1111	Sooltan Khan,..................	40	Ditto, ...	,, Ghazee, Brother of Omur Khan approver,...........	....	Bareilly, ...	Rohilcund.

No. in Genl. Register	Names.	Age	Caste.	Birth.	Place of Residence.		
					Village.	Pergunna.	District.
1286	Shewleea,........................	30	Sooseea, ...	Adopted of Komar Sing,	Pertabgur, ...	....	Indore.
1287	Sewa, ...	40	Ditto, ...	,, Omeid, ...	Ditto, ...	....	Ditto.
1542	Shumshera, ...	30	Moslem, ...	Son of Shafee,..............	Daenugger, ...	Hatras,.........	Koel.
1627	Simbhoo Jemadar, ...	45	Ditto, ...	....	Sopur, ...	....	Gwalior.
1628	Sewbukus, ...	40	Sooseea, ...	....	Ditto, ...	....	Ditto.
1630	Soobhaneea,.....................	40	Dheer, ...	....	Ootura,.........	Omroutee, ...	Hydrabad.
1632	Sadhee Khan, ...	50	Moslem, ...	Son of Badul Khan, ...	Utounjah,......	Khunrasa,......	Oude.
1638	Santhawun, ...	30	Rajpoot, ...	,, Gopaul,..............	Bulun ka Nawada,	Oonah, ...	Mynpoorie.
1644	Sawla, ...	30	Lodhee, ...	....	Bithoor, ...	....	Cawnpore.
1659	Sooltan Khan,..................	30	Moslem, ...	....	Korha, ...	Omroutee, ...	Ditto.
1665	Seeteea alias Soobaram,......	40	Sooseea, ...	....	Matcherree or Pertabgur,	....	Indore.
1666	Saddee Sing, ...	50	Ditto, ...	....	Rutlam, ...	Shahpore,......	Ditto.
1667	Simbhoo, ...	30	Ditto, ...	Son of Bhyroo, ...	Isurdha, ...	....	Jeypore.
1668	Sulga, ...	35	....	,, Surdar, ...	Jhular, ...	....	Ditto.
1676	Seuruttunna alias Nunda, ...	30	Gureereea,..	,, Khurpaie,...........	Sindouse, ...	....	Etawah.
1683	Sahib Raee, ...	35	Kachee, ...	,, Bindooa, ...	Jhalone, ...	....	Bundelcund.
1719	Sabit, ...	50	Moslem Facqueer,	....	Buchya, ...	Bhilsa, ...	Gwalior.
1760	Sona Khan Jemadar, ...	70	Moslem, ...	Son of Roorda Hussain Khan, ...	Utmorah, Sorapore Bedur,	Sorapore Bedur,	Hydrabad.
1804	Sahib Khan alias Sahib Ulla,	35	Ditto, ...	....	Sopur, ...	Khasrode,......	Gwalior.

1805	Sirdar, ...	32	Moghul, ...	Son of Namder Beg, ...	Kahar, ...	Lucknow,......	Oude.
1806	Shumshere, ...	40	Moslem, ...	....	Baroda,.........	....	Baroda.
1808	Sewla alias Ranjoe, ...	45	Sooseea, ...	....	Diggee Nalpee,	....	Jeypore.
1859	Sahib Khan,.....................	40	Moslem, ...	„ Kallee Meean or Abdoollah, ...	....	....	Hydrabad.
1878	Soonwajee, ...	...	....	....	Manoor, ...	....	Ditto.
1920	Sumbhooa, ...	25	Lodhee, ...	Son of Rumma, ...	Antha, ...	Seolee, ...	Cawnpore.
1922	Shere Khan, ...	34	Moslem, ...	„ Bhooree Khan Jemadar, ...	....	....	Bhurtpore.
1947	Sajourah, ...	40	Ditto, ...	....	Soopur, ...	....	Gwalior.
2035	Shunkura, ...	30	Lodhee, ...	Adopted son of Bhugwan,	Buraira, ...	Sindouse, ...	Etawah.
2089	Syud Allee, ...	30	Moslem, ...	Related to Shere Khan,...	Omroutee, ...	....	Hydrabad.
2108	Syud Emam, ...	50	Ditto, ...	....	Wakolee, ...	Nadgaon, ...	Ditto.
2130	Shumshere, ...	45	Ditto, ...	....	Boregaon,......	....	Ditto.
2132	Sahiba,..........................	40	Pathan, ...	Son of Moheeoodeen,......	Goorgund-gee Malkunda,	Ulmulla Telingana,	Bombay.
2148	Sheik Bheekee.	40	Moslem, ...	....	Barowna, ...	Araee, ...	Nagpore.
2187	Simbhoo, ...	35	Lohar, ...	....	Tillee, ...	Mungrolee, ...	Hydrabad.
2205	Serola, ...	...	Sooseea, ...	Brother of Surroop, ...	....	....	Jeypore.
2215	Sewa, ...	...	Ditto, ...	Son of Odda, ...	Onhearra,......	....	Ditto.
2229	Sirdir, ...	...	Moslem, ...	Son of Nuthee Jemadar and Brother of Motee absconded approver,...	....	....	Ditto.
2247	Sewlall Jemadar, ...	...	Sooseea, ...	Son of Peearjee, ...	Durreeaud, ...	....	Ditto.
2271	Shunker, ...	...	Ditto, ...	....	Jeypore, ...	....	Ditto.
2272	Soorut Ram, ...	...	Ditto, ...	....	Sampore, ...	Madhopore, ...	Ditto.
2348	Sewdial Baboo Jemadar, ...	50	Brahmun,...	....	....	....	Burdwan.
2370	Sahib Khan Jemadar	35	Moslem, ...	....	Omjeegurh, ...	Kalurka, ...	Mysore or Hydrabad.
2371	Sahib Khan Jemadar,.........	60	Ditto, ...	Son of Sheikh Nubbee, ...	Borwalla Bunarkota,	Sholapore, ...	Hydrabad.
2373	Sahib Khan, ...	30	Ditto, ...	„ Jaffir Khan, ...	Daksera, ...	Armore, ...	Ditto.

No. in Genl. Register.	Names.	Age.	Caste.	Birth.	Place of Residence.		
					Village.	Pergunna.	District.
2415	Sooliman,........................	30	Moslem, ...	Son of Moheeooddeen. ...	Hurkurmulla,.	Sholapore, ...	Bombay.
2425	Sulliman Nadof, ...	...	Ditto, ...	....	Neelkoree, ...	....	Hydrabad.
2444	Seboo, ...	...	Dhangur. ...	....	Masungur, ...	Sorapore, ...	Ditto.
2445	Sheikh Dara (doubtful Thug),	...	Moslem, ...	....	....	Sorapore, ...	Ditto.
2449	Saheben Sahib, ...	...	Ditto, ...	Son of Sha Bez Burree Sahib, ...	Najee, ...	Ulmulla, ...	Bombay.
2459	Surroopa,.......................	...	Sooseea, ...	Son of Dyaram, ...	Buntullee, ...	Puroree, ...	Jeypore.
2460	Suroopa, ...	36	Naek, ...	,, Hurnaut Sing and Brother of Khooshall (No. 1184,)	Mooachan, ...	Jhillae, ...	Tonk.
2533	Sheikh Emam, ...	...	Moslem, ...	....	Bandnall, ...	Sorapore Bedur,	Hydrabad.
2541	Sheikh Burreh alias Burree Khan alias approver Khan Jemadar, ...	50	Ditto, ...	Son of Nubbee Khan and Khan Jemadar,...	Heejara now Chittumully,	Afzulpore Shewmoga,	Hydrabad. Mysore.
2571	Sheikh Hoosain, ...	30	Sheikh,......	....	Sorapore, ...	....	Hydrabad.
2572	Sheikh Hoosain...............	25	Ditto, ...	....	Mooldee, ...	Ulmulla, ...	Bombay.
2582	Serusgee (Meena), ...	28	Moslem, ...	Son of Emam (dead),......	Purmore, ...	Beejapore, ...	Sattarah.
2586	Sahiban alias Sahib Khan,...	35	Ditto, ...	,, Makhun Putel (dead,).........	Balgee..........	Mundroop, ...	Sholapore.
2587	Sahib Khan,....................	40	Ditto, ...	....	Gugaw,.........	Akulkote,......	Sattarah.
2603	Sheikh Kalleh,.................	40	Ditto, ...	Son of Meean Khan, ...	Sonee, ...	Byapore, ...	Ditto.
2617	Sheikh Moheeooddeen, ...	40	Ditto, ...	,, Sheikh Kassim, ...	Ballondgee, ...	Afzulpore, ...	Hydrabad.
2643	Sahib Khan Bhowul, ...	50	Ditto, ...	Adopted by Mataule Khan,	Kullewur,......	Ulmulla, ...	Dharwar.
2644	Sahibun, ...	...	Ditto, ...	Son of Mahomed Alli,......	Kulkoomudgee,	Sorapore Bedur,	Hydrabad.

2659	Sheikh Hoosainee, ...	...	Ditto, ...	,, Buhdoor Meean, ...	Chuncholee,...	Afzulpore, ...	Ditto.
2671	Sheikh Ullee, ...	...	Ditto, ...	,, Sheikh Mukdoom,.	Munsingee, ...	Indee, ...	Bombay.
2677	Sheikh Futteh, ...	...	Ditto, ...	,, Sheikh Ismael, ...	Jooree Khoord,	Afzulpore, ...	Hydrabad.
2695	Sewo, ...	...	Moslem Dongur,	....	Mulinghee, ...	Sorapore Bedur,	Ditto.
2699	Sahib Khan, ...	...	Moslem, ...	Son of Burree Sahib,......	Hyperga, ...	Sorapore Bedur,	Ditto.
2702	Sahib Khan.	45	Ditto, ...	Adopted of Meean Khan.	Kulswar, ...	Ulmulla, ...	Ditto.
2711	Sadasookh Jemadar, ...	35	Nayek, ...	Son of Deva, ...	Sirwair, ...	Julai,............	Jeypore.
2738	Seolall alias Sholea, ...	25	Ditto, ...	,, Futteh and Brother-in-law of Omeid Jemadar,	Balapoora, ...	Oneeara, ...	Ditto.
2746	Surdam, ...	40	Ditto.	,, Odda, ...	Ainchire, ...	Bowrie,.........	Ditto.
2775	Saoonta (Botole,)	35	Ditto, ...	,, Futteh, ...	Balapoora, ...	Oneeara, ...	Hydrabad.
2785	Seoleea, ...	30	Ditto, ...	,, Balloo, ...	Gopalpore, ...	Bowrie,.........	Ditto.
2804	Sanwulleea Jemadar Jerasm,	...	Sooseea, ...	,, Boonda,...............	Phagee, ...	Jeypore, ...	Jeypore.
2831	Seeoleea (Sooteea,)	35	Ditto, ...	,, Bhoopa,...............	Surdop, ...	Buwara, ...	Ditto.
2850	Simbhoo (Meena,)	...	Meena, ...	,, Boodhoo, ...	Sudara,..........	Nawae, ...	Ditto.
2867	Seolall Suckloo, ...	...	Sooseea, ...	,, Bhowaneea, ...	Chandimhoolee, village belonging to the Thakoor Futteh Sing.		
2872	Shooja Sooteea, ...	35	Naek, ...	,, Nola,..................	Near Futtehgur,	Deolee, ...	Kishengur.
2873	Surroopa (Koran,)	30	Sooseea, ...	....	Phoolairee, ...	Dhoonie, ...	Jeypore.
2875	Sadanoo, ...	...	Ditto, ...	Brother of Nathoo approver, ...	Phooleta, ...	Oneeara, ...	Ditto.
2879	Sewa alias Dewa,...............	...	Naek, ...	Son of Boora, ...	Jhellayah,......	....	Ditto.
2899	Sewa Jemadar (Powar,)......	...	Sooseea, ...	,, Poora, ...	Pepulda, ...	Jhillie, ...	Ditto.
2908	Shera Dhardandun,............	...	....	....	....	....	Ditto.
2917	Sirdar Khan Jemadar, ...	40	Moslem, ...	Son of Jugdamal Jemadarnee, ...	Dawulpairee,..	....	Mysore.
2924	Sheikh Nubbee, ...	20	Ditto, ...	,, Alla Bux, ...	Sonee, ...	Ulsinghee, ...	Sattarah.
2983	Seochurn,.......................	40	Dosad, ...	....	Kunjee,.........	....	Patna.
3130	Sunker,..........................	50	Bagtee,......	Brother of Bhola, ...	Raeegaon, ...	....	Burdwan.

No. in Genl. Register.	Names.	Age	Caste.	Birth.	Place of Residence.		
					Village.	Pergunna.	District.
3131	Saum alias Sama, ...	60	Chundal, ...	....	Salkaghat, ...	....	Calcutta.
3136	Soogul,...........................	30	Dome, ...	....	Aunapore,......	Mungulkote,	Burdwan.
3137	Soobul,...........................	50	Chundal, ...	....	Buddeedaoga,.	....	Ditto.
3152	Sahib Khan, ...	30	Moslem, ...	....	Chitnullee, ...	....	Mysore.
3173	Shere Khan Jemadar,.........	50	Ditto, ...	....	Chotee,.........	Khurouj Khoord,	Ditto.
3184	Synd, ...	40	Hindoo, ...	Son of Burree Khan, ...	Parmullee, ...	Nuggur, ...	Ditto.
3322	Soorujmal, ...	45	Brahmun,...	,, Purusram, ...	Bunder Dooddee,	Mysore,.........	Arcot.
3385	Shewya, ...	...	Mahratta,...	....	Golegaon, ...	Ulmulla, ...	Bombay.
3443	Seetaram,........................	40	Hindoo, ...	....	Nelinghaut, ...	Chittoor, ...	Hydrabad.
3487	Seyboo, ...	55	Moslem, ...	Son of Abdoolla Bhai, ...	Near Mohunmedabad,	Cuddapah, ...	Mysore.
3587	Sreedhur Haldar, ...	30	Buneea, ...	Son-in-law of Bhowanny Havildar,............	Cheergaon, ...	Monoorsal, Thannah Keogaon,	Beerbhoom.
3589	Surroop Dome, ...	40	Dome, ...	....	Soondulpore, .	Ujmootsal, Thannah Sakoolee,	Ditto.
3669	Son of Gour Doss, ...	...	Kaet, ...	....	Burkapore, ...	Nazirgunje, ...	Pusmah.
3673	Surroop Dutt Ghat Manjee,	...	Ditto, ...	....	Pookooreea,...	Thannah Jafergunge,	Furreedpore.
3735	Surroop Luskur,...............	35	Ditto,.........	....	Koosa Hata,..	....	Ditto.
3738	Sheikh Leedoo, ...	...	Moslem, ...	Son of Sheikh Gohee, ...	Seebpore,......	Birahimpore, Tha. Muthowra,	Pubna.

3747	Sanwul Hoobanee, ...	...	Naek, ...	....	....	Todree.........	Jeypore.
3792	Syf Khan,........................	40	Moslem, ...	Son of Meer Khan alias Meerun Khan, ...	Secunderpore,.	Azimgurh, ...	Azimgurh.
3805	Sirjee Khan, ...	23	Ditto, ...	,, Meean Sahib, ...	Goolburga, ...	Umjunkheree,.	Hydrabad.
3813	Sooltaneeah, ...	60	Ditto, ...	....	....	....	Ditto.
3824	Sydoo Bhai,.....................	40	Ditto, ...	Son of Ismael Sahib, ...	....	Bedur, ...	Ditto.
3878	Shumohera, ...	32	Ditto, ...	Adopted son of Bahadur, and the son of Amee and brother of Shere Khan Jemadar, who was hung at Saugor,.................	In service with Raja Petumber Sing at Ayah, in the Muttra district.		
3879	Sheir Khan,.....................	60	Mehwattee,.	Son of Futteh Khan. Kurreem Khan's father's sister married Sheir Khan, ...	In service with Raja Petumber Sing at Ayah, in the Muttra district.		
3891	Sookheea,.......................	28	Lodhee, ...	Son of Chubba, ...	Phazeepoorwa,	Tirwa, ...	Furruckabad.
3900	Salabut, ...	40	Mooltanee,..	....	Suraba,.........	....	Khytul.
3958	Sheikh Hoosain, brother of Dewanjee, ...	50	Ditto, ...	....	Pitpurtee,......	Bagapullee, ...	Bangalore.
3959	Sheikh Daoo, ...	25	Ditto, ...	Adopted of Emam Sahib Lumboo, ...	A village near Kadamaen Kotah,	Cuddapah, ...	Cuddapah.
3960	Sheikh Hoosain Bellary walla,.......................	60	Ditto, ...	,, Emam Sahib Lumboo,...	Munpullee, ...	Bagapullee, ...	Bangalore.
3980	Sooltaun, ...	60	Moslem, ...	,, Hoosain, ...	....	Sattarah, ...	Hydrabad.
4010	Satteeah, ...	30	Bukall, ...	....	Surwall, ...	....	Ditto.
4024	Sirdara, ...	45	Meena, ...	....	Dudach, ...	Esurdah, ...	Jeypore.
4058	Sookhun, ...	80	Bhat,.........	....	Minoul, ...	Bansee,.........	Goruckpore.
4067	Sewa, ...	40	Naek, ...	Son of Chenima,...........	Jeypore, ...	....	Jeypore.
4077	Sahibeea Khochuck, ...	30	Moslem, ...	,, Mahomed Sahib, ...	Bunderkota,...	Mundrosse, ...	Sholapore.
4106	Syud, ...	60	Ditto, ...	....	Byrunkoss, ...	Shewmoga, ...	Nuggur.
4138	Shunker, ...	35	Rajpoot, ...	....	Ajeetmull, ...	....	Mynpoorie.

No. in Genl. Regis-ter.	Names.	Age.	Caste.	Birth.	Place of Residence. Village.	Place of Residence. Pergunna.	Place of Residence. District.
4144	Shamsoondur, ...	40	Rajpoot, ...	....	Toree.	Allumpore, ...	Indore.
4230	Sudhoo, ...	60	Lodhee, ...	Son of Gunga,...............	Seeseeae, ...	....	Cawnpore.
4265	Seetul, ...	35	Aheer, ...	,, Heera.			
4267	Sookhaiee, ...	...	Ditto, ...	,, Mahurban Raoot.			
4312	Shunkura, ...	30	Kunjur, ...	....	Kodtomedah,..	....	Gwalior.
4336	Sooleman, ...	30	Moslem, ...	....	Hureehur, ...	Halee Humar,	Nuggur.
4408	Sirdar Khan, ...	50	Ditto, ...	....	Rusoolpore,...	Durriabad, ...	Oude.
4451	Sookmee, ...	30	Kotal, ...	Son of Lochun Purdhan,...	Ramkistopore,	Ujmootsae, ...	Beerbhoom.
4482	Sooltan Khan,..................	60	Moslem, ...	Khaloo of Raja Khan approver, ...	Punderpore,...	....	Sattarah.
4489	Sahib Khan Ferozewalla, related to Meean Bhai,	30	Ditto, ...	Son of Bapjee Jemadar,...	Ojnee, ...	....	Hydrabad.
4492	Sooltan, Salla of Aproop Khan, Brother of Manoo Meean Bhai,..............	40	Ditto, ...	,, Burree Khan Kala,	Wadee near Moorad,	....	Ditto.
4497	Sathuppah, ...	30	Buneea, ...	....	Sanoul,.........	....	Ditto.
4509	Sooltana, ...	40	Moslem, ...	Son of Maxoodah, ...	Hautuputtee,..	....	Ditto.
4530	Sahibun alias Soobun, husband of Newazzee's sister,	30	Ditto, ...	,, Urzunna, ...	Bondageh, ...	....	Poonah.
4540	Seydha, ...	50	Ditto, ...	Adopted of Resoobha, ...	Kanapore, ...	Bedur, ...	Hydrabad.
4541	Sheikh Murteza,..............	40	Ditto, ...	....	Afzulpore, ...	....	Ditto.
4545	Sahib Khan,......................	18	Ditto, ...	Son of Hussun Khan,......	Goorgundgee,.	....	Dharwar.
4609	Surbee Sur Jung, ...	35	Chundal, ...	....	Gopalpore, ...	Shazadpore,...	Pubna.
4615	Setul Doss Budun Doss, ...	45	Kaet, ...	Son of Nowaedoss,........	Burkhapore,...	Khutoopoora, .	Ditto.
4810	Salar, ...	60	Moslem, ...	Related to Sahib Khan Ruhmut Walla, ...	Satholee, ...	....	Hydrabad.

4812	Sessoo, ...	30	Ditto, ...	......	Jour, ...	......	Dharwar.
4816	Sullime, ...	45	Ditto, ...	......	Sukhpoor, ...	......	Bancoora.
4843	Semboo Bhortee, ...	25	Gosaen, ...	......	Joipul, ...	Honsah, ...	Nizam.
4859	Sheikh Punchoo, ...	21	Moslem, ...	......	Elaheegunge, .	Rajbaree, ...	Moorshedabad.
4860	Sheikh Khyroo, ...	...	Ditto, ...	......	Tukhorah, ...	Shokooleepore,	Beerbhoom.
4862	Sheikh Kubeer, ...	30	Ditto, ...	......	Saddee Khan Decarah,	Jellingy, ...	Moorshedabad.
4863	Sookh Chand, ...	33	Kotal, ...	......	Ramkishen-pore,	Shohkoo-leepore,	Beerbhoom.
4868	Sulliman, ...	35	Moslem, ...	Nephew of Chabriah Mahtah Khan, ...	Nienna, ...	Allund, ...	Nizam.
4869	Surwar, ...	60	Ditto, ...	......	Wastoree, ...	Kullianee, ...	Ditto.
4873	Sahibeea, ...	60	Ditto, ...	Adopted of Noor Khan and father of Sheir approver, ...	Gudulomunee,	Moodibihall, .	Dharwar.
4954	Sampote Sirdar, ...	45	Goalah, ...	......	Manopore, ...	Godeseko, ...	Pooree or S. Cuttack.
4967	Sonrepate, ...	40	Ditto, ...	......	Pampora, ...	Runnapore, ...	Pooree or ditto.
	T.						
315	Thakoree, ...	32	Brahmun, ...	Son of Nundun, ...	Ajeetpore, ...	......	Etawah.
1239	Tejja, ...	40	Khangur, ...	,, Khanjoo, ...	Etowra, ...	Jhalone, ...	Bundelcund.
1439	Thakurreea alias Koosulla, hence received an injury in his right eye, ...	40	Gurreeah Shepherd	......	Deseeree, ...	Secundra, ...	Cawnpore.
1440	Toorab, ...	90	Moslem, ...	Son of Jowahir, ...	......	......	Oude.
1717	Tajeea, ...	20	Ditto, ...	Brother of Hubboo, ...	Burheira, ...	Seronge, ...	Gwalior.
2105	Taj Mahomed, ...	55	Ditto, ...	......	Papul, ...	......	Hydrabad.
3272	Toolshee Sircar, ...	50	Kaet, Bengallee,	......	Kulna, ...	Kutwa, ...	Calcutta.
3354	Tibboo Sahib, ...	40	Moslem, ...	Son of Abdool Ruhman, ...	......	......	Hydrabad.

No. in Genl. Register.	Names.	Age.	Caste.	Birth.	Place of Residence.		
					Village.	Pergunna.	District.
3582	Teencowrie alias Pauchcowrie Dome, ...	25	Dome, ...	Son-in-law of Surroop Dome, ...	Bamoonee Sundulpore,	Ujmootsae, Thana Sakoolee-pore,	Beerbhoom.
3659	Thunaee Coond, ...	...	Kaet, ...	....	....	....	Pubna.
3775	Thakoor Doss, (the fair,) ...	40	Dome, ...	....	....	....	Burdwan.
3777	Thakoor Doss, (the dark,)...	45	Bowree, ...	....	....	....	Ditto.
4025	Tonda, ...	40	Meena, ...	....	Edodah, ...	Oneeara, ...	Jeypore.
4284	Teja, ...	40	Lodhee, ...	Brother of Bulla and Bhowanny, ...	Seytapore, ...	Futtia, ...	Oude.
4456	Teencowrie, ...	50	Kotal, ...	....	Goureepore, ...	Gungowreea, ..	Burdwan.
4466	Ternee Bhai, ...	40	Moslem, ...	Brother of Bunjaree Ka Emam, ...	Boregaon, ...	....	Hydrabad.
4514	Toolka Buddya, ...	65	Nadof, ...	Son of Mobarick, ...	Ousa, ...	....	Ditto.
4619	Tublook Sah, ...	45	Sahoo, ...	....	Futtepore, ...	Pugla, ...	Mymensing.
4864	Thakoor Doss Bowree, ...	25	Bowree, ...	....	Lukhpore, ...	Bancoora, ...	Moorshedabad.
	U.						
667	Uppee Sheikh, ...	70	Moslem, ...	Son of Sheikh Bhikka, ...	Dareeabad, ...	Jaes, ...	Lucknow.
1357	Umrow Sing, ...	35	Rajpoot, ...	,, Aman Sing.	Dubo, ...	Jansi, ...	Bundelcund.
1526	Umria, ...	...	Moslem. ...	,, Omeid Sing, ...	....	....	Indore.
1546	Ullee Khan Jemadar, ...	28	Ditto, ...	....	Bykothpore, ...	....	Azeemabad.
1886	Unwur, ...	...	Burroot, ...	Brother of Khoda Bux, ...	....	Rukan, ...	Ojeyn.
2231	Umra Balna, ...	...	Naek, ...	Son of Koshal, ...	Sameea Khapprass,	Detoremgurh,.	Jeypore.

2366	Ulla Buksh, ...	50	Moslem, ...	,, Sirjee Khan.........	Dhokesura, ...	Armour, ...	Hydrabad.
2719	Umra, ...	40	Naek, ...	,, Mundroop, nephew of Omeid Jemadar, dead,)	Bentalleca or Pholeta,	Dhoona or Oneeara,	Jeypore.
2895	Ubba Utwar, ...	40	Ditto, ...	,, Huttheea, ...	Bhamuckpoora	....	Ditto.
3186	Ullee, ...	18	Moslem, ...	,, Maniek, ...	....	....	Mysore.
3356	Ulla Bux, ...	26	Ditto, ...	....	....	....	Hydrabad.
3433	Ulla Bux alias Dap Khan,...	35	Ditto, ...	Adopted of Ap Khan Emam Sahib Jemadar,	In the vicinity of Shemaya,	....	Mysore.
3830	Ullee Sha, ...	15	Ditto, ...	Son of Myan Saib, ...	Hidggeera, ...	Afzulpore, ...	Hydrabad.
3839	Ullee, ...	40	Ditto, ...	Adopted of Kutal, ...	Mooldee, ...	Sholapore, ...	Sholapore.
3921	Ulla Buksh, ...	60	Ditto, ...	....	Aseepullee, ...	Bhageepullee,.	Bangalore.
3962	Ullam, ...	55	Ditto, ...	....	Kurnakota, ...	....	Kurno.
3990	Urroo, ...	40	Koolee, ...	....	....	....	Hydrabad.
4009	Uttoo Baba, ...	30	Ditto, ...	....	Soorwal, ...	....	Ditto.
4022	Ullamee, ...	40	Ditto, ...	....	Budnoor, ...	....	Ditto.
4500	Uttoo, ...	40	Kooree, ...	Son of Halkattee, ...	Seroul, ...	....	Ditto.
4521	Ulloo, ...	62	Molsem, ...	....	Magurgah, ...	....	Ditto.
4621	Ullee alias Emam, ...	50	Ditto, ...	Adopted of Jungwall, ...	....	....	Ditto.
4622	Ullee, ...	40	Ditto, ...	,, Guddoo, Emam brother of NathooBoolakee (deceased,)...	Moree, ...	Nagnee, ...	Poona.
4851	Unnee, ...	16	Gosaen, ...	Wife of Manugee, ...	Umbullooar,...	Dhandasheo, ..	Nizam.
	W.						
444	Wuzeer, ...	30	Moslem, ...	Son of Turreeb, ...	Monowur Thanna,	....	Bhopaul.
1864	Wullee Syud, ...	40	Ditto, ...	....	Kunkee Deemee,	....	Hydrabad.
2286	Wullee Shah Jemadar, ...	40	Ditto, ...	....	Kunkee Deemee,	Hurdepette, ...	Ditto.
2965	Wuzee Khan 2nd, ...	35	Ditto, ...	....	Rudowlee, ...	Rudowlee, ...	Oude.

No. in Genl. Register.	Names.	Age.	Caste.	Birth.	Place of Residence.		
					Village.	Pergunna.	District.
2966	Wulleedad Khan, ...	50	Moslem, ...	Son of Dulel Khan,......	Kotehdeh, ...	Rudowlee, ...	Oude.
4425	Wuzeer Sheikh, ...	35	Ditto, ...	,, Ulla Bux, ...	Lugpoor, ...	....	Bancoorah.
4515	Wullee, ...	80	Ditto, ...	,, Mobarick, ...	Ousa, ...	....	Hydrabad.
	Y.						
1699	Yaseen,........................	45	Ditto, ...	Brother of Bolla and son of Sheikh Suddoo,	Chitnoo, ...	Sutrungpore, .	Gwalior.
3510	Yenka alias Hoosain,........	25	Ditto, ...	....	....	....	Hydrabad.
	Z.						
1524	Zoolfukur, ...	40	Ditto, ...	....	Agra Khass,...	....	Agra.
2814	Zalim (Barasheea)...........	50	Naek, ...	Son of Jurreeb Khan,......	Musurra.	Esurdah, ...	Jeypore.
3903	Zoolfee, ...	40	Belochee, ...	,, Jawahir, ...	Chandooa, ...	....	Hansee.
4273	Zoolfukur Khan alias Badul Khan,.................	...	Moslem, ...	,, Bheekun Khan, ...	....	....	Bundelcund.

List of Thugs still at large in Bengal to whom numbers have been assigned in the General Register.

Number.	Number of the General Register.	Name.	Parentage.	Age.	Cast.	Place of Residence. Village.	Place of Residence. Pergunna. Thannah.	Place of Residence. Zillah.
1	5088	Anund Sheikh, ...	Son-in-law of Meecho Jemadar,	,,	Mussulman,	Jooduh, ...	Thanna Dhurum-pore,	Pubna.
2	5089	Bewonee Dass Choin and Jemadar, ...	,,	,,	Kaet,.........	Khodarpora,...	Jheeneeaduh,	Jessore.
3	5090	Byragee Dass,.........................	,,	,,	,,	Ditto, ...	Ditto, ...	Ditto.
4	5091	Bhyrubchunder Dass,..............	,,	,,	,,	Gajeergantee,	Th. Salkeah,...	Ditto.
5	5092	Bholanath Jogee, ...	,,	,,	,,	Kentalbereah,	Ditto, ...	Ditto.
6	5093	Doorgachurn Dass Dutt, ...	,,	,,	Kaet,.........	Sreepore, ...	Kaloopul, ...	Ditto.
7	5094	Degumbernauth Jogee, ...	,,	,,	Jogee, ...	Kentalbereeah,	Salkeeah, ...	Ditto.
8	5095	Gooroochurn Mookerjeea, ...	,,	,,	Brahmun,...	Sateejooree, ...	,,	Burdwan.
9	5096	Huradhun Sircar, ...	Son of Sona-tun Sircar,	,,	Kaet,.........	Patrotore,......	,,	Bancoorah.
10	5097	Hurree Dass, ...	,,	,,	Ditto, ...	Khedarporah,	Jheeneeaduh,	Jessore.
11	5098	Jysutt Mojoomdar Jemadar, ...	,,	55	Ditto, ...	Ditto, ...	Ditto, ...	Ditto.
12	5199	Jynarain Dass,........................	,,	,,	Ditto, ...	Ditto, ...	Ditto, ...	Ditto.
13	5100	Kishan Dass, ...	,,	,,	,,	Ditto, ...	Ditto, ...	Ditto.
14	5101	Kaleechurn Manjee, ...	,,	,,	Ditto, ...	Ditto, ...	Ditto, ...	Ditto.
15	5102	Manick Kotal,.........................	,,	,,	Kotal, ...	Mateearee formerly Coolboreah,	Uggurdeep, ...	Nuddeeah.
16	5103	Nuffer Dome, ...	Sookmee Dome,	30	Dome, ...	Soondulpore,	Keogow, ...	Beerbhoom.

Number.	Number of the General Register.	Name.	Parentage.	Age.	Cast.	Place of Residence. Village.	Place of Residence. Pergunna. Thannah.	Place of Residence. Zillah.
17	5104	Netae Bowree,........................	Sookmee Dome,	,,	Bowree, ...	Kalee Myda Beburdah, formerly Luckpooree, ...	,,	Bancoorah.
18	5105	Rama Bunneeah,.....................	Roopnarain Buneeah,...	,,	,,	Koorgoon, ...	Shakoleepore,	Beerbhoom.
19	5106	Runnoo Bengal, ...	,,	,,	,,	Cutwah, ...	Cutwah, ...	Burdwan.
20	5107	Ramsoondur Kotal,..................	,,	,,	Kotal, ...	Ambeeka,......	Culnah, ...	Ditto.
21	5108	Rughonauth Jogee,.................	,,	,,	,,	Gajeergantee,	Sulkeeah, ...	Jessore.
22	5109	Ramsoondernath Jogee,............	,,	,,	,,	Goonagantee,	Ditto, ...	Ditto.
23	5110	Ramcoomar Paul, ...	,,	,,	,,	Kotlee, ...	Ditto, ...	Ditto.
24	5111	Sookhchaund Haldar, ...	,,	53	,,	Akreegunge,...	Raneetulla, ...	Moorshedabad.
25	5112	Seboo Haldar, ...	,,	,,	,,	Hajrahattee,...	Meergunge, ...	Rajshye.
26	5113	Sheikh Dhurmee, ...	,,	,,	,,	Sahebnuggur, formerly Dhunaepoorah, ...	Jellingee, ...	Moorshedabad.
27	5114	Sibchunder Sircar alias Seeboo Dass, ...	,,	,,	,,	Nuldangah, ...	Salkeeah, ...	Jessore.
28	5115	Sheikh Neeamut,.........	Sheikh Jumalooddeen,......	,,	Mussulman,	Narainpore, ...	,,	Bancoorah.
29	5116	Sheikh Bawool, ...	,,	,,	Ditto, ...	Jhooduh, ...	Dhurmpore, ...	Pubna.

30	5117	Teencowree Kotal, ...	,,	,,	Kotal, ...	Saldooleah Ajagore,...	Soleemabad,...	Burdwan.
31	5077	Asoreah, ...	,,	,,	,,	Foodkeepore,	,,	Bhagulpore.
32	5078	Bhuggeerut Jogee, ...	,,	,,	Jogee, ...	Gajeergantee,	Salkeeah, ...	Jessore.
33	5079	Bissessur Biswas, ...	,,	,,	Kaith, ...	Nuldangah, ...	,,	Ditto.
34	5080	Gungadhur Kotal, ...	,,	,,	Kotal, ...	Belleea Asapore,	Gongoreeah,...	Burdwan.
35	5081	Issurchunder Biswas, ...	,,	,,	Kaith, ...	Nuldangah, ...	,,	Jessore.
36	5082	Kishenchunder Mojoomdar, ...	,,	,,	Ditto, ...	Ditto, ...	,,	Ditto.
37	5083	Lochen Mittree, ...	,,	,,	Ditto, ...	Rampore, ...	Salkeeah, ...	Ditto.
38	5084	Mohun Dass, ...	,,	,,	Byragee, formerly Kotal,...	Majeergaow,...	Munteshun, ...	Burdwan.
39	5085	Ramsoondur Paul, ...	,,	,,	Kaith, ...	Gajeergantee,	Salkeeah, ...	Jessore.
40	5086	Sheikh Bhageman, ...	Sheikh Baroo,	,,	Mussulman,	Sonaekoomae,	Dhurmpore, ...	Pubna.
41	5087	Dookhee, ...	,,	,,	Ditto, ...	Ditto, ...	Ditto, ...	Ditto.

W. H. SLEEMAN,
General Superintendent.

MORADABAD,
GENL. SUPT.'S OFFICE,
The 6th November, 1840.

SUPPLEMENTARY

List of Thugs mentioned in the Moradabad General Register who have been disposed of or are known to have died.

Number in the General Register.	Names and Parentage.
1963	Allee Bux.
2496	Ameer Khan.
4028	Achumbut Aheer, brother of Ninhoot.
2354	Boodhoo Khansamah.
4091	Belass Khan, son of Bhaoo Khan.
3229	Belass Khan, son of Durgaee Khan.
4029	Bhoond Khan.
3420	Bhond Khan.
4238	Bridgelall Aheer, son of Luchmun Aheer.
4036	Chitroo, son of Zoomun Khan.
3397	Doollar Khan, son of Cheethun Khan.
3251	Danee Khan, son of Mustoo Khan.
4037	Danee Khan, ditto.
3260	Dahoo Khan, son of Munnoo Khan.
2494	Dan Khan, son of Badoolla Khan.
3399	Foudeea alias Foudee, nephew of Roshun.
4168	Fukeer Sing, son of Bhokoree Raee.
4266	Fyze Khan alias Gohur, son of Jaffir Khan.
2483	Ghassee Khan, son of Tanoo Misserie.
3276	Girdharee Bengalee
3401	Gooroos Kybert Bengalee.
3277	Geelafur Sircar alias Goolma Bengalee.
3423	Ghulabun Sircar.
3400	Guness, brother of Jewun Sircar Bengalee.
3226	Goolmeer alias Golam Meer.
4038	Goman alias Gomanee.
1972	Hosseinee Khan, son of Bukut Khan and brother of Khoda Bux.
4046	Khobee Khan.
2320	Nahir Khan, son of Bukut Bullee.
2497	Navoo Sing.
3243	Nizam Khan alias Jhowle Khan, son of Golam Allee Khan.
4055	Ninhoot alias Ninjhoot, son of Ruktoo.
3287	Sonephool Rae, son of Murdun Raee.
2984	Tingree, son of Jhikaree.

SUPPLEMENTARY

List of Thugs mentioned in the Bengal General Register who have died or been otherwise disposed of.

Number in the General Register.	Names and Parentage.
2996	Alum Doss Byragee.
3124	Alum alias Ulma.
3308	Anoopoodeen Sheikh.
4427	Azifa.
3004	Bhurut.
3005	Bohla.
3006	Bunda.
3011	Bhurut.
3012	Bhola.
3278	Bishunpersaud.
3293	Buhramalias Buhramdee and Bhowul.
3305	Buree Sirkar.
3306	Bhola.
3573	Bejah.
3574	Bejah Dome.
3757	Buddun Thakoor.
4855	Beijee Bowree
4944	Banka Bowree.
3123	Cheyn.
3310	Chota Sirkar.
3591	Chunder Mohun Paul.
3593	Chakur Haldar.
3609	Chenebus Chukurbuttee.
3616	Cheytun.
3758	Cheedbur.
3017	Dyanarain Mozoondar, Jemadar of Chotear.
3019	Dheena Ghat Manjee.
3618	Doonadhun son of Suddar Kisher.
4418	Doolal Sirkar.
4432	Doorgha Churn, Halder son of Buddun Halder.
4433	Doorgha Churn son of Gobind Ram Podder.
4834	Dookhoo Meeteea, son of Pubbun Meeteea.
4546	Edoo Sheikh.
3024	Gungahurree Mistree, Jemadar.
3025	Gopaul, son of Buddun.
3032	Golam, son of Golabdee.
3034	Gohee Muhuldar.
3296	Gudoo.
4434	Gobind Kotal.
2344	Hurree Sirkar, Jemadar.
3039	Hurro Sain, son of Mohun Sing.
3042	Hurree Meeteea.
3294	Hyder, brother-in-law of Kaleechurn, No. 3291.

Number in the General Register.	Names and Parentage.
3599	Hemaith Sheikh.
4437	Huldhur Kotal.
4454	Hyder Sheikh alias Teencowrie.
3045	Juggoo alias Kalee Juggernath.
3046	Juggernath, brother of Leeloo, Jemadar.
3047	Juggoo alias Burra Juggernath.
3048	Juggernath, nephew of Balee Kaet.
3050	Jhaboo, Jemadar.
3051	Jummun
3597	Jubbaree Sheikh.
4419	Jhubboo Bhuteeara, son of Kabil.
4818	Jooree Sheikh, son of Sheik Syfoo.
2346	Khuruk Baboo Jemadar.
3052	Kistoo.
3053	Konta, son of Buddun.
3055	Kattick, son of Netye Halder.
3056	Kistoo.
3058	Koodeeram.
3059	Kalee Churn.
3061	Khooshal Sheikh, son of Punchoo Sheikh.
3062	Kalee Churn Jemadar.
3063	Koora.
3064	Kashee Bukshee.
3065	Kishun Jemadar Haldar, nephew of Chunder Halder.
3066	Kumul Mundul.
3121	Keenoo Sheikh Jemadar.
3291	Kalee Churn alias Sheikh Kalla.
3578	Kumal Dome.
3579	Kanchun Doss.
3600	Kartick Ghose.
3602	Kunhae Kuhar.
3761	Kaloo Sheikh.
3762	Kunhye Dome.
3763	Kishun Ghose.
4439	Kumal Halder.
4442	Kishen Halder.
4444	Kumal Halder
4445	Kaleechurn Sirkar.
2493	Lall Baboo Bengalee Jemadar.
3069	Leethee Dutt Sircar Jemadar.
3071	Lall, son of Buddun.
3072	Larun Dome.
3073	Ludeea, son of Rampersaud Jemadar.
3074	Lethee Thakoor, brother of Ramkisore.
3075	Leeloo Jemadar, son of Kinneo Muzoomdar.
3076	Lookoor Meeteea.
3077	Lukhee Muhaldar.
3078	Sookool Meeteea, nephew of Leetie Meeteea.
3082	Lubbeen, son of Teloke.

Number in the General Register.	Names and Parentage.
3122	Laboo Sheikh.
3594	Leea Kotal.
3764	Lall Mahomed.
2341	Momen Jemadar Sheikh.
3084	Mathur, son of Mohun.
3090	Mulna.
3091	Muddun Jemadar, son of Surroop.
3092	Mohun, brother of Sunkur Tontia.
3093	Muggun Sircar, son of Seeam Sircar.
3094	Mohun Doss.
3132	Mechoo.
3292	Motun Sheikh, brother of Kalee Churn, No. 3291.
3307	Mooree Sheikh.
3593	Munsa alias Mohna.
3614	Moothoor Haldar.
3615	Manick, son of Surroop.
3765	Moonna alias Memsa.
4421	Mungulla, son of Khoosial.
4422	Mohun, son of Byjnath.
4547	Manick Jowardar.
3095	Naffer, son of Seeam Bowree.
3096	Nundkouz, son of Golam Doss Jemadar.
3115	Nehal Sheikh alias Tirbhoo, son of Momen.
3417	Niddheeram.
3582	Nunkowrie alias Sheikh Godee.
3608	Nuffer Kotal.
4446	Narain Kotal.
4825	Nussir alias Nuffer.
4858	Neetae Halder alias Chokur Halder.
3309	Puddolochun.
4423	Puddoo Doss, son of Gobur Doss.
3103	Ramkishtoo.
3104	Roshun Jemadar.
3253	Roshem Sheikh.
3271	Ramjewun.
3281	Ramdutt Sircar Jemadar.
3583	Rujoo Dome, son-in-law of Soobul Dome.
3585	Ram Mohun Sing.
3592	Ram Halder, brother-in-law of Kissun Halder.
3770	Rampershaud (the fair alias Pershaudia.)
3772	Ram Mohun, 2nd.
3773	Ram Mohun, 3rd.
4447	Roop Bagdee, brother of Suroop Bagdee.
4604	Ramcoomar Muzoomdar.
4894	Roop Bagdee.
3587	Sreedhur Halder, son-in-law of Bhowanny Halder.
3589	Surroop Dome.
3130	Sunkur Bagtee Mundul, son of Ramkishen Kotal.

SUPPLEMENTARY

List of Thugs mentioned in the Register of Thugs at large as having died or been disposed of.

Number in the General Register.	Names and Parentage.
4548	Adhoo alias Oodhoo.
4549	Aradhun Sein.
4550	Aradhun Deo.
4551	Aradhun Sircar.
3690	Boodhoo Sheikh.
3691	Bullae Chung.
3734	Bishenath alias Besoo Seikh.
3650	Dookheeram Chung.
4563	Dagoo Neogee
3674	Goopee Cupalee.
3742	Goluck Biswas.
4566	Gokul Nundee.
4568	Gorachund Biswas.
4569	Gopee Biswas.
4571	Goorpaul.
4572	Goopee Chung.
4573	Gokul Chung.
3698	Hurradhun Chung.
4575	Hookma Chung.
4576	Hindeea Sheikh.
4933	Hunneep Sheikh.
3741	Jyah Chung.
4578	Joogul Sein.
3652	Koluck Rahoot.
3699	Kissen Mistree.
3703	Kokoram Dass.
3706	Kaleepersad Chung.
3736	Kuramoodeen.
4559	Kashee Shah.
4561	Kashee Sircar.
4579	Khodba.
3709	Lochun Sein.
4582	Lochun Chung.
4583	Lochun Sonar.
4584	Mahomed Zumma.
4585	Meedoo Biswas.
4586	Munnee Kishen Shah.
3714	Neelmony Chung.
3715	Nubeen Toee.
3737	Nukee Sukdar.
4588	Neyn Nundee.
4620	Ootut Shah.

Number in the General Register.	Names and Parentage.
4594	Pundut Chung alias Papoosah.
3662	Ramnidhee Thakoor.
3722	Rajnarain Mistree alias Rajub Mistree.
4598	Rugoonauth Chung.
4600	Ramdhun Chund.
4602	Rajmohun Soom.
4606	Rungoo Bunwaree.
4619	Tublook Shah.

FINIS.

INDEX.

N. B. In this Index the name of every Thug whose name is recorded will be found, with the exception of the alphabetical list of Thugs at large and the supplementary lists at the close of the volume, the whole of which being already arranged alphabetically do not require to be transferred to this Index.

A.

B.

D.

E.

F.

G.

H.

I.

J.

K.

L.

M.

N.

O.

P.

R.

S.

T.

U.

V.

W.

X.

Z.